In an effort to re-organize society along Maoist lines, does the traditional

Is it fair to suggest that a primary target of Maoist

Was the old familial society targeted by maoist ideology out of a benevolent desire to 'liberate' women or simply to accelerate their consolidation of power in an end

Next Wave: New Directions in Women's Studies
A series edited by Inderpal Grewal, Caren Kaplan, and Robyn Wiegman

# THE QUESTION OF

# WOMEN IN CHINESE

# FEMINISM

Tani E. Barlow

DUKE UNIVERSITY PRESS    Durham and London 2004

2nd printing, 2006
© 2004 Duke University Press
All rights reserved
Printed in the United States of America on acid-free paper ∞
Typeset in Quadraat by Keystone Typesetting, Inc.
Library of Congress Cataloging-in-Publication Data appear
on the last printed page of this book.

# Contents

# Acknowledgments

This project became a book over the course of many years. Irene Eber, Charlotte Furth, Howard Goldblatt, Gary Hamilton, Marilyn Young, Wolfgang Kubin, and Don Price read some or all of the earliest portions of the research. During the 1990s, I found interlocutors in two long-lived, Bay Area reading groups. In Inderpal Grewal's "Feminism and Nationalism," I voiced my characteristic themes of the historical catachresis, the peripheralization of the sign, and the problematics of colonial modernity. I have developed these positions in various other venues over the 1990s. In Donald M. Lowe's "Marxism and Postmodernity" reading group, which ran concurrently, a sustained, critical, reading of Derrida allowed me to begin reframing historical and historiographic concerns that had preoccupied me in graduate school. Also during those years, Renli Wang read Chen Hongmou with me. Angela Zito, Jing Wang, Judith Farquhar, Jim Hevia, Wolfgang Kubin, Li Tuo, Francine Winddance Twine, Yitsi Mei Feuerwerker, and Dorsey Green all encouraged me to complete the book. I appreciate their unwillingness to accept anything less.

After I drafted the manuscript, Hiroko Sakamoto, Meng Yue, Jacqueline Berman, Dai Jinhua, David Palumbo-Liu, Uta Poiger, Li Xiaojiang, Deborah Porter, and Yi-tsi Mei Feuerwerker each carefully examined chapters where their expertise could best enrich my views and rectify errors. I acknowledge with appreciation the library support of Wenbing Peng, Brian Hammer, Scott Edward Harrison, Paul Walker, Sumei Yi, and Mengliang Zhang at the University of Washington, and the manuscript editing skills of Brian Hammer, Riki Thompson, and Tamiko Nimura during the process of revision. Liu Bohong, Dora Dien, Helen May Schneider, Tu Shaojun, Raoul David Findeisen, Lau Kin Chi, Liu Huiying, Yan Hairong, and Wang Zheng ensured that I found sources I needed. Christina Gilmartin, Chia-lin Tao Hiroko Sakamoto, and Chen Liwei answered my questions of fact. Claudia Pozzana and Alessandro Russo organized a 1999 seminar at the Project for

Critical Asian Studies that proved a good reminder of the pleasures of collective reading. The Modern Girl Research cluster, at the University of Washington, Priti Ramamurthy, Uta Poiger, Lynn Thomas, Madeleine Dong, and Alys Weinbaum, provided companionship as did Jean Allman, Susan Porter Benson, Dina Copelman and David Roediger at the University of Missouri-Columbia History Department. I gratefully acknowledge the support of Susan Jeffords, associate dean of social sciences at the University of Washington, and Judith Howard, department chair, for arranging a research quarter that allowed me to complete the draft. I have been improved as a scholar and a friend over the many years of intellectual companionship that Yukiko Hanawa and Jing Wang have extended to me.

Reynolds Smith was everything I imagined in an editor, and his legendary patience and kindness meant the readers he enlisted were superb. This book is far stronger than it would otherwise have been on account of the insight, persistence, and scholarly judgment of the Duke University Press readers. I am grateful to Lisa Rofel who has allowed me to thank her by name. I also acknowledge with appreciation the intentional and, sometimes, unintended contributions of others. Ding Ling warned me about the veracity of historical archives. Dai Jinhua provided manuscripts and new publications during the drafting of chapter 7. Zhang Jingyuan confirmed to me how she had translated key texts of French feminism into Chinese during the late 1980s and early 1990s. Joan Scott's intellectual probity and kindness have clarified my vision from the outset and contributed immeasurably to this project. The unfolding work of Gayatri C. Spivak and my engagement with it have brought welcome pleasure. At the Institute for Gender Studies of the Ochanomizu Women's University and at Hitotsubashi University in 2000–2001, I presented several portions of this work to colleagues. I am grateful for the responses of Tokyo scholars, particularly Hiroko Sakamoto, Akiyama Yoko, Masaki Miyao, and Ruri Ito. At the Press, Justin Faerber improved the manuscript with his meticulous reading.

Whatever in the long run I have succeeded in doing here, as elsewhere, I feel gratitude most strongly of all to my beloved partner, Donald M. Lowe, for his persistent belief in me and for his unstinting intellectual contributions to this book from beginning to end.

November 2003

The Question of
Women in Chinese
Feminism

# Introduction

Istory is not continuous but cumulative. The records of the past are left for succeeding generations to read or not read, to burn or efface, to ignore or to comb anxiously in search of signs of what the future will bring. Memories are annulled and trauma thrust back into the recesses of the unconscious, where each succeeding generation locates a new place to rethink its preoccupations against the background of a half-forgotten past. Progressive history is written retrospectively. This monograph draws attention to the intermittent quality of ongoing historical events. The book is a history of the discontinuous accumulation of feminist enlightenment in China in the past century and a consideration of the theoretical labor that went into forging each new element of the modern normative political order.

Over the years I devised a way of reading historical evidence for catachreses. Conventionally, catachresis refers to a particular misuse of a proper noun, where the term's referent is, theoretically or philosophically speaking, inadequate. A historical catachresis is my way of taking advantage of the ellipsis and making its analytic inadequacy a positive value. When reconsidered as *historical* catachresis, ubiquitous, descriptive, proper nouns become legible repositories of social experience. For instance, the catachreses *nüxing* and *funü* are pivotal in this history of women in Chinese feminism. I do not read these terms textually or intertextually, however. I read them historically: I stress their heterogeneous contents as well as their centrality and instability, what historians would call contingency. I also demonstrate the roles these terms have played in policy. This reinforces my contention that historical catachreses' power is political because these figures are mediated or thought experience.

Like Raymond Williams' notion of the key word, historical catachresis stresses the specificity and singularity of people's everyday norms or normalized experience. Like Foucault's genealogy, the histories of catachreses also focus on names; this way of reading is consequently nominalist. But as Foucault's method suggests, there is a difference between a history of ideas and a history of catachreses. The history of ideas might consider "the history of the body" and draw a line of development explaining the body's history in given eras or languages. The starting point for a history of a catachrestic "body" might be theories of corporeality and an investigation of the material conditions that contemporary theories presume. *Historical catachresis is an ideological entity*, in other words. It keeps open the possibility that "body" may be central to thinking and experience in one time and not in others.

Historical catachresis is like a figure of speech. The sign of its value to those who invested it with meaning remain; it retains the traces of the operating assumptions and normalizing strategies that characterize the other time and place. Therefore, locating loaded terms and calling them catachreses, as I do particularly with the terms nüxing and funü, means that I am drawn into a world where no distinction is drawn between experience and its ideation. Historical catachreses are highly ideated elements of lived experience. They are, to use Gayatri C. Spivak's notion, conceptual metaphors that have a diffused, powerful ability to explain everyday life and consequently to justify and define and stabilize our activities. This method of reading to locate historical catachresis stresses intellection. But it is intellectual in a certain way because the conditions for thinking are always embedded in the content of thought.[1] Because the thinkers that interest me are all modernists, an underlying hope of this study is that it will contribute eventually to explaining how modernist explanations of human social existence got to be normative in China's middle class. And why banal norms were so often—at least in theory—female-centered.

Seeking to accentuate the importance of the historical catachresis in the history of women in Chinese feminism, I have highlighted the future anterior tense in history writing. The future anterior is a verbal construction used to stress the covert or anticipated future embedded in the present moment (or in a moment that was a present in the past). One reason future anteriority is particularly useful in a history of feminist thinking lies with the heterogeneity of the past. Accepting that the present is always heterogeneous sensitizes us to the futuristic desires theorists and scholars addressed to readers. Writers, that is, have the future in mind. They may desire justice, strength, or power; all of these presuppose a future where legitimate claimants make good on their claims. But the central point about future anteriority in feminist historiography, which I take up in chapter 1, is that *the stress on "what women will have been," effectively destabilizes the referent of women in documentary evidence.* It shifts the way we look at women from a state of being to a name for potentiality. Reopening the future in a specific past helps to destabilize the assumptions historians may be making about the way past, present, and future flow in endless transition. It suggests that when, to use Benjamin's concept, time is brought to a standstill, what is blasted out of the past are possibilities. Historical catachreses return us to these lost possibilities or desires, and the future anterior tense invokes the horizon that people in another world confronted.

Thus, paying attention to the temporality of what women will have been, particularly in the work of feminist writers, does several useful things. First, it repeats and reinforces the truth that, like us, theorists in the past had motivated expectations and were not passively representing verities of "context," that is, things as they allegedly really were. Second, because future anteriority focuses on the activity of thinking and the role of the future in thinking, it calls attention to the creative capacity of even the most ideological or banal style of feminist thought. Third, it builds into the project of writing the history of women in feminism the quality that Joan Scott has written about in French feminism of being unfinished and chaotic.[2] Fourth, emphasizing future anteriority in analyzing historical events deepens the significance of feminism as an epochal but constantly unfinished, discontinuous project. The shift of emphasis, that is, accepting the truism that categories of women are historically variable, enables us to focus more carefully on how theorists intervened, shaping and crystallizing the ideological resources that characterized their moment. This is not a history of winners. Not only did some of the thinkers considered here become "history's losers," but others are just obscure and forgotten. Yet even when celebrated, like Ding Ling, they are memorable in part because their longings for a better future for women were not satisfied.

Feminist thinking in modern Chinese history is an integral part of contemporary deliberations about the nation and its development. That is not to say that it is always "nationalist," or that feminism has always been central to the concerns of male and female intellectuals in their daily work of study and writing. Rather, in composing this discontinuous and cumulative account of the question of women in Chinese feminism, what struck me is the remarkable way that feminist concerns return again and again into the critical spotlight. From the 1920s, when "the woman question" took genuine pride of place on the popular intellectual agenda, to the patriotic, instrumental recasting of women in the Communist Revolution's development discourse in the 1940s and 1950s, to the highly publicized and plaintive regrouping of social science feminism and gendered justice movements in post-Mao intellectual circles, feminist currents in critical theory have continuously effloresced into the general domain of intellectual life. Whether the problem is national culture and purity or the enculturation of nature, whether the stakes are mobilization of capital and labor power or race improvement, international competition, global equity, or critiques of gendered consumerism, feminist awareness and concerns have been an element of a national critical intellectual tradition.

The surfacing of a national tradition of feminism in China rested on highly complex preconditions that are not themselves feminist and that included disparate elements: the ethnographic surrealism of early sex theory, the eugenicist's will to power, modernist classification systems, bioscientific emphases on heterosexual normativity, Maoist ethics, and so on. Such foundational eclecticism also meant that although ordinarily it is a nationalism, Chinese feminism is always other things as well. Like founding national feminists elsewhere during the 1920s and 1930s, Chinese theorists engaged international biosocial, evolutionary, and revolutionary thinking both as nationalists and despite nationalism. As this study will show, once the contingent foundations of a bourgeois colonial modernity were settled into place, subsequent theorists in China would reargue women's liberation in other globalized theoretical venues. The international communist movement, global neoliberalism, and globalized poststructuralism has each flourished in changing relations of national to international state system and global capital. Two points of particular interest follow from this. A discontinuous, persistent record demonstrates how thinkers working outside of Europe, North America, and Japan have wielded the powers of universal enlightened Reason. Also, exclusive claims of the West to feminism feel less compelling once feminism's centrality to revolutionary modernization and development theory globally is asserted.

Social theory is this study's chief primary source archive. Some of the chapters look at explicitly theoretical writing, such as evolutionary or social Darwinism, or early patriarchal and psychoanalytic theories. Others consider, alternately, literary aesthetics and questions of revolutionary political ideology or ethics of mass movements. Nonetheless, each analysis privileges social theory precisely because of (and not despite) its ability to predicate abstract or general categories. In a history rooted in an archive that is not just generally theoretical in nature but is *generically* theory, categories of thinking are explicitly presented and intricately argued because the stakes are high: "theory" purports to be nothing less than truth. Enlightened theory and the social sciences are measured against the truths of social existence. This presumption—that truth is the register of adequacy in enlightened theory—itself compels historians (who are social scientists for better and worse) to accept universal claims even when they come from "Chinese." So mine is not a claim about situated knowledge so much as a brief suggesting that where claims are made in the name of truthful enlightened reason they must be considered universal no matter where they originate. Chinese feminism is indisputably Chinese and it is feminism, just as Japanese social science is Japanese and social science.[3]

These are some of the characteristics of a history composed on the evidence that theories offer. One last point deserves an explicit mention here. In openly analytic writing, it is necessary to clarify, where possible, the enabling assumptions at issue in one's own work and the work of other theorists. This sometimes leads to a stark staging of the relation of historian and subject, between my subject matter and my own intellectual positioning, because it is a historical fact that there are substantial areas of commonality potentially connecting us. This is not a matter of mere interpretation. The evidence I rely on is not particularly ambiguous and it is not primarily a narrative or story. The eugenicist roots of arguments about the freedom to love and choose a mate are equally present in Gao Xian, Charlotte Perkins Gilman, Margaret Sanger, Pan Suiming, and Nancy Friday, in the 1920s and the present day. Rereading century-old social theory is a reminder of the degree to which the assumptions animating feminism today are indebted to the enabling premises of an earlier popular eugenics. Popular eugenics persists as part of the structure of assumptions that stabilize high psychoanalytic feminism and popular culture feminism, in China and elsewhere.[4]

This book has seven chapters. "History and Catachresis" notes the existence of some useful lacunae in the recent efflorescence of a new social history of Chinese women in tradition. It highlights my question, How can social historians avoid making women into either an effect of social history's own procedural norms (e.g., Woman is always the same anatomical, social scientific subject) or a symptom of disputes among men and therefore dismissable on the grounds of male bias? This is a question of historical method. Accordingly, the chapter is absorbed with how historiographic regimes at the same time enable and limit what we can say about Chinese women categorically, which is to say, "as women." It takes the position that the subjects of gender histories are themselves embedded in the history of thinking, and it follows that the new terms for women in Chinese are points of access into the material history of the past. That is, the chapter is not particularly concerned with theories of agency. Its purpose is to establish the value of historical catachresis in writing histories that are evidentiary and archival, and to take seriously the ontological claims the evidence itself conveys. The most detailed example of how this works is my description of the role of women in eugenic feminism in the 1920s.

Chapter 2, "Theorizing 'Women,'" introduces in broad strokes the social and ideological background of catachreses that I develop in close detail in chapter 3, "Foundations of Progressive Chinese Feminism," and chap-

ters 4 and 5. "Theorizing 'Women' " establishes the historicity of the catachreses for women in Chinese politics chronologically. The point of this
exercise is to establish that repeated ruptures (colonial modernity, social
revolution, what Lin Chun calls "revolutionary modernity," or socialist
modernization, and later, market socialism) of social, intellectual life over
the twentieth century in China set in motion irreversible, cumulative
changes in the dominant forms of gendered subjectivity.[5] New analytic
categories and new scientific ideas about the natural conditions of human
existence were as material to everyday experience among China's new educated elite as colonial architecture, the technology of mass media, modes
of social organization, and styles of political expression. Yet, because colonial modernity affected the language of mass communication, ideological
novelties arose in contemporary written Chinese.

In chapter 3, I spell out the foundations of modern Chinese feminism
established in the middle-brow periodical press in the 1920s. They are
foundational arguments because contemporary theoreticians of sexed subjectivity and women's liberation ratified their claims and repeatedly described the implications for past and future social organization that these
theories raised. In China, as elsewhere, the new disciplinary knowledge of
anthropology, sociology, ethnography, and patriarchal theory imparted a
eugenicist urgency to the liberation of women because social sciences
intimated that the health of the Chinese nation and culture rested in part on
making natural selection more natural. This theory made nüxing—a neologism or newly coined word and a historical catachresis—into an evolutionary agent of natural selection. However, in the formative 1920s and 1930s,
nüxing seemed destined to remain tangled in an irresolvable knot. Her
social options were increasing, but her moral capacity was not developing.
Briefly, social theorists argued that the indispensable key to the evolutionary health of Chinese biocultural life was nüxing; yet nüxing turned out to
be a foundationally deficient person.

Nüxing, a catachresis, the first central figure in Chinese progressive
feminist theories, met international standards of enlightened truth because it participated in the globalizing episteme of sexuality. It was not a
unique invention of Chinese colonial modernist cultural life. I press home
the fact that Žižek's riddle—what accounts for the universality of the subject women over and above the allegation of women's social multiplicity—
which he appears to assume can be resolved only in psychoanalytic cultural
criticism, can be addressed historically. Indeed, as I suggest in later chapters, psychoanalytic theories are part of the ideological structure that stabilizes modernist concepts of womanhood internationally. In ideological
terms, under conditions of imperialist globalization, a eugenicist notion of

women unfolded in many places historically around the same time. Colonial and later revolutionary modernity conditioned the historic subject of
women in the Chinese Enlightenment, as similar projects in eugenic, biol-
ogistic, scientistic, and racialized styles of thinking were conditioning
other feminist traditions elsewhere in the world.[6]

Although "the people do think," thinking is not self-authoring.[7] Indeed,
quite probably self-authoring—women write women, men write men—is a
comparatively rare event. Chapter 3 argues implicitly that even when the
writing in question is generically feminism, self-authority takes place only
in relation to larger regimes of social truth. As I demonstrate, what caught
the attention of Chinese male and female social theorists were social Darwinian popular notions about human breeding. That is probably because
natural selection theories all require women and men to "select" their own
partners in procreation. The subject nüxing that colonial theorists predicated in their work based its claim to truthfulness on the universality of
science. Sexual science theory bound women's liberation to national priorities and to chauvinist fantasies of self-strengthening. But it also opened
up a strong argument that women's bodies belong to women themselves
because nature not only made us that way, but nature prefers individual
choice over all other procreative methods. Pervasive social and political
conflict over the century helps to explain why Chinese feminism is sometimes dismissed as an artifact of men. In my view, however, male and
female theorists shared the same key terms because they all tended to
ground the future liberated Chinese woman in a discussion of eugenic
sexuality.[8]

This book's earlier chapters contain relatively few examples of women
thinking. Chapter 4, "Woman and Colonial Modernity in the Early Thought
of Ding Ling," and its companion, chapter 5, present a detailed consideration of Ding Ling (Jiang Bingzhi, 1904–1986), a central figure in the
intellectual history of Chinese revolutionary women who would hold the
stage intermittently for fifty years. Colonial modernity is a term I have
coined to help me rethink the conditions and the features of enlightened
thought in Chinese intellectual circles after the monarchy ended in 1911.[9]
Dialectically fusing "colonial" and "modernity" accents what I argue is
modernity's essential doubleness, for modernity and colonial or imperialist projects are in material fact inextricable. Categorically, modernity cannot overlook the colonial dissemination of commodities, political and military technologies, governmentality, juridical norms, scientific and social
theories, and modernist styles. Ding Ling was a Chinese Enlightened intellectual. Her earliest fiction expanded even as it repudiated core colonial
modernist eugenic assumptions, including elements of progressive femi-

nism. Her creative fiction held up to scrutiny the inability of nüxing—feminism is a metonymy of Reason for Ding Ling—to meet the test of colonial modern Enlightenment adequacy.

Chapter 5, "Women under Maoist Nationalism in the Thought of Ding Ling," extends this line of argument. It proposes that the emerging framework of theoretical Maoism offered enlightened feminism a second chance. It enabled Ding Ling and other feminist communists to reconsider what the subject of feminism would be and how they, as agents of the revolutionary state, would pose the question of Enlightenment in a vast and war-weary rural environment. Colonial modernity to modern Maoist revolutionary mobilization, sexed subject women to the Maoist revolutionary collectivity and marriage to the state—what is remarkable about Ding Ling's long sojourn is the persistent way the question of women in enlightened thought continually surfaced for her even in the most painful circumstances. Ding Ling has reappeared on the platform of feminist theory in the People's Republic recently. This time however she is a mythic figure, said to embody rationalist principles first enunciated in Chinese progressive feminism in the 1930s.

"Socialist Modernization and the Market Feminism of Li Xiaojiang," chapter 6, examines the reinvention of enlightened Chinese feminism in the years right after the end of the Maoist government. Conditions for feminist criticism were very different in 1985 from what they had been in 1925 and 1945. Ending economic autarky not only reconfigured Chinese socialist development strategies, it also witnessed the revival of the university and the academic disciplines of sociology, anthropology, history, political science, and literary criticism. China's Enlightenment heritage of scholarship reestablished the ground for its institutional prerogatives. And academic restoration set the stage for another feminist resurgence as an experienced, politically savvy cohort of educated female citizens noted with growing alarm the state's withdrawal from affirmative action policies and the general disintegration of the Maoist public sphere. Writing directly on Enlightenment thematics in a feminist counterpoint of Li Zehou and Liu Zaifu (the era's preeminent post-Mao Marxist fundamentalists), Li Xiaojiang, the primary subject of this chapter, addressed a familiar question. She asked again, as theorists for fifty years had been asking, What is the proper subject of Chinese feminism?

The book's final chapter, "Dai Jinhua, Globalization, and 1990s Poststructuralist Feminism," addresses feminist theory in the despairing neoliberalism of the 1990s. In this discussion, which focuses on Dai Jinhua's theoretical project, I argue that global neoliberalism had opened up for feminist thought in China, as elsewhere, a new kind of internationalism and a new effort to square the circle of Enlightenment feminism. Where Li Xiaojiang had lashed out at the scandal of Reason for gendering humanity as masculine and had argued for a feminine subject of new Enlightenment feminism, Dai, who works at the intersection of psychoanalysis and history, looks toward the future. She anticipates, as others had before her, a future for a proper subject of women. Doubtless, in this book Dai is the thinker who best illustrates the feminist penchant for thinking in the future anterior, projecting what women will have been in a bleak past and her emergence as a whole subject in a future that has yet to appear. Certainly Dai's work illustrates the potential that the future anterior holds for realizing the constraints in our own thinking, for Dai is our contemporary. Still, my own position, a subtheme in each of the studies in this book, suggests that future anteriority has been a constituent of enlightened feminism throughout the century.

Part of the task of these four later chapters is to pose individual feminist theorists in agonistic relation to their moment's conventional beliefs about gendered humanity. The figures whose efforts I follow so carefully do not form a teleology and do not refer back to each other in a direct chain linking theorist to theorist. Quite the contrary, I have endeavored to situate each thinker in her moment of invention, unencumbered by the past or, perhaps more accurately, presuming a usable past and present that allow her a sense of futurity and possibility. Twentieth-century social and intellectual revolutions in China have rocked conventional gendered norms not once but many times. The discontinuous engagement of feminist thinkers with the project of women's emancipation illustrates my point that history is not so much continuous as cumulative. It also suggests that as the heterogeneous event that is women coalesces into a norm, it works ideologically as truism, as well as truth.

I am drawn to such remarkable moments when the heterogeneity at the moment of thinking is momentarily obviated in a great ideological or discursive move that reimposes what will henceforth be natural, establishes through some event or act a new, intransigent line of power. As I seek to show, that event comes about in many ways. The 1920s and early 1930s established the eugenic truth of evolutionary sexuality. The communist feminism of rural revolutionary and state power normalized a state of injury and created identity in the processes of mobilization. The new Enlightenment cultural fevers of the 1980s resulted in an eroticized, commodified truth of women in sexual terms. And so on. Such moments of consolidation come with the naturalization of a new logic. These can be effected when another truthful knowledge is secured or a new lexicon or dictionary holds out, again, the promise of translatability; it comes with the satisfaction of knowing that a question posed at the horizon of history has finally been exhausted. Once stability and clarity are achieved, the game is over. That is the historical moment that, in all its repetition, transfixes me.

Why? Specifically, because throughout the history of twentieth-century Chinese feminism (and no doubt other national feminisms as well) women who chose to occupy the newly naturalized category women have stepped into the arena. There they have worked the constraints and enabling conditions of the nationalized, feminist theoretical tradition. As I show most carefully in the case of Ding Ling, engagement with fixity after a time of reflexive heterogeneity unfolds as a wager of disappointment and hope. The hope is that the future will be an equitable one. Disappointments come in various forms. But hopes raised or hopes dashed, each of these feminist female thinkers maximally engages with the preconditions and presuppositions current at her moment. Particularly Ding Ling's life of writing illustrates how this process, which I call historical investiture, works. The core of progressive Chinese feminism is eugenics. Ding Ling's point, particularly in her initial gamble, appears to have been that there are limitations on a subjectivity rooted in eugenic rights, that is, the right to choose a sexual partner, a right vested in invisible, natural forces of evolutionary genetic selection. I suggest that she came to the early conclusion that the will of women and the Reason of natural law did not necessarily coincide. This insight appears to have instigated her to rethink the grounds of female subjectivity. But even in doing that, even in retracting certain parts of the commitment to "bourgeois womanhood," Ding Ling and her cohort by and large did accept the singularity of women as a universal subject. They were invested even as they questioned the terms of the present.

Why the foundationally deficient subject of women is repeatedly rediscovered is due in no small part to the fact that it is an irreplaceable platform. Even in its most objectionable forms, women gives Li and Dai, like Ding Ling, Gao Xian, Zhou Jianren, Se Lu, and others, a way to advocate for women. The adulterated quality of feminism's subject, women, is, as Wendy Brown and other feminist critics have pointed out, a problem that is common to political theories that are rooted in an identity. Progressive Chinese feminism is a historically novel predicate. Its catachrestic roots and the leverage it provides to theorists who discover and resurrect it out of the rubble of the past are testimony to its discontinuous persistence and continuing usefulness.[10]

Investiture, or the process of adopting the naturalized subject of universal women, links feminist thinkers to what Peter Osborne calls a "real abstraction" and Alain Badiou, an event. The advent of woman is a world-historical event in enlightened and revolutionary thought. The process of becoming invested in the historical event of women is, as many detailed histories have established over the years, part of the colonial, semicolonial, and modern colonial developmental processes. Lata Mani's pathbreaking study of colonial India, Laura Engelstein's history of reform liberalism in modern fin de siècle Russia, Philip Corrigan and Derek Sayer's early analysis of the English cultural revolution and its reliance on the subject women, and Sumiko Otsubo's history of colonial Japanese eugenics all follow lines parallel to those I trace in the final four chapters of this book. And this is only a sample of what is now available to nonspecialists. Each of these monographs, except Engelstein's of course, concerns the world-historical subject women and the investiture of women in the colonial modernist state revolutions of emergent capitalist state systems.[11]

Why write history this way? Even despite the fragility of the conventions of historical writing, historiographically reliable feminist historical writing has to struggle to keep the universal modernist category of women off-balance. Most gender historians and feminist critics now accept the argument that woman cannot be a stable category. But doing it, actually writing destabilized histories, is much harder than restating the comfortable truism that stable subjects are "essence" and thus by definition not really historical. Ever mindful of its doubled quality—History is always a part of history; history's subjects are always stabilized elements in contemporary ideologies—history writing actually has to struggle very hard to maintain instability. It is not easy to decline to know what a woman is before you start writing about women. As women has become, globally speaking, a universal truth of social science, an event or "real abstraction," writing feminist history means showing in detail how the norm of women is imposed, escaped, superimposed, displaced, reimposed, or perhaps exhausted. History, more than other ways of thinking about modern women, offers the possibility of working out the particular contingencies in play at each advent of women. Perhaps this is an aspect of what feminists Doria Cherifati-Merabtine and Madhu Dubey term "instigating and containing access to modernity."[12] Maybe one job for feminist history can be tracking down how the universal subject women predicated in dis/enabling modern humanism could possibly be thought to its limits.[13]

I hope this book will find several kinds of readers. It was written primarily for scholars who also confront the question of thinking about the question of women in feminism. These include readers who know a lot about China and feminist scholars working completely outside a specialization in China studies. My hope is that both communities of scholars will find my argument about global or international feminism another provocation for adjusting historical understanding of the ways feminism, colonialism, and globalization are linked. Particularly in national feminist traditions like those of Britain, France, Japan, and the United States, which were consolidated during each nation's imperialist project, this can be an awkward and prolonged process. For readers who may have little stake in the details of Chinese revolutionary history, I hope the evidence presented inspires more caution about claiming what is and is not "universal." For historians and colleagues in Chinese history, I hope my analysis of the multiple flowerings of the national feminism becomes an instigation for adjusting our general understanding of the relation of social change and gender politics. My stake is with strands in so-called feminist theory. This project may choose to read my study as a criticism of its increasingly exhausted reliance on psychoanalytic notions of desire and the alleged risk of essence.[14]

Enlightenment has had to figure out ways of negotiating its colonial heritage. In our time, this task has fallen largely to literary theorists. Much of their work is highly nuanced and has focused discussion on femininity and masculinity, eroticism, and desire and its fulfillment on literary representation and critical traditions. But as I read through various kinds of literary history over the last few years I have come to the position that feminism, in this case Chinese feminism, is not that abstract or amorphous. It also does not appear, in my reading, to be the effect of invisible desire working itself through a literary imagination. I make the case here that a simpler way to grasp the course of feminism is to read the ways it was and continues to be explicitly thought about. Reason's handmaiden, feminism, has made its case persistently, so persistently that it is an element of enlightened modernities virtually everywhere. A second common way of thinking about the global reach of enlightened colonial modernist ideas like feminism has been through a translation paradigm.[15] My stake is more modest and probably grosser. It rests on a notion of theory that is inextricably rooted in the abstract speculation of the people about whom I am writing. For me, the rationalist arguments that appear in translated documents are more significant than the processes of translation as such. In the end, it is the translation that remains.

Yet this book falls well within problematics that literature studies and translation studies have raised. That is one reason I find the 1928 image of the skull and candle that appears on the cover of Yi Jiayue and Luo Dunwei's The Chinese Family Question to be so emblematic.[16] Yi's blazing flame of the candle of Enlightenment sits on an inconsolably anxious skull. The candle is a sign of light and the absence of light. It signifies the stark contrasts that invest enlightened thinking with its particular intensity. Yi Jiayue was a male feminist sociologist. His work and this image are all about the contrast of a feudal family in historical eclipse and the dawning of the modern, gendered, individualized person. Yi's emblem hints at the quality of the repetitiveness that Simone de Beauvoir and Li Xiaojiang both note are built into feminisms, because to be useful at all, feminism must remain in thrall to arguments that are necessarily predicated on the secondariness and deficiency of women. No less than three formal moments of Chinese Enlightenment thinking mark the era covered in this genealogical history of the subject of women in Chinese feminism. Each time the question of Enlightenment is raised, a similar set of questions have unfolded: Where in "Chinese tradition" were women before modernity? How will Chinese women ever secure equal social standing with Chinese men? Do the deficiencies built into Chinese women by "tradition" still threaten the "modern" in women? Is feminism Western? What would a female enlightened Chinese subject look like?

Most of the people who drew sustenance from icons like this candle and skull are dead now. Vested in an eighty-year-old drawing, as in any physical residue of the way people once were, is a reminder of the persistence of the project and, because it has yet to end, of feminism's necessarily repetitive quality. The best story is no doubt not the unfolding of national traditions of thinking about women's liberation, though that is certainly a moving and important narrative. Another history is there to be told. It is about the specific and singular knowledge of thinkers who repeatedly forwarded the possibilities of modernist subjectivity through the constraints and enabling practices of feminist Enlightenment. Male and female feminist thinkers keep at the patient work of disenabling the conditions that make the questions When is Enlightenment? and When is liberation? necessary to go on asking.

There is a final point I want to make about Enlightenment. Yi Jiayue and Luo Dunwei's skull and candle is a symbol of the renewal of life. But it signals, maybe a bit ominously, the priorities that theorists tend to accord to intellect. This book is necessarily all about thinking. The archive that it reads consists of fiction, ideology, literary criticism, policy pronouncement, and political theory. As the skull-and-candle image suggests, historians of Enlightenment will probably always prefer to follow the line of abstract reason in search of signs of progress. How else can an emancipatory discourse satisfactorily measure degrees of emancipation? But it is important to keep in mind that human life passes through the bodies of women, not the skulls of men or even the skulls of women. This much is a natural as well as an ideological fact. The omnipresence of death and loss in the eras of imperialism, anti-imperialist and colonial wars, civil and politically inspired conflict, revolutionary transformation and postrevolutionary regrets underscores the pathos of an enlightenment sought outside the living body. This is also where twentieth-century feminism collides with eugenicist evolutionary sociology. Rationales for the emancipation of women from compulsory reproduction and socially enforced inferiority probably rest as much on dogma of race purity as on abstract ideas about enlightened reason. The successes of national feminisms owe as much to the eugenic requirement that women choose their own mates in the struggle of the fittest as it does to enlightened thinking about citizenship, suffrage, modernity, and human rights. If Enlightenment is ever superseded in feminism, the event will coincide with the declining potency of disembodied iconography that is so moving on the fading cover of a brave, old book.

What feminism definitively is I have infinitely deferred addressing. Rather than defining it categorically, I have sought to develop a descriptive method that portrays how, in specific archives, there has regularly arisen a discontinuous search for justice and the powers of self-representation. That is why it seems so ill-advised to claim feminism for the putative West. If feminism is just a word in North American English (a very recent one, according to Nancy Cott) for a much longer effort to put sexual difference and gendered inequality at the center of social theory, then feminism is itself catachristic, a concept in search of an adequate referent. Feminism and its subjects offer access points that critical theorists use to show how the way we think reinforces gendered inequality. And so, to discontinuous accumulation it is necessary to add the fact that feminism, understood as the record of thinking about what a truly just society will look like, has been from the start a shared resource and will continue to be a treasure trove of specific attempts until the end is achieved.

Once enlightened feminism is recognized to be international, then its depth and multiplicity become more clear. It is significant that the historical flexibility of colloquial Chinese has allowed for so many ways to phrase the name feminism or the movement to center female subjects. To this very day the process of reworking terms for feminism are part of feminist practice in Sinophone criticism. This suggests, as I have tried to show, that modern Chinese intellectual history, represented here in a study of Chinese feminism, is not a derivative discourse. The places of overlap, as I show in the case particularly of *écriture féminine*, suggest that origin is always aspecific and diffused; these debates are not of the West, but rather are debates undertaken now in the disintegrating "West" and other places about globalized world problems from specific perspectives and locations.

# 1 History and Catachresis

A concept-metaphor without an adequate referent is a catachresis.
GAYATRI CHAKRAVORTY SPIVAK, *Outside in the Teaching Machine*

The catachresis of women in modern Chinese intellectual history is the primary subject of this book. Analytic and descriptive material presented in this chapter sets the stage for arguments that will emerge in later ones. In reworking a literary philosopher's insight about metaphors and catachreses, I am looking for ways to decode the historical contents that are occulted in the kinds of categorical or proper nouns that historians routinely encounter when we read documents naïvely, closely, or "carefully."[1] There are consequently two major stakes in this chapter. The first is the question. What is the subject in a history of women? "women," as it is currently used in Chinese social theory, is an invention of the 1920s and 1930s, an era I define in later chapters as colonial modernity. Because most historians are sensitive to questions of anachronism and because women (like men) is always a categorical term, not a descriptor or social-cultural signifier of biological reality, the stake posed in the question What is the subject in a history of women? concerns how norms or categories are formed and stabilized. The problem of anachronism is most acute here. The second stake follows directly from the question of social history methods and concerns the status of signifiers. Currently, a rather common position in China studies is that neologisms are linguistic signs, rather than, as I contend throughout this study, access points into the "material" history of an era and consequently into the question of how the name of women itself becomes a historical artifact.[2] But if neologisms are entry points into social norms, how does the catachresis women work? How could writing about historical catachresis sidestep anachronistic assumptions about sexed subjectivity?

## The Future Anterior

Histories written in the present or simple past tense often claim to "ground themselves on the truth of women" precisely when they project contemporary beliefs about women's nature into the past.[3] They make a claim about women's reality or women's experience across time, place, modes of production, social relations of production, cognitive mapping, ideological conditions, and so on. They define what women are (e.g., procreative social beings) and then reassert this claim on the basis of evidence selected to support their initial generalization. This has the desired effect of demonstrating how women's work, ideologies, bodies, or desires are socially reproduced. Once a historian presumes that "women" are "in a society," a related claim becomes reasonable: that people in the past instantiated or embodied their own present and that their motives for action can be understood if we examine their social context with sufficient care. The authors of this kind of history presume that the subject represents the past because she was in it and also that the past explains the subject because she was in it. The conjecture that those who preceded us knew where in human time they were located when they acted historically is, I suggest, a potentially disabling inference that sometimes arises out of this general position. As is the assumption that past, present, and future form a stable sequence, either in abstract time or in the consciousness of historical actors, and the view that women is a definable, knowable category.

A history written to highlight future anteriority (as this one is) is not particularly concerned with what women *are*, that is, what women *must have been before, given what women really are* (e.g., agents of social reproduction).[4] Nor is it concerned with speculating about what women as a collectivity will be once patriarchy is abolished. Emphasizing future anteriority shifts attention away from ideal typical or representative women per se to writing and thinking focused on decoding women and their proposed future role. It takes less seriously the content of general claims and more seriously the politics of claiming. Potentially, this shift of emphasis adds flexibility and usefulness to investigations because it allows feminist scholars and advocates to identify what might have been the stakes in an immediate or singular moment. What ideologies condition the thinkable or writable and the real effect that written expression has on the environment are important concerns, too, but this book underscores the acts of invention. It is particularly interested in the ways that thinking infuses political events and may indeed constitute an event in itself.

Diane Elam's insight is that feminist history written in the future anterior mode would characteristically abjure or decline to use fixed definitions.

The work of feminist psychoanalytic theoreticians like Elam, Dai Jinhua, and Drucilla Cornell reinforce the suggestion that using future anteriority is a way of placing emphasis on the temporal heterogeneity of the present (how categorical or imperative knowledge about women emerges out of this heterogeneous unclarity is a more historical question). What they offer to methods of writing feminist histories is useful because although such studies must meet the criteria of materialist history writing (evidence, subject, contingency, periodization, specificity, etc.), they would justify declining to "claim to know in advance what it is women can do and be."[5] They would accept and even stress the value of doubting our own ability ever to know definitively what the limits of women's being are (and thus were and will be). Openness to inchoate or differently structured time suggests that history may accurately be written even in the absence of transhistorical theories about what women and men *are* or *were*. A history written in the future anterior, in other words, would not simply note the existence of a future encoded in every present, but would focus particularly on the capacity of this kind of present imagining to upset the sequence of past-present-future. Subjectivity, the province of feminism, is shaped in heterogeneous time.

For Elam, undecidability has the political effect of keeping open the category of woman or women to new strategies and subject forms. For me, Elam's insight offers a chance to highlight the lack of fit between the people and their times. It puts the premium on ways people are misaligned with their times, particularly when they are writing. Theorists, people whose writing is intended to make general claims, do not reflect or even represent their times so much as misread messages from the past, rethink received opinion, forget, embrace, accidentally contribute to it, and send messages from now toward the future. The processes of thinking and writing may or may not profoundly alter given conditions, but they are always aspects of a now. Future anteriority in history narratives puts a premium on this irrepressible force of thinking, where indecidability is most pronounced, and soft-pedals or questions the assumption of continuity in time.[6]

Rebuffing the temptation to know things in general about women therefore becomes a precondition for accuracy in history writing. Relieved of the need to specify or generalize in a universalizing or historicist fashion about what women really is, the problem of anachronism is less pressing (this does not affect the subject's own firm beliefs about what women really are). I am not arguing here for a return to empiricist history as a route around the problem of anachronism in feminist social science. The questions of how (or even whether) in the past women were collectively a biosocial entity or statistical norm (both modernist categories) or whether other, not modern collective nouns and governing ideologies were primary, becomes a feasible (rather than simply a theoretical) question to ask the historical evidence to answer. This leaves as an open question what sort of knowledge and experiences for and of women might appear in the future or, indeed, have appeared in the past. Much of this basic positioning will already be familiar to historians. What I am proposing is more like a shift of emphasis. Getting serious about future anteriority would, in other words, build into history writing itself a demand to retain contingency at the center of every description, every social category or interpretation.

In addition to its ability to reconsider the problems of anachronism and category, writing with an accent on futurity rather than continuity also helps in thinking about larger social events, such as women's movements. Women is often considered a special case because it is held to be at once both trenchant social fact and a political rallying point, the one politically irreplaceable, transhistorical feminine subject. However, as Rosemary Hennessy has definitively pointed out, feminism is not exclusively a project of representation. It should not become preoccupied with the politics of accurate representation. This is not only because the problem of anachronism defeats the quixotic goals of representation. For Hennessy, it is primarily because feminism's main task is forming political collectivities for future action.[7]

Presumption of the stability of women has led some social science writing about the Chinese women's movement to see the women's movement, modern Chinese women, or Chinese feminism as self-authored. Women and their movement are said to have awakened during the May Fourth era (1919–1927), of cultural revolution, declined under socialist patriarchy, and then revived in the post-Mao market economy.[8] Recast to take advantage of a more complex temporality, the question would become: How did this women's movement come to define its subject? "Women's liberation movement" would therefore be considered in more relational terms, contingent on complex relations with peoples, sexes, and politics other than itself.[9] Far from reducing a social movement's capacity to address injustice, however, disconnecting the subject women from political movements would actually allow the political question of Who is a woman? to be posed, as chapters 4 and 5 of this study demonstrate in particular detail. So, if we are able to disaggregate women because we do not know in advance what women is and we do not presume that women's movements simply represent the interests of women, other options are more feasible. It becomes easier to ask who the agents or authors of the women's movement were (as they cannot be presumed to be women) and whether feminism is really just "the thinking of women."[10]

This is, of course, not a book about social movements. It is a book about various cohorts of highly politicized people who claimed to know the truth of women. It carefully reads the theories of the feminists, Marxists, Maoists, social scientists, ideologists, fiction writers, Communist revolutionaries, and others who universalized the modern subject of women in revolutionary thinking, policy, and political mobilization during the twentieth century. The questions that such people—theorists and intellectuals, for the most part—raised suggests that the subjects women and women's movement are like ensembles or constellations, contingent entities formed in relations of "irreducible difference," in which a moment or term "inscribes the other in itself and is inscribed by the other outside of itself."[11] But what particularly concerns me in this study is that through their thinking, politicized intellectuals established women as a transparent category of knowledge. In the complex theories of Chinese progressive feminism and its feminist critics we see thinkers and policy analysis creating a valuable and unprecedented way to understand, and therefore to transform, social life. It is also in their theoretical work, which is aimed explicitly at the future of their present (and often as rooted in their analyses of the past), that future anteriority becomes transparently obvious.

## "Women" in Traditional China

If future anteriority is one way of stabilizing in historical time the volatility of the people who did the thinking, it is important to ask what conditioned them: What forces larger than consciousness acted on them? What sorts of assumptions did they make about past and future in their own uncertain presents? Over the past decade, new social history studies in the U.S.-dominated China field have established a vision or understanding of the general life conditions, life experiences, and expectations of elite Chinese women in core areas of the Yangtze River valley. A descriptive summary of these generalizations shows how the new social historians have displaced the earlier idea that Chinese women were condemned to lives of universal, permanent degradation. The new historiography of women centers on women of the gentry or shi da fu class, many of whom were literate. Few of the secondary sources I draw on for this summary suggest that the Song subject women in the social elite was distinct from the women of contemporary times. Indeed, some historians speculate openly that because they are themselves women and their subjects of concern are women, an intuitive bond exists that strengthens the analysis. I take up the implications of this assumption in the section following this one.[12]

Elite Song dynasty (960–1279) families grew up alongside and then superseded the aristocratic class of the Tang dynasty (617–907). Patricia Ebrey's pioneering work in the new social history of Chinese women clarified how the sexual division of labor contributed to the ascendancy of the new landed gentry class. The Tang aristocracy owed its entrenched position to its elaborate written pedigrees, preeminence on the national scale, and its adeptness at court politics. By contrast, the power of the new Song elites was the effect of their successes in the institutionalized government examination system (closed to women), competitive government office holding, and property ownership. Legal codes and other evidence in data on marriage politics suggest that Song protogentry elites were already vesting their daughters with substantial dowry wealth. In the property exchanges characterizing the emerging new-style gentry marriage practices, the husband's family provided bridal gifts to the bride and her relatives, and the bride's family, in turn, reinvested the bridal wealth (adding some of its own) into the daughter who was being exchanged. The exchange and consolidation of wealth as dowry heightened competition for daughters among elite families because all families sought useful political connections by all means possible. The parents of daughters who brought relatively larger portions of wealth from the natal family into marital family got, in exchange for their investment, larger, more powerful networks. Marriage politics was an avenue for raising the class standing of the bride's natal family.

Daughters consequently offered their own parents a host of opportunities to advance in all the arenas where gentry power really counted. Clear property law on the books regulated the exchange of daughters as wives (there also existed a large commercial market for buying and selling female concubines, servants, and slaves). Laws suggested adjudication of dowry claims and directly stipulated that brides would control their own wealth. According to Song law, daughters could legally inherit property from their father when the father had no sons, and daughters could be married uxorilocally, which is to say that the daughter could bring her husband into her father's family rather than being herself transferred to the family of her husband. Though this is also the era when elites began to use footbinding as a means to demarcate gentry families from mean or commoner families, men in the elite family were monogamous by law. Other household women, concubines, and slaves acquired for husbands had secondary ritual and economic status in relation to wives.[13]

Thus, some Song wives had advantages that other women (elites and subelites) did not have in the period of gentry class dominance that extended through the nineteenth century. Empowered Song gentry wives not only exercised control over agnatic property and retained rights to their own bridal wealth; they expected to undertake gendered, productive labor. Patricia Ebrey and Francesca Bray argue in the spirit of Jack Goody and F. Engels that in the Song period, high social status and property claims correlated. Elite female mothering skills (including responsibility to edu-cate children in basic literacy), productive labor as weavers and household and property managers, and key strategizing in the domain of marriage politics were all rewarded. Apparently, labor gendered as the responsibility of females in elite families had a high quotient of state-enforced ideologi-cal content, too. Until the middle of the sixteenth century, a state decree declaring that "men till [the land], women weave [the cloth]" maintained that noncommodified, domestic weaving for family consumption and cloth commodities produced in the commercial textile industry for the general market were separate.[14] Elite women profited from the overall positive valuation and necessity of textile work in the home, and subelite women benefited because their primary work was a prized form of labor. But all female kinfolk, regardless of rank or status or family resources, contributed weaving labor to the domestic economy.[15]

None of the positive conditions described above for female elites or subelites survived the Song dynasty, however. Using a sex or gender bi-morphic lens, prominent scholars in the new Chinese women's history are now reperiodizing the gentry era. They divide the so-called late imperial era of gentry class domination, the Ming (1386–1644) and Qing (1644–1911) eras, into two parts that do not correspond to either traditional histo-riographic or dynastic cycles. In this period, comprising the last decades of the sixteenth and the so-called long seventeenth century, powerful gentry families rose to dominate national culture and politics from a power base in the Jiangnan region of the country. Jiangnan is the name given to the region south of the Yangtze River, particularly southern Jiangsu province. The powerful Jiangnan gentry engineered their political ascent through a combination of examination success, landholding patterns, commercial-economic skills, and hegemony in the cultural spheres. A style of gentry, homosocial, domestic life consequently arose which had never existed before. Dorothy Ko, a pioneering historian of gentry women's lives and agency, holds that a so-called *guixiu* culture (literally, genteel young cloistered woman, more generally female upper-class gentility) took shape because of widespread commercialization of literacy in this era, which made feasible cultural niche marketing to cloistered women, the dissemi-nation of female- as well as male-authored popular books and poetry, and three practices that came specifically to define genteel womanhood: foot-binding of young girls, extremely high literacy among elite women, and strict female seclusion.

Thus, according to Ko, literate, cloistered female life practices and indi-vidual women themselves (though very, very few of them) entered the late Ming "public sphere" indirectly in several ways. Poetry and criticism emerging from the secluded studios of guixiu writers became commodities, which circulated locally and in some cases nationally, bringing great esteem to their families. Remarkably, wives, daughters, and courtesans who engaged in literary competition laid claim to one of the most significant debates in the contemporary intellectual agenda, which concerned the place of qing or human sentiment in social and cultural affairs. In another significant incursion into the public sphere, a tiny, important minority of superbly literate women established learned networks of their own; their parallel, female-only (as opposed to male-only) scholarly circles met regularly for rarified social exchange and widely reported literary pleasures. Wives and daughters were not the only female practitioners of the high arts, the new social historians argue. Female artistry also flowered in the late Ming era in courtesan culture. In the seventeenth century a vast marketing mechanism turned out women rigorously trained in elite gentle arts and made prostituted girls into skilled, sometimes brilliant and widely touted performers for entertaining at scholarly official gatherings. Ko argues that courtesans allowed what in practice was a functional division of spheres—erotic and domestic—to operate smoothly. It was far from rare that courtesans formed alliances with elite women, for wife and courtesan tended to share a similarly high degree of literary skill. This institutionalization of courtesan culture and the courtesan-wife relation apparently survived the immediate fall of the Ming dynasty but faded as the Qing authorities took over the reins of state power.

The new historiography of Chinese women clarifies a second era of gentry women's history, the High Qing or long eighteenth century. This period saw a striking change in elite women's lives as a consequence of the consolidation of the new state taxation schemes and the gentry's post-Ming strategy of retrenchment around family lineages (see below). A so-called high-level equilibrium trap emerged that balanced widespread female infanticide among the general population against an equally intense hypergamy, as the general shortage of women produced a situation where females in most strata were more likely to marry up the status hierarchy than down it.[16] Hypergamy, not surprisingly, did not interrupt the trend toward increasingly strict practices of sex seclusion. No longer the bearers of property themselves, even elite women appear to have lost all legal claim to property ownership. Many (although not all) scholars of this period concur that what one historian has called "Confucian ritualism" eroded the power of law per se and augmented the powers of patriarchal precedent or lineage codes in the great families of the Jiangnan region. As Susan Mann has established, this era also saw a century-long querelle des femmes accompanying the eighteenth-century classical revival of Confucian scholarship.[17]

Increasingly, family standing in the gentry class rested on ritual social practices that mushroomed throughout the era in scope and baroque social semiotics. The effect, Mann's pioneering scholarship demonstrates, was that elite wives did shoulder heavy household responsibilities, while at the same time the marriage market demanded a degree of female literacy so extreme that it made the burden of household management deeply frustrating to wives. Male and, indirectly, female literati debated the significance of this tension and its implications for women generally. That a dispute over the degree of education appropriate for women infiltrated national literati circles was to some degree a result of the efforts that educated women bearing the dual burden of elite housewifery themselves pursued. Such women seized on poetry as their vehicle of expression. Never challenging the conditions of their oppression, always endorsing the norms of the day, female literati reencoded poetry, making poesis a genteel preserve of the guixiu or wife and daughter. Scholarly house women critically edited vast compendia of women's poetry and wrote contributions to the poetic canon themselves. Wives used poetics to distinguish themselves from subaltern women and even their own husbands. Qing wives also used their literacy to discipline and disparage the courtesan culture. Guixiu literacy, according to this line of argument, augmented the power of wives because it gave them the literary means to reprimand husbands' erotic partners while showing up the husband in a veiled literary competition.[18]

## The Limits of Social History

Emma Teng has argued that this richly drawn new historiography of women raises the question of social history's epistemological conservatism.[19] Largely social historians by training, historians of China tend to draw a one-to-one correlation between the truths of society in the past and coded cultural representations of historical evidence. By and large, we have not considered as germane to our work the historicity of category itself. Geoff Eley criticizes this tendency in social history. In what he calls the "correspondence theory of truth," historians presume that the knowable past can be distinguished from what Eley calls "the forms of documentary representation, conceptual and political appropriations, and historiographical discourses that construct them." He recommends inverting our assumptions: Why not accept history as the "site of difference, a context of deconstruction," and compel ourselves to acknowledge the historicity of the category of "the social" in the social sciences, before we assume the stability of a context called "society"? The history of social forms must be written alongside the history of categories. What Eley is objecting to is not the use of categories like "worker" and "women," but the tendency among historians to not trace modernist categories like women and worker and to not consider how historiographic categories of analysis are necessarily also historical formations.[20]

Paul Rouzer raised this exact point in his laudatory review of Ellen Widmer and Kang-I Sun Chang's innovating anthology *Writing Women in Late Imperial China*. The position he takes is a good illustration of the alternative vision beginning to link cultural studies and historians in the China fields. Rouzer draws attention to a difference he sees between contemporary scholars' important discovery of the historical contours of a real event (e.g., seventeenth-century elite culture's ideological apotheosis of the female author) and the same contemporary scholars' universalist assumption that "woman as such" connects the past and the present together seamlessly:

> Educated women and men of the late Ming [late sixteenth, early seventeenth century] constructed "women's writing" as a category of analysis; many outstanding writers and anthologists, female and male, privileged "female authorship" and created an explicit ideology of the female writer. If this defines the parameters of our own discussions in the early stages of our research, then scholars should turn next to tracing the origins of this ideology and to see how it intersects with other cultural and social conditions and demands. Why would Ming writers start paying attention to women's writing, and seek to preserve it? How does one define "woman," let alone "woman writer," in the seventeenth century?[21]

Rouzer argues that the problem of anachronism in our current historiography is potentially crippling. He cites Joan Scott to the effect that even innovating scholarship tends to fall back on the presumption that Women is a stable category. This, Rouzer believes, obscures what is most significant historically: the unquestioned certainties or enabling assumptions that motivated such people in the past to write, to commit their ideas to paper in the first place. In Rouzer's and Teng's view as specialist researchers, seventeenth-century documentary evidence from the Jiangnan region does harbor a singular or characteristic female subject. But Rouzer is concerned that even as social historians have made the previously occulted lives of the literate gentry woman visible, the singularity of the category has been obscured.

But if the question of historical categories is endemic to social history, what exactly is it in the "social" that is making problems? To begin addressing this question, I look at three social history models: commercialization or modernization theory, ritual or social control, and a social class analytic.

suggest that where the new social history of women might be challenged for its apotheosis of women, canonical positions in social history that do not focus on this very subject tend to err in a different direction. Ko, Mann, Bray, Ebrey, and others may avoid the question of social-idealogical category but in the absence of this focus, society trumps women. Women become an affect of deeper historical processes. Obviously, I am staging a contradiction. My point is that even the best social history rests on anachronism to some degree. New women's history may present an ultrastable subject of women. But social history creates female subjects by default. The historical catachresis as a conceptualization of immediate social experience may help to resolve this impasse.

William Rowe's essay, "Women and the Family in Mid-Qing Social Thought," for instance, was primarily concerned with what he argued was "an unprecedentedly articulated debate within the [late imperial Chinese] elite over questions relating to women and the family." He is referring to the querelle des femmes that Mann's work has placed at the center of the new social history of Chinese women. Mann and others propose that the querelle des femmes fundamentally concerned questions about the visibility of women in the public sphere. They believe this visibility is linked to the agency of literate women. In Rowe's view, elite concern over women's education in ritual, or *lijiao*, was just one offshoot or effect of what he calls the almost cultural revolution of the late Ming dynasty. His primary interest is the almost revolution. Concurring with the new historiography of women at many points, he also argues that although the sixteenth-century commercial revolution upset an even earlier traditional gender hierarchy, it was not female agency or self-authoring that transformed gender relations. Rather, gender roles were transformed by a market economy and the commercialization of society in the Jiangnan region, where the almost cultural revolution occurred. Progressive change—transvalued human emotions, altered sexual behavior, and transformed family life—came about through "commercialization."[22]

Rowe's brief essay is not primarily concerned with either the conditions for the emergence of women as a subject or the agency of women in the era of Chen Hongmou (1696–1771). Chen was a Confucian state administrator whom Rowe employs as a prism for illuminating eighteenth-century Jiangnan society. But Rowe does weigh in on the question of women. He makes the explicit argument that not only in China but also in Europe, the subject women is historically stable, transparent, universal, and even congruent because the history of Europe and the history of China are on a parallel course from tradition to early modern consciousness and directly into modernity. He looks to the work of social historians Philippe Ariès and

Joan Kelly to make his case. This historic move enables all of the progressive ideals that Rowe attributes to Chen Hongmou: his preference for egalitarian families, approval of rising female literacy and companionate marriage, advocacy of women's participation in the public sphere, positive valuation of human sentiment, and a more universal and less parochial outlook. These are indexed to Rowe's assumption that women, or womanhood, like the experience of men and manhood, is translatable across time and space. Furthermore, Rowe interprets lijiao (ritual politesse; literally, "doctrine of ritual") exactly as many theorists in the early twentieth century in China's colonial modern sector did, to be the cultural practice of role playing. Below, I cite Rowe's analysis of lijiao for three reasons: it is a very good introduction to elite social practices; it illustrates how a social history absent an adequate category for women will tend to create one by default; and because I suggest an alternate reading in chapter 2.

Chen, Rowe argues, particularly emphasized the ancient practice of *fen*, or "social role." Fen are normative strategies proscribing relational behaviors (e.g., the Three Bonds connecting ruler to subject, father to son, and husband to wife). To police the functional orders of the patriarchy, social role philosophy drew distinctions (*bie*) between linked roles like father to son, husband to wife, distinguishing and fusing them in the same analytic gesture. A precise vocabulary of philosophic, ethical, and disciplinary terms accrued over the centuries of gentry dominance to reinforce the need for submission (*jingshun*), contentment with one's given lot (*dangfen*, *anfen*, *xunfen*, etc.), firmness in pursuit of appropriate performance of role (*jie*), and so on. As Rowe puts it, "By routinely acting out the duties of his or her role in a manner consistent with the li (ritual), each participant in this system of belief continually reaffirmed and reproduced the cosmic, the political, and the civilized social order."[23] In other words, and to slightly exaggerate his case, for Rowe, the lijiao did not produce women as a subject; it repressed real women. This model is precisely the reading that the new social history of women has attempted to ameliorate in, for instance, Ko's argument that women endorsed the lijiao even when it had a prejudicial effect on their everyday lives.

Interestingly, Kai-wing Chow drew conclusions similar to Rowe's. Where Rowe found a parallelism in liberal commercialization and considered its liberatory effect on everyday practices, Chow's study stresses the state's powers over society and explicit political strategies. He introduces the "sociopolitical matrix" and "kinship" as his examples. In his view, the political potency of the Qing rulers forced Chinese gentry elites to shift attention from achievement at court to cultivation of locality. They developed politicized scholarship around "ritualism." Ritualism, according to Chow, included the lijiao as a form of "social control" or obedience to rule.[24] Social control and male dominance regulate local society. Gentry created codes for managing correct marriage, burial, and funeral ritual organizations in new mortuary-related religious expression. This included necrographic textual scholarship and necromonuments that consolidated agnatic ties along with the more familiar family shrines (*jiazu*) and lineage halls (*zongmiao*).[25] But in this cult of necromonumentality, as in ordinary family cults, sexual purity was the only measure of women's value. According to Chow, it was the value that men placed on "ritual wifehood" (the term is Francesca Bray's) that centered female social experience.[26] Ritually good behavior for women, in the absence of outlets for productive labor or legal, female-controlled property, boiled down to sexual loyalty, Chow argues. Gentry men pressured female relatives to "maintain a good reputation by strictly observing all rules of proper behavior," including widow suicide, fiancée suicide, and bans on widow remarriage, known in the historiographic tradition as the "cult of women's chastity." In Chow's account, women is historically present as an expression of male social control, male desire, and male values.

The constituent elements of society condition what social forces produce the women in question. One social historian who has interpreted these "pressures" more positively as the mediated evidence of female-authored behavior despite an oppressive context is Benjamin Elman. In the seventeenth century the so-called Tung-lin-style of gentry political alliances composed of lateral, fraternal, cross-family, male-only members collapsed and a new social formation took its place. Elman calls the new formation "Chuang- and Li-style lineages" because these were the surnames of the families responsible for pioneering the new social forms. Unlike European elites of the same era, who rarely drew on wide networks of kinship ties, elites in China chose kinship strategies rather than political alliances to protect their class interests. Chuang- and Li-style lineages exchanged daughters as one of the means of forging tightly drawn family networks for perpetuating social and economic dominance. Consequently, the Manchu state recognized their utility and endorsed the new lineage-style kinship organizations. Until the nineteenth century, political dissent in China was channeled away from possible broadly based gentry associations and into primarily kin groups that in effect mediated class politics. Making a compelling effort to situate Confucian thinking in the material world of concrete social relations, epistemic fields, and ideological powers, Elman draws a link between new kinship forms and the empirical or Han learning (*kaozhengxue*) school of late Confucianism which rethought conventions inherited from Song and Ming eras, including the lijiao.[27]

For Elman, the social relations of kinship are the social and ideational basis of the late imperial epistemic order. In the context of these "institutions," women act and men act, though not under conditions of their own choosing and in differential relations to power. Thus, although "political and economic forces . . . made [patrilineal, *zongzu*] descent an ideological system as well as a social fact," still, lineages were "not passive reflections of, but rather dynamic contributors to, the political, economic, and social order."[28] Theory and practices of kinship, production of scholarship, home teaching, discipline in lineage schools, and, very important, the education and exchange of women strengthened lineage locally and nationally, via the examination system, where regional innovation influenced the national elite in the culture of government officialdom.[29] Yet this view, closest to my own vision of social formation, does not include an adequate description of female kin. This is surprising in light of the corporate strategy Elman describes and the importance it accorded to exchanging educated women. The categories of class and agency enable Elman to materialize thought while avoiding the "correspondence theory of truth," but he still finds it possible to write about kinship strategies without opening a fully developed line of discussion about female kin. In the end, social history method makes the category of women expendable to the social totality.

Dorothy Ko's pathbreaking monograph, *Teachers of the Inner Chamber: Women and Culture in Seventeenth Century China*, argues that in the period 1670–1730, what she calls, following Joan Scott and Peter Stallybrass, a "gender" or a community of women who identified themselves as belonging to a group composed of "women-as-same" emerged in Jiangnan's elite families.[30] Ko's book has broken fresh ground in Chinese social history because it demonstrated that even working inside the basic protocols of social history it was possible to write "women as a category" into traditional society. Ko launched her argument by linking traditional women's high "culture" to "commercialization," and then to the print media, which commercial publication had made available for the first time to female readers.[31] Seventeenth- and eighteenth-century commercial revolution transformed the boudoir, she suggested, and turned it into a workshop of gender consciousness (I return below to this significant claim). The agents of the structural adjustment of women to the market economy were professional teachers. Masculinized because they did men's work, female teachers left the "ideological and functional asymmetry in the gender system . . . unchallenged." Yet, achieving and teaching high literacy skills they also set an example that "inspired countless domestic women in the brave new terrains in person and in writing."[32]

These heroic female agents opened up a consolidated or essential gender of women and a feminine space of sexual difference "not by repudiating the old domestic boundaries [set by the lijiao, Three Bonds, Thrice Following, etc.] but by pushing and stretching them to new limits." Elite women turned conventional prescriptions (e.g., footbinding, moral education, the feminine virtues of talent, beauty, and goodness) into markers of "the parameters of women's domain." Furthermore, because a female literature of identity circulated among this "female gender" or "women-as-same (gender)" group, Ko put a face on the elite kinswomen. Their activities "hollowed out" the painfully severe constraints that social historians such as Chow had suggested were the common lot of women. An economic term referring to the maintenance of a form after the content has been extricated or transformed, the hollowed-out gender system remained intact but was thoroughly transformed. This change within the gender system, Ko argues, "was almost imperceptible," and "for this very reason it was most effective in undermining the restrictive old boundaries. The educated women were all still at home, but the content of domestic life had changed. . . . the gender system had managed to harness the continued support of the most educated of the womenfolk."[33]

The aspect of this rich study that is pertinent to my concerns is the case Ko makes for self-authored identity of elite women as a solidarity, or what she calls a gender. Ko rests her case for the gender analytic on Joan Scott's earliest attempts to define gender as "social relationships based on perceived differences between the sexes" and as "a primary way of signifying relationships of power [in] symbolic representations, normative concepts, social institutions, and subjectivity and identity."[34] In the seventeenth century among Jiangnan elites, "most women were . . . constituted as women in relation to men." Despite universal Han emphasis on internal kin differentials, literate female elites within the hollowed-out conventions of women's enforced seclusion created ways of establishing their commonality as women.[35] "Women" in that gender system was internally divided into wives and concubines or prostitutes. But by and large, conditions were sufficiently pleasant that elite women found no reason for direct challenge to the system, though Ko leaves that possibility open. Her point is that the *gender system managed to harness the continued support of the most educated* women, courtesans, and wives because it accommodated and satisfied them.[36]

Because her subjects are the upper elite and superliterate, Ko confronts the question of how class and gender operated in relation to one another. Her suggestion is that although elite female kin and concubines did recognize one another as belonging to the gender she names women, gender or women did not allow recognition across class difference. This is an interesting insight because it could suggest that the formula of gender is actually one possible class identity. Ko considers at some length the question of why elite women never acted more definitively on their understanding of their commonality. In part, she stresses the pleasures of the boudoir and the intimacy of women's cultures of poetry, passion, and footbinding. But the very conditions that made gender feasible also made elite women reluctant to challenge patriarchal norms, or as Ko puts it, "Women-as-same (gender) and women-as-different (class) worked to contain through empowerment."[37] This line of argument is strengthened toward the end of the study when Ko seems to correlate the rise of gender to literacy. Literacy itself becomes a material force in her general argument because it has the power to transform women of different surnames in the same class into social beings identified as "gender women." Thus, literacy made self-authoring or self-representation possible. Still troubled at this implication, Ko carefully qualifies her conclusion. It would, she comments, "be far-fetched to argue that women's communities . . . were social equalizers" in the sense of condensing all female subjects into the category women. Elite communities more similar than different (i.e., women of various surnames and educated courtesans) "were, after all, few in number and tended to hail from the same cultural milieu."[38]

The effort Ko pours into the problem of how to integrate gender and the social evidence is extremely useful. Among other things, it draws attention to the entrenched problems that attend the concept of gender itself for historians. What Ko tentatively and carefully establishes is, I think it is fair to say, a compromise. In her study, gender is not a kind of praxis (Trinh Min-ha's position) or a logic of relation (the Lacanianism of Drucilla Cornell), the social semiotics of sexual difference (Joan Scott's early formula) or even a complex means of materializing identity (the proposal of Judith Butler). In Ko's study, gender seems to be a utopian or desired recognition by women of commonality beneath the various differences that class, region, ethnicity, and rate of literacy impose on them.

## Historical Catachresis

Earlier, I proposed that Diane Elam's insight into future anteriority and historical undecidability was a useful mode for writing history. The previous discussion of a number of important social histories of the seventeenth through nineteenth centuries for information content (description, political background, analysis, periodization, focus, etc.) and for their methodological assumptions led me to identify an intriguing historiographic lacuna. In this section, I suggest possible ways of resolving the impasse Ko proposed for the relation between women and gender. It might help, I argue, to shift the notion of what is a suitable subject in history writing. Neither gender as such nor woman as such—what I call historical catachreses—emerges as a consequence of the historian reading literally and accepting that literal terms are ontologies or coded statements about social norms. Words that stabilize meaning momentarily, historical catachreses lack true referents and thus reveal their manifold analytic inadequacy. The task of this section is to begin considering why writing histories of catachreses may contribute to resolving Ko's double bind. Empirically speaking, if women appears as a gender only when women recognize themselves as women, their pre-condition amounts to either non-existence or what colonial Chinese feminist theory called being "the tools of men."[39] In both Emma Teng's and Paul Rouzer's view, the new gender history of Chinese women, for all it communicates about the lives of elites, is problematic because of its tendency to rest its case on an anachronistic female subject. Teng and Rouzer suggest that it should be possible to write histories that do not repeat a reliance on context and its presupposition that context is what "genders" people in the past. Kumkum Sangari and Sudesh Vaid have made a similar proposal to consider gender a condition of thinking rather than a social achievement. In their formulation, gender does not require that women recognize commonality across differences. It is, rather, a foundation or aspect of history method. "A feminist historiography," they argue, "rethinks historiography as a whole and discards the idea of women as something to be *framed* by context, in order to be able to think of gender difference as both structuring and structured by the wide set of social relations."[40] In their view, gender should both structure historians' questions (the method of history) and be shown to infuse or shape the social ideologies that typify the era being considered.

Yet another possibility is to redefine what is meant by context. This is the solution Rouzer proposes, and Angela Zito's work on ritual, though not about gender, illustrates how this might work. Zito argues that the Grand Sacrifice, the core of a "ritualist metaphysics," dominated eighteenth-century scholarly norms and ritual strategies. Second nature to late imperial Chinese elites, ritualist metaphysics was as powerful in its own moment as the Cartesian or bourgeois experience of embodiment was among elites in Europe. According to Zito, ritual metaphysics did not privilege an individual's inborn rationality, sexuality, or psychology. It emphasized instead something she calls a "process ontology." Ritual as process ontology required human bodies to signify in certain ways and body surfaces to set the stage for the performance of religious and political meaning. In example after example, Zito shows how performing the li and (importantly for elite women, as we have seen) the lijiao drew social boundaries and animated the material world through the elite praxes of writing, rewriting, editing, performing, and restaging the rituals of subjective embodiment. In Zito's hands, context becomes productivist and its terms of ideation become part of its material force.[41]

A third option is the one I advocate: to focus on historical catachreses and to write the history of them and their careers. I have adapted this notion from Gayatri C. Spivak, so it is necessary to introduce the catachresis's implications for writing history. I understand catachresis to be the occulted (i.e., concealed, hidden from view, condensed, made difficult to read) evidence of normalizing strategies which often appear as a subject form. Deconstruction and Marxist criticism are Spivak's preferred vehicles for negotiating writing, including heavily burdened paleonymic terms like "woman." To interpret the meaning of texts, she usually returns to the Marxist problem of ideology or "culture," which is held to connect humans in the larger world. Modern catachreses, while ideological and consequently grounded and not fully translatable (e.g., nüxing is historically distinct from "woman" or *femme*), are at the same time massified or universalized terms. They can be read both intertextually in the play of *différance* and as entities in value coding or normalizing ideology. That is because the one value available to all social forms under capitalist modernity is labor value. Consequently, for Spivak, as for me, catachreses are signs in a capitalist semiotics rather than symptoms of intrapsychic processes, although historical catachreses (like Denise Riley's "women" or my nüxing in chapter 3) operate as Lacanian chains of signification and are said to work in the unconscious as language. That we are as much spoken by the terms through which we know ourselves as we speak in those terms is by now almost a scholarly truism. But historical catachresis, for me, as in Spivak's use of the catachresis, does not operate freely in a Derridean play of signification. The term itself is simply a means of noting that ontological claims, stabilized in language, are both irreducible and yet understandable as value-coded or ideological demands.[42]

It is the persistent nominalism of the catachresis, more than a Spivakian preoccupation with its nontranslatability or its reducibility to abstract or capitalist value coding, that has made it particularly valuable to me in writing this history of the subject women in Chinese feminism. As in Foucauldian discourse, Spivak glosses the mother tongue as "something that has a history before we are born . . . is unmotivated but not capricious and is larger in outline than we are."[43] For my purposes, catachrestic language usages, what Li Tuo calls "mass signified [*jiti xiangzheng*] subject forms [*zhuti*]," are vivid players or agents in primary source evidence; they are what is most legible in the detritus of the past. Catachreses are ubiquitous key words or terms which appear repetitively in primary source evidence and seem to attract attention precisely because they denote a stable meaning that subsequently proves resistant, even aspecific. In the colonial modern era particularly, catachresis points to and grounds, archivally and materially, what China scholars have commonly glossed as "neologism." These are terms like society (*shehui*), self (*ziji*), and movement (*yundong*). Substituting the concept of catachresis for neologism (new word) adds analytic power and enlarges the possibility of thinking about these terms extralinguistically, as unexplored historical experience.[44]

For example, *xingyi* (sexual difference), *xing xingwei* (sexual behavior), *xingbie* (sexed-gender), and *nanxing* (male) are all neologisms for sure. Like many other neologisms, they were cycled through Chinese treaty port translations of European languages and Japanese in elite language reform, the work of proto-imperialist compilers of imperialist dictionaries and colonial treaty writers. But newly created words are also elements of modernist taxonomies. They are constituent elements in "discourses of modernity." Some words have greater depth and power. The modernist legitimation of a universal subject form woman (nüxing) is itself not just a neologism but in fact a conceptual and social subject, a real person with a body that can be photographed, stripped naked, used to sell commodities (and eventually dies, of course). Catachreses appear often as the subjects of generalities or theories, so in this case, women is a subject in a larger ontology, the key term in a truthful theory about human sexuality. Chapter 3 illustrates this point in relation to the claims of sex theorist and eugenicist Gao Xian, whose work (like the writing of many others) stabilized the subject women in the history of Chinese feminisms.[45]

Spivak argues that catachreses are a special kind of misuse of terms, where concepts are unstable because there is no one-to-one correspondence between concept and referent. This is a literary philosopher's critique of what Eley called the correspondence theory of truth. It is an important and sophisticated commonsense point. The catachresis or concept-metaphor without adequate referent is what she at one time called "a master word" to highlight general historical terms that have no literal, or particular, referent, because, as she put it very colloquially, there are "no 'true' examples of the 'true worker,' the 'true woman,' the 'true proletarian' who would actually stand for the ideals in terms of which you've mobilized" them.[46] Calling attention to how catachreses work is a good way to illustrate how universals and particulars operate in ordinary language and therefore how much historical and theoretical meaning simple terms carry. True woman is an ideological idea that is never fully reducible to the life experience of one individual, but does capture or stabilize categorically singular historical experience. It is consequently quite "real" and subject to history writing.

Yet catachreses link universals like Proletariat, Woman, Whites, and Enlightenment to tangible, immediate, irreducible, and concrete referents. Because of their occult or historical depth, catachreses may not be fully translatable, but when we use them we know what we are saying. Despite the fact that the terms are not stable or timeless, they nonetheless have real-world effects. Which is also to say that catachreses like the mass subject of Maoism, *renmin* ("the people"), or the place of the people, *shehui* ("society"), are historically datable or traceable. These are particularly good examples because each is both neologism, or newly minted word with an origin in time, and referentially inadequate because each refers back to an abstraction. Importantly, however, in history writing they refer to tangible and meaningful collectivities within a political economy where a Communist Party governed in part through the imposition of these self-same political terms or because, in precommunist eras, women and men understand themselves to be whole under their definition.

So for me, the absence of a true referent is precisely the characteristic that makes the notion of catachresis valuable. True referents are apparitions that live only in theories of representation. The absence of a true referent just means that the term stabilizes diverse parts or elements. That is how a historical catachresis such as women in feminist thought can contribute to writing histories that are empirical in the sense of being grounded in diverse written or other material archives, and yet read the archive as a repository of normalizing strategies. When particular signifiers are valued because of their ontological claims it becomes possible to write about the histories of the truthful experiences of women and men in the past and in places other than one's own.

A catachresis is, therefore, concrete. The concept refers to something irreducibly itself because people in the past have instantiated or testified to its veracity with reference to their own immediate experience. They say women is a certain way because they experience it to be so. The catachresis consolidates a universal as a particular and the other way around. Although we are indeed discussing a nominalist entity, *the catachresis is a figure in the social imaginary of the future anterior.* The catachrestic figure of woman anticipated in theory is a particular kind of universal, as well as a distillation of thinkable conventional normality. If catachreses are stable, meaningful terms of language per se, it is precisely because they are situated in inherited, burdened archives of writing, which Spivak, following Derrida, calls paleonomy. I expand from Spivak because my usage stresses not just the catachreses' historical sweep and their ability to exceed the capacity of sign systems or discourse to contain them but also their occulted quality; they are repositories of past meaning.

Benjamin wrote:

> A historical materialist cannot do without the notion of a present which is not a transition, but in which time stands still and has come to a stop. For this notion defines the present in which he himself is writing history. Historicism gives the "eternal" image of the past;

historical materialism supplies a unique experience with the past. . . . Thinking involves not only the flow of thoughts but their arrest as well. Where thinking suddenly stops in a configuration pregnant with tensions, it gives that configuration a shock, by which it crystallizes into a monad. A historical materialist approaches a historical subject only where he encounters it as a monad. In this structure he recognizes the sign of a Messianic cessation of happening, or, put differently, a revolutionary chance to fight for the oppressed past. He takes cognizance of it in order to blast a specific era out of the homogeneous course of history—blasting a specific life out of the era or a specific work out of the lifework.[47]

Gayatri Spivak's adaptation of the Derridean notion of the literary catachresis ("a concept-metaphor without an adequate referent") is not a wholly sufficient explanation for my purposes because it does not directly address the ways historians grasp specificities—subject, discourse, fact, socius—in history writing. Its sense of where deconstruction occurs is limited to certain kinds of texts: privileged genres. To write a history requires "blasting," in Benjamin's phrase, "a specific life out of the era or a specific work out of the lifework," while assuming "the notion of *a present which is not a transition, but in which time stands still* and has come to a stop."[48] Even when a concept-metaphor in Chinese feminism, nüxing, is the historical subject, materialist historical method in Benjamin's sense requires arresting time. The presumed sequence of past-present-future is unacceptable in Benjamin's view. Every moment is "pregnant with tensions," the tension of past trauma and future expectation, just to make a very obvious point. His "present which is not a transition" could—perhaps not in a way Benjamin intended—be understood as heterogeneous time on the human scale.

Bringing time to a historiographic standstill is difficult, however, because a present conceived of as precisely "not in transition" cannot explain itself. It must be explained (although, hopefully, outside restrictive, anachronistic political tropes like women or historiographic teleologies like commercialization). That is Benjamin's first point. "A historical materialist," he warns, "approaches a historical subject only where he encounters it as a monad," or, in my terms, the occulted figure of a catachresis. The historian cannot place the subject in time but must look instead to the contents of discourses and ideologies conditioning and situating a specific life, a specific era, a specific lifework. (This task is much easier when, as I have attempted to do here, the primary source is precisely theoretical resources that specific individuals and eras produced.)

It is in the discourse of the contemporary moment, Harry Harootunian has argued, and in the contents of discourse that we find the irreducible rules of play that once structured, limited, and enabled action in the past as an ongoing present, and thus conditioned, limited, and enabled subject forms. Because these contents of discourses—the material of history—are not, in Harootunian's words, "motivated by extradiscursive forces" but rather "are prompted" from within and take shape as "specific processes and practices of signification," historians face a difficult task. Historical work consists of deciphering and decoding discursive constructions or catachreses as they are frozen, arrested, or crystallized in the process of "establishing their own categories of adequacy" within the social, institutional orders of existence.[49]

## 2　Theorizing "Women"

Gender [is] . . . the very apparatus of production whereby the sexes themselves are established. JUDITH BUTLER, *Gender Trouble*

This chapter examines terms for women and their rules of play.[1] It introduces what are for the most part catachreses, or generic terms for women and woman in specific theoretical languages in the eighteenth, nineteenth, and twentieth centuries. The historical catachreses under scrutiny here are also subject forms. In the "prose of the world," as Harootunian writes, these subject forms are inextricable from the discourses that "open up a space for tenants to occupy," change, or alter as conditions are altered. Consequently, one thing historical catachreses encode is information about how, "in the act of appropriation, the subject is constituted by the matter of the discourse."[2] These historical catachreses are sometimes neologisms, but they are always conceptual statements and signifiers of a historical reality that is not a transition.

Between the eighteenth- and the early twentieth-century cultural revolutions, the dominant, formulaic historical catachresis in mainstream Confucian regulative gender theory projects was funü. Funü signified the collectivity of kinswomen in the semiotics of Confucian family doctrine. Confucian family philosophy was a specialized style of theoretical writing about being a person in the patriline, and the patriline in all Confucian thought was held to be the literal foundation of the central government. In the "semifeudal, semicolonial" 1920s, when self-avowedly post-Confucian cultural revolutionaries started rewriting the past as a dead "tradition," intellectuals, creative writers, and social activists invented the word nüxing in the rhetoric of global sex and eugenics theory. Chapter 3 is devoted to analyzing this nüxing catachresis and its implications during the era, which I am calling colonial modernity.

Early in the twentieth century the Chinese Communist Party (CCP) took over responsibility for the organized women's movement. Internal Party debates over what to call the subject women in revolutionary praxis actually continued for decades. An alternative, massified, politicized subject known in CCP diction as funü eventually superseded both the Confucian protocols of funü and the eroticized subject nüxing. In Maoist rhetoric, funü referred to a national subject that stood for the collectivity of all politically normative or decent women. Under the Maoist state's centralizing discourses, funü got resituated, first within the *guojia* (state) and then, secondarily, through the magic of revolutionary social praxis and ideological metonymy, in the modern *jiating* (family). In other words, Maoism reversed the older convention of woman within and man outside. It imagined a national woman, funü, intertwined directly in state processes over the period of social revolution and socialist modernization who, because of her achievements as a state subject, would modernize family practices.

Chinese states, like most states, had always regulated gendered norms.[3] But when Maoist thinking increasingly linked the catachreses of guojia (nation or state, depending on context), jiating (family), nanxing (modern man), and nüxing (all of these being both neologisms and new social formations), it empowered a modern rhetoric, a system of modern norms. Maoist funü existed as one element of a larger discursive constellation, with other modernist, universalist state categories, catachreses like "worker" (*gongren*), "youth" (*qingnian*), and "proletarian" (*wuchanjieji*). Funü, that is, formed a part of the "system of designations by . . . which," from the late 1930s until the Deng Xiaoping era of the 1980s, Party "political authorities regulate[d] all important social relationships."[4] (The centrality of this Maoist system is discussed in chapters 4 and 5 of this book.) Nüxing, by contrast, was reclassified in Maoist state theory to mean the reverse of normativity for women, at least in theoretical and political terms. No longer a universal term signifying women, nüxing meant a femininity that was "Westernized," "bourgeois," individualist, erotic. Until, that is, the post-Mao era of reform and market socialism, which saw the resurgence of feminist concern with the priorities of sexual difference and a return to theoretical acceptability of this older subject.[5] (Chapters 6 and 7 are devoted to this shift.)

A remarkable feature of Chinese feminist thinking is its persistence in the face of discontinuity and disruption. In the ruptures and discontinuous accumulation that returned the question of women's emancipation to the national agenda decade after decade lie the traces of enlightened optimism, diminished over the century but never fully defeated. Theoretical Chinese refined and sharpened its analytic vocabulary over the course of these violent ruptures. Perhaps the effect of revolutionary conditions on mass communication and literary expression, mechanisms for recasting gen-

Famine? political aw...

dered personhood, are particularly visible in theoretical Chinese. In any case, a working assumption in the discussion that follows is that these historically complex catachreses of women—*funü, nüxing, nüren, nüzi*—make it possible historically to evaluate the richly contingent, composite, or humanly made quality of regulatory concepts and categories. People thought in these terms, just as people contest, invent, accept, and refine them to this day.[6]

## The Subject Women Historically

Recall the question Paul Rouzer posed about the problem of writing a history of seventeenth- and eighteenth-century elite Chinese women. "How does one define 'woman,'" he asked, "let alone 'woman writer,' in the seventeenth century?"[7] Mid-Qing hypergamy, lineage retrenchment and family ritualism, commercial networks and niche marketing to female consumers, commercialization of media, female seclusion and footbinding, as well as the efflorescence of elite female literacy are all preconditions for grasping eighteenth- and nineteenth-century styles of womanhood. But, as Dorothy Ko's social history suggests, gender cannot be "read off" these data except through singular subject forms. Explaining the sexes historically would involve opening into scrutiny gendering processes and gendered subjectivities and treating them as "historically singular form[s] of experience."[8] A way that historians deal at this level of specificity is to read rhetoric naïvely. The guiding assumption is that key words or terms express something about the behaviors, expectations, and enabling constraints that they are describing.

Mou Zhengyun's genealogy of the key term funü is a good example. The study shows the centrality of funü in the Qing period and links it to funü's ubiquity in the Maoist era.[9] Mou, a classicist and Sinologist, tracked key signifiers of female subjects in the canonical works (*Shisan jing*) and dynastic histories or official post-mortems produced after the fall of a prime regime. Using this textual and intertextual resource, Mou establishes that in the period after the mid-seventeenth-century dynastic transition and before the era of state disintegration in the warlord era, 1913–1927, the key word funü surfaces in canonical texts more frequently than any other collective noun signifying women. Mou is particularly concerned with how key terms were defined in classical dictionaries and in the official histories. This helps to explain how specific eras may have understood key terms and allows Mou to track changes in definition, implication, and regularity of use. Her point is that between roughly 1750 and 1920, and only those years, the compound word funü arose to become the overwhelmingly preferred collective noun referring to female persons.

The transitional decades between Ming and Qing eras saw a meaningful shift in nomenclature. The two kinship terms nü (unmarried woman) and fu (married woman), previously separate nouns, were combined into a single word, funü, and were glossed as the collectivity of all women in the patrilineal family. Previously, particularly in archaic dictionaries, the word nü and its compounds, such as nüzi, nü er (girl child), and nüren (female person), meant unmarried girls, and fu and its compounds (furen, etc.) meant married women. However, although classic texts all use slightly different vocabulary and rhetorical strategies, none except the Liji ritual text (dated to the Zhou dynasty, circa tenth through third centuries B.C.E.), included the designation "funü," until, that is, the late imperial Confucian renaissance. In the High Qing and early modern eras a newly coined word, funü, had the novel, specialized meaning "women of the patriline." It would appear from Mou's detailed analysis that it was precisely these elements of analytic rhetoric that became, in Butler's terms, the "apparatus of production whereby the sexes themselves [were] established" in late Qing governmentability.

The historical event of linking married and unmarried female kin into the single collective noun funü was, in other words, a relatively recent development. Also, consistent with the work of Rowe, Elman, Chow, and Zito, who all discuss the surge in concern with ritual order in this era, the late imperial use of the term funü specifically defined fu in terms of ritual service to the husband and his family. Thus, Mou cites the Qing-era Kang Xi dictionary that the "already married is spoken of as fu, not yet given in betrothal is spoken of as nü. Parents and child, although she is married, still refer to her as nü [daughter]." Even more bluntly, "the already married nü [daughter, girl] is spoken of as fu. Fu means service [fu zhi yan fu ye], service to the husband."[10] Most of the evidence for this consolidation of terms, Mou notes, appears in the histories, where gradually the term funü overtook the two previously dominant common collective nouns in circulation for describing people gendered as female, furen and nüzi. By the end of the dynastic era, funü had become the most commonly used term for women in the Confucian theoretical language.[11]

Mou argues convincingly that marriage itself is the distinction or marking place between nü and fu because marriage is what makes a fu out of a nü. What also seems clear from her evidence is that in this unfolding of the historical term funü, there is no term present before the twentieth century that might indicate women as a group outside the family (i.e., another gloss on nüxing). Eventually, I will show that nüxing has as complex a genealogy in modernist sex theory as the terms nü, nüzi, nüren, nüdi, fu, furen, and so on in the Confucian canon that Mou sets out for analysis. Noting the absence in Confucian theoretical languages of a third term grounding all female kin is only the first step. These terms are, in a nominalist sense, signs of social experience.

Chen Hongmou, mentioned earlier in relation to the work of his biographer, historian William Rowe, was a celebrated government official in the 1740s, 1750s, and 1760s. In the course of his spectacular career, Chen showed particular interest in popular education and took the position that women best served the family and the civilizing process when they were literate. He expressed these views in one long chapter of a much longer work in which he selected and reproduced selections from earlier philosophic texts and appended to them his personal evaluations and comments. Chen's selected pedagogic texts concentrated on names and norms; he drew extensively on writing that established gender normativity by defining and naming things. Although, as Rowe pointed out, Chen took liberal positions, there are several ways that his preoccupations were not personal or idiosyncratic. The texts Chen cited were very familiar to educated readers and many were parables or posed ethical norms through old stories. The positions Chen took on female literacy and behavior in general were in response to the larger, unparalleled debates over womanhood that Susan Mann calls the eighteenth-century querelle des femmes. Chen's contribution to the dispute is explicitly normative and definitional. How elite women behaved in relation to these norms surely differed, but even the most refined *guixiu* could not have been unaware of them and to some degree acted in relation to their normative powers.

In the chapter of his *Wu zhong yi gui* (Five posthumous regulations) titled *Jiao nü yi gui* (Posthumous regulations on educating women), Chen spelled out what, in theory and practice, he means by women. The fact that he defined his terms as succinctly and bluntly as he does suggests perhaps that his interlocutors may not have shared his views. However, as is clear in the descriptions and instructions Chen attached to the text, he was very interested in how people behaved and what they should be called. He was preoccupied with the "very apparatus of production," which is the way "the sexes themselves are established." Below is Chen's core definition of woman:

> When *fu* [persons, sages, women of rank] are in the *jia* [procreative sublineage unit] they are *nü* (young girls, daughters]; when they marry they are *fu* [wives, married] and when they bear children they are *mu* [mothers]. [If you start with] a *xiannü* [a virtuous unmarried daughter/girl], then you will end up with a *xianfu* [virtuous wife]; if you have virtuous wives, you will end up with *xianmu* [virtuous mothers]. Virtuous mothers ensure virtuous descendants. Civilizing [literally, *wanghua*, or transforming through the influence of the monarch] begins in

the women's quarters [guimen]. Everyone in the jia benefits from the chaste woman zhennü. That is why educating women is so important.[12]

The first point about this definition is that it effectively forecloses the general, social category "all women." The citation presents a fu, who is either a fu, when she is married into a patriline, or a mu after she has children. Before her marriage, s/he (Chinese pronouns did not distinguish) was a nü, or a daughter in a patriline. Chen says that the fu is a person of rank who takes shape, is defined, because of differential positioning inside the patrilineal sublineage or procreative family, the jia. Quite simply, location says it all. Because the funü (Chen does not employ the term here but he does at other points in the Wu zhong yi gui) or generic women in the citation include fu, nü, fu, and xiannü, I could render the passage into English as follows: "Before [women] are married [they] are nü/female/daughters; when [they] get married they are fu or wives; and when [they] give birth to children, [they] are mu or mothers." As soon as I render it this way, I have substantiated a category, Women, that does not appear in the syntax of the sentence. The persons whom Chen's comment addresses and consequently substantiates are primarily wives and daughters, or funü. They are women, of course. But, as I will argue, they are gendered by virtue of the protocols specific to their subject positions and not necessarily or even in the first case by reference to the physiological ground they may or may not share with people outside the kinship group.

Funü is a collective noun shaped in relation to differential jia positions, whereas Women or Woman is a transcendental signifier. Chen defines what fu and nü mean primarily within the jia, because what defines and anchors funü is the ritual life of the family. Like the writers and editors in the theoretical tradition that Mou discusses in her survey, Chen does not assume a foundational status for Woman outside the relations of patrilineal kinship. This has practical, theoretical implications for the way the gendered person is defined. Rather than framing kin-specific situations as examples of "things women do," Chen is far more likely to explain that acting within specified ethical-practical boundaries produces a recognizable person. His overall argument in this edited and annotated collection of aphorisms, historical examples, poems, and family maxims is precisely that kinswomen should be educated not because they are educable, but because civilizing kinswomen raises the general cultural level of the family line and, through the family line, the nation itself.[13]

Funü, or "patrilineally related kinswomen," in Chen's family theory, is the context for highly complex subject positions like xianmu (virtuous mother); but funü is the lowest common denominator for female subjects.[14] The question is: How did Chen's writing situate human beings in kin and normative relations like xianmu and make them stick? Recall Elizabeth Cowie's early suggestion that rather than presuming that women are prediscursively *"situated* in the family," it is more accurate analytically to argue that it is "in the family—as the effect of kinship structures—that women *as women* are produced."[15] Cowie sought to understand kinship not as a system of exchange but as a production line that situated people in social or learned relations. Understood in this way, it is more obvious why abandoning the anachronisms of woman and women is useful to historians. Women may have suffered under the strict performance requirements of their stations in Chen's system, but they suffered as contemporaries of Chen and not as my contemporaries. Also, if the category of funü is an instance of gendering in a world where principles of rank and degree of relation to the patriline predominated, and if the evidence supports my interpretation, Chen's theory becomes more than a reflection of social reality. It is the coproducer, the signifier of historical or *real* signifieds. Cowie's willingness to consider the singularity of Victorian sex theory helps suggest that the exchange of actual women in patrilineal, patrilocal Chinese kin fields produced not the sign woman, but a profusion of signs with one thing in common. They are "real" women, but not in a contemporary "prediscursive" sense.

Yin/yang logic rather than the logic of strict opposition (male/female, either/or) characterizes gender theory in Chen's world, just as yin/yang logic can be found underscoring religious, social, governance policy, and juridicial theory. Chen used the Han Confucian Dong Zhongshu to reiterate his own views on positional inequality: "There is nothing that does not have a correlate, and in each correlation there is the *Yin* and *Yang*. Thus the relationships between sovereign and subject, father and son, and husband and wife are all derived from the principles of the *Yin* and *Yang*. The sovereign is *Yang*, the subject is *Yin*; the father is *Yang*, the son is *Yin*; the husband is *Yang*, the wife is *Yin*. [These are the three cords (*gang*), the foundation of civilization.]"[16] Putting this point negatively, Chen's texts do not refer to women's bodies nor to their body parts, nor to universal emotional qualities they all possess as proof of their social existence. Rather, his text argues that disciplined funü, stacked in hierarchical relations organized on the basis of yin/yang logic (e.g., funü inside the jia, men outside it; funü's job is filial caretaking, service to parents, moral instruction of children, and personal normative practice) guarantee the coherence of human culture.[17]

Calling these processes social-cosmological activities enacted on the never stable or fully boundaried primary site of the jia renders into contemporary analytic language the point late sixteenth-century physician Li Shichen made in his *Materia Medica*. "Normally," he wrote, "*qian* and *kun* make fathers and mothers; but there are five kinds of nonmales [*feinan*] who cannot become fathers and five kinds of nonfemale [*feinü*] who cannot become mothers."[18] Qian and kun are the first and last hexagrams of the I Jing or Book of Changes, which since the Song dynasty has been a foundational text of hegemonic Confucian studies. In the Book of Changes, qian and kun are forces operating in *tiandi*, the realms extrinsic to human culture, and in the realm of *wen*, or human social life. They are the paradigmatic forces of yin and yang. Yin and yang are many things: logical relationships (qian and kun, inside and outside, husband and wife), practical forces, and "designations for the polar aspects of effects," and so, in a social sense, powers inscribing hierarchy.[19] What Li is saying about these medical anomalies is that the dynamic forces of yin/yang do not "produce" women and men (themselves subject positions within yet another discourse) so much as the required civil projects of motherhood and fatherhood, husband and wife, brother and sister, and so on.

The anomaly Li reported had to do with the general instability of bodies in most Confucian discourse. The immediate cases of the nonman and the nonwoman, whose defective bodies forestall production, as well as cases of the castrated, impotent, or vaginally impenetrable and bodies known to change from female to male and from male to female, all present to the physician unstable surfaces that resist customary "gendering." In Li Shichen and Chen Hongmou's time, Simone de Beauvoir's peculiar notion that "women are not born Women but become Women" makes a lot of sense, since the surface onto which eighteenth-century Chinese subjectivities were inscribed (i.e., Li's fecund body) was more flexible than the (gendering) subject positions that producing sons and daughters enabled women to occupy and possess.[20]

What appear in Chen's texts are not the "sexes" as they are normally understood now, but a profusion of relational, bound, unequal dyads, each signifying difference and positioning difference analogically. A nü is a daughter, unequally related to parents and parents-in-law. A *xiaozi* (filial son) is differentially unequal to mother and father, yin to their yang. A fu is a wife, tied in a secondary or service relation to her husband. A *xianfu* is a wife who, grasping the powers accorded yin, masters her domain through her familiarity with the sort of protocols introduced below. Obviously (invoking Cowie's point), subjects got produced within the jia. Chen's definitions of nü, fu 4, and mu further suggest that although (good) women in the jia did have social relationships outside their immediate family, there was no legitimate or decent position for defining female persons (or male persons, for that matter) outside of the jia.[21]

Chen advocated education for women so that mothers could produce better filial sons and virtuous daughters, which would enhance the jia and solidify the Throne and foundations of civilization. In Chen's cosmology, female literacy meant moral philosophy, of course, and not poetics. For Chen, literacy, or learning to behave virtuously, and acting womanly were a single continuous arc in which acting normatively was the same as acting "as a woman."

The most important task for "acting as a woman" was the maintenance of difference. "Just as the yin and the yang are different qualities, so males and females should act differently," as Chen's text puts it. Citing Lu Jingxi, Chen underscored Lu's commonplace view that "there is a difference between the rituals of men and women. If you do not maintain the distinction, then you will cause gossip."[22] These protocols or gendering behaviors consisted of ritual or elite forms of courtesy. Behaviors, scripted physical motions, manners, and norms shaped what was decent, appropriate, proper, good behavior for each person. Intersubjective norms and gendered experience were inextricable. In the rigorous cadence of these kinds of text—when the daughters act on the protocols of daughterhood and married women act on the ritual expectations of wives, and so on—the distinction between men and women is accomplished and gendering is effected.

Funü itself was internally differentiated, and the educated funü learned how to retain a sense of appropriate distance in ambiguous situations and in conditions where ethical judgments were complex. According to one of Chen's moral stories, the state of Qi attacked Lu during the Warring States era. The Qi general encountered a woman attempting to flee with two young boys. At a certain point, the woman abandoned one child, who told the soldiers that the woman was his mother. When they finally captured her, the woman explained why she had left her own son behind to save her brother's son: in the relation of gong and si, the ethical extremes of selfishness and altruism, it would have been selfish under the circumstances to save her own child at his cousin's expense. The Qi general returned home and told his monarch that Lu was impregnable because even ordinary women behaved in a morally correct or righteous manner. The monarch of Lu, on the other hand, rewarded the woman with some gold and the title yigujie, or righteous elder paternal aunt, for he credited her with saving Lu from Qi.

Actually, Chen disagreed with the Lu monarch's actions. His commentary pointed to the fact that though she was indeed her brother's sister, the yigujie was also a wife to her husband and a mother to her husband's son. The yigujie, Chen insisted, had actually misunderstood the point of the distinction of gong/si. She could sacrifice her husband's child only under two conditions: if her husband had other sons (or could impregnate her, thereby replacing the dead one) and if her brother had died leaving only this son. Furthermore, the monarch of Lu himself undervalued the competing claims of sororal and marital protocol. The narrative assumed that one child must be abandoned. But, reasoned Chen, the better solution would have involved the death of the yigujie herself. Yes, the specific protocols of funü (i.e., "sister" and "wife") led in competing directions. Rather than fail either, however, the yigujie should have begged the Qi general to save both boys. This would inevitably have caused Qi to execute her, but what a righteous death it would have been! The parable and Chen's effort to reread it hints at its own complexity: not only were subject positionalities difficult to stabilize (it was difficult to "do" them correctly), but a person often found herself subject to simultaneous claims from multiple protocols.[23] Nonetheless, the example suggests how funü is the subject in this narrative and the importance of kin difference in normative performances.

Archaic ritual texts reproduced in Chen's textbook spelled out in detail how to behave decently: As a kinswoman [nüzi] you must establish yourself in life, for instance. Do not turn your head from side to side; if you wish to speak, do it without moving your lips; if you wish to sit, do it without moving your knees, and if you stand, do not wiggle your skirt. If you are happy, do not giggle, if you are unhappy, do not yell aloud. Inside and outside [the jia] kinswomen and kinsmen should be separate. These injunctions are lishu, or body etiquette, and Chen cited reams of text from ancient times listing them in minute detail. The protocols of funü are not mysterious or malignant. They seem mundane, practical, disciplinary physical movements and frequently personify behaviors, as Chen did when he reproduced the protocol of female host-guest relations using the historical example of Song Shanggong. Host-guest relations should be governed by a principle of purposefulness: walk gracefully in the company of your hostess; arrange your hands just so; accept tea; do not remain for a meal unless pressed, then only touch food to your lips; decline everything; keep your neck bent and head low; stay home whenever possible.[24]

The true mark of the educated funü, though, was not her discipline per se or her ability to master body etiquette (lishu), lijiao (social etiquette), and guiju (conventional behaviors), but rather her ability to devote herself through these codified behaviors to the service of her husband's family. Regulations for serving the parents appeared in canonical Han dynasty (second century B.C.E. to second century C.E.) texts, the Liji and the Zhouli, where they gave descriptive, elaborately detailed instructions. All funü shared some general behavioral norms, but they did so from specified locations in the family, and tied to each of those locations were precise service obligations. Chen included two parables that illustrate this point very well. The first involved Lu, wife of Zhang Daizhi, who was passionately attached to her *nü* daughters. She taught them about everyday life in great detail using the *falu* [law] concerning victuals and drink, well-executed food, handling meat and fish. Her *yunü* [youngest daughter] was married to Lu Yinggong. One day Lu went to see her daughter and felt unhappy when she saw that pots and pans were littered all over the room. She told her daughter's mother-in-law [*jiaguo furen*?] that she should not let the younger generation prepare its own food. Private preparations of victuals and drink ruin the *jiafa* [family law] [as they allow selfish privacy, to say nothing of bad housekeeping]. How strict the mother was![25]

This story distinguished between commendable emotional attachments and the disciplined behavioral protocols that the lijiao dictated. It is fine for a mother to indulge her beloved daughter, Chen noted. But "correct" or theorized family relations are not based on indulgences. The daughter's primary obligations were to the physical well-being of her husband's parents. The cult of self-abnegating daughters-in-law was, in fact, a testament to the expectation of service. According to the lijiao, the civilized person, a *gongmu* (exemplary mother), for example, should enforce the differences that must ritually separate her from her daughter once her daughter marries and becomes someone else's daughter-in-law. At that point, according to the regulations of the lineage, the daughter is subject to service obligation regulating the lives of her husband's *funü*.[26]

Civility or "correct" behavior rationalizes and scripts relations of difference among funü in the jia. Difference, or *bie*, has to be maintained among funü, particularly people who are as intimately connected as mothers and daughters. The protocols are, in other words, systems of regulating difference that set people in mutual, unequal relations and inscribe each in terms of correct behaviors. For instance, the general protocol governing *gusao* (sisters-in-law) in Chen's text followed a relation that specified a *shugu zhi nü xiongdi zhi qi* (relation of daughter of one's husband's younger brother's wife and one). A certain Ouyang married into the Liao family and had just produced a baby girl when her husband's parents died, leaving a girl called Runniang. Ouyang raised the two girls together but egregiously favored Runniang, her own child's aunt. When Ouyang's daughter asked why, the mother said, You are my daughter and Runniang is your aunt, the daughter of your grandparents. Besides, you have a mother and she does not. How could I treat you both equally?[27] Here, the bie (difference) is generational. Generation trumped the mother-child bond, just as the tension of public and private had trumped surname solidarity in the eyes of the monarch of Lu (though not in Chen's eyes) in the earlier example. Difference expresses itself and is adjudicated situationally. In the process, the discourses of difference blanket the field of play.

Chen's instructions rationalized joint subjects like mother-daughter, aunt-nephew. He also included positive descriptions. He cites, for instance, the Nü lunyu (women's analects), which states declaratively what protocols are required and how to enact them: The aweng/agu (father- and mother-in-law) are the heads of the husband's family. You are their daughter-in-law when you marry. So you must serve them as you did your own parents. When you serve aweng your appearence must be tidy. When agu sits, you must stand. You get your order from her and then you leave. Get up early and open the door, but be quiet and do not wake people up. Set out parents-in-law's towels and their soap and warm water, and then serve them. Retreat when they are finished. Their rice should be soft and meat overdone, because they are old and their teeth are tender. In the evening or late night put them into bed and leave the room. Do this every day. If others know that you do this they will say that you are a good and kind daughter-in-law.

It appears that in Chen's writing, protocols effect gender relationally because they link good behavior and correct performance of the written texts or recipes which have the primary task of situating and distinguishing kinship differences and service obligations inside the family. Performativity or norms materialized in performance, as Butler has suggested, situate the sexes through tactile differences of many kinds. In this case, the differences include age, rank, birth order, marital status, and thus gender. These protocols were neither mere codes or maps nor merely roles. They instructed people in the way advice literature does and they provided continuously reinforced personalities because they linked the theoretical traditions and contemporary behavioral norms. Protocols formed a bulwark of order against the undoing of difference and positioned subjects in social narrative.

If gender simply means the cultural clothing that women put on over their bodies, then Chinese women were only latent historical subjects or "invisible" historically. But if gender is the processes of the materialization of differences, including the difference of sex, then this Jiao nü yi gui shows women, or more accurately, funü, to be very much present in the historical record. Here the subject women is not the point. Chen did not have to provide his readers with fully enumerated charts of the differential positions through which the gendering of the sexes, the positing of sex difference, took place. By the eighteenth century the discourse on kin difference had been normalized into the foundational category of broadly shared experience.

## Producing Woman (Nüxing)

Imperialism forced into crisis the texts and the world of gendering protocols that Chen Hongmou and those like him had so strenuously attempted to stabilize and reproduce. The Manchu dynasty's long, slow implosion and the imperialists' relentless penetration of the heartland through the treaty port system transformed the political elites' social configuration and powers. Where previously the monarchy and bureaucracy had enabled Confucian officials to regulate the meaningful world, social upheaval dispersed these older powers. The old political order buckled in 1905, when the Qing throne abolished the civil service examination system. Eager to replace the old-style elites and their intellectual commitments, a modern, post-Confucian, professionalized intellectual emerged who oversaw the appropriation of foreign signs into the new, domestic, urban mass media.

In the early twentieth century a new social formation arose calling itself zhishi jieji (intellectual class), later qiming xuezhe (enlightened scholars), and finally (under the same forces that produced political funü or women as a political category), zhishifenzi, or Chinese intellectual under Maoist inscription. Zhishi jieji were the educated offshoot of the tiny, very significant new commercial bourgeoisie, who monopolized the appropriation of "Western" ideas, forms, signs, and discourses. In their hands, peripheralization of signs proceeded as new missionary-educated and college-graduated professionals translated, republished, circulated, and commented on texts in foreign languages. Historically, this group constituted itself as a colonialized elite. By that I mean two things. First, the colonial modernization of China forced into existence "new intellectuals"; these elements did not just "import" neologisms from Japan and the European West, but redrew the discursive boundaries of elite social existence. In this way, zhishifenzi occupied (and further valorized) the new, modernist, social field of shehui, or "society." Situated inside the treaty ports in a crude material sense— the palladian English banks and French boulevards, the German beer, American YMCAs, and Japanese factories—words like shehui acquired concrete referents. Shehui, a conceptual term, had, in other words, a visual, material, topographic referent in the new urban spaces of Chinese colonial cities. The powerful older theories and words from Chen Hongmou's time increasingly gave up their eroding referential ground. Once robust conventions were gradually reduced into something intellectuals of the 1920s would call "tradition" and regarded with either nostalgia, contempt, or fear.[28]

The rising importance of semicolonial urbanity or colonial modernity had a growing effect on conventional gendering practices. A rash of masculinist interest in the universal sign of woman had surfaced as early as the 1830s, when there occurred an efflorescence of what Mary Rankin calls "profeminine" male writing. The convention of men writing sympathetically about the needs of women was not new or remarkable; there were precedents in the various querelles des femmes of the eighteenth century. But by the 1860s male reformers were speaking admiringly of "enlightened" relations between women and men in Western countries. Already advocacy of antifootbinding and modern female schooling was part of progressive arguments that the male, new style intellectuals forwarded by the late 1890s and the first decade of the twentieth century.[29] Masculinist interest in nü initiated, according to Charlotte Beahan, an unprecedented surge in female-authored journalism discourses between 1890 and 1910 inside the slackening old world.[30] Calling themselves "sisters" or jiemei, these female writers reversed the strategy Chen adopted when he argued for female literacy on the grounds that ethical women in families produce strong states. "Why isn't China strong?" one woman writer asked. "Because there are no persons of talent. Why are there no persons of talent? Because women do not prosper."[31] Late Qing women sought liberty on "nationalist" grounds. The sisters' publications contributed to what rapidly emerged as "myths of the nation."[32] That is, writers positioned themselves as citizens of the Chinese nation, as advocates of national emancipation from Western imperialism and Manchu occupation, and as different from men of their own Han Chinese nationalist group. On those unimpeachable grounds they sought to mobilize China's "beloved but weak two hundred million women . . . the direct slaves of slaves."[33]

The expression "slaves of slaves" as a term for Chinese women signified a noteworthy change in the theorization of nü. "Slave" referred to male Han Chinese "enslaved" to the Manchu monarchy and thus signaled democratic patriotism. Women, as the slaves of slaves, reached into domestic units to recategorize all Chinese women in a patriotic unity against the myriad imperialists seeking to "divide China up as though it were a melon," as people put it then. The kin-inflected category of funü began a slow, fitful referential shift. In place of kin-inflected funü, some writers began to offer Chinese nüren (female person) as one specific instance of a universal category consisting of all women, and they did so under a patriotic inscription. An example of the mechanics of the referential shift comes from Zhen Ziyang's Nüzi xin duben (New study book for women), a 1907 collection of stories about virtuous women linked generically to narratives in the Chen Hongmou mode discussed above. The older texts celebrated "just mothers," "ethical stepmothers," and other situated kinswomen who managed the jia sphere well, thereby effecting, through their adept use of protocol under difficult circumstances, the space beyond their own jia, that is, the gong or general world. The modern text, in contrast, provided not one but two sets of ethical narratives about good women, set off from each other in two separate books.[34]

Book 1 retold stories familiar to readers in Chen Hongmou's time. These included the ancient story of Mencius's mother, who sacrificed herself constantly to provide her son an appropriate ethical environment; Yue Fei's wife, Liang, who personally fought the Nuzhen barbarians on behalf of the Song dynasty; and Hua Mulan of the Liang dynasty, who masqueraded as a filial son and fought as her father's proxy for twelve years. It also included examples of women who, in the hoary past, had transgressed unfairly gendered boundaries or had been unjustly ignored in masculinist histories. Huang Zongjia, for instance, was born a girl but did not want to be a woman (nüzi), so she masqueraded as a man and served as an official; Suo Maoyi allegedly taught the master calligrapher Wang Xizi his calligraphy style; and there were others.

Book 2 assembled a set of parallel stories about famous women of the West who matched or exceeded Hua Mulan's filial devotion because they served not father, husband, or patriline but the nation. Individual female heroes did not just contribute to the nation through their service to husband and in-laws, as the parables in Chen's compendium established. They served the nation directly. Charlotte Corday, or "Sha Latuo," according to the Chinese version of her story, studied at a nunnery for six years and became engrossed in a particular book by Girondist Charles Barbaroux about national heroes. The book's inspiration sent Sha Latuo to Paris, where she surprised the tyrant Mala (Marat) while he was with his concubine. In prison for his murder, Sha Latuo sent her father a filial letter declaring that tyrannicide was not a crime, and met her death with Puluhua (i.e., Barbaroux's book clutched in her hands). Another narrative venerated Madame Roland, who studied "the Confucianism of her country" but preferred the example of the Greeks and Romans. After marrying Roland for his politics, she inspired her timid husband to resist Robespierre. When Robespierre executed Madame Roland, her husband committed suicide and their servants, overcome, also petitioned for execution; their requests were carried out.[35]

The juxtaposition of "Chinese" and "other" stories engendered meaning in two significant ways. First, obviously, the reworked "Chinese" stories and the "Western" parallels jointly showed female heroes shifting their loyalties from husband or father to nation, without directly requiring that they abandon the prior object. A certain Frances (Frances Willard, perhaps) appears to have been selected because, following her father's death, she remained unmarried and devoted herself to the improvement of North America through a renovation of the family, the nation, and finally the entire world. Nation rose up to peripheralize Father, though never precluding his importance at the personal level.[36] Second, the bilateral mutual exchange of Western signs and Chinese narrative had the effect of producing a category of universal womanhood. Chinese narratives changed in a generic sense, that is, when the subjects of their interest became Western women. When Zhen located Chinese female heroes in the company of European women of the state like Joan of Arc, Charlotte Corday, and Madame Roland, the effect was to legitimate and universalize nüzi within a statist, universal (i.e., Europeanized) world history. Zhen sought to conjoin bourgeois state revolts like the Glorious Revolution and the French and Italian Revolutions, to the expected Chinese Revolution (the Xinhai Revolution occurred a decade later, in 1911). Giving such remarkable prominence to Western women in their national revolutions, moreover, granted universality to heroic female actions of whatever kind, at whatever time. Remarkably, the Chinese section of the text went so far as to legitimate Wu Zetian of the Tang dynasty, previously reviled as a female usurper and defiler of her husband's throne. Changes in pro-feminine discourses thus conditioned the form that nüxing eventually took.

Before the 1920s, however, female heroes continued to rest securely in the inherited binarism familiar from Confucian contexts of hero and the Throne. The term nüxing (literally, female sex) erupted into circulation during the 1920s, when treaty port intellectuals overthrew the literary language of the Confucius canon. Critics replaced the *wen*, or culture of the old world, with *wenxue*, or literature, inscribed in a hybrid (part colloquial Chinese, part European syntax that developed as people began reading Western fiction in Chinese translation) literary language. Wenxue rested on realist representationalism, and thus supported the production of modernist subjectivities. The field of wenxue unfolded in the 1920s as a general terrain of combat for intellectuals. The May Fourth movement of 1919 established wenxue as a field of realist referentiality: the second most significant major figure of that new textuality, after the "hypertrophied self"[37] of the writer himself, was nüxing.

Women by and large did not employ the term nüxing, or perhaps more accurately, there is no evidence that women developed this term to describe themselves. Like the recuperation of nü as a trope or symbol of nationalist universality in masculinist discourse that Rankin noted, nüxing constituted a discursive sign and a subject position in the larger frames of anti-Confucian discourse. When intellectuals overthrew the Confucius canon they sought the total transformation of "Chinese culture." The same modernist, semiotic revolution that invoked the new signs of society (shehui), culture (wenhua), intellectuals (zhishifenzi), individualism (geren zhuyi), and innumerable other new Chinese words gave nüxing or Woman wide and expanding discursive powers. Nüxing played a particularly significant role in two separate textual streams: literary representation and the body of writing known as Chinese feminism. Historically, women writers did not predominate in either one.

"Historical languages constitute classes," Talal Asad observed some time ago; "they do not merely justify groups already in place according to universal economic structures."[38] So nüxing coalesced as a category when, as part of the project of social class formation, Chinese moderns disavowed the older literary language of power. After the May Fourth movement (ca. 1919–1937), Chinese writers wrote in a newly modernized, Westernized, semicolloquial language in which nüxing played the part of a subject of representation and an autonomous agent. Nüxing took shape as one half of the European, exclusionary, male/female binary. Within the zhishifenzi as a class, this explicit sex binary had a lot of uses. Nüxing (like nanxing, or male sex) became a magnet. Its universal, sexological, scientistic core gave life to a psychologized personal identity. But nüxing was also a fulcrum for upending Confucianism and the older forms of social theory, with all its received categories. Chinese translations of European fiction, criticism, science, and social theory placed explicit attention on theories about sex opposition and sex attraction. In particular, colloquial fiction established sex as the core of an oppositional personal or individual identity and woman as a sexological category.[39]

In other words, the career of nüxing firmly established a foundational womanhood beyond kin categories. It did so on the ground of European humanism and scientific sex theory. That is, when it introduced the category of woman as a universal category of nüxing, Chinese feminist writing flooded texts with representations of women as the "playthings of men," "parasites," "slaves," as dependents of men or simply as degraded to the point of nonexistence. Feminist texts accorded a foundational status to physiology and, in the name of nineteenth-century Victorian gender theory, they grounded sexual identity in sexual physiology. Probably the most alarming of all of progressive Chinese feminism's arguments substituted sexual desire and sexual selection for reproductive service to the jia and made them the foundations of human identity.

The secret attraction of European texts was their emphasis on what Foucault termed "sexuality," a "singular historical experience" and a traceable regulative discourse: a historical artifact. When leading male Chinese feminists used the category women as a universal, biological fact and granted foundational status to the Victorian anthropological binary of male/female, it was often in terms of Chinese women's lack of personality or human essence. (I examine this question in detail in chapter 3 because it is one of the distinguishing factors in the national traditions of Chinese feminism.) In other words, when Chinese translators invoked the sex binary of a Charles Darwin or a Havelock Ellis, they valorized debates about female passivity, biological inferiority, intellectual inability, sexuality, and social absence through reference to the location of these "truths" in European social scientism and social theory. Thus, Chinese women became nüxing only when they became the other of Man in the colonial modernist Victorian binary. Woman was foundational only insofar as she constituted a negation of man, his other.

Ching-kiu Stephen Chan's exploration of nüxing in the literature of major male May Fourth realist writers makes this point at the level of literary texts. When the intellectual class, or zhishifenzi, turned to European-style realism, Chan argues, "the classical mimetic function of realism" required that the writer represent himself through his own representations of the Other, and the Other of male realist choice was woman. Nüxing was first and foremost a trope in the discourses of masculinist Western-inspired realist fiction. As Chan puts it, "Textually speaking," nüxing appeared in realist texts, "but as an innocent scapegoat, paying for the crimes that society has committed." Indeed, woman appeared within a cruel equation: "The root of your [female] suffering is to be found in my [male writer's] inability to right the wrongs that society has done me."[40]

Chan's point can also be made in a different way. When the modernist female writer Ding Ling began producing texts in the late 1920s, she too had to struggle with the self/other dynamic coded into the man/woman sex binary. Ding Ling's texts, as I develop fully in a later chapter, sought to take woman as a subject position and social psychology. Yet the work she produced during that period of her career invokes a nüxing who either must die, commit suicide, or lose herself in sexual excess and mental disorder. A universal woman independent of man had to be forged outside the terms of the simple evolutionary sex binary. In the end, Ding Ling, who continued to write but not as a eugenic woman, abandoned psychological realism.

The social history of nüxing is complex: I develop an intellectual history of its efflorescence in the 1930s. However, as it entered elite zhishifenzi discourses, nüxing as a representation took on a life of its own. Her image appeared in popular movies, in pulp fiction, in photographs and fashions, schools and parks. These representations of nüxing reinforced a universal category of woman emerging in the new consumer society. Accordingly, nüxing rapidly ceased to be a Western sign and became a sign of modernity in bourgeois New China. Once it was situated centrally in this new political economy and culture, the sign of nüxing took on a career and a politics of its own.[41]

## Reproducing Funü

The sex binary man/woman and the sign woman or nüxing never went uncontested. Carolyn Brown has vividly shown Lu Xun criticizing the initial formulation and arguing that the physical body of modern Chinese women "had become the repository of a meaning, the signified, that it did not rightfully bear."[42] Social critique from CCP theorist Xiang Jingyu contested what she saw to be a thoroughgoing irrationalization of Chinese new women, nüxing. In her extrapolations from international Marxism she forwarded funü as an alternative name for women as a collectivity.[43] Xiang lost no time classifying nüxing as a product of bourgeois preoccupations, and her comments in the early 1920s set the tone of communist theorizing for decades. Regardless, Xiang's early communist funü reentered modern theory the same way sexed nüxing had, in zhishifenzi recoding, usage, and rearticulation of social theory. In the process of transmission, communists, socialists, and social scientists systematically used the Confucianized, late imperial, collective compound funü to stand for women in social theory. The bourgeois social sciences, political rights theory, and the nineteenth-century patriarchal theory that left-wing intellectuals found so valuable also shared elements of the sex essentialism manifest in realist fiction. But enlightened social theorists shaped their critique to emphasize social production, and consequently weighted historical and institutional teleology over organic, biogenetic organicism. So, unlike nüxing, Marxist funü found its referential framework in revolutionary practice and in the historical woman that future world-historical teleology would produce.

The Chinese translation of Bebel's *Women and Socialism* is a foundational example of funü used this way. Its chiliastic tone and the systematic use of funü as the figure par excellence of general social revolution relied on a conjuncture of woman and society that attracted Chinese Marxists from the start. Later CCP theory would include Engel's "Origin of the Family, Private Property, and the State," Lenin's "Soviet Political Power and Women's Status," "International Women's Day," and "On the Freedom to Love," and Stalin's "International Women's Day."[44] The catachresis of nüxing testified to the sex binary's importance in what became a tidal wave of theoretical work and translation. The communist funü rested on other theoretical truths. It situated its subject of women in social production as much as in family reproduction. Women in Chinese Marxism took shape within an encompassing theoretical framework of Euro-Marxist modes of production, historical teleology, stage theory, the state/society and sub/super-structure binarisms, and, of course, the discourse's universal, international referentiality.[45]

State building supplanted bourgeois consolidation in both the "white," Guomindang or Nationalist Party as well as the communist camps, as the Japanese troops advanced in the late 1930s, occupying Manchuria and treaty ports and eventually extending their military hold into vast parts of the country. Socialist funü obviated nüxing once the right wing allowed the discourses of national salvation to become the special province of the left. The reactionary right rescinded its pallid remaining feminist rights arguments and dissolved the women's movement into a "feminine mystique." Socialist, Communist Party mobilization politics targeted funü strategically as a tactical object and eventually found methods of pulling women into the anti-Japanese struggle and social revolution by recreating funü as a third element or triangulating category mediating between the modern state and the modern Chinese family. But in the provinces during the late 1920s and 1930s an increasingly Maoist CCP grafted elements appropriated from local categories to its international Marxist teleology of women in social production/reproduction. The Communist Party's fugitive state projects (fugitive in the sense that during these years, the CCP abandoned territory under military pressure from the Japanese Imperial Army and the Nationalist troops and eventually undertook the Long March to Yan'an in the late 1930s) made the funü of Chinese Marxism into a category of political praxis.

In doing so, the universal female proletarian prominent in Bebel and other European Marxist writing relinquished theoretical centrality. In place of this figure, Chinese theoretical practice installed the village women engaged in various kinds of mobilization. Chinese communist liberation practices canceled out that older European subject of woman. To put it another way, the peripheralized sign of woman realized an independent local politics. The Jiangxi Soviet (1930–1934), for instance, identified woman as a political subject who met the following criteria: she was over fourteen years of age; had been emancipated from the fetters of tongyangxi (child marriage), prostitution, and female slave systems; had recourse from family violence; her physical body did not bear the marks of "feudalism" (no earrings or footbinding); and she named herself as a funü in liberating political praxis. This subject existed inside a structured sphere of politics beyond the rural calendar of fieldwork and beyond village social relations. She labored according to schedule and according to protective laws.[46] A rudimentary bureaucracy concerned itself with her welfare and ensured her freedom of marriage. Political networks, such as the Working Women's

Congress, operated to rationalize her political outlook. The symbolic center of this woman as a subject was undoubtedly the effort to propagandize Women's Day.[47]

The discourse of Woman under the fugitive state had a proto-mass-line role that allowed activists and Party Central Committee and rural women to speak in different voices and that opened a wide range of positions to local people.[48] These included *qingfu* (young women), *ludai de tongyangxi* (wives oppressed because they had been sold as infant brides), *dapinku laodongfunü* (great suffering women laborers), *nongcun zhong di laodongfunü* (the laboring women of the rural villages), and *nügong nongfu* (women workers and peasants). Even the heterogeneous *funü* of this period, however, was always already a subject-effect of state discourses and a by-product of its legal, ideological, and organizational apparatus. It is just that before 1949 the "line" did not attempt political closure. Funü consequently appeared to take a range of subject positions inside the Soviet state, beyond the reach of family and feudalism. For a Marxist feminist like Ding Ling, this was the arena for experiments in liberation. As one document put it, village women do not understand the agitation for liberation and need to have explained to them the link between victory in class struggle and the liberation of women. They must be taught that their self-interest is connected to the state, not the family.[49]

Thus, the ideological ideal was a healthy, semiliterate woman of eighteen to thirty-five years old who could "destroy her familist outlook and serve [the state even when called on to make] government transfers." She was expected to act out of self-interest (*benshen liyi*) for personal rights (*quanli*), "representing" herself through grassroots mass organizational work.[50] The funü encountered in these texts appeared never to have understood what was meant by "women's self-interest" until propagandists explained the stakes in concrete detail.[51] The natural interests women theoretically possessed, in other words, had first to be inscribed via the actions of recruiting, educating, nurturing, and mobilizing. Funü's proper field was "the organizational sphere of the Party" (*dang di zuzhi fanwei*), where she sustained herself in the political space of the CCP through election (*xuanju*), mobilization (*dongyuan*), and various organizational (*zuzhi*) practices.[52] Maoism in the late 1930s and 1940s constantly reformulated funü, always retaining the statist slant.[53] The formula that emerged in the early 1940s consequently involved a synecdochic process of exchange between two interpenetrated objects of political discourse: the state (*guojia*) and the family (*jiating*). Rather than posit independent funü as an agent of politics outside domestic closure, as the brief earlier experiments had done, the late Soviets' and Yan'an-style praxis emphasized production of funü through political processes that retained women and men in a sphere of politicized domestic relations.

After 1943 the CCP's party line turned to the transformation of the family itself. By 1947 Maoist state policy had shifted—in contradistinction to Marxist theory and socialist practices elsewhere—toward a reinvented family, which appears in these texts as jiating. The homily of the Zhu Fusheng family conference, for instance, treats the "history" of domestic politics as a Party historiographer might chronicle a Central Committee meeting. Published in 1949, this instructive story plays a role in structuring new citizens similar to what Chen Hongmou's text may have intended to play among educated female kinswomen. The women of the Zhu family, though oppressed, did not have the "habit of democracy, and did not know how to speak, ask questions, or actually say a thing." After Zhu Fusheng explained democratic procedure to them, they collectively transformed themselves from an autocracy (jiazhang zhuanzhi) into a "democratic family" (minzhu jiating). In subsequent months, family members instituted political democratic policies such as self-criticism (ziwo piping), domestic production of thread and cloth, and planning, all domestic production activities the CCP promoted at the time. The homily of the Zhu family nicely exhibits how statist political practices interpenetrated family relations, lodging funü through democratic rhetoric in a renovated statist jiating or nucleating family.[54]

The rhetorical recuperation of women into family required a politicized new family reconstituted in the language of politics. Leading Party officials promoted domestic political construction, as Zhou Enlai did, for instance, when he argued that women did not need emancipation from family, that what really needed to happen was for men to begin to take family responsibilities as seriously as women did.[55] Patricia Stranahan has argued that it was precisely this reorientation of woman policy that provided the stable base peasant women eagerly accepted; the resulting line both reflected "peasant realism" and achieved revolutionary transformation through social production.[56] The resulting collaboration of village women and Central Committee was, I want to stress, neither traditional nor universally Marxist. It was syncretic and as "modern" as any alternative.[57]

The Maoist interpenetration of state and family made the body of women a field of the state, at the same time that it opened the state to inflection by kin categories.[58] The entry point was reproductive science. Woman-work ganbu (cadres), armed with medical knowledge, brought to political activity the power/knowledge of sanitation, physiology, and scientific midwifery. Texts drilling village women in reproductive physiology ("It's just like your farm animals") dispensed information on bodily functions like the menstrual cycle and hygiene (don't borrow pads, don't drink cold water, stay away from the dirty menstrual blood that carries disease, don't have intercourse during your period, visit the doctor for irregularities, etc.). Scientific midwifery connected family reproduction to state politics.[59]

The dawning of the golden era of Chinese communist familism in the 1950s found the modern Chinese jiating sandwiched between a pre-1949 peasant-inflected formation and idealized revolutionary images flooding in from the more advanced socialist USSR. By that time the ideological norm or politically ideal jiating had become the nineteenth-century Europeanized family idealized by the zhishifenzi: mommy, daddy, and me.[60] So jiating grounded social production in a context heavily marked with traces of older formations, just as the nation did. The modern socialist jiating and Maoist guojia coexisted in synecdochic unity, as concept-metaphors of each other. That, at least, is how I interpret mobilizations like the 1957 campaign "Industrious and Frugal in Establishing the Nation, Industrious and Frugal in Managing the Family," where state and family are virtually synonymous; what operates in one sphere translates directly into the other. "The material and cultural life of our state's [guo] masses of people has improved substantially in the last few years. But the lives of many jiating are still not comfortable," the text reads. To raise the jiating's level the masses must "industriously develop our state's industry and agriculture." The work of housewives (jiating zhufu) must mirror the work going on outside the jiating, in the guojia. "Every housewife could be industrious and frugal in managing the family affairs if she institutionalizes a rational planning schedule. . . . Industriousness and frugality in the family labor strengthens industriousness and frugality in the nation."[61]

### The Women's Federation and Funü as a State Category

William Parish and Martin Whyte once commented that after Liberation in 1949, the Chinese state took no clear measures to transform family structure, and that Fulian, the state's Women's Federation, was an "amorphous" government bureaucracy, the only mass organization that people belonged to by virtue of physiology.[62] This does not explain the very real powers of the Women's Federation. The importance of Fulian lay in its power to subordinate and dominate all inscriptions of womanhood in official discourse. It is not that Fulian actually represented the "interests" of women, but that one could not until recently be "represented" as a woman without the agency and mediation of Fulian. That fact is a measure of its success and its importance.[63]

In late 1948 the government commissioned its leading female officials, dignitaries, and luminaries in the Liberated Areas with the task of planning the All-China Democratic Women's Association's (later, simply Women's Association) first meeting as soon as Beijing fell.[64] With formal gravity the Planning Committees and Standing Committee began directing the installation of new bureaucratic frameworks charged with deciding national policy and convening the association's first representative congress. In these initiating moments Fulian consolidated its power as a national state organ for responsibly representing "new China's women." With mechanical deliberation the bylaws connect representation of "female masses" to the international socialist women's movement through the accumulating processes of representation. "What is most deserving of pride," one document read, "is that the representatives [daibiao] from the liberated areas are all picked by election from the local area women's congresses. . . . We have been commissioned by the female masses. We must loyally represent their opinions." And the proviso: "Representation [daibiao] means representing the masses, [it does] not [mean] controlling [guan] the masses."[65]

This bureaucratization and Fulian's transformation from active production of funü to formally representing them in Beijing relied on past struggle. But it emanated from a new sort of definitional power. Representative bodies like congresses and the Federation itself did "represent the masses," but they also consolidated and mediated internal differences (tuanjiele gezhong butong de funü), homogenizing, so to speak, through political democracy. The inception of Fulian initiated for funü unprecedented participation in the rituals of state formation and promised bureaucratic power, but only so long as Fulian, the government, retained the power to determine what, in fact, constituted a funü.[66]

Speaking to this issue, Deng Yingchao laid out the official view when she argued that in the discourses of the state, woman had achieved "political, economic, cultural, and social elevation and elevation of herself in the family." Fulian's charge involved consolidating and expanding the political sphere carved out earlier under the fugitive state: a process, the document argued, that ensured equal status for women because it transformed them from consumers into producers.[67] By its third congress Fulian spoke in even broader, less autonomous terms, the gray, ponderous language of the state:

> The All-China Women's Federation is, under the leadership of the Chinese Community Party, an organization for the basic organization of every strata of laboring women. [It] has achieved enormous work success since the second National Congress. . . . [But now it] must improve and strengthen its mass viewpoint and its mass-line work methods . . . be concerned with and reflect the real interests and

demands of women, struggle energetically against discrimination and harming of women [etc.] . . . so that Fulian and the mass of women have an even more intimate relationship.[68]

The founding of Fulian, however, was not specific to women.[69] The same ritual unfolded in the mass groups that "reflected and represented" youth, trade unions, and other politically delineated constituencies. The Fulian organization (and its replicants) took part in a reinscription of the nation itself, and thus it represented at a subordinated level the processes of state building commencing at levels superior to itself. The socialist state consolidated gender difference on the material grounds of scientific physiology. Part of this scientism, clearly reflected in Fulian documents, is the notion that people are in literal fact material because their organic reproductive capacity makes them like animals.[70] Thus, under Maoist inscription, gendering located itself as a process of reproductive differentiation within "scientific socialism." The fusion of peasant realism and socialist scientism gave rise to texts like "People and Wealth Flourish" ("Ren yu cai wang"), which "encourage the people of the liberated areas not merely to work hard to get enough to wear and eat, but also to have more children, who, once they are born, must be supported [yanghuo]." Lyrically conflating "production" and "reproduction," the state policy vowed to train midwives, investigate infant mortality, propagandize for scientific sanitation, oppose feudal superstition, and publish popular chapbooks on infant care, all predicated on popularizing a modern understanding of reproductive physiology and sanitary childbirth practices.

Much work among women aimed at producing people who would collaborate in the biopolitical agenda of the state. Before the twentieth century, birth and death had possessed no direct link to the Throne or to state political economy. Life and death commenced in the spatial boundaries of the jia or sect and took form as matters of pollution, rupture, and reconciliation.[71] Although late imperial domestic and popular medical practices regarding menstruation, conception, parturition, suckling, and so on had been extremely sophisticated, they operated in the same neo-Confucian epistemic order as other gendering discourses. The socialist state, on the other hand, made clear the direct linkage of state practice and modern obstetric medicine in the process of popularizing the discourse of hygiene. The 1949 *Study Guide for the New Woman* straightforwardly declaimed that "the 27 lessons in this book . . . are for the exclusive use of village women in their study, literacy classes, and political lessons [which the CCP attempted to organize at the village level whenever possible]. It is appropriate as a refresher for teachers and active elements [representing the CCP's agenda at the village level] studying self-discipline." The book concluded each of its lessons (see "The *lijiao* [ritual etiquette] of the feudal society is the source of women's suffering," for instance) with an attached series of study questions, such as "How does the old power of the village oppress women?" Study, which meant learning the correct answer transmitted physiology as the foundation of gender difference. The textbooks inscribed sex physiological differences through their discussions of scientific facts and presented reproductive physiology as the foundation for the production of male and female. Thus, as has proved the case elsewhere, statist rhetoric inserted anatomical difference into a discourse on life and death. It assumed a binary base (the "physiology of the human female" versus the "physiology of the human male") for the reproductive biology that the science of physiology established or foundationalized. But the inscription of gender difference at the level of reproductive physiology elided something very interesting. It adamantly positioned material (re)production as the site of difference, but it did not theorize personality in physiological terms. Fulian writing has a tendency to inscribe difference at the level of physiology while curtailing attribution of difference at the level of personality. This latter, the realm of feeling and identity, until recently remained bound to conventions identified under Maoism in terms of social class, not sex or "gender."

It is easier to see the statist construction of funü under Maoism in the wake of post-Mao social critique. The post-Mao or Deng Xiaoping economic reforms aimed to transform or reform the relationship of the citizens to the means of production, systems of commodity distribution and consumption, and popular cultural and social life. After 1987, when it became clear that these changes in the economy and civil administration of the country would not be reversed, the forces unleashed a globally significant Great Transformation of the political economy, rewriting the national landscape and the relation of the nation in the reregionalizing, neoliberal international state system. This pathway is intensifying now as China accedes to the World Trade Organization (WTO) and as neoliberalism in the state's policymaking bureaucracies takes the dominant position. Major changes led to the end of the commune system, rollbacks in social welfare and social redistribution schemes, the rise of the new monied elites, and the government's support of domestic markets, where particularly urban populations are pressed to take up responsibility for compulsory commodity and leisure consumption. Since 1985 in literary and social science theory, questions of women's social and sexual subjectivity have become explosive.[72] The post-Mao state's efforts to reestablish mass organizations like Fulian brought on an overt conflict between the national subject funü and an increasingly sexualized, consumer-oriented, retheorized nüxing. The resurgence of the eroticized nüxing helps clarify the contradictory formation of nüxing and funü from a final angle. Under the previous statist protocol, funü allowed for the social production of woman in politics but disallowed any psychology of gender difference. The even older, initial May Fourth literary inscription of nüxing made woman the other of man, but proved insufficiently stable to resist statist inscriptions of funü. The recuperation of nüxing's heterosexist male/female binary does open up difference as "femininity," and thus it does provide the potential for feminist resistance. (This point will be developed more systematically in chapters 6 and 7.)

This sketches out the prevailing conditions of theoretical innovation in the late imperial period, the colonial modern period, and the periods of social revolution, socialist modernization, and the post-Mao reform economy. The next chapter describes in detail the rich and intricate arguments that put into play Chinese progressive feminism and its sexed, physiological understanding of the modern Chinese women, nüxing. Chapters 4 through 7 follow specific individuals and cohorts of thinkers who worked in the moments mentioned here in schematic form. In each case the question of women in Chinese feminist thinking describes a novel subject which is also a catachresis. I have read each to highlight the historical tense of the future anterior, which examines not what women are but what they will have been.

I n the early twentieth century, modern Chinese scholarship predicated—
it proposed in theory—"women, the sexed subject of Chinese feminism." Progressive feminist theory argued that human social and racial
evolution accelerated when individual women freely acted on their instinctive heterosexual drives and chose the best man available for social
reproduction. This eugenicist thread gave a hopeful, appealing legitimacy
to arguments about women's liberation, because it justified the autonomy
of women and their social liberation in evolutionary terms. Consolidating
nüxing, then, unfolded in a general theory of human sexuality grounded in
social evolutionary conjecture. Evolutionary theory, in turn, drew its legitimacy from anthropological observations that European, and later Japanese, and North American theorists made about non-European and primitive peoples. Of course, women was also a signifier of civilization and
modernity in internationally circulating theories. For purposes of this discussion, however, I highlight three key issues: (1) the foundational internationalism of Chinese feminism, (2) the analytic centrality of the sexed
subject of progressive Chinese feminism, and (3) the singular elements of
Chinese (internationalist) feminism.

Suffusing these arguments are several more general subthemes. First,
nationalism or nation narration does not explain Chinese feminism's singular qualities. National salvation was a grave preoccupation for intellectuals in twentieth-century China and elsewhere. In this regard, as Kumari
Jayawardena has shown, Chinese feminist thought resembles analogous
movements in Egypt, Iran, Turkey, India, Sri Lanka, Japan, Korea, the
Philippines, Vietnam, and Indonesia, which all developed national, nationalist, and anti-imperialist feminist traditions. The central problem Chinese feminist thinking confronted was to stabilize its own analytic subject.
To that end, a number of preoccupations became staple items. They were
the historical catachreses nüxing, or the sexual female subject, the social

problematic of *ren'ge*, or women's social-ethical-political standing, and the enduring nationalist trope of Chinese women's deficiencies or flaws, *que-dian*. These historical catachreses and questions in theory are irreducible to either Confucian precedent or strictly to the terms of the European and Japanese interlocutors whom Chinese theorists engaged in often imaginary dialogues.[1]

Second, feminism is an international discourse and not first and foremost a historical narrative about how Chinese women created their own local (national) feminism. I suggested earlier that feminism is a system of ideas, not the speech of women, and here I develop that point. In what follows I argue that Chinese theoretical feminism offers a distinctive kind of historical evidence, and that this body of preponderantly theoretical work on the "woman question" in the 1920s and 1930s was central to Chinese social theory generally speaking, including the new social sciences. The extent of speculation about the woman question is staggering in a brutal empirical sense. And, like other national feminisms, progressive, foundational Chinese feminism in the 1920s and early 1930s preoccupied itself with questions of subjectivity, citizenship, and women's choice. Progressive Chinese feminism was progressive because it presumed species evolution, arguing that once artificial social barriers to female subjectivity had been lifted, overall human development would accelerate.[2] It was a kind of feminism because it held that national evolutionary progress required the emancipation of women into citizenship.[3]

Lila Abu-Lughod has made a similar point about the Middle East, writing that, as a concept, feminism is "a particular constellation of ideas and political practices" that is "tied to a particular history—of capitalism, personhood, political and legal arrangements."[4] Abu-Lughod argues that feminism "disseminated" from Europe and, though I do not disagree, I would shift the emphasis somewhat. What the universalizing gaze of the European Enlightenment had seen, after all, were the disparate peoples of the world.[5] The dissemination of feminism returned the attention of metropolitan and colonial intellectuals to the same sites that had instigated the gaze of Enlightenment in the first instance. The logics of origin are not my primary concern; here, it is enough to propose that globally feminisms are constitutionally spectral. Generically they have arisen as gendered logics in relation to geopolitical others, which is to say that European enlightened feminism is inconceivable in the absence of colonialism, just as Chinese enlightened thought takes shape only in relation to the Great Powers and their various urbanities.[6]

The specific history of Chinese progressive feminism hints at the complexities involved. Zhou Jianren, Mao Dun, Wei Sheng, Gao Xian, and others were either contemporaries or were dragged into a contemporary moment with Margaret Sanger, Yosano Akiko, Havelock Ellis, Yamakawa Kikue, Dora Black, Ellen Key, Havelock Ellis, and Sigmund Freud. Bound to the same powerful ideas, albeit in relations of profound inequality, each was conditioned in part by the observations and concerns of Freud, Alphonse de Candolle, Wilhelm Schallmayer, Karl Jung, Thomas Herbert, Wilhelm Roscher, and countless other eighteenth- and nineteenth-century theoreticians, anthropologists, and theorists major and minor, whose generalizations had initially taken shape in relation to the alleged national characteristics of "the Chinese."[7] Theoreticians who figured prominently in Chinese foundational thinking about internationalized feminism in the late nineteenth and early twentieth centuries circulated unequally through theory projects not just in China, but in Japan, Norway, Denmark, India, New Zealand, the United States, France, and England as well. Chinese feminists were undoubtedly obscure under European eyes; nonetheless, they all participated in the globalizing project or event of progressive feminism.[8]

Yet theory is, in Balibar's phrase, "the impossible limit of an autodetermination . . . an effort to conceptualize the line on which we think."[9] And feminism is a modern theory. We know that the subject of progressive Chinese feminism was a sexed being. Like her counterparts elsewhere, the Chinese nüxing wore Tangee lipstick, exposed their arms and legs, and in fact set the visual template for self-adornment in the new consumer cultures of the 1920s in most parts of the world.[10] But nüxing is a novel scholarly category as well as a new social formation. Theoretical feminism in colonial modern China engaged people, mostly but not exclusively male, in a decades-long project of thinking about this new social phenomenon women that appeared to lie at the heart of the modern social, political, and representational order. I do not pursue the social history of nüxing here. My overriding point is that women, the sexed subject of Chinese feminism, predicated itself in relation to theories about eugenic choice that came into global parlance in evolutionary sexual theory. Eugenics theory puts the woman question at the heart of social science theory and theories of sociobiological reproduction. There it disseminates into the social science disciplines of anthropology, psychology, statistics, and other modern colonial scholarly disciplines.[11] This chapter establishes the basic framework of the contingent foundations of progressivist thinking haunting Chinese feminism, as it continues to haunt feminist criticism in many popular traditions to this day.[12] Chinese feminism is like other reflexive, contemporary, national traditions of feminism in this regard. Feminist theory is an embedded form of historical reflexivity or self-conscious thinking about perceived social crises. It is the evidence of thought. To think theoretically while acknowledging the historical specificity of theoretical work allows historians to focus on forces that might otherwise "simply act on us, imperceptible, outside of our consciousness and our grasp, mobilizing and disciplining us as subjects" even as we undertake theoretically informed projects of self-comprehension.[13]

## Citizenship and Internationalism

In the entry for "the woman question" in his monumental 1929 volume *Shehui wenti cidian* (Dictionary of social problems), social scientist Chen Shousun argued:

> The two most significant social problems of the contemporary era are the labor problem and the woman problem. The former makes sustenance its central issue and seeks to resolve that problem, while the latter takes the matter of sex [*xing*] to be the most central and fundamental question of human life. The woman question is not simply concerned with Woman herself, but broadly speaking with the lives of men and women, so that it has an intimate relation to social life generally. What is most important in this question is to reform current male-centered civilization and to abolish the slave status of women that has obtained, reestablishing a society with the objective of equal rights for women and men. To date, the social status of *nüxing* has not only been under the conquest of men [*nanxing*], *nüxing* has become virtually a class totally subordinated to men, seeming almost to constitute a second world to that of men.[14]

That is a capsule summary of key views in progressive foundational feminism in the 1920s: the centrality of sex to the question of women's emancipation, the sexed subjects nüxing and nanxing, and the view that women constitute a second order of subordinated beings, barely human, held by men in perpetual bondage. Earlier writing in the pre-eugenicist tradition of Chinese feminism was also internationalist, but it concerned itself more with citizenship than sexuality. To clarify the singularity of eugenicist or progressive feminism it is helpful briefly to describe the shape that its immediate predecessor took. This section examines thinking before the advent of eugenics and seeks to show that pre-eugenicist writing drew on alternative means of describing the female subject.

In their groundbreaking 1975 anthology *Jindai Zhongguo nüquan yundong shiliao, 1842–1911* (Documents on the feminist movement in modern China, 1842–1911), Li Yu-ning and Chang Yu-fa firmly established the fact that Chinese information about the international women's emancipation movement had been global from the beginning. "Taixi funü jinshi shi" (The contemporary history of Western women), published in 1900 in the magazine *Jinghuabao*, employs a pre-eugenicist vocabulary to describe female subjects.[15] Keep in mind that only twenty years separates the clarity of Chen Shousun's dictionary entry from the verities of early twentieth-century women's magazines like *Jinghuabao* and a journal I will draw on shortly, *Funü shibao* (Ladies' monthly). "The Contemporary History of Western Women" uses the terms *nü, funü,* and *nüjie,* though never in its many pages (or the other dozens of articles Li and Chang anthologized with it) does the neologism *nüxing* appear. "The Contemporary History of Western Women" had two objectives. The first was to qualify foreign achievements. Therefore, for instance, it reminded Chinese readers that sexual segregation had historically been as serious a problem everywhere, including the "West," as in today's China. Second, the narrative stressed how rapid the progress of Western women had been recently. It singled out American women worthies for their successful struggles to inherit and to will property. But it also approvingly described the efforts of anonymous women whose work had led to such milestones as the Swiss law of 1845 giving women limited property rights and the 1848 decision in New York and Pennsylvania to graduate women students from medical school. The essay optimistically suggested that Chinese women would experience a similarly rapid improvement of their condition after joining the global struggle for women's rights. "The Contemporary History of Western Women" is just one vivid illustration of the anthologists' larger point, which is that in the waning years of the Qing dynasty, literate women and men already had access to abundant information about the international women's movement.[16] Pre-eugenicist Chinese feminists also had an inclusive understanding of the international state system, and they did predicate a universal subject, women, that was rooted in the civil order of the nation-state system.

"The Contemporary History of Western Women" chronicles year by year the historical existence of a universal subject woman whose progress is measurable within an international matrix, held in place multilaterally through geopolitical or international states. A movement forward in abolitionist Boston is globally incremental; it contributes to the international women's movement in the same way as the banning of the sale of women in England in 1803 or establishing the 1810 Napoleonic code. Likewise, the first International Women's Congress in England in 1815 and the discovery in Germany that women's ova contribute to the fetus half of its genetic material continued to reinforce the essay's case that women are an international and a universal subject.

In other words, the argument for Chinese women's emancipation is not divisible from the discourse of nation in these sources.[17] The supplement of nationalism is always internationalism. Although women such as Frances Willard appear as national subjects, their achievements actually flow into the international elevation of women globally; so the nationalities of women are always noted, but their achievements register as international progress in an international arena. The same dynamic is working in the way "The Contemporary History of Western Women" structures the analytic category of *funüjie*, or "women's world."[18] Women's world included non-Han and non-Chinese subjects, in much the same way that womanhood is an inclusive category. It includes intra- and international difference across class, ethnic, and regional difference, both inside China's national boundaries and in relation to internally stratified classes of women of other nations. For instance, the third volume of *Funü shibao*, an early magazine addressed to female readers, contained three major articles—one on the Queen of Spain, another on an American woman balloonist, a third on Turkish women—all classified under the category of the womanhood question. Volume 3 was not a special issue on non-Chinese women; it was just another general issue about the world of women as such. It presumed the universality of funüjie and Chinese women's claim to womanhood, even when none of the particular historical instantiations it offered was in fact a Chinese woman. Similarly, the journal's seventh volume included several contributions about universal female suffrage, the U.S. struggle, suffragist actions in Britain, and Chinese women's claim to the right to vote after four thousand years of oppression, all appearing alongside an essay on the Queen of Italy. For there to be a specific funüjie with characteristically Chinese qualities, in other words, the category funüjie had to include women of the world at large. The journal *Funü shibao* did hold one group of nationals in highest esteem: American women.[19] But even in their estimable case, female suffrage was a distant dream, as women's enlightened parity was not reality in any country at that point.

It was thus relatively simple for Chinese journalists to lay claim to equal standing for Chinese women in a world where the emancipation of women into citizenship was still universally problematic. Subscribing to the suffrage struggle in this sort of world was a measure of civilized behavior. The internationalist context of nationalist thinking about women's liberation is visible in many other kinds of sources besides "The Contemporary History of Western Women." For instance, pre-eugenicist journalists situated China and Chinese progress inside the international colonial hierarchy of barbarism and civilization. Marriage portraits gracing most volumes of *Funü shibao* are a graphic illustration of this point; for instance, two plates appear in the center of volume 2. Doubtless these images deliver the shock of the new, and part of their importance may just be to model new wedding fashions. But the portraits are also significant because they put into civic or public, national, and even international circulation images of an event that previously had belonged to the interior space of the family (jia) and its ritual etiquette (lijiao). However, there is also a logic structuring the images that makes them more meaningful, in ensemble, than perhaps they would have been had they been printed separately. In the first plate a neon-green portrait of a Javanese marriage ceremony shows a traditional, royal Java couple from Guizu set in direct relation to a formal portrait of a "new style wedding" (see figs. 1 and 2). Unlike the "primitive" bride, the new style bride wears a modified Anglo-Chinese gown and a white princess veil and holds a bouquet of flowers. Her groom is wearing an elegant top hat and tux. In this second plate, old and new are presented together, perhaps indicating the inextricable relation of the modernist and nativist styles. On one hand is a high-society marriage party in what the photograph notes is a Chinese style. Flanking this portrait, which is captioned "Preserving the national essence: the old-style wedding," is a second image, captioned "The honey of freedom: the new style of European marriage," which shows only a bride and groom dressed in Edwardian garb. The message is complex.[20]

It is possible to read social evolutionary implications here because in social science theory from Morgan to Engels, marriage is a central event. Photographic technology allows the conventional happy family event of a marriage to be reproduced while also clarifying the marriage's importance not just to family continuity but to evolutionary development as such. Juxtaposition also implies that national essence and free or European marriage practices, though not mutually exclusive, may have a temporal or evolutionary sequence (see fig. 3). However, even when the photos are read ethnographically in a national evolutionary trajectory, the emphasis on citizenship and universality assumes the internationality of the very barbarism-to-civilization continuum that might situate China in a position of lesser development than France. Including China, it is implied that all nations operate on internal continua from barbarism to civility. A similar logic is at work in the discourse of hygiene. Here the point seems to be that Chinese feminine bodies are now measurable against universal standards of womanliness in the abstract, because this abstraction was an internationally established geopolitical norm. The continuing discussions of women's hygiene make the point in relation to women's modern hygienic practices, which authors claim are the foundation of the civilized family.[21] Scientific menstruation, cleanliness in relation to marriage, pregnancy, childbirth, and postpartum recovery are the elements of the ideal.[22] An article on aesthetics and the female body published in 1911 argued that there exists a universal, mathematical standard for calculating female beauty. Chinese clothes, English clothes, Japanese clothes—all are governed by a universal golden mean the author called "experimental aesthetics." The theoretical principle of experimental aesthetics is freedom of movement, because all bodies move and rest. Balance and proportion are therefore universal properties.[23] Experimental aesthetics are potentially democratic as well, because their universality means that clothes can be made to flatter all individual body types and are no longer simply functional social measures of rank and privilege. This is a universal female subject of a specific kind. Feminine hygiene and aesthetics predicated a material, scientific, procreative feminine body, but for all its emphasis on international norms and social development, this was not yet a sexualized body.

To pursue this point further would lead me too far afield. My basic object in mentioning feminist arguments before eugenics is only to suggest that there is no point prior to a geopolitical figuring of universal women in Chinese feminism. Women in Chinese feminism, no matter which analytic subject we examine—funüjie, funü, or nüxing—is constitutionally, in a naïvely literal sense, always already an internationalized subject. It seeks to liberate women into citizenship in a modern nation where the gains of Chinese women register as a national and international liberation movement. The predicate "Chinese women" in Chinese feminism seems to have begun life as an international subject, but not in the explicit discourse of sexuality. The recasting of the subject of Chinese feminism as a sexual subject occurred in the 1920s in an archive that was generically theoretical.

## Mei Sheng and The Chinese Woman Question

In 1923 the Shanghai New Culture Press began selling what became a multivolume series of pamphlets under the title Nüxing wenti taolunji (Collected discussions of the woman question). These pamphlets republished selected articles that had first appeared in the contemporary periodical and broadside presses. Between 1929 and 1934 Shanghai New Culture collated and reissued these pamphlets in six large volumes, containing 159 essays, under twenty topical divisions, and retitled the whole collection Zhongguo funü wenti taolunji or Collected Discussions of the Chinese Women Question (hereafter ZFWT).[24] (Close to two thousand pages by that time, these volumes were, in turn, photocopied and reissued by Fang Shiduo in 1977 in Taipei, under the title Zhongguo shehui shiliao jiyao [Abstracts of Chinese social history data.])[25] ZFWT represented an attempt to impose on the great disorder of Republican-era intellectual life a systematicity and clarity that had been missing in the ebb and flow of the women's periodical press, where each of the 159 articles had first appeared. Mei Sheng, the series editor, selected pieces from twenty-nine different venues, ranging in importance from Funü zazhi (Ladies' journal), his chief source, to lesser publications like Anhui xuesheng zhoukan (Anhui student journal) and influential coterie journals like Jiating yanjiu (Research on the family). Tables 1 and 2 chart

影攝之時婚結族貴哇爪

1 Wedding photo of Javanese nobility.
Source: Funü shibao (Ladies' monthly), vol. 2, interior front plate.

貞 定 史 女 陳 與 生 吉 君 劉
影 攝 之 時 婚 結 式 新 日 三 十 二 月 四 年 本

2 New style marriage.
Source: *Funü shibao* (Ladies' monthly), vol. 2, interior front plate.

3 Honey of Freedom: European-style marriage/Preserve the National Essence: Chinese old fashioned marrige. Source: *Funü shibao* (Ladies' monthly), vol. 2.

where Mei redacted the essays from and what these consisted of (e.g., translations from Japanese, English, French, and Scandinavian languages as well as local theory projects). The theory object, zFWT, that Mei created and marketed is the core of this section's discussion. It is, in effect, a feminist canon.

Biographic information about Mei Sheng is sparse, but some hypotheses can be drawn. Publishing under his given name, Gao Erbo, his pseudonym of Xisheng or Gao Xisheng, and possibly with his elder brother, Gao Ersong, Mei Sheng apparently edited or coedited three major projects. One is a publication tentatively dated to 1925, a collection of historical documents in three languages relating to the May 30th Incident.[26] The others are dictionaries, though this modest word understates the ambitions of the genre. *Jingji kexue da zidian* (A dictionary of economics), for instance, likely published in 1935, is an exhaustive listing of translated terms and analytic descriptions of the academic language of the international discipline of economics.[27] In 1929 Mei seems to have served as senior editor of a volume entitled *Shehui kexue da zidian* (The social science dictionary), published by the Shijie shuju in Shanghai. This remarkable dictionary of social science terminology translated bibliographic and biographic material and

Table 1   *Zhongguo shehui shiliao jiyao* (vols. 1–3)

| Journals | Articles | Journals | Articles |
|---|---|---|---|
| 1. Funü zazhi | 30 | 13. Shishi xinbao | 1 |
| 2. Funü pinglun | 9 | 14. Chenguang | 1 |
| 3. Juewu | 7 | 15. Chenbao fukan | 1 |
| 4. Xingqi pinglun | 4 | 16. Anhui xuesheng zhoukan | 1 |
| 5. Qianjiang pinglun | 2 | 17. Xueyi zazhi | 1 |
| 6. Laodong yu funü | 2 | 18. Shuguang | 1 |
| 7. Xin funü | 2 | 19. Shuguang zazhi | 1 |
| 8. Minduo | 2 | 20. Jiating yanjiu | 1 |
| 9. Xin chao | 2 | 21. Piping | 1 |
| 10. Xin qingnian | 1 | Other (no previous source) | 2 |
| 11. Gaizao yu yixue | 1 | | |
| 12. Xiandai funü | 1 | | Total 74 |

provided potted definitions of key terms in the social sciences along with capsule summaries of leading social science theories. In its flamboyant introduction, it stated that social science was the diagnostic tool par excellence for transforming the cruel, unjust global capitalist system. "Has today's social system," Gao asked, noting that 80 percent of the world's people were utterly destitute wage slaves, "reached the period of reform?" To which the answer was significantly that "to address that question, there is no other method than the method of the social sciences," for only it can reliably judge "how society is organized, how reformed," because social science method adroitly represents the complexity of society itself. Once the time is known to be right, human will (*yizhi*) is indispensable. Social science method however is what makes visible the conditions prevailing in the domains of economics, politics, law, religion, and philosophy, and visibility is the precondition of willed action. If Gao truly was Mei Sheng, then Mei Sheng considered social science theory to be prognosticative.[28]

This raises two important points in relation to Mei's probable editorial objectives in the zfwt project. First, for Mei, the woman problem constituted a central social category in radical social science theory. He therefore may have seen in woman theory an extension of social science method or another way of assaying what social science representation was prognosticating about real social conditions. The *Social Science Dictionary*'s very first entry is for *yi fu yi fu* (monogamy), which Gao describes in evolutionist, progressive, patriarchal theoretical terms as an event that correlated with the historical shift of human society from barbarism to agricultural

Table 2 *Zhongguo shehui shiliao jiyao* (vols. 4–6)

| Journals | Articles | Journals | Articles |
|---|---|---|---|
| 1. Funü zazhi | 36 | 11. Xuedong | 5 |
| 2. Funü pinglun | 3 | 12. Xin Zhongguo | 3 |
| 3. Juewu | 7 | 13. Jiaoyu zazhi | 1 |
| 4. Xin funü | 2 | 14. Nüjie zhong | 1 |
| 5. Minduo | 2 | 15. Wenhua jieshao | 1 |
| 6. Xin chao | 1 | 16. Tongsu yuekan | 1 |
| 7. Xin qingnian | 6 | 17. Xin taicang | 1 |
| 8. Xueyi zazhi | 2 | 18. Jiaoyu huikan | 1 |
| 9. Jiating yanjiu | 1 | Other (no previous source) | 9 |
| 10. Piping | 2 | | Total 85 |

and pastoral social systems. At this stage men sought to ensure paternity of their children and so they crushed the power of women by forcefully marrying them into patrilineal, clannish social formations.[29] The dictionary gives dozens of entries for terms such as "gender equality movement" (*xingbie shuping yundong*, 348), "the woman question" (*funü wenti*, 535–37), "women's labor question" (*funü laodong wenti*, 537–38), and "matriarchal system" (*muxi zhidu*, 178–80). The common presumption linking Gao Xisheng's social science theory to Mei Sheng's editorial project is that women are central both to social evolution and to social evolutionary or progressive theory.

Second, Mei's canonical social science theory literally mainstreamed gendered subjects. Mei is an exemplary figure because he stands at a crossroads of feminism and social science. In the outpouring of elite theoretical scholarship that led eventually to the apotheosis of social science, Mei was able to compile an attractive ideological object.[30] Partly he accomplished this goal taxonomically.[31] But he was also circulating material (e.g., key debates, general statistical information, major translations, personal histories, and other generic expressions of progressive writing) to a mass elite market, confirming the centrality of women in society. Using the power invested in the editor, he could repeatedly pose in distillated form the core dogma of progressive feminism.[32]

*ZFWT* provides a way to measure the viability of those modernist, predicative, theoretical categories. One can only imagine that the reissue project's duration indicates that the pamphlets and the compendium continued to make profits. (Advertisements in later issues quoted the price at 2 yuan for the new and 1.60 for back issues.) Mei Sheng's taxonomic ordering of a

Table 3    *Zhongguo funü wenti taolunji*, ed. Mei Sheng: Contents

*Tonglun* (General discussions)
*Jiaoyu wenti* (Question of education)
*Shenghuo wenti* (Question of life or livelihood)
*Jingji duli* (Question of economic independence)
*Canzheng wenti* (Question of political participation)
*Shengyu zhidu* (Question of birth control)
*Shejiao wenti* (Question of social intercourse)
*Liangxing wenti* (Question of the two sexes: Heterosexuality)
*Jiating wenti* (Question of family)
*Lian'ai wenti* (Question of erotic love)
*Hunyin wenti* (Question of marriage)
*Lihun wenti* (Divorce question)
*Dushen wenti* (Independence question)
*Zhencao wenti* (Chastity question)
*Daode wenti* (Questions in ethics)
*Xingjiaoyu wenti* (Question of sex education)
*Ertong gongyu wenti* (Question of public education of children)
*Changbi wenti* (Prostitutes and concubines)
*Nüzi xinli* (Female psychology)
*Jianfa wenti* (Question of hair cutting)
*Fuzhuang wenti* (Question of dress)
*Zhuanji* (Biography)
*Zalu* (Miscellany)

new field of social science knowledge about women apparently had an audience. When buyers presumed that women required emancipation—Why else buy the reprints?—they were predicating a subject called women in rich and philosophic detail. Each aspect or element of Mei Sheng's taxonomy is bound to the others in argument and juxtaposition, seeming to provide yet another slice of data or analytic insight. Essays with titles like Feng Fei's "A General Outline of the Woman Question," Yamakawa Kikue's "Gentry Families and Women's Liberation," and Luo Jialun's "Women's Liberation" appear, along with summary essays on August Bebel's *Women under Socialism*, in a privileged category called "General Discussions" (*tonglun*) indexing major universal questions about the history of the human race and ways to remedy social problems.[33]

Mei divided *zfwt* into a series of general arguments (see Table 3). "The woman question" composes itself in a grid of analytic subcategories. Some of these may have migrated into the academic theory project during the process of translating classics on the woman problem (e.g., August Bebel,

Charlotte Perkins Gilman's *Women and Economics*, the 1929 translations of Edward Carpenter's *History of Love*, or Margaret Sanger's eugenic birth control theories).[34] Or they may have arisen in speculative theoretical writing among social scientists like Feng Fei, whose 1931 "On Women [*nüxing*]" is as widely cited in Mei's sources as Japanese and European philosophic works.[35] Because its categorization of women as a eugenic, sexed subject rests on the assumption that there had been a founding act of criminality in the past when men brutalized women, many of the policy statements are attempts to reverse the wrongs men had done to women, starting from the alleged rape of matriarchy and the establishment of patriarchy.

One further point warrants reinforcing. Feminism is a theoretical apparatus. Evolutionary biology is a complex theory with cosmology, teleology, vocabulary, and predicated agents or subjects that are responsible for thrusting life forward on its course. Analogously, feminism is on one level a complex theory of how the social and political lives of citizens are distinctive and the curse or blessing of sexual difference plays out in specific times, stages, and places. Feminists in China predicated the theoretical subjects that I am reading here, with the benefit of hindsight, as historical catachreses. For progressive Chinese feminism (and perhaps other traditions as well), the question was how to understand the truth of women and how to produce women agentially.

## Gao Xian and the Subject "Women" in 1920s Progressive Feminism

The figure of nüxing initially caught my attention because it was a neologism. It combined the characters for "female" and "sex" in modern Chinese in a novel way. The term predominated in some places but not in others, and it operated in the historical field as a proper noun.[36] But as the evidence accumulated, I began to suspect that nüxing might be a central social subject or master word in the discourses of modern Chinese history.

What is at stake analytically in the catachresis can be illustrated by using the example of Gao Xian (no known dates). An engineer, businessman, cultural critic, and eugenic philosopher, Gao wrote tightly argued theories regarding sexuality, eugenic imperatives, and nüxing identity that distilled typical assumptions appearing broadly in many of Mei Sheng's redacted essays. Gao linked the woman's right to choose her sexual partner to the social evolutionary processes of natural selection, to China's national redemption, and to the universality of eugenic theory in general. He also, interestingly, placed the subject women in a contingent relation to the future. That is because Gao was truly reluctant to judge what women would become in the future, at least by the measure of what (in his view) they had always been in the past. His eugenicist arguments legitimated a feminist argument that women should authorize themselves and should represent their own needs as women. But he felt they should achieve these ends by extending into the social—and thus, for a progressive sociologist of that era, the natural—world women's erotic drives.

Gao Xian's two essays "Xing zhe" (Sexual selection) and "Lian'ai duli" (Independence in love) first appeared in *Xueyi zazhi* (The arts) in the 1920s.[37] They engaged the theoretical work of Charles Darwin and of the sociologist Lester Ward, a cheerful, optimistic, American social Darwinian who believed that human agents could, indeed should, actively control their own evolutionary destiny.[38] Gao sought to adjust Ward and Darwin to fit what he considered his own specific, social, and thus (by his reckoning) national evolutionary context. That makes him an agent of social enlightenment in the tradition of May Fourth Chinese scientific humanism. Gao's distinction was his conviction that "sexual intercourse is the secret of human life." In his view, sexual selection, sexual intercourse, sexual play, and secondary sex characteristics were central to social, national, and personal development.[39]

In "Sexual Selection," Gao argued that sex selection inscribed the difference between males and females (*zhuzhang nannü chayi qi zai xingzhe*).[40] It was therefore not just about the survival of the species but also, importantly, about the differentiation of each sex through the alchemy of male sexual desire. (This is, according to Lawrence Birken, a thoroughly Darwinian position.)[41] Not all species in nature propagate in the binaried sexuality of mammals, as humans do. But in higher-order organisms, sex selection orders evolutionary progress by requiring the exchange of essences between the different sexes. Gao was injecting into his own argument a very radical element in Ward's social Darwinian biogenetics. In Darwin's thought, sexual difference is construed to be both absolute and yet later or younger in evolutionary time than what Darwin had also theorized was an earlier, primary, originary androgyny of all life forms. Gao particularly valued theories about biogenetic evolution because it had the potential to upset the age-old centrality of the male in Chinese traditional thinking. "The origin of life is with the female [*nüxing*]," Gao wrote ecstatically. "Life continues through females. The biological agent [*shengwu zhuti*] is the female, because change requiring the joining of heterogeneous elements [i.e., male and female] involves the splitting off of a part of her self [i.e., the ovum] which makes the male [sperm, contrary to popular belief] a sidebranch, dependent upon [*fushu*] the female" (ss, 6). Actually, Gao argued, in nature the male is not central to life and the female is not the male's dependent.

But the mystery of egg and sperm in bisexual propagation was only one element of the centrality of the female in the reproduction of all life. Another part of the mystery was how higher-order organisms find one another and choose to mate. Here Gao argued that women needed to be allowed to choose their mates, and to make his point, he developed a eugenic logic. Sexual life, he began, is determined by scarcity—or hunger—and love (ss, 10; IL, 57–72): "Because people occupy a position within the natural world, in fact as an unconscious natural force, the impulse to leave behind progeny is an unconscious drive. . . . the two inescapable natural forces [hunger, ji, and love, ai, or more crudely put, gain, li, and sex, se] . . . are actually instinctive [bennengxing] and are the motive force [yuandongli] of human life [rensheng]. The source of these two instincts appear with the birth of each person. It could be said that the instincts are useful from birth and thus are a special condition of existence" (IL, 57).

A general theoretical problem is that, although progress rests on an exchange across (sexual) difference, it is not clear in nature or in human society who is choosing whom and why. Theoretically and historically, females have been known to choose males, males to choose females, and, last but best, male and female to choose one another.

Advanced modes of selection among highly developed social beings are cultural mediations of nature. They reflect and support and aid nature to take its course. Modes of selection, if they are progressive and civilized, ought to honor the centrality of the female in reproduction. This they would do by expanding attractive male secondary sex characteristics (dierxing ingzhi) and enlarging the woman's freedom to choose her mate on the basis of his attractive qualities. As Gao put it, What vies for primacy with desire is attractiveness or the development and maintenance of secondary sex characteristics that entice the other to select a mate (IL, 57). Theoretically speaking, then, if advanced societies acknowledged the natural tendencies inherent in the human species, they would "naturally" encourage females to be sexually assertive, because the determination of fitness in men rests with the intelligent—at least in evolutionary terms—desires of women.

However, not every human culture is equally developed. Indeed, some have not proved as capable as others at synchronizing social life with natural drives. Unfortunately, Gao argued, China was one of the less capable. It faced the task of entering the international struggle still confronting the need to set its culture back on the course of nature. He offered a complex teleology in explaining China's national failure, but his conclusion was not complex: "To sum up in one sentence," he wrote, "when women are lower and undeveloped, it is harmful to men. It is counter to Nature and degenerates the entire species" (ss, 16). Historically speaking, over the course of centuries, as Chinese society had become more complex, men came to dominate women economically and began to mediate hunger and lack: the men took over and perverted Chinese culture away from nature. Sex selection not only ended up the exclusive province of men; it eventually culminated in the degradation of all Chinese women in a prostituted economy of exchange of sex for subsistence. That occurred because Chinese society organized itself in terms of patrilineal descent, the very worst possible choice. The descent mandate required men to buy and sell women. That made all Chinese women into prostitutes. Also, it countermanded the natural order and degenerated the Chinese race.

This is a stark staging of commonplace ideas in Chinese progressive feminism. Gao's argument made a number of familiar points that are assumed or directly voiced in the work of theorists I discuss at length below. Thus, Gao's argument personalized sex selection and implied that the choice of whom to have sex with was, at least in nature, a matter of individual will. He also linked women and men in a logical double bind, which made the harm men do to women a self-inflicted wound to men. He just raised the stakes to an unusual degree. Instead of simply arguing that the chastity of women exemplified the cruelty of Confucianism, he claimed that the unchastity of Chinese women made China a world-class, international pimp. Rather than argue that China was uncivilized in relation to industrial cultures, Gao made China an instance of what happens to *overcivilized* communities, which of course allowed him to situate China centrally.[42] Chinese are not primitive, he argued, far from it. The more disciplined and civilized, the further human beings and particularly Chinese drifted away from nature or sexual physiology and thus the more incoherent, species-dangerous, and unjust Chinese social practices had become.

Male humans, who, according to Gao, hold autocratic powers over female humans in China, rely on various poisonous means of actually stalling social and female evolutionary development. For instance, they withhold education from women, or educate them in unnatural values like chastity. But although nature inscribes absolute difference at the levels of physiology and reproductive instinct, enlightened thinking suggests that culture potentially ameliorates difference; or it could if women and their male allies could lay claim to women's natural rights. At the cultural level, difference is enacted on the basis of relative abjection according to the power differential between men and women in China, and between men and women in the rest of the world. (The United States, he claimed, was more advanced, relatively speaking, because it allowed the education of women and female sex selection, though this had not always been the case there.) But artificially constructed difference is both unjust and necessarily remediable. When Chinese men degrade women, rendering them less than human, they rob women of personal being (ren'ge) and set back national and racial evolutionary progress.

The question of whether women in this construction were people *in a cultural sense* bothered Gao, as it seemed to bother a lot of May Fourth–era intellectuals and theorists:

> What is a "person" [ren]? . . . Speaking philosophically, a person is someone who can execute conscious acts and take on moral responsibility. These qualities are known as personality or ren'ge. Legally speaking a person is someone who manages his/her own existence and development. Those with such capacities are called people with ren'ge, and the power of personal social standing [ren'gequan] lies in vitality, reputation and freedom. Given this line of argument . . . There are those whom we acknowledge have a capacity to use their spiritual powers and act in conscious fashion, but we do not allow or recognize in them moral responsibility. In this case, does the person have ren'ge or not? When we disallow moral responsibility do we not disarm their ren'ge? (*ss*, 25–26)

The ren'ge problem obviously constituted a big gap in Gao Xian's theory. In practical terms, the critique required a female agent at the same moment that it appeared to disallow one. Consequently, Gao ended up arguing that Chinese women are degenerate (zhuiluo). They are culturally debased because in the absence of the power to alter their conditions, that is, absent sufficient ren'ge, women sell the only thing they have, sex, are encouraged to sell sex, indeed are rewarded by their parents for selling sex. Thus, "women completely lose their ren'ge, lose their powers of life and become worthless objects and sexual tools [qijü]" (*il*, 61).

Gao's antipatriarchal political plans for ameliorating bad social conditions are one reason he is such a good example of progressive feminism. His being male does not seem to preclude him from being the same sort of feminist as a woman might be, for women and men theorists defined themselves as subjects in relation to the same sort of evolutionary logic as Gao lays out here. As significant as his social engineering are two other matters: his modernist speculation about the naturalized order of organic gender difference and the social subjectivities or conditions of agency his kind of liberatory theorizing opened up.

One reason Gao Xian is such an exemplar of a May Fourth colonial modernist is his self-positioning in an epistemology that assumes that the laws of nature are truthful and transparent and that nature is an open book. Gao miraculates himself as the reader of that book. The idea that science adequately and directly represents reality, the assumption that human behavior has some complex relation to a natural or species-specific innate behavior, and the belief that natural law ascertained through rational reflection governs human existence all authorize themselves with reference to the nineteenth-century evolutionary canon. Gao Xian is, after all, a Darwinian thinker. But he is not just any Darwinian. He presumes the ground of what he calls *shengwujie* (nature), or sometimes *daziran* (nature), and participates in the social study of nature via the social science discipline of *shengwuxue* or biology. His political objectives are rooted in an organicist teleology that he reads off from the movement of evolutionary development, specifically the struggle of the fittest, the origin of the species, and natural selection.

But Gao also apprehends nature in normative terms. He argues straightforwardly that just as animals are better than humans (i.e., closer to nature), so women are better than men. His strategy of argument makes some discomfiting implications almost inescapable. First, because in these logics women tend to represent nature and because animals are better than humans, and women than men, then, maybe, women are like animals (*IL*, 62). Second, he suggests that *xingbie*, or gender as a way of signifying sex difference across species, is necessary because normatively human beings should conform even in their social lives to the laws of the jungle. Real normativity is an extension of nature. Third, because in nature difference is absolute, maintained through sexual selection (females prefer males with attractive secondary sex characteristics), therefore social gender is morally required to maintain natural, physiological difference, and that requires liberating natural drives to do the social work of the maintenance of difference. To put it crudely, it takes equality of access to sex to ensure the survival of natural difference. Thus, finally, sexuality is a moral imperative because sexual intercourse is the secret dynamo of natural development and therefore of social development.

Gao Xian's argument may be internally inconsistent, but his essays represent hard core argument in much social Darwinian thinking, in and outside China, in the early twentieth century.[43] Many of the peculiarities I am charting are as present in Ward's own thought as they are in Gao's reiteration of them. Or, for that matter, Margaret Sanger's neo-Malthusian reworking of many similar points. Whether these arguments are internally consistent or inconsistent is not the point. The effect of all the various weapons in Gao's rhetorical arsenal is larger than formal logic. The effect is an argument that makes sex the foundation of human life and the wellspring of personality. Reproductive sexuality is the normative foundation of human life, the core of personality, and, to a rather astounding degree, the ethical touchstone of human social behavior. Sexual desire (*xingyu*), sexual life (*xing shengming*), and their attendant frameworks of instinctive drives (benneng) are what constitute the realm of the "natural." Sexual drives make woman a metonym of sexuality because, as Gao argues, Chinese women are categorically prostituted. The prostitution of Chinese women derives not from promiscuity with strangers, but because they are forced by culture to barter sexual access for food and position. They *are* sex and *have* sex, which is why they can alienate or "sell" it. Under conditions where women are not forced to sell their sexuality, that is, in nature or in a just social world, women are (as they should always be in a state of natural justice) the heart of sexual and social reproduction.[44]

In Gao Xian's theoretical universe, to summarize thus far, sexual access and sexual reproduction (but not sexual desire, which is largely the province of males) are the defining characteristics of individual female persons. All individual persons participate in psychosocial life for better or worse, by selecting or being selected for sexual intercourse and reproduction. Socially, the natural impulses of sexuality and the desire to leave behind progeny are regulated or misregulated by institutions like the patrilineal clan (nanxi jiazu; *IL*, 62). Culture can reflect, deflect, or distort the instinctive nature in every individual being. The job of a social scientist, according to Gao, is to educate the reader to the underlying conditions of the natural world and to measure culture against nature. Nature constitutes the ground on which cultural differences are erected. Humans can judge whether their behaviors are sufficiently natural by measuring their own against the instinctual behaviors of animals (e.g., peacocks, wasps).[45]

The theoretical a priori for women's agency, therefore, is set out in the evolutionary disciplines (e.g., biology), which theorize a sexual difference between male and female society. Gao's essays draw a stark portrait of the neatly divided, biosocial, sexed dyads so thoroughly characterizing the modern age in China (as elsewhere) that most scholarship simply naturalizes into imperceptibility: man and woman, or nanxing and nüxing.[46] There is a one-to-one relation between the ground that Gao establishes, of shengwujie, and the agent nanxing and nüxing, who represent that ground, because not even the most mendacious mediations of culture can completely displace the natural drives of the "human animal." Although nüxing now simply signifies women or females in modern, colloquial Chinese, epistemologically speaking, nüxing is, particularly in a Darwinian or Wardian economy, the cover term for all organic females of all species of biological life. Nüxing is both a neologism but, more important, a catachresis because not only is the term new in twentieth-century Chinese, but Women in the state of nature is an impossible concept-metaphor. The point to be drawn out of this kind of writing is that when women are naturalized into "the female of the species," one way of translating nüxing, the so-called mediations of culture and society drop away and the text automatically performs the reduction of woman to organism. That is why, almost against his own inclinations, Gao seems constantly on the brink of arguing that Chinese women are so degraded they are nothing better than breeding stock.

The power of this logic also troubles Gao's attempts to argue on behalf of women's social equality. He establishes the irrefutable difference of women and men at the ground of nature. Sexual intercourse is the exchange of life across fundamental difference, the egg and the sperm. People exist to propagate life, and their propagative function, on the analogy of the sperm and the ovum, means that in the state of nature women and men are fundamentally different. The problem is that Gao has to maintain absolute difference in nature at the very same time he is promoting the common, progressive argument that nations prosper when gender equality is instituted and old-style seclusion dismantled. Thus, it would seem that the originating conditions of fundamental difference must be overcome at the level of culture. Or rather, the conditions under which males and females carry out their primary duty of propagating the species must be remade via modern cultural means to conform as closely as possible to nature so that the processes of nature go forward unobstructed. That requires ensuring the mechanisms of free sexual selection to proceed freely. And that, in turn, involves recentering Chinese women, presently derogated within the patrilineal descent ground, in general social intercourse.

This was a progressive and liberating position to take, if one accepts the foundational assumptions of social evolution, which are that reproductive sexuality is more natural than recreational sexuality, heterosexuality is normative, races are a phenomenon in nature, sexual selection is the internal motor of social evolution, and so on. But, as I have pointed out in my close reading of Gao's views on female ren'ge, institutionalizing liberation was hard to think about. If females are by nature the heart of sexual propagation of the species, then how is it possible to know what kind of education is appropriate for ensuring moral responsibility and thus the stimulation of ren'ge in women? And what if the education nüxing get is inappropriate? Who will make the decision about appropriate education for women? What would happen if educators mishandled women and produced social subjects who were even worse than the traditional, prostituted woman?

Another line of problems stretched toward the question of similarity bridging difference. If nüxing are allowed or encouraged to develop ren'ge of their own, will it be the same ren'ge as men's or a different kind? If women and men have basically the same personality structure (ren'ge), will their drive to bisexual species propagation (difference) be blunted? Because bisexual or mammalian species developmentalism rests on the meeting of sperm and egg (differences), how similar should women and men be (ren'ge = similitude) before women forget to choose sexual partners on the basis of men's highly masculinized secondary sexual characteristics? Can a sexually female woman with "masculine" social roles still attract the attention of highly masculinized men? Could biological nüxing turn themselves into nanxing at a cultural level? Or, to take up another line of reasoning, how can the normative or ethical ren'ge of men actually be measured in conditions where some people are characterized as *wuren'ge*, or those institutionally denied access to ren'ge, as Gao claims has been the historical fate of women in China? Under the terms of progressive feminism, to put it most simply, how is the liberated subject of woman, the woman who has personality or ren'ge, going to be constructed?

I have characterized Gao Xian's logic as progressive feminism and stressed how it situates in theory a primordial sexualized female ur-subject of nüxing. His preeminent problem is how to fill that subject with content. It was a question preoccupying contemporary intellectuals in the 1920s and 1930s. Of course, Gao and his contemporaries were establishing interlocutory, sometimes imaginary scholarly relations with Japanese theorists like Shimamura Tamizo, Yosano Akiko, Honma Hisao, Kagawa Toyohiko, and Yamakawa Kikue through Chinese translations. This is not even to mention European and U.S. social theorists such as August Bebel, Edward Carpenter, Ellen Key, and Havelock Ellis and sex-theory heavyweights like Henry Maine (*Ancient Law*), Bachofen (*Das Mutter-recht*), McLennan (*Primitive Marriage*), Zetkin, Engels, and many other, lesser figures. The subjects of great debates such as progressive Chinese feminism establish historical catachreses that propose and contain the possibilities for social subjectivity. Gao's discussion of the nüxing subject is an example. Ding Ling, Li Xiaojiang, Dai Jinhua, and the many other theorists who would embrace elements of half-forgotten foundations laid in Gao's time occupied but transformed this subject. That does not alter the fact that what are basically eugenics arguments had a legitimacy that could not be denied (i.e., natural selection). Natural selection is perhaps the philosophic ground women and men theorists could presume to be irrefutable and true and consequently a stable foundation for feminist revolution.

Making nüxing an identity or a social-discursive subject or a theoretical predicate is problematic, but only in the sense that *any* feminism potentially is.[47] For instance, Gao predicates an identity or subject category, nüxing, which is exclusionary in the sense that woman is not man, and explicitly normative on a number of counts: the measure of woman is the degree to which she is sexual; her contribution to national development is through her reproductive labor; there are good and bad, natural and unnatural ways of "doing nüxing," and so on. But Gao and others like him were nonetheless pioneers because they were establishing the viability of these modernist categories. Gao is self-consciously propagating what Judith Butler calls the "contingent foundations" of modernist knowledge about the relation of nature and culture.

A project of colonial modernity is the reordering of life at the center of discourses in the life sciences of biology, demography, medicine, and sexuality.[48] Gao and his colleagues must therefore be seen as collaborators in that general project. His gloss on Ward and Darwinian thinking contributes to thinking about liberation and the transvaluation of values.[49] In Gao's feminist theorizing, modern identity categories of race, class, and gender are central. The racialized biologies of evolutionary thinking made nüxing a social identity, a legitimate social fact. Gao's truth claims have an ideological charge. In the search for the conditions of knowledge about Chinese women and men, Gao concluded that Chinese women's characteristic was actually deficiency, the harmful effect of superculturalization and male sadism. At stake in progressive Chinese feminist thought, which I have exemplified here in Gao Xian's theories, is the centrality of eugenic choice and its alleged social evolutionary effects.

## Colonial Modernity

Colonial modernity is the term I have elected to use in order to rethink the conditions and features of enlightened thought in Chinese intellectual circles after the monarchy. I use it in the following ways. Colonial modernity as a term (1) intentionally restores to historical visibility the economic, political, ideological, and intellectual conditions for the emergence of discourses of modernity in China. (It also refers to modernities in those powers undertaking colonial projects in China, i.e., England, Russia, Germany, France, the United States, and particularly Japan, although the metropolitan focus is not my concern here.) Two decades ago, Edward Said showed exhaustively how "orientalism," or colonial knowledge, was a screen that obscured the economic, political, ideological, and ideational realities of modernity in colonizer nations. The periodization "colonial modernity" comes out of the orientalism debates, but it sets out a different task. Tacking the word "colonial" onto the ideologically charged word "modernity" is a way of highlighting the dialectical doubleness of discourses of modernity. Colonial modernity, in other words, shifts away from Said's preoccupation with hegemonic representation and concerns itself with conditions of modernity actually obtaining in colonies, subcolonies, indirect colonies, and semicolonies, under rubrics of "modernity" or "modernization."[50]

Colonial modernity (2) seeks to accentuate the political and ideological dependency, the intellectual interrelatedness of colonizing powers and colonial regimes. The commodity economies (e.g., opium, tea, sugar, and tobacco) that integrated international trade as imperialists sought to establish colonial domains also drew and reshaped political, administrative, governmental, ideological, and intellectual lines of power. Economic integration of the British opium industry between India and China opened up the drug trade to Japanese colonial and capital accumulation projects. It also altered Qing styles of governmentality and the relation of Chinese state and population, affected semicolonial styles of modern urbanization, and, to a degree, structured the diasporic movements of Chinese capital, capitalists, and labor power into Southeast Asia. Underdeveloped in the discourses of modernity are precisely these colonial commodities (e.g., opium, tea, labor), reordered styles of governmentality, juridical norms (e.g., international laws and treaties), administrative innovations (e.g., customs, extraterritoriality, treaty ports), and colonial trade in ideas that characterize colonizers (Said's emphasis) as well as colonial regimes.[51]

Colonial modernity is (3) cumulative. The colonial storehouse of policy and strategy could be and routinely was raided and its contents recycled. The relationship even between a colonizer and a directly colonized people is not exactly bilateral. Even a directly bilateral treaty rests on administrative techniques and policy that draw on past experience. Thus, for instance, the primary colonizing strategy of the unequal treaty system did not originate with China but was built on long experience with capitulation law governing relations between Europe and the Ottoman Empire. In other words, the European consolidation of Shanghai and Hong Kong, the United States' "open door" policies, Japan's indirect colonies in Manchuria and subsequent colonial empire in Manchukuo, Taiwan, and the Korean Peninsula have historical precedents. Each drew on older techniques developed over long periods of time in the unequal relationships built up over time between colonizers and colonized, the so-called capitulation system. The fact of multiple imperialist adventures in China, leading to the term semicolonialism, should not distract attention from the fact that already well-established colonial knowledge informed the Great Powers' experiments and contributed to "development" in their "spheres of influence."[52]

Colonial modernity is, consequently, (4) more a planar or spatial term than a temporal one. There is no direct line of teleological development connecting British, Dutch, or Spanish colonial occupation with the various overlapping semicolonial projects of the Great Powers in China two centuries later. That is because by the nineteenth and twentieth centuries most of the vast plane of the earth's surface had been colonized or partly colonized, and because of this spatial extension of the colonial project, colonial knowledge circulated through the colonial capitals. By the late nineteenth century the colonial agent was no longer necessarily the Imperial Navy or a policymaker.[53] Laissez-faire businessmen, entrepreneurial prostitutes, the joint venture media capitalists, anthropologists and sociologists, opium traders and missionaries brought with them as they scattered over the globe the assumptions and techniques that disseminated colonial knowledge without necessitating direct colonization.[54]

More than conditions or context (e.g., doubled quality, historically accreted framework, discursive traces, multiple or planar quality), colonial modernity (5) suggests avenues for thinking about Chinese Enlightenment. The European core of Chinese progressive feminism rested on Orientalist anthropologies, in Said's term. In the absence of arcane new knowledge about "Hindoos" and Iroquois, matriarchal societies and behavioral instincts, neither Gao Xian's nor Lester Ward's theories would have had purchase. Enlightenment social sciences of sociology, anthropology, and political science centered and authorized themselves with reference to these other places and explanatory drives. However, Enlightenment does not just float on a foundation of "knowledge" about non-European others. It is thinkable in far-flung places outside Europe. In this regard, gendered subalternity and the *aporia* or other that constitutes the self (ideas traceable to Said, Spivak, and the Subaltern Studies History Collective) may be only part to the story. The doubled quality of colonial modernity, in which modernity is colonial by definition, readdresses the reality that enlightenment itself is never unitary. Enlightenment (in this book, feminism stands in a metonymic relation to enlightened thinking more generally) may not require an other that is passive, rigid, or incommensurate since it can and does focus its powers of reason and social logics on an immediate terrain.[55]

Colonial modernist, enlightened intellectuals writing largely in Chinese developed characteristic strategies and specific tactics, which can be reread and comprehended. In virtually every decade since the 1919 May Fourth movement, in fact, Chinese intellectuals have reworked their commitments to enlightened thought: from the romantic 1920s to the revolutionary 1930s, to the Maoist Enlightenment of the 1940s and the post-Mao revolt against political dogma in the early 1980s (see chapters 5, 6, and 7). This is not a matter of abstract teleology. It is an accretion; ideas developed under specific conditions, in given social exigencies, always operating through the mediation of enlightened reason. To focus on enlightened thought, to propose its centrality as a colonial modernist discourse, centers attention on thinkers. Emphacizing the duality, both modern and colonial, of enlightened thought helps to free historical analysis from the burden of comparison. Chinese Enlightenment is neither derivative nor not derivative. It is the line on which new intellectuals crafted policy, ideology, social and scholarly critique, strategy, and all the practical theoretical projects of intellectual modernity. Focusing the spotlight on the thinkers and the content of their thought, accepting the variety of Enlightenment, revalues intellectual history. When a constituent element of enlightened thought, such as progressive feminism, is closely read, what emerges is the explicability of intellectual work.[56]

The question for intellectual history is not What is a colony? but rather, given the colonial roots of modernity per se, Is there anything singularly important about the way modernity is being thought here?[57] Colonial modernist fiction writers, new journalists, editors, sex theorists, social scientists, and progressive intellectuals reworked the relation of the people to language, law, citizenship, nation, and their own bodies. In the circuit of Japan, China, India, Southeast Asia, and Korea, one significant new element of social ideology and intellectual work was in fact discourses of sexuality, particularly sex theory as it related to the New Woman and "modern girl." The discourses of Chinese colonial modernity are consequently related to questions of eugenic sexuality, progressive feminism, the institutionalization of modern heterosexuality, and other social ideologies that make their appearance vividly in the publications of writers like Gao Xian as well as, I argue in chapter 4, Ding Ling's fiction.[58]

Theorists, then, in the disciplines of comparative anatomy, sociology, cultural anthropology, and sex theory, are responsible for engineering sexed identity, not just in semicolonies like China's treaty ports but, as Armstrong and Poovey and Young and Chakrabarty have made very clear, in London and Lancashire, too. The subjects that emerged out of the conditions of knowledge in Chinese treaty ports were, as Tomiyama Ichiro has shown for the subject "islanders" in Japanese colonial discourses, specifically and irreducibly themselves.[59] Like the "Japanese body," these scientized, biologized, evolutionized identities of woman and man are part of the sine qua non of colonial modernity. Where there is "sexual selection" one finds the modernist category woman. But each modernist subject, like each new factory-produced commodity coded in terms of capitalist value, is reworked within a semiotic political economy that can be read back into the conditions of its formation as legitimate knowledge. The identities of nanxing and nüxing are more than translatable tropes in Chinese evolutionary discourse. They were and remain political and social identities as well, because the theoretical project that accompanied the modernist transformation was gendered in new ways. Sexed man and sexed woman, historical man and historical woman as the representatives of genders about which chronologies explaining essences could be written, appeared with the era of colonialism and the flowering of the human sciences. Where nanxing or nüxing or man or woman appear, they are symptomatic of the conditions of colonial modernity.[60]

## Adequacy in Sexed Subject Theory

Gao Xian's theories are typical of the 1920s, and essays reproduced in *ZFWT* largely echo Gao's operating assumptions. In fact, Mei Sheng's whole editorial project presumes, coalesces, and no doubt therefore predicates the very subject that it is most preoccupied with explaining and defining. Nüxing operates as a feminist subject in general social evolutionary or progressive theory in three ways. The first is simply a matter of logic: nüxing is predicated in the theoretical assertion of Gao and many others that "women are the primary sex." Second, in a grammatological sense, nüxing is the subject that is not man; that is, woman emerges as such in the assertion that "woman is man's other." Third, nüxing takes on a material presence when complex theoretical statements are made in its name, for instance: Women under matriarchy controlled human destiny, but with the rise of private property were subdued under patriarchal constraints that conflated women with property. Such a statement is both a *definition* of what women are said to be and a public *affirmation* of the statement's universality, in the sense that the Oxford English Dictionary notes for "predication," which is "to set forth publicly, to preach, extol, commend."[61] These are the analytic bases of my proposal that Mei's compendium predicates women as the subject of feminism and as a tangible social subject.

Mei's *Collected Discussions of the Chinese Women Question* is also valuable because it illustrates how contemporary writing carved a "Chinese" theoretical tradition of feminism out of the heterogeneous flow of transnationalized sex theories current in the early twentieth century. Because so much feminist writing in the 1920s appeared in journals, the origins of progressive feminist theory are diverse and difficult to credit to one or two theorists working in an isolated university setting. One reason I have used Mei's collection is precisely because I can postulate who is doing the act. I cannot recreate what Mei thought as he selected articles for inclusion or exclusion, nor would that help me particularly even if I could. Rather, the historical activity of choosing this rather than that has the effect of embedding into the record the history of actions, if not their causes. In other words, shimmering out of this *ZFWT* taxonomy is a buried record of the decisions Mei made, the editorial acts he undertook; far more than thinking, the compilation or compendium marks taxonomic work with the indelible mark of a decision. That Mei was picking and choosing according to his inner lights is obvious once we look at the analytic categories—female character deficiency, heteronormativity, and ren'ge—normalized in the compendium and the relation of *Collected Discussions of the Chinese Women Question* to its primary repository of theoretical writing, *Funü zazhi* (Ladies' journal).[62]

*Deficiency.* In a long essay entitled "Women de jiemei" (Our sisters) first published in the journal *Jüewu* (Awakened) and republished in *ZFWT*, the feminist female theorist San Si predicated a female subject of history and society.[63] Since the fall of matriarchy, she argued, many thousands of years ago, women have lived "in the dark" (*zai heian zhong*). Their oppression was total. Stripped of control over wealth, women submitted to the patrilineal family. They became dependent on men, and because times were primitive and they did not know better, women as a subject group felt they had no alternative except to become beasts of burden (*nüma*) for men. They fell into a dream state of ignorance about their own victimization. Women were devalued in every era, in every social class, in every family. Educated girls from the higher classes were, if anything, even more blinded to the conditions of their own derogation than lower-class girls. They did not recognize how female literacy raised the status of the family at the expense of the interests of the educated woman. Middle-class women had a utilitarian rather than emancipatory or ethical grasp of education and differed by degree, not kind, from lower-class girls whose families used them as convertible sexual commodities in a fluctuating market. This total system of oppression was held in place by rites (li, lijiao), footbinding, filiality, compulsory marriage, and other social practices that deeply affect social actors. Even now girls endure a second-rate, male-dominated education. After graduation there is no option for them except marriage, where they face hostile in-laws, old-fashioned husbands, or men who purport to be modern but are actually wolves in sheep's clothing, false new men (*jia xinren*) who turn their modern wives into high-class toys (*gaodeng wanwu*).

By the time Mei Sheng republished this essay, the conviction that women were irrational, bestial, deficient, flawed, animalistic, passive, barely human, biophysically flawed, or lacking in character had become an ingrained cliché in enlightenment theory.[64] In its fantastic scenario, women is a foundationally deficient theoretical subject. "Oh, miserable fellow women," San Si writes at one point. "Can you know the reasons for your suffering? Fellow female dreamers, can you know why you are dreaming? Each day you do not see it is another day you remain in this bitter sea."[65] Cultural currents that empower men, San Si argues, also make women dependent, and individual men capitalize on this gender inequality to reinforce their dominance. But far sadder yet is the fact that oppression makes women stupid and despairing. That is the real import of San Si's essay. Yet, as though regretting the no-exit situation that her pitiless analysis of male cruelty and female masochism had opened up, she also equivocates in the end. The women of the past were stupid, bovine, salacious, male-identified, dependent, and ethically dubious because they were either illiterate or unduly influenced by tawdry literature, Confucius and Company, or they were simply broken in spirit. Though we cannot be blind to their deficiencies, neither can deficient women be blamed for their defects.

San Si's melancholy insight is that either women are despicable or they are nonexistent. She sees a no-exit situation when she looks at the collective subject women. Today, battered and tortured, women are blameworthy if they fail to cast off the very forces degrading their intelligence and ethical standing (e.g., customary practices, the tendency to accept orders from men, a vacuous sense of self, emotional and economic dependency), even though most have no concrete idea of what they might become. The conditions of their oppression make imagining an alternative future highly unlikely. If anything, the majority cast a pall on the minority of awakened women, who voluntarily sacrifice themselves to stir the slumbering female masses out of their customary indolence.

San Si's essay is typical of enlightened Chinese theory's predication of the analytic subject women (nüzi, nüxing, nüren, etc.). No matter what domain or subcategory of the woman question is at issue, this constitutional deficiency seems to emerge ipso facto from the conditions of the argument itself, as, for instance, in Li Guangye's "Jinhou de nüzi jiaoyu" (Women's education, henceforth) in the volume "Education Question." Li isolated two problems bedeviling Chinese women and consequently threatening the nation's prospects globally. First, Chinese women had been historically *maleducated*, causing them to overemphasize emotional moral character (*xinqing pinxing*), and second (though perhaps not necessarily as a consequence), women seeking education today do so only to sell themselves to wealthy, powerful men on the marriage market. Girls are both incapable of grasping the conditions of their own historical production and ethically incapable of assuming social responsibility for self or the larger social order. Li suggested that science might help Chinese women as a collectivity to overcome their constitutional flaws. Scientific knowledge improves women's capacity for reason. This supplies reasonable women to the nation, expands women's contributions to humanity and to women universally, and the contribution of each individual woman to herself. As it stands, women needs remediation because it is repulsive and distorted, unaware of where its true interests might lie, and seemingly incapable of conceiving its own liberation.

Li's essay also illustrates another presupposition structuring Chinese progressive feminist theory. Women as adequate *social* subjects are not available in the Chinese cultural-historical matrix.[66] Woman is a feminist theoretic subject whose sexual instinct, procreative agency, and evolutionary centrality potentially vest her with considerable power to do good. But since the historical era of primeval matriarchy there have been no female subjects who were both socially adequate and women. Why? Because in the old society the cultural matrix shaped females into subjects with only one social function: to serve their husbands and children. Harshly restricted to the domestic sphere, according to Li, the natural rights that women once possessed were lost when patriarchy replaced matriarchy. This loss has continued over a long period of sexist education, when men, or History or perhaps even evolutionary logos itself, inflicted domestic servitude on women. In any case, (mal)education is to blame because it "takes all kinds of women with different personalities [gexing] and throws them all into one model [moxing] and casts them as a kind of accessory or subordinate object [fushu wu] to husbands and children." Such a smelting and casting process prevents women's individual, moral character from cohering. What would a socially adequate female subject look like, according to Li Guangye? That is not altogether clear. Without a doubt, it would involve women's establishing ren'ge or personality, individuality, identity (Chinese ren'ge, originally Japanese jinkaku), a point I develop below. But in Li's conception, only the right kind of education could create an adequate female subject. It would be remedial and recalibrate the balance between contemporary women's unfortunate tendency to emotionalize and a new necessity for developing women's will (yizhi). In the end, self-representation was a chore that women had to undertake for themselves.[67]

The predication of constitutionally deficient female subjects appeared in standard arguments about economic independence (jingji duli), too. Baldly stated in Y. D.'s (Li Rongdi) "Zhiye yu funü" (Occupations and women) patriarchy rewarded men with the opportunity to create wealth and political power. The empowering of men registered as a foundational loss to women, who, relieved of responsibility for being self-sufficient because their husband supports them, are logically and categorically speaking parasites. Man is to woman, he argues, as human is to dependent, as host organisms are to parasites, and as achieving a personality is to its opposite: men:women :: human (ren):dependent (fushupin) :: animal:parasite :: ren'ge:wuren'ge.[68] Even where critics seem aware of the abyss this opens, still in arguments about constitutional differences between women and men within an economic frame, the female subject is deficient in spite of itself because women cannot participate in productive labor. Her economic parasitism is not simply a theft of her natural human rights; it is also a normative handicap because it makes her less than human. As theorists like Li Renjie, Gao Xian, and countless others pointed out, this is what made women dependent on the sale of their own sex.[69]

Y. D. reiterated a similar point in the domain of the sexuality question in an essay titled "Funü jingshen shenghuo" (The spiritual life of women), which expanded on insights in the work of eugenicist and feminist theorist Ellen Key. Key held that sex difference is anatomical, and that this accounted for why, in evolutionary terms, a division of labor was natural and necessary: males preserve individuality (*gexing*) while females preserve the race. Differentiation expresses itself at the levels of emotions, reason, and sensory capacity as well as in associative thinking. Their drive to preserve the species leads females to be more adaptive than males, more habituated and less innovative, and, as Havelock Ellis established in his sociological fieldwork, weaker in terms of the spirit of independence and capacity for creativity. Much as Y. D. seems to have disliked the thought, and as much as he cites Key's thesis that difference *is* equality, he could only conclude that "because women's and men's bodies have sustained difference, corporeal differences have led to the development of emotional difference." It was only a small step from there to establishing that the "reality of biology" is that men are more active, critical, changeable, and progressive, and women are constitutionally more repetitive, monotonous (*dandiaoxing*), and conservative.[70] In spite of their potential for evolutionary achievement, female subjects are inferior because they are different.[71]

This problem of the constitutional deficiency of the theoretic subject of women was difficult to evade. "Lian'ai geming lun" (On the erotic love revolution) by Shi Heng, published initially in *Jüewu*, is a case in point. This theorist sought strategies to reignite social evolution. The general problem confronting the Chinese race, Shi theorized, is that cultural archaisms have throttled natural social evolution. The primary culprit here is the lijiao, or social etiquette of the cultured classes, which is a culturally foundational, sacred, and seemingly unbreachable norm. But it is also the primary reason why national social evolution derailed. Evolution requires sexual selection, which in turn requires social intercourse between men and women who are social equals. Male and female are evolutionary and anatomically distinct members of the human species and should unite because they feel heterosexual desire for each other. The problem is that lijiao are an arbitrary "boundary between men and women," a barrier that artificially separates the sexes from each other and turns parents into breeding stock. The resulting social boundary is unnatural. Or, in the more flowery language of contemporaries, the obstacles to social evolution can be removed. The fix is sexual desire and the active, erotic bodies of both young women and men who can overcome the dead hand of the past when they choose and consecrate one another in the loving sacrament of the free-choice marriage bed.

Massive barriers stand in the way of this revitalizing erotic revolution, however, according to Shi. With regard to men, lijiao thinking has so poisoned and distorted their vision that they can see women only as servants or sexual prey. But far more troubling, the likelihood of women assuming agency, consolidating itself as a willed, passionate, erotic social subject capable of making a sexual selection, is not good. "When we talk about the revolution in erotic love," Shi argued, we are talking about evolution among the Chinese; to talk about evolution or revolution is "essentially to talk about women's liberation." The problem is that nüzi, the necessary agent of national liberation, must presuppose three absolute sine qua non—free social intercourse (shejiao gongkai), meaningful work, and equal education—none of which are actually available to women at the present moment. Put more starkly, Chinese women are, in this theory stream, primary actors in the task of transforming national history, but the conditions for their predication as adequate social agents do not prevail yet; they therefore remain deficient as subjects of their own liberation and, even worse, their deficiencies and predicative nonexistence may doom the progressive evolution of the nation itself.[72]

Heteronormativity. What I have referred to as a constitutive deficiency of the female subject in Chinese theory discussions has a complex relation to theory projects unfolding in other parts of the world at roughly the same time. Roz Coward has shown that in Europe in the second half of the nineteenth century, consequent on colonial expansion and the discovery that the European, patriarchal, nuclear family was not a universal norm, theoretical speculation posed two problems: How are social relations connected to state power? and What social evolutionary trajectory can explain the evolution of animal to human society, of barbarism to civilization? Publication in 1861 of Maine's Ancient Law led to almost immediate critiques of his so-called patriarchal theory from Morgan (Ancient Society), Bachofen (Das Mutter-recht), and McLennan (Primitive Marriage), all of whom criticized Maine on the basis of a concept of the mother-right society. Maine argued that all social relations were based on abstract, legalistic relations of non-consanguality (kinship was for him ideological), rooted in private property rights and organized around the absolute rule of the father. This made the state an extension of the patriarchal family but, more important, it held that father rights were originary. Mother-rightists rejected this connection of patriarchal family to state, contending that human social origins lay in the sensuous relation of mothers and children, which is in presocial procreation. In the view of mother-rightists, complex social relations must have been a later superimposition: blood was the obvious determination of matrilineal kinship and biogenetics trumped property relations. The base line of mother-right theory was the conviction that sexual relations had to have preceded social institutions, including patriarchy; the latter, it was suggested, had consequently grown up to regulate natural animal instinct and to organize property relations.[73]

The consequence of these theoretical debates was the emergence into visibility of "sexuality" as such. Between 1860 and 1930 social theory in Europe was preoccupied with questions of sexual organization. The force of these theories was to normalize the idea that social organization is always about sex. Yet, in supposing that the sex dynamic was the primary causal force in relations of kinship, family, sexual norms, sexual identities, and so on, theoreticians confronted enormous logical and substantive problems. For instance, did the Darwinian thesis of the origin of the species hold that human institutions *extend* innate human nature, or are social relations an imposition erected over nature? Edward Westermarck argued that the family was a natural social institution and proof of its universality was that it appeared not just in humans but in all species. Havelock Ellis and Betrand Russell, on the other hand, addressed what was widely held to be a mystery: How had men figured out their role in reproduction and how had they learned to control access to women to ensure patrilineal descent? Ellis and Russell's line of reasoning connected control of property and control of sexual rights. Some theorists conjectured that a paternal procreative family, where a patriarch claimed the labor of others, must have arisen at some point to surmount maternal promiscuity. Others imagined that individual fathers did not want to give property to men who were not their own sons, and so the fathers had had to seize control over all potential mothers. Yet another line of speculation suggested that males are by nature creative, females by nature procreative, so matrilineality was simply a primeval base of human evolution. In any case, by the mid-1920s there were two primary poles of speculation. One imagined progressive social evolution originating in polymorphous, promiscuous, maternal communism and evolving gradually into patriarchal monogamy and masculinized property claims. The other maintained that paternal family formation was natural, originary, and, most important, universally normative. Both major trends could assume that sexuality animated procreation and was the heart of property relations.[74]

But Darwin had never wholly explained the operation of the sex drive except to pose it as the motor of human and species evolution. The notion of natural selection, or incest avoidance in the interests of diversity in the gene pool, and Darwin's theory of sexual selection, allegedly the cunning formula developed among species to assure the ascent of the fittest, both presented social theory with a problem: How did sexuality get expressed in social relations? Was it extrinsic to social relations? Was it divisible or indivisible from social relations? Were all social relations erotic relations?

How did sexual desire fit into the picture of the human drive to procreate? Speculative ethnography was expanding Darwin's relatively underdeveloped notion of sexual division in several directions. Sexual division mutated into the theory that the human procreative sexes are in essence interest groups. Both maternal and paternal rights theorists presumed that the sexes had different interests (otherwise, how would they maintain their differences?), but increasingly the notion of difference tipped over into a theory of sex antagonism. Thus, Bebel, Engels, Zetkin, and Kollantai, under the banner of a diluted form of mother-right theory, proposed that the normative patriarchal family had been imposed on women *against their interests*.

It was logical to suppose on the basis of sexual interest theory that the relations of the sexes must be antagonistic, a "battle of the sexes." Unsurprisingly, conservative theorists in Europe took the war of the sexes and sexual selection in the direction we have seen Gao Xian move, which is toward theories that hold that male and female are emotionally and biophysiologically different to the point of incommensurability. Westermark, Heape, and Frazer, for instance, speculated at length on the psychosocial "characteristics" of the two sexes that they presumed to support primary social evolutionary and teleological procreation. Consequently, all manner of natural drives were attributed to each sex, from the natural promiscuity of men casting their seed widely, to the natural abjection of women, whose claims to civilization are attenuated by the role nature (i.e., procreation) imposed when it made women a separate caste with unique experience.[75]

These sorts of ethnographic and theoretic fantasies concerning sexuality and social relations theory presume the centrality of procreative sex. Until Freud, the question of sexual identity or the expression of sexual desire in individual choice lay folded within the discourses of property rights. To psychologize the issue and to attribute more flexibility to the problem of how individuals come to experience sexual desire, Freud contributed the notion of phylogenesis, or the thesis that the development of each individual organism recapitulates social stages. This initiated a more flexible understanding of how sexual desire got into the body of each individual. But it also pried open the question of the relation of desire and evolution. Did desire only forward human evolution? Was that its raison d'être and its exclusive function? The newly minted U.S. term "heterosexuality" is a symptom of this larger theoretical problematic and one element in the emerging sexological lexicon.

Jonathan Ned Katz has pointed out that for the United States, heterosexuality entered circulation first as a neologism in medical pathology, where it was defined as *perverse* desire for sexual relations with individuals of the other sex. In Krafft-Ebing's *Psychopathia Sexualis*, the term indicates pathology of sexual desire in individuals distracted away from social norms and obligations. The first entry for heterosexuality in the 1923 Merriam-Webster New International Dictionary retains the earlier sense, a "morbid passion for one of the opposite sex." Eleven years later, in the 1934 second edition, heterosexuality is a "manifestation of sexual passion for one of the opposite sex; *normal sexuality*."[76] On the basis of the initial negative definition, Katz argues that heterosexuality is a historical and ideological formation that took shape (at least in the United States) in the era of the shift from monopoly to consumer capitalism, and that is why it produced subjects alleged to possess an innate drive toward the consumption of erotic sexual pleasure.[77]

There are several points to raise about the cluster of theoretical issues that Mei Sheng placed under the umbrella terms of "(hetero)sexuality" (*liangxing*), "the family" (*jiating*), and "(hetero)erotic love" (*lian'ai*). First, when Chinese theorists put into play sexed subjects like Gao Xian's and Feng Fei's nüxing they were entering a long-distance conversation unfolding at about the same time in Europe over patriarchal theory and mother right, and in the United States over sexuality and personhood.[78] Anglo-American sex ethnography and theoretical projects unfolded synchronously with East Asian debates over the ethics and problematics of sexuality, because in each terrain the project was just being made, it was always under construction. Not only were these powerful theories being argued out and debated, but the claims they made to universality rested to some degree on colonial ethnography, which alleged to represent primitive or underdeveloped places like Africa or "overdeveloped" places like China. So, although it is probably more accurate to say that theoretical work aggressively incorporated these points on its own terms, diffusion does not do justice to the complex interchange that consolidated theory's claims to universality and enabled intellectuals in Chinese treaty ports to engage in international conversation about universality.

Second, though Chinese theorists were as engaged as European colonialists with sex theory and social relations, the project unfolded in China under different historical, economic conditions. The crisis of the national boundaries under the post-1842 treaty port system and the deepening problems of governmentality, legitimation, scholarly paradigms, and federalist command all led educated people to the exhilarating and tragic realization that they either needed to transvalue all received ideas or, conversely, that they would have to confront the possibility of ruin. From the mid–nineteenth century this led to increasingly more powerful waves of intellectual agitation. England, France, Japan, the United States, and Germany, the major colonizers, opened up new media and new places for foundational reevaluations of colonial modernity to take place. Cohorts of young students left the China mainland for study in Tokyo, Berlin, New York, London, and Paris, and the cultural crisis of semicolonialism deepened and became richer. Many men and women returned to treaty port China with cosmopolitan experience on everything from clothing and table manners to marriage practices and educational objectives. The first decade of the twentieth century gave way to the revolutions of the 1920s and eventually to the decades-long civil struggle to reclaim the state and systemically to modernize it. Among the new bourgeoisie and the scions of the older provincial elites there grew a cultural revolution that would shake deeply rooted assumptions about the work of intellectuals. The 1920s saw the rise of that characteristically searching narcissism of the professional literary and philosophic intellectuals who selected themselves to carry out the transvaluation of values.[79]

The impetus for Chinese feminism came, it should be said, from many sources. How a person is a "self," though frequently honored in the breach, had, as I argued in chapter 2, only yesterday rested on a habitus that was now disintegrating. The exhilarating possibilities of cultural transformation that characterize the great May Fourth movement came at a price. The price was the pressure to reconfigure what would constitute a person in the invasively urbane, semicolonial world of the treaty ports. As I argue in detail in the next chapter, not everyone was as self-conscious or sensitive as fiction writers were; Ding Ling is an instance of literary feminism that is infamous precisely because it was a singular expression of the problem of how a woman would henceforth be female. Because the crisis conditions for the theorization of Chinese feminism are as puissant as the theoretical resources Chinese intellectuals and ideologists read in the project of transvaluation, to that degree Chinese feminism is a Chinese project. One of the most illuminating long-term, ultimately revolutionary agenda items was to rethink gendered social relations as heterosexuality. That is, the doctrines and ideologies of scientific evolutionary heterosexuality became normative expressions of human nature.

Webster's Collegiate Dictionary with Chinese Translation, published by Commercial Press in Shanghai in 1923, does not include an entry for heterosexuality. This is not surprising, as the term had not yet been established in Anglophone theory and the dictionary originated in English. However, Mei Sheng's ZFWT contributors employ a plethora of terms in Chinese (some of them appearing in the 1923 benchmark dictionary) that *suggest* heterosexuality. Some, like the extremely significant ren'ge or jinkaku, are neologisms coined in Japanese. These terms suggested heterosexuality because in social evolutionary theory individuals choose the best mate for procreation. Getting women to the point where they could make the best choice meant installing a personality in them, and this success rested, as I suggested during the discussion of Gao, on the proposition that women get endowed with personalities that support correct erotic choices. In this respect, the poetics of ren'ge collude in the project of establishing heterosexuality.

Indeed, the third point to raise regarding Mei's inclusion of sexual terms is that many of the richest theories of sexuality and historical evolution entered into the debates in China already mediated through Japanese sex theory in Chinese translation. Shimamura Tamizo, Yosano Akiko, Honma Hisao, Yoneda Syotaro, Kagawa Toyohiko, Yamakawa Kikue, and others contributed theory streams which Chinese theorists translated, annotated, extended, or simply worked through in their own creative theories. Finally, subjects and theories alike, while specific in detail, are actually haunted by their own inexhaustible indebtedness. Universalizing sex theory in Europe already owed an inexhaustible debt to the Iroquois, the Aryans, the Hindoos, and all the other anthropologically significant, taxonomic human communities providing evidence for ethnographic theorists and their fantastic scenarios of evolutionary social development. Freud's theories of sexuality, for instance, are inconceivable without the existence of this sort of colonial anthropology. As William Pietz demonstrated, some of the key terms in the Freudian lexicon, such as "fetish," are linked directly to the colonial relation in which Europeans encountered the religious practices of others and sought through theory to make sense of difference. Analogously, the theory projects of Lin Zhaoyin, Mao Dun, Yi Jiayue, Zhou Jianren, and many, many others used resources originating elsewhere but vividly present in real time within the no-where space of colonial modernity.[80]

*Defining heterosexuality.* The most intensely focused of Mei Sheng's twenty-odd subject sections concerns the central theoretical questions pertaining to human sexuality. The primary term in play in these texts is *liangxing,* meaning the condition of being one of the two sexes, the relationship between two sexes, or perhaps simply the condition of being sexed. Lexically, the 1923 Chinese Webster's dictionary defined sexual as "opp. to asexual," but placed both terms in a capsule discussion of evolutionary sexual selection and natural selection. Being sexed, being in a heterosexual relation, or having a sex was inextricably linked, that is, to the theory (though of course it is not glossed as theory, but as fact) of "sexual selection (Biol) natural selection which results in the survival and development of certain characteristics, as bright colors or qualities of notes in birds," which enable "advantage for mating." In a way that mirrors much of the debate generally, sexuality is purportedly both distinct and yet subtly inextricable from evolutionary, procreative, teleological mating.

The term liangxing does not appear in the Chinese Webster's as a noun (i.e., "sex"). Under "sex" is listed "the character of being male or female or, of, pertaining to, the distinctive function of the male or female [suoyi cheng nan, nü, ci, xiong, pin zhi xing]" and "one of the two divisions of organisms distinguished as male and female [nanlei huo nülei, cilei huo xionglei, pinlei huo pinlei]." Or perhaps what sexes a being, makes it either one thing or the other, a descriptor that establishes sex in an ontological and anatomically very rigid fashion, as "the distinctive function of male or female" and therefore presumably having to do with procreation. Rather, liangxing appears as synonymous with the adjective "sexual" and is defined as "belonging to or pertinent to sex or the sexes [shuyu xingde, shuyu liangxingde]; peculiar to, or relating to, either the male or female or their distinctive organs or functions [guanyu nannü cixiong de, guan yu nannü cuxiong zhi shengzhiqi huo gongnongde]." Liangxing, then, is what people do, feel, or express on the basis of their distinctive organs or functions. And it is significant that the term encodes bimorphism. In twentieth-century English the term sexual is unitary and can be modified, thus bisexual, homosexual, heterosexual, asexual, and so on. The term in the Chinese of the 1923 Webster's, on the other hand, establishes sexuality as already bimorphic, including an originary opposition.

Obviously, dictionary definitions are one part of the emergence of key words, and this was particularly so during the 1920s. That was the era when, as Edward Gunn has established, the "rewriting" of Chinese means of expression, particularly its theoretical language, was in great flux. A good example is the glut of translations for the idea of the Freudian unconscious, which Zhang Jingyuan has traced in her Freud dissemination study.[81] The theoretical work that concerns me, significant because it is included in Mei's project, offers a range of variants on the dictionary term liangxing, words like liangxing fanzhi (liangxing reproduction), renlei de liangxing (human liangxing), and nannü liangxing (male and female liangxing).[82] Given the way these terms operate in context and the simple fact that the neologism liangxing includes two sexes, I translate these as variants of the term heterosexual. They are synonyms of a term, yixing, that appears in Yoneda Syotaro's "Love and Civilization." Another loan word, yixing became the root of the standard translation of heterosexual, yixing 'lian (literally, other-sex love). Yoneda's thinking was that "since the basic principle of sexual desire springs from sexual difference [yixing; literally, the other sex] we can now therefore research and investigate the truth of the matter—the love between the two sexes, male and female—through sexual difference [xiangyi de liangxing]."[83]

In theoretical Chinese, as in theoretical English, the term heterosexuality surfaced into visibility slowly. A number of pieces had to be in place before, as Katz found, the term could take on the powerfully universalizing and totalizing ideological force that it has in so many modernist discourses. In Coward's history of sex theory, Katz's history of institutional heterosexuality, Yoneda's theoretical speculations on the East Asian circuit, and theorists whose work I examine below, heterosexuality is considered a universal, normative, innate drive, expressed in erotic passion one feels for another of another sex, distinguishable from yet linked to the cunning logic of progressive procreation and consequently to human natural and social evolution. As Chen Dezheng put it, heterosexual love is "a natural madness . . . which individuals endure for the sake of the race."[84]

Do the contingent foundations of feminism presume heterosexuality? Feminism certainly rests on the availability of the collective subject women. Although "species" is the collective subject of social evolutionary thought (even in its nationalist form), popular evolutionary theories divide the collective subject into male-of-species and female-of-species. A dynamic thesis of sexuality fuels the assumption that all species are naturally heterosexual because nature visits heterosexual desire on them to get them to reproduce. The feminist subject women, shaped in relation to theories of social evolution, even in its nationalist articulations, demonstrates that women as a species have something in common. The subject of women stabilizes nationalist arguments about women's emancipation by rooting women in nature.

## Evolution, Heterosexual Poetics, Ren'ge: Shimamura Tamizo, Yi Jiayue, and Chen Dezheng

Three central analytic problems widely represented in Mei Sheng's compendium will help to situate the next discussion. These are evolutionary theory, heterosexual poetics, and the ren'ge problematic. Particularly the first two discussions, of the woman question and the theoretical project of understanding (or instantiating) heterosexuality, are difficult to extricate from each other.[85]

Shimamura Tamizo represents a typical position on the question of the relation of the woman question and the question of (hetero)sexuality.[86] In his essay "The Question of Heterosexuality" (translated as "Nannü liangxing wenti"), originally published in Japanese in 1921, Shimamura argued that it would actually be a mistake to continue subsuming questions of sexuality under the rubrics and problems of "the woman question." Indeed, his view was that heterosexuality should be the center of theoretical inquiry, no matter how upsetting the prospect. The woman problem was obliquely positioned in relation to the more deeply troubling question of what he proposed was a structuring relation of liangxing and liangxing *fanzhi*, or heterosexuality and heterosexual procreation. Before one could pursue the woman question, it was important to position women in a sex-positive theory that endorsed pleasure as prior to, or enabling, procreation and, consequently, evolution. Shimamura's theorization proposed, in other words, that pleasure has an evolutionary function. Tolstoy represented to Shimamura a tradition of Christian asceticism, which had taken a life-negating position. Accordingly, he argued that Tolstoy was an anti-materialist, whose sole rationale for heterosexuality was procreation and who aestheticized women outside that restricted domain. Tolstoy's renunciation of pleasure and his demonization of women's flesh and sexual fluids fetishized the eternal female (*yongyuan nüxing*) at the expense of real women.

Actually, Shimamura argued, procreation is not why humans have sex; sexuality and sexual pleasure are positive, progressive, idealist forces that have as lovely side effects procreation and racial improvement. It was not just that antimaterialist theorists of disembodied "spiritual love" were wrong: they were on the wrong side of history when they did not extricate sexual pleasure or sexuality (liangxing) from the discourse of procreation. The question was how to theorize heterosexuality and get it right.[87] Shimamura's point, echoed throughout these readings, is that Darwinian evolution situates sexual intercourse at the center of existence. Evolutionary sexuality is optimistic and life affirming, which is why, having used Tolstoy as the negative example, Shimamura turned to Ellen Key for the positive. Key's contribution was to point out that carnal and spiritual love are not divisible. Far from being exemplars of the eternal feminine, women are material beings, whose generous eroticism makes humans happy while at the same time improving the race. Key, Carpenter, and a theorist he terms Ni'Cai, probably Nietzsche, all enforce a eugenicist position that affirms sexuality as the enabler of procreation, and thus eugenic progress—but more than that, as the way humanity pleases itself.

Shimamura's point of the centrality of heterosexual pleasure echoes through the complex argument in Yi Jiayue's analysis of Morgan's and Engels's positions in an essay called "Jiating yu hunyin" (Family and marriage). Situating himself inside the mother-right debate, Yi began rethinking what was so often social evolutionary theory's default position: that family or kin relations are patriarchal because Nature and History made them that way. Holding up this position to critical scrutiny, Yi expressed more interest in theorizing a modified version of Edward Morgan's position, particularly Morgan's emphasis on maternity and female sexual desire. We saw Gao Xian's preoccupation with the power of the female of the species to choose how the race would be improved in free sexual selection. Yi was enthralled with pregnancy. Kinship, he reasoned, is, or should be, traced through the maternal line, not the paternal line. That is because in its originary state human society could not possibly have clearly distinguished paternity. Moreover, because the paternity of children cannot be established beyond doubt, but a child's maternity cannot be doubted, the founding of family as an institution would have to have been the effect of sexual desire and women's sexuality. Family, as he put it simply, could not be established by two men, even if those two men were father and son. Even sons and fathers—the paramount relationship in all forms of Confucian theory—had to be mediated through the bodies of mothers.[88] The question then is how to understand the historical descent of natural, primal heterosexual marriage.

Here Yi's position became quite complex. He recentered kinship relations in a modified version of Morgan's five evolutionary stages (consanguine-promiscuous, particonsanguine-group, paired-serial, patriarchal, and monogamous) and Engels's three-stage thesis (consanguine-promiscuous, particonsanguine, and pairing families). Quibbling with Morgan through references and arguments cited to Engels, Letourneau, McLennan, and others, Yi was balking at the notion that in its primeval state humanity had been promiscuous. Of course, when Yi took up a position within this problematic, he was staking out a claim to the theory project generally speaking. He was sorting through the implications for general theory while living in a (from the metropole's perspective) semicolonial outpost. But that is not the central point. Far more germane to the theoretical project and to Yi et al. as theorists is the fact that Yi was universalizing and particularizing the international debate. Yi and Gao might have been translating, but they were also laying claim to the universal truths that theoretical work in the traditions of Enlightenment reason and progressive history claimed for themselves. When theorists like Yi took over general theory projects, in other words, they were not so much searching for a way to redeem or consolidate the nation as they were demonstrating in praxis how the nation claimed a specific place within universal teleologies. The fact of Yi's participation not only strengthened his own standing as an enlightened intellectual; it also ratified enlightened reason, science, and modes of representation. It made the claim to universality truly universal.

The preponderance of the evidence, Yi reasoned, was that prehistoric humans had always structured their sexual relationships, they had just done so in a variety of ways. The evidence also suggested that the ancients had by and large been exogamous, and exogamic marriage was evidence that most predecessor societies had understood consanguinal clan descent principles (i.e., the paternal contribution). Yi did allow that a minority of ancients must have practiced endogamous and incestual family formations. That is how he argued his own synthetic position: that in prehistoric

times, when heterosexual unions (*liangxing jiehe*) were largely the consequence of sexual instinct (*xing de benneng*), sexual congress was not promiscuous, it was simply very brief, the "mariage temporaire" or *yi shi pei'ou
hun*. The various forms of marriage among the primitives had evolved
through stages of capture (the origin of exogamy); barter (*jiangmaihun* or
*par achat*, in which the single women of a defeated tribe were commodified
and sent as booty to the victors, a semienlightened form because patrilin-
eality is recognized); servitude (a complex form in which males indentured
themselves for set periods to the wife's matriline, returning to the paternal
clan with a wife after the terms of servitude were over), also classified as
semienlightened; negotiation (a truly enlightened form, based on understanding that marriage relations can be negotiated over time among social
groups of fluctuating relative power with each other); to the highest form
of marriage, the free love marriage, which is the preferred and future form
advocated by all socialists.

Actually, at base, Enlightenment was the issue because Yi indexed Enlightenment to historical processes. First there was the slow, progressive
move of humans from primitive, relative ignorance of instinctual drives,
toward realization that eroticism can replace violence, or sublimate violence in more sophisticated relations of sexual exchanges. The second
process was the slow, progressive realization among humans that neither
male nor female should be placed in a relation of servitude to the other.
Although all enlightened countries had by now adopted the negotiated
form, the free love option awaited future progressives. Heterosexual free-
choice marriage was the most natural and enlightened form because it
enabled the free expression of natural sexual desire. Only in free love
marriage could the "crystallization of spiritual and carnal" desire between
men and women be effected.[89] A third historical process at work in Yi's
theory was movement toward bolstering the individual, particularly individual women. Individuation meant evolving agency, but I take that issue
up in a later discussion.

The reason for focusing on marriage forms at all was that organization
of marriage determined the fundamental structure of the family, and the
family, by this argument, was the social origin of individuals. Yi consequently developed a frame for the historical evolution of the universal
family through three temporal stages of primitive or original and mother
right, or "maternal" (in English) family (*muxi jiating*); semienlightened
forms of transitional families ranging from matrilineal patriarchal family
(*muxi de fuquan jiating*) to patrilineal patriarchal (*fuxi de fuquan jiating*) and
so on; to the enlightened forms of the "modern family" (original in English). In its development, moreover, the modern family must have evolved
from temporary to polyandrous, polygamous, and so on upward and to-

ward the pinnacle of the monogamous, enlightened, contemporary family outlined in the theoretical work of Charles A. Ellwood.[90] "As I have argued in the foregoing," Yi wrote, "the family form depends on the reorganization of marriage forms; but marriage forms also rely on the reorganization of the procreative couple. For instance: (1) if the [social] form taken by the procreative couple is temporary, one cannot establish a family [because the relation is purely sexual; cf. 179]; (2) if the marital form is polyandry, the family form is of the savage type; (3) under the polygamous system, a semi-enlightened family is established; (4) if the procreative couple is organized monogamously then you have a modern, enlightened family."[91]

I will refrain from describing Yi's final analytic moves, which examine in some detail the property relations underscoring the family (e.g., patriarchal ownership of women and their reproductive capacity, systematic relations of subordination of women to men evolving toward a more mutual [xietong] relation of equality in which women and men "have a position of totally equal ren'ge" in relation to one another). Suffice it to say that he ends on the optimistic note that the evils of the present modern system must be swept away by reform of the procreative unit, its reestablishment on the natural ground of love. In conclusion, Yi quotes in English Engel's *Origin of Private Property*: "The family has been merely the temporary product of a particular stage of economic development, and that with the sweeping away of capitalism and private property the family also will disappear. The children will be cared for by the society as a whole, and man and woman will be free to enter into or abandon married life as their fancy may dictate."

I have elaborated Yi Jiayue's contribution at great length for two reasons: to reinforce the point regarding the erotic couple and sexualized woman's centrality in contemporary theories of heterosexuality and to show concretely how the project participated in analytic schemes that European and Japanese theorists were also considering. But Yi was only one of many intellectuals engaged in this theoretical project. Mei Sheng included two essays from Zhou Jianren, "Jiating Shenghuo de jinhua" (Evolution of family life) and "Zhongguo jiu jiating zhidu de biandong" (Changes in the old family system). Zhou's theoretical aim was to link the natural condition of maternity and mother right (i.e., descent recognized through the matriline) to evolutionary social progress and hence to two problems: first, that evolutionary change had ceased in China, particularly the rural areas, leading to a condition of ultrastability (*feichang wen'gu*), and second, that the consequence of colonialism and imperialism will be to trouble that stasis. Heavily indebted to the analytic concept of the "natural" and the idea that the "family is a natural organization, naturally organized," Zhou's interests lay with the problem of political citizenship.[92] Just as Rome had transformed Greece, the imperialists would influence China's developmental course. The example of progress will initiate in China a movement of the small family unit from secondary status in the lineage into the center of Chinese social organization. Colonial intrusion is thus progressive because, though "it is not possible to theorize exactly what system the national body [guoti/kokutai] will take after the establishment of the Republic," still there is no question in his mind that "the stability of this system will be undone once the education into Confucian patriarchal order [junchen fuzi deng jiaoxun] begins to be questioned."[93] Zhou was also preoccupied with female personhood. Because natural women had long been sullied, it was unclear whether women could ever learn to be "independent citizens" (nüzi nengfou zili de guomin) or whether the forces of malevolutionary rigidity had irretrievably habituated them to dependency. Nonetheless, underscoring his meditation on citizenship was the bedrock of eugenicist progressivism, which held that China had its own evolutionary trajectory that led from the primitive, natural family of the mother right to the ultrastable or unnaturally static paternal family to—through the mediation of imperialism—the love family that will progressively rejoin rural China to the dominant evolutionary strain of global progress.

A similar commitment to progress underwrote the schema of Chen Dezheng, who examined social evolution originating in nomadism and progressing through stages of agricultural production and the clan system, to industrial and family dissolution through the assays of sensual instincts (yuqiu benneng) and egoistic desires (liji 'yü).[94] According to this narrative, humans naturally became heterosexually intimate and established family relations for the sake of survival itself. Gender cooperation was indeed based on a division of labor (male outside, female inside), but it was only after the emergence of the private property system that "he who possessed power in the family" began to breed the children and egoistic desires turned to simple acquisitiveness. The private property system also originated the contempt that men came to feel for women because the sex difference (xing jian de qubie) determined that men had to work harder than women, and that in consequence, women become men's dependents. This contempt led men to prostitute women, and at the conjunction of the private property system, the emergence of species, the alienation of labor, and the devolution of human feelings, the cooperative family of the nomadic stage disintegrated into the autocratic family. Rules replaced genuine feeling in the family. The next stage after simple private property, industrial production and capitalism, further distorted the psychological drives of individuals. Although capitalism made possible independent life for women, this heritage of contempt and misogyny gave rise to inequality and lovelessness throughout the society. In terms of global development,

China had ended up with the worst of both worlds: a lingering, moldering clan system and a deracinated, exhausted, sexually perverse population.

Chen made two important points. First, natural instinct initially led women and men to live in harmony in the collaborative family and will lead them back to the garden once we dispose of capitalists, money culture, warlords, and landlords. Second, and more important, his narrative built on Engels's insight to explain how gendered interests had developed within the clan. The big family, Chen argued, took shape historically when capital accumulation became the raison d'être of kin relations. The elevation of men over women was rooted in private property. And, he implied, the conflicts between brothers was also rooted in economic competition, mediated through wives. In other words, Chen argued, family was actually an assembly of embedded interests competing along gender, class, and generational axes. Once again we see the notion that interests coalesce around gendered difference. Natural heterosexual desire brought human beings together for the sake of procreation; private property led males of the species to hold the females of the species in contempt. This in turn created women as a subject in need of enlightened emancipation, whose commonalities are, theoretically speaking, the product of both sexual species' being and oppression. This latter point, that women collectively possessed well-developed interests distinct from those of the patriline, came across explicitly in this essay. It connects arguments of this type to others, like those of writers Yan Zhongyun and Zhang Meili, who also are redacted in Mei Sheng's project and who spoke self-consciously as women, from the abrupt, compulsorily naïve, privileged position of awakened female subjectivity.[95]

*Heterosexual Poetics.* If, as I have been suggesting, eugenic feminism presupposes heterosexuality (one must conceive of women as a sexual interest group before their interests as a subject for emancipation can be formulated, and the sexual interest that women have in common is their common desire to procreate), how does this theorized heterosexuality work? Gao Xian made clear in his discourse on "Sexual Selection" that sexual intercourse itself in the higher species formed the apex of a law of progress that led from asexual through monosexual to cross-sexual forms of reproduction.[96] Yet evolution was only a scientific foundation and did not, in itself, explain how humanity gauged the direction of evolutionary flow or how individuals acted in ways that would forward the momentum of human or national evolution. It was a difficult problem. As Hoashi Osaro argued, the meaning of sexual reproduction appeared differently depending on one's standpoint. The nation saw in reproduction a way to replace citizens; individuals naturally considered it a means to a satisfying sexual life, whereas the theorist must raise to visibility the fact that marriage is a social formation that potentially bridges the gap between economic and spiritual values. Indeed, though presuming a natural community of women or natural interests of women in relation and opposition to men, evolutionism did not completely resolve the question of social regulation of heterosexuality because it was ambiguous about sexed subjects and their "natural" behaviors.[97]

Xi Leng's short essay "Yixing shejiao de taidu wenti" (The question of attitudes toward heterosexual social intercourse) raised what he felt was the confusion that occurred when people failed to distinguish between social regulation and the sex drive per se. He cautioned that the sine qua non of women's liberation, freedom of social intercourse (shejiao) or ending elite sexual segregation, actually had two levels: social intercourse and eroticized love. Though the second presumes the first, they are not the same thing: Heterosexual social intercourse and heterosexual love [yixing shejiao he yixing lian'ai] are two different things and this is not difficult to grasp, he argued. To get pure heterosexual love one must be active in a heterosexual society where social intercourse is available. But to use the argument for heterosexual social intercourse purely as a strategem for arriving at heterosexual love is incorrect.[98] In other words, sexuality or erotic drive situated women and men as attractive opposites. This required a domain that should be open and closed at the same time: it had to be open enough to encourage and support selection, but sufficiently closed to prevent promiscuous selection or sexual contact. There needed to be a space where the sexes located and chose one another, yet were prevented from collapsing sexual interest (good) into wild indiscretion (dangerous to natural selection). At least among elites where spiritual sexuality counted for something!

There were many ways to argue the point. Chen Dezheng, for instance, sought a model in primitive society where women and men mingled freely, while recognizing that modern social relations are far more complex, and therefore the key to understanding how our lusts can be mediated is correspondingly complex. So, although even in contemporary times, "social intercourse is natural and human society cannot avoid it," one also needs to distinguish erotic love from mere carnality (rouyü).[99] Mao Dun (Shen Yanbing) reinforced the theoretical position that the precedent for open social intercourse was the natural society of the past. Among primitives, he opined, social intercourse was the norm and people's sexual morality was quite adequate. Only when the sexes are artificially separated, ironically, does the unhealthy lust—what he called "a great idol for cheating people"—crystallize around romantic love. The masculine gaze that degrades and humiliates women has denaturalized what ought to be a fundamental social and thus public relation of men and women.[100]

Analytically, a related problem bothering some theorists is that sex morality presumed, without evidence, what was natural about sex. Wang Qingni's position is a good example of this matter. It was actually easier analytically to demonstrate social customs that were perverting heterosexual morality (prostitution, patriarchy, concubinage, harems, marriage law, chastity) than it was to describe the positive content of natural sexuality or where it would take humans who were not overconstrained. Wang made two attempts to say what was natural about sex. First, he theorized, "morality and sexuality are both natural instincts," which, when fused together, enabled something he called "heterosexual love" (liangxing de ai) to converge. Unfortunately, he was not too forthcoming about the content of heterosexual love except to say that sex morality and aesthetics are actually conjoined because all people naturally wish to have the most beautiful partner possible. This natural heterosexual desire has progressive effects in terms of sexual selection and national evolution. Then, however, Wang fell back on the common argument that to actually witness erotic love and ethical principles at work in naturally, progressive, and sexy ways was going to require creating the social conditions that would allow women to advance into subjecthood (economic independence, literacy, work, marital choice, equality of spouses, propinquity). After women became subjects or achieved standing socially, the naturally joined instincts for beauty and sex would be in a position to work together.

Lin Zhaoyin and Y. D. are examples of theorists who did theorize the sexed subjects quite forthrightly. Both men started from the same position, which is that "if you want to know the function of the two sexes then you must understand the *difference* between the two sexes." Lin's argument hangs on two insights. First, the very naturalness and flexibility of sex instincts leads to their sublimation. Second, enlightened people now know how logical and natural sexual expression is, which is why they would wish to overturn the social customs that have conspired in recent years to make sexuality a secret, private matter. The aim of progressive theorists must be to eugenically strengthen Chinese stock. That means finding better, more progressive avenues for sublimating the natural sex drive in people. Sex education at the levels of family, school, and society will undertake the reinscription of the individual desiring body (geren yüqiu shenti) so that knowledge about stages of development (infancy, latency, budding, blooming) can properly and ethically support the child's "natural" experience.[101]

Y. D. puts this notion even more baldly. Female, heterosexual subjects develop when a child's body reaches puberty. The child emerges from latency charged with sexual desire and the urge to procreate. The emotional life of women begins to change during the teenage years as she becomes marked by special emotions of wrathful indignation (fenfuxing), terrified shyness (kongbuxing), daydreaminess (kongxiang xing, where she indulges in reading mystery novels, makes intimate girlfriends, plans mass suicide, and has homoerotic sexual escapades), and affectlessness (wu ganjüe xing). These dangerous and latent emotions will disappear once the woman is pregnant, though one must watch her then for signs of melancholy and insanity. But although this developmental course puts unfortunate pressures on women, still there are reasons for the emotional differences that mark the two sexes. First, society has to be reproduced. The degree of difference between the sexes is a measure of civilization and biological evolution, and thus women will always be unfairly burdened. But second, haunting the sexed subject of heterosexual woman is the danger of the third sex. Masculinized women and feminized men threaten to upset the natural balance of the sexes. The sexed female body should be valued as a barrier against ambiguity. Eroticized, feminine female bodies are primarily heterosexual bodies because they are procreative bodies, so the more lushly feminine the body is, the more profoundly heterosexual the female is.[102] And as Lin argues, it is never too early to begin telling the story of sexuality to your children and showing them pictures of the beautiful nudity of women.[103]

I will not follow out in detail the question of where lian'ai (erotic passion) belonged in this analysis, except to note that most theorists seemed to agree with Kagawa Toyohiko that lian'ai was the beating heart of human subjectivity. It was something more than lust or instinct; it was a powerful force that nonetheless could "burst through the exterior of economic systems" and transform them for the better. Kagawa's view that "the birth of the self" occurred in the experience of passion because "without self lian'ai is impossible" certainly spoke for the views of many on the importance of making sure that the female heterosexual subject could come into being in China. The female lover had to appear first as a separate and centered self before anything further could be done to improve the racial stock.

In heterosexual poetics, my term for highly speculative writing about heterosexual drives, the effort to follow out the implications of theoretical terms and concepts regarding the centrality and power of magnetic sexual, social, and emotional bonds linking male and female lovers came to consider a large range of associated problems. For instance, how could the desiring woman be theorized in the disciplines of biology and psychology? How did sexual difference operate naturally and how socially? How could a scholar or a lover draw an ethical line between heteroeroticism and simple lust, which was not progressive because it did not enable women? How can the power of erotic heterosexual choice be put to use transforming stale, outmoded social conventions like the lijiao? Social theory could demonstrate the historically progressive dynamic of sexuality in the past, so why not use it to predicate future moves?

Theorists preoccupied with the centrality of heterosexuality typically began by claiming that heterosexual coupling is natural but that socially malignant forces—private property, autocratic family, patriarchal precedent, hyperstability, rural stagnation—had obstructed the unfolding of a natural dynamic. Oppressed by unnatural forces, women and men shifted from collaborative sexual harmony to the "struggle between the sexes" (*nannü liangxing jian de zhengdou*).[104] The interests binding women together with women, that is, outweighed the potential that exists for female and male to merge as sexual interest groups. Heterosexuality tended to devolve into conflictual groupings based on different interests, and that pitted male against female. The project of the Chinese theorists that Mei Sheng selected for redaction seemed to be working out how human heterosexuality could be harnessed *against* devolutionary social norms in China.

There are two final points before I consider the importance of the discussion of ren'ge to this foundational, national feminist habit of thinking. First, eugenic arguments are a progressive force in these texts. I do not mean to say only that eugenic arguments struck theorists of the time as progressive, though that is also true. Rather, I mean that in the construction and normalization of a progressive feminism, eugenic arguments provided theorists with a conceptual link between the great historical forces of social evolution and the specific problematic of individual, contemporary choice. Theorists made the assumption that individual-choice marriage would bring both partners sexual bliss. The sexual happiness of marriages improved the quality of children and therefore contributed to social progress. In the case of Chen, who reflected the earlier, more anarchist argument against the clan system and patriarchal family, the social effect of eugenically sound marriage choices was to improve the race by enabling the superior people to choose one another.[105] Also, of course, analysts like Xiao Feng and Chen Guyuan and many, many others often referred to racial improvement as a justification for individual marriage choice. That is because, as Xiao argued, children conceived in loving marriages are smarter and more capable than children from forced marriages.[106]

However one reads eugenically styled arguments, the notion that self-willed behavior on the part of men and women is racially wholesome because it forwards the greater good meant that the argument for female emancipation was linked not merely to social improvement but more foundationally to the human evolutionary trajectory. I am suggesting that far from an aberration, Gao Xian's theses regarding the capacity for humanity to intervene in its own social evolution were widespread assumptions in progressive feminism. The granting of women's liberation did not benefit only men (e.g., eroticizing procreation, centering the small family); it benefited the race as a whole. It seems to me that this is one of the tragedies of feminism globally. Its conceptual roots in retrograde, cryptoscientific arguments about racial difference and race improvement are not fully explicated.

Second, heterosexual poetics was one of those newly emergent places in the social landscape where the transvaluation of values was occuring. Theoretical work undertaken under the aegis and in the framework of "the woman question" became extremely complex. It was certainly a continuation of the eighteenth-century Qing debates on where in the social landscape the educated woman belonged. It was also an experimental course in the theoretical production of modernity. The proofs theorists contributed are often interlocking, supplementary, or circular. One influential essay argued, for instance, that evolutionary biology is legible in the written history of civilization,[107] which shows up in the record of national eugenic progress among citizens, that can be indexed through the people's spiritual culture, that reverberates in evolutionary biology, and so on and so on.[108] Without belaboring the point, I suggest that one of the reasons why these arguments have to be seen as foundational is precisely because they have struck some post-Mao contemporaries as well worth rearguing. But the central point to establish here is that heterosexuality in eugenic theories of national-racial development was visible in the 1920s because theoreticians made it visible.

*The Ren'ge Problem.* Of all the complex, foundational problems in Mei Sheng's collection, the most important is the ren'ge issue.[109] Ren'ge is a loan word from Japanese into Chinese. According to Chen Liwei, Inoue Tetsujiro coined the term *jinkaku* some time between 1887 and 1897, when Inoue taught at the University of Tokyo. The term does not appear before that time and seems to have been glossed for the first time in Chinese in the 1899 volume, *Xin Er'ya* (The new era) edited by a Chinese exchange student.[110] Apparently, jinkaku, like "society" (Chinese: *shejiao,* Japanese: *shakô,* particularly associated with the thought of Francis Gilman in the 1910s), had particular resonance in Japanese and Chinese work on August Bebel, Ellen Key, Havelock Ellis, and Henrik Ibsen.[111] *Hanyü wailaizi cidian* (A dictionary of Chinese borrowed words) defines ren'ge as "the sum and substance of a person's individual disposition [*xingge*], temperament [*qizhi*], capabilities [*nengli*], and special qualities [*tezheng*]." It is an interestingly redundant definition, as most of the definers are also synonyms; in vernacular Chinese, *xingge* and *ren'ge* are roughly interchangeable.

Wang Pingling raised the matter directly in his essay "Xin funü ren'ge wenti" (New women ren'ge question). Working in the domain of ethics, Wang argued that ren'ge had to be seen as more than simply the "form of the person" or even a moral quality, but in the context of the basic humanist question: What is human? or What is man? The conclusion he reached was that humans are animals who possess both reason and emotions. Whereas "rationality is the bright lantern that leads the emotions" and in effect disciplines them, "the significance of ren'ge is to use meaningful action to . . . establish a goal that is exalted, great and transcendent, aimed at creating a steady, appropriate life." In Wang's view, ren'ge was neither objective nor subjective, neither hereditary nor environmental, but provided a kind of spiritual essence with the capacity to improve on genetic heritage. The object of ren'ge is actual life, he summed up, not "vacuous theory." Ren'ge's objective in the last instance is to take the functions of reason and sentiment and to adapt them to actual life, to enter into actual life and to reform actual life. Ren'ge's eternal responsibility is not only to complete the life of a person but also to elevate human spiritual life. . . . So what is ren'ge? "It is the sentiment of reason and the thorough concretization of reason." Wang believed, moreover, that the rededication of ren'ge in women was the precondition for Chinese social evolution and transvaluation of new cultural values. "Masculinized civilization" prevailed in China, where women have "become accustomed to a slavish, dependent, parasitic life" and male dominance has led to an insipid unisex society (danxing de shehui). In Europe and the United States, on the other hand, "a climate of bi- or heterosexualization" is a "thrilling sight to behold," because the liberation of women's special genius into social expression was enabling rapid evolutionary progress. In the latter, the possibility of economic independence and social life was deepening the inroads made in the new culture movement, leading to women's moral refiguring outside the old ethics of "obedience, dependency, ornamentality, gentleness and chastity."[112]

Wang's thesis of masculinization is also similar to Gao Xian's. Society is composed of individuals who come in two kinds, male and female, unite and create new individuals, and maintain the continuity of evolutionary social progress. China's inhospitality to female ren'ge has derailed progression. This is not merely the fault of men, as women are indeed weaker than men in some key respects. However, evolutionary progress requires the full participation of women. "Henceforth," he argued, "women should have the brains of the philosopher, the attitude of the writer, the vision of the scientist, the hands of the laborer" (163). This is the objective for womanhood. So, in a manner of speaking, Wang called on women to voice their natural interests as a corporate entity. If the unconscious, social expression of the full subjecthood of corporate women would share with men a temperament that burnished reason with emotion and shone the bright lantern of reason on the effluvia of emotion, then female ren'ge seems most appropriately understood as a form of personal "standing" or social and ethical prerequisition. (In later chapters, I translate ren'ge in several ways: as "standing" or "social standing" or, in the translation that best expresses the intellectual sense of the term, as "personal standing.")

Personal standing is worldly in the sense Wang sought to attribute to ren'ge; the Oxford English Dictionary defines the word "standing" in terms of a "*manner of* standing." This manner of standing qualifies a "relative position (of a number of persons or things) . . . with reference to the other," and it characterizes a "situation, site, aspect" as well as "posture (attitude of a person); position (of a thing) as erect." In other words, it means "standing up." But personal standing also brings to mind the more legal sense, of standing under law: "one's place in the community in the estimation of others . . . relative position in social, communal or moral relations, repute, grade or rank."[113] It is in these two senses that I use the term ren'ge. Interpreting or glossing the theoretical term as personal standing also resonates clearly with the meaning attached to the term by Zhang Chenchang in an essay seeking to demonstrate how humanism addressed the qualities of personhood beyond the procreative role. He argued that the problem was not whether women were mothers but rather whether it was ethical to represent them exclusively as such. If, he argued, one represents women corporatively as mothers, they then become not human (*feiren*). To have standing in the representational order, women have to claim standing *with* men, though not *as* men.[114] It is also consistent with the sense conveyed in Feng Fei's "General Outline of the Woman Problem," where the question of the completion of women's personal standing in society appears in a global history of the corporate subject women. From colonial Africa and India and settler societies in North America to the heartland of the European industrial capital, it is the women of the world who hold the key to evolutionary development, and competitive nations make every effort to expedite their independent standing.[115]

Though theorists by and large presume the centrality of ren'ge, they often treat it indirectly. Feng's discussion is an unusually direct statement. Another obvious exception, redacted in the "Morality" section of the compendium, is Ye Shaojün's well-known essay "Nüzi ren'ge wenti" (The question of women's ren'ge).[116] Ye's position reinforced the sense that ren'ge refers to personal standing, as he begins his essay theorizing broadly about the relation of the individual part to the social whole. Ren'ge is the spirit which individuals amidst the masses ought to employ, he argued, as it is the sort of spirit that a sufficiently independent person or social element (*fenzi*) has within or in relation to the mass (*dazhong*) (149). To achieve this spirit of independence, one must build on natural instinct by loving truth rather than blindly following the masses. Yet, and rather to the contrary, people of the same era holding the same position should be equal, have equal ren'ge, precisely because each is equally an element of the same mass. Given the dictum that ren'ge expresses simultaneously both sameness with the masses and difference from them, it seems a logical extension in Ye's mind that women be recognized for ren'ge because they, like men, are part of the mass.

The question for Ye is why, to this point, women have been excluded from standing and whether at some earlier moment they had standing and lost it. His suggestion is that women as a corporate entity devolved historically, through no fault of their own, for two reasons: their labor was not considered productive labor and men unilaterally imposed on women familial roles or *mingfen*. (Mingfen are nothing less than the crystallization of the twisted male sadistic passion for keeping women ancillary and dependent on men sexually, socially, procreatively, and economically.) Men as a corporate interest group employ various strategies for retaining women in thrall, objectifying them and forcing them into secondary, slavish reproductive labor. Yet, although men corporatively appear to gain from this narcissism, actually they lose out, too. The real consequence of male sadism is the erosion of women's capacity for reason and sentiment. The degradation of women harms social evolution as it harms individual women, casting an artificial pall over what ought to be natural and spontaneous: human sexual life. It is in everyone's corporate interest, consequently, that women regain personal standing, that is, for men to "respect the ren'ge of the other," to see themselves in the gaze of corporate womanhood. Women's personal standing would enable them to disempower men, men whose sadism and inability to see anything other than a monochromatic succession of fathers and sons leads them to deride and degrade women's corporate genetic contribution to human reproduction. Revolutionary transformation of society must make social reproduction everyone's task. It must make the feminine central. Only through women is life reproduced, and individual women's genetic contribution to the fetus is a central social fact. That makes her labor, even where it is simply reproductive and nothing more, social production, not private exertion for private ends. Yet, for any of this enlightenment to occur, women must establish a perspective peculiar to themselves as a corporate interest group.

And that problem in turn ensnarls Ye in some of the same contradictions that bedeviled Wang Pingling earlier. Women as a corporate unit must be free to choose: men! Women are human (*ren*) and thus can claim ren'ge and qualify as persons of standing and no longer men's property, slaves, or housekeepers. But they are primarily free to choose men and to exercise their procreative powers for society at large. Their choices are severely circumscribed by nothing less than their own sexuality itself. Elsewhere, other theorists would argue strenuously that the choice of female chastity is not acceptable because the presumption for those who would extent ren'ge to women is that male and female are both equally important eugenic agents.[117] But psychosocially, the standing of women in society must rest on the reconceptualization of their work. Chen Qixiu put it quite definitively and concisely in his materialist historiography of the woman question: When women are in material [i.e., social] production, they are a part or an element [of society] and consequently men start recognizing the ren'ge of women.[118] But to Ye, whose vision was not as consistently materialist as Chen's, the problem posed was to rethink procreation, shifting it from the personal, domestic sphere to its true future as a broadly social event.

Where standing became most evidently problematic was in the matter of individual choice. Here, too, Mei Sheng represented a fairly broad range of discussion. The Wardian perspective (humans have the power to direct social revolution) that one finds in theorists like the high-spirited Gao Xian made ren'ge a frame for considering the ethical and legal question of human rights in conscious, willed subjectivity. For Gao, the ren'ge issue was connected to the social function of what he called the subject for or the agent of life (shengwu zhuti), what I called earlier the eugenic agent. You will recall that Gao argued that natural selection (a.k.a. struggle of the fittest) and sexual selection were different: natural selection is brutal and long-term species development, whereas sexual selection is more social and immediately malleable. But most significantly for Gao, sex selection means the female's right to choose suitable males for intercourse. Women are the shengwu zhuti because they care for the children of men, men whose interest in sex is, in evolutionary terms, primitivizing, selfish, regressive, even harmful. That is because men refuse to acknowledge that they are harming women, by holding that women are the objects of men, and claiming that women are cowardly, ignorant and incapable of independence. The truly foolish part is that "such men forget how they themselves achieved their contemporary independent testicles." In other words, the effect of being sexually attractive to women and thus being chosen for sex by women was that men came to possess pronounced secondary sexual characteristics solely in their relation to women (ss, 21).

But what Gao implies is that beneath the false, contemptuous, spiteful attitudes of jealous men, ren'ge is actually a matter of philosophy and law. He suggests that women already possess the building blocks for construction of ren'ge, by which he simply means a subject that is enabled to perform conscious acts of will and accept moral, legal responsibility for those choices. The problem that Gao saw in the discussion of ren'ge was a question of capacity versus entitlement. Because men did not recognize women's spiritual capacities, the men were the problem because they blocked women from expressing their innate capacity. The question became what the innate nature was. If denied expression, "do individuals have ren'ge or not? When we disallow them to consciously govern their own lives and development, and destroy their freedoms in life, do individuals have ren'ge any more or not?" (ss, 27). That is why for Gao, clarifying and distilling women's humanity out of the disorganized state that male dominance enforces leads to liberated subjectivity, ren'ge, and hence to the social mutuality of men and women in the future. The test of women's ren'ge will require men to abandon the lijiao, the most barbaric, ren'ge-destroying, deadly form of social criminality imaginable.

Because these theorists agreed so strongly that the lijiao or social etiquette of Qing dynasty elite life ruined women's ren'ge, they also tended to agree that one alternative means for regulating social intercourse among women and men was law. Mei included a series of articles on marriage and divorce that stressed women's standing in the domain of law or asked how women might best dispose of their own persons under the law. Yi Jiayue assumed this matrix in his essay "Zhongguo de lihun wenti" (The Chinese divorce question), which explicitly linked the questions of civilization in general, the law, and the natural inclination of women to exercise will in personal choice of sexual partners. To make this argument Yi, inspired by Ellen Key and Edwin Carpenter, advocated the institution of a new social system where natural feelings will legitimate individual choice and women will be free to choose to marry or divorce at will under the law.[119] Mei pointed out in an essay of his own that it was actually difficult to distinguish the ren'ge of the individual woman from the ren'ge of the married couple when considering the question of divorce ethics, law, and rights.[120] However, in matters of law, procreation, and domestic life, each individual member of the corporate entity still should have to develop the capacity to choose for herself.

The question of what elements of personality made progressive choices possible hovered constantly at the edge of these discussions. In Zhou Jianren's "Zhongguo nüzi de jüewu yu dushen" (Chinese women's awakening and their celibacy), for instance, the choice of celibacy is said to be open to the civilized woman, in fact signifies a degree of civilization in the nation or community. For Chinese women, however, it registers as proof of a viable individual will. The sign of the dignified woman of ren'ge is her ability to force her will to emerge into social action.[121] The viability of the will of women, the active force that will enable female individuals to transcend the problem that I term the constitutional deficiency of women's personalities, is a constant worry in writing about the sphere of the social and lawful. For instance, Wan Pu expresses her concern that although "women may have the will, they don't have the freedom to exercise it," and this has led to an atrophy that makes problematic their ability to secure legal political rights.[122] Zhang Xitan opined that the argument that only a minority of women are interested in the right to be political neglects the fact that only a minority of men are interested, too, and thus no matter what gender the person, representation boils down to establishing the principle of free exercise of will in all people.[123] In any case, what struck commentators like Yi Jiayue most strongly of all was the future: that women were now or would be in the future transforming themselves from dependency, parasitism, and hyperemotionalism into persons who use will to fight for their own independence.

Lawfulness in the sense of social propriety is another context or domain where the question of ren'ge frequently surfaced. In Xi Leng's "Yixing shejiao de taidu wenti" (Question of attitudes toward heterosexual social intercourse) for instance, a distinction is drawn between appropriate mingling of the sexes and the degenerate world of the dance hall where people become sexually besotted simply by propinquity.[124] A woman of personal standing "protects the solemnity of ren'ge during the period of transition from mere social intercourse to heterosexual love" and maintains an absolutely respectful attitude toward the other. But the new woman, the woman of standing, was also very explicitly theorized to be a sexual being who required a "new lijiao" to clarify appropriately ethical means of exercising her own legitimate will to pleasure. This liminal or theoretically proposed transitional stage led to tangible anxiety among theorists, and at no time more than when they raised the question of the politics and poetics of heterosexual eros.

A good example is Kuriyakawa Hakuson's "Jindai de lian'aiguan" (Perspectives on contemporary lian'ai), a prolonged discussion of how female subjectivity might be devised through a discourse of erotic heterosexual love. There are two voices in the text; the first belongs to the author and the second to the translator, Y. D., who interrupts his own translation to make the point that the Japanese conditions alluded to are more contemporary with European than Chinese conditions. Contemporary Chinese conditions, Y. D. asserted, would be more similar to Europe in the nineteenth rather than the twentieth century, as regards questions of marriage and free erotic choice. The essayist Kuriyakawa, on the other hand, is a romantic in the European style, and his essay rests on a tentative equation that links lian'ai with civilization in two ways. First, lian'ai (heteroeroticism) is the consequence of a historical evolution. In the barbarous past of prehistory people had sex merely for procreation; in the Christian era they romanticized love as a means of desexing and sacralizing women; the contemporary era is one in which women's flesh and spirit are potentially joined in ren'ge. But second, heteroerotic lian'ai is more developed in the West than in the East, because Orientals (dongfang ren) "look with particular prejudice at the relation of the sexes" and have not traditionally emphasized the beauties of the female. (Kuriyakawa seems to suggest that studying the nude and embracing the public representation of the fecund body of biological woman are progressive political activities.) Kuriyakawa also creates a magic quadrangle in which love and civilization form a match with heteroeroticism and the Occident, whereas animal procreation and barbarism are paired with carnal sex and the Orient. Orientals must therefore recognize the centrality of love in the evolution of civilization and allow love to boost the level of Eastern civilization.[125]

Here carnality, pure lust, in the absence of the heterosexual gaze of erotic love forms an obstacle to achieving equality.[126] And that is precisely where Kuriyakawa, and, one supposes, Y. D., too, raises and addresses the ren'ge issue. There are, he argues, increasing numbers of books and translations on sex now and though they are important, if we do not address the significance of the personal being in love relations [lian'ai shang ren'ge guanxi] and only popularize information about sex desire, not only will people not get the point, we will also have failed to dismantle ancient, vague prejudices.[127] Mediated through Key and Carpenter, his position is that "from the unity of two persons will consequently arise the total personality [wanquande ren'ge]" that female subjects require to be one with themselves. Kuriyakawa is well within the modernist domain.[128] But his point is that Nora's time is over. Ibsen's Nora, heroine of A Doll's House and symbol of the Chinese new woman, had entered into a slave marriage; she sold her sexual self in exchange for food. She left home for the "life of a person" and therefore she is, naturally, a precursor because "marital life in the twentieth century affirms the self [ziwo], making love its basic foundation and, in truly significant, unified marriages, no one person will sacrifice or worship in an unconscious, unreflective way." But what Nora neglected was the will of the self (ziji de yizhi). Though Kuriyakawa is aware of the point made in China by Lu Xun, that Noras have little economic recourse, he does not refrain from invoking Key, to the effect that the worst crime against humanity is a loveless marriage. And he castigates women, goading them to refuse all collusion with tradition and convention. Nora's century is over. Love is the acme of the new age. Enlightenment rests on the ability of the self to live in a mode of "self-assertion in self-surrender" (the phrase appears in English). Which is to say that the self is only visible in the unity of two completed individuals, each in possession of a ren'ge that he or she is willing to give over in exchange with the other.[129]

A term that contemporaries used in addressing a related issue is spiritual ren'ge or *jingshen ren'ge*. In an essay entitled "Xin shidai zhi xin zhencao lun" (On a new chastity for a new age), Hoashi Osaro takes a far more materialist and historically progressivist position than had Yosano Akiko or Hu Shih's response on reading Yosano in a Chinese frame.[130] Hoashi argues his position through the principled anarchism of Bakunin, citing particularly the Russian's speech to the Social Democratic Alliance in 1869. He maintains that one cannot but agree with Bakunin: the four major systems that anarchists must destroy are capitalism, the state, religion, and marriage. Marriage is psychologically perhaps the most daunting challenge because despite the fact that sexual ethics can easily be boiled down to eugenic concerns and the availability of sexual partners, the fact is that most societies at most times have imposed chastity on individuals. But Hoashi Osaro's point in outlining the spare history of the rise of the marriage system in Europe is that marriage coincided with the rise of private property and male dominance. Institutionalized masculinism (*nanxing benweizhuyi*) was the consequence of private property and the social organization of labor, society, which transformed instinct into regulated access to women. Now in the most economically advanced civilizations, marriage is contracted. Hoashi used the English term "marriage contract" and defined this as an agreement that women and men mutually agree to and employ will to establish through the mediation of law. Of course, the regulation of female chastity through the marriage contract is no bargain because it continues the contamination of human expressive life with capital, the state, and religion. It may grant some measure of equality to women in the legal domain, much as Western law has always fused civil and sacred law when it came to marriage. Nonetheless, these are compromised social relations.

The basis of chastity or loyalty in sexual congress can only be love and thus what he terms spiritual ren'ge. Human sexuality cannot be broken in two, spirit on one side and flesh on the other. Historical development has completely fused these two elements. That is precisely what makes human sexuality different from animal carnality. Humans have long since traveled from their animal roots to a more elevated life, from mere promiscuous lust to a spiritualized physical love. "This spiritual life is not the established fate of people," however. "It is rather created out of the negotiation of people's will in the environment. Thus the content of love is always evolutionary [*suishi jinhuade*]." That is because over the span of evolutionary time sexuality and human spirit have been enfolded, and as humankind evolved it made available a kind of sexual purity between women and men that opened up the doors of mutual respect, mutual admiration, and thus to a kind of chastity that is more like exemplary social loyalty of spirit to the chosen one. It is this unified body of corporate men and corporate women, or the two sexes as socially circumscribed sexes, that repollinates men with masculine attitudes and behaviors, women with feminine attitudes and behaviors. And that is why, Hoashi argues, "To press ren'ge upward and toward satisfaction is the ideal of married life and the only principle of married life." This is only to repeat in lyric form the truism that resounds throughout these foundational texts: marriage is love. "Thus my concept of chastity," Hoashi concludes, "is to endeavor to create a space for the ren'ge of mutual love."[131]

One final point should be made. There appears to be a difference separating analyses that stressed sexuality's latent or unconscious power to force progressive change in social formations, and progressive working within the frameworks of John Dewey, Lester Ward, and Karl Marx, who emphasized the need for conscious human agency even in evolutionary change. That is certainly the signal point in Chen Qixiu's "Nüzi zhenzao jinqian jiazhi (The monetary value of female chastity) which situates ren'ge in the frame of Marxian stage theory. When he applies the theory of historical materialism to the problem of chastity, Chen comes up with a four-stage evolutionary development of the mother right. His teleology leads from polyandry and abundant resources (matriarchy); to the uprising of men, polygamy over matriarchy, and men's emergence into the agents of material social reproduction; to the "liberation" of women into wage slavery (i.e., the contemporary stage); to a future in which the social standing of women is no longer measured by a man's control over her sexuality. As futurism, Chen's position is intrinsically interesting because it is a standard-issue, nonreductionist rendering of Chinese women's social worth.[132]

The thesis of the general will is expressed in a variety of venues, for instance, the Deweyan essay by C. C. (Xia Yun), which begins on a functionalist note ("Why get married? . . . To satisfy physiological need humans act on natural impulses to unite with the other sex, to continue the uninterrupted existence of the race and to extend their happiness and well-being") and ends on the cheery note that with sufficient social engineering, free marriage can become the key to liberation of women, which is in turn the key to social evolution.[133] As Dewey had promised, to build a progressive society, humans must act with volition rather than waiting for natural evolutionary changes. Change is progressive, incremental, and pragmatic. Hoashi Osaro reiterates the position more romantically when he criticizes the analogy of mandarin ducks standing for the married couple. Animals, he wrote, "marry" out of blind instinct, nothing more. More scientifically minded people might speak of ants as forming a society. This is incorrect as well, for ants cluster out of instinct, whereas human society is the product of consciousness and reason or intellect. Unlike insects, humans change the conditions of their lives and modify their environments. The basic issue for human beings is ethical because humans, male and female, always confront choices.

Ren'ge in emergent Chinese feminism was, as Raymond Williams noted in relation to the analytic category of individualism in England, a "fundamental order of being," what I would call an ontological presupposition: it is the analytic foundation of progressive feminism in China and the site where the feminist predicate "Chinese women" first appears. The problematic of ren'ge or women's personal standing is pervasive all through Mei Sheng's edited volumes. That is why I have been arguing that this ideological object, this spinal cord running down the body of feminist theorizing over the 1920s fetishizes women and their subjectivity. Like other analytic terms with great significance—individual, *meibun*, *wenhua*—ren'ge obviously has a very complex history and is ideological in the simple sense of connoting the political structure through which we are conscious of the world.[134] But analytic terms and theory generally speaking is a hymen of historical/theoretical meaning. In my historian's reworking, ren'ge has moved from a catachresis in Spivak's sense ("a concept-metaphor without an adequate referent") to being an effort inside an ideological formation that makes possible thinking about an emergent contemporary social formation.

Ren'ge is an irreducible term with complex historical provenance; that makes it both a universal and a specific. Yet, such a term requires the historian to refrain from dissolving all specifics into some precursor universal in the tedious game of the universal and the particular. Indeed, for a historian, the object is to retain for as long as possible the specificity opened up in the effort to rethink the line along which people in the past were actually thinking. Ren'ge is both like "individual" and yet not at all like it. Ren'ge is comprehensible analogically and it is a repository of complex reiterated meanings. But it is never reducible to a prior text. It is always historically new, future oriented, and socially embedded in significance and valences unknown to other domains where other, singular analytic catachreses may also be excavated.

## Conclusion

It may also be important to consider the question of historical difference: effusive concern with any given analytic term no doubt signals what Alessandro Russo calls an epochal epistemic impasse and defines as "growing uncertainty, not only about actual political value, but also about the cultural substance of historico-social categories."[135] Translation practice is not the key or the motive force in the study of catachreses. Far more is going on here than translation or the metaleptic extension of terms or simple neologism. The theoretical world that appears in vivid, repetitive, inventive detail in the pages of Mei Sheng's old anthology laid down the rational foundation of modernist thinking on a topic of central importance: What will the woman question mean and how should we resolve it? Nothing is more central to the question of colonial modernity than the questions of eugenics, evolution, and eroticism. Sexuality, as Foucault suggested, defines modernity as such. But, contra Foucault, this is no less true in Shanghai than in Tokyo, no less in Tokyo than in New York or London.

That said, what I have traced out in this chapter are some of the contexts in which the basic questions of heterosexuality, eugenics, and personality appear. I have begun to suggest that contextually the enormously elaborate discussion about ren'ge and the profusion of theories in which ren'ge appears as a central problematic actually is where predication of the modern woman took place. The question of woman in Chinese feminism is first posed and provisionally answered here. Each, the question and the answers, the subject and the theory, are inextricable from the others. Often, I call the resulting modern subject woman nüxing or "woman, a sexed subject." But it is not necessary that the term nüxing be present in the text to know that you are in the presence of the modern sexed female subject of liberation theory. Any time the theoretical subject is gendered female, appears as a sexual being at the center of human social creativity in evolutionary time, and sets off an explosion of anxiety about her capacities in the future, I can presume safely that the subject is nüxing. And, as I will eventually argue, this nüxing subject constellated around very specific elements of temperament which I have previewed here in my descriptions of theoretical language as female will (yizhi), feelings (ganqing, lian'ai), reason (lizhi), and so on.[136]

Earlier in this chapter, I argued that in the emergent conventions of Chinese feminist theory the subject woman was construed as constitutionally deficient. I cited a number of instances where women (nüxing, nüzi, funü, etc.) signaled a subject defined by its lack of standing in the human community, its absence of human qualities, and its underdeveloped grasp of personality. In many texts, ren'ge compensates for the dreadful incapacity of women, women's inability to establish a perspective peculiar to themselves as a corporate unit in China, except by default as a failed subject. That is how ren'ge stands as a future possibility for the social interest group women. Quite literally, it is the empirical evidence of what women will have been in one particular instance of predication in the apparatus of feminism. Feminist theory and theories of social science representation are probably indivisible in Chinese enlightened thinking. For inasmuch as woman signified deficiency in theory, she also seems quite necessary to Enlightenment generally. Indeed, many theorists tacitly or explicitly would have agreed with Li Renjie that "male and female liberation are the same question, not two questions, and women's liberation is men's liberation."[137] The discussion of ren'ge is very much about women as a category in feminism and women as a social mass, a singular instance of a community of concrete women. This was most easily visible in the range of debates where ren'ge played an important role in establishing the analytic standing of women as a category.

## 4 Woman and Colonial Modernity in the Early Thought of Ding Ling

The behavior of these "perfectly new" women on the historical scene was actually even more resolute and courageous than "her" appearance (even depicted in women's own narratives) in discourse. If as a type of linguistic existence, the "new woman" confronted the culture's and discourse's extreme barrenness, then it may be supposed that this type of lack, due to the temporary absence of . . . oppression, would at the same time create the opportunity for freedom. DAI JINHUA, "Gender and Narration: Women in Contemporary Chinese Film"

What sort of freedom? is the question Dai Jinhua's homage to the 1920s "perfectly new" women immediately provokes.[1] Previous analysis focused on the contingent foundation of progressive Chinese feminism's eugenic subject, nüxing, which I argued was historically heterogeneous in China, as it was elsewhere in the world.[2] Regardless of the theorists' sex or gender, the female subject in Chinese theory projects was sexual and its eugenicist certainties anchored feminist rights claims. The veracity of its subject nüxing was established in the sexual sciences. This chapter refracts Dai Jinhua's concern through the pre-Maoist writing of the canonical, revolutionary, Maoist Party writer Ding Ling (pseudonym of Jiang Bingzhi, 1904–1985). It also sets up the conditions for a later examination of the historical catachresis funü and Ding Ling's effort to recast the terms of the subject of women in Maoism. In the next chapter, I chart Ding Ling's apotheosis into an exemplary subject in a still vital strand of Maoist communist feminism. But here my immediate objective is different.

Yi-Tsi Mei Feuerwerker's pathbreaking *Ding Ling's Fiction: Ideology and Narrative in Modern Chinese Literature* demonstrated how Ding Ling's fiction operated in relation to prevailing norms of fictional narrativity.[3] Considered in relation to the intellectual concerns of the day, Ding Ling's work is also a persistent critique of Chinese feminism's core problematics.[4] With anguish, ambivalence, and cocky gravity, her literary narratives transformed an abstract elite feminist project into an elite, subjective, feminine impasse. Rethought in the world of feminist Enlightenment politics requires taking the writer seriously as an intellectual, for, like Doris Lessing and Tillie Olson, Ding Ling was also a cerebral, ideological, political writer. She brought to creative writing a left-wing intellectual's ethical preoccupations. And her polestar through the decades was always the debate over the tragic freedoms accorded the female subject of Chinese feminism. Ding Ling animated nüxing in a new colonial modernist representational order, she exhausted its capacities, and she raised the problem of feminine ren'ge in the framework of theoretical Marxist feminism. Her preoccupation with women's social standing culminated in the 1941–1942 Maoist crisis over woman policy. But in the late 1920s and 1930s, the period considered in this chapter, she addressed sexual drives and natural selection in relation to feminine character.[5]

Jiang Bingzhi (she adopted the name Ding Ling in the early 1920s, during her anarchist and cultural revolutionary period) is unlike most writers in the Chinese feminist canon because she became a power broker in the Party's cultural regulatory apparatus. Ding Ling joined the Communist Party in the 1930s and served under its governments through the 1940s and 1950s, until she was politically ruined in 1958, deprived of her political citizenship and her rights of representation, and sent into internal exile as a "Big Rightist," or severely blameworthy political criminal. She inherited the political concerns of her mother, a downwardly mobile, provincial gentry widow. Familiar early on with the picket line and the potent social space of the gentry women's school, Ding Ling passed virtually her entire adult life, until sentenced to the state labor farm, moving in the Chinese communist movement's cultural pantheon. She grew up in the remarkable world of educated, cultural, and revolutionary women leaders. This included figures like communist feminist Xiang Jingyu, a friend of her mother's, and Ding Ling's own beloved school companion, Wang Jianhong, whose misalliance with communist politician Qu Qiubai figured heavily in Ding Ling's early fiction. She lived her early maturity self-emancipated, a sexually defined "modern girl," in a common law alliance with the proletarian writer Hu Yepin, later martyred, while striking up strong, possibly romantic attachments to famous writers and critics like Shen Congwen, Feng Xuefeng, and Feng Da (whom she later suspected of betraying her to the Guomindang secret police).

Intellectually, Ding Ling moved from anarchofeminism into the left or Maoist wing of the CCP. In early 1931, after the state executed her first baby's father, Hu Yepin, she sought out political alliances with the most populist, culturalist, voluntarist wing in the Party hierarchy. Released from house arrest after the birth of a second child, conceived with Feng Da (Feng died while the couple was in custody), Ding Ling left for the communist-held northern outposts of the Border Regions Party-state in 1936. There she reached her political maturity, not just taking on increasingly weighty government posts but also consolidating her claims in communist cultural politics. Her activities during the Maoist Party Rectification Campaign of 1941–1942 figure in many attempts to explain her career as a cultural figure. But she was probably more significant to contemporaries in the 1940s and 1950s for her hard left positions on literary agrarian romanticism and her populist innovations among local folk artists than she ever was for leadership struggles over Communist Party affirmative action policies in 1942.[6]

The taut relation of erotic subjectivity and personal social standing—nüxing and ren'ge—is particularly strong in stories that Ding Ling, then in her twenties, wrote in the 1927–1934 era, though elements of the progressive feminist framework persisted well into her Maoist years. Her preoccupations, of course, were transformed during the punishing years she spent as a political prisoner. Yet, in the texts she prepared for republication as cancer brought death closer and in the pieces she published immediately after her release from prison, familiar themes connect the last years to the first ones: How can the citizen woman achieve standing in the community? What can revolution achieve for degraded rural women? Does the family or the state abet women's liberation struggles or do they overlook those struggles' claim to priority? How much must the individual or collective of Women do on their own behalf? How strong is the female subject of political practices? What are the boundaries in theory of socially sanctioned female autonomy? What is the relation of life force, nature, and social action to self-determination? To what degree can gender equity be addressed inside family formations? Where do love and romance belong in the struggle to achieve a good, politically ethical life? What accounts for a stable sense of self in female citizens? and other constant themes of Chinese progressive feminism.

There are several reasons to examine Chinese feminist thought of this era through Ding Ling's work. First, the truths of women sketched out in chapter 3 unfolded in her writing as a wager; disappointment with the female condition in a dark, barbarous society led her to gamble on a revolutionary future for women. Second, Ding Ling took seriously questions posed in feminism over her long life as a writer, calling into question eugenic feminist arguments and elements of Marxian developmental history. There is no question that she drew on the tenets of Chinese progressive feminism and never fully exceeded them. Yet her fiction is persistently compelling because it opens out the crisis points where nüxing (and later funü) did not cohere, despite high expectations to the contrary. Finally, Ding Ling's life of writing illustrates the point I made earlier about historical investiture. The core of progressive Chinese feminism is eugenics, and Ding Ling resolved that a subjectivity rooted in eugenic rights (i.e., the right to choose a sexual partner, a right vested in invisible, natural forces of evolutionary genetic selection) had its shortcomings. She seemed to conclude that the will of women and the reason embedded in evolutionary natural law did not reinforce each other, and that led her to rethink female subjectivity. Even so, she and her cohort largely accepted the catachristic singularity of the universal subject of woman. Perhaps in their era only the sexed subject guaranteed that they could actually "speak as women."

The New Woman

Rethinking the Chinese modernist literary canon to include female writers who wrote about women, Amy Dooling and Kristina Torgeson directly entered the debate over who authored Chinese feminism and its subjects. Was it Chinese male intellectuals and literary figures or Chinese women? I begin considering Ding Ling in the context of this issue because her themes were so central to the intellectual tenor of the era and because her example helps to displace this stark question and to redefine it.[7] The claim that men authored literary femininity was cogently pressed in Ching-kiu Stephen Chan's argument that the definitive event of literary femininity was actually the emergence of modern, anxious, literary masculinity. "The root of *your* suffering is to be found in *my* own inability to right the wrongs that society has done *me*" is how Chan most memorably described this despairing subject of modern Chinese man, who, narcissistically, could not envision a female subject beyond his own requirements.[8] Chan presumed the modernist position that the erotic bond of women and men is the primal creative force in cultural life. Rather than opening up female self-expression, then, Chinese modernism, according to this line of analysis, cut off the tradition of literary and poetic "femininity" that had given gentry writers as late as the nineteenth century a female voice irregardless of the writer's anatomical sex.[9]

I would suggest that this presumption of heterosexuality is both historically insupportable and the framework of Chan's remarks. The literary critic Jing Tsu has recently shifted focus from a presumed heteronormative relation of male and female to a homoerotic problematic. According to Tsu, the central achievement of the modernist new literature was to fuse individual psyche and national character. Ordinary, late Qing literary masculinism, previously an effect of the homosocial Confucian order, cathected into the nation under the stresses of big power imperialism and semicolonial-ism. In this fusion the preferred mode of male expression became masoch-ism. Now, masochism is the consequence of mourning the loss of an adequate national masculinity and a confident homosocial desire. At the center of colonial modernist male self-affirmation, in other words, there surfaced a disavowal and lament for what had disappeared (i.e., homo-erotic desire), a loss that literary modernism did not confront directly. Rather, literary modernism routed natural homoeroticism through the per-sistent trope of inadequate masculinity. The decisive factor in (male) iden-tity thus had little to do with women or the feminine Other. Indeed, the modernist, masochistic, masculine Chinese subject admitted into itself very little consideration of women at all in its historical process of male self-definition.[10]

Both of these arguments consider the historical event of Chinese colo-nial modernity as mediated through modernist literature. Both Jing Tsu and Chan suggest that a reordering of life processes, which I tracked in the previous chapter using eugenics, was also at work in the domain of mod-ern Chinese literature.[11] Social theories of eugenic heterosexuality sought to reorder organic life around the procreative couple at the expense of the bond of filial father and son and brothers, a point that Tsu's critical points echo. Procreative sexuality, as we have seen, was enshrined analytically as more "natural," to use Gao Xian's term, than fraternal love or the father-son bond. This much has been established and it suggests two further points. First, as Foucault and others have argued, the discourse of (hetero)-sexuality rests on a science of sexuality that includes what Foucault calls the "manifold sexualities," including various homoeroticisms.[12] Second, what other historians of colonial modernity in other places have noticed holds true in China: that the emergence of new women into "modern" sectors of social life is the hallmark of claims to modernity per se. For an elite that previously strictly segregated male and female space, the comingling in space of men and women in heterosexual relations was a social as much as a theoretical event. The loss of homoerotic desire and homosociality, that loss itself, participated in the modernist claims of heteronormativity. Tsu's insight into what we might call a mournful heterosexuality suggests a reason why the Chinese modern feminine literary subject was always off-balance, its coherence foundationally threatened and its representation fraught in both male- and female-authored fiction.[13]

I am not offering these arguments as causes. Literature and literary criticism did not cause colonial modernity. Rather, they opened ways of defining and understanding it. Tsu's shift of emphasis from the presump-tion of heterosexuality to the likelihood that heterosexuality was a histor-ical achievement in cultures of modernism is valuable because it opens the possibility of asking more questions about the gender of literature and gendered literary representations. For instance, if early Republican literary masculinity is at bottom masochistic (not heterosexist and despairing, as per Chan's view), the impasses in Ding Ling's fiction probably also speak to the institutionalization of a modern heterosexuality. The fact that feminism presupposes heterosexual interest groups, a theme in chapter 3, throws more light on Chinese progressive feminism's historical centrality. Perhaps the issue is not so much Who invented Chinese literary feminism? as How do feminist arguments invest women and men in the cultural politics of heterosexuality?

For instance, Ding Ling's first short stories were preoccupied with a nüxing that could neither speak for herself nor cohere in a meaningful fashion, not because female literary self-expression was unavailable to her, but because the incompatible elements of her own personality undid her. Nüxing has a difficult time stabilizing its erotic relations, not only because male partners are ultimately disappointing but also because one's own female self is so difficult to organize in the first instance. Particularly the "Sophia" figure suggests heterosexual dynamics' tentativeness and the instable ethics of heterosexual sociality. Recall that in progressive feminism, the problem of female ren'ge (social standing) returned analysts time and again to the position that women allegedly lack autonomy and humanity, and were consequently slavish and parasitic and the subordinate "playthings of men." Fixated on what she perceived were the failures of women to organize themselves adequately in the face of a hostile society, Ding Ling still placed at the center of every story a debilitated female self (ziwo) charged with telling its own tale. Not surprisingly, this was often the story of women's failures and deficiency—but it was a self-disclosure. The relation of female narrator to this nüxing subject, or bildung, finds the narrator determined to fully disclose the erotic needs of the desiring woman agent, but equally set on measuring her instability as a social subject. This, then, is what I call Ding Ling's hopeful wager. In conditions that, echoing social theorists and social scientists, she simply called social "darkness," Ding Ling's earliest fiction repetitively gambled on a possible future where, live or die, women do achieve self-determination, with men and without them, even when sympathetically cast protagonists compulsively fail to live up to authorial expectation.

This feminine willed existence as an autonomous subject, the goal of enlightened Chinese feminism, rested on the presumption that society was formed of libidinous, self-interested, juridical individuals who stood equally before the law.[14] The terms or qualities of personhood stipulated in progressive feminism are, to put it bluntly, the same elements of subjectivity that appear in the characters populating the early Ding Ling story collections. They were feminine in an acceptably recognizable form while at the same time self-directing their own procreative, sexual choices and exercising their own will. It was not that, with a little effort or good luck, a Ding Ling new woman could "pull herself together"; stability and an accurate sense of self seemed to be constitutionally or foundationally impossible to achieve. Although the eroticism that her stories so famously express is often the desire of a female subject for a male object, the consolidation of that desiring subject is tentative. Her defining eroticism remains a chronically incomplete project. This may account for the fatalism that comes over the female figures in many stories where the goal is self-narration inside a strict heterosexual binary of desiring male and desired female. But this sinking feeling also afflicts women protagonists who take men as their desired object and women who take other women for their erotic ideal. Consequently, these figures cannot become women of ren'ge because as new women, no matter how hard they strain they never strike an adequate emotional balance. This does not exculpate the social oppression that predatory, sadistic males inflict on females. But it does extend the analysis of why, despite good intentions, new Chinese women could have foundered so badly. In Ding Ling's fiction, emotion and will, progressive feminist nüxing's defining characteristics, fail to cohere in a stable, workable, active female agent.

Virtually all of Ding Ling's stories in the late 1920s can be considered feminist in the sense that they showcased "the woman question" as a social problem. "Xiao huolun shang" (On a small steamer) traced the internal monologue of a woman who has sex with a colleague and, under the iron law of the double standard, has just been fired from her job.[15] In "Yi ge nüren heyi ge nanren" (A woman and a man), a man has to rape his wife to clarify his exclusive sexual rights to her.[16] A lot of these stories were harshly critical of men. To some degree, they all reduced masculinity to a matter of incomprehensible male sadism in which an abusive man seduces and betrays a "new woman" who has dared to choose him for her sexual partner. Quite a number of these new woman characters reflect on the question of whether they have actually prostituted themselves when they have sexual affairs without marrying. In one story, Ding Ling romanticized a whore because of her frank appreciation that at rock bottom all women prostitute themselves to men, whether they marry them or not. In "Qingyunli zhong de yijian xiaofangli" (In a small room on Qingyun Alley), a cheerful young prostitute decides between her career as a sex worker and a recent marriage offer. She chooses the lesser of the two evils, reasoning that in the sex industry she at least has individual freedom and sexual variety.[17] In "Mengke," a character denounced free-choice marriage, arguing that it is essentially no different from arranged marriages because it sanctions yet another form of female prostitution.[18] Echoing the popular eugenic theorist Gao Xian (see chapter 3), Ding Ling's romantic story about a prostitute may even raise the mocking suggestion that the regret of new women who repent their erotic choices puts them ethically beneath the realism of the prostitute. Still, the position had a double edge. Natural reason holds that erotic choice ought to be the prerogative of the self-willed new woman. That truth should hold no matter how perversely the male-of-the-species behaves or how pathetically incompetent the female-of-the-species proves to be.

The nüxing in Ding Ling's earliest, founding progressive feminist fiction suffered a lot from male sadism, the unfathomable meanness of male lovers, and the male-dominated society at large. But they were perennially torn between the competing drives of feminine will (yizhi) and female emotions (qinggan). Internal irresolution and passivity made unlikely the female claims to ren'ge. Stories and story fragments raise for compassionate comment symptoms of female depletion and inertia. Holding out the candle of Enlightenment against the overwhelming darkness, Ding Ling was asking an immediate post–May Fourth question: Why has nüxing still not achieved social and emotional standing?

In passionate and affecting fiction Ding Ling showed the new subject inflating herself with emotion only to discover that excessive emotion atrophied her will. At other times, she developed a strongly willed sense of self, but, inexplicably, found that action contaminated or corrupted most genuine expressions of feeling. This made women self-conscious, stagy, and manipulative. Individual nüxing subjects, who begin a narrative listing strongly toward one pole, the willed, for instance, might end up mired in the other extreme, in passive self-destructive emotion. Mengke initially appeared as a dramatic, highly willed character, but the terrible dénouement of her story belied the initial construction. This shifting, unbalanced, quicksilver vacillation reinforced the sense Ding Ling's early texts convey: nüxing can never escape the constraints of sexed subjectivity because the core of "female" personality is wuren'ge, or lack of what it takes to establish a personal standing in the society.

Most of her first stories were character portraits of women whose strong emotions frustrated or undercut their will. "Zisha riji" (Suicide diary), a deeply affecting, short fragment, traced the internal monologue and diary entries of an exasperatingly self-critical writer, Elsa.[19] Because she cannot overcome the dark social stagnation around her and cannot claim to be better than the normative women around her, Elsa feebly plots suicide. It is not that she is lonely or lacks friends or potential lovers or a loving parent. She cannot find a reason to stay alive, except that she is afraid of dying. In the end, she even barters away the very manuscript that records her decline. Also cast in the widely used feminine literary form of the diary, "Shafei nüshi riji" (Sophia's diary) charts the mania of a fervid new woman whose expectations of erotic love and life are too extreme for her circumstances.[20] Like Elsa, Sophia is surrounded by loving friends and models of equanimity, whose more modest life expectations make it possible for them to accept the darkness surrounding them all. Calmly loving heterosexual couples and the passionate love of her girlfriends, even two persistent male lovers, one she disdains and the other she eroticizes, make sure that Sophia is rarely alone. Yet despite the love of friends, Sophia allows her erotic fantasy about Ling Jishi to transport her; she chooses him for her lover and when she sees more clearly that he is a pompous fool, condemns herself to death. Mengke, in the famous story by the same name, the innocent art student who seeks a pathway for herself in the new society and is thwarted at every turn, is perhaps the most hapless and isolated of all Ding Ling's early heroines. The central figure, whose name means "dreamer," refused to accept the real world and willed herself to ignore it. More than Ah Mao in "Ah Mao guniang" (The girl Ah Mao), the lower-class version of a girl whose erotic fantasies outweigh her will and rationality, Mengke is forced by increasingly harsh events into a corner where self-prostitution as a common cinema actress is her only choice, excepting suicide. In "Ah Mao guniang," wherein the title character falls in love with a bourgeois neighbor and whose fantasy of romance overwhelms her small, insignificant but potentially happy life as a wife and daughter-in-law, the flaw or weakness of character drives the plot forward. But in all of these cases, the central figure in the narrative faces the collapse of a great dream of overtaking mundane life, the female lot, and in despair seeks death.

For the most part, these heroic and ludicrous characters paint portraits of what occurs when new women allow their passions to frustrate or undercut their capacity to will themselves or to will change in the world, or even to live in a world where change is inimical to will. Many things flash through the mind of a female character momentarily paralyzed in this situation. For instance, a character might be suddenly overwhelmed with a feeling that interrupts action, preventing her from doing something else. She might recall that at one time she could move on her own command, or, lapsing into a reverie, in the thrall of some false, hypercritical hindsight, she might imagine herself to have been more powerfully self-willed in the past than she ever really was. The protagonist Elsa in "Suicide Diary" realizes she needs her will at exactly the moment it appears to have vanished. She meditates at length on the horrible lethargy and ennui that prevents her even from deciding if life is fundamentally good or bad. This forces her to reflect on why she seems to have paralyzed herself. "Since I am not a whore," she reasons, "why do I need to cater to so many people? I ought to have a will of my own. I am well within my rights to simply eject people I don't like from my presence" (21).[21] Something inexplicable prevents her from doing it. This paralysis precludes even the simplest acts, like leaving the room, cleaning up the garbage, truly loving, changing the subject, ending a fixed smile, showing her true feelings, and killing herself.

At times, the text's narrator allows a female character enough insight to recognize that in part, her problem involves the failure of will. At other times, the narrative merely describes in detail a character's experience, dwelling on the horrible languor associated with a sickened will and allowing the entire experience to remain extremely vague and unfocused for both reader and character. Ding Ling used this second technique extensively in "Mengke." At first, Mengke appears to be a daring, sentimental new woman (xin nüxing) figure who seeks her fortune and a chance to realize her talents in the big city. Frustrated by scheming colleagues and her own tendency to dream away her time, she dissolves into passive frustration. She is unaware of the judgments the narrator is leveling against her, and knows only that something is connecting her powerful feelings and lack of will to the awful sense that immobility is making her sexually dirty. "I'm leaving, I'm leaving," she thinks to herself, feeling trapped and helpless. "And she was indeed thinking such things to herself, but there she remained." She feels the vulgarity of the actresses and blushes when the movie crew exchange knowing looks and eye her body. "She alone was astonished . . . as if . . . she had become a prostitute and was there letting those utterly disrespectful eyes roam over her" (68). Mengke knows that under such circumstances she should act; she knows she has acted in similar situations in the past to avoid being used by other people. But in this circumstance she cannot even get out of her seat until someone prompts her. "The injury to her feelings was really enough for her to have refused this importunate request," the narrator remarks at one point, "but now she consented. It was not clear even to her why, to her surprise, she was demeaning herself" (70).[22] Somehow, feelings choke and paralyze Mengke's will.

A similar pollution of the feminine will unfolds in "Sophia's Diary." Sophia confesses to the diary after an encounter with her beloved, Ling Jishi: "Why is he able to respond only to my helplessness, my vulnerabilities? . . . I wished I could kick him out, but a different kind of feeling dominated me. . . . [and] once again I yielded to his shallow affection and listened while he talked animatedly about the stupid pleasures he enjoys so much. . . . I even acceded to his insinuation that I try acting more feminine. That made me despise him even more than before, and I cursed him and ridiculed him secretly, even as inwardly my fists struck painfully at my heart" (58). The remarkable thing about this story is the clear message it conveys: Sophia's will is twisted because her lust is frustrated. Intuiting that her obsession is at bottom sexual has made her a more self-aware and self-directed figure than the relatively passive nüxing character Mengke or the outrightly improvident Ah Mao. Each is periodically trapped in miasmic eroticism, and all Ding Ling's nüxing characters at some point report the sensation Sophia voices directly in the diary: "I want something, but I'm not willing to go and take it. I must find a tactic that gets it offered to me voluntarily" (58).

Nüxing characters often find it difficult to take things directly, even at those rare moments when they know what it is they really want. Ding Ling rarely used parable in her early texts; the story of "Wait Patiently," in "Shujia Zhong" (Summer break), is an important exception. The tale illustrates the xin nüxing's ability to feel things strongly at precisely the moment she loses control of her will and so prevents herself from acting on those emotions:

> In a great swamp where reeds, beautiful grasses, and duckweed abounded, swallows and small birds often liked to fly about and sing. There were also many beautiful fish there and so the birds that like the taste of fish also gathered. Among them was a type of bird called "Wait Patiently." Because she looked very much like a gray cane, she often assumed a haughty attitude of disdain while she waited and watched. Perhaps because of this attitude or perhaps because she hadn't the courage to make an attempt at finding the fish she really liked, she spent all her time standing immobile in the middle of the pond. As she stood watching other birds snap up the fish one by one, she was consumed by envy. All she did was dream that the fish themselves would offer themselves up into her mouth. But the result was, after standing for who knows how long, that "Wait Patiently" moved from feeling exhaustion to feeling despondent, and from despondency she came to realize that she would have to search the fish out for herself. Therefore, stifling her rage, she bent her long neck down; but the fish had all been snatched away by the braver birds. Now she realized that it was too late to do anything about it.[23]

The nüxing "bird" appears in the terrain under false presence and floods herself (the text explicitly genders the bird as female) with feelings of envy, disdain, haughtiness, despondency, and rage. She somehow convinces herself that she can have what she wants, accomplish her desire, without ever willing anything or lifting a finger for herself. Desire notwithstanding, she discovers too late that without a will she becomes immobile, has immobilized herself, and that the passive person loses everything in a bourgeois world of competition. All Ding Ling's nüxing subjects trace themselves back to this parable. They all want something: true love, sexual ecstasy, affection, a mother's love, fame, or just secure happiness. But for so many reasons, with the social chaos outside them in the world at large and the stubborn incoherence of their own personalities, they simply cannot take what they want even under the very best circumstances.

In Ding Ling's earliest creative fiction the same character that at one moment expresses passive frustration often moves fluidly into an exaggeratedly willed mood the very next. Such a character contaminates her own capacity for genuine emotion. This becomes a problem because the hypercritical nüxing places enormous value on having unsullied or pure emotions. Consequently, in a feelingful mode, she tends to act out what turn rapidly into very ugly needs. Instigated to frantic action by the undisciplined capriciousness of her own will, such a woman might try to use her sexual self, to turn herself into a femme fatale and forcefully manipulate everyone: husbands, lovers, friends, enemies, and, most deadly of all, her own emotional self. Women who feel the internal need to manipulate others end up making themselves false, self-conscious, and hollow. Femme fatale characters appear happiest when they are pretending to be someone else: a movie star, their own best friend or sister, or the heroine of a French romance novel. Ding Ling gave many of these nüxing characters Western names, such as Nina, Marian, Mary, Elsa, Sophia. A foreign name does not signify bad faith in itself, but it does seem to indicate a character's commitment to febrile, sexually expressive femininity.

In one story, the protagonist Wendy, the governing presence in "A Woman and a Man," actually has a whole range of phony names she employs to promote a vision of herself as a charismatic, sensuous, commanding, irresistible, and devilish lover. This Wendy, if that is indeed her real name, "was a woman of excessive passion, yet one who should never be able to experience real love. She lived in a constant state of perverse deviancy" because, while she loathed sentiment for its erotic charge and thought that "the desires of the flesh" corrupted innocent sincerity, "she would risk everything to pursue a conversation about such exciting topics. [Talking about sex] seemed to have become an addiction" (12).[24] Wendy chose her conquests carefully. When the story opens, she has just singled out a wonderfully phony poet, with the mock Japonesque nom de plume "Ouwai Ou." She concocts a lie and leaves her husband at home so she can go to the park to meet, and possibly seduce, the fake poet. The story delineates all the strategies Wendy develops to mentally possess and dominate Ouwai. Why? Because, the narrator explains, Wendy needed to "have other people love her," and so "the more casually you treated her, the more insistent she became" (17). The problem is that Wendy had long ago lost the capacity for warm, sensuous feeling. She had actually chosen to have an affair of the heart with Ouwai because experience and expedient calculation assured her another in a host of thrilling, secret conquests. "It was as though," the narrator sneers, "she was acting in a play—something which Wendy understood very, very well." Only theatrical staginess and love of risk remained genuine emotions to Wendy; the only thing she had genuinely felt in a long time was the predatory movement of her own perverse will.

Other early Ding Ling texts show female characters that actually slip back and forth, from the solipsism of "Wait Patiently" to the sexual aggression of Wendy. Sophia best exemplifies the experience of entrapment these fluctuations impose on protagonists, forcing them into obsessive, repetitive, deadly cycles. For instance, on the one hand, Sophia feels an awkward, unaccustomed, passive need to wait for the objectified other to make his first move. At other times, she struggles not just to anticipate but to master Ling Jishi, to "teach him a lesson in love." When she acts under the influence of her misdirected will, she struggles to command Ling and best him with her daring lies, her skilled acting, her calculated sexuality. She knows that when she acts the femme fatale she corrupts the experience of love, but though she calls this trap "artificiality in love," she is unable to prevent herself from doing it. Sophia's ambivalence is particularly acute because of her mortal illness.

The protagonist of "Ta zou hou" (After he left) confronts the same problem. Nina feels that she should force her lover to leave after they make love because she fears that if he stays, her love for him will weaken her. After he leaves, she realizes that she polluted pure love because she allowed herself to be swept up in obsessive recalculation. She is ruining the spontaneity of erotic play because she is so thrilled that she possesses the power to command him to leave her once they finish the sexual act. The further she obsesses over her compromised love, the more self-conscious Nina becomes, until finally she despairs. "Why, since she didn't love him, had she gotten so close to him, disregarding all the rules of propriety. . . . she'd done it, she'd done it all and couldn't blame anyone else."[25] Importantly, the narrator sustains a vision of the affair separate from Nina's and reassures the reader that Nina does in fact love him. But even the narrator grasps Nina's contradictory formulation: when she acts on her will, she pollutes her feelings, so if she wills sexual pleasure, then the more she loves, the greater her bad faith and the more she compromises herself.

Illuminating in fiction a terrible dilemma, previously only theorized in the searching heterosexual poetics of progressive social theory, is one of the remarkable achievements of Ding Ling's feminist literature. This is the ultimate double bind that her version of the new woman confronts. It is a double bind because no matter which direction ego turns, the results will be the same. On one scale lie corrupt sentiment and an impulse to painful self-consciousness, immobility, lethargy; on the other is the contaminated, overly febrile will that turns relations with other people into cold and manipulative exercises in self-aggrandizement. The upshot, and this is why it seems to me that beneath these dramatically unrestrained texts beats a moralist's conscience, is that terrible consequences are visited on women caught in the cyclical, instable flux of sentiment and will. The poisoning process of will to sentiment, sentiment to will, means that no female character can distinguish between dreams and real life. They all either delude themselves in a theatrical fantasy of omnipotence or dissolve in passive, sexual dreamworlds. Lost in the fantasy such confusion breeds, nüxing characters sometimes will decisions, though they never establish emotional calm outside the realm of their own turbulent feelings. Decisive action only leads to regret over what they think they have done in the past. But by the time a nüxing understands enough about her situation to have regret, she is close to self-destruction.

This fundamental temporality is most acutely drawn in four stories that made Ding Ling famous and were collected in a volume titled *Zai heian zhong* (In darkness). At one level, "The Girl Ah Mao," the story of the peasant girl who desired more than fate had assigned her, was a simple political allegory. Ah Mao left her father's rustic cottage for her new husband's urban family. There she discovers that she possesses a feminine core within. Her burgeoning sense of individual selfhood makes her a "class heroine" to the story's narrator because Ah Mao's new sentimentality brings her to the eventual realization of her own oppression by the patriarchy. Self-consciousness does not immunize her against pressure from society, the city, or family, and when she understands she will not be able to escape her in-laws, Ah Mao kills herself.[26] But remarkably, the narrator upsets this simple-minded morality tale with a bitter judgment against the protagonist. Ah Mao has a toughness that makes her able to endure beating for her new convictions; she possesses an organic will. Her strong desires mark her as a nüxing character. But she fails to invent some way to connect the two qualities in her personality, and so the targets or objects of her desire are not awe-inspiring, but simply tawdry. She wants pretty clothes, money, the admiration of male strangers. When she realizes these objects are outside her reach, she retreats into a universe of dreams inside her own mind: "All right, she thought, I'll just live this way all my life. . . . Still, she does not stop her fantasies. Previously, a living, beating heart had persisted at the center of the fantasy. But now, now she simply schemed to be able to taste the sweetness of a little joy within the fantasy, to use the fantasy as consolation against the dismal feelings she had when sober. But when night fell, could that little pleasure offset the signs that followed after she awoke from fantasy?"(254).

Something in Ah Mao prevented her from seeing the world outside as it really was. Narration drew a hard line between her displaced dreams of fantasy and the reality the text established and all other characters confirmed. Despite poverty, lowly position, and ignorance, all of Ah Mao's in-laws clearly saw reality. Only Ah Mao mistook the dying woman next door for a contented, pampered bourgeois wife and the desperate young concubine for a cheerful bourgeois "lover." Worse yet, Ah Mao expected a phantom lover to rescue her; she poisons herself when she realizes the folly of her dream. Ah Mao, seemingly the most degraded of Ding Ling's early heroines, is many things, including a parody of the ideology of free love and sexual selection. There is no way to ignore her courageous leap into self-determination; at the same time, her dreams and their social impossibility make her a fool.

Ding Ling employed the same plot structure in "Mengke." Mengke lives for a while in the home of a wealthy relative. Her talent for fantasy leads her to transform her cousin into a romantic figure; she ignores the fact that he befriends her for instrumental sexual ends. Narrative again proposes two perspectives: the knowers (all characters plus the narrator) and a central figure, blinded to reality. The narrator enlists the reader's sympathy for Mengke but is not willing to overlook Mengke's complicity. Something in this character encourages her to spend her time "lying in bed . . . thinking of her future life" and "fantasizing herself as a hero, a great woman, a revolutionary" in lurid detail. Inattention and predilection to fantasy cause her to idle away months doing nothing but socializing, flirting, dreaming. When the moment of truth arrives and the sexual threat materializes, she turns to movie acting, becoming a figure of fantasy for others: "And so her decision was made, for after all [she was a creature of] illusory dreams" (58–59).

Mengke had the capacity to act on her own will; perhaps, once upon a time, she might have (the narrator insists in a flurry of her own self-delusion) made herself over into a brave, heroic woman. But Mengke paralyzes herself. When romantic feelings cripple her daring will, her character becomes so muddied and impure that she simply fails to distinguish between the light and the darkness. She seeks relief from passive dreams, not in purposeful acts, but in waking dreams, which take the form of play acting: "Night fell. Mengke got up from the cot, and with a light bound, she stood by the table, and warmly and tenderly combed her short hair. Gazing into the mirror she saw her own soft fingertips as they stroked each other in front of her bosom. By this time her own longing had captured her. She forgot the unhappiness of the day. She made a seductive face into the mirror, then an indolent smile, then she began to playact for herself. Her acting did not follow a plot line, nor had it any background. It was simply Mengke sitting by herself in front of an eight-inch mirror, in front of a table, making a series of different facial expressions" (65).

The kind of sexual expression that consolidates subjectivity and supports will is different from the life that Mengke settles for. Sexual self-determination as such is not at stake, for Ding Ling did not give up on the progressive, modernist, biogenic faith that sexual desire is the motor of human social existence. The question at stake remains the issue central to progressive feminism in the 1920s: How should women themselves conduct their erotic lives? If, as the narrative voice seems to think, the modern women are handling their own eroticism badly, how should this problem be remedied?

"Summer Break" shifts emphasis slightly from how women make wrong choices to how women fail to reverse wrong choices even when they have regretfully understood their own accountability. During the summer vacation, the teachers of Independent Girls' School have each concluded that they erred when they chose to live as a free, new woman (xin nüxing). The three major figures, Zhiqing, Jiaying, and Chengshu, succumb to what Ding Ling later identified as neurasthenia (shengjing shuairuo), a nervous disorder presented here as the outcome of sexual repression and regret. Each woman senses her own personal failure and, following a spate of bitter quarreling, each retreats into individual lonely fantasy. In her regretful reverie, Chengshu considers why she insisted on getting an education (against her mother's advice), why she refused marriage, and, a source of particular regret, why she has to work for a living. In this vein, she begins to fantasize about an awkward sexual encounter years in the past. With the magic of romantic hindsight, Chengshu transforms the experience from a near rape into a romance. Gradually, the narrative problematizes her understanding of her own past experience.

This technique of narrative sabotage operates more obviously in the case of Zhiqing. This character's mind disintegrates completely and she condemns herself to emotional darkness. Because the portrait links sexual repression to the nüxing's decomposing sense of self and presents this as the cause of her vitiated ren'ge, it is helpful to quote the relevant passage at some length:

> Zhiqing simply developed a sense of intense self-hatred, particularly when she looked at that stack of account books; what was money worth! . . . She didn't lack money, what she lacked was greater power, which would allow her to feel life itself. She thought of everything, but

she couldn't think of a way to save herself. Permeated with regret she became absorbed with her already departed, lovely youth . . . But time was something that could never be retrieved, and so she was even more disheartened. She . . . locked herself in her little room, where she lay with disheveled hair, wrapped in an old, wrinkled garment, staring out of a pair of eyes that sank further and further into her face every day, thinking as though in a dream, of things only possible in daydreams. Thus, the realm of glory and the realm of sexual love in many ways eased that uneasy realm of her heart for a short time, and shone radiantly without surcease from the top of her bed canopy. And at the center, on the throne of that glory and love, sat Zhiqing. She gave a little smile and then at times laughed out loud; the laugh startled her back to consciousness. In an instant those things seen in the dream receded far, far away. . . . For this reason she realized more clearly what it was that had her so tightly in its grip. At times she would even say to herself, "If only I could prolong my dreams longer."[27]

This character knows a great deal about herself. She "knows" that in the past she had a will, that it eroded, that her hoarding and vaunted economic independence are a result of her capacity for sexual repression. Most horribly, she realizes that she is to blame for her addiction to the twilight world of dreams. Self-knowledge heightens her pathetic sense of regret. Zhiqing finally has enough sense to fall in love with Chengshu and sleep with her, which apparently redeems her somewhat in the narrator's view. Homoeroticism might not have been Ding Ling's first choice, but she dignified it as a real expression of sexual love. Ten years into the debate over the woman question, Zhiqing still struggles with sexual shame and, perhaps more gravely, does not possess "greater power which could make her feel life itself." Love momentarily secures her emotions, but her will is not strong enough to save her from a self-defeating, dead-ended, solitary life.

"Summer Break" illustrates the severe penalties Ding Ling's stories imposed on nüxing. Zhiqing and the rest, the blind and the sighted, those in darkness and those who saw the light, exist inside a repetitious cycle that they compulsively initiate: neurasthenic collapse, rally, fantastic erotic pleasure, dreams of self-directed change, disappointment, self-loathing, relapse. Although the stories do not explicitly address what is fueling the repetitive cycle, Ding Ling and her circle were aware of Freudian-style arguments about the dangers of erotic repression. So while social repression forms the backdrop, in the late 1920s Ding Ling's stories hinted that individual sexuality is at issue in many ugly behaviors, ranging from female Don Juanism, to homoeroticism, to masturbatory sexual phantasmagoria.

I dwell on these extraordinary stories because they illustrate the analytic difficulty confronting the writer. Ding Ling was also a new woman. Her sense of self came in part from occupying to the maximum limit all the theoretical preoccupations of progressive Chinese feminism familiar from her politicized teen years and early adulthood. The stories take the position that the Chinese new woman cannot be stabilized or centered. There are several reasons offered to explain why. The society truly is in darkness, and consequently no amount of will, feminine or masculine, can ever overcome the surrounding filth and degradation. But the political possibilities initially held out in theories about the proper subject of the new woman turned out to be too weak to support the realities that these modern women faced. Here the undertow of despair is most pronounced, I think. The writer Ding Ling herself is a doubled version of the characters she painfully sketches. She is consequently not the autobiographic subject at stake. But certainly she is akin to these characters, is predicated as a social being in the same theoretical style as Ah Mao, Sophia, and the rest, for Ding Ling, like them, also identified herself as a woman.

The biggest obstacle for women in the In Darkness stories is that woman is the equivalent of sexuality as such. The sexed body is what makes women what they are. Its eugenic claims are the royal road to modern personhood. These sexed subjects of feminism have adopted the critique of male domination and write their difference from men as incommensurate sexual difference. Yet many women (and men) found it difficult to tolerate sexual expression in good women, just as Ding Ling's early heroines cannot accept either their own power to signify sexuality or society's efforts to deny their eroticism. That basic contradiction accounts, in my view, for the tension inherent in Ding Ling's most compelling story of the period, "Sophia's Diary." This is the account of a nüxing character who realizes, yet refuses to embrace, a reality the narrator eventually imposes on her. Sophia understands her obsession: she offers her diary because it analyzes "the psychology of a woman driven insane by the way a man looked."[28] So, though she courts the dark consequences of love and calls on love to make her too passive, too aggressive, too lustful, humiliated, false, and confused, Sophia always knows that her feelings for Ling Jishi are not real because they conjure up a fantasy man. Sophia becomes a woman only when she chooses the phantom reality of erotic love. She calls up a polluted will, flooding herself with self-contempt and self-hatred, and finally indulges in the familiar delusions of the stalemated woman. She relies on her delusory self-image to attract the object of her desire. Yet even in such extremity she retains her grasp of the reality principle: "I've been living an illusion, an illusion which Ling Jishi created for me. . . . Because of him, I can drink the sweet wine of youthful love to my heart's content and spend the morning basking in the smile of love. Yet also because of him, I now appreciate this plaything "life." I've been disenchanted, think again of death; the self-loathing I feel at my own willingness to fall is the lightest punishment. Really, there are times when I wonder whether I have the strength to kill him in order to protect my romantic illusion" (69).

Let me restate the conflict Sophia embodies: to love requires me both to enchant myself and to kill my beloved. The new woman of sentiment embodied "the sex," the male subject's desired object, his Other, within the erotic gaze. Nüxing can become an eroticized woman subject only when she becomes an object; to be the chosen requires her to present herself as her sex, or at least an emotional facsimile of appropriate emotions. This desiring object (surely the fantasy of Ling Jishi's pure erotic love for her is as much an illusion as her eroticization of herself as his object of desire) imagines herself into the heterosexual delirium Ellen Key and Shimamura Tamizo had proposed in theory. Yet, the willful nüxing predicated in progressive Chinese feminism has at the same time to make choices, because her "individualism" requires her to extend her modern will. Sophia therefore feels impelled both to attract Ling Jishi's attention, making herself a sexual object, and, to retain her willed sense of self as an active subject, to act purposefully as a normative agent. She cannnot do either one thing or the other, or both at once, so she does each in turn. That act cancels her claims to be a person of standing (ren'ge) for several reasons. Obviously, she is constantly changing her mind about who she is. Also, when she compromises herself in ways that she deeply regrets or allows herself to be indecisive, she trifles with the feelings of other people. Unable to see what ethical stakes drive the vicious cycle of her life, outsiders accuse her, perhaps unfairly, of being insincere and untrustworthy. Nothing Sophia does is in good faith except the task she sets in her diary of total self-disclosure.

"Sophia's Diary" is an example of Ding Ling's characteristic bad faith new women. As Sophia successively ignores her health, deceives her friends, embarrasses herself in front of strangers, she never doubts the truth that Ling is her own desire's creation. She knows she has made him up. As the affair grows in intensity, Sophia has more and more trouble living out the fantasy that love justifies her eroticization of Ling because at some level she knows her desire is illusory and requires her to constantly redefine her will in sentimental terms. When she strategizes to capture Ling, however, she feels so self-conscious and false that she makes herself uncomfortable. The harder she tries to make Ling love her, the more insincere love becomes, until she cannot hide from her own insight: love is only a strategy for dominating the beloved. When she finally subdues Ling she hates herself. "What did my heart feel when lips so warm and tender brushed my face? . . . 'I've won!' I thought 'I've won!' Because when he kissed me, I finally knew the taste of the thing that had so bewitched me. At the same moment I despised myself" (80).

These stories are structured to increase the narrative distance of author from protagonists, in part, perhaps, to delimit the new woman's subjectivity. For instance, each diary entry represents a moment when Sophia sits down alone, stops the delirium, and reports directly what she knows about the truth of her condition. She writes to monitor her own feelings, to inscribe her own history, to renew her own regret, to speak her own truth. "Sophia's Diary" is Ding Ling's premier nüxing portrait and the most accessible, sympathetic sketch of the conflicted female experience. But in fact, all the early texts share the same logic and narrator. The narrator relates action sequences or directly criticizes things the protagonist thinks or feels. Characters allied with the narrator represent the "reality," which the storyteller affirms as the true reality, but with which protagonists either cannot, as in Ah Mao's case, or will not, in the cases of Zhiqing and Sophia, align themselves. So, for instance, Ah Mao's in-laws and the storyteller know what concubinage is, but Ah Mao does not. The narrator and Mengke's cousins all know Mengke's virginity is in peril, but the character does not. Sophia's friends and the narrator know how corrupt Ling really is, but Sophia allows herself only a partial knowledge. It is the narrator who can claim to balance subjectivity and personal standing, for it is she who possesses both the ability to see clearly the reality of social life and the stability required of an ethical agent to judge social morality.

Although she acknowledged using personal experiences, Ding Ling always claimed that her writing was not autobiographical.[29] These stories back up her claim. As narrator, she repeatedly clarified the distance separating the storyteller and the nüxing in the fictions. For instance, she relied heavily on third-person narrative, while at the same time including narrative introjections at key plot points. She restricted the amount of dialogue allotted characters. She disciplined the text narrator and forced it to adopt the most critical stance possible against its own characters. All of this increases the regretful temporality of the text and intensifies the regretfulness of the protagonist; it also means that the narrative and the narrator withhold information from the protagonist until the last possible moment. This is an issue because of the narrative strategies that frame the question of the nüxing psychology. When a female narrator reprimands or criticizes female characters, there are not one but two "feminine" subjects in the text. One of them, as I have shown using the example of Sophia, can create only fantasies and regret. The other is most evident at moments when it directly voices disapproval about the more eroticized, "feminine," aroused female subject, but its presence shapes the narrative as a whole. Ding

Ling's earliest stories negotiate this split. Technically, the device generates an extrasubjective position and pushes the problem of the nüxing's internal contradiction into explicit crisis.

In Darkness may be a sophisticated rereading of Flaubert's Madame Bovary.[30] If so, Ding Ling apparently used the story to forge a way of writing the truth about nüxing that would not implicate or paralyze herself. As the female author of a story about nüxing, anything she might say about female character flaws would, if she were not very careful, redound to the narrator's own "self" and obliterate the claims on reality she herself was making. Several intertextual parallels link the two texts. Like Emma, Ah Mao is married to a man she likes well enough until she glimpses city life. The bourgeois family living next door kindle in Ah Mao dreams she can never realize, partly because she is low class and also, linked to her class standing, because her appreciation of bourgeois life is implausibly far-fetched. Recognizing finally the hopelessness of her vapid desire, Ah Mao takes poison and dies in agony. Some parallels are exact: Ah Mao's father and the farmer Roualt, the d'Andervilliers' ball and the glittering vision of the city, Ah Mao's fantasy lovers and Emma's Leon/Rudolph. Some are more like gestures. As Flaubert had, for instance, Ding Ling infused her story with dispassionate insight and critical disapproval. She sealed off the character's inner thoughts, provided the implied narrator with allies who defined the communal solidarity of the protagonists world, and so on. Distinguishing the narrator's trustworthiness increased her claim to ren'ge.[31] Take, for instance, this passage:

> Right now [Ah Mao] reckoned women to be pretty unremarkable and figured they must all be much like herself, with only one idea on their minds, a sort of limitless yearning born of vanity and aspirations to pleasure. That was foolish, rustic, Ah Mao's error! Did Ah Mao just not know there were capable women working as officials or minor functionaries? . . . That at the same time there were women cooking and washing for themselves, who were bleeding their hearts dry to write works which others took, totted up by the mere number of words and then exchanged the words for money, on which these women then had to live. . . . These women took what in their isolation they came to perceive and the words they had no friends to share with, wrote everything down for the world to read, only to derive from their work an indifference equal to death itself. Yet these women continued, patiently, along the literary path, which this materialistic time with its scramble for profit disdains to notice. (243).

Here the narrator overreaches a bit and credits foolish, rustic, idiotic Ah Mao with stupidity beyond redemption; she has a habit of "thinking very little of women, while . . . crediting everything womankind created to men" (234–35). That is Ah Mao's greatest error: she supposes that "the entire fate of women" is somehow irrevocably "linked to men" (235). But this direct reprimand is an exception, a rare instance of finger pointing. More commonly, the narrator slips in the other direction, and expresses untoward sympathy for the nüxing she proposes to evaluate. Once in a while, the narrative unravels completely because a storyteller simply cannot bring herself to blame the protagonist for what she herself agrees is the protagonist's own mistake.

That was the problem contemporary critic He Yubo noted when he pointed to an obvious anomaly in "Mengke." Why, he asked, given the overwhelmingly censuring way the character had been drawn, had the narrator smuggled so much sympathy into her evaluation of what was, in every respect, self-inflicted suffering?[32] He put his finger on the instability of the relationship of storyteller and protagonist in most of Ding Ling's early texts. In the early 1930s Ding Ling began talking and writing explicitly about this relationship, and she provided two metaphors to rationalize her technique. In the first, she made gender and class interchangeable; in the second, she stressed the danger posed by the similarity of female writer and female subject.

In Ding Ling's view, the basic similarity of protagonist and narrator is always a potential threat to the literary text. As a writer, she argued, she failed when her narrator identified too strongly with a character's point of view. The story "Yecao" describes such an event. A writer named Yecao reaches a stalemate with the story she is writing because "she had injected some very fervent feelings into a very cool rational woman and had, moreover, introduced a light layer of melancholy. This was not really the character that she had imagined but it was precisely the shortcoming in women she understood best." The writer reconsiders whether she should "tear up the manuscript and rewrite it, or go on but without being sympathetic to this woman." Vexed, Yecao's mood disintegrates as she "thought of the social environment that caused women to overstress emotions. She reflected on how pitiable women were. As she reflected, *she began to loathe herself*."[33] For some reason, Yecao cannot solve a simple technical problem, recast her protagonist, and save her piece. Rather, her dilemma raises in her own mind the larger social question of the female subject per se. It is bad enough that she fails to imagine a woman character that is both rational and sentimental without being excessively either. Worse by far, the writer cannot prevent herself from identifying with the subject she accidentally invented. At that point, a botched sketch becomes a reminder of "female weakness." If generically all women are essentially flawed, the fictional author herself must also share these flaws. Yecao is no different from all women, and that is what rekindles her self-hatred.

This is apparently the dilemma Ding Ling believed she faced in the early years of her writing. She offered an explicit analogy to that effect. "In my past stories," she noted, "the protagonist is frequently a woman, and this is natural, because I am a woman and have a clearer understanding of women's weak points. But because of this people have come to misconstrue me. Actually I loathe the weakness of women. It's the same with Fadeyev's Metchik. . . . [Fadeyev] exposes Metchik's weaknesses very powerfully, but it looks to us as if Fadeyev tends to defend Metchik. I do not sympathize with the women in my work, but I do not always succeed in conveying my views in my writing."[34] Everything about this argument is odd, however. Ding Ling said that women writers "naturally" wrote stories about other women in order to criticize them. She did not explain why. She drew on the Fadeyev/Metchik analogy to explain why she sometimes failed to be critical enough of them, by her own lights, while she claimed at the same time that although she failed she always tried her hardest. The problem for Fadeyev was that he and Metchik came from the same social class, which meant that Fadeyev could not but identify with his character's consciousness. Ding Ling claimed that her ability to distance herself from her protagonists was similarly compromised, because women would naturally identify with one another just as people from the same class do.

Both these claims—one analogizing class and gender, the other inventing a natural relationship of female narrator and her female subjects— actually reinforced the foundational instability of the feminist subject women. Under this inescapable logic, half of Ding Ling the author was inevitably "like a woman" in the pejorative sense, and so shared women's weakness. The other half wrote narratives and empowered herself when she criticized generically female or nüxing characters. The problem, it seems, is that Ding Ling feared that her literary work did not consistently or effectively subdue one aspect to the other. Actually, there appeared to be a battle raging between the superior element, Ding Ling the writer, who knew all, judged, criticized, and held political views, and another, socially, perhaps even biologically determined, pitiful, weak, excessive Ding Ling, whose "common" experience of femininity claimed to be the truth of female women appearing as embodied characters in the stories.

To illustrate the relationship structuring these two expressions of female subjectivity I return briefly to "Sophia's Diary" and the problem of regret. Sophia wants to ensure that at her death she will have no cause for regret. But she knows she has no way to ensure this wish, because she makes all her decisions in her dream world. "As for me," Sophia confides to her diary, "my time is brief, so I love life with greater urgency than most. I don't fear death. I just feel that I haven't gotten any pleasure out of life. I want . . . all I want is to be happy. I spend days and nights dreaming up ways I could die without regret. . . . But how can I name what I really need?" (56). Yet, when Ding Ling named her famous protagonist Sophia she was signifying more than individual idiosyncracy. No one connected with the Chinese women's movement could fail to know about the two great heroic Sophias, Sophia Perovskaya, hero of the Russian revolutionary movement, and Sophia Zhang, hero of the 1911 Revolution in China that had ended the Qing dynasty.[35] Each of these figures signified to Chinese readers the power of feminine will in revolution. Yet Ding Ling used the sign Sophia to address a category of womanhood that was not victorious or revolutionary, but reduced, regretful, self-absorbed, self-pitying, and privatized. Stories like "Sophia's Diary," I am suggesting, predicated a universal category of Women but only in the end to advertise its alleged instabilities or deficiencies. Indeed, early Ding Ling texts represent not just a regretful but a regrettable female subject. Each and every element of the enlightened feminist vision—female education, economic independence, freedom to love, eroticization of personhood, heteronormatizing procreative relationships, sexual hygiene, self-determination in sexual life, the fusion of will and sentiment—turned out to be more promise than deliverance.

Perhaps regret accounts for the immediacy of Ding Ling's early fiction, the "something" her readers agonized over as "so moving that it must be the author's own experience."[36] Progressive feminism and political anarchism framed the way Ding Ling grew up and how she began writing about femininity. The eugenicist position in modern evolutionary biology that requires women to select their sexual partners was more problematic than it seemed. The dogma that individual sexual life influenced biosocial formations seemed less convincing in practice than in theory. For instance, the choices made by new female schoolteachers were grounded in modernist views on women's obligations to the social totality. The fact Ding Ling laid bare in "Summer Break" is that such women had little immediate social effect and were, in fact, immobilized, their stubborn self-respect and bravery unappreciated even when they could manage to achieve it. Progressive forms of feminist theorizing had made a wager. But rather than healthy independence, ameliorated oppression, and social investment, it seemed that liberated women confronted excess, rejection, disappointment, and failure. Certainly the larger society was primarily to blame. But individually and collectively, nüxing chose fantasy over reality and fantasy led them to act in ways they later regretted. No nüxing ever knew if her choice had been based in truth or illusion, reality or fantasy, and because women allegedly acted to avoid realities, chances were good that all choices were wrong. Even the nüxing who sought to leave the darkness could not, because the original choice was made from inside, not outside her own fantastic mind. All most nüxing ever realized was that yet another decision was ill-fated. Most could expect only to endure the endless consequences of wrong decisions: the harder women struggled, the more willed they became, the more regretful they would end up being.

Yet, to create the illusion of regret in the narrative, the author had to invent an omnipotent storyteller. The first four texts Ding Ling produced conformed to this same shape. In "Sophia's Diary" she signified reality with those elegant commonsense allies, Yufang and Yunlin, who, stalwart to the end, wait for Sophia's dream palace to collapse. And the reader waits with them. Maybe the tension the story conveys tapped into Ding Ling's own regret at forcing her character Sophia into such a regretful mode (a move that Yecao could appreciate). It is impossible to know. However, until Ding Ling the writer framed her narratives as a means of producing regret, she had difficulty separating her self as a writer from her self as a woman. Ding Ling, writer and revolutionary, established a place for herself outside of nüxing, a light, "real" place that provided the necessary leverage for her effort to rework the gendering of modernity. If there is one sentence in Ding Ling's earliest texts that must be taken as absolutely central to this project, it is the cry she placed in Sophia's mouth: "How can I then express all my regret and self-hatred with my pen?"

## The Subject of Marxist Feminism

Ding Ling's apparent disappointment with women's struggle to achieve social standing, the ren'ge matter, did not lead her to abandon the problem of women. One reason she is a significant figure in writing the history of the catachresis women is precisely that she remained vested in the question of the truth of women's singularity. Ding Ling's *In Darkness* writing inhabited, criticized, and yet could not wholly exceed a key assumption of progressive Chinese feminism: that nüxing was the Chinese female subject of the future. Certainly these early Ding Ling female characters are brave and enigmatic. They are also troubling and disappointing. But Ding Ling did not abandon the project of thinking about the problem of women from her own position as a self-identified woman. What she confronted head-on after this literary critique of women's weaknesses was how to fashion a remedy. Between her sharply critical enthusiasm for highly eroticized modern girls and new women and her early communist writing, which reconsolidated heterosexuality as evolutionary life force, she rethought the subject of women in clear and significant ways. Particularly the novel *Wei Hu* (1930) sought to provide readers with an alternative female subjectivity, defined this time in terms of women's work or praxis.

Ding Ling could make this leap because, as Christina Gilmartin has established, progressive feminist assumptions were widespread in the 1920s in the academic, literary, and political circles—anarchist, socialist, communist—that Ding Ling frequented in these years. Not only did terms for women like funü, nüren, nüzi, and nüxing circulate in a highly contested signifying economy during the 1920s and 1930s, but the Communist Party was a place where self-identified women addressed the woman question directly. Indeed, between 1922 and 1927, female theorists like Xiang Jingyu, Yang Zhihua, Xiao Chunu, and Cai Chang were considering the theoretical subject Women as part of their organizational responsibilities. Their determinations drew on many of the same assumptions as those of other progressive Chinese feminists. But they downplayed eroticization of the subject women in liberation theory and drew instead on the strain in progressive feminism that situated originary difference sociologically, as class difference, and equally important, geopolitically as national historical difference. When in 1929 Ding Ling began to reconsider how nüxing might overly privilege eroticized emotion and personal choice as the heart of eugenic improvement schemes, social-theoretical speculation was already widely available. It surfaces in two of Ding Ling's important novels, *Wei Hu* and *Muqin* (Mother).[37]

The early formulators of the Chinese communist women's movement explicitly rejected the nüxing formula. Their theoretical subject Woman emerged with reference to Soviet Russia and German Marxist texts, and they tended in their writing to use the term funü. The Marxists' theoretical subject was not primarily erotic or psychodynamic; it was not composed of will, emotions, consciousness, or lust; it did not refer back to female characters in European novels. Funü was economic, historical, theoretical, and overtly political, and it redefined itself in revolutionary social praxis. Funü's referent was the "workers of the world," in all their historical specificity. So Chinese funü possessed originary difference, but this primary difference was national and international. Historically, early Marxist theorists writing during the First United Front between the Nationalist Guomindang (GMD) and the Communist Parties (1923–1927) foreclosed on the notion that sexuality defined difference and identity. They did retain Woman or Women as a global historical category. Indeed, national difference seemed more significant when the question of how individual sexual choice drives natural selection was sublated into social revolution and the cutthroat world of international politics. Eugenics, social biology, sexual anthropology, and the other elements of international social theory continued to influence Marxist women's liberation theory, which drew heavily on the foundational theories of Bebel, Engels, Morgan et al. The question CCP founders confronted was where natural sexual drives ought to be vested in political terms, rather than the question of sexual drives as such.

In 1923, Xiang Jingyu, the CCP's most interesting theorist of women's liberation, had already divided the literate, Chinese female elite into three types: (1) those living in small, modernist families; (2) those pledged to "independent lives where they were free to use their own wills" (yizhi) professionally in the service of society; and (3) "romantics" (langmanpai), who sought absolute freedom to please themselves, filled their minds with fantastic anxiety, wallowed in self-congratulatory feelings, and ended up becoming "sentiment maniacs" (ganqing wang). Xiang, an old friend of Ding Ling's family, was centrally concerned with the quality of women's subjectivity. "Opening up social intercourse [shejiao gongkai] is their fashionable slogan," she wrote in a famous essay. "So they leave their books unread on a daily basis, but never, ever forget to meet their boyfriends." She continued: "The freedom to love is their sole objective and so long as they have their lovers, they require nothing else! They live totally aimless, vagabond lives and so their nerves become coarse and indolent and their mental facilities inert so that they read nothing, do nothing, and all the while proclaim endlessly: this is women's liberation!"[38] These figures of the "intellectual woman" (zhishi funü) or romantic, the individualists and the girl students (nüxuesheng), and so on fell under the category of xin nüxing, or new woman, and thus served as excellent foils. In Xiang's famous view, the romantic's mistake was her conflation of "liberation" and sexual desire. The romantic was happy to spend her time indulging her sexual instincts, now rendered "natural," if not downright respectable in the wake of Darwinian ethical transvaluation.[39] But, as Ding Ling was concluding and left feminists argued, erotic expression could not be taken literally as a widespread liberationist objective because it did not address male sadism, restore national sovereignty, provide defense against imperialists, reverse semicolonialism, or relieve the suffering of the poor.

Particularly sexual liberation bypasses the objective, material, political, and economic oppression of subaltern women. As Yang Zhihua argued in the wake of the May 30th Incident, the Chinese women's movement in the 1920s retained its class restrictiveness and its colonialist (zhimin zhuyi) Christian missionary focus, which meant it specially privileged the "question of oneself" (zishen wenti).[40] This had strategic drawbacks because not everyone had a chance to cultivate the erotic self in freedom. But also, the self of nüxing rested, in Yang's view, on the question of sexual difference. She agreed with the position of Xiao Chun, who argued that an inescapable derogation occurred when the syllable nü got fixed to the word ren, or person. Even the best men could not escape sexualizing women (nüren) when women defined themselves as other than men, because the movement of the binary nüxing/nanxing (female/male) automatically made it appear "as though women [nüzi] were some other kind of animal [lingwai yizhong dongwu]," which is to say that they were other than human.[41] The self of nüxing could consequently only be Other, an individualized plaything of man, his brutalized, degraded sexual toy. Women's liberation would be well advised to discontinue its single-minded concentration on sexual liberation, eugenic choice, and "personal rights" (zishen quanli) because this emphasis reinforced sexual othering or alienation and reiterated the sexual double bind. A possible way to neutralize the repetitive cycle that "others" women because it makes them not-human was to recontextualize the woman question and to reinscribe all women as historical agents. This is the theoretical subject that I have suggested appears most frequently in Marxist texts as the noun funü.[42]

Xiang Jingyu, particularly, sought to shift the direction of thinking about women's liberation from the female subject's own desire (for self-representation, erotic pleasure, personal rights) to exteriorized frames she called history and nation. The problem Marxist feminists confronted in a highly potent eugenicist atmosphere where Marxism competed with other theoretical paradigms to explain sex oppression is the question of where the sexual drive should be vested. And the point to which Marxists, including Ding Ling herself, eventually gravitated is that sexuality is sublated into racial necessity and is situated in the demographic whole of the nation. This is a position securely in the internationalist eugenicist mainstream. Chinese 1920s Marxist writing advocated a national inscription of woman as funü, as a category of Chinese historical modernity, and placed the female agent and her praxis at the center of China's revolutionary project. All this was in place by the end of the First United Front (1923–1927). Historically, Xiang argued, the woman question and the "labor question" (laodong wenti) always occurred together and were characteristic of bourgeois configurations, first in Europe in the eighteenth century and more recently in all of Europe's colonies. Each historical epoch produced gender relations appropriate to its mode of production. The mode of primitive communism, for instance, organized female labor for social as well as reproductive ends, and so ancient women enjoyed equality with, or even superiority to men.[43] Only under the regime of private property had women suffered a reduction to sexualized domestic slavery. Likewise, material conditions and modes of production determined what kinds of liberation were historically available to contemporary Chinese women.[44]

What then, according to Xiang, was the historical epoch facing the contemporary Chinese movement? The period of national revolution underway was unfolding in a global colonialist economy because in the twentieth century what effected the capitalist metropole eventually shook the peripheries. As had the strategists of the Indian women's movement, Xiang argued, activists in China should keep the European imperialist project of global domination in mind when calculating strategy. Xiang believed that Chinese women collectively should ally with the USSR and strengthen resistance to imperialism.[45] This did not mean abandoning the commitment to women's liberation. It was not wrong, a young, Marxist feminist Deng Yingchao (later a state official and wife of Premier Zhou Enlai) argued eloquently, to demand political rights and inclusion in history. For, she continued, despite the fact that the Chinese women's movement will take India or Soviet Russian models rather than European ones, still feminism's core notions—universal human rights, women's rights, modern critiques of naturalized inequality—are part of the European Enlightenment heritage that, with capitalism itself, are the historically positive triggers for China's political, historical development.[46] He Xiangning placed the woman subject on a theoretical grid. On one side lay semicolonialism, semifeudalism, unequal treaties, and economic imperialism, and on the other side the lijiao (Confucian social regulations), which erased women altogether. In He's thinking, women's liberation undertaken in a colonial context required that women join the national revolution. Participation would elevate women's social standing. You cannot blame women for failing to achieve the levels of struggle and sacrifice of Chinese men, she reasons with a characteristic twist, because the colonial, capitalist, imperialist, treaty port culture conspires to keep women ignorant.[47]

In a key 1925 article, "E'guo geming yü funü" (The Russian Revolution and women), Cai Chang, just returned from five years abroad, including time spent in the USSR, described how the Bolsheviks had linked the autonomous women workers' movement to the Leninist revolution. Propaganda efforts and direct lobbying by the autonomous women's movement had resulted in the institutional merging of women into the dictatorship of the proletariat. Her point was that this event actually made women theoretically and practically central to national reconstruction. Cai had seen for herself that "Russian women now have absolute freedom and equality with men at the level of politics." Chinese women could expect the same. Historically, Russian women's context before the October Revolution and the current conditions of Chinese women were strategically indistinguishable. Both contexts trapped women categorically as nonproductive (bushengchan) family members, or kinfolk (e.g., "good wives, virtuous mothers"). Cai's intervention in the debate also turned on a characteristic logic. In Russia, she wrote, you will not find an independent women's movement or an independent women workers' movement because the working women's movement is a part of the larger proletarian class movement. In all of the Soviet republics there exists a common federated proletarian movement. What binds the social movements into one is the effort to consolidate the struggle for the dictatorship of the proletariat. Thus, all political work aims at establishing the labor principle as the foundation of the new society. That is why "there is concern only for the proletariat, and they pay no attention to sex differentiating between women and men [nan nü liangxing de qufen]."[48]

Cai Chang's point was not that differences between men and women had disappeared after the Revolution in the Soviet Union. Rather, strategically speaking, political subordination of sex/gender to class difference foreclosed on the autonomy issue, defused hostility between female and male workers, and rewarded women by bringing them into the dictatorship of the proletariat. For her, the point of theoretical work seemed to be to "establish the labor principle as the foundation of the new society." And because nüxing was the subject of sexological discourses, it had built-in limitations. In Cai's essays funü is an alternative female subject inside the proletariat, situated in relation to the labor principle rather than in opposition to men as an undifferentiated humanist category.[49]

It may be that a lacuna in this early historical work became the mother of invention. The lacuna—that national modernity requires gendered subjects and a demonstration of gender equality, but Bolshevik modes of production frameworks downplay the ground of gender difference in nature— encouraged these early Chinese Marxist theorists to conceive of women strategically as a collective, internally stratified, political subject. Because they insisted on thinking through where the woman question belonged in Communist Party strategy from the perspective of self-identified women, these CCP theorists positioned in discourse a flexible, "empty" ideological subject they usefully referred to as funü and which they filled up with practical data. For instance, a 1926 official document summarizing United Front organization of women and the practical consequences to Marxist woman theory noted that the women's movement was lively and strategically useful on a national scale. Activists should gather real information about laboring women (laodong funü), the female masses (funü qunzhong), and the peasant women's movement (nongfu yundong).[50] The historical and analytic vacuity of the category women in theory was precisely what made it valuable. (Given what Ding Ling's widely read fiction was uncovering, it may also be the case that the Marxist position promised a future that the nüxing temporality actually closed off.)

Xiang Jingyu's essays of the early and mid-1920s, which served as the theoretical basis of CCP woman policy until 1942, are the best resource for how this theoretical subject worked. In the view of Xiang, who was ex-

ecuted by the Nationalist Party government in 1928, nationalism and national revolution are what bind funü to the state. "Women's movements
arise along with national movements," she wrote. "Without a national
movement it does not matter whether there is a women's movement or
not." Self-interest (*benshen liyi*) dictates women's participation in nationalist politics, as it had historically in the 1911 Revolution and 1913 federalist
effort. The reason the women's movement must ride on the back of nationalist movements is simply because the nation is what entitles citizens
to their rights and powers (*quanneng*). Though now it is a commonplace,
Xiang held a modernist's historical view of nation.[51] Most significant for
my purposes, she presumed the subject of the Chinese women's movement
in the context of global politics. The Chinese national female subject was
suspended between local warlordism and foreign imperialism. This national subaltern subject, funü, had to participate in beating back foreign
capital's domination of China's national infrastructure and recentralizing
power because without a place to extend national sovereign rights, the
freedoms promised women in eighteenth-century European Enlightenment theory would be meaningless.[52] In Xiang's view, the civilizing mission of what she clearly demarcated as the European Enlightenment was a
welcome project. She did indeed hypothesize that China's national revolution would resemble the Indian model and that China's future proletarian
transformation on the Russian model was historically inevitable. But this
did not change her belief that sovereignty and socialism ensured enlightened human rights on the European model, so the Chinese women's movement best served itself by serving the nation.[53]

However, because the nation had not yet taken shape, women's work
should focus on national consolidation. Specifically, according to Xiang,
funü should act politically because their positioning was doubly valuable:
"Women in the national movement can, on the one hand, represent the
demands of all the nation's people to save the nation and its people [*jiu guo
jiu min*]; on the other they can represent the desire of women as a whole
[*quanti funü*] for women's equality with men."[54] This dual ability of funü to
represent self to state and state to self was her special characteristic and
signaled funü's essentially statist construction in this stream of strategic
theoretical writing. When funü acted politically to represent others or herself, in other words, she was actually consolidating her own liberation.

Funü's second task was to produce herself. More than Cai Chang or
Yang Zhihua, Xiang Jingyu addressed women's education and culture. Take
for instance, "Cong pingmin jiaoyu zhong huafen nüzi pingmin jiaoyü de
wojian" (My opinion on dividing plebeian women's education from common folks' education). There she argued that for pleb women "common
folks' schooling" (*pingmin jiaoyu*) was problematic because they did not

consider themselves to be a class fragment; thus, although the objective of transforming "dependent" females into political subjects was good, the means had fallen short.[55] Xiang's larger point was that education could as easily produce good wives as good citizens. If educational processes were not monitored for nationalist content, then bad instruction would reproduce modern dependency in the same way women's education in the past had reproduced "models of women like Mencius's mother." Mediocre education of women simply "produced excellent dependents [fushupin] or ornaments [zhuangshipin]" for men.[56] The nation loses, as do individual women and women collectively, because dependent women sacrifice themselves to individual men and thus deprive the nation of their services.

This last insight led Xiang to the notion that women are an oppressed class (bei yapo jieji). In the course of the twentieth century all oppressed classes—women, workers, and the citizens of all weak nations (ruoxiao minzu)—would walk the "road of freedom and equality." This future, more than anything, should determine the shape of female education in the modern age. Liberation for women in these terms had to mean the production of subjects who possessed not "feelings" and "will," in the rhetoric of progressive feminist psychosocial theorizing, but rather "independent judgment [duli panduan]" and "developed reason [fazhan lixing]." Awakened woman (juewu nüzi), who concerned herself with historical probabilities, would invest effort in a liberatory curriculum strong in the physical sciences and the social sciences, for she would use her knowledge to grasp her own status in rational terms and use herself as a lever for overthrowing the rotten old society's definitions of women.[57]

Taking Xiang and the others seriously as theorists as much as political strategists clarifies the intellectual stakes in Party policy. The subject of women in these theories fuses the mode of production narrative and anti-imperialist nationalist discourse. The subject funü (and nüzi and nüren, but never nüxing) of early Chinese Marxist writing about the category Women prior to 1942 never disputed European rights theory. Indeed, it stressed the potential of twentieth-century national and proletarian liberation movements to women as a means of fulfilling women's claims to these rights. Nor do the interests of the state in these theories collapse all of funü's autonomy into itself. As Cai Chang herself pointed out in an essay titled "Su'E zhi funü yu ertong" (The women and children of Soviet Russia), no matter how close the collaboration of women and the Bolshevik Party, the real equality of women and men will not be achieved until such time as motherhood is socialized and becomes the state's responsibility, the nation's responsibility, and not the property of individual families. In 1925 this goal had still to be achieved in the USSR. As of the late 1980s, voices from the Chinese state's own Women's Federation were still calling for the socialization of housework, to say nothing of motherhood.[58] However, there is no question that the project begun in the early 1920s in the Women's Department of the Chinese Communist Party was to recast the universal subject women in historical terms as a subject of history. Women are not essentially subjects in nature, they proposed: the subject women is itself historical and consequently emancipatable.

In spring 1929, Ding Ling began to publish her stories about female writers. "Yecao" appeared in May, "Nianqian de yitian" (The day before New Year's day) in June 1930, and "Busuan qingshu" (Not a love letter) in 1931; *Wei Hu*, composed between spring 1929 and spring 1930, was her first full-length novel and shows the extent of her early effort to mold the implied, critical monitor of her earliest fiction into an embodied writer.[59] This figure of the clear-sighted woman writer is a marker of Ding Ling's investiture in the theoretical feminist subject funü. Just as her initial stories emerged as commentary from the margins of progressive feminism, this female writer entered progressive literature from the hinterland of the Chinese Marxist cultural movement. Ding Ling's struggle to redeem this figure unfolded on several fronts simultaneously.

First, a spate of stories dramatized how a writer, reflecting on her previously undisciplined life as a new woman, takes from that experience a reinforced conviction that natural feminine impulses must be controlled. Yecao is an explicit example, and so is Xin in "The Day before New Year's Day," described as solid, dark-skinned, with intense eyes and bushy eyebrows (not unlike Ding Ling):

> As a natural condition, although not a physical one, the women knew that her nerves were not altogether sound. So when she felt terribly oppressed, as she often did, she thought about all kinds of terribly heartbreaking things and would cry hysterically. She intensely and profoundly hated behaving this way and felt it an expression of weakness. Often she tried to restrain her emotions.
> "What are you crying about! [she would tell herself]. . . . Bury yourself in work—that's all."
> Her friend, who was also her lover, couldn't help finding her overly nervous, so often with a moan and a smile, he'd say to her:
> "Women will be women." (154–55)

Writing alleviates Xin's emotional claustrophobia. Yecao's crisis is less amenable to resolution. She is the more eroticized version of the female writer subject who uses fiction to recover memory and rechannel desire into manageable forms. Like Xin, Yecao knows about the life outside her mind and what effort went into retaining her writer's handle on it. Yecao forces herself to write about "wild excitement and passionate love" because she does not want to relive it. Trapped in a stuffy room writing on a luxurious day, she catches herself toying with a "return to intoxication," and she pauses, with the thought that "she had no further need for all that pleasure." Too much pleasure too soon had ruined her. Only writing lets her make a harmless facsimile of her fantastic past and its "mad, passionate, poetic world." Only memory makes it seem attractive at all in retrospect (95). When, to test her own resolve, Yecao gives in to "unwanted contrary impulse" and meets a man in the park, she keeps him from witnessing her erotic desire. He has a seductive pitch. "Your heart is much tougher than other women's," he cries at one point. "You can't be swayed, for you love only yourself and your work. . . . It's precisely because of your attitude, so dignified and honorable, that I love you" (103). And he is right to the degree that Yecao shares that nüxing temperament joined to a normatively better character. Yecao has more self-respect than Mengke; she does not use love as a shield against life, as Sophia had. Although from Nanxia's perspective Yecao seems "tough," she does not manipulate men for pleasure, as Wendy and the femme fatale protagonists do. The Yecao figures restrain themselves before they inflict self-damage, rather than realizing their transgressions after the fact. Newly minted, judicious female storytellers Xin and Yecao are, in other words, embodied versions of the reality principle that Ding Ling's earliest writing had insinuated into the machinery of the narrative.

A second level of Ding Ling's struggle involved changes to her writing style itself. Recall that in "The Girl Ah Mao" a bitter, judgmental narrator speaks knowingly about what characters are thinking but does not have independent subjectivity of her own. It would appear that Ding Ling's literary objective, certainly not anticipated consciously but sought after vigorously nonetheless, was to establish a genealogical line for the independent female author. "Yecao" gave the storyteller the ability to judge and discipline herself and could be read as a rewriting of the pathos of Elsa in "Suicide Diary," whose writing, if it can be called that, reinforces the protagonist's inability to see difference at all. In the culmination of these experiments, *Wei Hu* separates the monitor from the nüxing formation completely, breaking her earlier tense or divided feminine subject into two elemental feminine characters. Each receives a separate history and fate. It took Ding Ling two years and a massive revision to complete *Wei Hu* to her own satisfaction.[60] But once she finished it, she seemed to have written an autobiography, and certainly her style of writing had fundamentally changed. *Wei Hu* is therefore a genealogical novel. Nothing explicitly tells the reader that Shan lived on to become a famous writer, but the implication was there and Ding Ling never repudiated Shan's yearning for discipline, order, vocation. The fictional proxy, Shan, is positioned to become in her future Ding Ling herself, a famous revolutionary writer. The novel served this purpose. Personae after *Wei Hu*, the "Ding Ling" of the 1933 novel *Mother*, the 1936 narrative "Chen Boxiang," and the 1942 short story "Wo zai Xiacun de Shihou" (When I was in Xia Village) all trace themselves back to Shan and her position in Ding Ling's personal genealogy as the idealized reenvisioning of a recently discarded new woman self.[61] If this interpretation is accurate, then *Wei Hu* is, among other things, a justification. And it is valuable in a larger sense as well, because it recasts progressive feminist subjectivity in relation to revolutionary normative practice.

Nominally, *Wei Hu* narrates the story of a revolutionary man. It represents a three-month period in the life of a brilliant, middle-aged, communist intellectual recently returned from several years' study in the Soviet Union, whom the Communist Party assigns to work at "S" University in Shanghai. In Nanjing briefly, a friend introduces Wei Hu to a collective of "free" women. The friends are arrogant, anarchistic, feminist women; they appear to have little interest in men, but Wei Hu feels drawn to them anyway. He returns to Shanghai. The group of women disperses to find some individual direction in life. Their charismatic leader, Li Jia, and her best friend, Shan Shan, follow Wei Hu to Shanghai, where Shan, by then hopelessly infatuated with Wei, enters "S" University. The friendship between the two women sours as Shan's new disciplined regimen limits their free time together. Shan's search for meaning in her work shames Li Jia. Because Li cannot temper her desire for mindless "freedom," she experiences a terrible ennui and then decides to solve her problems by seducing Wei. Li's decision places Wei in great jeopardy, and morally he betrays himself twice: first, he drops all of his political work to spend time at home with her; then, when he can no longer bear his comrade's criticisms or his own guilty feelings, he abandons Li.[62]

In what Ding Ling called a "dialectical narrative structure," character depictions and plotting style in *Wei Hu* differ even from the short stories about female storytellers she was producing as she cast and recast the Wei Hu story. The narrator of the novel seems to have no stake in the story's outcome. All autobiographic content present at the level of plotting is purged of tense and affect. The narrator relays the characters' feelings through tediously mechanical shifts of perspective, engineered to present the views of each protagonist as "objectively" as possible. This mechanistic narration contributes to the feeling of stopped movement emanating from the story and drains all tension from the plot. The dialectical method ended Ding Ling's stylistics of regretful retrospection and heralded her new interest in estrangement and alienation. Everything about this novel speaks of alienation, from relations between protagonists to the narrator's own apparent detachment. Thus, for instance, the novel's narrator moves protagonists from location to location and builds up a feeling of cumulative dislocation. Section 1 inserts Wei Hu into the women's collective at the moment it begins to disintegrate. Section 2 unfolds in the apartment building where Shan Shan and Li Jia live across the hall from their friends Fu Sheng and his wife, Wen. The relations between the cohabitants get tense when Wei intrudes to court Li. The final section unfolds in Wei's elegant, solitary bachelor apartment, where the lovers indulge their romantic and sexual fantasies in total isolation. Then, of course, Wei leaves Li his rooms and simply walks out the door into the underground world of Communist self-sacrifice.

Particularly *Wei Hu* describes the sensation of estrangement phenomenologically. It conveys the experience of being alone for the first time; realizing that your friends have their own lives and cannot always take care of you; the appalling realization that morally responsible decisions are not easily made and require work; the odd feeling that people may represent pieces of a character that never come together, or that two persons might each be half of one single, unstable, historical personality. But mostly, the novel's organizational structure conveys emotional estrangement through the mechanism of the romantic triangle. Exactly unlike the deeply subjectivized and tense relation between character and narrator in Ding Ling's earlier work, *Wei Hu* discounts the narrator's introjections and foregrounds the shifting and tangled relations among three characters in three different combinations. This achieves distance because it imposes three different perspectives for the reader to consider and provides merit for each, thus forcing readers into a choice. In each relation, Wei Hu is the common element.

In the narrative foreground Ding Ling places the primary triangle of Wei Hu (a fictionalized portrait of Qu Qiubai), Li Jia (a fictional rendering of Ding Ling's close girlfriend, Wang Jianhong), and Shan Shan. Below, the narrator describes how Shan, who, given the actual relation of Ding Ling and her friends, can only be a fictional representation of Ding Ling herself, thinks over the impact that Wei is having on her relationship to Li. Of the three of them, only Shan grasps how potentially unsettling the triangle is:

> Shan Shan had her own troubles. . . . Even in the light of her personality, which lacked Li Jia's fiery recklessness, still she of the two of them should have been closer to Wei Hu. She had come to study precisely because of her rather vague personal attraction [to him]. . . . Shan Shan had not yet examined herself very thoroughly, but she understood Li Jia. She realized that her own unhappiness was unjustified, yet, without knowing what she had done, she had pulled

away from her best friend. Why couldn't she bring herself to be as open [as Li Jia]? How could she feel at ease when she was on bad terms with Li Jia? (91–92)

Neither the passionate, Sophia-like Li Jia nor the older man, Wei Hu, can match Shan's insightfulness. Still, both Li and Wei express anxiety and irritation attributable to the oppressive pressure that the other two, Shan and Wei or Li and Shan, stimulate in them.

But the novel also develops a second triangle linking Wei and the two other characters of Fu Sheng and Wen. When Wei begins to visit this couple every night hoping to catch sight of Li, he provokes Wen's suspicion. One night she teases him to his breaking point, and, out of fear of having his motives revealed, he grabs Wen and kisses her to throw her off the scent. This stimulates a flurry of angry feelings. Fu Sheng resents having to work with Wei, who has just "confessed" to having a crush on Wen, while Wen's suspicions only increase. Because the narrative does not push this incident any further, it seems likely that it exists only to underscore the general sense that the triangle signifies social alienation, misunderstanding, estranged sensibility, the loneliness of one's own motives. Finally, Ding Ling included in the shadowy past a third triangle composed of Wei Hu, Illya, and Illya's Polish lover, who is not named but is referred to only as "the Polish guy." The narrative never reveals directly what Wei himself thinks about the old Moscow romance. Illya exists in narrative terms only because Li reports to Shan Wei's vague memories of having had an affair in Russia, and the suggestive photograph of the Russian woman conveys unspeakable significance to the two young Chinese women.

The love triangle as a sign allows plotting to engage alienation at several levels. First, complex, conflicted relations of heterosexual and homoerotic desire bring to the surface the question of where sexual love and expression belong in the life of women and men. Second, the sign of three as the sign of choice means that triangulation forces each subject to exercise will, to decide his or her own fate, inside the cauldron of personal conflict. Third, the ultimate choice is always a moral choice between indulging the self and organizing the self's potentials in service or praxis. Her privileging of tension between indulgence and praxis (or love and revolution, in the language of that time) was Ding Ling's first stab at the question of how the liberated or post-traditional female subject defined a normative self in the service of national politics.[63]

Ding Ling's sensitivity to erotic currents between women surfaces in the portrait of Li Jia and Shan Shan, too. Shan feels jealous when Li catches Wei's attention. She wishes her friend no harm, but recognizes clearly that Li is "blocking her way" to Wei's affections. Shan also claims to understand Wei's mechanical, "male" sexual drive and his need to "play around" with women. On top of all this intuitive erotic knowledge, Shan senses the sensuous, physical connection that links her to Li. That precious, strange bond would rupture no matter which of the two women Wei chose. "You and I will always be connected to each other," she murmurs to Li as she strokes her sleeping friend's bare neck. "I'll never let any bastard harm you" (96). Shan's fear that Wei might indeed be a *mogui*, or bastard, however, causes her concern with the realization that she can no longer protect her beloved against sex with a man. Indeed, one night Shan even begins seeing Li's sexual beauty through Wei's eyes. "Jia," she remarks after she has stared at her friend's body so long that Li has lost her temper. "You really are beautiful. If I were a man, I'd love you, too" (154). On his part, Wei honors the low-key erotic bond between the women by petitioning Shan for permission to sleep with Li: the night he consummates the affair, Shan relinquishes Li to Wei, saying, "Fine. I'm giving Jia over to you" (155, 161).

But Shan also discovers in the transaction that sexual initiation estranges her from erotic dependence on Li *and* her low-grade fever for Wei. Though she endures Li's betrayal stoically, waiting for the affair to end, and though she never deserts Li in the interim, Shan simply does not feel the same way about her when Wei returns her. "Thank you so very, very much, my dear friend," Wei murmurs to Shan as he opens his door to leave Li for the last time. Shan, ignorant of his planned betrayal, replies with what is ostensibly a polite request to prolong their visit. "No," she says. "I can't wait for you. Why don't you stay?" (210–11). The unintentional double meaning expresses Shan's reluctance to take over his commitment to her friend. Shan can no longer "wait" for a number of reasons. The sexual solidarity of women exists for her only in the fantasy world of the homosocial collective, before heterosexual division. In choosing each other, Li and Wei both betray Shan, open her to the larger world of work, and thus disrupt their triangular, enclosed, hermetically circular flow of libidinal energy. Li's power over her friend no longer claims priority over Shan's commitment to her work, no matter how ill-defined the nature of the praxis. Once she is in a position to, Shan chooses praxis rather than erotic love as a way of defining her life and consequently herself.

*Wei Hu* is thus partly a novel about how Shan makes herself into the sort of woman capable of such a decision. After all, Shan gives up her erotic attachment to Li's beautiful body, but she also abandons her desire for Wei and so, in the economy of this narrative, for a male lover, too. (At the extreme, one could say that Ding Ling was giving up on the heterosexual project, though of course, never on the importance of sexual expression.)

Initially, *Wei Hu* presents the girlfriends as inseparable complements, over-lapping halves of one single subject:

> This left just the two, Li Jia and Shan Shan. Of the women who [had] made up the group, they were even closer than the general rule, al-though each was animated by a different personal makeup. Further, Shan Shan really envied Li Jia's openness and her self-indulgent lack of inhibition, while Li Jia adored Shan Shan's intelligence and her talent for devoted friendship. Both equally loved art and freedom passionately (although it would actually be more correct to say that they loved to play). They had spent the past two years studying music and painting. Initially Li Jia always showed greater talent for the arts because of her exorbitantly passionate boldness; but it was also Li Jia who always tired of them first, and so finally their interests had turned in yet another direction. Now Shan Shan secretly wrote poems be-cause she was more deeply melancholic. And Li Jia, who dreamed of shedding her blood for others in heroic sacrifice, had gotten deeply involved with the so-called Chinese Anarchist Party as a means of winning for people the liberty she so adored. Still, when she talked with Shan Shan about such passionate poets as Shelley, Byron, and Goethe, she felt the same admiration and passionate absorption as her friend. Li Jia often sensed running in her veins a similar profound *Weltschmerz* as that of the poets. It wasn't that Shan Shan felt dif-ferently, but that she did not face life with Li Jia's courage or boldness; her conversation also had an acerbic bite to it. From the outside, Li Jia appeared the more attractive of the two. But deep in her heart, when Li Jia analyzed things, she had to admit that no matter where she looked, at knowledge, personality or the way she lived her life, Shan Shan was her superior. Very few people, she had to admit, could compare with her friend. So as a result the two women lived together even more compatibly than ever. (25)

In this revealing passage Li claims Shan as her complement, even, one might say, her better half. Indeed, Shan appears to have the superior ele-ments in her person and yet remains strangely oblivious to her own virtues. She depends on the exuberant, flashy, sexy Li. "I really need you to provide excitement and give me courage," Shan tells her in the midst of their first major quarrel. "Really. So many times I realize that things are important and interesting only when you are by my side, full of happiness" (102). Each woman looks to the other. Neither sees the need to be separate until each recognizes the other as a sexual threat rather than a complement.

The need to divorce each other emerges when the story forces each to decide between play (*wan*) and work or praxis (*zuo shi*). Formulating a binary, nonexclusionary, ethically structured relation between wan and zuo shi was, in fact, the task of the novel. Recall that initially the friends are like one person, open to love and literature, content to live in unstructured, self-gratifying play. The encounter with Wei Hu opens the initial rift between the two parts of this complementarity; but as their dissimilarities take more pronounced shape, the narrator increasingly sides against Li and with Shan. "I'm not saying—I mean—of course, you are bound to be a bit reckless—what I mean is," Shan stutters as she struggles to change Li's mind. "If you go on playing like you are now, you are really going to regret it in the future" (103).

The more differences between them Li and Shan discover, the more like Sophia, Mengke, and Ah Mao Li turns out to be. For instance, Li deeply resents Shan's pressure because "the one thing she particularly did not want to do was to think about the problem which at present most demanded resolution." Although she had given the problem some vague consideration, Li "knew her thinking represented no more than impractical dreams." Finally, Shan delivers the ultimatum: "Originally we were too innocent, and I can forgive that. But *now*, Li Jia! *Now* I'm already twenty-two years old and you are twenty. . . . We must really decide which avenue to take." When Shan insists that the choice be made, points to the many existing possibilities, and refuses to make the decision for Li, Li flies into a rage. "You're wrong!' she cries. "You're dead wrong. Everything you say may apply to you, but you have no call to include me in with you." For the first time, she is treating her friend as an enemy (102, 106).

After this explosion, the friends find each other emphatically alien. Qualities of personality previously latent clarify abruptly. Li sags into passive lethargy and feels Shan's "defection" keenly. "She seemed to feel she ought to take back the throne she had lost," because without Shan's uncritical love, Li feels unimportant and, anyway, she loathes being alone. After waffling for a long time suspended between outrageous dreams of glory and the need to work, Li does what Sophia had done; she substitutes love for work. Her unwillingness to choose disciplined study or labor agitation among Shanghai's female proletariat sets the tragic romance in motion (127–29).

Shan feels guilty at leaving Li behind but knows her choice is best for her, even though she cannot really say why or even what it is that she has chosen. Shan studies, but she never studies with any great commitment. More than anything else, she seeks discipline even in the "old arts" like ink brush painting, for which she has little aptitude. Mostly she wants a way out of the gaping hellish hole that has opened before her and that threatens her and her friends. One thing is vividly clear: "Now she was alone, relying on the will or purpose that she had resolved on over the last half year to get her through" (96).

The insight Shan gains in struggle is that all women need to do something: women need work. Love, desire, sexual pleasure, fantasy: none of these require effort, except perhaps the energy it takes to keep intact self-delusion. It is not enough to be what lovely, amusing, brilliant Li Jia became, Wei Hu's fascinating Other, the object of his desire. When Wei happens to compare the solid, hard-working women he met in the Soviet Union to the febrile, unstable modern Chinese women, Shan repeats to him the criticisms she made to Li directly. "Chinese women," she tells Wei abruptly, "[are emotionally unstable compared to Soviet women] for no other reason than they have no work to do" (81). The comparison of women by nationality, of course, had resonance in the formulation I discussed earlier in relation to theorists Xiang Jingyu and Cai Chang. "Chinese women" are a historical subject formed in relation to the erotic relations among Wei, his insatiable Russian lover, Illya, Illya's lover, "the Polish guy," and Li.

Indulgence is an overtranslation of the word *wan*. Yet in the novel, Ding Ling used it to describe a range of activities, from playing with children to flight from responsibility. Wan in *Wei Hu* means all endeavors not directly bearing on social progress or personal discipline. Zuo shi simply means work, but in the context of this narrative it forms an opposition to wan, and consequently takes over the deeper meaning of praxis, or a creative act for transforming an agent and the agent's surroundings. This narrative opposition structured around the dialectic of wan and zuo shi is reiterated through the character of Wei, a technique that makes for a rather mechanical reading experience, but a thoroughly clear message. The Wei Hu character embodies both tendencies, in much the same way that Shan and Li are two elements of one woman, or two tendencies within the gender as such, Shan representing work, Li play. Wei states this theme bluntly in his farewell note to Li. "On the one side," the note reads, "stood my unwavering commitment to work, on the other the natural needs of my life," by which he means his wan-life of sex, literature, romance, aestheticism, personal safety, and individualism (215).

In Ding Ling's hands, "love" was becoming a catchall for all personal indulgences balanced not against revolution, actually, but against a large, diffuse matter of praxis on behalf of all progressive communities larger than the self, including the revolutionary avant-garde. The novel was Ding Ling's first major exposition of a theme that became commonplace in cultural circles during the late 1920s called the tension of "love and revolution." Just as she habitually did and would continue doing, in *Wei Hu* Ding Ling made it difficult for characters to make a "correct" decision. As in the stories of Sophia and Elsa in the 1920s and Zhenzhen and Lu Ping in the late 1930s (see chapter 5), *Wei Hu*'s internal dynamic is posed through the tension that the need to choose imposes on the protagonist. It is a hallmark of ethical fiction that confounds the character with an moral dilemma and then judges her decisions compassionately.

In this novel, as in key fiction throughout the 1930s, Ding Ling placed sexual politics prominently at the center of the ethical question of how to understand love and work, how to strike a balance between them. Take, for instance, the case of Fu Sheng, who chooses "revolution," a choice represented in the novel as a decent or ethical form of work. Yet, the narrator and most of the novel's protagonists criticize even this good man because his Stakhanovite work pace and superficially selfless commitment have actually shackled his wife with all the child care and domestic labor, which effectively cripples her moral development. This is a typical example of the problem of balance that the novel proposes. *Wei Hu*'s characters must decide, often case by case, the significance of each personal action, must interrogate the consequences of every act both in relation to personal communitarian life and measured against the suffering and political turmoil unfolding outside their immediate circle. How much relaxation does a revolutionary require before play becomes selfish gratification, for instance? How do you measure personal commitment? What is the difference between genuine praxis, selfish ambition, generous joining in struggle, calculated cruelty to others in the pursuit of a larger good? What is and is not politically significant work?

It is important to stress that although *Wei Hu* did place sexual desire in a new relation to female subjectivity, nothing in the novel suggests that love is unimportant or morally questionable by definition. Rather, the message that this novel conveys is that romance poses an ethical problem because it generally pulls individuals away from their own creative transformation of the world and into dependent, regressive, selfish, personal lives of retrograde indulgence. The subject's moral dilemma alters the meaning of romance. That is because this subject is charged with the task of finding a way of making personal pleasure into something socially useful, or at the very least, a way of fusing personal necessity to socially meaningful work. How the need for love and the need for work are ideally one and the same surfaces in the figure of Illya.

"It's because of [Illya] that people are bad-mouthing Wei Hu," Li Jia says. It seems that Illya and Wei had cohabited, but in the three months of their liaison had failed to find happiness because he could not satisfy her sexually and she took to spending nights with "the Polish guy." Wei felt drained (*pibei*) by her and asked that she release him, but she wouldn't allow it. She complained to other people that the Chinese guy had deceived her. Then Illya cursed him and she cursed China. Wei left her. But even then Illya refused to let go and returned to Wei as he was preparing to leave Russia for China. The Russian revolutionary asks Wei if he will take her with him and expresses her jealousy for the future Chinese lover he will certainly find at home. Although he does not fully satisfy her erotic needs, she still feels a strong emotional bond to Wei.

> Shan Shan studied the photograph carefully for a while. Then Li Jia said: "You don't suppose this was why people reproached Wei Hu, do you? Can they really be considered to have been in love at all? Wei Hu said that the whole affair made him doubtful because he never, at any time, felt any anguish or ecstasy; just that he had a woman and that was that. They each did their own work during the day, miles apart. At night they ate and slept together. On Sunday the two of them went to the opera or took in a movie. So he felt no pain when he left her." Shan Shan sighed: "What's wrong with that? Quite to the contrary, I really love this woman."
>
> "So do I," [Li Jia agreed.] "There is something about her we will never be able to match." (186–87)

It is not clear with whom we should be sympathizing in this important subplot; the lusty Russian woman, after all, has called Wei's sexual stamina into question, and worse, the vigor of the Chinese people when she betrayed Wei with "the Polish guy." Also, Wei cared so little about her that he left her behind too easily, a lapse of feeling that might reflect as badly on her as on him. But the emancipated, revolutionary Illya appears to have another significance to Shan particularly. Perhaps in Illya Shan sees that erotic love, far from being categorically immoral, might be compatible with revolution; perhaps revolutionary praxis is a way to redeem and recalibrate love itself. Illya is, after all, the only character in the novel who grasps how private feelings could become one with revolutionary obligation and commitment. Illya offers Wei sex, but not at the expense of her work (10). This "Russian triangle," then, has further implications. Wei rejects Illya's offer of an integrated, antiromantic, sexually open liaison because it does not suit his taste for "anguished" and "ecstatic" love affairs. The onus is on him. When Shan says that she "loves" and wants to emulate Illya's example, she seems to be voicing the idea that a good choice for engaged women, women as a subject of theory, may be the resolution of wan and zuo shi in a loving, open, mutually engaged revolutionary life.

*Wei Hu*'s characters turn out to represent a highly schematized set of moral choices, set in a framework where the overall task is to renegotiate the ethically most acceptable relation of erotic congress uniting women and men. Each character embodies the difficulties this negotiation poses.

Wei himself, for instance, has two distinct personalities, according to the narrator. The first he inherited from his parents, the second he created for himself through revolutionary praxis (199–200). But unlike Illya, or even Shan, Wei is never able to integrate the competing demands of wan and zuo shi; he chooses them both at once and so the story shows him tearing himself in half. Ding Ling crammed the novel with concrete evidence of Wei's dualism. She had him appear dressed in crude workers' clothing and then in spiffy Western suits; he cannot decide whether to flee with Li or abandon her; when he chooses politics, he struggles to forswear poetry, but then slips back to poetry at the expense of politics. His "two kinds of characters and two personalities" determine that he will never choose a woman like Shan over blissful torment with Li (199). Wei never disrupts his impulse to associate women with love, sexual angst, poetry, privacy, suffering, and thus with wan. But, of course, the point of the novel is not to train Wei Hu. It is to bring the female characters in the plot to an appreciation of their own worth to themselves rather than their use as love objects to him.

Another level of this normative theme unfolds in Wei Hu because Ding Ling worked into the plot a character, Shan Shan, to serve as Ding Ling's own proxy. Though Wei Hu is not really a novel "about" one individual character, we realize from the beginning that the third-person narrator tends to favor the Shan character. Shan, it notes, "naturally considered human feelings more solicitously than Li Jia," and "The longer one lived with the delicate-minded Shan, the more deeply one got involved with her," the more profoundly "intelligent" and "sweet-natured" she seemed to become (91–92). So although Shan appears less essential in plot terms at first, the central business of the plot always ends up revolving around her. She disciplines Li Jia, she forewarns about Wei Hu's perfidy, she gives Li to him and takes her back from him, she loves a man and a woman, and she decides to work for a revolutionary future in spite of herself. In normative terms, Shan, of all the characters, makes the most correct choices, though almost accidentally. Li realizes this foundation of Shan's superiority in the closing sentences of the novel, when she remarks that Shan at last has established a "career" and that Shan's avenue is her own last salvation. My hunch is that Ding Ling accomplished a great deal for herself in this exercise. When she reinvented herself as Shan Shan, she rectified the nature of her early personal dependence on her girlhood friend Wang Jianhong, with whom she had fled Hunan. Jiang Bingzhi began creating a genealogy for her writing self, Ding Ling.

This chapter began by discussing how nüxing linked Ding Ling with the problematic of female ren'ge, first predicated in eugenicist ethics and the evolutionary sociology of the 1920s. The argument examined the internal psychology of the Sophia character and suggested that Ding Ling's first writing rested female subjectivity on a characteristic temporality of regret. This regret, it turned out, actually opened up a normative space where a superior woman, capable of overcoming her foundational weakness, could emerge in the redefining processes that revolutionary praxis offers all subordinated subjects. A historical mode of anteriority gradually replaced the regretful instability of the nüxing protagonists, a historical narrative that proposed that we cannot know in advance what women will become because, like colonized peoples, racialized minorities, and proletarians, women must fashion themselves in the future. For a feminist thinker this is an exemplary position, in the sense that Ding Ling's intellectualist, moralist fiction connected in a self-reflexive, sustained way to larger projects and problematics in progressive Chinese feminism. "What can be demarcated, defined and determined," Balibar usefully summarized, "maintains a constitutive relation with what can be thought." Thinking or putting into question the notion of the border or the discrete differences separating things from each other—men from women, for instance—gives rise to the praxis that Balibar defined as "the impossible limit of an autodetermination . . . [the] effort to conceptualize the line on which we think."[64] Ding Ling's literary consideration of the catachreses nüxing and funü never quite exceeds the conditions of their own production. That is not a criticism or a condemnation; it is recognition of the limitations of criticism and the limits of thinking. What can be said is that Ding Ling's literary rethinking of the catachreses funü, nüxing, and so on draws our attention repeatedly back to the crisis of ren'ge, or how the standing of women and their normative personal being will be handled: by women themselves, by the society, however defined, by the politics and politicians of the future.[65]

The accelerating disintegration of life under the Chiang Kaishek government's extermination war against the Communist Party apparatus and the Japanese imperialist erosion of Chinese sovereign integrity, the Communist movement's search for a theoretical, practical, and military avenue to revolutionary consolidation of the state: all of these momentously destructive events form the backdrop of what emerges in Ding Ling's fiction as schematic, formalized, ethical problems. In these circumstances, and as events became even more complex and dangerous, the effort to continue thinking about a revolutionary modernism where women will be represented and represent themselves encodes priceless information and human resolution. In the torment Ding Ling documented in other stories that I do not showcase here, she also continued to think about what people, but even more, what women will have become in a future that the entire Communist movement fought to put in place.

Gradually surfacing in Ding Ling's work is another subject of revolutionary feminism. Funü and its cognates furen (e.g., Bebel, *Women and Society* in

Chinese translation) and nüren are generally associated with sociological discourses of modernist heterosexuality in sociological writing and political theory. As previously noted, the term funü predominated as a category of gendered social relations in late Qing dynasty language. It took on a novel, historical specificity in twentieth-century CCP revolutionary rhetoric and social revolutionary practice. In Maoist theory and practice of revolutionary war and social mobilization, pioneered during the CCP's hiatus in the far Northern Border Regions during the late 1930s and 1940s, funü would become a foundational enabling constraint of social policy. I take up the subject and its entitlements and stalemates in the next chapter. I want to conclude this chapter, however, by demonstrating how Ding Ling's intellectual efforts to define war and social revolution's constitutive relation with thought contributed to moving the ground of women's social standing and elementary subjecthood, their ren'ge, from the eugenic domain of Nature into a regime of History. This is not to argue that eugenic modes of thinking dropped out of feminist theory streams altogether, any more than literature "caused" social change. Much is preserved in Ding Ling's thinking that is familiar. These include the priorities she accorded erotic drives, to the by now completely normative belief that women serve the nation and themselves when they choose their own procreative partner. Ding Ling's job during her period of transition into Communist revolutionary struggle was to edit Beidou (Great dipper). This journal's name signaled to readers the present impasse and the way out of it. The same can be said of the dead ends or feminist impasses addressed in her imaginative fiction.

It is worth repeating that although no one denies that nationalist objectives were at stake in anti-imperialist national struggle and consequently in writing that predicates funü, in and of itself "nationalism" is not a sufficient causal explanation for the Chinese communist women's liberation movement.[66] In my view, Xiang Jingyu was correct that "women's movements arise along with national movements. Without a national movement it does not matter whether there is a women's movement or not." But Spivak is also correct when she adds, "Consciousness of national identity is marked by the use to which it is put."[67] The point is that there can be no general typology of the relation of nationalism and the women's movement. The uses to which nationalism is put range too widely for that. What analysis in the nationalist paradigm generally leaves out of consideration are the specific objectives that establishing the nation ensures along with objectives that are held by nationalists to transcend nation.

With this proviso in mind, my final task here is to demonstrate how Ding Ling put women in History. The unfinished novel Mother retrospectively proposed what women must have been all along, that is, the product of national and international revolutionary history. It was retrospective in a personal sense as well as an ideological one. Certainly the novel reworked core assumptions that appeared in her early fiction, but we have also seen how fluid her thinking had been from the beginning of her career. Nonetheless, the novel is significant because it so directly thematized History. Ding Ling set the story in the pre-1911, late Qing era of national revolution and stated that it was to be one chapter of a longer history of women in the Chinese revolution over the course of the twentieth century. *Mother* did two things: first, it told the story of Ding Ling's own revolutionary roots; second, it suggested what the future might have looked like to the author's own mother, who had been left, like the author, a newly widowed woman with an orphaned child. *Mother* drew explicit attention to Ding Ling's version of the historical national subject "Chinese women." In this regard, *Mother* took over and cannibalized the subject that Xiang Jingyu was predicating in her theoretical writing; recall that this is the same Xiang who appears as a character in the novel itself.

Why Ding Ling began relocating her female characters away from the darkness, proletarianizing them, situating them historically "in life," is not a mystery because she also began in these years to offer advice about what is good literature. She first raised this matter as a question of "content" (*neirong* or *cailiao*) in 1930, *Spring, Shanghai*. But resolving the problem of truthfulness in representation or closeness to life took time and thought. She had been ambivalent in 1931 when she wrote, "I did not oppose pieces that were incarnations of the author, but I have come to oppose things written out of illusion." Her immediate problem as a writer, she continued, was that she lacked experience outside her own class. She had criticized Chinese proletarian fiction for this deficiency, saying that it generally lacked an experiential core. In 1931 she was willing to settle for fiction rooted in the experiences of students, whom she recognized as her core readers. "I feel," she continued in one well-known statement on the topic, "that writing about peasants and workers is not necessarily good and one can really use material from any part of society when one writes. I have plans to write a long piece on my own family."[68] She certainly understood the stakes of the debate, but this resolution, to write about social groups she knew intimately, left unresolved a host of questions. What, for instance, was the difference between writing under illusion (whether erotic or class-induced) and experience? Why shouldn't a proletarian writer privilege romance, for even subaltern boys and girls fall in love? Why not go directly to the masses and experience their lives and thus create a foundation for proletarianized fiction? (The short answer to this question was that you could be exterminated for this sort of activity.) There is no way of knowing what Ding Ling's literature might have done if her life had unfolded otherwise. As it turned out, in May 1933 the GMD secret police seized her and she lived under house detention for the next three years; she was widely presumed dead.

Mother was Ding Ling's final publication before she disappeared on 4 May 1933. She began the novel in May 1932 and finished it in April 1933. Between the death of her child's father, Hu Yepin, and beginning Mother, she had produced virtually nothing but the breakthrough realist story "Shui" (Water), a canonical text. She resolved the earlier writing block with Mother, and in the subsequent eleven months it took her to complete the historical fiction also wrote three long realist stories, a handful of shorter experimental fragments, editorial directions to Beidou's readers, and several major statements about revolutionary literature. Hu Yepin's death virtually beggared her and Ding Ling wrote Mother for money. Dalu xinwen (Mainland news) published the more or less completed first third of the serial, but when the censors shut the newspaper down, the text appeared in book form under the Liangyu imprint. For all of the reasons above, though part of an unusually large flow of writing, Mother was even more fraught, transitional, incomplete, and fragmented than the canonical "revolutionary" pieces that granted Ding Ling her place in the pantheon of revolutionary Chinese fiction writers.

As she made clear several times, Ding Ling herself believed that Mother represented real, objective, historical circumstances. She believed she had written a historical, realist narrative. Employing strongly materialist language, she explained, "I first started thinking about writing this book when I returned from Hunan to Shanghai" because people in Hunan told her about the "collapse of the rural economy, the landlords and the particularly horrifying news about the doomed official class." The incursions of machine production, warlord and official government oppression, and local gentry decadence each had taken a toll on the already depressed rural economy, deepening the national crisis. So, she said, she decided to write a book that would expose "the historical process of change" in rural Hunan. Mother would cover "the period from the end of the Xuantong reign, through the Xinhai Revolution, the Great Revolution of 1927, down to the most recent widespread rural unrest in the villages."[69]

Mother tells the story of a recently widowed provincial gentry woman, Yu Manzhen, who finds herself alone on her decrepit estate with two small children. Heart-sickness, cold weather, physical depletion, and the bleakness of her fate nearly kill her, but she recovers a will to live once spring arrives. Her slave, Yaoma, convinces her to settle down in the country by promising to transform the pleasure garden into a productive farm. Yaoma and Yaoma's slave family will support the household on their profits (the text considers use value, barter, and sale parts of the local economy) while they all wait, oblivious to the historical irony of their choice, for the infant boy, Da, to grow up, take the imperial exams, and become an official. News of her mother's death takes Manzhen back to the Yu compound in the town of Wuling, where she learns about a modern school for elite women. She wins her brother's permission to attend it and then liquidates what remains (after her in-laws have pillaged it) of her husband's estate in order to support herself and the children for the duration. At school she befriends other patriotic women of her class and the group transforms itself with dress reform, foot unbinding, rigorous discipline, and discussion about national salvation. As they grow bolder, the women realize that their brothers are part of something called "revolution." They try to join this revolution individually but the men rebuff them, and so, lacking other recourse, they gather in Manzhen's garden to swear an oath of sisterhood. During the summer of 1911 the sisters go home for vacation. A comet appears in the sky. The revolution breaks out. The novel ends.

*Mother* forms an exclamation point. The new woman subject and the literary aesthetic supporting it are nowhere to be seen. Rather than Ding Ling's vaguely untrustworthy narrator-in-process, this novel produced a peculiarly inflected female subject, who was partly an invention of national historiography—a revolutionary nationalist feminist—and partly a sort of tacked-together personality knit out of conventional kin obligation, recuperated into a new historical teleology. Ding Ling's turn to the nation's past was also a turn to Marxist teleology. Like other communist writers in the League of Left-Wing Writers (organized 2 March 1930 by leading left intellectuals and cultural workers, including Ding Ling), Ding Ling set out to reconstruct indigenous, subaltern cultural practices that were nationalist but not feudal, and modern but not Western. Although her hero, Manzhen, starts out a veritable paragon of feudal, cultural, Chinese womanhood, she ends by standing for Chinese modernity in ways no other figure possibly could: Manzhen is not born but rather becomes modern, she is not born a woman but becomes the modern nation's woman when she comes to political consciousness.

The novel is a national allegory in a feminist sense. Where it allegorizes, it is interested in demonstrating how, under Chinese family feudalism, gentry women must be counted as a subaltern group along with slaves and bondservants. At the end of the story, the heroine Manzhen advocates transvaluing kin protocols into patriotic sisterhoods.[70] However, *Mother* created in Manzhen a subject of prerevolutionary history who marked a place of precolonial, uncontaminated *Chinese* female subjectivity. The lijiao are the mark of her Chineseness and her authenticity is further attested by her nonheterosexual status. Manzhen is not one half of an internally divided humanity. She is not a sexual Other, nor does she sexually other others, because she has no erotic life at all and is no one man's erotic "plaything" or "slave." Although, arguably, Manzhen others her own slaves within the category of funü itself, for the most part Ding Ling's historical and cultural China de-emphasized the importance that progressive feminism had placed on the eroticized, heterosexualized nuclear couple in order to highlight the future anteriority of the feminist political sisterhood.[71]

In other words, Ding Ling enculturated (i.e., explained what is essentially "Chinese" about Manzhen) and historicized (i.e., explained the ways Manzhen was an agent of History) the literary narrative, and in doing so she associated preheterosexual styles of personhood with Chinese cultural authenticity.[72] Mother consequently renegotiated the conditions available for imagining female actors. In the novel, Ding Ling knit the eugenicist theoretical world of natural selection into a larger logic of historical modes of production. She did not dismiss progressive Chinese feminism; she sublated it into a larger, encompassing theory of historical development. Of course, the mode of production narrative does not necessarily sustain any particular female historical agent. In a general theoretical sense, in fact, Woman is problematic in classical Marxism, unless, that is, special attention gets paid to supplementary assumptions. That is because women (just like men) is a class subject in Marxism and because, practically speaking, there is an apparently irresistible tendency to masculinize class and make men the subject or agents of History by default.[73] When Manzhen takes the oath of revolutionary sisterhood, she demonstrates that oppressed women have in their possession an irrepressibly spontaneous consciousness that, barring actual historical effacement, women can put to use for communitarian, often national, interests. Ding Ling eventually had to confront criticism that her agent of History was actually insulated from the heart of historical change because the writer's class status made it virtually impossible for her to grasp reality. Be that as it may, Mother did offer an alternative to masculinized Chinese modernity and did call into question procedures that had made over modernity and history itself in a masculine mode.

Mother's critical reception is a good way to examine both the narrative structuring of the story and the legitimacy of some of the points I developed above. Recall that Ding Ling insisted that she wrote Mother in response to a visit home and with the desire to expose the "historical process" of change in one Chinese province. Apparently, she thought of the novel as a provincial study, a local color narrative, of the sort, according to Marsten Anderson, that offered an alternative to "critical realism."[74] Contemporary critics did not agree. Quan Ma said that Mother was a bad book about the Republican Revolution, written by a bad writer who had lost control over her narrative and had let nostalgia for her gentry class back-

ground undermine her politics.[75] More sensitive to the feminist implications and thematics, Yang Gang read the story as a saga of Chinese
women's liberation related through the figure of Manzhen, who represented "how our 'previous generation of women' broke through . . . feudal
ideology and power."[76] Though structurally the novel had serious flaws,
Yang argued, the moving descriptions of Manzhen's liberation process (the
scenes of her unbinding her feet, for instance) rescued *Mother* from complete redundancy.

But even Yang Gang could not quarrel with critics of all kinds who
agreed on one point: "The main theme the writer sought to present—the
change in Manzhen's character . . . is not well written."[77] As Ding Ling's
close friend Qian Qianwu explained after her May 1933 disappearance in a
kindly "posthumous" review of the novel, he could accept *Mother*'s focus
on Manzhen and could endorse Ding Ling's desire to write about the
"decline of a large family." But he remained unconvinced that Manzhen
had transformed herself from a "virtuous wife, good mother," the Confucian ideal, into a revolutionary mother and sister.[78] It was not so much that
Ding Ling's colleagues in the League of Left-Wing Writers, like Qian,
disapproved of her project (insofar as they understood it), but rather that
they were perturbed that her wish to write historical narrative did not jibe
with what they saw as an "unconvincing" tale of personal, female, ideological transformation.

In fact, Yang Gang was highly critical of the narrative's alleged failures.
Yang held two key twists of plot responsible for the novel's vacuity: the
epiphany in the garden illustrating Manzhen's new will to live and the
inexplicable though moving passages in which Manzhen confesses her
jealousy of her brothers and of all men and takes her first step toward
personal liberation. Yang felt that Ding Ling relied too heavily on these plot
points to carry the burden of her central theme, personal transformation,
and had not been able therefore to connect questions of identity to objective movements of History outside the world of the cloistered gentry
woman in the inexorable movement toward the 1911 insurrection. Ding
Ling's peculiar way of linking subjective Manzhen and objective History
was baffling, Yang felt. And "since there is relatively little written about
Manzhen's character and her [personality] is placid to the point of lacking
all obstacles," neither the garden scene nor the meditation on inequality
mustered sufficient explanatory force.[79]

It is the case, as Yang and the others pointed out, that as a saga of
Republican revolution *Mother* lacks historical detail, and given Manzhen's
strangely opaque subjectivity, the novel also works badly as a historical
romance. The intellectualized linking of social revolution and women's
liberation is not a sufficiently compelling explanation for Manzhen's re-

markable behavior (liberating her feet, risking her reputation, swearing an oath to serve her country, transgressing conventional expectations of chaste widow behavior). So how should we understand this apparent contradiction? It is possible to read the causes of *Mother*'s alleged failures as a rich fund of knowledge, not so much about women as such, as about how woman operates as a category in a historical narrative. In that regard, the novel suggests an inversion. Rather than, as Quan Ma would have it, "lacking" anything, *Mother*'s narrative actually works positively to prevent something else from occurring. That something else is the foregrounding of a hypostatized feminine personality whose motivation is explained in relation to her natural endowment or her sexual difference from man.

If *Mother* is a prophylactic narrative, how does it work? First, the narrative is explicitly diachronic and implicitly teleological. It presents itself as a bildungsroman, a historical romance about a gentry woman and her friends who are awakened to history and enlightened about the possibilities that history holds out to progressive elites in bourgeois revolution. The story intimates, therefore, that its referent or lodestar is the political events of 1909–1911. Written in the 1930s, of course, the historical saga set at a decisively revolutionary moment suggested that history was continuing to unfold toward the writer's own present and beyond into the reader's future, à la Pasternak's *Dr. Zhivago*. Beyond pressures of censorship, *Mother*'s characterization and plotting also suggested that because they were cloistered, oppressed, and maleducated, elite women, the novel's protagonists could not know either present or future with any clarity. In other words, Ding Ling cloaked historical inevitability with characters who had no way of "knowing" about the imminent 1911 Xinhai Revolution.

*Mother* referred to the past in a second way when it borrowed Ming-Qing narrative conventions to organize and situate female characters. It abounds with references to gardens, and Ding Ling did say at one point that she had used *Dream of the Red Chamber* for her prototype in writing *Mother*. As in older Chinese novels, *Mother*'s action unfolded in the women's quarters and Ding Ling lingered over descriptions of drinking and poetry contests, tracing out the intricate relationships binding the major figures and their families. Kinship ties, the rituals of friendship and social status, and rural propriety are all filtered into the picture of the awakening to political consciousness of a remarkable yet typical Chinese gentry woman.[80] *Mother* thus draws equally on literary European Romanticism and the Ming-Qing pattern of ceaseless recurrence in fictional narrative.[81] For instance, it foregrounds organic time and subordinates characters' time to the revolution of the seasons, going out of its way to attribute emotions to protagonists that seem seasonally "appropriate." A novel in four parts, in each the periodic seasons underwrite both the characters' internal temporality and the chronological, political events that finally and somewhat inexplicably lead to revolution.[82]

But *Mother* was by no stretch of the imagination a "traditional" narrative.[83] Obviously, the bildungsroman-style plot kept the narrative focused on a "traditional" female subject in a way conventional narrativity did not often do. Life education produced new knowledge of self for Manzhen, as she literally learns to live her own life. But Manzhen is a singular subject emerging out of one historical stage into a new one. The plot moves her "from tradition to modernity." At the conclusion, the protagonist is no longer what she began as, a feudal woman. She steps forward out of the colorful, decadent, cruel world of the elite great family and into the lonely struggle of her own solitary road of her singular life. In short, the Sino-bildungsroman gave Ding Ling a way to historicize women. In the process, Ding Ling, a fiction writer, made subjective femininity the effect of objective forces, and thereby presented Manzhen to the reader as an iconic portrait of a general category in Chinese Marxist aesthetics. Because it was historical allegory, the education of Manzhen recapitulated the mode of production narrative's movement from Chinese feudalism to the bourgeois period and the movement of Chinese women from object to agent. Because it was historiography (it represented real History), *Mother* also suggested that because some agents of the revolutionary movement were female, the past should not appear to be exclusively the project of men. But there were other useful effects of this plot strategy. First, when the internal life of protagonists is linked to the seasons, a Ming-Qing trope, or to the historical unfolding of key events in revolutionary history, consciousness is no longer the source of volition or will. Relocating will from individual subjects to objective historical forces suggests that it is unnecessary to dwell on the psychodynamics of sentiment and will. Second, neither Manzhen's inside (vacuous, to be sure, but conscientiously "historical") nor the world outside her self points toward struggles over marriage, social standing, footbinding, women's education, or literary reform.

*Mother* is a history of the allegedly authentic Chinese female subject before the advent of eugenicist progressive feminism. And this is its remarkable achievement. It refuses to analogize revolutionary or national salvation in masculinist terms. But more than that, it reaches back into a feminist tradition of writing that had not yet, looking at this history from Ding Ling's own generational perspective, flowered into eugenicist styles of scientism. The project set out for Manzhen is not free choice of a mate or even the improvement of the race or the contribution that erotic expression potentially offers human development. The ground of the argument, if a novel can ever be said to have just one argument, shifted the matrix from national evolutionary developmentalism and its reworking of the relation of nature and culture to a relatively uncomplicated idea of historical causality.

Manzhen and her revolutionary classmates are historicized in the sense that they are alleged to represent Chinese women's transition from feudalism to bourgeois capitalism. They are cultural specificities because family feudalism is their immediate oppressor. They are national subjects because, as members of the gentry class, they, just like their brothers and husbands, identify their own desires with national salvation. The Manzhen of the early novel is the passive embodiment of literary cliché. The later Manzhen achieves modern self-consciousness, but only as a joint subject or collective embodiment of a historical subject of national womanhood. Over the course of the novel, the contours of a political femininity emerge, though in the absence of personal will and feminine temperament. Chinese women's consciousness is always held to be remediable in this oddly optimistic reworking of Ding Ling's oldest concerns and uneasinesses about female subjecthood. "Women" changes, as History changes it. Funü is an agent but not of a class-woman for itself; Manzhen is an agent in the national historical telos.

For instance, Manzhen's pre-enlightened consciousness reads like bits and pieces of the elite lady's literary cliché grafted onto internalized, elite social restrictions: "Manzhen raised her eyes and looked around. Everywhere she looked joyous colors returned her gaze. It made her feel that she should stop talking about suffering. She had lived in this joyous place for so many years but had never truly known it until now. It was just this sort of ambience that appeared in so many of the ancient poems she had read. . . . She must strip off the gown of the great mistress and take up the garb of the farmer's wife and capable mother. Manzhen straightened her back, looked proudly out into the distance, then back at the house; her meaning was clear: 'All right, I'll show you all!' " (63). Given this strong endorsement of life as "farmer's wife and capable mother," the narrative appears to reverse itself when, paragraphs later, Manzhen leaves her comfortable idyll on the strength of the following transition: "Oh dear, how time has flown. It's been six or seven months, hasn't it? That's how long Mother's been dead" (63).

In plot terms, Manzhen has more reason to stay than leave Lingling Hollow. She has discovered the extent of her property and the labor power of her personal slaves. Her household is threadbare, to be sure, but as a member of the rural gentry class, in residence on the remaining farmland her husband left her, she commands social position and certain conventional protections. As Yaoma, that font of conventional common sense, points out, the most "reasonable" course and the strategy of most repute would be for Manzhen to remain at home on the farm while her son matures. Again, in terms of *Mother*'s foreclosures, the crude way the transition from country wife to grieving urban daughter occurs cannot be attributed to Ding Ling's lack of skill. In "Sophia's Diary," for instance, Ding Ling vividly demonstrated her mastery of foreshadowing and motivation. That story relayed the protagonist's every movement reflexively through Sophia's own consciousness. *Mother*, on the other hand, relates the facts and peremptorily moves the protagonist from location to location. So neither Manzhen's first decision to stay on the farm nor her later, sudden departure finds an internal correlate in her personal qualities. In fact, the novel makes little attempt to explain why, beyond simple happenstance, it is Manzhen who selects revolutionary transformation rather than some other oppressed woman. To suggest a reason would be to imply the preexistence of a hypostatized or generic woman, and this text refuses to admit that possibility. Manzhen wants revolutionary knowledge, not a greater emotional or erotic range. She exchanges one normalized protocol, "virtuous wife, good mother," for another, previously out of reach: "teacher."

*Mother* treats the disadvantaging of women in relation to men at greater length, as contemporary critics recognized. But it also made Manzhen's gender a simple sign of disadvantage rather than a real sexual difference. Manzhen is not constitutionally different from her brother; rather, she represents a privileged element within the category of the oppressed and thus is like tenant farmers of both sexes and family slaves. It is on that basis that Manzhen lays claim to revolutionary subjectivity. But, to phrase my point another way, nothing in the way *Mother* represents women suggests that women have a greater need of liberation than other oppressed peoples. First, women is a heterogeneous category, a point worked out at length below. But second, Manzhen does not have a "female" personality and therefore makes no claims with reference to her ontological status. Absent a deficient female subjectivity, Manzhen's motivation lies outside her "self." Yaoma, *Mother*'s voice of tradition, often reinforces the point that as wife and mother, Manzhen had always met the expectation of feudal society. Quiet, gentle, scholarly, proper in etiquette, unwilling to quarrel, responsible and chaste, Manzhen embarks on life education in large part because the feudal family betrayed her. "She had," the narrative claims, "two children dragging her down, her estate was gone, her husband's brothers had ravaged her like a pack of wolves, and everyone else was sitting back, hands in their pockets, to see what would become of her." Even when modern education changes her, the text accords little space to the quality of those transformations. It simply states that Manzhen "didn't want to go on being the same person she had been before" (28).

Why? "She wanted to forge a road for herself and was willing to ignore the laughter and opposition. She didn't want to be controlled by others any longer" (96).

Interestingly, *Mother* casts subjectivity primarily in kin terms. Or, in the rhetoric of progressive feminist theory, it describes individuals in terms of their "roles." Manzhen is a widow, mother, daughter-in-law, friend, teacher, national sister, but never a centered, sexed, bourgeois subject. She does remap how an individual woman might respond to the demands these roles impose, both in the sense that she embodies them for much of her life and then determinedly slips out of them without disintegrating emotionally. In this regard, *Mother* appears to relocate the site of women's oppression. Rather than male sadism or the sexualized society or even the deficiencies of women per se, the novel has Manzhen state what oppresses Chinese women: "It's the rules of conduct [*guiju*] that are the cause of our [women's] suffering, and with us Chinese, the richer your family is, the harder it is to be a woman" (62). *Mother* repeatedly illustrates how lishu and guiju form the core of feudal oppression of women. Entire episodes of narrative appear to be examples of this point. Digressions like the one below show the long-term effects of convention on women's daily lives:

> Since you have a lot of relatives, a great deal of socializing is required of you. In the space of a single year, there are countless weddings and funerals you must attend. For every social function you host there will be another you must attend in return. And judging how much or how little to send in the constant flow of gifts that is dictated by life in Manzhen's social class is a fine art. If you make a mistake out of a lack of familiarity with the lishu, you become the object of scorn. Of course, if you treat the whole business lightly, you will be off completely from the social life of your peers. No one can live totally apart from others, for there will always come a time when one needs to ask a favor. For example, when Lo Nainai came home for a few days, if they were short of servants and things were a bit too casual, no harm would be done. Lo Nainai herself would never make a point of talking about it, but it was hard to avoid the eyes of the maids and elder servants. . . . There were too many relatives and sisters-in-law, too many women servants, all waiting for a chance to criticize something. Thus, Manzhen's household had their hands full, despite the fact that they had only two guests arriving and both were members of the same family. (154)

Because lishu structures social relations, *Mother* describes a world where women's lives are distinctive because certain opportunities are unjustly and conventionally denied to them. But *Mother* also hints that women and men are essentially similar. The lishu are objectionable not only because convention is unjust, but also because lishu draw the difference between women and men conventionally in the first place. Essential difference is nowhere even on the horizon, and its place has been taken by mere historical habit, what Ding Ling might call the feudal culture. To emphasize this point, Manzhen has a male double, her brother, the successful, vital, revolutionary scholar-official Yu Yunqing. Manzhen not only resembles this brother physically, she is also like him temperamentally and intellectually; only lishu have denied her the education, freedom, and social connections that paved his way to power. "In this society she was not even allowed to meet alone with her aging eldest brother-in-law," Manzhen reflects during her reverie on inequality. "Restrictions were fixed by all the rules of common etiquette. What single individual could break all those restrictions?" (68). Because oppression is the side effect of systematic patriarchy rather than the immediate result of individual male sadism, Manzhen's relations with Yunqing are remarkably friendly. Even when she is negotiating with the avaricious Jiang family she sees how the very formalities that oppress her also protect her against their depredations. "If I do things according to the rules and never breach the lishu," she argues, "I have nothing to fear from them" (49). A large part of Manzhen's heroic stature lies precisely in her equanimity: she does not blame men as a sex for the systematic oppression of Chinese women any more than she blames her own personality or, for that matter, women as a sex.

If feudal lishu are to blame for women's sorry state and if woman as a category is historically mutable, then, Mother's reasoning suggests, the most direct route to equality would be to mobilize women out of confinement and enforced idleness. This suggested political resolution is consistent with Ding Ling's argument in Wei Hu, set in the historical present of the 1930s, that women need work. The mutable, unconscious, prerevolutionary force of women trapped in lishu represented in Mother, at least from the perspective of the future looking back into the alleged immediate past, a useful heterogeneous social category. The category women in Mother is heterogeneous because the text offers not one but many different ways to be female. Examples range from slaves like Yaoma to the capable merchant wife Lo Shuzheng, from powerful older wives to exhausted middle-aged daughters-in-law, eccentric gentry girls, foolish young brides, girls just reaching puberty, ugly and beautiful women, wicked, cruel landladies, competent women, insensitive women, and opium addicts.

Mobilization depends on a pioneer avant-garde. Obviously, Mother did not pull Ding Ling toward a readymade Marxist position on subaltern women and resistance. Ding Ling chose to write about the national revolution, an event the elite had, theoretically speaking, led, a revolution that in any case had not required a subaltern vanguard. When the novel considers the impact of economic class oppression it does not really focus on the suffering of commoner and slave, but on the provincial elite. Yaoma's suffering aside, little challenges Manzhen's claim that rich women suffer more than poor ones. Although Yao is a slave, she is the most prominent spokesperson for upholding lishu and has, unlike passive Manzhen, relatively healthy feet, a strong will, and tremendous authority in her restricted little world. The historical account of Ding Ling's mother's generation of feminists made women's emancipation the subject of Chinese history and Manzhen a part of the cadre of pioneer women who (if Ding Ling had finished writing the trilogy) led the women of China in revolutionary self-emancipation.

The lishu and guiju, moreover, are not internal weaknesses but feudal, ideological, or superstructural elements; if female weakness is primarily historical, it is also mutable. Lishu determines the pattern of social relations and the ranks, degree of servitude, family status, and economic access that conjoin to enliven individual characters. Even the most superficially advantaged, unpleasant gentry woman commands pity because, until the present, History has denied her access to the means of resistance. Third Mistress Yu, Manzhen's sister-in-law and Yunqing's wife, is a particularly good example of this point. Third Mistress is Manzhen's Other in several respects. She is the prototypical "virtuous wife, good mother," whose strong, intelligent children will never want for anything. But her limitations and oppressions are clear when her own husband forbids her to accompany Manzhen to school, arguing that lishu and his own comfort militate against it. Yunqing, who supports education for women as long as it is not his wife, argues that the family loses if she violates the gentry custom of female seclusion. Third Mistress responds bitterly that she, unlike her "unfortunate" sister-in-law Manzhen, or even her own daughter, is fated to spend her "entire life being your household slave" (99). All Third Mistress's clichéd faults, her shrewishness, minor cruelties, mistreatment of inferiors, and pettiness, can be traced to family feudalism, that ugly combination of lishu, high status, and female powerlessness.

Readers pity Third Mistress rather than condemn her because of her bound feet. "Third Mistress Yu," the narrator says, "had suffered a great deal over those feet. That she could very easily lose her reputation if small feet suddenly fell out of fashion remained an unspoken, heartfelt fear with her" (36). Feudalism deformed the woman's feet, yet made feet the marker of her worth. Manzhen the widow, the unmarried girls that she succors, and her new friends, the bizarrely "modern" new female schoolteachers, are all worthless in the eyes of the feudal family. But Third Mistress is not, and in the end she will support lishu because they are part of her body.

Third Mistress's misfortune is to be wealthy and comfortable and consequently under the domain of guiju and lishu. Only the pitiful widow Manzhen is free to reinvent herself as a new woman, an agent, and a national subject (61).[84]

*Mother*'s last chapter is organized around the problem of bringing the political sisterhood into existence so that the sisters and brothers can combat this foreign imperialism and the oppressive feudal government. Initially, the women students just work at their primary task: rehabilitating their feet, athletic drills, calligraphy, and examinations. The female academy is transformative. As they learn geography, they also learn more about imperialism. They read Western science and political theory and find themselves falling under the influence of new literary and educational journals their brothers and husbands are importing from Shanghai. In the end, they conclude that unless they put into practical use what they are learning in school, they and the new womanhood they represent will count for nothing. "If all we do is study," one female student queries the others, "isn't that just another name for writing 'eight-legged essays'?" (158).

After they consider political assassination and armed insurrection, the women finally select Manzhen's more modest proposal that they form a national salvation sisterhood. It is not a conventional kin relation, though the appearance of sodality apparently suggests that we should read these relations as a sign of gentry China's particularist culture. *Mother* actually offers three different styles of sisterhood and suggests that only one is politically progressive. The first illustrates conventional sister relations among educated women. When Manzhen was a girl, she reminisces, her parents encouraged her to form a circle of female friends. They noticed that "when her 'sisters' came over they not only discussed needlework, but talked of novels, played chess and drank wine as well." Nothing came of this relation because once they were married, the obligations of lishu prevented the women from continuing intellectual connections outside the family. Manzhen "often thought about these childhood friends" and even invited them back once, but "they had all changed, and even their cordiality seemed false" (167–68).

Between the hackneyed and ephemeral girlhood literary club and the patriotic sisterhood of women revolutionaries, Ding Ling went to great pains in *Mother* to illustrate another possibility: the sisterhood of conspicuous consumption. Perhaps this grouping, which Du Shuzhen, the merchant wife, organizes for the cloistered elite women, is intended to represent the female side of the bourgeoisie in *Mother*. Du is a rather laudable character. She runs a business, for instance, and is the only woman character in the novel who really grasps how capitalism works. But Du's kind of social proto-feminism is not adequate or equal to the nationalism of the gentry sisters because it ignores national salvation and focuses on drinking, enjoying the gardens and gewgaws that money can buy, and consolidating women within the bourgeois class. Du offers nothing new. The "oath" she suggests as a way of binding the women together is nothing more than a second-rate version of the gentry man's poetry society. The revolutionary sisterhood is essentially different from either elite girls clubs or bourgeois pleasure seeking. It is a vehicle for national salvation and the transvaluation of all conventional notions about women, while at the same time historically loyal to the past and focused on establishing a national female essence. The revolutionary sisterhood binds nationalist women into a collective unit. As Manzhen puts it, she "never imagined that she would entertain her new sisters in that old back garden (the site of her first sisterhood) again. Much less that these new sisters would want to meet not just for talk and laughter, but as a means to unite in common cause as one body, in society and in their every pursuit" (168).

The significance of the oath of sisterhood, a literal rewriting of the relations among enlightened or awakened women, is taken up in great detail in the novel's final chapter. The ceremony takes place in a scholars' garden, abandoned after Manzhen's father's death, which she, now a female scholar, has returned to its former elegance. The swearing takes place in late spring, too late to signify youth, but early enough to connote the fact that the women's decision symbolizes the initiation of a long, historical, revolutionary struggle. There are references galore to the blooming flowers and the female scholars of *Flowers in the Mirror* and to the peach garden oath of national brotherhood in *Romance of the Three Kingdoms*. And always, the story carefully distinguishes between how the new women can draw on available cultural forms (national essence) while stripping the decadent patina of meaningless, conventional, and oppressive lishu.

> Now, in late spring, although some of the flowers were beginning to fade, others had just burst into exuberant bloom, such as the magnolia on the trellis, the peony on the terraced flower bed, the hydrangea quivering like a great snow-white ball, and the tea roses and Chinese roses, which exuded a heavy scent; besides those, purple iris grew along the path beneath the trees. . . . [The women] sat in the room struggling to express their rather ceremonial opinions. The scarlet oath splashed with gold lay on the desk, waiting for the skillful Yu Minzhi, who would fill in the blanks. Third Mistress Yu had also sent over a pair of tall ceremonial candles and a great number of firecrackers to congratulate them, as well as some refreshment. Qiuchan and Lamei [*yatou*, or little slave girls] had bound their plaits with red string. Later, out of respect for the opinions of Manzhen and Xia

Zhenren, they omitted the ritual and just exchanged a simple, common vow that went: "We vow to work together and help each other in the spirit of comradeship. Anyone who does not will be cast aside by Gods and humans. . . ." After placing lit candles and some sandalwood incense on the desk, Yu Minzhi reverently bent over the paper and carefully wrote for two hours. Everyone signed her name and that was the end of it. Since the firecrackers would be wasted if they didn't use them, they set them off in the garden. (169–70)

*Mother* shows prototypical female sisters in revolution who select out elements of received convention, yet avoid both of two possible reductions: self to family position and self to generic sexed subject. Though the novel retains an emphasis on social relations of kinship, it transvalues them in a revolutionary vow to work as one.

Finally, when *Mother* made Manzhen both a widow and a revolutionary sister, it raised the question of a matrilineal family. A revolutionary sister, Manzhen is alone, in the sense of not having a patriline, but not lonely because her very sense of self comes out in her oath to her sisterhood, the band of female scholars, the collectivity Modern Chinese Women, lying beyond the realm of patrilineal convention. As the novel ends, Manzhen concludes that "there really was no place she could call her jia. She was a person without a jia. Wherever her children were, that was her jia" (185). Privileging the band of sisters over the patrilineal family, *Mother* even hints at the existence of a matrilineal family, a mother-centered jia.[85] As we have seen, Ding Ling often returned to rework her own apparently endlessly flexible personality in a string of retroactive autobiographies or autobiographic portraits. Like *Wei Hu*, *Mother* includes an explicit Ding Ling proxy, the child Xiao Han. *Mother* probably also conflates the events of Ding Ling's own recent past at the time she wrote the novel, with the imaginary life history of her own, more politically correct mother. The author appears in this narrative as a version of her own mother, in other words, as well as her infant self, and, by implication, as the devoutly filial receptor of prescient revolutionary wisdom. The novel is genealogical in the more pejorative sense of being a mystification, a stable place for starting over in the endless explanation of who I am or what is my self and femininity. It seeks to reestablish a new public biography in an earlier, less ambiguous time. This strategy distanced Ding Ling from the modern girl psychology and framed her concerns in a familiar sentimental tribute to a suitable object of desire: the parent.[86]

Parallels between Ding Ling's immediate experience and the way she represented Manzhen in *Mother* are obvious. Both women had just been widowed, each immediately after producing an infant boy in the dead of winter. Each loves her newborn but must reckon with the inconvenience he imposes. Ding Ling's accounts of the new revolutionary disciplinary routine she developed after Hu Yepin's death—to get out of bed immediately on waking, work long hours, bathe in ice water—are echoed in her portrait of Manzhen's agony as she bathes her newly unbound feet after having risen at dawn to study (112, 135). Perhaps this conflation of mother and daughter meant Ding Ling could distance herself further from an increasingly (in the eyes of the CCP) unsavory past. Manzhen had, in actual fact, sided with the communists over the anarchists. The novel also suggests that Ding Ling had grown up in a politically nurturing environment, where the political sisters, including Xiang Jingyu, had given her a rich, collective, proto-communist female education.

Xiao Han plays a relatively insignificant role in plot terms, but her appearance intensifies the novel's complexity. Because she is always the perfect daughter, Xiao Han infuses the story with a lingering sense of prelapsarian romance. She loves her mother unconditionally. Manzhen "loves her Xiao Han because she pities her" (90). The likely fate of the orphaned daughter is the marriage market, even concubinage, and that contributes to Manzhen's decision to seek schooling. Manzhen takes the little girl to school with her each day so that at least she will grow up educated. Even though Manzhen periodically forgets all about her daughter, she has Xiao Han's needs in mind, and Manzhen's intentions at least are above suspicion. And even though Xia Zhenren suspects Manzhen of preferring the son and slighting the daughter, Manzhen gets off with just a mild criticism and the suggestion "Xiao Han is so adorable. Elder sister Manzhen, we must educate her well. You must not favor the boy over the girl" (162).

Less expected, *Mother* seems concerned to strike up a quasi-sororal relation between the characters of mother and daughter. Periodically the narrative reviews why Manzhen's classmates all adore Xiao Han: her intelligence, devastating cuteness, winsome playfulness, sensitivity, independence, charming nature, and so on. (Beginning with *Wei Hu*, the temptation to romanticize her alleged previous selves as a way of heightening her own attractiveness apparently became increasingly difficult for Ding Ling to resist.) Xiao Han spends her time with her mother's sisters and fits effortlessly into the world of the revolutionary sisterhood. In fact, as the women draw up their plans for the flower garden oath, Xia Zhenren—the portrait of Xiang Jingyu—turns to Xiao Han and, with generous excitement, says, "You join us, too" (166). *Mother* allowed Ding Ling to make herself into her own mother's sister.[87]

The question of women haunts colonial modernity as this formation effloresced in China during the interwar years of the 1920s and 1930s. When, through the vivid feminist writing of Ding Ling, we look into the question Dai Jinhua raised sixty years later, "What sort of freedom?" for new women and we read the texts through enlightened feminism, its modernist sexual codes, and representational strategies, what becomes evident is the stubbornness of the feminine impasse. In the decision young Ding Ling made to commit herself to the communist movement there is that gamble, characteristic of Ding Ling and many others. It is a gamble on a future that has not yet precluded what women will become. It seems clear that many of the problems posed in colonial modernist literary practice and feminist progressive theory were not superseded or even truly abandoned. But that impression crystallizes when time is not a transition and the moment is blasted out of the flow and stabilized in the future anterior tense of a singular world in play. Ding Ling never learned better. The present impasse always led her to a future gamble. Other core problematics might shift, but the enlightenment project of women's emancipation remained intact; only its subject changed. In the years that followed her incarceration, the internal subject of women in Chinese feminism was reconsidered and Ding Ling again forwarded her claim to freedom in a new way, in Maoist nationalism and the subject of funü.

## 5  Woman under Maoist Nationalism in the Thought of Ding Ling

Oh, Party! Mother! I've come back. DING LING (1978), cited in Song Jianyuan, *Ding Ling Pingzhuan* (Critical biography of Ding Ling)

My most heartfelt words of thanks are to the Party. Without the comrades of the Central Committee I would not even have a today, the right to speak from this platform, or the right to compose essays. . . . I [also] want to thank the Party for my long education, which gave me the will to continue to endure [*yili duguo*] this endless twenty-year period. DING LING (1979), "Jiang yidian xinli hua" (Some words from the heart)

Sexual love [*lian'ai*] is fire. Fire is not something that can be played with casually. DING LING (1980), "Lian'ai yü wenyi chuangzo" (Love and artistic creation)

Feng Xuefeng was perhaps the first to note Ding Ling's talent for advancing ideas while altering them.[1] In the previous chapter I highlighted Ding Ling's early fiction, which favored stories about a woman writer critically reconsidering the analytic subject women in a historical frame I called colonial modernity. This chapter illustrates how, in an episteme of revolutionary modernity, Ding Ling's writing embraced while calling into question the national subject of Chinese Communist Party feminism. Funü took shape in an ideolect or ideological dialect of Chinese Marxism, and harbors complex historical debts to internationalized theory streams that flow from Bebel, Marx, and Engels, USSR internationalists like Lenin, Clara Zetkin, and Stalin, and May Fourth figures like Xiang Jingyu, Mao Zedong, and Luo Qiong.

The revolutionary modernist subject funü is not primarily a linguistic event. Funü, a category of state mobilization and normative class liberation, was embedded in a semiotic system that explicitly linked theory and practice. This raises four points that are woven through the chapter's exposition. First, Chinese feminist preoccupations are central to modernity however it is defined. In Ding Ling's literary centering of the women problem during key decades of the Republican era (1911–1949), colonial modernity, and well into the apotheosis of revolutionary modernity, the anxiety that women is always more than the representational order could accommodate set off bitter debates at irregular intervals. In the late 1920s, the early 1940s, and again in the 1980s, Ding Ling drew the subject women into crisis.[2] Second, when feminist problematics merged into Communist Party social planning schemes during the era of New Democracy, the signifiers for women in Party ideology became, in addition, real descriptors in mobilization policies.[3] Communist Party policy terms are ideological in the contemporary, cultural studies, or Althusserian sense, as well as the Maoist sense where discrete historical eras are believed to possess exemplary, typical, or normative characters (renwu). Third, while statist categories like Maoist funü rested on specific political practices that include and disclude constituencies (particularly in legislation bearing on land reform and class status assignments, for instance, or political citizenship itself in the case of rightists), other, heterogeneous possibilities persisted. These unfolded in counterhegemonic and disenfranchised spaces, or in unincorporated areas that lay beyond the machinery of state.[4] Fourth, woman in the communist state matrix was a normative entity defined in communitarian social practice. Progressive, eugenicist feminism with its concern to understand women as individual sexual agents in a struggle for social standing (ren'ge) gave way in Maoism to two key concerns: When does a historical moment become a typicality requiring a new political truth (e.g., when is May Fourth antifeudalism anachronistic and what should replace it)? and What is the inherent human potential of the true daughters of China (i.e., the masses of underrepresented, often brutalized and starving laboring women) that a Communist Party agent can reflect back to the collectivity of funü, legitimating while confirming the Party's political authority?[5]

In late 1941 and early 1942, CCP Marxists transformed Maoist ideas into a Party line. Gregor Benton was the first to note the degree to which the publication campaign Ding Ling approved for the Party's official newspaper, Liberation Daily, was a "Maoist" phenomenon, in the sense of forming a "united front with Mao against the bureaucracy."[6] Most scholars credit her "mini hundred flowers campaign" with instigating the cultural rectification and Mao Zedong's summary statement of Party cultural policy, the canonical "Talks at the Yan'an Forum on Art and Literature." The Yan'an Rectification, a political performance of differences and the reconciliation of differences among the revolutionary elite, is a significant crossroads for intellectual and political history. Its implications far outstrip the points I raise here about its stakes for feminists. But the fact remains that Ding Ling did authorize public discussion of questions about sexual politics when she raised questions about the relation of writing to the mass line. In other words, even as women were interpolated into the new Maoist representational order in terms of their labor value, value to the state, capacity for enlightenment, and so on, the question of sexual norms remained problematic.

Most of this discussion of the Yan'an Rectification pertains to woman policy. However, Ding Ling played a role in precipitating another debate over culture during that crucial event. Besides policy on women's labor touches on problems of representation, I also include several points here that are central to my understanding of Yan'an Maoism. The 1942 Rectification established the primacy of Mao Zedong Thought on cultural expression in the arts. Collaterally, this ratification of Mao's thought on culture instigated the creation of a group of cultural workers whom Ellen Judd calls ideological intellectuals. She means those among the "entire social category" of the intelligentsia who were specially tasked with "shaping the dominant lines of a culture and its consequent importance for ideological and organizational work in a revolutionary movement."[7] Ding Ling was a central figure in the carving out and charging of this group and can therefore be termed a collaborator in the Maoist institutionalization of culture.

The institutionalization of this new revolutionary culture and its ideological intellectuals occurred in a specific framework. The Chinese Literary and Artistic Association (Zhongguo wenyi xiehui) and the Shaanxi-Gansu-Ningxia Border Region Cultural Association (Shan-Gan-Ning bianqu wenhua xiehui), also known as the Literary Association (Wen Xie), which Ding Ling founded in 1936 and 1938, respectively, formed the institutional backbone. But I also include as institutions the communist university system, the Lu Xun Academy of Art, literary salons, Sunday schools, publications like *Xingqi wenxue yuan* (Weekly literary garden), which Ding Ling cofounded, and a number of informal poetry workshops.[8] Formal Party Rectification or thought reshaping sought to discipline what by 1942 was a mushrooming cultural bureaucracy. Ding Ling, Ai Qing, Lo Feng, and Wang Shiwei most probably initiated their high-profile literary debate over censorship with Mao's support and in the context of a creeping bureaucratization of the Party arts.[9]

The most convincing explanation for why Mao then abruptly turned against his own lieutenant in this strategy, Wang Shiwei, appears in an interview of Wang Ruowang that Kyna Rubin published in 1981. Wang Ruowang told Rubin that Mao had always supported critical publications like *Qing qi dui* (the *Light Calvary* broadside), the venue that preceded Ding Ling's literature column in *Liberation Daily*. According to Wang Ruowang, Mao also supported Ding Ling's call to use critical essays (*zawen*) in the Communist Party's newspaper, until, that is, Wang Shiwei's "Yebai hehua"

(Wild lily,) criticizing the "dark spots" in communist social and political life, resurfaced in a hostile Xi'an Guomindang newspaper. That and the fact that Wang Shiwei's refusal to offer self-criticism or to embrace the new policy of minimizing social problems led to his being scapegoated and, during the evacuation of Yan'an, summarily executed.[10]

The political faction that Ding Ling headed in 1942 consisted of writers affiliated loosely with the All-China Writer's Resistance Association, or the Wenkang. Zhou Yang spoke for writers at the Lu Xun Academy, or what is called in Yan'an studies the Luyi group. Although the two groups concurred on many specifics, the Luyi group appears to have eventually moved toward a principled emphasis on "praising brightness," whereas Wenkang placed relatively more emphasis on "exposing darkness." Of course, because Party Rectification itself rested on both exposing and praising, and because both tendencies are visible in most of the study documents disseminated under the names of Liu Shaoqi and Mao Zedong, the theoretical emphases themselves are unremarkable. If anything, Ding Ling seemed most preoccupied with the Maoist doctrine of the unity of theory and practice and its adjunct literary policy that representation should be rooted in personal experience.[11] Ding Ling, however, had been appointed to edit page 4 of *Liberation Daily* in May 1941. Whether or not she had the unqualified support of Mao Zedong and Chen Boda, as she seemed to think, Ding Ling did control access to the paper and she solicited manuscripts encouraging Party members to publicly voice criticism.[12] On 9 March 1942 she published her own "Thoughts on March 8." The essay spoke directly to the question of the women category in theory and praxis and vigorously contested the idea that women best served the Party when they contributed their domestic and sexual labor to it.

Party disciplinary action began in early April at Luyi, at the Government College, in the theater world, and at the *Liberation Daily* offices.[13] In early June Ding Ling's previously well-received story "Zai yiyuan zhong" (In the Hospital) was prejudicially rereviewed, and she faced a number of hostile charges. They included oversimplification, identifying herself with a bourgeois female protagonist, and misusing literary realism in a way harmful to educated youth.[14] A week later, she apparently reconciled with the emerging dominant group. Not only career bureaucrat and literary critic Zhou Yang, Ding Ling's bête noir in later years, but writer-administrator Ho Qifang, the mercurial novelist Xiao Jun, and many other old comrades were on the other side. Ding Ling chaired an abortive struggle session against Wang Shiwei and then resigned her editorial post at the Party paper.[15] Almost by rhetorical sleight of hand, Mao Zedong's "Talks at the Yan'an Forum" then caused many of the admittedly legitimate issues that ideological intellectuals and writers were raising to virtually disappear into broader problems. They dissolved into the core concerns of Mao Zedong Thought, which, besides cultural ideology and art, included national defense, political economy, and questions relating to governmentality and military authority. The state, in other words, had disarmed the cultural critique and incorporated problematics of literary representation into problematics of political representation.

After these traumatic events, Ding Ling reapplied herself to questions of literary-political representation in the parameters that Mao (and, as a Maoist, arguably Ding Ling herself) had established at the Forum. By the mid-1940s she was pioneering yet another battery of literary techniques for producing texts that accurately forwarded the needs of the Maoist nation. Certainly her own responsibility as a writer and her ideology encouraged the perceived need to represent the *as yet unrepresented* poor. But even then, she did not have an answer to the question of how women should be handled categorically in Maoist literary or political texts. I leave for later in this discussion the question of literary representation and concentrate for a moment on the role Ding Ling played in shaping women as a foundational category of Maoist socialist modernity in the communist discourse of woman in development.

Between 1934 and 1986 Ding Ling drew on the immediate conditions of her life to project a future for women even when her own future seemed hopeless. In 1958 her considerable powers as a culture broker were curtailed as she was charged and convicted of political crimes. Her sentence was banishment into the gulag or state economic sector of the Great Northern Wasteland (Beidahuang), where her husband, Chen Ming, joined her on a labor farm. For twenty years she remained a political prisoner. She lived under a loose regime in the first years and then, during the Cultural Revolution which erupted in 1966, as a convict, often in solitary confinement. As the Cultural Revolution wound down in the late 1970s, negotiations began that would eventually bring her back to Beijing and write her case back into Party history. When I met her in 1982 at a beachside hotel in Beidaihe, she had recovered the life that her achievements, her loyalty, and her history of wrongful persecution entitled her to have. In 1984, when she died, she had been cleared of all political crimes except for the Feng Da matter and the unclarity surrounding the charge that she had betrayed the communists to the nationalists in exchange for her life.

## The Subject Funü in Maoist Nationalism

The late 1930s are noteworthy because they began a long-term shift in Ding Ling's normative subject and in the future that her narratives projected. Increasingly she painted a future where the liberated communist subject

Women would no longer require critical or political special attention.[16] U.S., Japanese, and European historiography on this shift used to assume that Marxism in China and Maoism were ideologically incompatible with what critics termed Western or bourgeois feminism in the 1940s. Christina K. Gilmartin has demonstrated that, on the contrary, Party formation in the 1920s and after never clearly distinguished Marxist women's policy from progressive feminist theory, because most cultural revolutionaries had always been both.[17] Naihua Zhang has confirmed that for the post-1949 era, the institutionalization of the Chinese women's liberation movement under the Chinese communist state sublated the feminist heritage into its political policies.[18] Ho Kuo Cheng, who presciently argued as early as the 1970s that the issue was never Communist Party hostility toward the women's question, has been proven more right than wrong.[19] War exigencies restricted what the Communists could do for village women during the anti-Japanese struggle beyond legitimating their citizenship claims on the Border Government. In other words, although women's liberation has an episodic intellectual history, post-Mao women's liberation theory is unthinkable in the abstract of the communist tradition of feminism. Ding Ling is a central figure in this Communist tradition because the catachresis woman in communist Chinese feminism is so obviously consolidated in her literature and political philosophy.[20]

Du Wanxiang: Ren'ge Redefined. In 1980, after the 1958 verdict was reversed, Ding Ling began discussing her short story, "Du Wanxiang." The story is a parable of the Chinese Communist Party's claims to political legitimacy. A quiet, prosaic, dirt-poor young peasant bride comes to the Great Northern Waste with her husband, a tractor driver. In the most harsh environment conceivable—poverty, illiteracy, punishing weather, cultural deficiency, military discipline, her civil status as a "dependent," and the kindly patriarchal chauvinism of family and government officials—Du Wanxiang comes, through good works and self-help, to embody everything that is good about the CCP. This was unmistakably Ding Ling's voice. A strange mix of sentimentality and understated criticism, the narrative insinuated that while the Central Committee might have forgotten that its claim to legitimate power rested on the ethical agency of subordinated nonentities like Du Wanxiang, Du (and Ding Ling) had not forgotten. In the immediate years after the catastrophe of the Great Proletarian Cultural Revolution this was not a risk-free position to take.

In "About 'Du Wanxiang': A Talk at the Face-to-Face Meeting with Readers Organized by the Beijing Library," Ding Ling made a significant claim. When I wrote about the emotions Du Wanxiang had for the Great Northern Wastes, she said, "I was actually also writing about my own emotions, emotions that all people of the Great Northern Wastes have. In the end I could not write enough, but had I not had exactly the same emotions [as she] I could never have written about the emotions of Du Wanxiang."[21] This was an exact reversal of the distance Ding Ling had insisted characterized her as the author of literary writing and the subjects represented in her fiction during the late 1920s and early 1930s. More significant, it was also a statement that her years of forced proletarianization had earned her subaltern status; her feelings could no longer be distinguished from the feelings of the subjects among whom she had been condemned to live. The story Ding Ling told at the library event in 1980 was that Du Wanxiang was actually a real person, a model woman soldier on the state farm where Ding Ling had lived. The unit leaders introduced them. Du, a women's work cadre, was to learn about culture and political theory from Comrade Ding, while Ding Ling should study Du in order to restructure her own not-yet-proletarian consciousness. In any case, they had become friends and worked together to raise the local farm women's cultural level. Ding Ling had not consciously considered Du a literary subject. Still, she had learned what she could about Du's history and work, particularly what made her a normative or model woman soldier. When the Great Proletarian Cultural Revolution broke out, Du was punished for associating with the Big Rightist Ding Ling and Ding Ling put to good use some lessons of her own she learned from Du. When the Rebel Red Guard humiliated or enraged her, Ding Ling thought about the normative, quiet heroism of her friend Du Wanxiang to pull her through. So close was this identification that when Ding Ling recovered her political right to self-expression she wrote about herself through the subjectivity of Du, the ren'ge of a fully realized, proletarianized, daughter of China.

The stake here is what Ding Ling claimed she learned in this relationship. She had never had any difficulty, she wrote in another of her postimprisonment essays, writing about the weaknesses of women.[22] In the case of the model worker, however, what she confronted was an example of women's strength enduring unendurable injustice. What were these strengths of Du Wanxiang? An ability to bear hardship uncomplaining, adapting, but also never complying fully with unjust demands. Self-awareness, even in conditions of extreme poverty and deprivation. The drive to excel in one's work, yet never at the expense of others and always in the service of other citizens or society as a whole. A seasoned response to humiliation, which sought to alleviate the causes of torment rather than to react against it. The stubborn drive to speak her truth beyond the representations of others while at the same time showing what is most truthful about the majority experience of revolutionary transformation. While the fictional Du serves the people as herself, as a bride, a daughter-in-law, a mother, and a dependent, her normativity is the effect of her ordinary goodness.

The long quotation below shows allegorically the power that Ding Ling was assigning to ordinary goodness. To get a sense of this reversal and the distance Ding Ling had traveled, it is useful to recall that other parable, of the "Wait Patiently" bird in "Summer Break," that she developed to showcase the deficiencies of nüxing:

> They had cast off their traditional consciousness and with unbounded fervor and full hearts, had established a modernized socialist agricultural base, tempering themselves to become new model workers of the highest moral qualities. They had produced great wealth and created a new proletarian culture. Although these were China's border regions, they were still linked tightly to the heart of the nation. . . . [Du Wanxiang's] speech helped them see, hear, and feel things they had never seen or heard or been moved by before. It was as if she had transformed these ordinary things and made them suddenly more significant. Du Wanxiang had not recited the classics like a pedant. The maxims and wisdom of those classical [Maoist] works were diffused throughout her simple speech. Just as crops absorb sunlight, rain, and dew, good people, good works, and good precepts had slowly saturated her very soul, worked into her blood, and made her a living thing deeply rooted, with abundant foliage, able to resist all contagion. Du Wanxiang did not have a lofty, bigger-than-life spirit. She was simple and affectionate. No matter how much people looked up to her and were guided by her, in the end she remained the same amiable, straightforward, simple and honest, modest, incandescently fervent Du Wanxiang so comfortably familiar to all of them.
>
> The Party secretary walked over and grasped her hand tightly. "Comrade Wanxiang," he said with joyous sincerity, "you've taught us a wonderful lesson. I want to thank you on behalf of all of us from the bottom of my heart."[23]

A strange story, set on the eve of the outbreak of the Cultural Revolution, shows a normative woman modeling for an audience of her peers the very oridinariness of the people's goodness and their good longing for development. This, Ding Ling said in her memoir of the "real" Du Wanxiang, was what she thought about when Rebel Red Guard students forced her to clean their latrines. In Du's spirit Ding Ling complied with Red Guard demands, while at the same time refusing to accept their view that she and they were enemies.

The parable of Du Wanxiang holds out the possibility that ren'ge for even the most dependent of all women—a motherless child in the case of Du, the Big Rightist and anti-Party element in Ding Ling's case—is always possible. A major shift of focus is that in the parable ren'ge is necessarily a communitarian achievement. Normative ren'ge for Du is achieved when the entire community is mobilized toward a future of Enlightenment. This was certainly the conclusion Communist theory and practice reached during the anti-Japanese war, and it rings through a 1947 policy statement Chen Boda, then Mao Zedong's secretary and chief intellectual interpreter, made on the combat view of women's liberation. "The so-called combat view of life," he wrote, "implies that women must eliminate all such slavery traditions as compliance, cringing, and to bow and submit in order to please a few persons, and that they must be independent, self-respect [sic] and self-confident, unyielding, highly spirited, and opposed to every injustice—national oppression, social oppression, and family oppression." Ding Ling's own lessons from Du cast a peculiarly ironic light on the "combat view" of women's liberation. "Previously, the endurance of oppression was the virtue of women," Chen continued. "Now, the reverse is true: to resist oppression is the virtue of women. Previously, women's duty was to live a dependent life. Now the reverse is true: their duty is to lead an independent life. All this means those women must stand straight up. They can not only speak and walk loudly but also lift up their fists and shoulder rifles to pursue whatever task which, in their opinion, is rational. *In other words, women ought to stand straight up, secure their individuality, manage an independent living, not to be the slaves of their parents-in-law and husbands, and to oppose every system and form of prostitution.* . . . The main theme is to fight: to fight alongside all those oppressed men."[24] Thirty years of this sort of rhetorical mobilization refracts through that ironic postrevolutionary moment in which Ding Ling rewrites the real Party history through the figure of Du Wanxiang. In Ding Ling's parable of the communitarian struggle of woman to establish ren'ge, it is the risk of socialized labor, the opportunity to be mobilized outside even the most loving feudal family, the chance to become literate, and finally, the opportunity to lead others through one's own example that transforms Du from dependency to independency.

How Ding Ling arrived at this position must be explained. By the 1980s she had been a Party writer for fifty years. Of course, like most powerful, senior cultural revolutionaries, she had proved to be vulnerable. But as she herself pointed out from time to time, it is not appropriate to minimize her powers because representing the people is a form of discursive domination.[25] All communist writers participated in the extension of revolutionary citizenship to disenfranchised peoples by rearticulating the state's order in political allegories, narratives, dramatic performances, literary criticism, and outright guidebooks about allowable norms, behaviors, and techniques of personal transformation. A good example is her 1951 publication *Kua dao xin de shidai lai* (Stride into the new age).[26] Her first collection of zawen (critical essays), the volume included well-known essays such as "Cong qunzhong zhong lai, dao qunzhong qu," (From the masses, to the masses) in which Ding Ling, a confident Maoist functionary, offers her official view on the need to plan for the cultivation of the new generation of vernacular or proletarian writers. The essay exudes the benevolence of an empowered elite writer instructing art workers and readers about "appropriate" experience and voicing positive enthusiasm about a future when the masses will produce writers who can represent themselves.

Ranking officials in the regime's new cultural bureaucracy in the 1950s had the authority and no doubt the responsibility to express themselves formulaically on a range of topics. In the essay "Tan 'laolao shishi'" (Speaking on "honesty") she argues that the old society scorned and condemned honesty as a civil virtue. In the new society "there is only one road to serving the people and that is honesty."[27] Excusing herself as "not an expert in this area," she parceled out advice on romance, arguing (in a line she held for many years) that love is a progressive emotion, so in the new society romance should be openly considered and never confined to the hidden world of personal fantasy. In a calm, authoritative tone she disposed of questions she said young people were posing: "Does love interfere with study?" (A little, but not as much as repression does.) "Should you get married before you graduate?" (A silly question because marriage is a matter between the two people involved.) "Should courtship be long or short?" (Women tend to prefer long courtship because they had such a bad experience in the Old Society with forced marriages, but that is a matter best left to individuals.) "Is love just something that makes life less boring?" (Ridiculous idea.) "Who should lead, the man or the woman?" (Neither and both, but generally women tend to lag a bit behind because society still honors the old feudal notion of respecting the man and despising the woman.) "How do you find a partner?" (Broaden your contacts, as young people in the Soviet Union have done, but never consider using a go-between!)[28]

Of course, her authority derived from her willingness to perform the role of petit bourgeois intellectual-in-transformation. Many of the essays address the question of how elites can enter pleb life and truly experience the "people's emotions."[29] In "Zhishifenzi xianxiang zhong de wenti" (Problems of intellectuals going down), for instance, she shares her personal experience of the problems intellectuals encountered in poor villages: the everyday harshness of life, the effort required to translate theory to practice and mobility reforms in the lives of the people, the struggle to disrupt the intellectual's habit of moodiness.[30] But there is a characteristic way that

Ding Ling made public use of her "private" life in writing, as she did, for instance, in the afterword to her collection *Shaanbei fengguang* (Scenes of Shaanbei). The afterword begins by acknowledging her errors in 1942 and explains how missteps actually lead revolutionaries out of their ignorance and into understanding, from impressionistic emotionalism to Marxist theory and from insecurity to a secure sense of knowing the truth. The heart of the narrative is her studied confession that "some people are born revolutionaries" and others, like herself, have to get there slowly, step by step, becoming revolutionary with difficulty and earnest effort. In other words, Ding Ling's standing as a writer or engineer of the soul had become bound up with her ethical standing but only in relation to the new civil order and civil subjects' struggle that doctrine and revolutionary mobilization mustered.[31]

Ethical political authority gave Ding Ling leeway to reflect on the ways that in a mobilized rural society female ren'ge might eventually express itself. She was writing a lot about this question in the late 1940s and early 1950s as she began her big project of writing a Maoist novel that would narrate the entire significance of land reform (I return to this novel, *The Sun Shines over the Sanggan River*, in a moment). However, in two preparatory *sanwen* (descriptive essays), she specifically focused on this question of what to narrate about the standing of women characters in the new society. The first sanwen dealt with a normative Maoist new woman or *funü*, Guo Jinqing, who became a military hero while impersonating a man. The tale of Guo was remarkable, Ding Ling wrote, and that made it easier to narrate, but the novelty of cross-dressing was not the story's essence. The real story was Guo's "particular strength of will." At first, she just wanted to avenge her father, but eventually she learned to transform personal grievance into a desire for class vengeance, and that was what motivated her to suffer and fight like a man in the company of men. Moreover, in battle and even under the most grueling of conditions, Guo fulfilled her responsibilities to the Party. "In this way she emerged victorious over her environment," able to endure more even than the men around her. What is instructive about Guo Jinqing is "her courage, her fearlessness, her stubbornness and her impressive manner."[32] However unfortunate or sad this masquerade was, Guo's will and endurance are what justify Ding Ling's decision to write about her, to elect her into the circle of heroes of the Revolution.

The second essay is a highly coded or ideological story about a central relationship in Ding Ling's project, which is the fraught relationship of a female author and her subject, a categorical woman. "Yong yuan huo zai women de xin zhong: guan yu Chen Man de jizai" (A person who will live forever in our heart: record of Chen Man) considered a real character who was the seeming polar opposite of Guo Jingqing, Chen Man, an impoverished, self-representing, revolutionary funü without any particular élan at all. The piece stages an encounter rather similar in many ways to Ding Ling's 1941 short story "When I Was in Xia Village," which caused great controversies in 1942 and then again at her show trial in 1958, when it was used as evidence of crimes against the Party. "Chen Man" tells the story of a female cadre-writer and a peasant woman who meet in Song Village, where the writer is part of a land reform work team. The team spends its first days searching for so-called active elements among the oppressed poor peasants, who must, according to the policies or theory of land reform, form the base of the violent seizure of landlord property. Nothing much happens until an intense older woman challenges the silent village men and is elected for a moment to chair the organizational small group. Yet this woman, Chen Man, cannot herself believe that it is appropriate for a woman to head a group of men. The narrator assures her that it is but finds out later that a man has replaced Chen. Fallaciously, a consensus replaces her on the grounds that Chen is not a native of the village.

The narrator investigates. She finds that Chen does have a questionable, controversial reputation. It stems from several things. First, Chen had drifted to Song Village only to move in with an old man, Li Laodong. Particularly since the arrival of the land reform work team, Chen endured constant abuse from her common law husband, who shelters her only to exploit her labor. Other villagers also abuse her, calling her a whore and hitting her primarily because her late first husband had been a female impersonator in an itinerant opera troupe. The story's narration draws several points out of this situation. The arrival of the communist government work team actually jeopardizes Chen because with their ideological support she has become a real person and demands personal standing in the hostile community of the oppressed. The old man is murderous because she will no longer serve him. And she has promised to tell all the village secrets to the land reform team, which will multiply the numbers of her enemies.

The story's second important conclusion regards how the female narrator thinks about the mind of the other woman. When rumors initially circulate that Chen has fallen ill, the narrator decides it would not serve the interests of the organization to visit the old woman. But the narrator cannot help thinking about the older woman's situation, and so several days later she decides to pay a call, only to meet the widow halfway as Chen is making her way toward the narrator's temporary quarters. It turns out that Chen has fallen ill from thinking. She has decided to break with the oppressors and open up the wedge the cadres need to puncture the complex web of oppression holding feudal village relations in place. What Chen discovers, what brings her over to the side of the Revolution, is her own spontaneous insight that "your mind is the mind of Chairman Mao, and Chairman Mao's mind is a mind that's for all of us." The narrator reacts in astonishment at that explosive creativity of the oppressed, beaten outcast who transforms herself into a mobilized, politicized female activist. For her part, Chen seeks out the narrator because Chen can neither read nor write. And so she sings her ideas and the narrator promises to "write them down for you and send them to Chairman Mao."[33]

In the end, Ding Ling embraced this peculiar revolutionary subject funü at the same time that she treated its deficiencies critically. She was both advocate and critic of state policies on women. The questions she raised for public discussion in "Thoughts on March 8 (Women's Day)" about categories and subjects of women never disappeared from her fiction, even in her National Defense literature of the late 1930s or social realism of the late 1940s.[34] Similar concerns about subjectivity and Chinese womanhood recur in the stories, essays, reportage, and travel diaries she published between 1980 and her death.[35]

*The Context of Normative Womanhood and Yan'an New Democracy.* Ding Ling's national defense literature suspends its agents between the domain of the family (jia) and the domain of the nation state (guo) in the context of what David Holm argues was a discourse of Maoist cultural nationalism. In this framework, she posed the problem constantly of how praxis or political work liberates the obscured powers of the oppressed. This included the powers of women as a collectivity, so her National Defense stories fictionalized Party policy and merged the impoverished women into the heterogeneous subaltern subject of "the people." This constituted both a gain and a loss in later calculations because, while it downplayed the singular qualities of suffering that are specific to women as a collectivity, it also granted to women social standing of their own, female ren'ge.

In almost all of Ding Ling's stories in the 1930s the prerequisite to personal empowerment had been either that a political agent exist outside the control of a conventional patriarchal family, or that she endure some sort of personal violation. To remake her fiction to the specifications of National Defense literature, Ding Ling had to heighten themes that had already played a role in earlier stories. One of her first efforts after arriving in Yan'an was "Yi ke wei chu tan de qiangdan" (The unfired bullet) and it became her best known war sketch of all time.[36] Enormously popular it may have been, but the influential "Bullet" and "Dongcun shijian" (The affair in East Village) also seemed to sharpen her literary vision of the revolutionary socius or human society in mobilization. In Ding Ling's National Defense stories, all people, but particularly the weak, female, immature, and helpless, initiate forms of praxis to defend the nation. The trade-off is that their loyalty to nation makes them superhumanly powerful political agents.[37]

"The Unfired Bullet" is an indescribably simple-minded short melodrama about a "little devil" (xiaogui) or war orphan, whose adopted Red Army unit (duiwu) accidentally abandons him in a poor village where he takes refuge with an old widow. Good boy that he is, the child is fond of the village granny, but wants more than anything to rejoin his comrades because "he is used to [his unit] and only that kind of life can nurture [yanghuo] him." He is not a feral boy, for he does have a military-political unit to return to. One day, a pillaging band of White bandit soldiers captures him. A moment from death, he announces quietly to their leader, "Commander! Save the bullet! Save it for fighting the Japanese. You can use your knife to kill me instead!" (26–27). Such astounding patriotism and courage in one so tiny stops the commander in his tracks. He reconsiders not only the murder he is about to commit, but the fact that his victim is a fellow Chinese rather than a Japanese enemy, and he ends up joining the little devil. With the boy's help, the bandit chief recruits his own gangsters into the Red Army.

One of the sources of the little boy's power is the fact that he is an orphan and therefore not beholden to any selfish, individualistic, paternal authority.[38] The duiwu disciplines him, and in a peculiar trade-off, perhaps because the nation expects it from him, this boy breaks out spontaneously into political activity. All alone in a strange village, constantly fearing he will be betrayed to the enemy, he begins to do simple patriotic, nation-building, anti-Japanese propaganda. He gives lectures, narrates patriotic stories (shuwu or shushuo), sings Red Army songs, and gives explanations about the fact that serving the nation means serving his own social class interests (163). The child magnetically attracts people to himself and to his ideas. They love his songs and easily learn his stories. His charisma and the homespun way he exemplifies communist social morality are fused when he offers his own life to the nation, and the power he embodies transforms the heart of the bandit chief.

Elements of "The Unfired Bullet" returned over and over in Ding Ling's wartime fiction. She almost always structured her National Defense narratives around the central opposition of utopian nation-state (guo) and a distopic family (jia). Things that are categorically like the guo include nonkin social collectivities, Party cells, army and propaganda units, patriotic crowds, and groups of anti-Japanese artists. That move made the socius an offshoot of or part of the state. Feudalistic and jia-like social elements surface in the form of decadent rural power holders, paternalistic rapists, helpless patriarchs, evil political reactionaries, and selfish people who protect only their own kin. It is within this ever-present, haunting opposition of jia and guo that women, weak people, old people, children, cripples, victims, and oppressors allow themselves to be ideologically transformed into ethical communists, and appear, like the little devil, to be powerful instruments for creating a better, postfeudal, modern society. The powers of these agents are not personal, particular, or local. Charisma, moral example, self-sacrifice, and spontaneous political praxis are only side effects of revolutionary modernity because antifeudal, anti-imperialist mobilization frees the weak from the very irrational feudal obligations that required them to destroy their wills to serve the cannibalistic old family.

Indeed, Ding Ling's portraits of rural patriarchal cruelty show the family as an evil second only to Japanese imperialism. "The Affair in East Village," the best early example, focuses primarily on the systematic misuse of Chinese women in a feudal village political economy. Tightly controlled, tensely ordered, the narrative prefigures issues that resurface in Ding Ling's lengthy, compelling social realist novel, Taiyang zhao zai Sanggan he shang (The sun shines over the Sanggan River), which also relies heavily on a suspenseful narrative that resolves itself in a conclusive paroxysm of violence.[39] Unlike the novel, however, "The Affair in East Village" focuses on how women become sexual commodities and therefore items of exchange. Local power broker Landlord Zhao has imprisoned patriarchal poor peasant Chen to force the family to forfeit the chastity of its innocent minor daughter-in-law (tongyangxi) Qiqi. Because son Chen Delu cannot endure the crime of "unfiliality" (buxiao), he agrees to leave his beloved Qiqi in Zhao's household as collateral against a loan of bail money for the father. When Zhao rapes her, Chen Delu, the unwitting dupe of his own feudal mentality, blames innocent Qiqi. Later the peasants revolt against Zhao's tyranny with the help of the visiting charismatic underground Communist organizer. Only Chen Delu feels too compromised to join the others beating Zhao to death.[40]

"The Affair in East Village" and "The Unfired Bullet" are examples of Ding Ling's persistent theme over these years that nationalist mobilization is not just a temporary, necessary evil (an anti-imperialist stance), but rather a long-term, positive resolution to Chinese feudal social relations (an antifeudal stance). In her Yan'an fiction, the mobilized nation is the modern nation. Ding Ling's national defense propaganda fiction at Yan'an reworked mythology that she had first introduced in Mother, insinuating that she was not just any old daughter, but the daughter of Revolution. In general, anti-Japanese, antifeudal mobilization appeared in her fiction in terms of its value as a precious moment of social chaos. Anti-imperialist action made personal, community, and national transformation possible, because Japanese occupation expanded the compass of Chinese subalterneity and made all Chinese—children, old folks, students, women, and the masses of the impoverished—homologous of each other, which, in turn, tended to reduce the importance of internal, national social inequality. There also appears in her fiction of the late 1930s a new realm capable of supporting social forms that are alternatives to patrilineal family relations. In this realm, which I think was probably a vision of the future Maoist society, political action held the key to personal and national redemption. The collectivity of the weak empowered each person to represent the national interest and to liberate the self in the process.[41]

For Ding Ling, the collective was the ethically unimpeachable social form mediating between past and present, jia and guo. In line with the growing role of ethical discipline in her writing since *Mother*, and the question of self-transformation infusing even her earliest creative work, Ding Ling's *Yinian* (One year) focused on the collective she organized, the Northwest Front Service Group (Xibei zhandi fuwu tuan), and illustrates where she was headed with emancipation through collectivity and the relation of individual to collective. The publication is called a *shilu*, or life record, and is not classified as a literary work (*zuopin*). Her designation of genre suggests that she wished to depict herself representing life directly, without resorting to literary artifice. During her travels with the Service Group, she explained, she divided her group into four, setting out the responsibilities of each subunit—magazine, news, acting, and singing committees—on an elaborate flow chart. She imposed a strict protocol of seventeen regulations, including prohibitions against drinking, quarreling, and insubordination. Group members were to remain disciplined, courteous, serious-minded, unfrivolous, self-critical, and clean at all times. Those who broke rules got demerits, then warnings; the program included "struggle sessions" to correct nonconformity.[42]

This power of the collective to restructure social relations and the ethics of the revolutionary subject surfaced most vividly in case studies of three marginally older, male, bourgeois writers: Wang Qi, Tian Jian, and Tian Shan (74). Ding Ling's troop voice their objections to Wang during a struggle session with him. Wang's subjective failings include pessimism, ignorance about the strategic aims of the United Front, lack of faith in the army, individualism, "low feudal taste," and a preoccupation with sexual matters. Consequently, at the farewell meeting staged to send him on to his new assignment, Wang claims to have died and been reborn morally. He uses the Party's political language for the first time and commits himself to the "unrelenting, harsh, unceasing struggle . . . until death" (77).[43] Each case study differs in detail, but the plot never varies. Ding Ling allows a literate man to join the group. She worries that he will not fit in because of his previous undisciplined life experience. The moral example of the collective wins him over and he realizes why he must sacrifice his individuality (or his creative freedom, complicated political ideas, or sexual preoccupations). The group is successful. The compromised individual transforms himself. The nation is served. In each case, an empowered collectivity of obscure, ill-educated young people humble a relatively more powerful man. (Wang Jian was already a fairly well-known poet in the late 1930s; he committed suicide when he was implicated as part of Ding Ling's "kingdom" in the antirightist campaign of the late 1950s).

A reverse version of this conversion experience also appears in the records of the troop's work. In "Haizimen" (Children), Ding Ling suggests that once they are liberated from family, children find it easier to identify with the nation than their parents do. A number of pieces ranging in genre from the quick sketch to the short story reinforce the point that the identification with nation made children into political agents. The case of Li Qianglin is the most vivid example. Old Mr. Li brings his little boy all the way from a remote mountain village to join the Service Group because little Qianglin insists on fighting for the nation. Then Old Mr. Li changes his mind. He and his brothers only have this one male child among them, and no matter what the boy or the people around him say, Li just cannot risk losing the boy. But the boy is intransigent. "Even if I am killed by the Japanese in the future," he declaims, "it's still better than dying here now." To which the old man finally says, "You are right. Go on, go on. When the Japanese come, I'll go up into the mountains. I'm not much use. In the future, when you have won the victory, come back and see. You know your grandfather only has this one grandson to continue our family line. The ancestors are completely dependent on you for their incense" (69). Whether the text describes a powerful male figure brought low by the Service Group or elaborates the theme of the morally transformative child, Ding Ling's war stories always list the ways mobilization empowers the weak because anti-imperialism undermines feudal relations and sets people on the road to modern, revolutionary social forms.

After Ding Ling returned to Yan'an in 1938 she still applied these same transformative politics, this same vision of the mediate collective, to the woman question. For instance, "Xin de xinnian" (New faith) links an old woman's anti-imperialist defense of the nation to her antifeudal self-invention. The Chen brothers' village sustains a Japanese attack; the enemy kills many family members and abducts the old mother. She returns eventually but has apparently been shocked into insanity: raped, forced to be an eyewitness to the rape and murder of her grandchildren. Yet, like the helpless child in "The Unfired Bullet," Granny begins spontaneous praxis by telling stories to the villagers. The family decides she has lost her mind and plans to tie her up. Despite enormous embarrassment, she actually expands her performance and incorporates new tales of the Red Army, soldier heroes, and the sadism of the enemy. Eventually she comes to the attention of the Party. Women's work cadres appear and make her an official recruiter. At the story's close, the politically empowered old woman addresses not just her neighbors, but a crowd of strangers—society in the abstract—from the stage. Even one's most precious sons, she testifies, must be sacrificed for the good of the country and the community (77).

This version of the narrative links mobilization and national defense to the policy of liberating female kin out of the family and into society. Granny mobilizes men into the army, but as for herself, she "just does not want to stay in the house anymore" (69). After the enemy ruins her, she ruptures the old ideology of female chastity and socializes her own rape; she liberates and makes herself a metonym of the nation in the same instinctive political gesture.[44] The all-round consequence is excellent, of course. The fusion of Granny's storytelling with the aims of national salvation and political transformation infects the entire kin group: "The whole family had never been so united and loving" as after she began her work. They just "did not realize . . . the old woman was the cause of it." The women of the family join the Women's Association en masse.

In yet another version of this plot, women characters experiment with social labor and shift themselves out of the domestic sphere into the national sector. The story is "Shouhuo di yitian" (Autumn harvest day), written for the Yan'an periodical *Chinese Women*. Two bourgeois students have left their families to live in a political unit. One woman plans to climb a mountain and do "light labor," helping with the harvest work. The other suffers from neurasthenia (*shenjing shuairuo*), a debilitating disease of the spirit, which expresses itself somatically. She will have to stay "in the kitchen." At the end of the day, they meet to talk about the problems of individual praxis. Because they both come from the bourgeois class, they share a problematic subjectivity, signified by the neurasthenic. Both consider physical labor the index of their political development.

> Liu lay next to [Wei Di] holding a copy of *Chinese Women* but she wasn't reading the magazine. Rather she was watching Wei Di's sunburned but peacefully composed face. Liu Se was thinking about Wei Di's history, for the course of Wei Di's life had been far tougher than her own. Why then did Wei Di appear so open, so happy and strong willed? . . . She could not restrain herself and out tumbled the words.
>
> "Wei Di, I remember you saying once that happiness is a kind of

virtue. . . . the extent of your happiness makes me feel I don't quite understand. Wei, none of life's vexations seems to have made an impression on you. Where did you ever discipline yourself and cultivate this kind of mentality?"

Wei attributes her spiritual growth to labor in the public sphere and to collective life. "I used to be an extremely melancholic person," she reminds her friend. "Since I've been here my spirit has been liberated. . . . I don't have to fear anyone and I dare talk and act. I believe I am very suited to collective living. . . . How could I not be happy?"[45] Significantly, Wei ends up convincing Liu that all work for the nation is praxis, even what would appear on the face of it to be just housework.

"Xianzhang jiating" (The county magistrate's family) is a final example. The story combines the power of the politicized child, the antifeudal effect of anti-imperialist mobilization, the political unit's mediation of oppressive family and modern nation, women's liberation, and productive labor. The narrative brings Ding Ling and her by now famous Service Group into a local administrative center during the first tense months of the United Front. The wife of a Guomindang (GMD) magistrate approaches them and insists they take her only daughter into their children's acting troupe. Ah Ling proves a remarkable girl. "Although this child had not cried and had not said a word about her family she was already experiencing the kind of rationalized life an eight-year-old child should not have to live," Ding Ling reported, adding, "I really loved the child." Several days later, the magistrate himself shows up and tricks Ding Ling into surrendering Ah Ling to him. He can accept his wife's leaving him to join the guerrillas, but his retrograde filial devotion to family makes it impossible for him to let go of his child. As he carries off the screaming Ah Ling, Ding Ling regrets the loss but can do nothing because the United Front, and thus the nation, are at stake.

The story problematizes the moment of mobilization when every person—man, woman, and child—must sacrifice family to nation. The patriarch who is simultaneously father, husband, and official in the GMD government has set himself against national and personal liberation and is reduced to abducting his own child. Not only does the child refuse to go with her father; the father himself regrets what he recognizes to be a personal weaknesses. "She should stay here," he cries in anguish. "Her mother will fight me over this!" Even so, at the age of forty he simply cannot give up his only child, though in betraying such weakness he is "no better than a woman." The magistrate's family is spontaneously more progressive than he is, in other words, and more aware of their responsibility to the nation. Ah Ling's mother had sought out the well-known leftist Ding Ling because she is a patriot. "Good, go along," she tells her daughter. "Now each of us must go out on our own, and none of us should brood or worry about the others."[46] Unlike the father's need to possess his child, the mother's service to nation is unselfish. Sacrifice pays an unexpected bonus, because Ah Ling's extraordinary latent talents cannot surface unless her parents give her up to Ding Ling and the national collectivity.[47]

Ding Ling's war literature obviously exemplifies larger contests arising in the late 1930s over questions of Marxist theory and Chinese state policy under conditions of civil war. Wartime Maoism's difference from Euro-Marxism lies particularly in its explicit culturalism and nationalism. Some critics have criticized these elements of Chinese Marxism—precisely what distinguishes Maoism as a system—saying they are insufficiently Marxist. Ding Ling's fiction is symptomatic. These deceptively childlike narratives are conjuncture points where the Maoist Party's statist, nationalist, and culturalist concerns can all be observed. After all, Ding Ling had been a collaborator (not a central figure but an important secondary collaborator) with the progenators of the Maoist literary project, ever since she had started associating with Qu Qiubai in the 1930s. At that time, it would appear, Ding Ling's girlfriend Wang Jianhong both linked and alienated Ding Ling and Qu, for according to Wei Hu, Ding Ling's proxy, Shan Shan, truly understood her fate only when Qu stole Wang away from her. The available evidence suggests that Ding Ling's specific concerns at Yan'an probably unfolded inside what later became singularly Maoist frameworks and not, as used to be supposed, in opposition to them.[48] But Ding Ling's identification of her own project of cultural work with Maoist nationalist mobilization theories and practice is only half the story. The question of what Maoism was and was not rests on a complex historiography of its own; in this stream, Ding Ling's creative work is a mere tributary.

Mao language was a language of order, a language of command. The CCP in the late 1930s and 1940s in the Northern Border Regions was a localized Bolshevik organization preoccupied with seizing state power. To accomplish this, it had to stave off the Japanese enemy. More important in its own conception, it sought to construct modern revolutionary government at the hamlet level to extend the state's powers beyond the older Qing and GMD parameters. Yung-fa Chen's local study *Making Revolution: The Communist Movement in Eastern and Central China, 1937–1945* gives a richly detailed example of how the Communist Party reinvented and mobilized a modern state during the war of resistance.[49] Discourses of the nation, Chen demonstrates, were thoroughly insinuated into the Maoist political project of state construction. Nationalism at Yan'an formed a diffuse and flexible discourse that justified the CCP's claim to sovereignty and its right to exploit the wealth and population of the locales or Border Regions, while explaining the need to resist the imperialist enemy with a variety of sophisticated means. The Maoist discourse of nationalism was inextricably bound to the Party's statist political project.[50]

Drawing primarily on internal documents to illustrate his point that Maoist organizational rhetoric was vivid, concrete, imprecise, and free of cant, Chen stresses at the same time its ambiguous construction. Maoist language of command, he argues, remained imprecise precisely because "ambiguous language enabled the CCP both to maintain its Marxist point of view and . . . [to achieve maximum] flexibility in strategy."[51] For instance, local ideologists knit amorphous, relatively abstract terms like "democracy" and "nationalism" into meaningful short narratives about the need for class struggle in resistance. The result was a form of knowledge that made it impossible for local speakers to distinguish between class war and national defense.[52] This made good on the CCP's promise to dislodge feudal relations, at least at the level of semiotic or cultural conditions. It also conveyed specificity while opening up a realm of ideological tropes like class, rights, and nation to common popular usage. The imprecision of concepts like class exploitation and imperialism gave the new signs a polyvalence that appealed to speakers at many different levels.

It is important to reiterate this point because the Mao language of command really worked: it actually did make available to the government the wealth and power of the local people. It may appear intriguingly polysemic and certainly it was a linguistic event. But it is a language of command because it is not extricable from the overall state's policy of population mobilization. When individuals are classified according to social class terminology, their labor power can be extracted in ways that benefit the state. The sensitive local project of fitting a general language of command to local conditions, which Chen illustrates extremely well in his discussion of the significance of the struggle session and class analysis, effectively realized in concrete terms what are abstract or theoretical political categories. Class categories and class identities were not only tangible; they enabled the officials of the government and Party to mobilize real people for work. Cadres inducted people into military service or put them to productive work on the basis of class categories. Villagers were punished or rewarded depending on where they fit into the classification categories of middle peasant, worker, or landlord exploiter and what strategic necessity the leadership decided to pursue. Classification and categorization, therefore, were enabling and empowering practices that made the state manifest, made it real, in a way that sheer military brute force could never accomplish.[53]

However, as a language of command as well as a series of positions staked out in relation to international Marxism, Maoism, perhaps because its foundational experiences required that language command, had a particular concern and theoretical need to explain the sphere of *wenhua*, or culture. Rather than popularizing the cultural achievements of the Chinese or European bourgeoisie, a Trostkyist choice, or simply waiting until a proletarian alternative finally surfaced to unmask hegemony, a Gramscian position, Maoism instrumentalizes culture, holding that there is virtue to instructing the underclass in appropriate nationalized, revolutionary, and modern cultural forms. Translation of rural practices into the modernist categories of the Maoist state practices and economics occurred in this realm of culture. After providing for the common defense and extending uniform taxation through land reform, the Maoists' greatest civil initiative, by their own lights and objectives, was to regulate cultural life. In this venue of cultural initiatives, how Ding Ling thought as a woman in the era of revolutionary modernity became more significant because her literary representations and personal positioning in cultural life as an internationally known figure always had implications in terms of broader questions of governmentality. It also suggests, though it is not my concern in this book, that Ding Ling was a doctrinaire Maoist writer, who was devoted to the mobilization of the people's cultural forms.[54]

The Maoist emphasis on culture emerged gradually. From the 1929 Gutian Conference, throughout the Jiangxi Soviet era (1930–1934), and into the mid-1930s at Xi'an, leaders sharing this view of culture gravitated toward one another. They identified themselves as Maoists only at Yan'an, where they harbored the "long-term aim of building a modern Chinese nation state by educating the masses in literacy, modern scientific knowledge, and loyalty to the CCP." To early Maoist thinkers, culture offered a medium for mobilizing human energy in the service of state building. By the time Mao published "On Democracy" in the first month of 1940, this vision of cultural mobilization was fully formed. At its heart lay what the theorists termed "national forms" (*minzu xingshi*). As David Holm shows, this formula originated in the New Enlightenment movement of 1935 among communist intellectuals dissatisfied with the League of Left-Wing Writers and the CCP line on cultural issues. These New Enlightenment theorists believed that the historical era demanded an indigenous, popular, national movement that would accept old cultural practices but "enlighten" them by placing them in the service of proletarian revolution. Leading cadres in the New Enlightenment group Chen Boda and Ai Siqi came to Yan'an, where they began advising Mao. Out of the collaboration came several key insights that would later guide state policy: (1) enlightened practices can be developed from native cultural habits (i.e., revolutionary modernity can emerge out of feudalism without necessarily erasing all characteristically "Chinese" elements), but (2) since Communists must take it on themselves to do the enlightening, activists needed to be trained to recognize promising cultural signification, and (3) skillful cultivation of cultural initiatives would be required to realize the Maoist vision of a modern, New Democratic polity. In Holm's view (and most recently the view of Wang Hui as well), this belief of communist intellectuals that they could shape a progressive, popular, nationalist culture out of crude, rural mass was the "artistic counterpart of Mao's base building strategy."[55]

Maoist cultural ideology was effective with the peasant and popular audience because it required activists and propagandists to literally perform nationalism. Holm painstakingly lays out the sequence of decisions that led the CCP cultural bureaucracy to adopt the *yangge* dance drama and make it symbolize the modern Chinese nation (according to Ellen Judd's ethnography, Ding Ling was instrumental in developing the Party line on popular theater). Drawing a direct analogy with Yung-fa Chen's study of local government rhetorical and real effectiveness, the evidence suggests that the government's emphasis on cultural practices in mass mobilization relied on a collaboration of universal and particular, general and specific in reiterative ideological language. The point for Holm is that Mao's general theories were successful governance precisely because they were rooted in Chinese Enlightenment culturalism. The Chen Boda–Mao Zedong–Ai Siqi theoretical position, which made "culture" the public sphere and the arena for effecting revolutionary transformation, was an effective tool in the struggle to modernize the rural, impoverished Border Regions. Particularly after 1942, Maoists made their targeted interventions into local culture on the basis of real knowledge about local conditions. This helped them educate villagers to grasp what the state had in mind for them and their locale and what a national objective meant locally. Not only was the category of culture foundational, Holm argues, but the Yan'an Maoists presumed the existence of a cultural sphere lying somewhere beneath the political arena, cementing the economic substructure into place. The Maoists made the cultural worker into a kind of glue (Holm's word), a social adhesive that united antagonistic social-economic elements when necessary and reconciled them to work in the same harness for well-defined nationalist ends.

Two further qualifications remain. First, the universalizing claims of Mao Zedong Thought and specific literary representations that embodied it were normative because their subjects—funü, for instance—had protocols or ethically correct behaviors attached to them. The example of *One Year* provided in the previous discussion of the Northwest Front Service Group included specific examples of Ding Ling's own view about how in political struggle her collective could produce "good people." This was a norma- tivizing practice. So were the little devils and rural figures that appeared in Ding Ling's war fiction in the 1930s and her reportage of the 1940s. Their behaviors and alternatives were crudely hewed, highly charged fusions of local common sense, often cloaked in a feudal kin patois, and enactable modern alternative cultural practices, and each one had a nationalist future policy objective attached to it. They resembled stories like the very late-era "Du Wanxiang," that is. Emphasis on the performance (biaoyan) of ideo- logical subject positions grew out of the requirements of war mobilization. This emphasis reverberated in the Maoicization of the performing arts. By the end of the Yan'an period, the dance drama had emerged as the model of modern Chinese mass art.

Second, culture problems predominated in the Party Rectification move- ment, it would appear, because of the ambiguities inhering in the idea of a cultural sign itself. The naturalization of Yan'an cultural categories aligned May Fourth Sino-European notions of the national folk culture to the larger domain of the guojia state or nation. Assigning such fundamental powers to the cultural realm raised unique problems. (Even for a Maoist it is sometimes hard to decipher what a particular cultural sign indicates.[56]) All signs in a Maoist culture regime would, by definition, always have two potential referents. In theory, all national forms pointed backward to the national (and thus feudal) past and simultaneously forward to the bright potential of socialism. The Maoist framing of culture institutionalized this instability. For a Party writer, the instability meant that the potential for misreading and misrepresenting increased. Some responded with silence; some engaged immediately in a struggle over what the object of literary representation ought to be for themselves, Maoist writers; and some took on the task of policing representation. A minority, like Ding Ling in The Sun Shines over the Sanggan River and its prototypes, used every possible means to carry out the mission stated in Maoist theory and transform old narrative devices into modern national forms.[57]

Ding Ling's female fictional characters went "into society" and "into life." Each arena of society or life was a tangible spatiality with normative lessons to teach.[58] In the war fictions I discussed above, Ding Ling consis- tently advocated a space—the revolutionary social unit—where social life outside family but within the nation was possible even for women. Exam- ples of these alternatives to the feudal family were the raped Granny's public sphere of address, the world of the female cadre dorm, and the performance troupe. But shortly the question would become, as it does so often in Chinese feminism, Where does the woman with ren'ge belong in this new society, in this new, new life?

In the wake of the famous Party Rectification of the arts in 1942 (and her role as critic of the "dark spots" on the bright sun of Party life), Ding Ling spoke directly to the question of the instability of Mao-style representation in her own response to the Chairman's talks. The essay, entitled "My opinion on the problem of class stand," exemplified the shift in Ding Ling's position away from her earlier 1930s view, which had resolved questions of literary representation into "life," to the statist position that she would take in later years, which mediated literature through the state-representing-the-people. To invoke life or personal experience and make it the primary ground of progressive literary representation, she argued, was naïve. It overlooked the fact that peoples' experience is an end product, not an initial, original essence. Experience is mediated through class and, in the case of intellectuals, through complicated histories of reading books. "We have read feudal literature, bourgeois literature, we have studied the ancients, the romantics, the symbolists, and the realists," she wrote. "And at the time we read them we did not necessarily possess a very thorough critical vision."[59] Literature that most people would consider ridiculous had shaped writers in earlier years, she continued. The problem is that such books bred in Chinese bourgeois literati an ecstatic strain that, over the long run, proved ruinous. In this 1942 essay, which was frequently anthologized in later years, Ding Ling complexified her understanding. Mediated experiences, social class convention, and cultural norms mobilize life and consequently mediate literature, too.

Interestingly, though, Ding Ling was refining rather than abandoning her frequently expressed belief that the writer's special preserve is emotion. To create great Marxist-Leninist literature requires writers to exploit older literary sensitivity and to feel emotion, she argued, but they must also transform the origin and qualities of the emotions involved. Reaching that objective meant establishing a new proximity to class-mediated life experience:

> That which is equally important as study and indeed cannot be separated from it is life. You absolutely must live with [the masses] if you want to understand their feelings and thoughts and write about the proletariat. You must change yourself, and rid yourself of the old feelings and consciousness [ganqing yishi]. You must absolutely spend a long time tempering yourself in the struggling life of the masses. Only by dissolving your own emotions into the emotions of the broad masses will you be able to intuit and represent [reflect] the emotions of the great masses. This is not merely a matter of modifying our outlook (perspective), rather we must change our emotions, we must thoroughly change our entire being [geren]. Only living among the

struggling masses will enrich our emotions, heighten our emotions; only then can we cast off our individualist sentimentality, our dreams which seem so exquisite but which in actuality are such frivolous emotions, only then can we develop a passionate attachment to mankind, a passionate attachment to the undertaking of the proletariat. . . . [And] if you cannot commit yourself to and live a high level of emotion you cannot write great works that will move people. (49)

The Maoist writer, like any other creative writer, aims to represent feelings. But for Maoist writers at that time, the feelings represented were the feelings of an *other*. Later, Ding Ling would invest energy to nurture the sort of young proletarian writers who did not need to distance themselves from their class of origin. But in 1942 there were few writers who were not petit bourgeois. Most of them needed, therefore, to abandon their "armor" and give up the class privilege that protected them from the suffering and the ignorance of the oppressed. Only this would make it possible for nonproletarian writers to accurately represent the other class without hollow arrogance or self-aggrandizing pride in both the realist anticipatory or revolutionary temporality that is communist literature's distinguishing characteristic.

Ding Ling's second preoccupation in "My Opinion" concerned the proper balance in literary representations between bright and dark. Y. T. Feuerwerker has shown that Ding Ling was arguing a sophisticated point here: if the writer has a correct overall viewpoint, she can be counted on to do the right thing, and therefore, whether she praises or criticizes is less important than whether she is right or wrong in her choice of target or subject.[60] But it is also here that the question of the instability of the Maoist cultural sign is most pronounced. Ding Ling seemed to be arguing that the cultural sign is subject to multiple, competing interpretations. We don't look at things in isolation nor do we look at one particular stage but rather we look at development, she wrote in "My Opinion." Moreover, when we see contradictions in the midst of this transformation, when we see the struggle between the new and old we must positively point out to whom the truth belongs. This is a problem fundamental to literature. But by the same token, many problems result from it. Whether we should write about the light or the darkness is just one example (46). Debates over darkness are indeed debates over how to phrase things, how to represent them accurately in written texts. But prolonged exclusive focus on such questions trivializes more abstract yet compelling issues. Measuring whether something called "darkness" is present and how much of it there is in relation to another thing called "light" reduces literary representation to a question of whether a datum can be said to really exist or not. The question, she said, is not as simple as "whether something is real or not real, seen or not seen" (47). Because progressive literature necessarily reveals the oppression and suffering of the laboring classes and points the pro- letariat to the means of alleviating its suffering in the future, progressive literature cannot be said to directly represent—or directly desire to repre- sent—anything so concrete as "reality."

Ding Ling's ease with the Mao group's dictum that writing and repre- sentation have a culturally aggressive role to play in the CCP political arena is illustrated clearly in this essay. Her position reflects the view that repre- sentational orders, that is, culture (wenhua), come into existence through struggle, and therefore (a Mao position), whoever controls the ideological apparatus controls the immediate reality. What does not get addressed directly here is the problem of what to do when experiences for some reason are confounded, exceeded, or somehow ignored in the practices of cultural representation. Ding Ling was posing the question of what hap- pens when the suffering of individual women exceeds a unitary category of oppression. How can the special characteristics of female suffering be distinguished from the subaltern's oppression in general? If culture is malleable, if it is indeed the arena of revolutionary transformation, then how is it possible to address the special vulnerabilities of women as a group within necessarily general policies across the differences that sepa- rate women? Is the right place for solving this dilemma certain specific normative practices? Is it in the work of normative representation that writers call "character" (renwu) or "normative characters" (dianxing renwu) or characterology? What needs to happen before the term "women" no longer requires special attention? These are all questions that presume a great deal of political sophistication, to say nothing of strategic savvy. They point to complications that arise in any projected government policy. The Party's job—"our" job as Party leaders—is, Yan'an communists concurred, to represent the people, all of the people; the ethical boundary of the people is reflected in the mirror formed of the enemy, the reactionaries, the land- lords, traitors, rightists, and so on.

Communist women and other feminists faced the real problem that women really was a troubled subject in political representation and public policy at that time. In the Party newspaper, where policy matters were openly debated, a series of essays and reports on domestic and marital affairs appeared rather abruptly in late 1941 and early 1942. One worried out loud that social pressures and the exigencies of war were forcing female cadres back into exclusively domestic lives, another that family rectification and family policy ought to liberate women out of domesticity and into society, and thus no special domestic education was necessary for women.[61] In the tradition of progressive Chinese feminism, the newspaper ran reports illustrating the range and complexity of modernization of domestic affairs reminiscent of Funü zazhi (Ladies' Journal) and Funü shibao (Ladies' Times). Essays appeared on Islamic marriage and divorce law, the education of girls and their ideas about marriage, results of an investigation into the age of marriage among Yan'an's female peasantry, and a two-part short story on the themes of love, marriage, and child rearing and their effect on educated Yan'an cadres.[62]

It is difficult to know what immediate events led Xie Juezai to publish his "Let's Listen to Village Women Speak Bitterness" on 9 March 1942.[63] Nor the anonymous critics of "Dedaole xie shenma jiaoxun" (Attaining some instructions), who "voiced criticisms of Party policy for women as strong as Ding Ling's" and gave female comrades the same advice as had Ding Ling and other critics: delay marriage and childbirth, avoid the double burden of child care and party work.[64] Zeng Ko published "Yuanjiu muqin" (Save the mothers) on 8 March 1942. She argued that although women at Yan'an had made some gains, domestic responsibilities undercut political enlightenment. Party policy should address the material conditions of female cadres so that good mothers could continue to also be good revolutionaries.[65] On the same day and in the same venue, Cao Ming argued that marriage might even signify the abandoning of individual responsibility. Women needed to create their own individual destinies not only for their own benefit but for the nation's behalf, too.[66] Bai Shuang contributed the thought that there was no theory that could convince progressive women to accept baby making and child rearing as their singular contribution to national salvation.[67] But of course, the zawen that most riveted reader attention on the question of the subject Women was Ding Ling's "Thoughts on March 8."[68]

According to Patricia Stranahan, whose monograph Yan'an Women and the Communist Party is the most comprehensive account of the social history of this obscure period in communist feminism, the less immediate problem for these elites was also their long-term question. The political goal of the Central Committee and the Women's Bureau of the Party remained as it had been in the Jiangxi Soviet era (1927–1934): the emancipation of women from feudal oppressions, including domestic tyranny. The conditions of life in the Border Regions made restructuring such a policy extremely difficult. Arguing primarily on evidence available in Liberation Daily, Stranahan says that official decisions about women policy parameters in the Border governments went through three stages. In late 1941 Party elites debated the weaknesses of work with rural women, stressing the tensions between outsider cadres and local villagers and between patrilineal interests and the efforts of local cadres and outsider cadres to shelter oppressed female family members. But between 1942 and 1945, senior cadres responsible for women policy long-term planning, defensive after Ding Ling's critique, finally settled on a loose policy of women's emancipation through mass line-style production. In these years, wealth and human managerial and cultural capital were all invested in the task of organizing female labor into weaving cooperatives, which produced a commodity at the same time as they mobilized a kind of mass subjectivity rooted in common work. This policy goal provoked feminine self-interest: women producing, taking profits, and reaping rewards for their work came to outweigh all other considerations. Balanced against small producer self-interest was the modernizationist and egalitarianizing policy of female literacy training, which, Stranahan notes, was in fact a part of the production policy and did perhaps more than anything else to prepare women to claim social equality with men—that and plans for retooling democratic family ideology to mobilize women within domestic economies rather than attempting to establish an economic alternative to it. In a third phase, Stranahan points to the twelve months between March 1946 and March 1947, when the Communist Party prepared for civil war and, confident that it had integrated women into society and met even Ding Ling's stringent criteria of success—that women would no longer be specially privileged over other derogated subjects—policy shifted. The new line encouraged the participation of female labor in conventionally male work, reactivated proscriptions against cross-class organizing of women, and, of course, land reform.

As Stranahan presciently pointed out in a footnote, however, "The material published at this time *did not define the term 'woman.'* Obviously, mothers-in-law were women, and had suffered just as much under the traditional system. [But] after the policy was revised in 1942–1943, one rarely found mothers-in-law mentioned. The new policy promoted family harmony and sought to include women of all ages."[69] It certainly is the case that CCP policy discouraged more avant-garde formulae and that its incorporation of the ren'ge problem differed slightly from earlier, progressive feminist canonical writing. Policy did not vest ren'ge in individuals. Rather, it contained emancipation in the political economy of the family. However, as the fictional examples of Chen Man and Guo Jinqing and later Heini (in *The Sun Shines over the Sanggan River*) make certain, Ding Ling's own position did not polarize individualist feminism against familist communism, either. The avenue she suggested in her critical essays and in her fiction was that women forms an internally stratified, future possibility. It is a future political subject that is necessarily mediated through Party agency and Party policy. This future subject would be funü. Its present emotional realities and labor value would coalesce as such (be "tempered" and "steeled," "disciplined" and "burnished," to use the idiom of the times) only in a modernist relation to the revolutionary state formation.

By the logic of Ding Ling's own thinking, this project of communist feminism would require the extension of a subject women. That is, women would need to offer future possibility, a revolutionary temporality beyond the quotidian oppressions of the past. Rather than a stable entity, according to "Thoughts on March 8," women would have always to possess enough flexibility to disappear back into the social totality if, when, practical political practices and policies dictate. Now, it is true that Ding Ling wrote a self-criticism of "Thoughts on March 8" and excused herself for alleged lapses into individualist thinking. Indeed, in the early 1980s she was still cautioning second-generation readers, who were just then encountering the essay for the first time, that true emancipation of women would rest on social, not individual transformation.[70] In the "struggle between the new and old" in 1941, however, the state (i.e., the place where the work of emancipation would take place), as Stranahan's study helped clarify, had yet to articulate a content for woman. This policy matter casts an important light on Ding Ling's contribution to the rectification of Party feminism and particularly her focus on how its subject of Women should be evaluated. The literary version of this same question was how revolutionary writers should represent the complex cultural and political signifier funü. Ding Ling elected to open up the question through the normative aesthetics of character, or what I call characterology.

## "Thoughts on March 8" and the Literary Question of Funü

Ding Ling's authorial tone in "Thoughts on March 8" is familiar. The essay makes three points. First, it measures against its own revolutionary promise the Communist Party's most powerful representatives and finds that they are not doing enough to recognize the special circumstances facing elite, activist women. Female revolutionaries are criticized when they leave home and when they stay home. They are measured and judged against the unrealistic expectation that they excel in political and social or domestic and reproductive labor without sustaining losses in either sphere. The meretricious argument that domestic service is political praxis—"Isn't giving birth to children also work?"—has little persuasive power because childbirth gets no official recognition and it takes more work to dismiss a cadre than a wife. Second, political authorities are not appropriately addressing regressive social attitudes. Women's special circumstances are not being properly represented (i.e., as an affront to the behavioral norms of the revolutionary community) or addressed in policy. Unfortunately, these deficiencies will remain undisturbed because male comrades are refusing to give up their right to divorce those they consider their political inferiors or who just get old and ugly looking after men and children. Ding

Ling's third point has to do with what she called "women themselves." I want to pay particular attention to this point because it speaks indirectly to the question of what the political content of woman or the state's funü would be, or should be.

"I myself am a woman," she wrote, "and I therefore understand the failings of women better than others. But I also have a deeper understanding of what they suffer. Women are incapable of transcending the age they live in, of being perfect, or of being hard as steel. They are incapable of resisting all the temptations of society or all the silent oppression they suffer here in Yan'an. They each have their own past written in blood and tears; they have experience of great emotions—in elation as in depression, whether engaged in the lone battle of life or drawn into the humdrum stream of life."[71] The essay went on to address "women themselves" directly in Ding Ling's characteristically semilaudatory, semicritical tone. She cautioned women to husband their own health, to claim happiness, to think rationally rather than emotionally, and to learn to endure what they cannot change. But, as usual, her advice came with a fillip of criticism of "modern women's" weaknesses, which she summarized as the tendencies to loaf around, romanticizing and obsessing, their emotional passivity, vulnerability to flattery, and blindness to self-deceptive illusions.

Ding Ling presented the question of equality, in other words, in the context of character, character weaknesses, and personal behavioral norms. This is certainly the way she developed the case against the male cadre's patriarchal sexual attitudes and behavior. The hypocrisy of men, she pointed out, led them to cloak sexual predation in ideological language, which was a double offense. Character in the sense of normative behavior was as much a problem for men as for women because men, too, had weaknesses. This point is worth stressing because the fiction Ding Ling wrote in the early 1940s raised in fictional form ideas that appear as zawen writing in "Thoughts on March 8." The difference is that questions of character or subjectivity can be more complexly considered in fiction. With her characteristic habit of embracing the idea while changing it, Ding Ling endorsed the goal of the Communist Party to deliver a future where the political subject women did not require special attention. She particularly stressed the problem of women's deficiencies (quedian). But her writing kept open the problem of the difficulty in literature or policy writing of ever getting women properly represented in the final instance. Only in the context of cultural and social grids mediating direct historical experience can female subjects be definitively and correctly represented in policy and in fiction, she seems to say. And even then, women as such—in all its emotional content and social burden—has yet to be specified. As a social, historical category, funü poses a question but does not provide definite solutions.

In three major stories drafted at the same time as "Thoughts on March 8" Ding Ling worked through the themes she would directly address in the essay. The strongest criticisms "Thoughts on March 8" levels concern sexual ethics and the problem of divorce law. (In the late 1970s Ding Ling claimed that she had actually written the essay because the husbands of two of her women friends were planning divorces to marry prettier, younger girls.)[72] In this regard, she seemed to be making what in our time is a conservative argument that state marriage legislation ought to protect vulnerable women from the social and economic catastrophe of divorce. This was certainly the overwhelming point in her 1941 short story, "Ye" (Night).[73] "Night" examines the fate of a truly backward wife. The narrative concerns a hard-working, poor peasant, who, through his own labor and patriotism, has become a local cadre. He Hanming's dilemma is that his erotic desire is colliding with his political responsibilities. He derogates each of the women he encounters because he has no political reason not to, no line to guide his judgment, and just enough political language to justify his own appetites.[74] When he chances on a pretty girl he conflates sex and social class, and rather than acknowledge his feeling to be simple lust, he projects onto the girl a political epithet of "backward" and an angry feeling that this girl deserves to be a landlord's daughter. With no real understanding, He has no way to separate his own normalized, feudal carnality from his own jumbled-up political rhetoric. Then He encounters Hou Guiying, his village representative to the National Congress of the Women's Association, and Hou uses her Party position to solicit sex from him. There is only one thing preventing him from obliging and that is his fear that others in the village Party unit will criticize him and that this would threaten his local power. Hidden in the house while He waits in his barn for his cow to calve is He Hanming's wife. The story revolves around his realization that he is free to divorce his old, politically backward, powerless, and wrinkled-up wife, who now has not only to do her own work but, because He is now fully occupied with politicking, He's farmwork as well.

Initially, Ding Ling represents the wife through the eyes of the husband. But as the narrative unfolds it points to the political reality lying beyond or occluded in He's perspective: "She cursed him because he didn't make any money and because he wasn't a family man, and he cursed her for being old-fashioned and backward. Conjugal relations had become increasingly impossible for them since he had begun to work as a county official, and now they lived in a state of irresolvable enmity." Then, "he had been getting progressively more morose so she felt worse than ever before. It seemed to him that as his disposition was improving hers was getting worse, though actually it was he who was growing further and further away, and she who had no way to hold onto him" (7). Unless the writer intervenes, of course, the oppression that He's wife endures will remain unseen because there is no one there to represent her suffering. This is not because she cannot speak for herself; she can do that, though only in the bitter, local, feudal language of enmity. But the very people politically empowered to represent her in the future have every reason to not do so. In the complex geometry of the plot, He Hanming's wife is blameworthy, as she does nothing to improve herself and everything to exacerbate the problem; yet, unlike Hou Guiying, she is caught in the double bind of the older wife. And reading one step further, the political or normative category of Women in the political policy of the government does nothing to protect He's wife from Hou and He. "Night" makes the very same points as "Thoughts on March 8," in other words. But it does so in Ding Ling's familiar critical realist vein in the context of everyday village life. And to my knowledge, it did not attract criticism. Indeed, "When I Was in Xia Village" and "In the Hospital," stories that eventually had a large impact, went over similar ground, also through the idiom of character.

The political problem for He Hanming's wife is that her labor has not been socialized yet. It does not register on any future index of value. In fact, her labor is devalued in the gaze of the nation, and that, in Ding Ling's view, is a loss to the nation as much as to the nation's women. Ding Ling presumed the revolution an unquestioned good; by this time, her preoccupations centered on "how the really backward peasants became the new people," as she put it in 1954.[75] In "Night," He's wife is excluded from this story of renewal, and that is the central problem the plot confronts. In this regard, all Ding Ling's critical realist stories are rather similar, as each is framed in terms of what ren'ge (personal standing) would have to be for all women citizens in a Party state. The work that female citizens do and how the state should "see" or witness their contributions is at stake. Ding Ling's 1942 normative framework is already statist. In her critical writing the state is central and it is derelict because it has misrepresented or is failing to adequately grasp unfolding but as yet unresolved conflicts that women face. Evidently these same women must, nonetheless, be measured against their potential to the future of Communist China, their weaknesses notwithstanding their representative value.

Zhenzhen, heroine of the controversial story "When I Was in Xia Village," and Lu Ping, protagonist of "In the Hospital," are good examples of Ding Ling's problem of futurity and normativity, or what women can expect to become if they commit themselves as a gender to the revolutionary future. The question of futurity is difficult. Each story requires the political authorities to make good on the claim that all women have on enlightenment and emancipation, not just some who are pretty enough or young enough or lucky enough to be married to indulgent husbands. The Party state is beholden to women's future and must ensure that its own language is properly used, is placed in the hands of those whom it will benefit. These stories are quite obviously the work of a Communist Party writer. But the question of normativity is more complex. Specifying who the subject women is in theoretical and thus activist or practical language can be done. That was Stranahan's point when she highlighted unclarities before 1941 about what the signifier women included or discluded. Who gets included into the simple mobilization of women in a mass action or in a spinning cooperative is actually a key organizational problem. A good policy, the policy on women in the mid- and late 1940s, for instance, specified clearly that the term "women" included all laborers in the spinning and weaving drives, all participants in the production drives, all model labor heroines and those who emulate them. Chen Yung-fa's point that Communist language in the Border governments was precisely calibrated to extract the maximum usefulness from the people is worth reiterating here. The subject funü is not, I want to stress, a simple linguistic datum. Normative mass-line writing in labor heroine propaganda or exemplary women in political organizing, for instance, explicitly set out the extent of this mobilization category. As I will argue shortly, so did Ding Ling's novel *The Sun over the Sanggan River*, which, in her usual fashion, adopts the subject category funü and points to its lacunae at the same time.

"When I Was in Xia Village" recounts how an elite female cultural cadre arrives in Xia Village to rest and learn about everyday peasant realities.[76] This first-person narrator gives a detailed account of meeting a young rural girl who has returned from the enemy lines, where she was working as a prostitute and spying on the enemy.[77] Events swirl around the older woman and she monitors what there is to know, commenting constantly on village opinion, relationships, gossip, and activities. Before young Zhenzhen, promised to the narrator as "material" for writing, actually arrives to meet the visiting cadre, peripheral characters report on what sort of person Zhenzhen is. Each representation is different. Progressive village cadres see her patriotism; feudal village women blame her for having refused an arranged marriage and thus inviting punishment (rape by Japanese soldiers); her female relatives affectionately yet implacably try to force her back into a community that will never forgive her for the rape or her devastating service to the nation.

A major shift occurs when the narrator meets the protagonist and finds a brave and forthright girl who, without "bitterness or dejection," is determined to make her own way in the world. From this point onward the narrator's primary concern is the quality of Zhenzhen's character, her personal nature. How does Zhenzhen (whose name, of course, translates as Chastity) compensate herself emotionally for the trauma of rape? How does she explain her willingness, her ability to sacrifice herself repeatedly to spy against the Japanese enemy? What feelings does she have toward her father and her lover who did not support her antifeudal demand that she be allowed to marry whom she chose? When the less progressive villagers spite her for events she cannot control, does she spite them back? What explains her even temper, her phlegmatic acceptance of her fate, her ability to endure? Certainly no one in her community can answer these questions that the internal narrator poses, for each of them is implicated in the events of the tragedy. And so the narrator decides to refuse all commentary from bystanders.[78] But the question of Zhenzhen's being is complex. Even the young girl herself must consider whether the tragedy has altered her character in any fundamental way, perhaps ruining her beyond repair: "More than a year has passed since I was raped but everyone is so curious. Now look at the people of this village. Some are very kind to me, but many try to avoid me. Take my family. They too behave like the others. Everyone wants to have a quiet look at me. No one takes me for the former Zhenzhen. 'Have I changed?' I ask myself over and over again. No, I have not changed. If I have, the only difference is that my heart has become a little harder" (263).

In a sense, Zhenzhen weathers what a peripheral character, Comrade Ah Gui, refers to as Zhenzhen's "unspeakable suffering" in a better form than the villagers do. It is Ah Gui and not Zhenzhen who voices the sentiment "It is wretched to be a woman" (263). It is Zhenzhen who can think benevolently of the village's best interests, and it is the villagers who miss the opportunity to learn and change by emulating Zhenzhen's valiant struggle. The narrator believes that neither rebellion against her feudal family nor rape and indignity have essentially altered Zhenzhen, who, on the contrary, has suffered and grown. Indeed, the narrator prizes Zhenzhen's "calm and quiet" manner, her independence and self-respect (264). She "never expressed the need or desire for a man's care and comfort," the narrator reports at one point. She simply wanted "warmth" and a comfortable place to wait while her wounds healed over (265).

After a tremendous, principled struggle, however, Zhenzhen realizes that the villagers simply cannot accept her back on the old terms. The rape and her work have not changed her character, but they have permanently altered the perception others have of her. "Follow their wishes!" she finally decides. "Why should I? Have they ever listened to what I wanted? . . . I have made this decision not for myself alone but for everyone. People say I am young, narrow-minded, and obstinate and bad tempered. Well, I'll not bother to explain myself. There are many things which they do not have to explain" (269). Zhenzhen must leave and go to Yan'an City, where she will get medicine and political support. What sort of work she will do is unclear. Possibly (this is controversially left open) the nation will misuse her.

But insofar as the question of ren'ge for women citizens is concerned, Zhenzhen and the narrator share the expectation that the state (represented by the Party and its policies) knows that chastity is not the measure of womanhood. In fact, staked out in the story is an ideologically progressive position endorsing Zhenzhen's decision to leave the feudalized village on the chance that a kind of citizenship exists elsewhere that authorizes her tragedy and her independence. At least the narrator, herself an agent of the state, is witness to Zhenzhen's sacrifice. Reflecting Zhenzhen back to herself, the narrator exceeds the gaze of the villagers' disapproval or patronizing acceptance. By the ethical code of Chinese communism being hammered out in the caves of Yan'an, Zhenzhen is a miraculously good person.

Ding Ling directly referred back to the question of Zhenzhen's character in a famous statement in 1954 on writing from life. The context was a discussion about character formation and historical accuracy in literary texts. She argued that for Marxist-Leninist writers, actual characters—prototypical (dianxing) characters (renwu), or historical typicalities—must be in the moment. There can be no anachronism in good Marxist-Leninist literature, for its special strength is historical accuracy. Yet character is an effulgence of emotion in two ways. The writer reflects back to readers emotions appropriate to the character, and emotions also come up out of writers, for it is the writer's emotions that determine why some kinds of characters are legible, representable and others are not. The latter emotional dynamic is why Marxist-Leninist fiction is not written by committees. In any case, to connect interior of the writer's emotional life to the interior of hypothetical characters requires a kind of emotional surgery in which the writer establishes intimacy (shuxi) and understanding with the type of person determined to be typical. Good writers start from their own childhood preoccupations and passions and continue to change with the times, adding experience and theoretical acuity through participant observation.

Ding Ling offered herself as the example. When she began writing in the May Fourth era, a time of great sadness and despair, her most beloved (zui xi'ai de) characters formed a sort of interior entourage which she drew on when she composed characters typical of the time. But life changes, and characters typical to the moment also change. Gradually, the "characters that flowed out of my pen slowly changed their nature [xingge]," although traces of earlier prototypes certainly lingered:

> For instance, [Zhenzhen], the female protagonist in "When I Was in Xia Village," is a peasant girl, not an intellectual. Her composite elements have changed, she is more optimistic than Sophia is but spiritually there are still some places that are similar to Sophia. I know

that this sort of character has already passed from the scene. The nature of the social system has been completely changed, and the content of the spiritual life of characters has also completely changed, so I have done my utmost to seek new characters, the interior lives of new people. The only people I want to write about now are new people. For example [the characters in] *Sun over the Sanggan River* are all completely new people. This is to point out that with regard to my literary oeuvre, these types of people were rather scarce in my previous work. But still I wrote into that novel a Heini. Though this character does not have a really important position in the novel, the readers like her because there is something there. Most of the letters that I get from readers ask about Heini. Even though the author paid little attention to and did not develop her character, because of the author's previous intimacy [*shuxi*] with the character type, past affection [*xihuan*] is what the readers at once turn their attention to.

When I was in the land reform I saw a girl coming out of the landlord's door one day, a very beautiful girl. She was the landlord's relative. She turned her head and gave me a glance. I felt that manifested in that gaze were very complex emotions. In that one flash, my mind suddenly had in it a character. Later, while I was chatting with a comrade at another place and we were talking about how to manage the landlord's sons and daughters, I immediately thought about the girl that I had seen. I thought of all the unknown tortures this girl would have endured in the landlord family, tortures that other people have no way of knowing about. My emotions were suddenly just bestowed onto this character, feeling that this character ought to have experience different from the landlord. But when I actually began writing about her I rethought the fact that this character is not easy to handle. . . . This is to clarify that after a character forms in the mind of the writer, it is deeply and firmly rooted, and so not easy to change. This can allow us to understand something, which is that our minds must have new characters and to stabilize them requires constant attention and nurture. Characters do not just suddenly appear. It is quite incorrect to say that I went to a village and saw a person, came home and wrote about him. The character that you want to write about must have long since been inside your brain already.[79]

Beneath the theory of emotional identification Ding Ling developed here and the suggestion about authorial projection that I leave for analysis later lies what interests me in the context of "Thoughts on March 8": her implicit belief that what will count to *readers* is character.

The narrator's admiration for Zhenzhen is based largely on the girl's ability to withstand physical torture and to endure contempt from those she loves without losing her emotional balance. Zhenzhen is a normative character. Refracted through the narrator's comments and reports about what judgments others pass on her, the story centers on the character of the girl. And because of that doubled quality of female narrator and female character there is an echo effect reinforcing the normative value the story places on coolness, brightness, intelligence, and self-reflection in a woman's temperament and the premium placed on generosity even when those around you are narrow and feudal-minded. Zhenzhen is a thoroughly modern character in the revolutionary sense. She measures her sense of self, her *gexing* or ren'ge, against her own claims on citizenship. She absolutely fits the prototype outlined in Chen Boda's exhortations on the combat style of life for revolutionary woman: "independent, self-respect[ing] and self-confident, unyielding, highly spirited, and opposed to every injustice. . . . their duty is to lead an independent life . . . to stand straight up, secure their individuality, manage an independent living."[80]

Unlike the model of Heini, whom Ding Ling said she saw in a glancing moment emerging from the landlord's gate, Zhenzhen was pure abstraction. The only life models the author had for Zhenzhen were the positive reports friends passed on who had been to the hospital to see the girl spy. And so it is not surprising that in retrospect, Ding Ling would agree with her critics and put Zhenzhen into the camp of protagonists who retained traces of the Sophia prototype. The question is, which characteristics? Zhenzhen has Sophia's stubbornness, but to a degree that is almost unbelievable she is a complacent and phlegmatic subject. The closest Ding Ling came to describing a scene like her older, censorious position on women's weakness is Zhenzhen's single emotional outburst. Then the internal narrator comments simply that "Nothing could be more terrible . . . than a woman who has lost all pride and self-control" (266).

Ding Ling then published a story about a woman who did lose all pride and self-control. It is useful to compare these two stories and their protagonists. "When I Was in Xia Village" reprised Ding Ling's commitment to the centrality of normative characterization in fiction, particularly in Marxist-Leninist fiction. The characterology or scrupulous concern with character elements (*chengfen*) showcased several matters. The very goodness of the character meant that the feudal outlook of normal villagers becomes unjustifiable; if in wartime women must make sexual sacrifices, how can it be ethical then to blame them for sexual crimes? But character focus also meant Ding Ling could showcase the ethical complexity of a backward village and suggest, as she argued explicitly in "Thoughts on March 8," that the future victory of the nation and the Communist Party had to rely on mobilizing precisely the durable ethical potential that the rural female citizen, among other proletarian subjects, possesses. At this level, "When I Was in Xia Village" is not so far away from the basic wartime story "The Unfired Bullet," in which the goodness of the proletarianized agent wins over hostile, feudal elements. "In the Hospital," on the other hand, while also a characterology, centers on a dubious subject, Lu Ping. This story repeats Ding Ling's authorial commitment to character, but it reverses the equation she had established in "Xia Village." Lu Ping is consequently a systematic study in feminine weakness.[81]

"In the Hospital" also fictionalized the questions Ding Ling posed in "Thoughts on March 8" regarding the future facing educated female elites in the Border Region. Lu Ping, an ardent and independent but inexperienced girl, is the normative character. She summarizes the problem of petit bourgeois educated women and the undisciplined potential they offer to the future. In the immediate plot, Lu, a dreamy, literary sort of midwife, reports to a Communist lying-in hospital to begin her assigned duties. Even with only middle school training she is better educated than most of the other women working there. Also, she assumes the importance of basic hygiene, modern medical techniques, sanitary work conditions, and other modernist reforms, and her rural comrades do not. Indeed, the lying-in hospital is like all work units: rife with sexual politics, factional differences, simple ignorance, lack of forbearance, and other quotidian annoyances. On top of that, the physical conditions of the hospital fall far short of Lu's rosy expectations of what the revolutionary life is like. There is little light and much damp darkness. Lu works hard to remedy the deficiencies around her: she associates herself with the more progressive young doctors and nurses; she tries with little success to serve the masses with cheerful fortitude; and she struggles to ignore the gossip that her efforts are just to attract men rather than to improve medical care. After a miscalculation that nearly kills her, she has an emotional breakdown and recovers very slowly.

"It doesn't seem to surprise anyone," Ding Ling wrote in "Thoughts on March 8," "that women make up a big proportion of the staff in hospitals, sanatoria, and clinics." Perhaps this offhand comment had resonance among the very girls and women reading "In the Hospital" and identifying with the struggle of Lu Ping, perhaps even learning "strategy" from Lu's personal failings. When the senior cadre corps at Yan'an finally required Ding Ling to make a public self-criticism for publishing "Thoughts on March 8," she directed this audience to withhold their sympathy. They should realize that although she had poured into the essay the "blood and tears" as well as "sorrow and fervent hopes" that she had held "for many years," she had not expressed her point well.[82] Perhaps the same group of men and women who had drawn attention to the weaknesses of Party policy on women also knew how to read the metaphor of the hospital as a place where women make up the greater proportion of the staff. The character Lu Ping certainly expresses disappointment at her assignment. She would rather be a famous writer or, if that is out of reach, at least a famous mass leader. In the relative obscurity of the unheroic gynecology department of an out-of-the-way lying-in hospital, however, she is forced through hardship and disappointment to accept the "iron discipline of the Party" and some genuine wisdom in the process. The lesson she learns is that her standing in the community must certainly be compromised if she cannot control herself. Few comrades will be able grasp what is implied by the independent life of women. "You are a good person," says Lu's mentor, a soldier who has lost both feet because of bad medical care. "But you have no notion of strategy" (264). This, too, echoes the advice Ding Ling would offer female and male readers of her zawen. Having no strategy means that Lu contravenes the four maxims that "Thoughts on March 8" directly specified were the keys to how the "modern, aware woman" of the future learns to deal with adversity, misunderstanding, and injustice.

Lu Ping's characterology shows how countermanding the maxims brings catastrophe. First, overstrung and at a constant fever pitch emotionally, she willfully ignores her own health. Though shivering with cold, she imagines that it is more "revolutionary" to suffer than to ask for a thick quilt. She works and plays to excess; indeed, the less satisfaction she gets from her compulsive work pace, the more extreme her behavior becomes. Her grand-standing consequently has the opposite effect of her intention, turning the comrades away from her. Second, Lu has no conception of what happiness might mean under her circumstances. "Make sure you are happy," Ding Ling had written to readers of the zawen. "Only when you are happy can you be youthful, active, fulfilled in your life and steadfast in the face of all difficulties. . . . This sort of happiness is not a life of contentment, but a life of struggle and advance."[83] In theory, Lu knows (as Zhenzhen seems intuitively to understand) what Lenin said: "Being unhappy is the greatest insult to life." To Lu, oscillating between frantic and aggressive desire to prove her revolutionary optimism and neurasthenic despair at her disappointments and failures (to say nothing of the flaws and insufficiencies of those around her), happiness is chimerical. She cannot know what Ding Ling already knew and had already expressed in another short story, "Zhandou shi xiang-shou" (To struggle is pleasure): that happiness is created out of a realistic appraisal of one's real circumstances.[84] Lu's struggles go awry because she cannot see outside of her own self-enclosed emotional limitations, just as Sophia is trapped in her own consciousness. And she cannot think rationally at all when she is caught in the downward, neurasthenic spiral of unhappiness. So she contravenes another of Ding Ling's imperatives. "Yes, one ought to struggle!" the narrator declaims, but "with whom ought she to struggle? With everyone?" The more irrational the character becomes, the more unrealistic her demands on the hospital to provide her patients with supplies unavailable anywhere in the Border Region. Eventually, even her close friends Liya and Zheng Peng criticize her; her former allies among the orderlies tag her as a "romantic."

Consequently, Lu cannot remain resolute in the face of hardship. "Not to suffer," Ding Ling told her readers on March 9, "is to become degenerate. The strength to carry on should be nurtured through the quality of perseverance" (320). The Lu Ping character illustrates what happens to an "aware, modern woman" who fails to "cast off [her] rosy illusions" in a hostile world. "Real life made her feel too frightened. . . . She took a critical look at her everyday life; in the end, what good did it do for the Revolution? Since the Revolution was for the greatest number of people, why were even the closest of comrades still so lacking in love? She was wavering; she asked herself, am I not faltering in relation to the Revolution? The neurasthenia she'd had before came back to bother her again, she had insomnia every night. . . . The labels of petit bourgeois consciousness, heroism of the intelligentsia, liberalism, and so forth were all pinned on her" (262).

Lu Ping is not an admirable character. Comprehensible in context, she is obviously a negative model sympathetically drawn. But the Lu Ping Bildung is sufficiently ambivalent that it, along with "When I Was in Xia Village" and "Thoughts on March 8," was classified as a poisonous weed in the show trials that convicted Ding Ling in the mid-1950s. The tragicomedy of critical opinion is not my point.

As she had in the "positive" characterology of Zhenzhen, Ding Ling made character the central issue in "In the Hospital," too. She in effect ceded to ethical criticism the question of what constitutes a woman. This is not to deny the strain of moralism in Ding Ling's earliest portraits. But there is a qualitative difference in the revolutionary fiction. Everyone has a say in these stories. Gossip abounds; allies and enemies express their opinion of the ethical-political value of the character and measure her behavior on primitive axes like emotional liberalism, heroism of the intellectuals, and other mediated virtues. There are not even the normative tensions that I argued characterized the progressive Confucian dogma of a Chen Hongmou, although I think that discernible in Ding Ling's sketches is a dilemma plot very similar to the parable of the woman who sacrificed her son to save her nephew.

My point here is two-pronged. First, these communist feminist or revolutionary modernist morality tales reverberate with the kind of tensions that are familiar from earlier eras. The deeply psychologized portraits of female subjects that Ding Ling developed in response to the question posed in progressive Chinese feminism and eugenics theory proposed an interior for femininity that simply had not existed in fiction before. That is one reason why Dai Jinhua and Meng Yue positioned Ding Ling at the beginning of the female tradition in modern Chinese vernacular fiction. Second, Ding Ling herself participated in a recalibration that linked the interiorized female characterology to the moralism of communist nationalism. Increasingly, her own narrative persona got caught-up in the dilemmas of good behavior. This is explicit in *One Year* and its ratification of self-criticism sessions. The Maoist moralization of politics makes the revolutionary record notoriously difficult to read. In 1999 a researcher named Gu Man published a short report in the *Ding Ling yanjiu tongxun* (Ding Ling research newsletter). In the three-page document, Gu reported on an older comrade who had reinitiated a rumor after Ding Ling's death in 1986: "On Ding Ling's body was collected all the defects of all bad women."[85] Not the case! Gu Man said. To the contrary, Ding Ling's body was the concentrated place where moral integrity and the bitter suffering of the Chinese intellectuals and upright Party members had unfolded.

## Writing, Feelings, and funü

I want to return briefly to the question of the normative female subject, funü, and the instructions Ding Ling gave Marxist-Leninist writers who wanted to write about funü. Recall that Ding Ling had once seen a girl exiting a landlord's house and had cathected the girl in a single glance. Eventually, Ding Ling used this surge of emotion and the image of the innocent girl to expose the darkness of the lives of girls and women growing up in elite families. Her emotions, she had explained, became invested in the feeling that this character ought to be different from the landlord. The nub of the problem was that once a writer develops insight into a character it is difficult to change that initial, intuitive apprehension. Writers do not just go to a village, see someone, come home and write up the character. The character "must have long since been inside your brain already."

Ding Ling made this point in 1954. Later in her published statement, she tries to justify her treatment of the middle peasant character in the novel, *Gu Yung*, saying that she had met a real person just like Gu Yung during the land reform. In the antirightist campaign against Ding Ling, her generosity to the representative middle peasant character in the novel ranked with allegations of sexualized disloyalty in female characters as major "crimes" deserving judgment, punishment, and reform. But in 1954 Ding Ling was arguing that in the struggle to properly represent the truth of land revolution the writer had to write intimately from life. Over twenty-five years later she ratified the same point. Chairman Mao was correct about literature's need to reflect life and right about the requirement that writers "enter into life" (*shenru shenghuo*), she explained. Her own practice involved a struggle to break out of her original tight circle of experience and reach into the greater social universe. Her unceasing efforts meant her skills had improved. Skill meant she could describe what lay close at hand, the immediate life of the people, without error or distortion. There were two further implications. First, good literature requires critical commentary (she seems to mean the process of passing political judgment) because that keeps the writer on the straight and narrow, and anyway, no one writer can see everything accurately. Second, good writers must love what they endeavor to represent.[86]

I want to address the question Ding Ling stressed here of loving what you represent because it will help me to explain what I mean when I conclude that Du Wanxiang (the paragon young wife, orphan, and army dependent whom Ding Ling memorialized in the immediate post-Mao years) is a parable of communist feminism and the apotheosis of its female subject, *funü*. In "Shenghuo, sixiang yü renwu" (Life, thought and character), Ding Ling explained that good Marxist-Leninist writers will each have an individual style, but all will share the need to establish intimacy with the object of reflection or representation and make that object (*duixiang*) as familiar as one's own family. Like childhood friends, you must make the masses so immediately present to your imagination that no matter how much time elapses between when you first see an individual and the next time you see her, the comfort level remains and you can draw her up to the threshold of representation with ultimate ease. But dialectically, the representer is within the same process as those whom she seeks to reflect in fiction. Your own character must be tempered and influenced in the very process of becoming intimate and learning to love the people who stand beyond the immediate circle of your own life. In other words, the people may be changing rapidly in the era of mobilization and land reform, but so are the writers, reshaped in the emotional surgery of countertransference. The problem is that the writer ultimately is going to do something with the emotion that she exchanges with the subject of her writing.

This is how Ding Ling described that exchange in 1954. "Let's say I go to a village where there is an old granny," she wrote, and develop an intimacy with her. "I treat her as I treat my own mother. But what if she does not treat me as her daughter? Then I still do not understand her. *You absolutely must get to where you treat her as a mother, and she treats you as a daughter, and only that is the mutual emotional relation.* To get this you must give her something over a long time, give her emotion [*ganqing*], swap a piece of your heart [*jiang xing suan xing*], look for her, care what she's doing [*guan ta de shi*], pay attention to her, help her, and treat her with harmonious feelings and intentions. There will come a day when you and she are equals, when she completely trusts you. Then your friendship is confirmed [ni zhe ge pengyou cai suan jiao dingle]" (171; emphasis added). You absolutely cannot, Ding Ling continued, cultivate such people to extract their stories. Ethically, writers must not abuse the trust of the people they learn to love or nurture them in emotional bad faith. Writers are part of the project of establishing the truth of Marxist-Leninist theory, truths stemming from the accurate representation of a historical moment. But writers cannot write merely from theory or cold observation. They must create inside a flow of true emotion. A reciprocal motion of love between the granny and the writer ensures accuracy and literary quality beyond formula or formalism.

A basic problem is that the "object" of the writer's attentions knows that the writer has special powers. The relation between writer and object is consequently very complex. Not only are the people afraid that you will write about them (pa ni xie ta), but they will lie to you if they know you are a writer or reporter and if you have no emotional bond with them. They will simply give you the false story they have concocted for officials. They know that you are "not an ordinary person," that you are not simply one among many, but rather that "you constitute a representative. You are there" in the village or on the state farm "to enter into the struggle, to lead the struggle, interfere with life and become one with the people there [da cheng yi pian]." Perhaps they also know that you must withdraw and reflect on the dialectic of knowing before you can write meaningfully, critically, and compassionately, as is your obligation. Nonetheless, the opportunism of the writer and the subaltern's fear of being represented will mutually subside if the writer passionately loves life, the people, and the slow, ardent work of coming to know them (170).

When the Central Committee restored to Ding Ling the right to publish under her own name, she said that the twenty years she had spent "under," floating along beneath the surface of mass life in places that are rarely lifted into literary representation, had a few positive aspects. "I saw," she said, "many people and many things that would not have been visible to me from the surface."[87] Having made character itself the site within fiction and political representation where ethics is enacted or performed, and the place where historical accuracy (i.e., the writer gets it right) and correct action (the people get it right) are open to measurement, Ding Ling had nowhere to fall back when she herself was accused of betraying the people and committing the sin of historical anachronism. She herself had made an open book of the question of women's character and behavior. This transparency of self and literature opened the writer and her product to scrutiny. Writing or bringing into representation degraded subjects, characters engaged in socially distasteful acts, and sexualized subjects was held to degrade the writer, too. Part of Ding Ling's moral charge in "Thoughts on March 8" called on the government to support the Zhenzhens and discipline the potential of Lu Pings. Of course, Ding Ling embarrassed individuals in 1942 and called attention to their sexual lives. That move itself made more transparent yet another problem. To rescue He Hanming's wife from the status of "under"—to enable the wife to speak for herself in the idiom of the enlightened state—meant drawing attention to He's girlfriend. The lustful exchange between He and Gui filiated with their new political power to exploit others. Another thing this description of sexual power did was to criminalize lust because it made sexual fidelity a matter of state policy. At the very least, Ding Ling was herself positioning sexuality in an ethicopolitical frame: What responsibility does the Party have to abandoned wives?

There is an element of the right to represent the proletarianized Other that Ding Ling returned to over and over even during her internal exile. Recall that He Hanming's wife, Chen Man, and Guo Jingqing (the cross-dressing revolutionary female soldier) all come from the same social strata. They are among the most degraded, proletarianized subjects in the entire rural context. Chen and Guo learn to represent themselves. Through their actions and intentions they appeal to the state's representatives directly, bypassing the local patriarchal family and village structure, which in part is responsible for their continuing oppression. Chen breaks into spontaneous songs to Chairman Mao, rather like the "little devil" child in "The Unfired Bullet" when he recruits the local people into the anti-Japanese resistance. Ding Ling consistently made the Chinese Revolution and Communist Party the agents of liberation to these most oppressed of the oppressed, slaves of slaves multiply enslaved, the destitute, the sexually ambiguous, the often prostituted, raped, and degraded rural woman. The evidence suggests that during her twelve years of hard labor reform on state farms in the Great Northern Wastes, Ding Ling came to see herself as one of them.

Evidence of a slow authorization of herself as a state's subject, funü, in ethical and revolutionary transformation comes in an interesting piece Ding Ling published illegally and pseudonymously, by taking the name of the woman allegedly telling the story. Entitled "Wo de shenghuo huiyi" (Recollections on my life) it is the autobiography of a real person, Ren Guangrong, who had worked with Ding Ling in a chicken breeding operation. Ren was also a Hunanese, like Ding Ling herself. During a famine when she was a child, she and her family set off to beg sustenance and work. Homeless, threatened by dogs and cruel children (themselves only marginally better off than she), reduced to shit-gathering to buy grain, the family was saved from perishing in 1949 when Ren's uncle, with the Communist Party's guidance, led the poor to take over the Peasant Association. As the story opens, Ren is a genuine worker in the advanced sector of the state farm, receiving a wage for her social labor. She has two pairs of clothes and money in the bank and is learning how to read. The simple first-person narrative account of her suffering and her revolutionary redemption concludes with a praise song, which she sings to the great benefactor (*da'enren*) of the poor, the Chinese Communist Party.[88] Ding Ling, of course, no longer had the legal right to represent this other woman. She was a Big Rightist, and so she had the liberty only of teaching the other how to read, a fact that is elided in the story of Ren Guangrong. Out of love for the other, her object and her subject, Ding Ling decided to illegally supplement Ren's achievements and to compensate for her not quite adequate literacy. Ren appears to represent herself, just as Ding Ling appeared to not be ghost writing "Recollections on My Life." What interests me in the relationship struck here between Ren and Ding Ling is that emotional exchange forms the core of normative representation. In actual fact, the "I" in the narrative is a fusion of literate and illiterate, represented and writer, for there is literally only one model of womanhood left and it is Ren Guangrong. Ren Guangrong is a shared or partible subject where the writer and written meet and fuse into a single subject, *funü*, that will enable one to surface into representation at the expense of the other.[89]

The verdict against Ding Ling in 1958 was "Big Rightism," an ethico-moral crime against the people. Whether she accepted the judgment against her or not, her life depended on personal improvement calibrated in normative terms. In the late 1980s, Zheng Xiaofeng based his account of Ding Ling's farm years on newspaper-style investigation and reportage. He went to visit the units where she had worked to find out what her record had been over the dozen years she spent in labor. His 1989 account suggests that for whatever reason, strategy and moral reflection had long since fused in Ding Ling's self-presentation. The subject she became was the moral embodiment of precisely that ethically rigid, ideologically defined, political subject *funü*, which, as a Party member and a woman, Ding Ling felt it her duty to teach the Ren Guangrongs of the world. Take the example of an anecdote that Zheng Xiaofeng gathered from a certain He Fuyou about Ding Ling's ethical self-presentation:

> One day Ding Ling's stove went out and started leaking fumes. She came and got me to help her fix it. Ding Ling asked me: Lao He, do you think I am a bad person? I was startled. Lao Ding continued. Some folks say that we are Big Rightists. How do you take it? I said: Rightists are sent to us from the central government. When you came into our midst and once we connected with you, heard what you have

to say, saw what you do, we knew that you were a good comrade and not a bad person. Look, when something goes wrong on the chicken line the leadership always says: Call Lao Ding. Everyone is very assured around you. Is that so? Yes that is the case. They are all very assured. Ding Ling's two black eyes sparkled with tears of emotion and she said: From now on I'll serve you folks more courageously. I came here to be reformed and so please raise any point where you see my incorrect spots and I'll reform them. I thought happily: She truly is a revolutionary of the old guard, so modest and humble. Every year the masses appraised her and everyone said that Lao Ding should have had the hat [of political criminality] removed. In 1961 Chen Ming's hat was removed, but not hers. In 1962, others, and still not her. . . . This person utterly devoted to the Party with all her heart, why does her reform never end?[90]

It is an interesting question. In fact, it suggests that Ding Ling's entrenchment around reform of self had the strategic aim of alleviating danger, relaxing the people surrounding her. The strategy proved useful when outside agitator Red Guards attacked Rightists in 1966 and the local people protected her from excessive abuse. But it also hints at another, slightly different message. If the Big Rightist Ding Ling herself spoke the idiom of self-reform, and if the people around her judged her, as the people of Xia Village had judged Zhenzhen, on an index of reform, then continuing the judgment against her reversed the relation of criminal and judge. Who better to judge the crimes of the central government than the undeservedly criminalized icon of revolutionary feminine endurance?[91]

Funü in the Future Anterior

Sustaining the peculiar rhetorical integrity of Maoist ideolect and its world is difficult. Irony and sarcasm threaten it, as Commander Wang Zhen did when he advised Ding Ling in 1958 to put in her time, wait for things to blow over, and just go back to Beijing. Local police can punish and otherwise threaten even a left-wing, Maoist, Big Rightist like Ding Ling, a reminder that far more than an ethical deviation, "rightist" is a dangerous, criminal, legal status.[92] Between cynicism and actual vulnerability, Ding Ling's strategy appears to have been to recreate a Yan'an-style modernity in her new, backward, bedeviled rural borderland. Whatever her immediate motive, this stance became explicit in the early 1960s, when her chief accuser, Zhou Yang, invited her to return to Beijing. Ding Ling wrote back to the Writers Union saying that as the Central Committee encouraged writers to go down to the grassroots (jiceng) and she was already there, she had decided to remain so she could bring the Yan'an revolutionary tradition to the Great Northern Waste.

Her reference to Yan'an models in the Great Northern Waste is significant for two reasons. First, over the past two decades, Ding Ling has become the apotheosis of "the Yan'an way." Wang Zhongchen and Shang Xia's study of Ding Ling's political "crimes," for instance, argues that she was innocent of all charges against her in 1942. "Thoughts on March 8" was just "a little one-sided." The error in that essay was immoderacy, her inability to see the bright with the dark, and consequently the author's exaggeration of the need for women to struggle independently of the revolutionary state effort to ensure women's emancipation within the revolutionary state. Historically, contemporaries had not considered the zawen a threat to the Revolution. On the contrary, principled criticism was the hallmark of that heroic era. Ding Ling, they alleged, had felt sufficiently comfortable with the criticisms of her position that she generously admitted to more responsibility for the rash of critical publications than she honestly had to. She had nothing to fear or to hide in her record at Yan'an. All the more reason to recreate Yan'an in Chahar and cast herself as its very embodiment.[93]

But also in Ding Ling's actual practice the measure of revolutionary modernity turns out to be funü. In the several gulag villages where she lived for many years, Ding Ling developed a series of projects targeting female illiteracy, women's labor, women as heroic material for revolutionary arts, and the revolutionary transformation of backward female subproletarians into modern, productive citizens. Ren Guangrong brings home a salary. Her labor is socialized. Though remaining a mother, daughter, and wife, she is also a worker. Zheng makes the point that Ding Ling refused the chance to establish a relationship with a young woman named Xiao Wang Gang who wanted to become a writer, saying, "In the past we have relied on literature to develop a relationship with the people. Now I want to develop a relationship with the people by relying on labor and immersing myself in them."[94]

Yet there is something flat in Ren Guangrong, Deng Wanrung, and the other heroic rural female workers who populate Ding Ling's manuscripts of her last thirty years. This moral flatness had precedent. Critics called attention to the vacuous goodness of Yu Manzhen in Ding Ling's 1933 novel, *Mother*. Her very best critic, Feng Xuefeng, also noted the "abstract" characterization of Zhang Yumin, secretary of the Party branch of Nuanshui Village in the Sanggan River valley where Ding Ling set the Stalin Prize–winning novel, *The Sun Shines over the Sanggan River*.[95] Actually, this description holds true for many of Ding Ling's funü characters. What she said in response to the characterological criticism of her novel is that Zhang

Yumin "represents a positive progressive character [*daibiao zhengmian liliang de xianjin renwu*]."[96] The writer seemed to be suggesting that goodness as a quality of character or a quality in normative characters has little real content. Goodness is not a known quantity, but an untested potentiality. Perhaps Ding Ling was suggesting here that the positive content of characters who are caught up in revolution (i.e., in the progressive, forward movement of revolution) can be judged only in retrospect. Only when the character is judged from a standpoint in a future retrospection can we know for sure what is the positive content of the "positive progressive character."

Ding Ling's notion of the "positive progressive character" evaluation holds true in her writing about the Maoist category funü, and consequently is a good example of the historical status of that sort of feminist subject. I have already suggested that funü was a notion stabilized in the mobilization politics of the New Democracy, and that consequently it persisted as a social fact within the Maoist ideolect. This made funü a social fact in policy terms. I invoked Chen Yung-fa's monograph to support my argument that political categories really were finely calibrated to social realities, and consequently that funü must be grasped as a subject within state's discourse and not a linguistic curiosity.[97] But now I want to argue that funü was also an ethical ideal, a projection of possibility or, in Ding Ling's terms, a "positive progressive character." To make this case I turn to a brief analysis of Ding Ling's famous 1947 novel which won the Stalin Prize for Literature in 1951, and to the way the character Heini operates there.

*The Sun Shines over the Sanggan River* (hereafter *S G R*) recounts how a Chahar village, Nuanshui tan, carries out its land reform struggle.[98] With fifty named characters and scores of others in this long novel, subplots proliferate on the model of *Tale of the Three Kingdoms*. Eventually, each subplot feeds the main force of the story, the problem of how to overthrow the village hegemon, Qian Wengui, and his feudal allies. Animating the novel and providing a genuine psychological intensity is the question of whether the spontaneity of peasant rage will finally be able to connect with the rising consciousness of characters who represent the abstraction of the Communist Party and its revolutionary technologies.[99] The members of the village Party branch, the Land Reform Work Team assigned to Nuanshui, and the masses all working intensively still require three campaigns before their accumulated, mobilized rage breaks out into open accusations and a demand for land and justice. Beneath the great arc of the waves of mobilization structuring the novel proliferate complex subplots demonstrating the extent and nature of Qian's dominance, the complex intersection in the village of class and kinship differences, the anxiety of how to assign differences between the poor and the more poor in class categories, the history of the revolutionary movement in Nuanshui, and the strengths and flaws of its core cadre in the Peasants Association, Party branch, militia, Women's Association, and other government institutions. Marriages figure into the subplots and so does the secret romantic connection between Cheng Ren, chairman of the Peasant Association, and Heini, "landlord" Qian Wengui's niece and serf. Yet the struggle session in which the Liu brothers finally spark the assault on the landlord and the exultant sharing of the spoils of the struggle leave many questions unanswered. The future remains an open question.

In a 1980 reevaluation of this long-forgotten novel, Cai Kui Zhenhai argued that *SGR* was more than anything a staggeringly Maoist text. Not only did it reflect the Chairman's thinking at the time it was written, but its thematics of process instantiated and reflected the Mao position on land reform theory generally. I agree with Cai Kui, and would add from the distance of a post-Maoist world that the analysis is also marked by Maoist habits of thinking. For instance, the microhistorical events in the village unfold contingently. This quality of contingency within the great revolutionary overplot of History seems to emerge from the way the narrator returns readers to the repetitive relation of theory and practice. The necessarily endless unfolding of willed revolutionary action comes about in the evaluation of the successes and failures of specific actions and their effects. At various levels of Communist awareness, the various flawed characters who populate the space of the novel—the village Party branch, the government cadre, the members of the Party land reform Work Team, the county party chief—contribute their experience and their vision as well as their weaknesses (*quedian*) and failures.[100]

Ding Ling, as I showed earlier, insisted that she wrote literature from life. This meant two things. First, living people were the objects for character and plot. For instance, after leaving prison in the early 1980s, she returned to the Sanggan River basin to meet again the people she had observed and worked alongside during the writing of the novel. But second, "life" referred back through the Maoist ideolect as a claim to objectivity. By the time Ding Ling wrote about revolutionary modernity in the microcosmic space of Nuanshui village, life had come to mean something quite different from unmediated personal experience.[101] Life meant that complex and fleeting moment when the conscious, willed, active agency of a common people thrust History toward enlightenment. To "enter life" and write about it was, consequently, a battle constantly waged against anachronism. The ideological grid that gave writers and mass leaders their ability to anticipate, initiate, reflect, criticize, regroup, and reanticipate—the mass line in land reform—also gave a writer like Ding Ling the optic she needed to reflect (we might say represent) what is significant in historical life.

Every detail in this concentrated narrative broadcasts the immediacy of the political event filtered through the meaningful language of Maoist dialectics. Every detail, from the acreage Gu Yong passes on his way into Nuanshui village to the kind of paper he uses to wrap his land title deeds, signifies only one thing: that Gu Yung is not a rich but rather a "well-to-do middle peasant," as his true character and the accretion of concrete, vivid, accurate detail will eventually go to prove. Gu has to emerge as a correct or accurate version of the ideologically constituted person of his class so that his misclassification can be put to rights as we read the concrete evidence of his actual class nature. In the novel, Gu (like all the other characters except one) is a sign of the larger order, his character composed of other signs that we learn to trust and that deepen the hermeneutic interpretive possibilities the novel and the land reform event itself provide. Revolutionary literature and art reflect the reality of the "concrete form" of life's basic characteristics and protocols.[102]

I noted earlier, on the basis of David Holm's exhaustive study, that Maoist policy on the arts in Yan'an held culture to be the glue keeping the social structure intact. This "new Enlightenment" position is central to the way Ding Ling organized *SGR*. Specifically, the break with the old order and the beginning of the mass's movement toward the New Society comes when the villagers collaborate in the effort to speak Qian's true name out loud. Qian's power is rooted in his ability to make strategies and extract knowledge out of people. He is "spiderlike" in his ability to weave compromising nets involving many people, complicating the real conditions of people's oppression with the old cultural or feudal outlooks. He draws on his kinship relationships with Heini, for instance, to obscure the fact that she is his slave.[103]

The Qian character embodies what passes for elite opinion in this tiny miserable village. *Qian* (wealth, money), *wen* (culture), *gui* (value, expense, dearness, cost, honorable)[104] holds the power, and yet the masses collude because they are unwilling or unable to speak out against him. The core of the plot is the lesson of how the people learn to recode Qian's old sign system. When their own counterhegemonic, minoritarian cultural norms finally erupt out of their feudal constraints during the struggle session, they crush the despot because they nullify his language. Ding Ling broke the novel into a series of cycles that illuminate the stalemate of peasant speech and clarify its "cultural" or semiotic force. Thus, for instance, chapters 1 through 7 mark out one long rumor cycle as female kin visit each other's courtyards seeking intelligence and checking out rumors that a struggle against the landlords is being planned. A second cycle stretches from chapters 18 through 23, balancing the domestic cycle against an exterior, male effort among the Party cadre to set a political language into currency so the poor peasants will have a filter that allows them to represent themselves as the oppressed. Yet the masses still fail because they cannot find a political word for Qian and they fear the unspeakable. For their part, the outside Party cadres who have arrived to oversee the village land reform simply do not understand the coded language the village cadres use when they call Qian Wengui a "landlord." Qian has virtually no land! How can he be a landlord in its absence? But in fact, this outside work team injects into the village a discourse that has little relevance to the way Qian actually maintains his feudal position. It is not that the poor misunderstand the nature of their oppression; the problem is that theory and practice have not yet struck a unity. Ding Ling's episodic narrative pulls the reader spasmodically toward that essential political moment: the popular naming of that power and the politicizing struggle session against Qian.

Of course, it requires some very skilled outside intervention in the person of Zhang Pin, the county Party committee director of propaganda, to show the land reform team and village Party branch how important it is to speak the name of the oppressor. Only Zhang seems to understand that when "nobody brought up" Qian's name, it means that "the people didn't dare speak out" (237; 250). Zhang explains to the work team and the reader that the villagers must face the oppressor and speak his name, and in that speech their relation to him will be reversed. But even when Qian is paraded in front of them, his hands in fetters, the people are still at a loss and silenced by his look, the memory of his cruelty. "The peasants hated him, and had just been cursing him; but now that he stood before them they held their breath and faltered. . . . The longer the silence lasted, the greater Qian's power became until it looked like he was going to win" (272; 286).

In staging this encounter and placing such weight on the matter of the peasant's need to name the oppressor, Ding Ling was certainly playing on the Maoist view that the cultural sign always has two potential references, one pointing backward to the national (and complexly feudal) past, the other simultaneously forward to the bright potential of enlightened, international socialism. The silent confrontation between Qian and the masses, "like the pause before two game cocks start fighting," reminds us that speech is part of the Maoist notion of cultural glue and consequently portends progress or reaction, depending on who dominates the speech act. The drama of how the peasants burst open the despotic language of the old order and begin to speak in their progressive mass voice lies beyond my immediate argument here. Suffice it to say that beneath the old and resolvable order of legible signs that will make possible the correct resolution of class categories and consequently the just division of land lies another, abstract way of understanding how the villagers behave. This second level is the populist, national character of the people. They must live in a world of life choices and ethical possibilities that are available to the revolutionary writer as the positive future content of a progressive peasant collectivity. In this subliminal form of ideation poor peasants become a collectivity synecdochically along the axes of oppression and oppressed, sanity and insanity, honesty and corruption, old and young, male and female. *SGR* is a synecdoche of the future of the People's Republic of China at this level.

But I raise the issue of speech and its centrality in the novel to make two further points. First, this is a Maoist novel. It expresses the concrete Maoist theoretical aesthetic worked out among the Yan'an cultural elite in the early 1940s. Second, a single character out of hundreds remains speechless even after the resolution of the standoff between the villagers and the despot, the oppressors and the oppressed. And that is the character of Heini. I think a good argument can be made that Heini is also a representative "positive progressive character" (*daibiao zhengmian liliang de xianjin renwu*) in Ding Ling's special understanding of the unspecified and untested good embodied in future perfect characters like Manzhen and Meilin, who passively indicate what women shall have become in a future order.[105] In the context of Chinese communist feminism there is more to be said about the character of Heini.

As Ding Ling was to remark many times over the years, Heini is a minor character in the vast canvas of the novel; she appears infrequently. But what readers could not help notice was that whenever Heini does appear, it is in the context of some ambiguity. The sweetheart of Cheng Ren, she complicates the easy line the Party cadre wants the poor peasants to draw between themselves and the oppressors. The niece of the poor peasant Wenfu, Heini complicates the problem of affect, for she loves him and would prefer to live a life of poverty in his household than be sold to the highest bidder. She is chaste and good, unlike the villainous landlord wives and running dogs of Qian, though of course she seems to belong to the same class they do. Her life is easy and comfortable because she is clothed and eats well, unlike the poor peasant women who own nothing and may even be trapped in their courtyard hovels because they have no clothing to cover their nakedness.

In 1980 literary critic Yang Guixin repeated, perhaps unknowingly, the citational practice Ding Ling employed when she wrote under the name of the poor peasant woman Ren Guangrong. "My surname is Qian," Yang's essay begins. "My given name is Heini. I am the niece of the hegemon landlord Qian Wengui, a character written down by the old writer Comrade Ding Ling. In 1946 during the land reform movement in Nuanshui tan I began to not have a voice at meetings. Now, in the presence of one and all, I want to defend myself."[106] I was not allowed to speak in Ding Ling's novel, Yang's "Heini" continues (and throughout this essay Heini speaks in the first person). It should be said that in this lament, Yang remanded a line of criticism that began with Feng Xuefeng and runs through the antirightist movement and Zhou Yang, the ultra-left line of the Gang of Four and into the late 1970s, during the Dengist rehabilitation of Ding Ling. Critics had nearly universally pointed to the Heini character as "weak." The presumption was that Ding Ling had not known what to do with the character, and most critics cited the author's offhand remark that she had kept the Heini figure in the novel because readers liked her.

Yang Guixin asked the question Why wasn't my oppression dignified? Heini is an orphan, a motherless child. Her oppressions exceed the domain of the merely economic because she is a slave and consequently a sign of superexploitation; like a cow, she is being raised for the marriage market. Her oppression exceeds the political categories that other progressive female literary characters like Qun Lan and White Haired Girl embody because, though he robbed her of wages and freedom itself, Qian implicated her in his power when he sent Heini to school for four years to become literate. This increased her value in the marriage market and it shut her off from the collectivity of village women, who are virtually defined by the tragedy of their illiteracy and who, in a memorable scene, refuse to allow Heini to participate in their mobilization as the Women's Association.

I cannot join the Women's Association, "Heini" continues. I do not dare to approach the male "outside cadre." I would like to have married a poor peasant, Cheng Ren, or even to have lived with my poor peasant uncle, Qian Wenfu, but the hegemon would not allow it. At the time Ding Ling wrote about me it would have been anachronistic for her to have done anything more than she did because girls in those days were far too ashamed and unsure of themselves to speak openly about topics like marriage, must less love. Now I am fifty years old and I have endured enormous suffering and injustice under the incorrect lines on status and classification. I will speak out. Critics today only reconsign me to living hell when they repeat the earlier notion that I am passive or a Sophia character. I probably needed the Liberation more even than the male poor peasants did because I was a slave, imprisoned in the family of the feudal hegemon, suffocated in a net of relationships. Yes, I am typical! I am a "normative or typical character of a normative or typical environment" (*dianxing huangjing zhong de dianxing renwu*), but in another respect I am indefinable (288). And I am a sign of superexploitation. The key question to ask yourself is: "Have I got a family? Is Qian Wengui's family really my family?" (277).[107]

Before proceeding to examine the emergence in the twenty years since Ding Ling's death of a critical tradition that now has made her an exemplary communist feminist, I want to draw one final point about temporality out of Yang's essay. In the progressive Chinese feminist conventions of the 1930s, I have argued, the eugenicist tradition established the natural right of women to play an evolutionary progressive role in choosing their own mates, and it opened up the question of what sort of social character women should claim when they exercised that right. The problem of lacking ren'ge was a central concern in this body of theory. Yang is posing a similar question, in a different way: What will women become, given how dubious their solidarity is now, if it is so difficult for others to recognize their social abjection? How can an Enlightenment open emancipation to women collectively or individually and allow or enable them to legitimately represent themselves? If the poor peasant women nominated themselves as funü but refused to admit into their body the ambiguous and compromised figure of a Heini, who consequently was misclassified in the state's grid, what should happen now that retrospection allows the rectification of errors like this one? Surely the fact that Yang is herself a woman critic and notes in her monograph, Ding Ling chuangzuo zongheng tan (Speaking on the breadth and depth of Ding Ling's creations), that she herself grew up in a village just like Nuanshui, participated in the processes Ding Ling described in the novel, felt a shock of recognition and decided to go into literary cultural work because of having read SGR, is not beside the point.[108] But it is not the only issue. For Yang is a strong advocate of what she calls "our tradition of revolutionary literature." To Yang, there is no contradiction between the nascent communist feminism that she sees in the figure of Heini and Ding Ling's loyalty to the Party state.

## Post-Mao Ding Ling as Icon of the
## Communist Women's Movement

In 1998 Hong Zicheng published his definitive judgment of what he called the "strange phenomenon" of Ding Ling's dismissal from office. His overview, 1956: Bai hua shidai (1956: Era of the Hundred Flowers), one of the volumes in Xie Mian's retrospective series Bai nian Zhongguo wenxue zong xi (One hundred years of Chinese literature), concluded that the show trials and struggle sessions proved to have no substance. As Hong points out, there is no question that Ding Ling was a Maoist.[109] Thirty years after the fact, Hong concludes that the purge stemmed from a confusion, rampant among the writers at the time, between "the Party" and individuals speaking in the name of the Party. This led to hyperpersonalization and the criminalization of personal failings. The personal histories of individuals became maps full of clues to social-political "crimes" against history. Also in the mid-1950s, when Ding Ling was finally sentenced for the crimes of anti-Partyism and Big Rightism, the events of the 1942 Yan'an Forum were being dragged into play and had become retrospectively the imaginary measure of what was acceptable for a normative communist writer. Documentation of this verdict makes very depressing reading.

But Hong Zicheng and Zhou Liangpei's reversal of the verdict on Ding Ling is not my central concern. Here I only want to make one minor and one major concluding point. First, the minor point. The nightmarish writing that made up the bulk of the public campaign to smear and ruin Ding Ling's standing in 1957 as (in Hong's view) China's best living writer of literature capitalized on a refusal to distinguish among a literary character's personal failings, an author's personal history, and what I call historical anachronism. A good example is Zhang Tianyi's long, 10 October 1957 *People's Daily* accusation that Ding Ling's Sophia was an ethically bankrupt character whose legitimacy as such could only be accepted on the following "historical" grounds: (1) if Sophia truly represented the reality of the time, and (2) if no other representation of a piece that more accurately represented the real reality could be found. Neither exculpatory condition prevailed, Zhang insisted. Miss Gan's story "Geju" (Separation) was more representative of the moment, and anyway, chronologically speaking, "Sophia's Diary" had arrived on the historical scene nine years late! Ergo, in the eyes of History, "Sophia's Diary" must be an anachronism. If it was not a simple "reflection" of the times, it had to be something else. That "something," in Zhang's view, was highly suspect. As Miss Sophia "in no way resembled the young people who played roles in the May Fourth era and since in no way large or small did Miss Sophia play the progressive function of those May Fourth youths," what role did she play? Sophia, who in theories of anachronism becomes not just a literary but a real historical player, "lacked all reason, had no spiritual life and had no principles. She thought only of herself. She wanted only to make herself happy, so she could pleasure herself. That is why she is afraid to die . . . wanting only uninterrupted search for new pleasures to satisfy her own desires—such as desire for profit, fame, glory, 'will to power' [quanli yizhi] and even sexual desire." She, Zhang charged, was the embodiment of Hu Shi's humanism![110] Worse, she is an expert in the techniques of love. Not just a romantic, Sophia is a practiced seducer, a woman who wants to "occupy the other, toy with the other to satisfy her own lust."[111] Worse still, she cannot even describe the objects of her desire clearly as she is so completely narcissistic that she loves only her own mirrored self-representation. Zhang then poses the question of why, given her status as mere historical anachronism, anyone would be attracted to Sophia at all. The only people supporting this woman must be people who "completely agree with her." And because by no means whatever could Sophia have ended up joining the revolution, and because she signifies Ding Ling as much as Sophia, the essay concludes with the thought that the current campaign uncovering Ding Ling's secret anti-Party activities is simply the next chapter in the unfolding story of "Sophia's Diary."[112]

In relation to the subjectivity of women in emancipation theory, this preoccupation with anachronism is odd and noteworthy. Of course, when writers and critics adopt Engels's position on literary realism and suture historical and literary time, they can presume further that there exist correct and incorrect ways of representing women. This ideological aesthetic presumes that history will condition and restrict the shapes that concrete women take. The notion of anachronism can be a policing mechanism, in other words. But anachronism also keeps open the question of what women truly are and what they will become. The discovery of anachronism may be as rich a source of emancipation thinking as the charge of anachronism in Zhang is patently a disciplinary one. Maybe Zhang's question, Why privilege Sophia?, requires an answer. Maybe the very capacity of anachronism (this is Zhang's idiom) is to trouble each reduction of women to any one thing. Perhaps what Zhang and so many others after him were to argue was that Ding Ling's crime of anachronism stems from the incapacity of the signifier women to ever completely be exhaustive because no matter how capacious it is, it can never contain everyone.

Zhao Yuan's analysis of SGR expanded a line of criticism of the character Heini that Feng Xuefeng and others in the late 1940s and early 1950s had initiated. Ding Ling, Zhao argued, had not provided Heini with a "process of ideological thought" (sixiang guocheng), and that is why Heini seems so bland and nice. Heini has no capacity for reflexivity; consequently, she has no moral life. Thus, her character has no historical valence beyond "goodness." This was at odds with Ding Ling's own commitment to a literature that reflected the political economy of the times. In other words, Heini was anachronistic. In the broadest sense, then, what commentors read as anachronistic (because they overwhelmingly accept the Engelsian framework for realism, holding that the real in literature is revealed in fidelity to historical processes) is the capacity that some of Ding Ling's female characters have for sliding out from under Marxist-Leninist theory's drive to universalize and its alleged capacity to capture in words a photorealist moment. And surely Marxism-Leninism is not unique in its universalizing drives. Perhaps what I have been calling Ding Ling's characteristic ability to embrace to the limit the given condition of agency in the theoretical framework of her shifting times, while simultaneously calling these representations into question, is registered in the language of critics as a question of anachronism. Even in Ding Ling's complicity with the movement toward characterology, readers encountered enigmatic female figures like Zhenzhen who are both exact vehicles of the new discourse of state womanhood, funü, and yet are still irreducibly complex. In a fascinating twist, what struck critics as anachronistic in Ding Ling's female characters from Sophia to Heini (and what could be more anachronistic than Du Wanxiang at the end of the brutal and devastating Great Proletarian Cultural Revolution?) has come increasingly to be prized in the emergent feminist appreciation of Ding Ling as a female writer about femininity.

The larger, second point regards a drifting movement in Ding Ling criticism, from the historian's preoccupation with reversing an unjust verdict of malfeasance to Ding Ling's eventual resting point now as an icon of feminine endurance and suffering in a narrative of the Communist golden years and, therefore, of national potential squandered. With the exception perhaps of Meng Yue and Dai Jinhua's Lacanian counternarrative of the Chinese women's literary tradition in *Fuchu lishi dibiao* (Surfacing onto the horizon of history; see chapter 7), however, the preponderance of Ding Ling iconography comes from a cohort that embraces the Chinese Marxist-Leninist tradition of revolutionary literature. The formation of the Ding Ling Research Group and the flow of foundational, rehabilitative publications from the Chinese Literature Association (Wenxie) led in 1980 to the surfacing of an entire community of Ding Ling scholars. This scholarly cohort has gone on in its own trajectory, largely unaffected by the initiatives that I describe and analyze in the next two chapters of this book. This recuperation of Ding Ling's literature is quite separate from the new wave feminist initiatives of the 1980s and 1990s.

Communist feminism, on the other hand, as I have suggested here, was a matter largely of mobilization policy and the invention of conventions in ethical portraiture that I have called characterologies. Ding Ling was active in both these domains. Indeed, a case could be made that "Du Wanxiang" is a brilliant caricature of the worker heroine and model women narratives of the Yan'an era. After the Cultural Revolution the enlightened Chinese feminist project was taken up by others whose work is unthinkable in the absence of communist feminists like Ding Ling, but who did not continue these initiatives. When young internationalist theorists like Li Xiaojiang make their forays into literary representation, they turn to their own contemporaries, such as Zhang Jie, rather than to the older Liberation generation and its preoccupation with "entering into life" or its obsession with ethical protocols of communist social revolution. The preoccupations of Dai Jinhua are split between the modern Chinese women's literary tradition, which in her view Ding Ling founded and betrayed, and the contemporary, 1990s domain of sexual difference in film representation.

Nonetheless, filaments of the progressive feminist moment of the 1930s persisted well into the revolutionary period, and the category *funü* was nothing less than a contentious key element of revolutionary modernity. I have presented the case for this argument through Ding Ling's fiction and politics. And, in a sense, the recuperation of Ding Ling as a writer and as a communist feminist reinforces what I am implying is a thorough compatibility of revolutionary Maoism with what are often termed feminist objectives. Xia Kangda's "Zhong ping 'Wo zai Xiacun de shihou' " (A serious critique of "When I Was in Xia Village"), for instance, refuted the charges that the story was a "poisonous weed" (ducao) or an "anti-Party fiction."[113] On the contrary, Xia argued, the story is the reverse or antidote of "poison," because Zhenzhen is both a real character (i.e., the literary representation of a real contemporary) and, more important, she historically represents the broad tragedy of all Chinese women wounded in patriotic warfare during the anti-Japanese war. As Naihua Zhang has confirmed, the category of political mobilization, funü, which Ding Ling did so much to establish in both her embrace of its revolutionary mobilization of villagers into the category of women and her reservations and cautions regarding its weaknesses as a future for national womanhood, kept open the problem of women in the nation-state throughout the Mao period.[114]

The first wave of scholarship reversing the verdict on Ding Ling and returning her to her place in the history of Chinese literature illustrated, too, what the Deng Xiaoping critique of ultra-leftism would entail. After ten years in jail cells, Ding Ling was a poster girl for victims of the Gang of Four. The move to redeem her owed much to the need for loyal victims. On her own part, "seeking truth from facts" seemed to suit her objective of publishing as much as she could to right the record on her political, literary, and personal life. That much is plainly visible in retrospective essays on the Yan'an years and other controversial life experiences, as well as the recalibration of her literary standing by critics like Xia Kangda, Zhao Yuan, Hao Shendao, Yan Jiayan, and Cai Kui Zhenhai.[115] Far more was at stake in the early 1980s recuperation of Ding Ling's fiction than Ding Ling's fiction. The critics and Ding Ling herself built up the new portrait of her as an icon of everything worth monumentalizing about the Yan'an experience—its literary world's freedom from cliquism, the powers it gave the politicized writer to work for the mobilized people, the actual work of going to the popular base of new colloquial Chinese literature, the proletarianization of the tradition of Qu Qiubai's baihua fiction, the ethical seriousness of writers at the heart of the state formation—and joined to that apotheosis of Yan'an an argument that nothing in the Gang of Four period could justify the injustice that this good woman endured on the basis of her principled politics.

Interestingly, these critics also raise the problem of anachronism. Their collective objective is to restore to literary criticism a sense of reality about context. Editors of the volume Ding Ling zuopin pinglun ji (Collected commentary on Ding Ling's work) make this intention vividly clear. Each essay establishes a theme. Xia Kangda deals with politically ominous complexity (fuza) in realist literature, Yan Jiayan with the question of the surrounding environment (*zhouwei huanjing*) or context in the process of literary and historical representation. Cai Kui takes up the issue of historical process (*guocheng*) in order to argue that no literary representation that takes seriously history's processual reality or flow could ever claim to be fixed. Each critic is self-consciously building a case against the sort of logic and reasoning that I illustrated in Zhang Taiyan's attack essay on Ding Ling's Sophia. To that end, Xia pointedly disputes an attack that Yao Wenyuan made in which Yao claimed that Ding Ling used Zhenzhen to express Ding Ling's own hatred of the Yan'an Border Region and its Party government. On the contrary, Xia argues, it is *Yao's* point that is anachronistic, for what Ding Ling actually did was to demonstrate the complexity that she and her contemporaries encountered; to deny this complexity with benefit of hindsight is precisely to misrepresent historical reality. Yan Jiayan's theme of the surrounding environment is organized in the same way. Fiction, Yan argues, discloses the contents of the surrounding environment that produces it because literature represents the sensations people of the time actually endured, their hardships and life struggles. Actually, Lu Ping, the flawed heroine of "In the Hospital," was, Yan argues, a modernizationist whose efforts to bring modernity to government medical services made her an antifeudal revolutionary girl, despite her petit bourgeois temperament. To believe otherwise, according to Yan, is anachronistic because no historical figure can avoid the challenges of everyday life, momentary weaknesses, and unclarities (a Dengist theme). Zhao Yuan draws an acute line to separate today's readers and critics from people a generation earlier in order to argue that Ding Ling was, if anything, *antianachronistic* because she took as her project the job of writing contemporaneously about her own times. She imposed even more stringent pressures on herself because her literary realism required her to understand the historical moment as she lived it and observed it; her technique built into itself the requirement that she would have to have been right *in retrospect* about the Party line and its future consequences. Indeed, the success of her land reform novel, measured against others in its genre, is due to her very prescience.

Thus, early post–Cultural Revolution criticism echoed many of the initiatives that the Deng Xiaoping regime sought to reinstate in public, civic, and cultural life. This wave of post-Mao interest in Ding Ling also seemed to be arguing that in rectifying Ding Ling it could somehow reverse the damage, and salvage what Yang Guixin treasures as "our tradition of revolutionary Chinese literature." As researchers had increasing access to Ding Ling herself and to the records of her past, they became increasingly concerned to get right the details of her personal history. This is clear in the 1982 volume by Wang Zhongchen and Shang Xia, *Ding Ling shenghuo yu wenxue de daolu* (The path of Ding Ling's life and literature).[116] What these authors ran smack into was the woman question. In the spirit of the Deng Xiaoping regime's strategy of reversing the verdicts, they used detailed autobiographic information to establish that Gang of Four–style charges against Sophia were unprincipled and historically inaccurate. But, when these avatars proceeded a step further to endorse Sophia's rebellion as truly progressive, they ran into Engels's discussion of why bourgeois love and marriage reform, with its scandalous presumptions about sexuality, are actually historically progressive and therefore positive and good. Sexual desires really are motivating Ding Ling's Sophias, they acknowledge. Still, this is a pure sexual desire. It is pure because Sophia's grounds for rejecting her lover are that he has no idea of what true love is all about. True love may be lustful, but it is also progressive. Anyway, even when Sophia got a bit unclear, Ding Ling knew it. Hence Ding Ling escaped being contaminated and was never degraded, even when she dared to describe a female character's erotic feelings. How would Sophia register true love's absence if she did not have the desire for its presence (27–30)? Once they made Sophia a core personality of the age, Wang and Shang went on to broaden their analysis. The question of the liberation of women is one of the most important questions that the new colloquial literature raised, they pointed out. That is precisely why Feng Xuefeng rated Ding Ling's "Sophia's Diary" along with Lu Xun's story "Mourning" as the two characteristic works of the era (39). More than Bing Xin and other female pioneers, Ding Ling had actually produced a character that represented the Chinese "new woman" through the author's uncanny ability to use subjective reflection (ziwo guancha) to create objective representation (51–53).

Along with this renewed interest in Sophia as the historical apotheosis of the "personality liberation" (gexing jiefang), critics in the early Deng Xiaoping era also began to redeem the Sophia character as the epitome of antifeudalism and to recognize the modern girl's importance in antifeudal liberation. This is a minor theme in Wang and Shang, but it is a major thesis for Yang Guixin. Truly the most exciting of the new Ding Ling critics, Yang accomplished a number of important transitional moves in her monograph, Speaking on the Breadth and Depth of Ding Ling's Creations.[117] First, she went directly to the historical question of how to think about female subjectivity in relation to Ding Ling's representative fiction. Do Sophia's male lovers, Yang asks rhetorically, really understand her? The question of whether the lovers recognize the woman as a subject enables Yang to argue that in fact Sophia, like the Yan'an-era fictional characters Lu Ping and Zhenzhen, represents the historical theme of Chinese women's "coming to consciousness and thought awakening" (sixiang juewu he renxing de suxing) because what antifeudalism does is to expose the restrictions placed on women (26). When Sophia refuses to become the lover of either suitor she splits herself into the desiring woman and the other woman who "demands sexual equality, who demands that women have independent personality" (*duli ren'ge*) (27). The remainder of the long chapter links into a continuous historical chain the question of duli ren'ge as it surfaces in the characters of Lu Ping and Zhenzhen.

Second, Yang directly raises the question of anachronism that I am arguing should be interpreted as a signifier of the impossibility of ever accomplishing what Engels promised, that is, any conclusive representation of what women actually is. After all, Yang argues, Ding Ling had not read Engels before she started writing! Analogously, whether or not Wang Meng and Liu Binyan had ever read Ding Ling's "In the Hospital," each had nonetheless written a famous story redolent of similar themes. That is precisely, Yang points out, what constitutes a modern tradition of literature. Precedent and anachronism may in fact be signifiers of the deeper reality, which is that historical materialists should continue their historicist analyses of literature, for at least in Chinese feminism and progressive humanism it takes a long, long time to fashion a new revolutionary person out of the detritus of the feudal past (55–60). Foreign scholars, Yang writes at one point, have represented Ding Ling as a Chinese feminist (45–46).[118] So long as they recognize this advocacy position from within the context of Ding Ling's commitment to literature and the value of her literary texts as such, this interpretation is correct and appropriate. It is through her skills and sensitivity that the record of revolutionary women's history can be read.

It would appear from Yang's position and from Song Jianyuan's strongly argued *Critical Biography of Ding Ling* that by the late 1980s, Ding Ling criticism was moving toward anointing Ding Ling native daughter and exemplar of the revolutionary tradition in Chinese literature.[119] Published in 1989, during the height of the student movement and politics of culture, Song's massive volume, as the introduction of Du Pengchen puts it, places Ding Ling's oeuvre "in Chinese society, Chinese history and the significance of Chinese literature."[120] Song makes two points: (1) that Ding Ling was in fact the outstanding heir of Lu Xun because of her contributions to forging the correct path for proletarianized literature, and (2) that Ding Ling's position in the battle for women's standing, ren'ge, was the consequence of this apprenticeship to Lu Xun and an outgrowth of her primary commitment to the proletarianization of Chinese literature. In other words, like Lu Xun, for Ding Ling literature was a weapon. Following his lead she used the weapon to overthrow masculinist, feudal attitudes. Song cites "Thoughts on March 8" as evidence for his position and as a key datum in his argument.[121] What is significant about Song's book, in my view, however, is how Song joined these two positions in a way that in essence feminized the Chinese revolutionary tradition in literature. Song's historical narrative privileges the transitional fictions in the early 1930s over the late 1920s, and he is particularly attentive to what (no doubt in the spirit of the humanist tradition among intellectuals in China) he called "proletarian humanism" and "revolutionary humanism."[122] Enfolded within the love she harbors for the subaltern is always to be found Ding Ling's concern with Chinese women's progress. In Song's view, this is the decisive point for arguing Ding Ling's historical adequacy to serve as modern Chinese literature's paradigmatic figure.

In the 1990s Ding Ling studies proliferated. Xu Huabin's *Ding Ling xiaoshuo yanjiu* (A study of Ding Ling's fiction) complained that he had to constantly revise his own text to keep up with secondary publications and the release of previously classified materials.[123] In *Ding Ling xiaoshuo de shanbian* (The evolution of Ding Ling's fiction) Peng Shufen stressed Ding Ling's role as a representer of the masses (*daiyanren*), a spokeswoman of the time and of the people. Tucking the question of women's liberation safely into her "evolutionary" framework, Peng's volume provides more evidence of the growing inextricability—within this emergent Ding Ling critical tradition—of Ding Ling and the Maoist Communist Party. Both Ding Ling's vitality and her status as an icon of national suffering suggest to Peng that for older Marxist-Leninist scholars, nonelite cultural workers, secondary schoolteachers, and perhaps even readers (who are buying the dozens of reprinted collections like the 1995 two-volume reprint of Ding Ling's greatest hits, *Ding Ling nüxing xiaoshuo jin zuo* [Ding Ling's best writing on women[124]]) the Party had increasingly become a maternal force. For Peng, Ding Ling is the creative heart of a softer, gentler Communist Party. Li Daxuan's *Ding Ling yü Shafei xilie xingxiang* (Lineage of the form of Ding Ling and Sophia) focused on the national tradition, which he traces back to antiquity and forward into the colonial diffusion of Western influence in order to write about Ding Ling's construction of national womanhood.[125] Zhou Liangpei's massive, absorbing, and detailed literary biography *Ding Ling zhuan* not only collated the historical detritus of the writer's life, but also published reams of Communist Party evidence of the details of her political persecution.[126] Just recently I received the conference volume from the seventh Ding Ling conference, entitled *Ding Ling yu Zhongguo nüxing wenxue* (Ding Ling and Chinese women's literature), which contains essays on "Ding Ling, Nüxing Literature, Feminism," "The Discontinued Thinking of Ding Ling's Feminism," "'Miss Ah Mao' and Ding Ling's Nüxing Literature," and more.[127] Safely encapsulated in the national tradition, Ding Ling is now Chinese literature's leading communist feminist thinker.

# 6 Socialist Modernization and the Market
## Feminism of Li Xiaojiang

Ding Ling is the founder of modern Chinese feminism. LI XIAOJIANG, Nüren: Yi ge yaoyuan meili de chuanshuo (Woman: A distant, beautiful legend)

The woman question reignited at the end of the Maoist regime in 1976. Over the subsequent twenty-five years, theoretical feminism has continued in popular academic and elite research institutes and universities. In this chapter, I address the foundational work of philosopher-politician Li Xiaojiang; in chapter 7, I take up Dai Jinhua's mediascapes of the neoliberal 1990s. Li and Dai voice different concerns. They are positioned differently in relation to the Chinese great transformation in the late twentieth century and the rapidly receding horizon of revolutionary modernity. As I hope becomes clear in the course of these concluding chapters, neither the fact of their sex nor their distinctive thinking has fully extricated either one from progressive Chinese feminism's initial assumptions or psychic investments or its accumulated, conventional, Maoist statism.[1]

Li Xiaojiang's 1980s oeuvre consists of a Chinese feminist critique of Chinese revolutionary modernity undertaken in conditions of rapid marketization, with the objective of pioneering a commodified subjectivity for women organized around the duty and pleasures of domestic consumption.[2] There are several reasons to characterize her thinking in this way. First, Li in essence drew on a feminist critique of reason to rework 1980s Marxist humanism, to supplement humanist cultural criticism in the immediate post-Mao moment, and to relocate the feminist subject women in a postpolitical market economy. Her fantasy project—what theorization is not partly fantasy?—would have fostered national development by enlisting women in self-betterment schemes, including lessons in good consumer practices. Second, Li's market-centered consumer policies were intended to recover women's real, natural, feminine singularity. Women express this femininity, heeding the government's accelerated policies of domestic consumption, when they commercialize their forms of self-expression. Market feminism does not pick up where progressive Chinese feminism allegedly broke off in the late 1930s. It does not bring about a restoration, and it is not the resumption of an interrupted national tradition. Li's work is as much about contemporary Maoism and the political depth charge of the Great Proletarian Cultural Revolution (1966–1976) as it is about progressive eugenics, sexual selection, and the chronic question of women's social standing. What Yan'an-style Marxist feminism did in the 1940s to disinter and rethink historically significant social, theoretical problematics in relation to the present, thinkers like Li did in the 1980s. The present is never a repetition or even an extension of the past; we are always thrust into a future in search of pasts that we are barely equipped to understand.

Li Xiaojiang's feminism reengaged an explosive contemporary intellectual scene. In the 1980s, journalists, writers, filmmakers, scholars, editors, critics, and post-GPCR elites began carving out a semiautonomous cultural order in relation to but distinct from existing state government mass organs. Li's earliest creative work took place in this intellectual nexus. Over the course of a long, astonishingly pervasive, public discussion about enlightened reason, immediate post-GPCR intellectuals achieved, among other things, the renovation of a high Marxist but pre-Maoist general theory project. Marxist humanism was in part a revulsion against Yan'an styles of cultural criticism. The debates culminated in the late 1980s in waves of civil society activism called the cultural fever (wenhua re), hastened, no doubt, by processes rearticulating China's universities and elite school systems to international orthodox social science curricula and standards. Li's efforts at establishing a university discipline of women's studies are best understood in this broader context of wholesale academic retrenchment. Finally, Li undertook her projects in a resurging commercial media. Polemicists like Li, able to reach a mass-market readership, fed the consumer's desire to address gender equality, gender difference, and sexual expression.

In the last half of the 1980s a nationwide network of female feminist scholars coalesced around a Beijing-centered dispute over how a theory of women's liberation, or theoretical feminism, could be developed that would stabilize a proper subject Women. Li was a key player in this event. She pioneered what rapidly became a cliché: the accusation that revolutionary modernity, particularly the Maoist cultural formation, had denaturalized women's bodies. Other contemporary thinkers voiced similar criticisms, and I am not claiming that Li's thinking is wholly unprecedented. What she did appear to recognize long before others was that Deng-era Marxist humanism was the philosophical wing of a set of new institutional practices. No matter what is said now about the pitfalls her thought exposed for contemporary feminists, there seems little question that Li accurately diagnosed the political stakes when she hit on the strategy of criticizing masculine humanism in order to stabilize the theoretical subject of modern Chinese woman in social science scholarship. In its patterns of chronic loss and recovery, feminist thinking in China and elsewhere is always done in the present. Li was thinking toward the future in the 1980s, and it is pertinent to keep in mind that the future of the past rarely connects with the past of the present. This chapter's treatment of Li is consequently limited to her thinking and its preconditions in the 1980s. I do not investigate the inventive contributions she continues to make to the women's movement in the PRC and internationally. As much as possible, I have tried to read her creative early work without benefit of hindsight, as a message to the 1990s. Clarity of hindsight must never be imposed from the outside; it must be confronted, as Ding Ling sought it, from within. The constraints theorists encounter and the conditions of possibility structuring their world are present, in distilled form, in the content of their thinking.[3]

## The Popular Foundations of 1980s Feminism

Between 1986 and 1989 a skirmish began in the Chinese press. Virtually everyone involved in the debate rejected the Communist Party's claim to have established social, political, and legal equality for Chinese women. The key players resisted (i.e., their thoughts took shape around) an effort that the post-Mao state had begun earlier in the decade. That effort was to restore the Women's Federation, make it truly a mass organization, and embed it in a revitalized government ideological and social service apparatus. The two political events—the restoration of a Maoist Women's Federation and the growing attack on its Mao-style concept of women's liberation—unfolded at around the same time.

At the end of the ultra-Maoist 1970s, the Central Committee of the CCP began reassembling a bureaucratic infrastructure. It included in the process mass organizations like the All-China Federation of Women (i.e., Fulian, the Women's Federation, or ACFW). The ACFW's instructions were to regroup and "steadfastly protect the interest of the masses, which it represents," while reestablishing the Central Committee's prior definition of what constitutes a woman.[4] In 1978, when the National Women's Congress gathered for the first time in twenty years, restoration took place in the name of Comrade Mao Zedong. Arguing that the Gang of Four had usurped the work of the Federation and smeared the organization with the epithet "revisionist," longtime Party official and women's policy advocate Kang Keqing protested, saying that it was not possible to call her organization revisionist. Mao Zedong personally and the Communist Party generally speaking had "helped the female masses to establish their own organization." "Women's mass organizations," Kang charged, "were initiated [only] because Mao was concerned [to liberate women]."[5] So it was perhaps not surprising that, as the economic reforms of the early 1980s began wreaking change in women's and men's lives, ACFW officials and strategists decided to recycle liberation and social welfare strategies from the earlier, allegedly simpler and more pure era of the pre-GPCR decades. Although it could point to a distinguished record, the ACFW ran into problems as soon as it tried to reclaim exclusive authorship of Chinese women's liberation.[6]

By the early 1980s the political stakes were rising. Economic reforms announced in December 1978 at the Third Plenum of the Eleventh Congress of the CCP repudiated Maoist social-economic development policy. These reforms mandated changes in agricultural economy, industry, employment, and flows of population and resources across urban and rural sectors. A new development policy was beginning to take shape and major sectoral shifts were shuddering through the political economy. On the heels of these 1978 mandates and over the next five years there followed intra-Party rectification, decollectivization of the rural economy, and other major reversals. The end of the rural commune system saw the collapse of the national social service infrastructure (the so-called iron rice bowl) and rapid devolution of responsibility for old age, social housekeeping, disability, education, and welfare onto the domestic or household unit. The velocity of these changes suggests reasons why the ACFW decided, in 1980, to establish archives and research centers at each county and urban basic unit. Achievements gained in the past were slipping away; future collective gains were hard to imagine. It was decided that a comprehensive, heavily documented history of the Chinese women's movement might help mediate the transition.

General confusion about the Federation's future appeared to heighten the anxiety that Deng Yingchao expressed when she considered not the value of this history project but its dangers. She warned audiences that her campaign to document the indivisible relationship of the Maoist state and the women's movement required reauthorizing the Federation and remembering its valiant history. She recognized the complexity of this maneuver. Local-level, data gatherers needed to reestablish that, in fact, there had been an inextricable relation between proletarian national revolution and communist women's liberation. Corroboration would redeem the achievements that the Gang of Four had sought to wipe out in the intermediate past and, it was hoped, feed popular efforts to recuperate the necessity of collective redress for women. Meanwhile, the Federation would reinsert woman back into official discourse and consequently back into the official machinery of political representation.[7]

Deng Yingchao, Kang Keqing, and Cai Chang (each an elderly, decorated personification of the Communist women's liberation movement) oversaw the effort to document and reinstall the subject of women in Chinese Marxist feminist institutions. On her release from prison, Ding Ling drew on similar rhetoric, but unlike Ding Ling, Deng, Kang, and Cai were senior government officials. The national subject appears in their writing not in the shape of narrative or parable, but as the correct or objective repository of vast historical forces. In their official description, funü is shown categorically resisting feudalism, imperialism, and bureaucratism (standard fare) and upholding the thought of Chairman Mao. She is a homologue of the working class in the sense that those who qualify as funü are also proletarians (though not all proletarians are, of course, funü). As a theoretical subject, this national woman embodies neither bourgeois feminism nor ultraleftist Gang of Four stereotypes about absolute equality. Gang of Four partisans had erred when they denied the special characteristics of females, the Maoist revisionists argued. On the other hand, national woman's consciousness is inessential; it is enough that she be politically flexible and open to recalibration according to new norms of state development policy and general human nature. The goal of the Federation is to prepare China's women citizens to participate in the commonweal as funü. In this genealogy of this instantiation of historical funü, Deng, Kang, and Cai argued that Chinese women had reached the apex of liberation during mass mobilizational high tides, when the state dictated that domestic labor be socialized. These included the land reform of the 1940s and early 1950s and the Great Leap Forward of the late 1950s and early 1960s.[8]

According to these remaining Mao-style administrative policy goals, funü was not just a nationalist trope. Rather, funü embodied the progressive historical elements within the people's history generally speaking. This formula worked in reverse, too. Any period could be judged progressive if the national subject Chinese women could be said to be a revolutionary force, fully mobilized into productive labor, and its liberation truly a necessary condition for full proletarian, national, and thus global revolution. Women's liberation was, in Cai, Deng, and Kang's view, the bellwether of revolutionary success. In other words, funü in the early 1980s administrative thinking looked a lot like Ding Ling's fictional portrait of the rural farm woman, Du Wanxiang, though it lacked that story's nuance and critical subtheme of political injustice.

The official history project that Deng Yingchao and her colleagues were promoting seemed clearly aimed at rescuing and repositioning a Maoist revolutionary, modernist female subject in the new post-Mao regulatory political apparatus. It seems fair to say that ACFW was reasserting its claim to represent the nation's women at the very moment when the political consensus that had bound women to the state was collapsing.[9] There were good reasons why cadres like Kang and Cai were proud of their mass organization's achievements and would not countenance any diminution of their administrative power to police the ideological term women. Their immediate problem was that to reinsert national women into post-Mao political ideology ended up requiring the official administrative sector to paper over increasingly more noticeable gaps between the state's representational practices and the everyday life of citizens. As economic reform deepened in the mid-1980s, charges of sex inequality in the Party and society became commonplace.[10]

The Women's Federation seemed to unravel as the problems it confronted exceeded its mandate. One could say that a latent crisis was taking shape because the relation of womanhood and misogyny was difficult to explain in the statist language of the Federation. The ACFW seemed stymied and offered little rhetoric or legislative will to address discriminatory practices in state-run sectors even against women workers. Discriminatory practices that may or may not have existed in the state sector during the listless late Mao era were increasingly hard to overlook in the post-Mao era of decollectivization and withdrawal of state subsidies. Given the degree to which women's achievements legitimated socialist development, the erosion of women's gains ratcheted up existing doubts about the governance project itself. As Li Xiaojiang would put it, before "I knew I was a female [nüren] but I didn't recognize that this implied special characteristics, that a difference existed between me and other people, or rather between me and men." It was this liminal or obscured sex difference and its damaging political effects which finally called into question the representational labor Fulian claimed to be doing on women's behalf. "Fulian," wrote Pan Suiming, a man, a sexologist, and a longtime ally of Li Xiaojiang's, "at times just sees itself as an institution of social administration when it really ought to be out there representing [daibiao] women. The cost of this self-effacing phenomenon comes about because Fulian lacks an independent will."[11]

Major doubts about the Federation finally coalesced around precisely this question of political representation. A wave of popular writing surged through national venues, from semiofficial Federation journals like Zhongguo funü (Chinese women) and Hunyin yü jiating (Marriage and family), to academic outlets like Xuexi yü shijian (Study and experience), and even into the Party theoretical organ Red Flag. Generally, the arguments broke around the question of whether Fulian "represented" anything at all. Pan's blunt essay summarized a pervasive sense that perhaps the Federation's failures of "will" were due to the fact that "women's liberation" meant as little to ordinary women as womanhood itself did. That was because ordinary women saw women's liberation as a gift from on high, a meaningless political endowment. Confronting the old guard ACFW efforts to document the plebeian woman's participation in revolutionary transformation, Li Xiaojiang and her allies offered a new counterargument. It boiled down to the charge that because the CCP had awarded liberation to Chinese women, logically speaking, women must never have sought it for themselves.

This was a significant point for several reasons. First, it cast women as constitutionally disabled rather than simply politically disenfranchised. Pan Suiming's writing on this point, which I use because it economically combined so many of the era's preoccupations, included an argument that 1980s women's movement strategists should organize women along the same lines as disability movement strategists were doing among their core constituency. This odd association of physical disability and femininity echoed the concerns that Li, among others, was voicing about women's bodiliness. Second, when they claimed that women had neither sought nor welcomed Party-mandated liberation, critics like Pan were predicating a Women, often the relatively neutral or extra-Maoist term nüren, which lay—as yet unrepresented, but nonetheless *representable*—beneath the official terminologies that for years had commonly designated womanhood in the communist and nationalist ideolects as funü. In Pan's professional view as a sexologist, for instance, policymakers should accept the special needs of women. Either the government would grasp the singularity of women, or those real women, those ideologically pre- or unpredicated fleshly women, would, in their turn, continue to dismiss it. They would not under any circumstances identify themselves with it. As Pan put it, most women felt that "representing funü is Fulian's business and has no connection to me." When the Federation finally did undertake structural reform in late 1988 it did so still refusing to relinquish its political subject of funü and its powers to represent her.[12] Third, the debate over the failure of the political establishment to correctly represent the nation's women forced critics not only into considering more embodied theories about the constitution of the human person, but also into new thinking about more complex relations between the Chinese women's movement and revolutionary modernity as such. This emerged in a discussion among theoreticians over what the proper subject of women's liberation ought to be.

Pointing out the disjuncture separating women's interests and the representational practices of Fulian was the single most important move critics like Li Xiaojiang made as they sought to undo late Maoist policy's exclusive hold over Chinese women's liberation discourses. That and the ancillary point, that women's liberation had been imposed on women by men, put on the table debates that were impossible to resolve analytically. That is to say, when critics reversed Kang Keqing's historical narrative defining Chinese women as most truthful or potent during mobilization high tides like the Great Leap Forward, they imparted a logical twist or double bind to the problem of stabilizing the subject of Chinese women. "If," their counterlogic went, "the feudal 'women's way' [fu dao] had turned women into the inferiors of men, then the high tide of leftist thought obliterated sex difference, making it impossible for women to actually be women."[13] This idea that leftist mobilization had obliterated natural sexual difference became the most powerful critical slogan of the 1980s women's movement. It is as powerful in its political context as the slogan "The personal is political" was for the revolutionary women's movement during the 1970s in the United States.

The idea that "the high tide of leftist thought [had] obliterated sex difference, making it impossible for women to be women" redefined womanhood categorically as a marker of "difference from men." Women and men theorists argued this point, as the case of Pan suggests. But those in the best position to demystify the alleged denial of women's core psychology and physiological singularity were women willing to identify themselves "as women." These women had to, in effect, own their sexual identity, as Li did when she noted that knowing herself as female was one step beyond recognizing a gap separating women and men. Such women drew on their firsthand experience with political masculinization during the vaunted ACFW high tide mobilizations of the Great Leap Forward and GPCR. Daughters of the founders of the proletarian women's movement, they felt they had sustained the full onslaught of the state's forces of sexual evisceration. These "masculinized" women felt themselves to be in what they believed was a teleologically untenable position. After all, history's developmental stages linked progressive social struggle to evolutionary social reproduction. How could any decent liberation theorist countenance a leap-frogging of the stage of the struggle for women's (or workers', or the disabled's) self-representation in favor of some doomed and chimerical Maoist high tide labor mobilization campaign?[14]

Feminist arguments hinging on a logical proposal that woman is either man's Other or that woman is an ersatz man have a familiar ring. It is a staple in feminist theoretical projects, not just in China and not just in the immediate post-Mao era of the initial Deng Xiaoping economic reforms. However, read in context against both ultraleftism and the even earlier archives of 1930s progressive Chinese feminism, this burgeoning post-Mao feminism seemed to be predicating a fresh subject. She was a natural woman who lay submerged beneath denaturing social forms waiting for her chance to step forward into the ethical community of social subjects.

As Li Xiaojiang's contemporaries Ruo Shi and Feng Yuan argued explicitly, the task of women's liberation in the late 1980s was to reinstate an appropriate sex difference that is fundamental to a healthy humanity. Reinstating difference meant realigning the genders on the basis of natural logics. Natural logic is grounded in human evolutionary progress and must trump all logics of social engineering. A century-old debate on female ren'ge reverberated in Ruo and Feng's point that "women's liberation does not mean obliterating women's special characteristics. It does not require forcing women to be not female. Rather, it wants them to be women and also to be persons."[15]

Any reassessment regarding women's liberation practices in the 1980s had to concern itself with the category of the person. That was unavoidable. Once that threshold was passed, however, the question of how to cast the subject Women found theorists doubling back to unresolved questions about the relation of women in culture. For instance, borrowing Ernst Cassirer's notion that *culture* gives access to the category of the person, Huang Hongyun argued that fully half of Chinese humanity found personhood inaccessible because traditional culture was producing Women as "vulgar, passive, dependent virtuous wives and good mothers." Gender difference, Huang argued, should imply separate but equal cultures: one female, the other male. In China, the traditional culture (*chuantong wenhua*) had failed to do even this. Unaware of the great debates of the colonial modern 1920s, and denied access to the history of the Communist Party's own internal debates during the 1940s, Huang and other culturalist critics opted for the subject nüxing. This theoretical problematic of a separatist women's culture commanded sufficient interest that in 1989 a Women's Culture Study and Discussion Association (Nüxing wenhua yanjiu taolun hui) began to meet for talks.[16]

Another noteworthy debate ensued that placed into discursive tension three hallmark tropes of 1980s feminism: women (nüxing), personal standing (ren'ge), and social roles (*jiaose*). Female roles, according to this argument, specifically "virtuous wife and good mother" (*xianqi liangmu*), repressed women's standing or personality. When women did organize a sufficiently stable self (ziwo) and began to emerge socially with "independent social standing" (*duli ren'ge*), men either recoiled from them or sought to marry and subdue them into the demeaning, emotionally laborious female roles of wife, housekeeper, and child care nurse. Lin Gang's "Xiandai nüxing jie fang zhi lu zai nali?" (Where is the path to modern women's liberation?) is a manifesto against this kind of contemporary thinking. To a masculinist society, Lin charged, women translates into sister, wife, and mother; the duties conventionally attached to those roles are custodial. Pro forma liberation, that is, CCP diktat, had done nothing to interrupt a social definition of womanliness that is measured in relation to role-defined, expropriated labor. Society claims to have liberated women, but it still derogates women who have children because it continues to privatize their labor. Such condescension might have worked in the past, Lin argued. Women in the 1980s, however, possess a sufficient sense of self that they will step forward and demand an end to these unjust social roles.[17]

In the view of these analysts, modernization had simply increased the numbers of roles available to women outside the kitchen door, beyond the domestic sphere. A generally positive development, it had successfully undermined older, stricter sex divisions of labor. The problem in the contemporary period was consequently not too few but too many roles, in the sense that ultraleftism compelled women to add male roles on top of their own "female" domestic duties. To Ruo Shui, this tipped the appropriate balance of self (ziwo) and roles too far in an unnatural direction. That is because in Ruo's argument, some sexually defined roles ought to be recognized and retained. The reason was that "roles are the positions that people make out of the net of relations [guanxi zhi wang] in nature and in society. Roles make people into people." In Ruo's construction then, roles both oppress and liberate females "because that is the double nature of roles." Strategically, moreover, a female person should play a range of different roles. But, beyond tinkering with appropriate social role structures, woman's paramount object would have to involve nurturing her own female ren'ge. Setting this priority meant that women themselves would have to reject both exclusively masculinizing roles and old-fashioned protocols that categorically oppressed female individuality, such as "virtuous wife, good mother."[18]

In the view of these theorists, then, Chinese women needed to recover the ability they had lost at the fall of matriarchy to "recognize the social standing of the self" (ziwo ren'ge renshi). Li Ying proposed to do this through a history of the relation of self and role. A matriarchy had once existed, she argued, where female ren'ge flourished. Patriarchy came to power on the back of historical necessity and imposed a sexual division of labor that effectively quarantined women in the family. There the emotional expectations associated with maternity and wifeliness sapped women of their self-consciousness and destroyed their personality. Women survived, but they were enslaved to a "traditional psychic consciousness" (chuantong xinli yishi) for thousands of years, until the rise of capitalism and socialism. Wei Bingji and Li Ying felt that there was only one real solution to the problem of roles undermining ren'ge: to develop in women themselves a stronger sense of their "essential consciousness." Women consistently fail because they have an underdeveloped sense of their own gender consciousness, or consciousness of themselves as women. Having little sense of themselves as women makes it difficult to maintain balance. Indeed, ren'ge is incompatible with feminine roles as these are presently organized.[19]

This general line of argument informs Li Xiaojiang's strategies and her attempts to resolve it helps explain her importance to these debates. The general formula has inherent problems. When you argue, as Liu Lihua did in 1990, that liberating nüxing from roles is good but that, also, the problem with ultraleftism was its *overvaluation* of women who, stripped of female roles, were insufficiently female, had "no female ren'ge" or social standing *as women*, then you not only build into your critique an automatic contradiction (nüxing need feminine roles to make them feminine, i.e., female ren'ge, at the same time that they need to reject both feminizing and masculinizing roles that would adulterate female ren'ge), you also open the argument to endless regression. You posit a category of female persons who have no ren'ge because they lack feminine roles, but then include others who lack feminine ren'ge because the roles they assume are unacceptably masculine. You set up a contradiction between roles (which confer "gender") and personality (empty until it is filled with gendered "roles") that cannot be sustained within the context of the theory. Unless you resolve the categorical problem it will regress endlessly into the question of what constitutes an essentially female woman. It is not difficult to end up arguing tautologically, as Liu did, that "men have male special characteristics, women have female characteristics, and mixing up these special qualities blocks the realization of latent talents and vitalities native to each."[20]

The effect of this kind of argument was momentous and invaluable. Illogical or not, it had the result of prying women out of its exclusively statist context. The argument over difference, equality, and personal standing (ren'ge) posited the subject women in 1980s feminist debates as, at least potentially, an independent vehicle for subjectivity. By the late 1980s, a post-Federation project took shape around the "discipline" of women's studies. Women's studies, under any of the competing terms then in circulation (*funüxue, funü yanjiu, nüxingxue,* etc.), posed an institutional alternative to domains like the Women's Federation. Whether it adopted nüxing as role theorists advocated, and freighted the new women subject with the eugenic heritage, or funü, in the parlance of the ACFW, or nüren, as more historically inclined and social science theorists advocated, the effect was actually the same. The dismantling of the link between the Women's Federation's subject and the nation in the latter half of the 1980s transformed how gendering operated in theory and consequently transformed how the subject women could be predicated. It is possible to trace out in greater detail the debate that unfolded between officials seeking to reestablish an older institutional order, even as the Maoist order crumbled in the face of marketization, and freelance critics like Liu, Pan, Li, Ruo, and the others I cited above. But the semipopular press was not the only place where the post-Mao feminist intellectual movement was being fashioned.

## Social Science and Women's Studies in the 1980s

As a relatively accessible popular debate over women's studies and Li Xiao-jiang's central role in framing it proceeded to unfold in the media, elite scholars from national think tanks and universities also were redefining something they came to call *funü lilun yanjiu*, or women's "theoretic studies," or just policy studies on women. The formula of theoretic studies (contributors gave their own English translation for lilun yanjiu) initiated a major efforts to gender scholarship and social policy while recovering pre-Mao, academic social science normativity. Those publishing under the rubric of theoretic studies took the position that the post-1981 economic reforms were causing an upsurge in women's theory writing. Women's elite theoretic studies had national implications for reform, in their view, because such studies were a symptom and an effect of national processes of social transformation. Interestingly, these upper-level discussions of disiplinarity and theory routinely footnote Li Xiaojiang and acknowledge her as a significant founder, but they do not include in their canonical volume anything Li ever wrote. Perhaps her worker-peasant-soldier education made her unacceptable in the rarified world of elite academic theory. It is unclear whether Li in fact declined to participate in elite projects or whether canonical scholars, for their part, found her work overly rooted in the give-and-take of popular journalism.

In any case, a huge compendium of exemplary theoretic writing published in 1991, Zhongguo funü lilun yanjiu shinian, 1981–1990 (Women's Theoretic Studies in China from 1981–1990) pressed elite scholars to accelerate theoretical research on women for several reasons. Theoretical writing opened a critical platform for reflection on social events, it framed female subjects in research and practical politics, and it stabilized professional niches for scholars like the theorists themselves. Reconsecrating a humanist social science that stressed social fact over ideological or cultural revolution, the editors of the volume argued that "the times" were responsible for "hailing" the reawakened Chinese women's theoretical movement into action. The volume posed what is for this era a conventional relation of theory, society, and history to explain its interventionary moves. "Women's theoretic writing is a response to the reality of the women's movement," the editors argued, and consequently, "it can also reflect on [*fansi*] history, traditional culture, the entire history of civilization." Far less explicitly preoccupied with the question of the category of the female person, the elite version of post-Mao feminism stressed instead the representational capacities of enlightened social science theory.[21]

*Women's Theoretic Studies in China*'s call for the theoretic study of Women was part of a movement in the elite academy to reconstitute all of the traditional social science disciplines. In much the same way as Li Xiaojiang's project appears to have emerged in relation to efforts at revitalizing the Women's Federation, feminist social scientists began presenting a case for gendering the human sciences at the instant that the elite academy was reconsolidating its foundational disciplines. Reports from feminist and womenist scholars Tan Shen (sociology), Yu Yan (anthropology), and Chen Ping (demographics) echo thematics raised in humanist scholarship by Li Meige (psychology), Luo Qunying (ethical philosophy), and Li Huiying (literature). These long, bibliographically rich discussions reveal a theoretic scholarship staking out protocols for gendered research at a moment of wholesale recuperation of the pre-1966 academy. Yu Yan's explicit criticism of Li Xiaojiang's women's studies model, "Nüxing renleixue: Jian'gou yü zhanwang," (Anthropology of Women: establishment and outlook) for example, argues that the academic discipline of anthropology, previously quiescent in the PRC, already possessed all necessary intellectual resources for gendered scholarship. This not only vitiated the need for institutionally independent departments of women's studies, but it provided established disciplinary frameworks that were older, better equipped, and when gendered, would be intellectually superior to women's studies.[22] Li Meige's "Nüxing xinlixue yanjiu jianjie" (A brief introduction to research on female psychology) echoes Yu's disdainful criticism of the subdiscipline of women's studies. It seems likely that she, too, had Li Xiaojiang's innovations in mind when she laid out the theoretic claims about female subjectivity made in the discipline of women's psychology. Yu's endorsing of psychology's claim to be a globally or universally truthful regime rested, in her own view, on psychology's resurgence in the PRC in 1981, its tested canon, and its significant subdisciplines (e.g., the study of gender difference, family psychology, psychophysiology, and comparative psychology).[23]

As they participated in retrenching the various disciplinary standards and subdivisions in Chinese elite universities and research institutes, these scholars—among them, Li Xiaojiang's critics, competitors, and interlocutors—undertook their own project. They were proposing to situate the gender analytic as an open question for research in globalized social science scholarship. In itself this was a remarkably powerful move. First, it cast doubt on what I will momentarily characterize as Li's pessimistic, fundamentalist, heterosexualist matrix. Second, it writes women into the project of restructuring the social sciences. Of course, these theorists did not question the basic assumption upholding social science scholarship, which is that theoretic work is an analogue of scientific theory. They assumed that women in the social science disciplines is a source of obscured truth; the project of including women in the representational order is remedial and practical for them, because once the truth of Women is revealed scientifically, efforts at social remediation can be undertaken. (This assumption is why I prefer to overtranslate funü lilun as "policy on women.") Third, the gendering of the social sciences and traditional disciplines might, as Tan Shen argued, have had little practical effect on increasing the number of female sociologists in the discipline or numbers of sociologists working on sociology of gender. But what it could do is render conventional disciplines foundationally uncertain. Female scholars such as Chen Ping and Tan Shen could easily demonstrate that a good sociologist cannot proceed in demographic work or basic sociological research without a clear grasp of the split subject of disciplinary knowledge.[24]

As these critiques of women's studies suggest, the academic elite's move to reconsolidate disciplinarity in the human social sciences and the apparently more populist preoccupation with the subject women in liberation theory overlapped in discussions over the institutional drive to establish women's studies in Chinese universities. According to Wan Shanping, the term women's studies first entered into the picture in a book review of Shirai Atsushi's Women's Studies and the History of Women's Movements, which appeared in the PRC in a journal called Studies of Social Sciences Abroad. The topic of women's studies consequently became an agenda item for the 1984 Federation-sponsored academic meeting of the First National Conference on Theoretical Studies of Women.[25] Male journalist Deng Weizhi's advocacy in 1985–1986 is often credited for bringing the discussion to a more popular constituency.[26] It would appear that by the mid-1980s women's studies, like women theory, was beginning to coalesce as a place where academic political activity might be developed.[27]

Possibly, scholars associated with the women's studies initiative were more concerned with rewriting national histories of Chinese women than were mainstreaming social scientists. The conventional categories of popular stage histories could always be used to explain why an empty space called "women's studies" had opened up outside of China and was worth emulating. Li Min's complexly argued Zhongguo funüxue (Chinese women's studies) illustrates this point.[28] Instead of the loyalist project Deng Yingchao had called for, linking Chairman Mao and the women of China, historians like Li Min instead provided innumerable, heterodox, historical rereadings of the premise that Chinese women owed their liberation to Mao Zedong. But elite social scientists were also positioning themselves to acknowledge the degree to which a women's movement predated the proletarian, anticolonial, anti-imperialist war of national liberation. This was consistent with their general consensus that existing academic disciplines could handle the problem. Rather than defining women in relation to revolutionary norms, revolutionary practices, or the question of Party political representation of the subaltern, elite historians were framing their projects within previously banned orthodox social science protocols such as statistics, demographics, and social surveys. The claim of the Deng Xiaoping cohort of modernist social scientists to "seek truth from fact" also rings through women's studies scholars' claim that they represent women historically.

When the women problem is redefined under the auspices of social science, the question of representation ceases to be primarily about personal ethics or even, as the case of Ding Ling illustrated, a matter of heroic ethicoliterary expression. By the mid-1980s historians Xiao Li and Xiao Yu, for instance, were reperiodizing women's liberation from an origin point in the Manchu reforms of the last decade of the Qing dynasty to the 1911 bourgeois revolution and subsequently the May Fourth movement.[29] Cai Yu proposed that contemporary Chinese women's studies and its history projects draw on the work of overseas Chinese women scholars (who were just producing a first wave of doctoral dissertations) and the arguments of earlier Chinese colonial modernists like pioneer historian Chen Dongyuan.[30] Chang Ying baldly attributed the women's rights movement's origin to the revolutionary bourgeoisie, in contradistinction to official hagiographies and Deng Yingchao's Federation genealogies. She also claimed that historically speaking, the independent women's movement did not flourish because the proletarian movement had overridden it. Chinese women had sacrificed themselves for the national good, Chang argued. These patriots had abandoned their own struggle for rights in order to forward a nationalist agenda. But the proletarian movement had not in fact freed women. Proletarian politics had aborted the entire autonomous women's movement and had given women nothing in return.[31]

According to a scholar named Qing Ren writing in 1989, "If one could say that the period of the early 1980s was concerned with researching the woman question as it affected women's employment, safeguards, and other concrete matters, *the mid and late years of the decade saw increasing focus on research into women themselves* as a consequence of the elevation of research and the lavish attention paid to it."[32] Qing's periodization is accurately reflected in the publications I have read. This is not surprising, as women's studies constituents and those social scientists who were advocating a women's theoretics were highly reflexive communities of scholars. They were constantly scanning their own products, positioning and repositioning themselves in relation to the broader movement to reestablish the academic social sciences, and increasingly in relation to peers outside China. In this contrast self-surveillance, scholars and journalists were producing an academic subject, nüren (woman). This nüren formed an irreducible "identity" or anchor for advocacy politics. In practice, it offered researchers, theoreticians, and political cadres like Ruo Shu, Wang Jinling, Huang Hongyun, Du Fangqin, Lin Gang, Li Ying, and the others a working subjectivity that efficiently papered over the more destabilizing problems that any subject women inevitably introjects into theoretical work. Yet, if "women themselves" is a universal subject of social science, then where does "we" fit into the picture? If we is just "we Chinese," then how can Chinese women's studies handle the question of the particularity of Chinese modernity in the universal of Enlightenment?[33]

## Li Xiaojiang's Market Feminism and 1980s Liberal Theory

It is not possible to cast Li Xiaojiang or Chang Ying, Xiao Li, or, for that matter, Tan Shen, Chen Ping, Li Meige, et al. as "native" or "local" feminist theorists. Whether in an effort to finesse gender logics at work in humanist Marxism, as per Li Xiaojiang, or to sketch in bas relief a subject women against a dismal historical record of proletarian revolution, as Chang Ying had, the common historical horizon was a monolith called "the Revolution," and while they may be nationalist, the proletarian and Marxist traditions in China are also internationalist. Knit into all of them is the presumption that in the last instance, historical determinants exceed nation. The revolutionary tradition takes a national form, in other words, but its nationalism presumes an internationalist matrix. Analogously, as I will clarify shortly, for 1980s intellectuals like Li Xiaojiang, enlightenment is always by definition trans- or international. Again, this is true although enlightenment naturally unfolds according to this view in specific national frameworks.

As a new generation of feminist scholarship in the PRC consolidated around the social science and historical subject of nüren, Li Xiaojiang commandeered center stage of the debate for several reasons. Born in 1951, Li has the familiar profile of the rusticated, educated youth: years in the countryside, a Great Leap mentality valorizing human will in the Maoist struggle to transform the physical and cultural environment, a claim to embody the crimes of the state against womanhood, and a willingness to perform as a woman. Her native abilities (she specialized in physical science topics before shifting to the human sciences) and praxis-oriented education gave her an outsider perspective in the new elite educational order. Li started early and published widely. Six volumes of her work appeared in the late 1980s: *Funü yü jiazheng*, 1986 (Woman and domestic science), *Xiawa de* tansuo, 1988 (Eve's exploration), Nüren de chu lu, 1989 (The way out for women), Nüren: Yi ge yaoyuan meili de chuanshuo, 1989 (Woman: A distant, beautiful legend), Nüxing shenmei yishi tanwei, 1989 (Inquiry into women's aesthetic consciousness), and Xinggou, 1989 (Sex gap).[34] But the essays composing these books in many cases appeared much earlier in semipopular venues before reissue in respectable, academic-style book volumes. Li also founded the Enlightenment Series at Henan People's Press to develop the curricula for her invented discipline of women's studies. A risk-taker in the academic women's movement, through her entrepreneurial efforts key organizational meetings convened. She established a women's studies program at Zhenghou University, and she became a liaison between the Ford Foundation and the Chinese feminist intellectual community in funded projects seeking to bolster formal women's studies programs in Chinese universities. Certainly, there were other important innovators active at the same time, but assumptions and conflicts in the 1980s seem to crystallize around her and around her work.

Li's national prominence also rested on her accessible, marketable, feminist take on key features of the debates over Enlightenment as she understood them. She was at that time an intellectual wholesaler or popularizer to a female constituency that might otherwise have found little to identify with in the debate. The debates were putting the spotlight on "culture," to some degree to reverse Maoist theoretical preoccupations, and that certainly overlapped with broad-based feminist concerns. Marxist humanists advocated demobilization and cultural reflexivity (wenhua fansi) rather than, as I demonstrated in relation to Ding Ling, mobilization and cultural revolution. A primary question theorists posed was what in Chinese culture had sanctioned and created Maoist excesses. These initial discussions unfolded primarily among progressive communists and democracy advocates who were enraged at the injustices and squandered hopes of the Mao era and hoped to return Chinese history to its "natural" course. Their concerns echo in a slightly different form through arguments over how to theorize female ren'ge.

Often overlooked in historical accounts of the Cultural Fever years is that participants were engaged in efforts to establish an ideological grid that would legitimate the new government's economic modernization policies. A frequent characteristic of Chinese governmentality has been the close relation binding academic ideological work and political power. Intellectuals engaged in theoretical production during the late 1980s had every reason to think that they would govern the country eventually, and so the renegotiation they undertook of the terms of Chinese national modernity in theory was not a purely academic offensive. Like philosopher-critics Li Zehou, Liu Zaifu, Jin Guantao, Gan Yang, and Su Xiaokang, Li Xiaojiang also set out to establish a benchmark sense of what pre-Maoist Chinese modernity had been in order to theorize the relation of past and present in a discourse of post-Maoism and enable contemporary state policy formulation. That expectation helps account for the tone of authority infusing general theoretical work in this period.

To recuperate a viable Chinese Marxism, progressive Marxists turned to earlier pre-Mao, radical social science norms. As institutional retrenchment proceeded, academic theorists began reengaging a Chinese socialism that had already assimilated enlightened theory in the era 1890–1930. This was a socialism redolent of eugenic sociology, progressive history, evolutionary developmentalism, and the ideal of scientific objectivity. Li Zehou exemplifies the immediate post-Mao return to the foundations of Chinese Marxism. And it is not possible to interpret Li Xiaojiang's pioneering feminist thinking, in my view, unless one reads her positions back through the Marxist humanism suffusing the scholarly world in the era of de-Maoicization. In other words, Li belongs as much to the cohort of Marxist humanists like Li Zehou and Liu Zaifu as she does to the cohort of new feminists.

Li Zehou's primary strategic move in theory was to measure Maoism's apostasy from Marxism. This he did in several ways. He rewrote Chinese Marxism's relation to enlightenment; he replaced Mao Zedong's voluntarist exaltation of mass subjects with his own reading of Kant's vision of the centrality of a creative, modern, individual subject. In this way, he explicitly criticized what he and most other post-Mao intellectuals charged was the destruction of individual agency. He also assaulted all theoretical systems (Maoism, Frankfurt School, colonial discourse theories, etc.) that, in his view, overvalorized culture or made culture an autonomous, discursive critical space of action. Indeed, he targeted all theories that in any way seemed to rely too heavily on superstructural elements. This fundamentalist revival of pre-Maoist Marxism seemed crafted to undercut the voluntarism of ultraleftism and to expedite the reworking of Chinese Marxism into an ideology that would support national modernization. Modernization, that is, the purposive transformation of the national social-economic base, could, the theory went, prevent future Cultural Revolutions because it could install, in a grossly materialist sense, a public sphere that grounded Reason and empowered creative individuals. Individuals in the public sphere (a domain resting on the foundation of the socialist market economy) would push historical development forward in what Li Zehou called "practices" (i.e., "material production and the practice of tool making").[35]

In the course of outlining his extremely influential critique, Li Zehou developed key terms that others, Li Xiaojiang included, simply adopted without citation. "Cultural-psychological formation" (wenhua xinli jiegou) describes the effect of the heavily coded superstructure grounded in the Chinese agricultural mode of production and its ability to forestall the autonomous development of capitalism in China. "Sedimentation" (*jidian*) depicts the process of archaisms accumulating in the social unconscious of the people. "Internalization" (*neihua*) is a notion Li Zehou developed using Piaget's theories of affective and cognitive development to describe how subjectivity is circumscribed in cultural-psychological formations. "Humanization" (*renhua*) refers to the process of human praxis acting on nature in the dialectical processes of sedimentation. "Subject" (*zhuti*) connotes the self-sufficient, activist, social subject available only in the process of progressive modernization that must transform the substructure, which is to say the agricultural mode of production, and the ideological superstructure, or popular cultural-psychological formations.[36] Li Zehou also pioneered a crucial modification in how modern Chinese history was periodized. In his teleologies, the "thought revolution" of the first Chinese Enlightenment of the 1920s becomes the key moment in modern Chinese history, replacing an earlier, Maoist historiography that privileged popular peasant uprisings and the vanguard actions of the CCP's rural social revolution.

So the pivotal action in modern Chinese history, according to Li Zehou and his followers, was not class revolution, but the forging of humanist values in the May Fourth–era Chinese Enlightenment. One further step took this line of reasoning from privileging consciousness to privileging thinkers. For complex reasons, the question of the subject (zhuti) of modernity eventually came to dominate theoretical work among intellectuals of all schools of thought in the late 1980s. The effect was the popularization of a rather cunning teleology, which held that immanent efforts at enlightenment and modernization were acting on a historical imperative: to make "a concerted and self-conscious effort to redefine the intellectual self as an autonomous, self-determining, self-regulating, and free subject."[37] What is utterly missing in all of this discussion is any admission of a sex continuum or a gender differential or any social or biological difference that might allow a request to be lodged for redress rooted in a claim that oppressions are gendered. Into this vacuum stepped Li Xiaojiang. Like Ding Ling, she, too, would endorse the general philosophic framework she encountered while calling into crisis the formula itself.

"The conflict between economic efficiency and principles of fairness is concentrated on women's bodies," Li Xiaojiang wrote retrospectively in 1993. "But women's liberation has prerequisites; even if social conditions permitted a high level of material and cultural development, there must always be the subjective condition of women's conscious desire to develop, that is, the awakening of women's subjectivity."[38] Li was calling attention to the fact that Chinese theoretical modernity (like homologous discourses elsewhere) was as "male" as what had preceded it. Marxist theory, like other Chinese cultural narratives of modernity, rested on the immobilized or underdeveloped female subject burdened with illustrating the other side of masculinized universals of modernity, civility, humanity. Yet Li embraced the modernist argument. She took the position that to address inequality, women's economic standing and subject formations should be improved to the point that women would enjoy different but equal subjectivities and powers equivalent to (though, of course, different from) the subjectivities that men had enjoyed historically since the capitalist bourgeois revolution. Li's retelling of the familiar narratives of capitalist modernity, however, kept intact the strict division of male and female essence because in her understanding, sexual difference was exclusively and extensively biological and corporeal.

Just as Li Zehou saw no incongruity in forwarding himself as the legitimate heir of European Enlightenment, Li Xiaojiang apparently never considered the possibility that conventional Chinese theories about women's liberation in China, now a century old, might be derivative or secondary in any way. The positions she took were not an attempt to emulate or reproduce what she claimed was "Western feminism." She had read Beauvoir's The Second Sex in Chinese translation and felt its arguments were empowering, but she did not consider Beauvoir to be her better; she did not consider Chinese women or Chinese feminism secondary in relation to Beauvoir; indeed, she did not acknowledge any fundamental or ontological gap separating her own context and that of postwar France. Li's claim to European Enlightenment is rooted in an equally certain belief in the legitimacy and primacy of Chinese thinking about women's liberation for Chinese women. Her thought is therefore not grounded in cultural specificities per se. Rather, it is her allegation that all women everywhere share an organic, scientific, corporeal body—and are therefore bound together beneath the skin in a logic of bodily similitude. History may make women superficially different, she argued, but our material bodies make us similar in the last analysis. This theoretical investment goes some distance in explaining Li's messianism. The ideologically and scientifically correct appreciation of the centrality of the material body will enable Chinese women theory or feminism to universalize its theoretical findings to all women, just as easily as French feminism lays its claim to universality. Reasoning in this fashion authorized Li to assert that Western feminism itself had erred in recent years because it had tended, in her view, to minimize what is in material fact an ineradicable sexual gap or ontological divide.

So-called Western feminism, insofar as its canon and tenets were understood among Chinese thinkers in the 1980s, and the history of the Chinese women question in Chinese thought were important factors in Li's thinking. But even these may not have been her central preoccupation. I make this suggestion because Li does not appear to have considered her justice argument to be a minoritarian position or to address women exclusively. On the contrary, her work seems to point more at mainstream theoretical problems than at specific contemporary feminist positions. Her line of reasoning seemed to be that Li Zehou and Liu Zaifu were, like other philosophers, overlooking an obvious point: they neglected the fact that the subject of modernity is a split subject. Li Xiaojiang's critique, that is to say, originated in intellectual concerns that were not definitively or exclusively feminist or womanist but she made them feminist in a way that her cohort in general did not do. Concerns about general epistemology, psychodynamics of public expression, and the institutional framework—schools, publishing houses, social welfare, collective scholarship—that support modernization are elements of Li's philosophy. Thus, accounting for her importance involves briefly introducing the conditioning elements that lie outside the content of her thought, beyond the province of feminist thinking per se in the 1980s.

In their exposition of Maoist epistemology's limitations, Australian Marxist scholars Michael Dutton, Paul Healy, and Bill Brugger point out how mass political subjects became a core element in Maoist philosophy when Mao Zedong turned Stalinism upside down. Rather than accepting Stalin's economism, Maoism privileged mass politics and formulated mass subjects in relation to differentiated experiences of exploitation. "The determination of experience" in Maoism "shifted from the workers' relationship with scientific technique, to the people's level of exploitation and degree of participation in struggle; it was no longer 'read off' the economic instance but rather off the political."[39] This privileging of *relations of exploitation* is the heart of Mao's thesis of continuous revolution, because the experience of the exploited provides the basis on which political ideologies and actions are judged true or false and on which purposive action is plotted. The starkly troubling point, suddenly evident in late 1980s Chinese cultural theory's preoccupation with the problem of subjectivity (zhuti in Li Zehou, ren'ge in Li Xiaojiang), is that Maoism is as rationalist as Stalinism is. It, too, posited a knowing subject capable of envisioning totality when correctly positioned in relation to the political.

The difference between Maoism and Stalinism, then, was that Stalinism retained intact a Euro-Marxian individual knower, whereas Mao Zedong Thought substituted for this individual Bolshevik knower massified subjects like "the people," "the peasantry," "woman," and so on. These were precisely the mass subjects that critical theorists in the late 1980s sought to undo. As I suggested earlier while reviewing popular and elite feminist theory projects, Li Xiaojiang and her associates concentrated on the mass subject of women, or funü. Their extensive critiques argued in effect that the Maoist mass subject of Chinese womanhood, funü, did not properly represent existential reality and would have to be replaced institutionally, socially, and epistemologically.

In the late 1980s post-Mao modernization theory sought to jettison the political, this theoretical imaginary that Chinese Marxism had specially privileged, and return the economic field to ontological priority. In the new vision, bottom-line economic concerns should regulate viable politics. This was as true for an institutionally less powerful theoretician like Li Zehou as it was for very powerful politicians like Ye Jianying and Chen Yun, major architects of the Deng Xiaoping economic restructuring policy. Modernization cultural theorists like Li Xiaojiang and Li Zehou shared with national planners the view that the more sophisticated the national productive forces and the more scientific the experience of the people generally, the better able the nation would be to grasp itself in thought and monitor its own progress into modernity. That is because these thinkers, given their institutional commitments to statist governmentality, had little reason to call into question the foundational conventions shaping up in reform doctrine. Inside and outside policy-formulating bureaucracies, theorists shared the assumption that theoretical work requires a ground or field of objective knowledge on top of which certain kinds of knowing subjects are established in theoretical work and practical experiments. Both Maoist and post-Mao versions of Chinese Marxism, in other words, retained a largely empiricist orientation.[40]

To make the point directly germane to Li Xiaojiang's critique of masculinist modernization narratives, when theoreticians dismantled the elements of Maoism that they determined had been most responsible for the brutality of the earlier regime, they left in place a range of assumptions about the relation of subject and object fields. While they shifted from a political to an allegedly economic ground for theory making, they left intact the centrality of the knowing subject. Although faith in the legitimacy of a specific agent or subject, Party cadre, for instance, went into crisis, a place remained in the new philosophies for the mechanisms of agency, new agents, perhaps theoreticians or educated men.

In the case of polemics on woman, Maoist epistemology had stabilized that singular mass subject of funü. As Li argued from time to time, the Maoist subject of woman actually has advantages. She herself had drawn on it to claim legitimate access to public revolutionary life and she worked on equal terms with men because of it. Funü gave Chinese strategists the advantage of an already emancipated female citizenry that could be drawn into efforts at modernizing the economy and stimulating subject consciousness in somnolent peasants and workers. It was not that the collective mass subject woman was wholly regrettable, in Li's view, so much as that Maoist woman had no body. The ideologically constructed funü's body did not menstruate, give birth, feel sexual desire, or seek out pleasure. If the positive features of funü were that it enabled individual women to achieve and affirm the rights of women in positive terms, the negative features of massified woman were that she could not confirm her difference from man affirmatively. That was precisely because she was not different from man: she was the same, and that was a problem.

Epistemology and embodied reason are obviously not exclusively feminist questions. Neither was the second immediate conditioning factor, psychodynamics, shaping Li's theoretical work. Troubling psychodynamics presented themselves to post-Mao woman theory in the shape of specific literary texts and debates about literature in the 1980s. As Meng Yue was the first to argue, Chinese literature from Mao Zedong's Yan'an Forum on Art and Literature to the fall of the Gang of Four had worked in a peculiar fashion that did two things simultaneously. First, it disrupted what Meng believed was a natural, evolutionary, historical development in modern Chinese fiction of a "gendered eye." Second, it made Chinese literature into a mere vehicle, which statist ideologists had in effect hijacked and used to collapse all signification of difference into a paranoid recoding machine that did nothing but repeat the same master trope—triumph of the Party-state over the people-nation—over and over again.[41] In any case, in the early 1980s a cohort of writers started publishing stories about female protagonists enduring de-Maoicization. Fortuitously, these female writers—Zhang Jie, Yu Luojin, Zong Pu, Wang Anyi, Dai Houying, Zhu Lin, Zhang Xinxin, and Shen Rong—created what Li Ziyun termed the first truly psychological fiction of the post-Maoist period. What they did in the most general sense, to follow Meng's analysis, was reinsert into literary representation the differences that properly characterize social exchange, and, eventually, they provided enough evidence that the natural "gendered eye" of feminism reasserted itself.

As Li Xiaojiang started thinking about political remedies for institutionalized injustice in the early 1980s, major female literary figures like Zhang Jie were writing simple sociological fiction about previously banned subjects that would soon be classified as a "woman question." In fact, these writers were raising more general issues. They addressed, for instance, emotional pathologies born of the lack of personal life, sexual despair and the pain of sublimation, homosexual desire, and the psychologies of people forbidden to love or, on the opposing hand, compelled to marry by the stifling force of social convention. These have as much to do with the lives of men as with the lives of women. Still, it was female literary figures like Zhang Jie, Dai Qing, Zong Pu, Wang Anyi, and Zhu Lin who pioneered discussions about politics and personal life and caught the imagination of readers in the years just before the cultural reflection movements broke out in the late 1980s. They continued to address questions— in fiction and the suddenly popular genre of oral history—that in male-dominated academic circles were articulated in enlightened vocabularies as the projects of "theorizing subjectivity," "modernity," "nationalism," and so on. It was not a strictly policed division of gendered labor. Women theorists and male-authored literary texts explicitly negotiated questions of bad subject forms in early efforts at literary de-Maoicization. Everyone seemed to recognize that in this early fiction lay an unasked question that had deformed their own thinking: How did subjectivity work outside the state-dominated theater of the political?[42]

Besides embodied reason and epistemology, another major factor shaping Li Xiaojiang's thought in the mid-1980s consisted of debate over how modern women should be represented scientifically (as opposed to politically or ideologically) and what role institutional knowledge about women might play in efforts to alleviate them of oppressions particular to their sex. I have already suggested that the critique of the Maoist order involved an attempt to reground reason in real experience, in scientifically reputable and materially tangible conditions. As de-Maoicization accelerated, Li and other educated, well-positioned, Party-educated intellectuals aggressively pursued institutional change. Some launched public criticism of the past record of government bureaucracy; others sought to innovate in socially useful scholarship. Li's initiative was to write pedagogic aids, teach ordinary women, publish simplified language critiques of mass-line women's policy, and, most important of all, found institutional free zones where knowledge about women (real knowledge) could be written, published, and disseminated.[43]

In terms of knowledge, emotion, and the institutions of scientific rationality, Li's position is distinctive but not unique or singular. Where she parted company from both the nonfeminist Enlightenment project and feminist theoretical disputes has to do with the question of women's status in philosophy. In other words, she was innovating particularly in the area of female personality or subjectivity. Her critique addressed deficiencies of Chinese women's ren'ge, which, she argued, were the result of women's exclusion from the regimes of historical representation under feudal, semicolonial, and Maoist regimes. To remedy this epochal exclusion, as I show momentarily, Li pursued a certain subject form in her scholarly writing and by virtue of her rising social influence. This affirmative female subject could not help but derive in part from the social and political legacy of ultraleftism.

In an essay titled "Wo weishenme zhubian Funü yanjiu congshü" (Why I edit the Woman Researches Series) Li put the significant founding moments of her Enlightenment Series publication project respectively at her own first attempt to teach a course on women's literature and the first ever post-Mao Women's Research Conference held at Zhengzhou University (both in 1981). She also mentioned 1985, when exclusionary pressure on young female academics became so acute that she and several friends initiated a scholarly discussion group about the problem at the Henan Provincial University. These experiences and meetings led to her desire to found a scholarly publication, which eventually became the Henan University Enlightenment Project Series, devoted to scholarship on women. The extraordinary take-off phase of the Communist Party's market reforms in 1986 and the ensuing surge of social pressure, including markets for women's media, seemed to guarantee the project's success. Consequently, during the cultural reflection years, scholarship on women and Li's Woman Researches Series (Funü yanjiu congshu) were nearly synonymous, and most of the leading lights in women theory, sex theory, and the critique of women's literature tradition published volumes in the series.

The mission statement that prefaces each volume reiterates Li's founding impulse. She sought to establish a new discipline of women's studies through her publication list and to support the discipline with an academic scholarly field built on the foundation of reflexive, enlightened scholarship:

Research on Women [funü yanjiu] is the outcome of the move toward synthesis in the human sciences in the era following the "sixties" which resulted in an era of great studies in humanity and scientific self-reflexivity. Research on women could open a new discipline—women's studies [funüxue]—which uses "women" as its object for proceeding to specialized study to supplement the blank left in traditional humanities and sciences; it could create a kind of method which investigates all of human existence from the angle of sexed persons historically and currently, naturally and socially. . . . Its charge: to use scientific research as its method to reach subdisciplines to deeped specialized knowledge and understanding of people, especially men and women in China.

The people are in China, the books are in China. This Series' basic characteristics are all Chinese!

In 1988, when she wrote the mission statement, Li anticipated in the encyclopedic spirit of the European Enlightenment, that the project would disseminate truthful, specialized, and scientific knowledge.

Like Li Zehou, Li Xiaojiang was explicitly raising the question of enlightenment. But she began from a fundamentally different starting point. Her point of origin was the incommensurate relation of masculine and feminine; to her the sex gap was as foundational as tool making. To establish a contemporary study of gender she needed to theorize a legitimate method that recognized the gendered subject(s) of modernity. She settled on women's studies. The choice, she realized, brought with it some deficits, though the field itself was simply a branch of the social or human sciences. Women's studies, Li noted, first emerged in the United States and then spread to Europe, Canada, Japan, and the rest of the globe, where it had had a salutary and transformative impact in humanist studies. The problem confronting Li and other Chinese women who sought to vernacularize women's studies in China was that "in our nation," unlike other arenas globally where women's studies had been integrated into customary humanism, the scholarly and theoretical worlds still have a tendency to despise and discriminate against questions having to do with women, making it necessary to go to the extreme of establishing a special scholarly emphasis.[44]

This put Li, philosophically speaking, in the difficult position of simultaneously affirming Chinese centrality, the singularity of women, and the universality of enlightened humanism (once it recognized the sine qua non of the "gendered eye"). Despite her perception of specific Chinese hindrances to the development of women's studies, Li also recognized that to be politically useful, women's studies must have for its principal object the study of women in China. Why raise the issue of Chineseness in this context? she asked rhetorically. "Because the first principle of the founding of the human sciences is the principle of nationalism [minzuxing]." Indeed, Li argued, "there is no such thing as abstract Humanity." Except for the primary difference of sex/gender (xingbie chayi), nothing is more absolute in the thought of Li Xiaojiang than national origin (5–8).[45] The dialectic between the abstraction embedded in the very category woman and its specific national and/or local realizations is crucial to her thinking. "The starting point of research in a Marxist women's studies must be movement from all of Humanity [renlei zhengti zhong] into greater abstraction," she argued. "Insofar as abstraction is concerned, it must be able to investigate Woman as if it were one element of the totality of Humanity; at the same time, Woman must be seen as a special case in the social life of Humanity— one that contains all of the categories of totality—and from it this abstraction must determine the relative basis of its own Self. Only in this manner will it be possible for us to raise a scientific theory on the basis of the multiple totality of the human sciences to address the practicalities of the women question and women's liberation" (87–88). Thus, in spite of its national focus, Li rooted her feminist Enlightenment project in the supposedly universal medium of social science theory. Most of the projected titles listed in a 1987 introduction to the series are indeed basic texts in scholarly method and disciplinary regimes: Funü jingji huodong lun (On the economic activities of women), Nüxing yü chouxiang kexue (Women and the abstract sciences), Guoji fudong liangbai nian (Two hundred years of the international women's movement), and so on.

Its social science foundation situated Li's Women's Research Series in the fevered world of cultural theory. Li intended to elevate corporeal difference in the social Real and use it in a wedge movement to unmask masculinist bias in mainstream Enlightenment theory. The first section of what is certainly her most famous collection, Eve's Exploration, is titled "Lixing de shulou" (The Oversight of Reason) for obvious reasons. "Oversight" performs a Chinese Marxist feminist groundclearing for Li is preoccupied with abolishing speculation about women under socialism. Marx and Engels, she argues, were more progressive than their contemporary utopian or bourgeois rights feminists because they did address the material origins of gender and class oppression and their critique did provide Chinese communism with a winning strategy. After 1949, the CCP ran into trouble, however. Its woman theory failed to adapt; it made the women's liberation movement synonymous with proletarian emancipation, and it reinforced a move that Chinese women themselves had initiated to abandon femininity and to adopt a strategy of "human first, female only after." Li seeks in this discussion a revitalized woman theory and a revived, autonomous women's liberation movement that accommodates women's femininity and mobilizes a less flawed (quehan) female subject who will be more self-conscious (ziwo yishi de).

Li's target is not materialist forms of history, it is Maoist state policies. Women's work foundered during the Great Proletarian Cultural Revolution, she argued, because Maoists had declared scientific Marxism (i.e., Stalinism) itself off-limits and refused to allow theorists to mobilize science for exploring new social phenomena or establishing fresh social truths. It also prevented woman from emerging into Marxism as an abstract category, which made it altogether too easy for the Gang of Four to disable work among women. They just banned the Women's Federation and undermined the potential of even the mass subject of woman to effect changes in women's lives. Now Chinese women must recover their femininity and Chinese Marxist woman theory must prove again that, indeed, Marxism is an open philosophic system as well as a worldview and stands at the apex of progress in terms of its starting point. The solution to the weaknesses of Chinese classical Marxism, insofar as the woman question is concerned, Li argued, is to take up the Deng Xiaoping slogan "Seeking truth from facts" and simply declare no limits on the very areas that Maoism had made taboo: sexuality, the analytic divisibility of gender and class, and the global history of bourgeois feminisms. So, in fact, Li's willingness to engage standard Chinese Party historiography is as marked as her interest in the previously off-limits topics of feminism and establishing the analytic foundations for the subject she calls total or universal woman (zhengge funü) in this first essay and nüren elsewhere.[46]

When she enjoined Chinese Marxism to reconsider the woman question in theoretic work, Li argued that "woman theory essentially belongs to the human sciences" (Eve, 25). In "Renxing de shenghua" (The sublime of humanity), her frontal critique of Li Zehou's philosophic masculinism, she developed this point at great length. With that declaration she placed herself in the camp of the Kantian-Marxists and particularly inside Li Zehou's project to spell out a Marxist practical philosophy, which would lay the philosophical foundation for a notion of subjectivity as the main conceptual framework with which to examine Chinese culture and history.[47] Indeed, much of Li Zehou's familiar vocabulary of subjectivity, the sublime, reflection, consciousness, sedimentation, interiorization, and so on appear without comment in her volume. Marxism, she argued in (perhaps imaginary) dialogue with Li Zehou, indeed ought to reinvent itself in terms of academic discourse of the human sciences, but neo-Marxism must surpass classical schemes by making sure that its subject, Humanity, is sexed. It is no longer acceptable that Man (ren) obscure the femininity of one half of Humanity (renlei). Because the human sciences are broadly theoretical and their subject, Humanity, is doubled, in the scholarly practices of the human sciences the representation of woman is the measure of accuracy. The measure of a theory's viability is whether or not woman appears there as an abstract category. In classical Marxist theory the position or question of woman is the same as other social problems, Li argued, in a position redolent of Mei Sheng's, since in Karl Marx's time the woman question had not attained abstract theoretical status or become an aspect of the bourgeois social structure or even become the subject of historical examination. Theory (abstraction) and scholarly representation (practice) are inextricably linked: the woman question must be raised in each for the human sciences and neo-Marxism to fulfill their potential. Just as Marxist human sciences must include the split subject of Humanity, so all research and theorizing about woman must appreciate the degree to which representation is the representation of Humanity and the progress of Humanity is a historical development toward enlightenment. (24)

This explains the apparent contradiction between Maoist funü and modernizationist nüren in Li's work, and the dialectic she engages when she considers the universality of enlightenment through the particularity of Chinese experience. The revolutionary subject of Maoism emphasizes (to some extent, actually produces) an equivalence between men and women. Effectively, then, Maoism produces a female subject akin to but historically beyond the point of enlightenment feminisms. Its negation in turn by the fully gendered subject that emerges in post-Maoist theory (nüren) opens the space theoretically for a synthesis between the public, civil woman as political subject and the subjectivity of woman in all her difference from male subjects. This possibility would realize the claim that the specific Chinese revolutionary experience not only continues the enlightenment but raises it to greater levels of human/universal potentiality than are available to Western feminism. (The actual probability of realizing such a synthesis under the economic and social conditions of Chinese modernity will be discussed later on.)

In the first place, however, the theoretical project itself will prove to be difficult because in the academic domain there is an indifference to theory on women which in actual fact is impeding the establishment of a systematized human science. That is to say, Li Zehou and the masculinists had unconsciously tainted their own advances by leaving out of their critique the central and explosive problem of gender. So "theoretical research" (lilun yanjiu) may indeed constitute "a kind of science," and may indeed be an expression of reason. But none of the current theoretical exercises have undertaken to ensure that the enigma of woman is unravelled. Neither the theoretical world, which excludes women, nor the women's world, which does not deign to engage theory, has come to terms with the challenge posed by the human sciences on the one hand and the real-world progress of women's liberation on the other. Until now. "What is woman theory [funü lilun]? Plainly put, woman theory is the abstractions about woman made in philosophy. In practice, women's theoretic research can oppose two different objects, forming its own relatively independent theoretical category [lilun fanchou]." So far as women's liberation is concerned, practice itself constitutes the first concrete object of women's theoretic research (Eve, 19–20). In the history of the human sciences as in all other academic sciences, according to Li, truth is established step by step in an orderly progression: from simple to complex, from phenomenon to essence, from analysis to synthesis. To make the human sciences complete a newly wrought truth about woman must interrupt the assumption that humanity is male. As in all other human sciences, this truth must have a place in theory (i.e., as the abstract category woman) and be a subject in history (i.e., the universal historical movement toward women's emancipation and thereby toward the true apotheosis of Humanity). Once Li authorized woman theory in the human sciences, her next move was to plot out the field of knowledge that the forging of an abstract category woman in philosophy made available.

Li elaborated this outline at great length in *Eve's Exploration*, inviting Chinese scholars to draw liberally on international theorists like Simone de Beauvoir, Ellen Key, Betty Friedan, Alexandra Kollantai, and August Bebel, as well as Chinese research of the 1920s and 1930s on Chinese women pioneered during the May Fourth Enlightenment. She also stated in diagrammatic, terse language where she thought research ought to head. To those who might object that this notion of women's studies is too heavily indebted to Western and specifically American prototypes, Li replied that "our women's studies [*funüxue*] is not a ready-made textbook copy of theirs," because it is also taking shape within the historical context of Chinese discussion and Chinese concerns (29). But it also has more potential than non-Chinese forms do, for the simple reason that Chinese scholars and Chinese women have already experienced revolutionary change; though Chinese women's studies presently lags "twenty years behind Western nations," it exceeds, at least in potential, what non-Marxist and non-Chinese scholars are doing now because Chinese women's studies can begin with an always already liberated subject, *at least in theory*. Thus, despite the fact that the Revolution fell short, the cumulative effect of liberatory legislation and experience is that Chinese women's studies is in a privileged position globally; nationally, its position is also redemptive because it can assume new responsibility for those who would continue social progress today (98).

To this point in her argument Li Xiaojiang had foregrounded a critique of the masculinism of Li Zehou–style Marxist humanism. But as soon as she began making affirmative arguments about the positivity of woman as a category in the privileged scholarly regime of Chinese women's studies, she encountered problems, because it is analytically more difficult to sustain affirmative accounts than to offer up critiques of the masculinist positions of others. Partly, this is because she set in motion the logic of the Self and the Other. (This is a matter I will raise in the conclusion of this chapter, which examines in detail Li Xiaojiang's metaphysics.) But also, when Li authorized the subjects woman and China, she confronted multiplying questions of difference. One in particular recurred for her: the question of how, if the subject women always emerged, even in the foundational human sciences, in nationalized form, one should answer the universalizing question What is a woman?

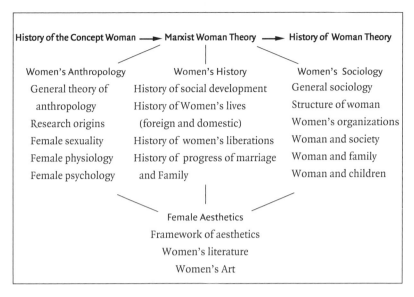

History of the Concept Woman ⟶ Marxist Woman Theory ⟶ History of Woman Theory

Women's Anthropology
General theory of
  anthropology
Research origins
Female sexuality
Female physiology
Female psychology

Women's History
History of social development
History of Women's lives
  (foreign and domestic)
History of women's liberations
History of progress of marriage
  and Family

Women's Sociology
General sociology
Structure of woman
Women's organizations
Woman and society
Woman and family
Woman and children

Female Aesthetics
Framework of aesthetics
Women's literature
Women's Art

4 The Systematic Framework of Marxist Women's Studies.
Source: Li Xiaojiang, *Xiawa de Tansuo* (Eve's exploration)

Li's solution was to embrace the absolute incommensurability of males and females. The virtue of this position is that it enabled her to unfold historical teleologies inside specific national modernities, with appropriate attention to the differences of each nation-state's experiences in global capitalism, yet allowed her to mediate historical differences through a trans- or supranational incommensurable gap of sexual difference. And it made possible the argument that Enlightenment shifted ground like mercury on an uneven surface; emerging in Europe, it had shifted eastward through Russia and finally, in the present, to post-Mao China. In one of her earliest major statements, "Nüxing ziwo renshi" (The self-comprehension of woman) Li introduced the basic formula of the sexed, universal subject of nüren, reiterated and elaborated in many other essays.[48]

Nüren, she argued, exists within historical evolutionary flows that govern the laws of development for all national formations and thus all peoples. Regardless of nationality, all women share a universal history and certain synchronized, historical stages through which their sex, nüren, must pass; specificities are secondary and advances in one region stand for advances for all women. But specific differences among women do exist, and all women, regardless of nationality, will undergo those stages even if at different moments. The universal stages of the evolution of nüren are matriarchy, slavery, and liberation. The important point here is that nüren's evolutionary path is dissimilar to that of men (nanzi), whose trajectory follows the more familiar Marxist sequence of matriarchy (the one stage the sexes share, though on terms of inequality), feudalism, and bourgeois dominance. This sex-historical, evolutionary difference (*chayi*) is both a positive and a negative thing; it is positive in the sense that it corresponds to the physiological reality of sexual difference, but it is negative because in modernity Chinese women have yet to achieve full subjectivity and thus differ from Chinese men by virtue of their insufficiencies, their lack of cohesion, their presubjectivity.

The motor driving history is therefore not just class struggle à la Marx and Engels. At an even more profoundly organic level, what drives progressive history is the immutable and natural sexual division of labor that began in the transition from matriarchy to patriarchal small families in the period of slavery and that modern history must both mediate and preserve. The claim is that, left to its own devices,[49] history can socialize nature and forward the slow, evolutionary development of equality. Or at least that is the implication of Li's dialectic of Nature and Culture: "Therefore, we can say about the starting point of human civilization that the social division of society into classes was absolutely natural. The social division of labor forces in fact maintained for a considerable time the natural division of human labor—what ensued historically was the socialization of appropriate natural divisions" (*Eve*, 40). This is where the implications of Li's critique of Li Zehou begin to surface quite vividly. Because the natural divisions determined by procreation are normatively immutable, Li is forced to conclude, there have been eras when the forward progress of humanity *required a historical degradation* to be visited on nüren. In the slave stage of history, for instance, men set about resolving the problems that history had set for them: they built a rich material and social existence. Li is very clear on this: men created civilization and the marvels of social production are the product of men's work during the era that men enslaved women, that is, from the rise of patriarchy to the era of Enlightenment. The creativity of men rested on a cruel but necessary devolution of women into "tools of existence" (*cunzhong de gongjü*).[50]

This leads Li to draw the obvious yet peculiar conclusion that over the entire history of civilization, although men and women have lived together on this earth, they have experienced two totally different evolutions.

> Man—[exists] in opposition to Nature [*ziran*]: in the struggle with Nature he gradually manifested an independent subject consciousness [*zhuti yishi*]. It is Man that transformed nature and created wealth under the urging of this subject consciousness. In the process of continued accumulation of wealth, men felt and have got the power to be outside material changes. . . . Women—detained by Nature, continue their own

individual physiological destiny and the collective natural mission of humans as a collective whole, using their very dehumanization to reproduce humankind. In the development of civilization, the importance of woman is to be concretized in relation to man and in concert with other natural phenomena, to passively endure the great transformations of humanized Nature, that is to endure the power of being alienated by men. Thus have these two obviously different tracks [guidao] deeply yet often invisibly and unconsciously inscribed the inestimably deep "sex divide" [xinggou] into human life. (Eve, 42)

In the end, it is not precisely clear whether nüren is the feminine of the species or the missing, abstract feminine element of a Li Zehovian humanity. Perhaps both of these things. In crediting mankind with the development of civilization, however, Li Xiaojiang unfortunately undercut strategies for equality based on justice claims and reinforced such commonsensical nationalist arguments as that ameliorating the lot of women contributes to national wealth and power.

So the implication of Li's thought in the 1980s was that national development and justice for women are agonistically opposed, at least to some degree. Amelioration of women's suffering presupposes economic reform. Economic reform will make the pleasures of consumption available to women. Women are consequently rendered able to realize fully their own reduction to bodiliness under the demands of the history of enlightenment. With modernization an equality that retains bodily difference will be brought about. The logic of an argument centered around the physicality and women's disabling reproductive responsibilities certainly led in that direction. The other implication of Li's sort of market feminism was that it predicated the completion of women as a subject in feminism exclusively in the context of consumer society. Civilizational and economic development toward a future free of want is the only way out, in the long run at least, for women and their chronic problem of subjectivity.

The next task for Chinese women, then, must involve the stimulation of "the subjective condition of women's conscious desire to develop, that is, the awakening of women's subjectivity." Women's studies' rationale in this framework is nothing less than to encourage Chinese women generally to ask themselves Who am I? and What is nüren now?[51] The answer to this latter question has already been explored: nüren is a universal, evolutionary, anatomical, physiological, menstruating, and parturient procreative body. In her popular writing, as had progressive feminists in the 1930s, Li described the corporeality of woman's body in elaborate anatomical detail, beginning with the fetal matter's constitution in xx and xy chromosomal patterns, through birth and childhood (yüerqi), youth (qingchunqi), maturity (chengshuqi), transition (gengnianqi), and menopause (jiejingqi). All nüren are universally reducible to this body, which signals its genuinely natural difference from man's body by flowing, changing, erupting, and reproducing.

Li strongly cautions those women who would evade the demands of this body and either fail to marry heterosexually or refuse pregnancy and childbirth. Women who do not use their body in sexual reproduction have been misled into thinking that equality can be purchased at the expense of difference and have betrayed their physiological destiny as nüren. There are two noteworthy aspects to this construction of nüren's body in this context. The first is the significance Li attaches to menstruation. In her personal experience, menstruation was equated with political trauma. In their theoretical work, negotiating the difficulties of menstruation is the greatest danger nüren face and leads potentially to moral and developmental failures (a preoccupation in sexual studies during the 1920s as well). Second, each biophysiological stage in Li's description of the anatomical specificities of nüren are related—foundationally related—to moral developments in female subject formation. Nüren who successfully negotiate the dangers of the onset of menses and enter the period of psychosexual and reproductive maturity can, given their historical era, expect to achieve an "I" or wo of some sort, be this a traditional, selfless I (wangwo), contemporary not-I ( feiwo), or future Greater I (dawo) in which the nüren finally achieves what men have enjoyed since the beginning of the slave era: the prize of individuality or individual being, of ren'ge.[52]

This is the overtly physiological or corporeal heart of Li's critique of funü and Maoist woman policy generally. It echoes in eerie detail the preoccupations of 1920s progressive feminist theory without any clear indication that Li was aware of the others—largely male others—who had predicated the priorities of the body in similar ways five decades earlier. When the CCP ignored the body of nüren, she theorized, it encouraged the socialization of women who had neither the individuality of men nor the femininity of women. They were, in Li's parlance, neither true nüren nor nüxing because they sought liberation only in a public realm and in ways that denied fundamental bodily differences. To resume their progress toward enlightenment (and therefore their historical mission to move humanity toward the end of history), women must achieve selfhood through the struggle to achieve the natural stages of their psychosexual maturation (Domestic, 12–23). Awakening women's subjectivity is in part a matter of making women aware of the nature of their own physical being.

The problem for women's studies, the barrier it must overcome, is that women as subjects, in China particularly, are simply underdeveloped in comparison to men as subjects.[53] To illustrate her general thesis of female deficiency, Li argued a teleology complete with causal factors and elaborate, multistage temporalities. To each evolutionary stage of humanity's history there belongs a corresponding "model" (matriarchy-*natural*, slave-*domestic*, liberation-*social*). Corresponding to each model is a form of female consciousness. Under the matriarchal formation, for instance, woman's consciousness took form as a spiritual, selfless love of mother for child. However, during the slave era, woman's consciousness atrophied. Attendant thereon, she lost all possibility of human agency because without a consciousness, personal will is not available. Woman presently confronts the problem of how to negotiate a transition from slave consciousness to consciousness of liberation. Lacking a sense of self, or a socially appropriate place, a standing, woman finds that history is forever exceeding her capacity for agency. (Women's liberation, for instance, is not actually the invention of women at all. It is the product of a global industrialization that quite simply tore women out of their domestic sphere and placed them willy-nilly into the social sphere.)

The key issue for Li is not that liberation for women initially "just happened." It is not even that women should have been able to put the state's imposed liberations to better use, but rather that because of the differences in their separate historical evolution, men and women confronted the present with very different resources for achieving subjectivity and social standing. Whereas men-in-history have always had a class nature and enjoyed subjectivity as masters or slaves, landlords or tenants, capitalists or workers, women, living an evolutionary course outside men's history, have stagnated for a thousand years because they were constitutionally unable to achieve "independent being" (*duli de ren'ge*; Domestic, 53). Women had no consciousness of individual subjectivity because they vegetated within the natural-historical roles necessarily conferred on them historically, the kinship roles (jiaose) of mother, sister, wife, and daughter. This meant that women as a species entered the modern era inherently disadvantaged. Whereas, during the European Enlightenment, men achieved the necessary, modern "self-consciousness as complete or essential Self" (*zuowei ren de zhengti zijue yishi*), women have had to wait for a full century before certain foremothers seized enlightened reason and established an abstract subject woman on women's behalf. How did this opportunity make itself available? History working through imperialism initiated the global women's liberation movement and thus imperialism laid the ground for the historical reconciliation of the sexes in the progress of humanity.

Enlightenment for nüren requires self-recognition, and the process by which nüren comes into consciousness of herself for herself is precisely the liberationist project of women's studies. I underline this element of Li's argument because I think it is significant that at this point in her thinking she simply assumed that women in industrial and postindustrial countries were successfully negotiating their own Enlightenment. At least they had a sufficient handle on it so they were no longer burdened with a self stitched together out of semifeudal "roles." Because the particular instantiation of nüren and the specific consciousness or mind in question is always concrete, it is necessary to turn to the consciousness of one specific instance of woman—Chinese woman—to proceed any further.

"Oriental Woman" (dongfang nüxing) is a stereotype deployed in some of Li Xiaojiang's most Li Zehovian expositions. It represents her analysis of the consciousness possible for contemporary Chinese women and begins from an analysis of the "sedimentation" (jidian) of historical qualities that have historically led to Chinese Woman's present "disposition" (qizhi). The sedimented formation of the Oriental woman is the consequence of three lines of causality: the social structural (great feudal–great family system), economic foundational (the small peasant cultivator's self-reliance), and the ideological (Confucian, Daoist, and Buddhist), which, through the vehicle of aesthetic consciousness, produces the traditional elements contributing to the consciousness of Oriental woman: restraint (kezhi), steadfastness (jianren), reserve (hanxu), and dignity (ningzhong).[54] While women globally in the modern era are torn between desire to procreate and the need to work outside the home, Oriental women felt the contradiction most heavily because of semifeudal semicolonialism. Later, robbed by the Communist Party of her essential difference from men, yet bearing within her sedimented feudal remnants as the shards of a failed subjectivity, Oriental woman could not enter public life. The so-called liberation imposed on women during the GPCR reinforced rather than solved the problem, which is why equality without difference lead Chinese women to despicable subject positions: lack of self on the one hand and loss of self on the other. In any case, Oriental woman currently possesses neither the powers of the old female roles under feudalism (jiating jiaose) nor a coherent subjectivity in postfeudal modernity. That, more than anything else, is why women's studies is central to the reemancipation of Chinese women back into their psychoanatomical difference and thus central to China's progress as a whole.

The peculiar circumstances of the underdeveloped personal being of Chinese woman led Li to perhaps her most famous thesis of all, the notion of the double burden. The double burden has two aspects. First, it means that, whereas in Europe women gave up feudal social formations and took on the contradictions of the modern era, in China women simply added modern roles (jiaose) to the feudal roles they already had inherited, doubling their alienation from personal being or social standing (ren'ge). More commonly, the double burden refers to Li's belief that when the CCP prematurely "liberated" Chinese women by fiat, the result was that women engaged in social production while at the same time doing the necessary and essential work of domestic reproduction. To "awaken to self-consciousness," contemporary Chinese women must resolve the crushing contradiction of the double burden in their own particular fashion.[55] They may take advantage of the maternity leaves given Chinese women under law, or they may choose to retire completely from social production to focus on the domestic sphere. In any case, they will have to take some time off of work to obey the central imperative of sexual difference, which is simply that women must procreate:

> We must clearly recognize that now, under the present conditions of our country, due to restrictions on the kind of economic development domestic labor cannot be swiftly reduced, yet the responsibility of child rearing is still something that women must undertake and the work of upholding family responsibilities still rests for the most part on the shoulders of women. The anxiety of dual roles is a heavy millstone around our necks, but it is one that we must continue to shoulder. *This is the price we must pay for the advancement of History and women.* (Eve, 133)[56]

The model of liberated Chinese womanhood under the current economic reforms is a repatriated, modern housewife in Li Xiaojiang's 1980s formula.

It helps to keep in mind the explosive quality of 1980s debates on sexuality. Feminist polemics revolved around a sense of bodiliness that is conveyed best graphically. The legend beneath the image in Figure 5, which appeared in the January 1987 issue of the glossy popular periodical *Xiandai jiating* (Modern family) says, "The human body is most beautiful. The beauty of the human form is in a category of its own and no matter if it is animals, physical objects, flowering vegetation or scenery, other images simply cannot compare, because the beauty of the human body is Humanity's sensual self, it is Humanity's direct self-appreciation. Photographs of the models of the human body are one important aspect of the photo arts, which are in the same category as sculptures and painting of the human body." And of course, the artistry of the photographer in highlighting the girl's posture, bosom, and upward gaze embodies youthful and harmonious femininity through meticulous composition, lighting, and use of shadowing. The legend implies that the photographer's creative intentionality rescues the nude from nakedness, socializes her, and transforms her animality into art.

Redeemed from nakedness in the rhetoric of lofty humanism and spiritual uplift, the image was still remarkably fresh in a visual culture that a mere five years earlier had automatically banned nudes as obscene. The

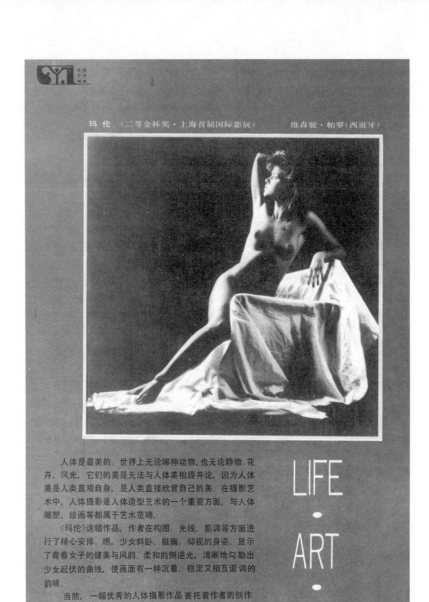

5 Civilized nude. Source: *Xiandai jiating*
(Modern family), January 1987, inside front cover.

young nude is undeniably sexual. It reflects the cusp of an advertising image just then infiltrating a new, urban, commercial culture, as well as an older, 1920s-era ideology about the naturalness of sexual nature. But it also forms an argument in itself. The image insinuates the materiality of a time just adjacent to itself, when ultraleftism, indeed revolutionary modernity itself, held sway, and it argues that art representation, not political representation, is the conduit to truth. That is because, according to this legend, the human body represented in art is itself a self-reflexive appreciation or apprehension of the Self of humanity. Thus, the graphic echoes the characteristic linkages on display in Li's *Sex Gap*. Enlightened self-reflection, the preferred cultural objective among the wounded intellectual class in the 1980s, included quite centrally a consideration of human sexuality, anchored in the physical body.

The image in Figure 6 appeared in *Modern Family* in February 1986 and is of champion weightlifter Xu Qinhua. No legend accompanies the photographs. The extraordinary posture of the dominant image of Xu flexing her arms, standing motionless on tiptoe, head cocked back over her left shoulder, is arresting. Subordinate images of Xu running down the side of the photo layout are of a clothed, ordinary-looking woman posed by the sea amid natural rock formations and in conventional domestic configuration with husband and parents. It would appear that the physicality of Xu's championship body, muscled, naked, speaks powerfully for itself. I read the photograph to say that not only is the woman's body healthy and strong, but it is representable, indeed appropriately reproducible in nearly any social context. The corporeality of the body beneath the social skin of clothing is the foundation that supports social reproduction of cultural forms across materiality, that enables the bridging or necessary humanizing work of transforming Nature into Culture. There is nothing unclear or unlovely or even intimate about this nearly naked body. The smooth, polished, hairless surface of the oiled skin gives off a glittering reflection that exceeds and monumentalizes the otherwise unremarkable life of an ordinary-looking Chinese woman. The scientifically distinct and easily discerned female body of the modern Chinese woman advertises post-Mao social theory as obviously as the legend of the art photo, with its philosophically freighted banner of "Life–Art–Explore." Not since the 1930s dissemination of sexualized female bodies in advertising images had anything approaching contemporary levels of semiotic freight been attached to images of women's naked or nearly naked flesh.

In retrospect, the force underlying this great transformation of social ethics and theoretical preoccupations was certainly the policy decision to develop a socialist market economy. The Deng Xiaoping consensus and its reintegration of China's economy into the neoliberal international arena

一九八六年上海市健美比赛
女子全场冠军获得者——许勤华

陈钢 孙建国 摄

现代家庭 MODERN FAMILY

报刊代号 4—410 定价 0.45元

6 Weightlifting woman. Source: *Xiandai jiating*
(Modern family), February 1987, back cover.

retrenched the idea that social regulation involved law, individual competition, domestic consumption, and other elements of the dominant international order of development. Unlike the 1920s (to which the era of the 1980s is often compared, particularly by people active in the 1980s), the great social transformation of de-Maoicization unfolded as an erratic and violent policy of state reform.

The subject of Li Xiaojiang's post-Mao feminism rested on this shattering recuperation of the physical body and its legitimate, irrepressible (if recently rediscovered) desires. Her theoretical work called for justice on both grounds: that political crimes against nature had made her generation of women into men, and also that the new market economy, though key to women's eventual liberation, was inflicting its own patterns of discrimination. Li's early theories leave relatively underanalyzed the implications of the new market orientation. Market culture situated women as producers of children and value, but more important, it transformed them into consumers. The market is where, at least for the foreseeable future, women would remain unless and until history allowed the sexing of reason. That was how Li positioned her theoretical sociology and it gave her a way to justify her criticism of the institutional ACFW women's movement. Market feminism is not rooted in past mobilization campaigns. Rather, it teaches women the skills they will need to make the best use of their resources—sexual, domestic, personal, and intellectual. The wise use of resources in Li's educational schemes meant that women's human qualities would improve faster, and that would positively affect human emancipation. Social development leads to historical progress, to the eventual reconciliation of the competing drives of equality and national progress, and consequently to the very historical progress of enlightenment itself.

Li opened an obvious lacuna: Where would the unreflexive (feiwo), passive, misdirected Chinese women go to find appropriate knowledge? What mirrors can she find that will allow her to recognize herself as a biogenetic, human, and nationalized yet still wholly universal subject, nüren? Certainly, the women's studies materials Li wrote and edited addressed that question. But not all women are sufficiently well educated to find abstract academic work interesting, and a range of pedagogies would be needed. Li was raising, in a new way, in a new context, the perennial question of women's ren'ge. If Chinese women are presently defined by their lack of personal being and social standing, then what is present within them that can stimulate desire to redress this fundamental lack? How can one affirm the potential subject of Chinese woman while one defines the present subjects in terms of their lack of ren'ge? The volume *Woman: A Distant, Beautiful Legend* illustrates the shape of Li's contradiction. Dedicated to nüren everywhere, no matter what their color, race, nationality, profession or age, the opening passages of the introduction reiterate in simple language many of the points Li had raised in more academic writing. She particularly emphasizes the devastating effects that male dominance (using the euphemisms "masculine consciousness" and "masculine will") have wrought on women. As a consequence, women are lost to the world and forgotten even by themselves; their centuries of enslavement have devastated their ability to act, and women by and large are in fetters that bind them; they have lost sight of their track (guidao), and so on. The narrative takes a rhetorical stand:

> But what is the historical course of women [nüren] then? If we search the historical classics and archives for her, the consequence is this: nüren has no history! . . . It appears that nüren is a distant, beautiful legend. In this world where the sacred and profane, dream and reality are all mixed up, in the realm of literature one finds the marks of nüren's existence and actions left behind. Literature is like the mirror of the life of Humanity, reflecting more or less the reality of society. . . . This book [of mine] is written for woman. It is a paean to beauty, and the greatness of the feminine; it is a paean to love, the faith of women; it is a paen to the children and to humanity; to the selflessness of women and to peace, the strength of women. This book seeks to employ a great, boundless maternal humanism to use the past experience of women's shame and glory to enlighten today's women into consciousness of Self. To be a person, a nüren, requires that we find an imperial subjectivity for women![57]

*Woman* is a secret history of presubjective woman created by ransacking the subterranean world of global myth and literature. You must recognize that you are indeed a nüren, and you need to see clearly your female identity, Li argued. If you really want to understand yourself, then you must understand this first: *you are a woman*. Yet, woman, that category does not belong to you. Woman is sacred and she is the enigma wrapped in the shroud of a hundred thousand years. Yet if you really wish to grasp this you must begin with the recognition that you are woman![58] The subsequent three hundred pages consolidated Li's evidence. Starting with myths and stories about woman in the ancient world of matriarchy (in the "West," the Queen of Sheba; in the "East," Xiwangmu the western matriarch), the narrative relates stories about women in the era of slavery when women's sphere was exclusively domestic, then follows the course of woman from the awakening in the European Enlightenment, the Russian and Chinese Enlightenments, to modern woman's struggles with modernity. The final section, "Woman," focuses on the liberation movements of the 1960s in the United States, relaying information in chatty, anecdotal style. The volume set out to convince a female reader that she must abandon the Maoist attempt to make Chinese women into Chinese men. She must admit that her historic mission as a universal historical subject woman is, in descending order of importance, to be a mother, a creator of life, a warrior for justice, and, in the familiar May Fourth metonymy of the nascent, modern Chinese woman, to embody the historic qualities of brave Sophia, Ding

Ling's partly awakened, modern Chinese female subject, in the final historic step toward global women's liberation.

## Li Xiaojiang and Sex

Li Xiaojiang has always seemed to be a polarizing, controversial figure. I do not know if her imagined male philosophic interlocutors, Li Zehou or Liu Zaifu, ever responded to her critique of reason. Over the years, she has offended various constituencies within the women's studies and gender studies communities inside the PRC and outside of it. She continues to place herself in an agonistic relation to some feminist scholars in the Women's Federation and to other scholars in the Chinese expatriot scholarly community in particular.[59] Some of this ill will may have to do with Li's ability to instinctively dramatize the predicaments that she writes about so vividly. An example of this sort of popular self-dramatization is her essay "Zouxiang nüren" (Towards woman), which conveyed her shock and terror at coming to consciousness as a woman. All of a sudden, Li wrote with a flourish, she had ceased being a person and initiated her life as a woman. She had always excelled in the meritocratic, Maoist world of her youth. It gave her an androgynous, almost masculine will, which meant she was capable of extreme ultraleftist volunteerism and could go to any ends to reach her goal. Her marriage, heterosexual procreative life, and the birth of her child forced her to confront, more vividly even than at the onset of her menses, the natural singularity of women and her own sexual particularity. She had to live out what she would later theorize as the "typical Eastern woman's fate" of selfless domestic sacrifice and the second burden of salaried work. She realized that "the double roles" of mother and worker imposed "a double standard, like a double-edged sword," which disturbed her sense of self and threw her off balance. "I failed to understand why this only happened to women, only those who had female bodies." And that was when it occurred to her that womanhood is precisely this experience.[60] Li's personal narrative of life in sexual reproduction put a face on the experience of an entire cohort. Her autobiographic writing particularly is fundamentalist in the sense that it makes her own persona the touchstone of her theoretical claims. If you do not live it, you cannot claim it is the tacit message. Yet Li was performing for others an experience that only women in her own cohort, at her educational level, with her frustrations and accomplishments could claim to know intimately.[61]

This prevalent argument that Maoism had reversed nature when it forcibly liberated woman has become a truism over the years. Li's vivid popular performance of nature at the heart of subjectivity centered sexual subjectivity. It made her own experience a datum in feminist theory. Though her market feminism links economic reform, female subjectivity, domestic service, the erotic agency of women, and the question of consumer choice to macroeconomic concerns about labor surplus, political demobilization, and urban development, still Li's core concern is the power of sexuality in social evolution. That makes Li Xiaojiang not so much an "essentialist" theorist, in my view, as a "sexualist." If I am right, she properly belongs in the theory stream of Ellen Key, Gao Xian, Chen Dezheng, Xi Leng, Kagawa Toyohiko, Shimamura Tamizo, and other theorists of heterosexuality (see chapter 3). Li's favored tropes and theoretic problems—the procreative body, the inversion of nature and history, the problems of equality and difference, social teleology and natural order—shimmer with the preoccupations of sex theorists and past eugenic feminists.

That is why it seems correct to end this chapter with an analysis of Li Xiaojiang's most explicit and polemical theoretical work on the 1980s *Xing-gou* (Sex gap).[62] Although she has repudiated some elements of the argument, it is still a remarkable piece of writing. *Sex Gap* is a heterogeneous pastiche of policy strategy, personal experience, and theoretical riddling or play. It intervenes radically and rhetorically in the great debate over national development policy that culminated in the event of June 1989. In that regard (and because it is preoccupied with the relation of the universal and the particular), I would call it a prescient form of Chinese neoliberalism. But *Sex Gap* is bluntly about sex. It theorizes Li's claim that she was not a woman until her body presented her with the signs of difference—bleeding and childbearing—and the society began to extract the crucial surplus (domestic) labor that necessarily will power China's national, social evolution. Finally, *Sex Gap* merged the singular experience of Li's generation to a theoretical strain in international feminism, Betty Friedan's *Feminine Mystique* and Simone de Beauvoir's *Second Sex*, particularly Beauvoir's Marxist existentialism.[63]

*Sex Gap* considers the logic of sexual congress in an agonistic relation to logics of sexual emancipation. Although it may be the case, Li argues, that under the conditions of the social emancipation of the sexes a logic of "substantially the same" prevails, this logic of similitude rests on a subordinated recognition that in fact the sexes are *not* the same. The allegedly universal principle (*gongli*) of equality is thus foundationally unstable. Equality is contradicted by the very sexual gap that makes the notion of universality seem a hoax. The objective of Li's tract is precisely to unmask this hoax and to argue that universality in the logic of sex is not, in fact, similarity but difference, difference rooted in the nature from which every human community must wrest its humanity. Equality in principle is belied by human praxis. Rather than obscure the fact that the ground of human universality is natural sexual difference, she argues, a better strategy is to admit that male and female emerged historically in a differential evolution. In a counterdiscourse (*luoji beilun*) like her own, not only are the histories of woman and man not synchronous, but woman's colonization by man and the imposition of a male-centered standard has led to the de-individuation (*feiren'gehua*) of women as a historical sex.

Citing Beauvoir, Li argues that the "process of humanization of Nature is also a process of the objectification of women" (9). If universality is anything, it is the ground formed when women were necessarily degraded into extensions of man. Although its roots are in nature, the universal degradation of women is nonetheless expressed historically, which is to say that the human sexes evolved on independent tracks. Accordingly, "the nature of the evolution of the two sexes is dissynchronous and that is the first principle of the foundation of the history of human civilization" (7). It is only because this historical datum has been overlooked that we can then speak of an artificial [*renweide*], logical counterdiscourse. Logical rationales are not purely objective and do not spring purely out of logical speculation, but rather are submerged in the collective unconscious as the end product of the movement of history. In other words, Li seems to argue that nature determined the secondary status of women until women could themselves achieve subject status and give history a reflexivity that emancipation would truly demand. *Human emancipation rests on the evolutionary development of women.*

*Sex Gap* sought a way to mobilize feminine difference against what Li, like many Marxist theorists, concurred was the Communist Party's instrumental use of a practical logic of similitude to reinforce Chinese women's degraded, masculinized status. And yet Li did not distinguish ontology from the existential logic that one is not born, but becomes, woman. Her concern lay with establishing the foundational status of biological difference and the creative potential she felt lay in natural, sexed embodiment (50–57). It is, Li argues, "in her existence as a biological entity that Woman concretizes her link to the increase of human population; which is to say, Woman's natural destiny is to guarantee the biological continuation of humanity through time" (10). If anything is universal, this is the universality of human existence. The biological or natural continuation of humanity through time is the one certainty of nature and history.

Nonetheless, until a female personality (ren'ge) emerges that is sexual and social, practical and theoretical, humanity as an undifferentiated whole will have to remain unselfconscious. The dissynchronous evolutionary paths of male and female will continue to diverge. Genuine female emancipation will remain just out of reach. The transition from nature to social emancipation rests on the project of establishing social standing for women. Objectively, therefore, not only will social development and human evolution have to retain the impress of the sexual gap, but it will have to build into its teleological future a social standing for women that is feminine and equitable. Until that time and until that emancipatory event, women will remain men (95).

Li's overarching philosophic project in this remarkable book, therefore, is to link her discovery of the universal foundation of difference (the sex gap in nature and history) to the familiar historical teleologies of Mao, Bebel, Marx, and Engels. She had to move the reader from the social division of labor to what she argued was the natural division of reproductive labor. Much of *Sex Gap* is devoted to tracing evolutionary historical stages from matriarchy to patriarchy, the middle eras to modernity, and on into the premature or pseudo-emancipation of women into productive labor, and so on. At each step, Li goes to great pains to point out that because masculinity-humanity-history coincided and because it is the duty of the unpredicated female body (feiwo or *feiren'ge*) to provide a material base for mindless human reproduction, there has been no historical uprising of women. History for women lies in their infinite particularization within the regimes of social gender (*shehui xingbie*), where the immobilizing and particularizing reproductive functions—wife, mother, daughter—substitute for any female autonomous subjectivity. Objectified and in thrall to this patriarchal web, women not only contribute nothing to history, but they have not benefited even now from the efforts made by states on their behalf—for a host of reasons, beginning with the fact that woman as a subject does not exist for herself in theory in any sense.

Yet, woman, even in a latent state of prepredication, is an irreducible, albeit ahistorical entity. And this particularity preoccupies Li in her odd and compelling book. Analytically and theoretically, the particularity or particularism of the feminine is momentous. Women cannot be enfolded into mere class abstraction nor reduced to a simple category of social or political economy. The task facing Chinese women and theorists is, therefore, to articulate a feminine place of subjective standing that is appropriately gendered, that is truly feminine and not an ersatz man, a Maoist "liberated" and therefore castrated woman. Men will be men, and women will be finally and truly women only when the special, sexual, particular difference of women is acknowledged as universal, foundational fact (40–43). The law of heterosexual dualism prescribes no other nature for the (two) genders than the one grounded in sexual reproduction.

Li Xiaojiang's *Sex Gap* precisely parallels Simone de Beauvoir's *Second Sex*, it should be pointed out. In *Sex Gap*, Li contemplates briefly but bluntly the priorities of the sexed body, particularly its grotesque physiology, and provides an extraordinarily negative characterization of what she judges to be feminine deficiencies, nurtured and fed by women's secondary status in the established, masculine order. Like Beauvoir, Li dwells at length on the interiorization relation that man establishes with his projected Other, woman. Li claims the same scholarly and political tradition and vocabulary (Engels, Bebel, Victorian ethnography, and stage debates) as Beauvoir had. Both theorists pose an agonistic dilemma of feminist pseudo-emancipation and presume that history is a global flow of economistic transformation that somehow ranges through time and space in a barely differentiated, globalized, "universal history." And yet they are not the same book. Li employs the terms "active" and "passive" rather than the existentialist terms Beauvoir employed, "immanent" and "transcendent" (16–17). Li also overlooks questions of difference in social, national, or cultural codes, choosing instead to fold social difference into her big corporeal anatomical divide. "There are only two social sexes [xingbie] in humanity," she concludes, but "in different societies at different times, gendered behavior of [those] two genders [liangxing xingbie] has been remarkably different" (24).

In *Sex Gap* Li seeks to reencode a logic of the universal and particular in a postrevolutionary gender crisis. She describes the gap in social terms in great detail in a chapter called "Yin yang da lie bian" (The great fission of yin and yang). There she notes that globally (or at least in all nations that really count), the 1960s was a time of conflict between the sexes (registered in rising rates of divorce and sexual promiscuity, problems stemming from the same cause). She attributes a historical failure to resolve the gender of humanity, to gender the human personality (ren'ge) as most likely cause. The evidence, she asserts, is all around. Pessimistically, she points to a famous passage from Zhang Jie's "Fang dan" (The Ark):

> Probably they [the women] would all remain single until they died. Why was it? There seemed to be a yawning abyss where there should have been reciprocal understanding between themselves and men, an abyss similar in nature to the "generation gap" plaguing older and younger people. Could it be that a gender gap troubled the relation of women and men? Could it be a "sex gap"? In this stage of historical development it might well be that women were simply more evolved than men, or perhaps the reverse was true. Or was it that men were so much more evolved than women that they had forfeited the possibility of engaging in any dialogue from the same starting point?

Zhang's story denotes an unbridgeable sexual antagonism and "The Ark" became the touchstone fiction for feminists in the 1980s. It expressed the profound alienation from sexual life and heterosexual norms the Cultural

Revolution had imposed. It was also central to the task of rethinking what socially appropriate kinds of femininity and masculinity would allow sexual connection between women and men without at the same time enslaving women to men.

But Li's citation of this story raises other significant points. Certainly, first, in her articulation of fiction into theory, she was suggesting that philosophy is the proper regime for thought in the present moment. Literature's function in her work is usually to illustrate a theoretical point. She does not stay with "The Ark" for long because her imaginary interlocutor is Li Zehou, but there is little evidence that she had any real interest in the contemporary women's literature movement. Not the sort of searching engagement that Meng Yue, Dai Jinhua, and other literary critics had as they undertook at that moment to establish a canonical Chinese women's literary tradition. Second, Li's preoccupation with the play of universal and particular lends this book a predictable familiarity. The universal takes on clarity only within a web of historicist categories: civilization, Man, historical progress, individuation, liberty. The particular coincides with the Other and remaindered, female, the barbaric, static, de-individuated, material, and passive. Like Beauvoir, Li makes this logic of male primacy and female secondariness historically, theoretically, and psychoanalytically foundational.[64] Third, Li's theory of the sex gap situates the question of female subjectivity in geopolitics (the relation of "China and the West") as well as a presumed relation of evolutionary descent between the past and the present. Perhaps the ensuing instability of the signifiers is part of what provoked her anxiety.

There is a fourth significant point that *Sex Gap* raises. Just as Gao Xian had in the 1920s, Li was predicating a human person driven to social performance out of sexual, instinctive, desire. Her intellectual framework is not squarely or exclusively eugenic. But in *Sex Gap* the subject women is nothing less than the pure sexual subject because Li made women's procreative body the mother lode of all historical progress. She was not joking about the corporeal body's centrality. *Sex Gap* fixates in a manic drive to repredicate or reencode all received, social subjects—"man," "mankind," "humans," "humanity," "woman," "women"—and to reduce all historical teleologies to a base line of sexuality, sexual desire, and sexual reproduction. For instance, halfway through the work, Li stipulates that humans are concrete entities; that is, there is no sacral "humanity" à la Chinese Marxist humanism. We are all, to the contrary, (1) biological entities with (2) sexual drives produced in (3) social relationships (52). This abrupt challenge to the disembodied ethical idealism of the ultraleftist period and no doubt the Marxist humanist emphasis on abstract humanity, which once again overlooked the descent of man out the bodies of woman, echoed in theoretical language popular attitudes that were conditioning and drawing inspiration from projects like Li's Enlightenment Series. It is a remarkable achievement. At one and the same time, Li was pointing to a foundational lack in Marxist humanism and also reflecting through her own theoretical prism the powerful move emerging in educated circles to redeem nature.

## 7  Dai Jinhua, Globalization, and 1990s Poststructuralist Feminism

When Ding Ling went along with the epochally current process of turning toward revolution, it was not without suffering loss; the consequences of her abandonment of the female consciousness and the intellectual consciousness not only resolved that intimates that intellectuals abandon their own historical value, it also intimates that they abandon, repress and lose the initial elements of the May Fourth critical tradition, that is to lose their power to criticize the feudal ideology and narrow stupidity of the mass psychology that had sedimented in China's masses (the mass of rural and urban lower orders) in the 1930s. MENG YUE AND DAI JINHUA, *Fuchu lishi dibiao* (Surfacing onto the horizon of history)

[We] are living through a movement from organic, industrial society to a polymorphous, information system . . . from the comfortable old hierarchical denominations to the scary new networks I have called the informatics of domination . . . [this includes a shift from] Freud [to] Lacan. DONNA HARAWAY, "A Manifesto for Cyborgs"

Chinese women's studies, strictly speaking, began in the 1980s. Professor Li Xiaojiang did most of the original creative work. The exact meaning of her creation is *funü yanjiu* (Women studies) [original English]. . . . It is possible to say that Li Xiaojiang is the creator of contemporary Chinese women's studies [*nüxingxue*]. DAI JINHUA, *You zai jing zhong* (Still caught by the mirror)

D ai Jinhua has a unique place in 1990s Chinese scholarship. Marxist film critic and cinema historian, Lacanian literary critic, adversary in the sharp public debates characterizing Chinese cultural studies elites, fixture on the international Asian lecture circuit, and a pop icon with a national TV audience at home, Dai is also—perhaps even primarily—a feminist thinker.[1] She credits her core insights in film and literature to European avant-garde critical theory; Lacan and Althusser are obvious interlocutors. At the same time Dai also recast so-called French feminism in a national historical frame. Working with Meng Yue and

Zhang Jingyuan, she has established an *écriture féminine chinoise*. Dai's allies do not come from either the social science establishment or Ford Foundation or Fulian-style NGO feminists. Rather, she and historian and critic Meng Yue, historian and editor Wang Hui, literary critic Li Tuo, sociologist and editor Huang Ping, and literary critics Chen Xunxin, Zhang Jingyuan, and Liu Jianzhi (Lao Kinchi) form a small but significant neo-Marxist, scholarly avant-garde. Linking them is a common reservation about the Chinese government's globalization strategies and their own efforts at providing theoretical alternatives to neoliberalism.[2]

Dai Jinhua began her remarkable scholarly career working on gender and the politics of cultural representation. Meng Yue, now a U.S.-trained historian of China teaching in California, and Dai coauthored the influential book *Surfacing onto the Horizon of History: Research on Modern Women's Literature*, published by Li Xiaojiang's Enlightenment Series. Their project established analytically the canon of Chinese women's modern literature and presented an argument for why certain texts had canonical status and others did not. A distinctive, female tradition of modern Chinese literature had emerged in the twentieth century, they argued. This literary tradition had historical significance because it crystallized in literary representation a larger, urban, emerging historical and social subjectivity of women which the authors called by its May Fourth name of nüxing. *Surfacing onto the Horizon of History* was the single most influential work originating in Chinese of poststructuralist, feminist literary criticism in the 1990s (though arguably it appealed to readers because of its "1980s" idiom).[3]

As Dai became a national and then an international celebrity, her scholarly preoccupation with canonical women's modern literature gave way to her work in Chinese film and film cultural criticism, the 1995 *Jingcheng tuwei: Nüxing, dianying, wenxue* (Breaking out of the city of mirrors: Women, film, literature).[4] *Breaking out of the City of Mirrors* addressed the question of how the subject of feminism, nüxing (neither eugenic nor a biogenetic or social scientific) is resituated in film culture in a singular framework of visual representation. Her objective in her highly theoretical Lacanian-Marxist film criticism was apparently to read the category of women into the social text. The name she gave to this social text is "the 1990s." Now in midcareer, Dai focuses her scholarship on how the ground beneath her continues to shift and buckle under relentless, rapid social and economic transformation. Consequently, the beginning of the new century finds her pioneering yet another academic specialization, of cultural studies. Because Dai participates in international cultural studies streams as a mature scholar rather than as an overseas student, her vision of what cultural studies might be expected to accomplish in the current conjuncture rests on national political exigencies, and the prism she uses to refract "the 1990s" is the new social movements of the 1980s and their violent dénouement in 1989.

Dai's metaphor of "the 1990s" has taken shape between two momentous events. The first is postsocialist development, the second is the mass culture of consumption; both are attendant on state planning. Aimed at the national political economy, its regimes of production and its patterns and policies of consumption, the Deng Xiaoping policies of gradated or unequal development has been transformative. The national economy sustained an annual 10 percent growth rate beginning in the early 1980s, with dips in 1997 down to 6–7 percent per annum and more recently up into the 12–13 percent range. A postsocialist development policy of systematic inequality on national, regional, and intraregional levels has meant accelerating growth in the coastal provinces and decelerating inland development. Redistributive social and economic policies associated with Mao Zedong are gone, and the unequal policies associated with Deng have given rise to explosive change in the megacities Shanghai, Canton, and Beijing, where class stratification is acute and growth involves the influx of a massive, impoverished rural labor force that cannot be wholly absorbed into urban development.

Second, the garish coloration and underlying tinge of nausea that suffuse Dai's work on the 1990s are the effect of encountering this bureaucratically controlled culture of consumption. Chinese cultural studies scholars conventionally use 1992 to mark the division between the 1980s (a golden era when critical intellectuals still predominated even in emergent popular venues like TV) and the 1990s when Deng gave his Southern Excursion Talks regarding the State Council's decision to expand the Chinese national market economy and promote a mass or popular commodity culture of consumption. At least until its accession to the World Trade Organization, Chinese development policy has linked export production to a structured, more or less controlled, internal consumer economy. Patterned consumption (e.g., advertising, vacation shopping, internal tourism), the burgeoning of a so-called leisure culture fostered in the Chinese national context, has led to the emergence of a popular or mass culture. Commercialized relations to the means of production, controlled consumption of pleasure, and the commodification of basic needs have reshaped the late 1990s physical and ideological landscape. In Dai's latest work, the 1990s is a shorthand, imagistic reference to this new terrain, a world that her mature cultural studies describes and judges.[5]

To cinematic spectacle and women-authored fiction Dai has added a new preoccupation with the mass culture industry's impact on the social text and the progress of Enlightenment. At the behest of general editor and entrepreneur Li Tuo and in his innovating series *Contemporary Mass Culture*

*Critique* (Dangdai dazhong wenhua piping congshu), Dai has already published two volumes, *Yingxing shuxie: Jiushi nian dai Zhongguo wenhua yanjiu*
(Invisible writing: Nineties chinese cultural studies, 1999) and *Shuxie wenhua yingxiong* (Writing culture heroes, 2000), which advance her project of
engaging the Zeitgeist. In other major publications, *Still Caught by the Mirror*
(1999), *Pintu youxi* (Mapping/Playing the game, 1999), and an edited volume introducing new women's fiction, *Shiji zhi men* (Gates of the century),
she continues to ask how a theoretical subject of woman can make its way,
agonistically, through the minefield of post-Mao commodity culture.[6]

A discussion of *Surfacing onto the Horizon of History* begins this chapter.
Because June 1989 was as much the beginning of the 1990s as it was the
end of the 1980s, I want to distinguish between the developmentalist current in mainstream Chinese feminism and the theoreticist current of écriture féminine chinoise Dai Jinhua typifies. Dai's method is agonistic.
Rather than critically trace Reason's progress in history as enlightened
sociology in the fashion of Li Xiaojiang, Dai has attempted to theorize an
epochal break. Her project has increasingly targeted whatever in the carnival of the contemporary scene might be grasped in analytic, psychoanalytic, and political terms. In the frantic years of the late 1980s, when the
third great Chinese Enlightenment repudiating the utopian tragedies of the
Mao years swept the intellectual world, no one anticipated how thoroughly
the social, cultural, and material world of 1990s China would be affected.
Buried in the heated rhetoric of the fevered 1980s were complications that
surfaced into visibility (to use a favorite metaphor of hers) only in the
1990s.[7]

Dai's sensitivity to what Donna Haraway named the informatics of domination is clearer in relation to Li Xiaojiang's market feminism. Each theorist, near contemporaries who belong to different intellectual cohorts, is
equally preoccupied with the historical catachresis of nüxing. Li's early
work, as we have seen, used the eugenic, heteroerotic and corporeal, abject
female body to resolve the question of women in feminism. Dai, too, is a
feminist and hallucinates an imaginary collectivity of real women. But in
Dai's universe the traces left by past and present women as women cannot
yet be represented in the contemporary social text. Their traces will be
representable only at some future time when patriarchalism's long Oedipal
trap is sprung and women themselves resolve the question of women, both
in theory and in practical, everyday feminism. Anatomy is still destiny in
Dai's formula, but she makes two foundational assumptions that Li does
not. First, for Dai, originary difference structures psychodynamic divisions
of power, yet the nature of the division forecloses on the possibility of a
genuine female subject form or consciousness. Second, it follows that for

Dai, expression of sexual difference rests on the period or the time of representation. Women's history is pure futurity for Dai, who is intent on retheorizing the riddle of female subjectivity and social standing. Where Li would return existing women to a lost matriarchal fullness that history itself cunningly required women to sacrifice on humanity's behalf, Dai argues that, lacking a subjective social form, women can become female only in the labor of self-writing and invisible writing. Ren'ge is futurity because the question of women's standing has yet to be solved socially or psychically. But how gender difference and women's standing appear will always be a function of the historical era and the organization of modes of production. In the 1990s, global, electronic, mass-mediated representations are the only fully legible text.

Dai respectfully shares Li's position that the Chinese Revolution violated the logics of history and nature by masculinizing equality under socialism and transgressing foundational sexual difference, but Dai's politics are distinctive in three ways. First, while Li's market feminism connects her to national development policies because female agents are primary consumers in a commercialized, state-defined, domestic sphere, Dai's feminist Marxism is an anticapitalist politics of utopian resistance. Second, as Li endorses development ideology so long as it recognizes the distinctive needs of women, Dai expresses bottomless reservations about the socialist market economy and its feminization of desire in what she considers a crass, massified, commercial commodity culture. Third, where Li still appears to endorse the split subject of universal reason, Dai has invented a cultural critique rooted in revulsion, which wants the truth of women to remain unresolved and woman's relation to reason aporetic or unrepresentable.[8]

In the deeply contradictory knots of enlightenment set on a disturbing map of global capital, cultural criticism of Dai's kind rings true. Her arguments are homologous with intellectual movements unfolding in re-regionalizing "Asia's" metropolitan core cities of Taipei, Tokyo, Seoul, and elsewhere. Indeed, Haraway's argument (published as Meng and Dai were writing their own Lacanian-style feminist negotiation with revolutionary modernity) is that everywhere the new world order consolidates it does so ideologically with informatics, communications networks, futurist utopias, and Lacanian theories of gendered subjectivity. Whether Dai's hot, contestatory, "postmodern" style actually signifies the displacement of early twentieth-century Chinese progressive feminism depends on many outcomes, including the continued viability of the Chinese national economy and the development policies she opposes so vigorously. Now it is only possible to say that in Dai's hands, these ubiquitous and mundane signifiers of a new global order have come to include the following: (1) Chinese women's subjective self-authorization unfolds primarily in fiction because the new subjectivity of regnant masculinism resurges in visual media; (2) the real subject of women is nüxing, whose hidden history can be excavated out of the unconscious of masculine culture, but whose historical existence in the social text remains for women to write into existence; (3) gender (i.e., the logic of sexual difference) is foundational and primordially heterosexual; (4) Chinese cultural and communication studies must develop its own arsenal of critical techniques for exploiting whatever enlightened national emancipation opportunities remain, against the 1990s wave of transmigrating capital, labor, liberal developmentalism, and Hollywood cultural flows; and (5) an alternative to elitist écriture féminine may be aural writing or, simply, the speech of women who perform femininity.

Dai's writing is confoundingly heterogeneous. Its performative, frenzied quality rests on sentence structures in which steepled clauses reach, imitatively, toward the very rhetorical heights they themselves are proclaiming, while the spatial poetics of her prose makes of the intellectual scene a material, topographic diagram of a tangible, semiautonomous, discursive space she calls culture. This space of culture is not wholly reducible to nation. Nor is it a cultural text in the sense of being a mere habitus. Dai's space of culture is more like an intellectual tableau populated with historical players. Her writing echoes with the rhetorical experiments of Gao Xian, the May Fourth eugenicist, and Yi Jiayue, Gao's contemporary and a modernist family theorist; Lu Xun, the father of Chinese modern literature, and Bing Xin, a mother of Chinese women's literature; Lester Ward, the influential U.S. eugenic social scientist, and Charles Darwin; Mei Sheng, entrepreneur of Chinese progressive feminism, and Mao Dun, novelist, feminist, communist; Shimamura Tamizo, the Japanese sex theorist whose works in Chinese translation are part of the foundations of Chinese progressive feminism along with Margaret Sanger and Ellen Key; as well as Dai's own near contemporaries Julia Kristeva, Teresa de Lauretis, Laura Mulvey, Christian Metz, and Jacques Lacan.

What I called progressive Chinese feminism in chapter 3 and connected to a globalized circuit of eugenic sex theory rematerializes here. In an altered, displaced form, Dai's psychoanalytic feminism extends and departs from Chinese progressive feminism. She still assigns foundational powers to sex difference, as Gao, Yi, Mei, Shimamura, and Key did three-quarters of a century earlier. Dai, however, detaches and amplifies sexuality away from reproduction. Sexual difference is the key to personhood, never national racial vitality. Her theoretical landscapes cannot be reduced to the national melodrama. Like eugenic philosophy, her psychological universalism is part of a broader trans-, post-, or international event. Even at the beginning of the twenty-first century, nineteenth-century sexual anthropology is still the medium of rarified theories of sexed personality. But écriture féminine chinoise considers the nation to be an extension of patriarchy. In Dai's language, the nation is a carnival of sons. One day she and her collaborators may appear to have affected a truly epistemic shift from structure to dynamics on the order of Freud to Lacan. But it is equally possible that their brilliant cultural criticism, so similar to that of Joan Copjec, Teresa Brennan, and Luce Irigaray, is, like theirs, too deeply in thrall to the progressive, feminist, eugenic theories of the early twentieth century to achieve the longed-for goal.[9]

## Psychoanalytic Feminism Is All About Heterosexual Sex

Even analysts like Judith Butler, who contest Lacanian theory in the name of queer possibilities, still must take issue and thus engage the foundational heterosexualism of Lacan.[10] Because psychoanalytic feminism in Chinese theory circles, as elsewhere in the 1990s, presumes a working knowledge of Lacanianism, I will lay out its basic positions to open an avenue into écriture féminine chinoise. There are three assumptions in the general theory that bear directly on Dai Jinhua's concerns. First, and most broadly speaking, Lacanian or post-Althusserian psychoanalysis understands social relations through concrete metaphors that assume a drive, called desire, held to consolidate social life and bind us all sexually to other people. The primacy of sexuality is the sine qua non, the basic assumption that enabled Dai and Meng and their colleagues to theorize an écriture féminine chinoise in which nüxing is the national sexed subject that surfaces out of the masculinist representation of desire and onto the horizon of history. This primacy of sexual desire in turn is rooted in complex arguments about the ways that humans become subjects, or how, to put this in an older language, nature becomes culture. For Lacan, human culture is a scrim or impenetrable text that directs, shapes, folds, and knits desire into normative forms of human existence (or, as Butler showed, leaves subjects who are homosexual bereft or abject and lacking human subject forms). This story of the emergence of human or male personhood has become an article of faith in cultural criticism, particularly in literary neo-Marxisms, which must locate in theories of subjectivity some way of connecting human social relations to extrahuman economic, social, and cultural forces.

Desire, a presubjective flow, this theory stream argues, connects infants and their mothers in a postnatal, imaginary facsimile of the fetus's primary attachment to the mother's body. Eventually, a third or paternal term enters this primary sexual-affective bond. The father's presence undermines the imaginary mother-child relation because it poses an alternative to the child's fusion with the mother. When psychic elements that are "not-mother" interrupt the infant's fantasy that he is still a part of mother's body, the imaginary dyad of mother and infant turns into a triangle. Revelation of the triangular ordering of desire resituates the infant in a new context, where, for the first time, he sees reflected back to him, as in a distorting mirror, the contours of his own self, mediated through the grid of paternal authority. This grid is called the Symbolic order. In Meng and Dai's initial formulation it usually appeared under the term "patriarchal culture." In the Symbolic, the father is authoritative, though not in the way that he desires because his own male privilege is conditional; he is, after all, just a grown-up infant whose primary drive is to reunite with his mother's body, to live once again in a presubjective, Imaginary relation to a mother's love. This love is erotic because it is bodily and preconscious. Nonetheless, mother must place her child under the father's authority because she needs to use her baby as a power source (that is why the baby is her phallus) and as a way of compensating for her own exclusion from the Symbolic order. When she submits her child to the law of the father, the child, who previously saw mother as whole and complete, perceives mother's deficiencies in relation to father.

After this so-called mirror stage of Oedipalization, in which he has a glimpse of what he might become, the child gets conditionally independent of mother yet remains affectively dependent on her. The child moves into life with others (i.e., he "enters the Symbolic"), where the old dream of fusion is sublimated in language; language (or "male language," as women cannot be directly represented in it) structures his experience. As the child enters the Symbolic order, speaking a patriarchally structured language, drawing and being drawn by others into psychodynamic relations, the Oedipal process of becoming a human subject sketched out above in intrapsychic terms as a series of negotiated drives in his imaginary relation to mother is reconsolidated in *social* terms. The child's unobstructed love of mother remains intrapsychically imprinted in the pre-Oedipal stage, in the era of his life before he began struggling to become a subject (the psychoanalytic term for a person), and this intrapsychic world will supply energy that drives the subject in his efforts to be himself through others. In most theory associated with Lacanian psychodynamics, to become a subject requires the child to overcode the older, interrupted, or lost love of mother with a new recognition, absorbed within the Symbolic, that mother is actually derelict (i.e., she has not achieved and cannot achieve subjectivity within the Symbolic order). The child's disappointment in mother only intensifies the difficulty that mother is having. For mother sustains a sense of self only with great difficulty; indeed, *her only choices within the Symbolic order are either to be defined in relation to men or to accept that she is nothing more than a male projection of what she is to them.* Lacanian theoretical projects cannot provide a subject form for women that is not mediated through male language, male Symbolic orders, male desire, and male developmental norms.

Second, because desire (the invisible, erotic force routing people's later everyday perceptions through, the theory goes, their earliest, infantile bodily pleasures and needs) propels all the delicate processes that allow people to become or not become subjects, people are actually never finished or fully stable. They are always provisional, lacking and wanting, pulled into the orbit of the very others that define them, the subjects, and make them possible as persons. The Oedipal child wants to compensate for what his mother feels as a lack (she is not a man, does not have a penis, cannot author a family) because he loves her with an originary and necessarily estranged (because he can never fully reunite with her body) love. He experiences desire as lack. She needs him to compensate for what she never has. She is defined around lack. The boy who aspires to be a subject, a man, must transgress mother's desires to use him as her phallus, in order to remain independent of his mother's lack and to sustain his difference from her. The theory is less clear on the question of the female Oedipal stage, which requires the girl, who is fundamentally like her mother, to play out over and over again the ambivalent drama of her own status in the Symbolic (which is to say that she is foundationally lacking and never in a position to be female or feminine in the absence of men and masculinity). Nonetheless, the erotic force of desire is gaseous, sticky, and complex; it usefully offers a way of understanding human subjectivity as never fully stable, always contingent on other people, always in process.[11]

Third, the theory is also about sexuality in psycholinguistic or discursive terms. In language, which the Lacanian, psychodynamic, and feminist theories consider to be provisionally under the control of men, a one-to-one relationship or "phallic economy" determines that there will be only one signified assigned to every signifier. All terms will be said to have one meaning and one meaning only. This masculine desire to control language is, of course, a hallucination. How do we know it is a hallucination? Because women (or the psychic fantasy men have about what women *is* or what women *means*) actually is always more than the term woman could ever possibly accommodate. The very nature of women is extralinguistic, in other words. She is there in the world. She is central to the dramas of personhood. But women exists outside of the language that shapes and names social relations because no place exists in this "phallic economy of language" (phallologocentrism) for something that is purely and simply woman. Real subjects (momentarily integral, balanced, valued, heterosexual, etc.) are culturally constructed out of the need of men to believe that only they can author the world.

Now, outside of this hallucinatory perimeter of male language there actually and truly does exist, according to this theory, a sexual pleasure (*joissance*) that is not unitary or penislike and consequently is unavailable to men. Because joissance is multiple and feminine, it cannot be packed into any one-to-one relation of signifier and signified. So, although woman is never able to be a subject outside the dominion of men, woman is also a guarantee that the totalitarian language of men will be forever called into question, off-balance, incapable of describing everything in the way it pretends it can. Women—who can never become real subjects—nonetheless guarantee that subjectivity for men is and always will be illusory, that an exterior to male domination will always exceed the capacity of men to dominate, and that subjectivity even for men will always be an uphill battle.[12]

These three principles of (1) erotic desire, (2) decentered subjectivity, and (3) phallologocentrism are the foundational structure of most psychoanalytic or Lacanian feminism. As earlier academic theories about sexuality and anthropological stages of development in colonial modern European intellectual history rested on the colonial discoveries of human difference, the global reach of these newer psychodynamic theories of human personality are linked to events historically, too. A case could be made about neoliberal globalization and the collaboration of consumer capital in eastern Asia through Japanese, European, and U.S. multinational corporate capitalism, of course. But as pertinent to international forms of feminism is the impact on theory of the Chinese Cultural Revolution. The case of Julia Kristeva is an example of what might be called a lateral convergence of an international theoretical feminist and scholarly practice in the global 1990s.[13]

The point of overlap in psychoanalytic feminism between French Maoism and Chinese post-Maoism is *About Chinese Women*. In this influential book, Kristeva describes her trip from Paris through China's major tourist sites and home again during the late Cultural Revolution. While she was visiting the prehistoric Banpo village excavation site and taking in a lecture on historic Chinese matriarchy, Kristeva, a Parisian Maoist, speculated that the matrilineal, orgasmic, truthful language that she felt Chinese women had spoken in the archaic past had somehow survived into the present. She "theorized" that the Chinese Communist Party had emancipated this archaic joissance when it liberated women from Confucianism and returned them to native prehistory. Kristeva felt strongly that Chinese women had something to offer "Western" women. That was, first, a means of joining somebody else's less phallic, more feminized, still archaic symbolic order somewhere outside France, and, second, a means of opposing the monolithic capitalist, patriarchal exclusion of woman from the Symbolic order *inside* France. As she wrote about Chinese women, in other words, Kristeva magically found herself able to envision a way of reversing prohibitions against mother, daughter, and woman glossolalia *at home*.[14]

Obviously, the book *About Chinese Women* was also about, or more accurately, it was primarily about two theoretical matters that Lacanian feminist thinkers in the late 1980s confronted. First, reworking Freud into a Lacanian formula, Anglo-European innovators, from film theorists Christian Metz to Laura Mulvey, adapted Kristeva's notion of women's joissance to establish a new position on how people's intrapsychic drives get expressed socially. Their operative assumption in the late 1980s and 1990s was that cinematic image worked just like the Freudian dream text: it presented symptoms of unconscious drives that could not be directly accessed. The theorist's critical study of film culture and film criticism was increasingly assumed to be a direct analogue to the psychoanalyst's confrontations with a living client (though of course, Kristeva herself really was a psychoanalyst). As the belief that cinema texts allowed critics access to real human symptoms became commonplace in critical theory, literary critics began to see texts "symptomatically" as well.

The second matter *About Chinese Women* confronted (and through it, Kristeva scholars at large) was the genealogical problem of the historical elaboration of Freud criticism. In feminist studies a so-called second debate about sexuality and sexual difference erupted over the elaboration of Freud theories. At stake was the question of which of the various early-century Freud interpreters had developed the master's insights into an acceptable general theory of human subjectivity. This question was central because Freud himself had never clarified how subjectivity for women might work or even indicated whether it was a possibility at all. This gap in the theory led to the question that Kristeva posed during the second debate over sexuality in Freud theory: How can women voice their being directly (rather than indirectly through "male language")? If in language and culture women are representable only in male terms as the projections of men or by stealing power (the phallus) from men, which effectively turns women into ersatz men, what women need is some way to voice their difference from men directly. The popular or vulgarized version of this complex idea is the truism of finding "women's voices."[15]

What came to preoccupy psychoanalytically inclined feminists, including Dai Jinhua, throughout the global 1990s were questions related to the concerns Kristeva had raised in *About Chinese Women*. One does not need to be a Kristevan philosopher to pose such questions; many are obvious absences in Freud's theory. But once the second debate on Freud, mediated through the Lacanian problematics of desire, subjectivity, and phallologo-centrism, had elevated the importance of the father and the Symbolic, the question of where the feminine resided became pressing. Feminists, including Dai and Meng, raised questions inside the Lacanian worldview that Lacanian theory had not resolved, or even in some cases ever posed outside feminist circles. For instance, how specifically do sexual-linguistic economies structure language so that it is impossible for woman to speak her difference from man? What historical events placed this ban in effect? What currently prevents women from speaking as women? Does patriarchy's power differential mean that women cannot ever have their own "women's speech"? Is language by definition masculine? If the Oedipal constrictions were lifted, would women still be sophisticated ventriloquists, speaking the language of men? Would a "women's language" be a pale imitation of men's (i.e., human) language? If there had ever existed a women's language, did it leave traces? Where? To be truly female (rather than just a phallic or "fake" woman) must women remain silent? Should they (be compelled to) speak a naturally poetic language that refuses any one-to-one relation with signs? Psychoanalytic feminists all over the world concluded that an answer to these analytic questions might lie in an écriture féminine, an invented way of calling attention to the disruptive potential of language in the hands of non-men. The emerging practice of écriture féminine in France, Britain, the United States, Japan, China (all places where Lacanian-feminist projects consolidated), and probably elsewhere, too, held the common view that actually, the feminine resides in the breaches or gaps of language.[16]

The horror and the gift of this theory to feminists is its corollary that woman is not a subject. Let's start with why it is a horror because, from the point of view of its advocates, the promise it offers is more valuable than the horror is confounding. The horror is the problem of female dereliction. Alys Weinbaum's simple definition of the Lacanian term dérélicfion is useful in explaining the position that Meng and Dai take in their history of the subject nüxing. "Déréliction," in Weinbaum's aphorism, "is the state in which women remain in the absence of symbolization of their subjectivity and intersubjective relationships."[17] Horribly, though it offers a way to grasp how male sexual subjectivity works in relational terms, psychoanalytic feminism has great difficulty thinking about women except in the state of déréliction. That is because when women's subjectivity and intersubjective relationships are symbolized, the process can take place only within an order (the Symbolic) that is already shaped to accommodate men's Sisyphean struggle to become subjects. This suggests that collectively woman is a medium, not a subject. As a mother, she is the fullness he must lose in what Dai calls the "coming of age ritual" of sons becoming fathers. Woman is what compels sons to become subjects under the father's threat of castration. Woman is a name for what the male subject lacks, in other words, the Other he has lost, the thing that makes it possible for him to become a potent father when the cycle repeats itself and he takes over control of the fantasy that he is ruler of the universe.

Why might this theory's argument—that women are by definition not subjects—be analytically useful and consequently a gift? Because it can be seen to hold out the possibility that a richer, more admirable reality of women might exist in a Real that lies beyond the totalitarian fantasy that men control women. Or it could be argued that woman's abjection keeps open the possibility that the future will be different. It also offers in the place of women's subjecthood the notion of joissance, a conceptual resource that projects feminine pleasure into another place, where phallic sexuality does not dominate. These openings turn women into a theoretical resource. A task of literature studies—because literature in psychoanalytic theory is assumed to encode desire—is to search out literary texts where elemental pieces of the ineffable offer a genuine femaleness not fully colonized in the phallic economy. If women do not have even the provisional stability that men can achieve, albeit with great effort, through the repetitive personal and historical Oedipal cycles of father-son castration, then perhaps the ineffability of women is a source of hope.

Meng Yue and Dai Jinhua developed these resources in a direction that best suited their needs. In a densely written, fifty-page theoretical preface to Surfacing onto the Horizon of History, which they jointly conceptualized and Meng wrote, and which they published just as the popular political movements of 1989 crashed and burned around them, they argued that "the fate of Chinese women and the fate of Chinese history were intimately and irregularly entangled." Meng and Dai transformed History into an analytic, male, human subject. According to their theoretical-historical exegesis, in the era between the founding of the feudal order and its overthrow by capitalism, Chinese women remained a defeated gender, harbored in the unconscious of history. To obscure the brutality of their symbolic victory over women, men erased women's sense of self (nüxing zishen), and with it women's ability to express their own genuine countertruth, or difference from men. Men not only replaced women's sense of self with the patriarchal name of nüren, but they actually took over the phallicized subjectivities they had bestowed on the women directly under their control. Nüxing retained the secret of her own social domination, of course, and with it a latent capacity to reverse patriarchal ideology at an opportune historical moment. Drawing on the same familiar body of anthropological and sexual theory as late nineteenth-century sociology, modulated now through Kristeva, Meng and Dai concentrated on developing a historical overview of what history had bestowed on women and how women had used the opportunity.[18]

Feudal Chinese modes of production appropriated women's symbolic surplus value, the two theorists argued, and built a patriarchal edifice over what had been a primeval natural physiological division of labor. Banpo (where Kristeva had fatefully visited) and other prehistoric villages had indeed been matrilineal, or natural social formations. When patriarchal logic effectively barred women from subject status, it absorbed them into social cultural life as a mere utility. Feudal women, in Meng and Dai's conception, was "a function [zhineng], a tool without subjectivity; she is only a daughter [nü], mother, wife, daughter-in-law, grandson's wife [xi] and never Woman [nüxing]."[19] The consequence of women's exclusion from historical subjectivity was a clan system organized to regulate male succession. The name given to these processes of expulsion and erasure is "civilization." Civilization is a tissue of ideological forms obscuring and justifying domination, and men's domination of women is the origin of this system.

In short order, the concentration of female symbolic surplus coalesced into a singularly *Chinese* historical culture. A shift from the natural or originary sexual difference of male/female to the social distinction husband and wife (i.e., woman defined maritally in relation to patriline) placed primary civilizing processes under the domain of the feudal clan. Social distinctions separating men from other men (e.g., fathers and sons) outweighed the sexual difference of women and men, so this characteristically Chinese symbolic system emerged around men. The corresponding speech universe handed men "the creative codes, the power to make forced interpretive moves, the power to speak and to explain things" (13). Attributing their insight directly to Kristeva, Meng and Dai argued that under these circumstances, when women want to enter into this male-supporting and male-serving discursive system there are only two channels: she can borrow his tone and inherit his concepts, standing in his position, speaking in the style of his normatized symbolic system, entering into discourse as a male homologue; or using speechless 'speech,' she can draw on extraordinary language to "speak" (14). That is how feudal culture robbed women of the capacity to speak through their own flesh about the truth of female experience. Only écriture féminine restores to women their power to signify bodily difference, to speak a speechless language.

The true perversity of the feudal gender discourses took root in an elite literature that coded desire in China metaphorically. Here the problem lay in the surplus of cultural residues that sexualized and objectified women, commodifying already objectified females and dividing women into two types: pliant objects circulating among men or, in the case of women who resisted, extruded embodiments of un-reason. Because the feudal Symbolic (i.e., male culture) employed culturally specific yin/yang logic to explain inequality, castration was relative (fathers are castrated by emperors, as sons are by fathers). This relative flexibility, however, points to the loss of physiological or real sexual difference and its reduction to a cultural gender misattribution. Male writers used female heroes metaphorically to project their own ideal relations with other men. They colonized their own metaphors. The metaphor of woman expressed homosocial relations of difference. This colonization of high literary signs accelerated the evacuation of content from metaphor, further hollowing out the language until women was nothing but an empty signifier (20). Indeed, feudal men so thoroughly plundered the subject forms available to women even in the Symbolic that they left women in what Meng and Dai termed the "chaotic sea of the pre-Symbolic" (21).[20] In life and in literature, feudal women had only two avenues out of this pre-Symbolic: they could inhabit an empty signifier women and thus enter the Symbolic as men had prescribed, or they could die (21).[21] Otherwise, female was nothing, chaos, nameless, incapable of assuming identity or subjectivity.

Two patricides—the Revolution of 1911, which ended the monarchy, and the May Fourth movement of 1919, which ended Confucianism—brought a close to the eviscerated feudal sign system. Out of the chaotic "cultural unconscious" and against the odds there emerged an entity that Meng and Dai term "women as a group," or *nüxing qunti*, which established itself on the horizon of history in a problematic but ineradicable fashion for the first time in Chinese history. It is women as a group that preoccupy Meng and Dai for the remaining 250 pages of their book. Why? Because once the totalitarian façade of feudal culture had ruptured sufficiently to allow the partial formation of subject forms for women, the struggle of actual women turned to wresting away a representational space and representational practices that would allow self-naming. Self-naming is the job of the female tradition in literature. But it is a difficult job because women must reestablish the primacy of originary sexual difference over what Dai would call in her later work "the circular dance" of homosocial temporality. Only the latent countertruth of women (écriture féminine) can reverse the historical, cultural, ideological masculinism of the Chinese Symbolic, according to the authors (5).

The balance of *Surfacing onto the Horizon of History*'s introduction shows why postfeudalism, or Chinese New Culture, was also male-dominated. Following the double historical patricides of 1911 and 1919 there arose a desire to recentralize and reorder the nation, leading, in turn, to pressures forcing women out of the center and into the historical margin. Marginalization of women succeeded in great part because capitalist urban markets erupted out of rural China and these urban markets recommodified women into either housewives or sexual commodities, placing them once again in a peripheral position in the male Symbolic or cultural order. Psycholinguistic dynamics also played a part in this patriarchal restoration. The May Fourth women's movement did take up the slogan "I belong to myself," and that did cause uproar in the language of the Symbolic order because it signaled the appearance of a women's struggle for subjectivity. But although the May Fourth rebellion sanctioned the primacy of heterosexual difference for the first time since Chinese prehistory, heterosexual difference remained, according to Meng and Dai, irremediably phallologocentric.

The example Meng and Dai offer to support this claim is the central importance in the New Culture's literary world of Henrik Ibsen's Nora. It is true, Dai and Meng argued, that Nora is the icon of liberation in the May Fourth patricide, but Nora actually chose a male-defined model for herself. Ibsen, a man, has Nora respond to the question "Who am I?" with the statement "I am a person, just like you." In other words, in Meng and Dai's interpretation, the humanism of May Fourth encoded a subject for women that was indistinguishable from male subjects. "I am a person like you" collapsed all possibility of women speaking their difference from men and still remaining human. What this lost for women was "the gender characteristics and entire historical significance of women—the true interpretation of women by women." As Dai and Meng put it:

> On the one hand, women are not dolls, women are not the gender roles that society stipulates, but women are also still not themselves. That is because the referent of the so-called "I myself" is none other than a replica of maleness. . . . This is a naming without a referent, so that the relation between "I" and "I myself" is only synonymous, emerging from a sealed, cyclical repetition, as though facing two opposing mirrors, neither face of which can signify a reality of the outside world or open up a meaningful space. . . . To fill in this great absent referent is the most pivotal and complex step of women's process of developing into subjecthood. . . . or their hearts knew they were not the same as the single standard, yet they had no language of their own, they could not give that "not the same" thing a name; could not even locate the vocabulary. (34)

Consequently, women also failed to become an appropriate subject within the powerful modernizing discourses of science, politics, Marxism, and Darwinism. But mostly, Meng and Dai are at pains to show how the colloquial literature project that made a women's tradition or écriture féminine thinkable also, in the hands of male authors, powerfully reencoded the signifier woman in a way that discounted women's remaining differences from the male subject of humanism.[22]

Examining male writer Lu Xun's female characters, Xiang Linsao and Zijun, and the male progressive feminist and novelist Mao Dun's "new women" characters, Meng and Dai argued that May Fourth male writers continued to colonize signifiers of women. This time, masculinist writers used the sign of woman to illustrate the inhumanity of feudal history. In this respect, May Fourth or "modern Chinese literature" was little different from the male-dominated creative fiction of earlier ages. Lu Xun, Ye Shengtao, Ruo Shi, Wei Jintao, Mao Dun, and all the other mainstays of the male tradition of May Fourth colloquial fiction sacrificed the sexual singularity of women. When, as in Mao Dun's fiction, the sexuality of women did appear, it was never as itself. Female sexuality appeared either as a criticism of women's alleged unreason or, more frequently, female sexual expression stood as a sign for the febrile quality of bourgeois revolution. Mostly, women remained trapped in male metaphors and what Dai would call "hollowed-out signifiers." The value of a Xiang Linsao or Xi'er (in the revolutionary drama White Haired Woman) was purely metaphoric. She could never mean just herself as a subject because women signified either an item sacrificed in feudal culture or a great reservoir of sacrificial fluid that fueled the male rebellion against the father, or women became a lost resource rescued by Communists: never did women rescue other women in the name of women. The remasculinizing, modern Symbolic tried to sweep into its vortex all signifiers of women and women's foundational sexual difference.

The special introduction to Surfacing onto the Horizon of History paid particular attention to the relation of phallologocentrism and twentieth-century Chinese women's countertradition of écriture féminine. It hinted at ways psychoanalytic feminist scholarship might analyze the special configuration of Chinese contemporeneity (Dai would take up this question extensively in Breaking Out of the City of Mirrors). But it also noted that Chinese women were enjoying the fruit of the revolution, ren'ge, in the sense that they had indeed theoretically achieved de facto rights and independent social standing.[23] The problem, from Dai and Meng's perspective, was that Chinese women had achieved these gains within a Symbolic order that crystallized and consolidated male cultural figuring.

Men and their allies, phallicized or phallic women like Ding Ling, had defined, decreed, and institutionalized a ren'ge that defined womanhood in post-1949 PRC. This thoroughly masculine revolutionary culture precluded joissance, or the sexuality proper to women. Mao Dun and Lu Xun (and, by implication, the entire male literary canon, the pantheon of the

CCP's Women's Bureau, and all Communists of both sexes who supported women's emancipation), Meng and Dai argued, were as much a part of the ideological mainstream that continued to dislodge and displace sexual difference from its rightful place at the center of the cultural order as Confucius & Co. had been in feudal times.

As Gao Xian had two generations earlier, Dai and Meng were supposing sexuality to be the core of human culture. Like him, they were sanctifying the natural life processes through the magic power of sexual attraction and sexual exchange of egg and sperm. However, Dai and Meng passed a mixed judgment on the May Fourth Enlightenment. Where Gao and his cohort had expressed exuberant optimism that cultural policies could intervene in natural processes, Meng and Dai tempered enthusiasm with complexity. Modernity had inflicted a painful split on the new women writers, they argued. Female literary pioneers had suffered because the May Fourth cultural revolution called on them to be both awake to their own tragedy and oblivious to it: clarity in the face of Oedipal exclusion is so alienating that blindness becomes for some the preferred option. Castrated in a sense, nüxing (i.e., the historic subject of woman born in the death throes of the dynastic tradition) suffered the same imposed, internal split as present authors of écriture féminine did. The historical subject of nüxing and its authors, whom history had charged with the task of revealing the buried traces of women invisibly written into the totalitarian male culture of the Chinese, suffered great torment. Nüxing's task of forcing subjectivity up out of the unconscious of the masculine Symbolic and onto history's conscious horizon began in the early part of the twentieth century. At century's close, Dai and Meng mourned, women still confronted the hollow mystifications of a "liberated" political order.

Yet, a Chinese tradition of women's writing since the May Fourth era had still managed to accumulate a significant record of female subjective experience. *Surfacing onto the Horizon of History* claimed to illustrate how écriture féminine, the nüxing tradition of women's writing, had broken through the constraints of the neopatriarchal Symbolic when it configured subjectivity for women in psychodynamic and cumulative forms. Their argument was ingenious and "historical." The new female literature written as a consequence of the patricidal crisis in the cultural sign system hinted at the existence of another reality within the crevices of phallologocentrism.

For example, women's loneliness, which previously could not register in a male Symbolic because women were not subjects and had no self to alienate, is actually the hallmark of May Fourth female fiction. Acknowledging female psychological states in literature makes feasible subject forms that are female. For instance, how it feels to be objectified and passed among men is usually obscured in male writing about marriage markets.

This very experience materializes in the new women's tradition. Experiences of fatigue, of pre-Oedipal merging with the mother's love, the pain of gendered labor on the marriage market and visual sex objectification, the terror of being a woman rather than a daughter or wife: each is a real event in the writing of the new women's tradition of literature. Indeed, the option of denying the singularity of women, returning to the painful comforts of phallologocentrism remain an open choice in woman-scripted normative literature. Meng and Dai, however, are out to canonize writers who choose the mode of écriture féminine. They are unsparing about the burden of the choice imposed on those who wrote their difference from male-defined norms. Denoting female singularity is painful, they argued, because it commits writers to the cultural margin and so to a horrifying loneliness. And that is why, they propose, even the founders of the Chinese female tradition in modern literature could not bear to pursue the course for long.

Dai and Meng admit writers and individual texts into their tradition of écriture féminine on the basis of what each writer did to surface the historical subjects Woman and Women. This is not just a matter of how writers describe female experience in general. Only those who pinpoint the surfacing into historical visibility of the singular (i.e., female loneliness, horror of commodification, fatigue, fusion) subjective being of women, unmediated through a masculine lens, figure into this genealogy. History at this level of their argument is psychodynamic and has a developmental trajectory. They presume that the history of Chinese women cannot be distinguished from the subject of the nation, but not in the mundane sense that women serve the nation in its competitive struggles with other nation-states. New China is founded on the Oedipal crisis of patricidal sons. It has its developmental, historical trajectories to negotiate. Because New China has neglected to consolidate the modern subject of women onto the horizon of historical consciousness, écriture féminine recapitulates development, must stand in for a female, Oedipal stage. The Chinese women subject-in-potential must pass through, or perhaps more accurately, establish a means for experiencing her own mirror stage. This developmental requirement is not individual but civilizational and therefore in this theory stream, historical.

The story of the Chinese female tradition, as Dai and Meng tell it, is consequently a story about the consolidation over time and into the future of a normative and singular feminine subjectivity. The discussion of this norm and its allegedly historical formation and fruition falls into three historical periods. Women writers awakened to women's difference in the May Fourth era (1917–1927). They placed nüxing at risk during the national urbanization and resurgence of masculinist political ideology of the 1930s,

Oedipalizing nüxing in a heterosexual male gaze (1927–1937). Writers in the key tradition of écriture féminine granted the nüxing subject full self-awareness of her female subjectivity during the Japanese occupation (1937–1947). Then history ended. Put another way, infantile nüxing separated from the mother's body and the father's Symbolic in the May Fourth Enlightenment. It recognized the full implications of its sexual difference in a direct relation of heterosexuality during the period of the rise of communism. And it courageously weathered the terrors of heterosexual difference as a fully realized subject when the phallic state was itself emasculated during the Japanese occupation. The implication is clear and ferocious: only the emasculation of Chinese patriarchy in colonial terror could have opened the gap in the phallologocentric order that allowed a female, national subject to mature.

These are the insights that lend *Surfacing onto the Horizon of History* its power. I will outline Dai and Meng's argument a bit more fully because similar psychoanalytic moves are at stake in later works Dai authored and there is a reason why Dai, a film critic, expanded on the reasoning that she and Meng pioneered in relation to literature. The analysis applied equally well to the film culture Dai saw reemerging around her. Films are extremely expensive to produce, and particularly in socialist countries they are considered a national resource. Making visible female subject forms is less likely to occur in film, because women have fewer opportunities to control what cinematic means of production are available. The critique of phallocentrism in the national film tradition is therefore necessarily a part of film criticism. But the project of écriture féminine is easily available to women in literature; literature, which costs nothing to write, offers means of production that are widely available. Because it was open to any woman who desired self-expression, the most fragmentary literary evidence has, from Dai and Meng's perspective, enormous significance. Yet, historically speaking, only two kinds of women had relevance in the May Fourth era: rebel daughters trapped in the orbit of the father, and daughters who could not resolve their fusion with the mother.

Meng and Dai draw on early twentieth-century figures Lu Yin, Bai Wei, Feng Yuanjun and Chen Hengzhe. Each gave to écriture féminine chinoise portraits of women as daughters in revolt against patriarchy and as daughters in search of mothers. Torn between the promise of heterosexual desire and the constraints of enlightened reason, pioneering writer Lu Yin in the end rejected her own sexuality, that is, the reality of sexual difference. She chose to remain a phallic woman, defined not by anatomical difference but by her desire to be like the father, male, "just like you." Feng Yuanjun, in the same historical period, also attacked the feudal tradition, but in the name of an overly idealized heterosexual romance. Her female characters emancipated themselves from the father's desire and his provisional control. But in her heterosexual romances the female lover fuses herself so tightly to her beloved male lover that she cannot see the ideology of love from a gendered perspective.[24] Feng illustrates the painful difficulty involved in stabilizing the subject nüxing. Her fictional alternatives of the weak and male-defined mother or the masculine girl rebel fixes women in the signature of an identity that is not a gender; that is, their personalities still owe what coherence they achieve to the new male Symbolic and in fact betray the role that sexual difference must play if women are ever to become capable of accurately speaking women's countertruth. In short, Feng's female lovers are still too male-identified. They cannot achieve full feminine subjectivity. Consequently, although they bravely initiate a sense of self in relation to the heterosexual lover, in the end they retreat from the anxiety of self-definition into maternalism.[25]

In what can only be called an imaginary or theoretical teleology of the history of the real subject of woman, Dai and Meng are laying out the stages of historical development leading to the achievement of subjectivity. They offer Lu and Feng as success stories in a teleological sense. Both creditably initiated the Oedipalizing of nüxing. Their literary writing placed nüxing on a historical stage, where her effort at self-making could continue to unfold outside the ersatz or male-defined Symbolic order. The example of Lu's and Feng's failures, as much as their triumphs, underlines two important points: first, it demonstrates that a woman's relation to the paternal order can be observed; second, it awakens readers and writers to the profound problem that (sexual) difference poses.[26]

To overcome the problem Feng's fiction allegedly posed (i.e., her characters have no access to a pre-Oedipal stage), Dai and Meng turned to what they considered May Fourth écriture féminine's extreme opposite potential.[27] Here the symptomatic writer is Bing Xin. Her standing in the pantheon of écriture féminine is assured because her oeuvre as a whole mediated the female pre-Oedipal (recall that this is the stage of development prior to the necessary recognition of sexual difference). Bing Xin moved nüxing a stage forward in the cumulative development of the historical subject of nüxing. She was oceanically contented. She lived out her days as a contemporary of the May Fourth cohort, yet she never undertook patricidal rebellion, so she avoided being mired in the paternal order. She also avoided becoming an Oedipal woman who privileged sexual difference on the condition of abjecting the mother, of accepting the male view that mother is derelict. Bing Xin confronted no paternal prohibitions that limited her fusion with the body of the mother. She therefore negotiated a bridge between the self-enclosed worlds of maternity and paternity. Her fiction described a world in which the cycle of mother and daughter (like the cycle of father-son) never ended and wives always became mothers and never became women. But she validated this world. Particularly her poetry, according to Dai and Meng, retained the pleasures, a kind of joissance, that come from prolonging the unitary fusion of daughter and mother. The fusion was progressive in a teleological sense because it projected the unconscious content of women's pre-Oedipal feelings into a general philosophy of love. Although this move may have retained women in a state of refusing difference, it also historicized women's unconscious life, pulling the unconscious out onto the horizon of history.[28]

Recall that for Dai Jinhua and Meng Yue, the decade 1927–1937 was *retrogressive*. In this decade, the leading national economic development sector, the city, endured colonial occupation. But far worse, the lagging or rural economy devolved into a paralytic stasis. The new male intellectuals crudely readapted theories of political rationality to use them simplistically in mass agitation. They created a popular social Imaginary of mass omnipotence. This developed further into a gross formation that the disenfranchised and castrated mass could easily cathect to. A political crisis subsequently unfolded when, with the successful patricide against the feudal father, the May Fourth generation of sons actually failed to replace the castrated old patriarch with a new, modern father. A historical struggle among the sons broke out in the national arena and the underlying social dynamic shifted from father-son or patriarchal continuity to a conflict among a chaotic range of male claimants to power. Deluded, the left-wing intelligentsia reflected back to the hallucinating, oppressed masses a re-sacralized, hollowed-out or false image of a good political father. The pertinence of this sketch of patriarchal history in crisis to the tradition of women's literature and the maturation of the historical subject of Woman lay, according to Dai and Meng, in the chastening that écriture féminine endured over that fateful decade.

When enlightened intellectuals turned to revolution they betrayed nü-xing. That is the gist of Meng and Dai's argument. This "turn" to mass politics betrayed the epochal power of the historical subject of woman. It erased gender consciousness of difference (*mosha xingbie*) and eviscerated the feminine ego (*xiao wo*) of the cumulative female subject. While promoting an idealized representation of increasingly brutalized and murderous rural masses, the left-wing or mainstream revolutionary ideology subjected intellectuals, through the project of proletarian literature, to idealize women in the image of laboring, mythic, working-class earth mother. As subjects and as writers, women were split into two alienated possibilities. On the one hand, the subject woman could collapse back into a male Symbolic. On the other, writers could renegotiate a style of self-brutalization that mimicked the truth of women's Real, offered a chaste facsimile. In each case, the tradition of écriture féminine registered a great alienation. But it chronicled as well and with great clarity a profound problem that all women confront: in the words of Bai Wei, that women have no Real: "If you say 'woman' [nüren] to a man then it means the dominated object of his desire. If you say it to a woman it means the part of herself that is already alienated."[29]

Meng and Dai staged what amounted to an unmasking of mainstream ideology largely through a comparison of the work and careers of Ding Ling and Xiao Hong. In the case of Ding Ling, alienation is expressed in two ways. Early on, she had written about the necessarily carnalizing power of the male gaze, but her text showed that what was reflected back to women was not women's own singularity in heterosexual exchange over difference, but rather their alienated body in an economy of commodified sexuality. Consequently, Sophia is a beacon because she achieves a victory over the alienation of her own sexuality. Looking into the carnal gaze of man, she opts to become her own toy rather than his. But Ding Ling could not live with the consequence of her insight. Under the historical circumstances, the claim of self condemns the female writer to utter loneliness and marginalization at the edge of life and death, and so, fatefully, Ding Ling chose to join her husband, Hu Yepin, in the camp of the left-wing writers and undertook the task of erasing gender difference in her own self and in her texts. The further into the left-wing camp she sank, the more deluded she became about the true nature of the Chinese masses, Dai and Meng argue. When in the late 1930s Ding Ling saw the peasantry correctly, defined in terms of its hostility to sexuality and of sexual difference, it was too late for her to recover herself or her literary project. Her self-betrayal meant that she could only snipe at ideological aporia. Eventually, she aborted the responsibilities of the critical intellectual.[30]

It was Xiao Hong, not Ding Ling, accordingly, who kept intact, at great personal expense, the earlier gains of écriture féminine. Repeatedly abused, beaten, and abandoned, Xiao embodied in her own childhood trauma the larger historical discontent of the female collective unconscious with the conditions of its habitual enslavement. Her decision to leave the left-wing camp, like her choice of lovers, involved Xiao in a self-victimization that was appropriate to the historical moment; positioned by rather than within the Left, she chose integrity of the female self over life itself.

This choice of death makes Xiao's texts and example more valuable than Ding Ling's in the history of the female tradition, for Xiao kept alive the larger historical project at a most difficult juncture. Xiao lived squarely in the Imaginary of literature and the Real of gendered slavery (for if there exists a Real for women it is a Real of gendered slavery). Thus, the great novel *Field of Life and Death* represents the reality of the Chinese masses in every detail of their brutishness, cyclical animalistic pleasures, and tragic inability to distinguish even the boundaries of the nation itself, which explains their failure to defend it. Because Xiao retains her link to the Imaginary of women through her literary vocation and her desperate clarity about the Real of women's oppression, she is capable of avoiding the betrayal of a Ding Ling, who opted to become a phallic woman, a woman as defined by men and through a male Symbolic. Xiao's fiction represents the singularity of women's sexed experience.

The way forward for écriture féminine chinoise in Meng and Dai's "history" came neither in the Chiang Kaishek camp nor in the Mao Zedong camp. It came in the barren landscape of Japanese-occupied China. In the triply divided world of the late 1930s and 1940s, the national situation became progressively more complex. Enlightened intellectuals in the nationalist-held regions retained the May Fourth style, while in the Communist liberated zones a new de facto liberation obtained, but Communist liberation meant in practice that women were freed to become men. It occurred at the level of political economy.

At each historic step forward in the struggle to consolidate male (and phallic female) subjects, a genuinely female self was erased and its historical trajectory eroded. This loss to women of discursive power meant that women could not write their difference; the national culture entered a devolutionary condition of sexless differentiation of women and men. And with the disappearance of the possibility of a singular femininity, the conditions of later tyrannies were locked into place. That is because—as Gao Xian and theorists like him in the 1930s had initially argued—when the phallic economy wholly colonizes the signifier women and empties it of any real, female experience, there is no possibility of resisting the process of totalitarianism. To Gao, this meant a devolutionary trajectory of racial, sexual degeneration. To Dai and Meng, it meant that the joissance of women, the possibility of a feminine Real beyond the singularity of phallicized signifiers, was lost.[31]

Only in the Japanese-occupied areas did female writers embrace the luxury of the freedom that comes from detention. They were free to focus on the self or individual in an extreme situation; as they lacked social choice, they were left with only the riddle of woman's self. Emancipation from indigenous patriarchy enabled Su Qing and Zhang Ailing to continue the development of the tradition of écriture féminine and its movement of the historical woman from daughter to male-defined woman to self-consciously singular self-representation of women by women. What characterizes Su's and Zhang's fiction in Meng and Dai's eyes was their abandonment of victim status. Women appear in their fiction as mature players in explicit heterosexual relation, always self-directed and so capable of making bad decisions; they are never simply weak. Moths drawn to an erotic flame, these protagonists cast themselves into experience. Existential choice for better and worse moves them beyond the prison house of patriarchal femininity and into a singularly female discourse. In the work of Su and Zhang, according to Dai and Meng, the Chinese women's tradition revolted for the first time against the male literary canon, developing its own plot structure, modes of expression, and vocabulary. Only in the poisonous garden of the Japanese-occupied areas could this occur, could woman as a singular gender truly enter heterosexual (*liangxing guanxi*) desire as itself.

Particularly in the work of Su, Meng and Dai see an explicit record of women's actual experience or experience in the Real. Su's scorching self-mockery exposes the rituals that attend the exchange of women among patrilines, particularly the hollow empire of the feudal mother-in-law. Self-awareness about conventional women's lives strips away from womanhood properly speaking all ideological mystifications and consequently clarifies how male domination works. In the words of the literary critics:

> According to the male Professor Lacan's theory, women in patriarchal society will always be subjected to the anxiety and shame of the lack of the *fei le su* (phallus [English in original text]) a portrait of the male generative organ, it is not the real, reproductive, biological penis, but rather a sign [*fuhao*]; it is father's power, a symbol [*xiangzheng*] of father's power, they can only go through the male to get an Imaginary phallus, and with this enter into the Symbolic. Thus it is giving birth and not marriage itself that ritually transforms women into persons and names them. And it is the child rather than the man that enables women to shake free of the anxiety of lack as well as the situation of namelessness. *But what is repeated in Su Qing and is concealed in Lacan is that which constitutes this imaginary phallus is not an androgynous child, but a gendered one: a son, a boy child.*[32]

Motherhood is the work of women. It justifies the enslavement of women to men. In that realization, a self-realization or self-awakening or self-reflexive consciousness, Su opens up a crevice in the ideology of patriarchal maternalism, arguing, albeit largely unconsciously, according to Meng and Dai, that even the "choice" of a husband is nothing less than women's reinscription into the conventions of motherhood unless the singularity of sexual desire can break out of the prison of reproduction. Ren'ge, then, achieves a stable social subjectivity only in the status quo (i.e., the Symbolic that is organized around male control of the phallus). In Meng and Dai's view, Su's literature shows precisely the irredeemable quality of this naming of woman. Until the subject of woman is reorganized around the Real of women's singular sexuality, the universe Su describes will persist.

In opposition to Su's mocking derision of women's secondary, cowlike existence, Zhang Ailing, Dai and Meng argue, introjects a cool concern with spiritual culture into an inhospitable and already psychically evacuated national tradition. Zhang's female characters do not choose a feminine role but land, like guests or aliens, in unstable social positions, looking around themselves at a strange topography as a foreigner might see it. This weirdly corpse-like, feminized national identity distinguishes Zhang's oeuvre. An ageless, embalmed beauty standing in for the national tradition, romantically linked to some hapless mother's son who will never truly become a man (can never possess the phallus even in his waking fantasies), moves in a ruined country where there are no fathers left, where a postpatricidal calm has descended. Zhang's is a world where evasion of the exchange of women takes priority and time passes as the bride waits for word of her lover.

And on that note, Meng and Dai end their volume with a reminder that the historical liberation of women onto the horizon of history actually led, for unspecified but overdetermined historical reasons, to the death of difference. Of course, it is obvious that their critique is as apropos of the Maoist era as of Japanese-occupied Shanghai and consequently addresses the mishap of the historical subject of women in their own time. Their point is that in spite of socialism, a tradition of écriture féminine was established for the Chinese woman by Chinese women themselves. The historical tradition of the tentative coming-into-consciousness of a singular subject, women, on the horizon of national history announced the possible end of male totalitarianism.

In perhaps the only published scholarly review of *Surfacing onto the Horizon of History*, Zhang Jingyuan, writing in *Xueren* (Scholars) in 1992, noted that until the reform era of the 1980s and the renaissance in women's literature and criticism, no contemporary, major work on the topic had ever been published in the PRC. Meng and Dai's history was the most innovating development since Tao Qiuying's *Zhongguo funü ya wenxue* (Chinese women and literature) in 1933 and Tan Zhengbi's 1935 *Zhong guo nüxing wenxue shi* (History of Chinese women's literature), she concluded. Zhang was placing *Surfacing onto the Horizon of History* into the history of Chinese women's literature studies. But she also contrasted it to several other contemporary studies that Li Xiaojiang's Enlightenment Series had also published. The question puzzling Zhang was why, even discounting their overly exuberant language and analytic difficulties, only Meng and Dai's volume had risen analytically to an international standard of excellence. Meng and Dai had restricted their focus to nine authors, Zhang noted, because their object was not historical excavation of modern women's writing as such. Rather, it was to expose the two millennia of phallologocentric writing preceding and contextualizing modern écriture féminine. Their target was culture, not "men." Zhang also noted a second breakthrough that she felt Meng and Dai's study had achieved: it had convincingly argued the thesis that history's conscious (male) and unconscious (female) coexisted in the same temperality, in the same historical moment. I mention Zhang's second point because it anticipates what I think is the central role that écriture féminine plays in Dai Jinhua's analysis of cinema.[33]

Surfacing onto the Horizon of History emphasized women writing women and thus the singularity of the sexed female literary subject in the embryonic, Chinese, historical tradition of écriture féminine in women's literature. Dai takes the position in her cinema and cultural studies work that the subject women exists or will come to exist only through a project of translating or surfacing the unconscious significations of women's Real into a conscious or historical record. The unlikelihood of the emergence of a female cinematic auteur in the People's Republic seems one reason why Dai, who is after all a pioneering film critic, keeps intact her long-term critical engagement with écriture féminine. Also, because of the very successes of film as the paramount medium of male subjectification, it is incumbent on her to provide in literature the patient example of alternative media that, because they are cheap and available to anyone, remain open to female self-invention.

Dai Jinhua's 1998 edited volume Gates of the Century, for instance, introduced what she called "1990s women's culture and écriture féminine."[34] This volume presents the literature of Wang Anyi (a self-reinvented 1980s author) and newcomers on the 1990s scene Xu Lan, Meng Hui, Jiang Zidan, Lin Bai, Chi Li, Tie Ning, Chen Ran, Xu Kun, Chi Zijian, Zhang Mei, and Wang Yan. In Dai's extensive introductory comments, "Strange Encounters and Breaking Out: Nineties Women's Culture and Écriture Féminine," she makes the case that the tradition of Chinese women's writing established in the first half of the twentieth century had reemerged in its last decade. The 1990s were witnessing the "reappearance of the original picture," she argues. New authors had literally returned to the transgressive styles of pioneers like Lu Yin, Feng Yuanzhun, Zhang Ailing, and Su Qing and were continuing what Dai called with a more cinematic theoretical flourish, China's gendered "field of vision." So Xu Lan's fiction showed the influence of Zhang Ailing, just as Chi Zijian's historical writing reminded one of Xiao Hong's narrative preoccupations.

Remember that for Dai, écriture féminine is the most highly gendered form of cultural expression available, and to her, "gender" means the logic proper to sexual difference. So écriture féminine helps readers to recognize the irreconcilability of gendered difference and to capitalize on it. Women writing difference wrenches male literature out of its resurgent (the effect of commercialization and globalization) but contagious, deadly, lethargic entropy. Why is this important? Because male culture always positions women's subjectivity and female sexuality in a sinister rather than a pleasurable or benign light. In fact, left to itself, male literature would return women to déréliction, the rapt immobility that is their functional position in the totalitarian representational order of phallologocentric writing. Feminism's contemporary resurgence has value, Dai argues, because "écriture féminine draws on a clear, gendered identity [making possible women's] entry into a cultural field of vision."[35]

My point is that Dai never substantially changed this core position staked out in *Surfacing onto the Horizon of History*. Women writing women remains for her a privileged form of cultural expression. She has added increasingly more reasons why écriture féminine is invaluable. For instance, because feminist theory is necessarily parasitic, nestled in the elitist cultural effusions of the theoretical 1980s, écriture féminine has the ability to morph in a game-like relation to the culture of the new Chinese Enlightenment, and therefore it keeps alive an otherwise defeated 1980s critical comprehension. Without écriture féminine, not only would women's surfacing into subjectivity be effaced, but the record of achievements of the 1980s would be lost. Writers in the women's tradition also unleash what are equally preserving (because feminism is unthinkable in the absence of enlightenment conceptions of man) and contestative (because the obvious aporia in humanity is woman) initiatives. In this, Dai's position parallels Li Xiaojiang's critique of enlightened reason. Only feminist writers can rupture and extract out of 1980s enlightened thought cultures of resistance to globalization that had been embryonic in the older, chaotic, incautious moment of their initial expression. In the 1990s, game logics prevail. It is the dubious privilege of gendered women to haunt the margin of mainstream mass culture, even as the mainstream cannibalizes positions that earlier seemed to threaten status quo thinking. The subject women in feminism and those critics and writers who take up the position of women have the potential to keep one step ahead of the game.

I underline these points because women's literature continues to bear what may seem at first glance to be disproportionate weight in Dai's overall theory project. The Chinese tradition of écriture féminine, having resurged in the late 1970s, offers readers and cultural critics the sharpest, most observant, disruptive possible openings, according to Dai. For what purpose? It gives critics like herself the traction they need to contest the new, suffocating commercial mass culture. A male-dominated Enlightenment culture critique is limited and has not achieved anything close to the facility of writers in the écriture féminine tradition. Even when he repackages narrative that transgressive female writers like Xu Lan and Zhao Mei wrote and uses them for his commercialized purposes, male cinema auteur Zhang Yimou cannot divest the stories of their latent and inherent power to disturb the phallocentered culture. Victory in the long, siege-like struggle for cultural enlightenment ongoing in the "cultural city of mirrors," Dai argues, depends on an écriture féminine strategy in which female-authored feminist literature enables women's subject formation.[36]

Cultural studies is the primary field where protracted war against mass culture unfolds, and écriture féminine is arguably its paramount battlefront. In Dai's hands, the discourses of women are a weapon or tool for transforming Chinese culture. Because the symptoms of success and failure, advance and retreat in this battle are often indirectly apparent, Dai must read constantly and diagnostically, and must exploit all resources available for enlarging women's psychic capacity, their possibilities for subjectification. Feminism, that is to say, is part of elite cultural criticism. It proposes an epochal struggle and it is that strategic imperative that has compelled Dai to "extend" the "academic territory" of her reading practices from film studies to literary criticism to cultural studies and its mass culture critique. Of course, she legitimates her own position as a feminist critic with reference to the real emergence of actual or concrete women. But the only place where the subject women can be said to have indubitably appeared is in fact in écriture féminine.[37]

## Cultural Studies

In the ten years separating Surfacing onto the Horizon of History from Gates of the Century, the tasks of the feminist critic and the cultural realities both changed. The feminist project at the "gate of the twenty-first century" was profoundly and tragically distinct from the catastrophic advent of "the 1990s" in June 1989. So, although it is important to keep in mind that écriture féminine is the unspoken ballast in much of Dai's writing in the 1990s, it is equally important to distinguish, as she does, between her 1990s perspective on feminism and her earlier, 1980s vision.[38]

First, when Dai writes in Gates of the Century about the revival and extension of the tradition of écriture féminine in the 1990s, she literally projects that revival onto a startlingly visual, topographic grid or map. Her work has a breathtakingly spatialized quality. It is not that her political investments had changed since her initial collaboration with Meng Yue. But, as Dai pointed out in a 1998 interview, in the 1980s, particularly when it came to theoretical feminism, she had always taken the position that theory should insist on distinguishing itself from developing practices in the mainstream women's movement. This attitude made her, she said, an unadulterated "elitist"; of course, it made her a philosophic idealist as well.[39] But by the late 1990s Dai's analyses were set in a primary field of "culture" that seemed hardened into a tangible relief map. Her cultural terrains are vivid and manifestly material, as though she envisions all cultural forms through the optics of cinematic media. She undertakes even literary criticism in a "field of vision" now, where arguments take on an objectlike quality. Now her powerful language and its tightly controlled sadness present breaking historical events as though they were being screened in front of our very eyes. Agents transgress her fields, break out of mirrored cities, or, memorably, trespass the "balustrade" (yue jie zhalan) separating theoretical domains from one another.

Second, the persuasiveness of her argument about the historicity of nüxing in women's literature rests on her creativity as a poststructuralist feminist. She and Meng developed the position that a Real for women lay in the unconscious of history. The prerogatives of theory (by definition, an enlightened and privileged form of thinking) are what enabled them to claim to see a tradition at all and to claim so much in the name of a tradition of women's writing. Importantly, however, Dai's understanding of theory changed over the course of the 1990s, though her commitment to the political power of écriture féminine did not. In a famous roundtable in April 1988, "Dianying: Yahnise shidai" (Cinema: The Janus period), for instance, Dai declared that "the normative standpoint of theoretical workers" should be to concern themselves with reflexivity, but never with application. Though conditioned historically, the Faustian theorist is concerned with pure rationality and the self-critical awareness that only Enlightenment opens up. Theorists are analogous to creative artists in this particular respect. Theorists, she said then, engage in the project of "shouldering the burdens of history, its contradictions and difficulties."[40] In the sadder, less hopeful late 1990s, however, she argued that the eruption of globalized mass culture into Chinese cities in 1993 had left intellectuals stupefied, ill equipped to handle the moment, and bereft of adequate theory or critical vocabulary. History had outstripped pure theory. Only theory's valuable game-like quality remained. My point is simple: whereas Dai's conception of what theory is and what it does changed significantly over the 1990s, she never revoked her belief in the centrality to history of the surfacing into visibility of gendered historical subjectivities, female and then, consequently, male. In that respect, the 1998 introduction to Gates of the Century took up exactly where the 1989 Surfacing onto the Horizon of History left off.[41]

Third, in her many articles, interviews, and dialogues over the ten intervening years, Dai drew attention to post-Mao feminism and how feminist writers had coped with the intensifying social derogation of women, the erosion of gains made under socialism. As she puts it, if the tradition of écriture féminine in the 1980s was an ark or vessel for fording the rushing water, and if it was a burden that women shouldered with male colleagues who were engaged in complementary praxis during the heady days of the historical reflection movement, in the 1990s women are on their own. *Gates of the Century* is a differently wrought portal. It is a way out of the mirrored city. The rules of the game for feminist action are changed.

For instance, Dai evaluates highly a Jiang Zidan story because it has "a female-constructed female character—in the process of writing a gendered self, as well as the reality of female existence—a character in search of an author, in the process of searching for the author who will narrate her speechless condition."[42] The topics contemporary writers must address (e.g., historicality, precommunist fictional pasts, the weapon of historical genealogies, methods of foiling narrativity) are different from Zhang Ailing's time. In the new, global, massified, domestic cultural economy of the 1990s, commerce and development in economic globalization have disrupted all continuity. The accumulated historical burden is, on the one hand, a great imposition. On the other hand, adverse conditions actually burnish écriture féminine, which now has a sharply whetted ability to grasp society and social change quickly and accurately and to offer destabilizing alternatives. The tradition of female literature has not been simply reestablished. Women writers take it up again because écriture féminine chinoise is a valuable weapon. Only this literary women's intervention can excavate the real experience of women in history and, consequently, potentially, alleviate the condition of Chinese men, who are themselves mobilized in phallologocentric cultural relations.

Finally, Dai has an oceanic feminist objective. Her aim in each of the fields she entered in the 1990s is usually the same: to locate historical evidence for any movement in the unconscious material of women's experience out of the interior or submerged strata of male discourse, history's unconscious, and into the consciousness of historical representation itself. Much of her theoretical adaptation of the "white foreign fathers" (Lacan, Althusser, Foucault, Hegel, Marx, etc.) feeds into her foundational project of documenting the rise to subjecthood of a previously abject pre-Oedipal or undifferentiated Chinese woman. Her view in *Gates of the Century* seems to be that fiction still offers the best opening, the best portal for this transfer of psychical matter to the socius. That is how I interpret her argument that écriture féminine did not fully mature as a tradition until the 1990s. As she wrote, "1990s écriture féminine has the special characteristic of gendered self-consciousness, [of providing] the obstinate labor of adventing female life and female experiences from out of the gloom of a drapery of mist."[43] This is so because the commercialized and globalized discourse of the mirrored city is itself a male discourse, a projection of masculine defenses. Dai's deceptively simple language in the late 1990s tends to cloak the psychoanalytic framework that organizes her insights. She says only that commercialization of the city has brought with it gross sexualization and commodification of women's bodies and that, as before, men are attempting to use women to "pay the price" of modernization, to act the part of its sacrificial victim.

In the 1990s Dai Jinhua invented and popularized her own cinema-cum–cultural studies program at Beijing University. She had become a film theorist and film historian by chance. Educated in an era when the state decided what and where students studied, she had been assigned to film school, and when she graduated she found herself, through a series of rather accidental moves, inventing film studies in order to teach it.[44] Dai has recently isolated two primary commitments that she believes have characterized her work from those early periods of invention to the present. First, feminism has been her "basic position and research method" since beginning her film theory specialization in the early 1980s, though it was only when she proclaimed herself "to be a feminist and conducted research on women writers and female directors" that she "encounter[ed] loud applause and condemnation." Once out of the gray zone intellectually, she came to think that "feminism cannot be recognized (or maliciously resisted) until it comes out on a banner. For me, feminism is an important position, an integral part of my theoretical position. *More important, it is an experience and a way of life.*"[45] I emphasize the last sentence because it clarifies Dai's first imperative that women's experience is universally sublimated into the male Symbolic and that the task of feminism is to desublimate and represent it. This is the historic task that makes feminism a way of life as much as a mode of thinking. Desublimation and reinscription of space around freshly desublimated subjects is the first underlying logos in her project of describing cinematic topography and aggressively gendering cultural space.

The second long-term element visible in her cinema theory is her effort at resetting the relation of écriture féminine, a literary project, and the critical study of cinema in light of the special problems that cinema presents to critical theorists. In this pursuit, she distinguishes the protocols proper to literary studies and cinema studies. Literature, she argues, crystallizes the experience of the Other. In feminist literature or écriture féminine, the Other is therefore induced into history as woman, or nüxing, a historically new subjectivity that exists only because of the authorial practices of female feminist writers. The medium of film and film studies as the rationality proper to the medium have different responsibilities from literature and literary criticism. Desublimation and self-authorization are not the tasks of cinema. In cinematic media, according to Dai, the problem is how to think about the *diegetic signifier* (i.e., the purely filmic sign which is systematic and meaningful in relation to other signs in the film itself) in tension with complex *extradiegetic realities*. Film is singular precisely because it rests on confusion between what is strictly within the frame of the film as such (the diegetic) and what film signifies about the world outside the frame (the extradiegetic). The extradiegetic is the domain of cultural studies proper. It is what Dai vividly describes as "culture in general" when she is undertaking film criticism. She sorts extradiegetic cultural phenomena into a taxonomy of cultures, such as mass culture, elite culture, literary culture, and film culture. As I suggested above, one of her strengths as a literary critic in scrupulously distinguishing film and literature is her ability to set literature's social text in an extradiegetic framework that is visual or topographic because it is in fact the Real of the camera eye.

What are the analytic strengths that are proper to film? One stems from the fact that cinema was from the outset a social (i.e., not-theoretical), compromised, and heterogeneous popular form. Speaking about what makes the cultural history of film thinkable, Dai has argued that while cinema in China is chronologically older than the new literature, film is more like a cultural scrim than a tool of transformation.[46] (Largely, that is because film cannot desublimate or self-authorize.) Not only is film a modern technology, but it cannot enter social circulation except as an industrial commodity. Another particularity of film is its complexity. In movies there is almost always a narrative, but the characteristic of cinema is that it projects a visual field where disparate elements tend to appear without explanation, thus pointing outward to undigested social events unfolding in the extradiegetic world. Not all elements of the mise-en-scène have significance in the picture that is projected on the screen. A good example of this special quality in film is an illustration Dai gives in the interview regarding the early silent film *White Rose, the Chivalrous Heroine*. Certain visual elements, Chinese actors dressed like U.S. cowboys and Indians, intrude without comment into a neotraditional Chinese melodrama. The question for film studies is what these elements are doing in a "Chinese" film in the first instance.

So, third, film studies properly speaking is defined by the degree to which it can take advantage of film's heterogeneity. That is why film, and its essentially worldly involvements, is amenable to cultural studies in a way that literary criticism, by its very nature elitist, historical, progressive, and for Enlightenment, is not. "I do not intend," Dai said, explaining how her distinctive method differs from the earlier work of others, "to rewrite film history the way history of literature was rewritten in the 1980s. This is of course due to the difference separating the media of literature and film from the specific cultural role each has played in modern China. If in the realm of literature one can regard practices of aesthetic judgment or criticism of pure literature as significant in itself, establishing such coherent criteria would be difficult in the context of Chinese film history . . . in as much as film is an art of modern industrial civilizations, whatever remains—once we remove all 'impurities'—as pure art may be so insignificant that we wouldn't be able to amass sufficient material for writing a history."[47] This resolute position illustrates Dai's commitment to the elitist or Enlightenment tradition of cultural politics. But it also makes a final point. Because cinema is constitutionally impure, incoherent, effluvial, it actually allows us greater access to the fields of life and death where the drama and game of feminist cultural recoding must continue.

Dai's film critique is preoccupied with how historically male, dominant culture and male subjects reinvent themselves cinematically. In the bitter days after the failure of the cultural reflection movement of the late 1980s, Dai turned toward the question of how the Janus-headed Enlightenment tradition of Chinese intellectuals could be salvaged. Perhaps one of her major concerns was why, historically speaking, heightened, even self-defeating intellectualist styles of masculinism seem almost cyclical. In the first half of the 1990s Dai's cinematic work focused on the question of the resurgence of phallologocentric cultural coding in film practice. This effort positioned her in what she would come to call the Sisyphean project of cultural criticism. An agonistic attempt to see and to question new forms of masculinist power required her, for reasons I discuss at length below, to pay close attention to the significance of male-authored new film culture in a geopolitical framework. If, for the most part, her studies of literature have stressed transgression and the rise to historical representation of women, her film work was deeply engaged in a feminist, Frankfurt School–style critique of the constraints on processes of "breaking out" for male and female subjects. Of course, her concern with cultural studies of mass cultural space in the late 1990s required her to pose afresh the question Breaking out of what?—for by that time and by Dai's reckoning, the tectonic cultural terrain had once again been shifted in the earth, shattering a great transformation of the global economy.

An instructive example of Dai's preoccupation with logics of masculinity is her critique of female director Huang Shuqing's film Ren, gui, qing (Woman, demon, human). "Ren, gui, qing: yige nüren de kunjing" (Woman, demon, human: A woman's dilemma) examines the dynamics of female subjects in cinematic space and first appeared in Dai's *Dianying lilun yü piping shouce* (Film theory and criticism handbook) published in 1993. Two years later she reissued it as a chapter in *Breaking Out of the City of Mirrors*, paired with a study on écriture féminine and feminist gains in film practice. Remember that according to Dai and Meng's historical periodization, the women's literary tradition had ended in the 1940s and, at least according to Dai's reckoning, had reemerged only on the horizon of Chinese history in the 1990s. Dai set out a parallel theory of cinema periodization. According to her stage theory of development, filmmakers had successfully liberated Chinese films produced in China in the first half of the century and created their own idiom by adapting Hollywood norms. Socialist filmmakers beginning in the 1950s, however, had not exploited the cinematic or technical resources of older, popular, Hollywood-inspired films. Communist film practice instead sought to extirpate the heterosexual gaze. To that end, the state-controlled industry buried its older prehistory and started over. Yet, Dai argues, immobilizing though it may be, for female viewers Laura Mulvey's "gaze" is still an integral part of any adequate, filmic, representational order.

When, in Dai's view, women are no longer an object of male desire, they cannot represent themselves as Other, and consequently they cannot fulfill their emancipatory potential as the sign of gendered difference. What Mulvey wrote as a critique of Hollywood cinema, Dai took as a necessary historical, developmental step. In the absence of the male gaze, Dai argued, woman becomes an empty signifier and women's actual experience within the sexual logic of difference cannot be expressed. The empty signifier woman is open to ideological packing at the whim of prevailing ideological formations. The emasculation of film is one reason why nothing in Chinese film history corresponds to the gains women registered through écriture féminine. Because most of Dai's exquisitely detailed film-based studies focus on how castrated sons patched together a postsocialist, lapsarian, neopatriarchal, transnational cultural Symbolic through the process of self-authorization they pioneered in their collective subjectivity as Fifth Generation filmmakers, her essay on female director Huang Shuqing is an exception generated to prove her own rule.[48]

Huang's *Woman, Demon, Human* is the story of a woman who plays male roles in the Beijing Opera. The filmmakers, whom Dai and Mayfair Yang interviewed in 1993, based the movie on the life of a real female opera star named Qiu Yun, who plays herself in Huang's film. In her reiteration of the traditional ideal of masculinity, the actor Qiu's nostalgic performance of masculinity made it possible for Huang, the filmmaker, to explain to an ordinary, mass viewer why merely translating gender logics or "roles" does not yield emancipation. Doing man's work does not liberate woman's self. Contemporary women, who work as men do, are caught in a trap where they both long to and yet cannot achieve a social ideal of womanhood. Dai calls *Woman, Demon, Human* the only genuine women's film ever made in China, because it desublimates the psychodynamic fix of women who are compelled either to masquerade as men or to capitulate their subjectivity altogether. Only *Woman, Demon, Human* accomplishes for film culture what écriture féminine and the tradition of women's literature is doing to recode phallologocentric literature and criticism.[49]

Huang's broader theoretical importance to Dai lies in how Huang reconfigured the Mulan archetype. *Woman, Demon, Human* took the Mulan myth of a girl who pretends to be a man, acts valiantly, and then returns happily to being a girl, and turned it into a real story about a woman in the male Symbolic who pretends to be a man, succeeds all too well at that, and when she finally tries to become a real woman can only simulate gender because no real men exist to "see" her as a real woman. In the film, Qiu is the daughter of an adulterous mother whose cuckolded husband raises Qiu to be an opera singer. In the course of her career, Qiu stages a series of attempts to escape from her fate. Each of these is an attempt to break out of the city of mirrors (Dai's dramatic, material metaphor of the male Symbolic). First, she tries to escape the conflation of womanhood and whoredom, but this leads in the end to the loss of the heterosexual gaze that can confirm her subjectivity as a real woman. She then attempts to escape simple misogyny by refusing to play female stage roles. But what she discovers through this strategy is that choosing to *not* play women does not actually change one's real sex. When her own teacher falls in love with her and she rejects him, the Qiu character signals her acquiescence to the fate of normal women, which is to live with lack—of heterosexual completion, of suitable gendered subjectivity, of power to express and power to determine. Enlarged spheres of choice cannot overcome the psychodynamic limits around which female subjectivity is formed. In fact, the traditional male roles Qiu performs on stage immure her even more tightly in this trap, because the ideal male she plays is a figment of her own thwarted heterosexual desires. Here Dai seems to argue that Huang was inverting the strategy of the male auteur, the primary subject of Dai's brilliant *Breaking Out of the City of Mirrors*. Dai saw in Huang a female artist expressing what women want in a man by telling the story of a female artist who performs the role of a vanished ideal of masculinity *from a woman's perspective*. Huang's ultimate insight is tragic, according to Dai: what a woman performs she cannot posses. That is because her performance consolidates the incommensurability of subject and object.

And yet, in this historical moment, the metanarratives that Qiu recycles through her loving performance of a vanished style of masculinity are so decrepit and defunct that they actually offer a way out of the double bind that women face. To outmaneuver the bind contemporary Chinese women find themselves in, Dai suggested, a woman must instantiate the trap itself: she must make the problem visible to herself and others. The performance or reiteration of subjecthood in the domain of cinema practice is not gender drag. It is a way of exemplifying what is at stake for women who seek to put the Real of women onto the horizon of history. If, that is, words do not exist for self-expression, then performativity can, at the very least, open up our eyes to possibilities. In other words, Dai's essay is a despairing use of cinema practice, deeply indebted to literature's priorities, to open our eyes to future strategic possibilities.[50]

Because *Woman, Demon, Human* is the exception that consolidates the rule, the question of the subject women posed in literary self-authorization is never far from view. But although Dai notes that "women" is the answer to the riddle, her case study, *Breaking Out of the City of Mirrors: Women, Film, Literature* is particularly fixed on the Sisyphean struggles of the male cohort that reestablished the film industry and placed China's semiautonomous cinema culture into the global industry during the 1980s and 1990s. Sons are the chief protagonists of the study. Its primary motive historical force is global capital. Its drama unfolds in the national and international domains where the logic of sexual difference is the primary metaphor organizing social relations among women and men, ordering ideological formations, and structuring the relation of stronger and weaker nations, castraters and the castrated. For the media or film critic, the primary social text is national cultural life in a postrevolutionary context. The great narratives of the 1980s are eroded and superseded in the roaring 1990s globalized culture of consumption. Dai poses the Foucauldian question of power's enabling constraints. The feminist asks: If women's emergence onto the horizon of history is such a short story, how do we account for the power that minimized or prevented this event in the past? Dai's response is characteristically complex. But for my purposes, it consists in the following.

Historically, according to Dai's *Breaking Out of the City of Mirrors*, Chinese cultural reality since the mid–nineteenth century is castration. The supremacy of the West is the Real for the Chinese. The Real confronts Chinese intellectuals with a split between their cultural practices and the reality of their historical emasculation. The spiritual exile of a cohort of young men who, immediately after the Mao era, claimed the name of "Fifth Generation" cinema auteurs, gave rise to an explosive creativity. Their project tried to bridge the disjunction of history and culture, to resume the May Fourth movement of the 1920s while at the same time reconstituting a historical archaic before the time of that traumatic emasculation. Also, Fifth-Generation cinema sought to confront the historic trauma of the Great Proletarian Cultural Revolution at a personal level. The auteurs— Zhang Yimou, Tian Zhuangzhuang, Chen Kaige—shared a personal biography that marked them as men and as artists. They belonged to the Communist elite. When the GPCR broke out, these young men found themselves caught. They were Red Guard sons, banished to the rural periphery in the name of that transcendental father, Mao Zedong. But they were also the sons of their own real, damaged, and emasculated fathers, whom they adored and had castrated in Mao's name. As filmmakers, the Fifth Generation therefore used their vocation to seek an entry point back into the symbolic order as men (i.e., the sons of their fathers). This project could not succeed. Their endless spiritual exile from the symbolic order meant they remained aphasic sons, trapped in the circular dance of father-and-son succession, in colonialism and Maoism, lost in the preconscious labyrinth of language and representation. Dai focused relentlessly in this study on the static condition of aphasic sons in the ideological double binds of the post-GPCR era.

Exiled from the Red Guard generation and their own defeated fathers, these artists replayed over and over a single narrative of the exilic son's effort to rehabilitate the Name of the Father in mythic prehistory. Eventually, their new cinema language, purged of disrupting ambiguity and effeminate glossolalia, renarrated a national subject but vested it under a feminized gaze in a Westernized field of vision. To achieve this position, the auteur had to recolonize the film signifier woman, as Chinese male artists had done from the beginning of their civilization, only this time in a globalized frame. The capacity of male auteurs to do so further escalated the difficulties that women auteurs faced employing film media for self-representation and self-authorization.

In Duan qiao zi yidai de yishu (Severed bridge: The art of the son's generation) Dai sketched out the new technical "language" of the exilic son's film practice.[51] The piece rests on close readings of films like One and Eight, Horse Thief, The Black Cannon Incident, and other classic Fifth-Generation movies. But its primary lesson is to expose the psychodynamics of the auteurs and their art's historical predicament, which is their failure to breach their way into the father's Symbolic and thus to express the traumatic content of their own historical and individual experience. This failure is overdetermined. What are the underlying determinations? First, according to Dai, there is no Chinese convention for representing "individual experience of shock as legitimate" (12), which is to say that the lingering feudal tradition hinders the efforts of women and men to establish sexed, heterosexual subjectivity as the primary social bond. Recall that this is the heart of Dai's psychoanalytic utopianism. Her normative measure in the end is always whether heterosexual bonds and gender difference, the logic of sexual incommensurability, occupy a primacy over father-son cyclicity. Dai often hints that something in Chinese culture makes historical movement toward this emancipatory goal very difficult to achieve. Second, the weakness of intellectuals as a collective subject continues through the art practices of the Fifth Generation because Chinese intellectuals abandoned the old order but have yet to create a new one. Fifth-Generation films only reiterate this weakness. The aphasia of the sons and of Chinese intellectuals is the same aphasia. Third, the measure of the failure of this project (i.e., the failure of the sons to achieve a linguistic symbolic order that is in synch with history's Real) is in fact a clarification of the spiritual distance intellectuals and Chinese men still have to travel. But even in its ultimate failure (it does not achieve a historical expression of individual trauma and does not foreground the dynamic relation of heterosexuality), the cultural project is also an amazing achievement. Why? The film language of the Fifth Generation, Dai points out, did create antireality, a new mythos. In doing so, it detached linguistic signs and real signified, leaving a simulacrum of the Real. This phantasmagoria in fact clarifies the remainder, an element of experience that cannot be represented as such in any symbolic order. Thus, Dai calls the nonlinguistic image (16) the ineffable and unrepresentable noise of a trauma that, preserved and conveyed in Fifth-Generation film language, is the historical male unconscious.

But in Dai's vision, history always writes the script. Arguing in regretful retrospection, she realized that China had been recastrated in 1987, when the national culture ran into the buzz saw of globalized, "Western," commercial culture. Unable to withstand the anxiety of inexpressible trauma, the sons not only buried every utopian possibility that the G P C R carnival of mayhem had presented to the nation, but they manufactured, in the face of the new global threat, a mythic paternal hero charged with papering over all castrations, ruptures, and losses. Dai presents her reading of Red Sorghum to show the atavism of the generation of sons' nationalist response to globalization. A counterhistory, the film indulgently brings the sons back into what she calls the "circular dance," or the cycle of masculine history. The film Red Sorghum presented a resolution of the aphasia of sons. It brought history back onto the visual field of signification. It purged anxiety by carrying out in the safe confines of a movie another ideologically contained, psychodynamically necessary patricide. Why necessary? Because only the justifiable patricide can anoint a new hero, absolve the father's threat of castration, and cathect anxiety to a nationalist ideology. Of course, the cinema narrative has another, final bloody task: it must sacrifice the father's women (for all women belong to the father) on the altar of history. This final act, this reiteration of the story of the son, ensures the abjection of sons and the nation. It is the sacrifice of his own Other that makes the Chinese man a real son and reinserts him in the ideology of national historical survival in the international stuggle of the fittest. The utopian moment of discontinuity is betrayed, lost as the circular dance of death—father to son—makes yet another pass around the dance floor.

"The Severed Bridge" formed the ground base for Dai's study. The "Jiji de xuangi-zai du shi de biaoxiang xia" (The quiet uproar: Urban representations), is on the lookout for fissures and networks of fissures that the 1987 onset of globalized mass culture set off. There the argument unfolds in the context of the surfacing of the mass culture and is exemplified in the "Wang Shuo phenomenon." The historical preoccupation with fabricated primeval ur-societies, an important motif in Fifth-Generation films, gives way in the discourses of urbanization to films like Huang Jianxing's *Black Cannon Incident* that reworked the signifying chains of city, worker, village, peasant into the new metropolitan surge that accompanied globalization. In an argument heavily indebted to Fredric Jameson, Dai argued that Huang's film registers the surfacing of an autonomous realm of culture, where older formulas and people are set into new contexts, into modern, metropolitan spaces. The supplement is no longer prehistory but the city. Wang Shuo is the greatest exemplar of this shift and earliest advocate of urban culture's priorities and possibilities. Disconnected from the avant-garde masculinism of the Fifth Generation, a purely entrepreneurial and commercial writer, Wang is nonetheless as dependent on the sacrifice of women for his access to the cultural Symbolic as they are. Chapter 3 of *Breaking Out of the City of Mirrors* poses the logical question: If at both avant-garde and mass cultural levels the subjective self-authorization of male cultural auteur requires the degrading and sacrifice of women, is there an alternative history unfolding where women authorize themselves in cinema practice? As I argued above, Dai's response to the question she posed to herself was that important counterdiscourses appear in the tradition of women's fiction. In the cinematic Fourth Generation, Fifth Generation, and in mass culture generally, women is an empty signifier. It is empty because women either bears no relation to the actual experience of real women or it is obviously a stand-in for the emasculation of Chinese men under the gaze of the West, the Maoist state, and now "the market." As a signifier, women is empty because except for Huang Shuqing, Zhang Nuanhua, and Hu Mei, no female filmmakers have stepped forward to narrativize their own emergent experience.

The logic of the sons, developed with such incredible force in "The Severed Bridge," is of course an analogy for the predicament of contemporary women in the prison house of language. That is the topic in "*Women, Demon, Human: A Woman's Dilemma*," which Dai placed in *Breaking Out of the City of Mirrors* as chapter 4. In this context, Dai's theoretical point is that the trauma of history effects male subjects in a different way than it affects female (pre)subjects. The mirrored city of women does not rest on psychological trauma suffered in tragedy (castration, patricide, taboo), but on what Dai calls civilized violence or the evacuation of experience from the bodies of women. Women actually suffer in the process of the emptying out the signifier women. Psychodynamically, men must endure the traumatic journey that leads from aphasia or déréliction into conditioned maturity (or the failure to achieve it). Women only endure the pressures of the flux of empty signification. Unless, that is, they take up feminism and the historical tasks of writing self and consequently writing a real history of their gendered difference from men (a move that will also, it bears repeating, redeem the utopian possibility of heterosexuality).

In later chapters, for instance, "Liegu: huihuang yu xianluo" (Abyss: glory and ill repute) Dai analyzed how this wretched impasse fared in the unfolding of globalized 1990s culture. Under the "interpellating gaze" of a West, the Fifth Generation's retrospective obsession with the archaic and paternity became anachronistic. Economic and political urbanization, massification, globalization, and the rise of the mass urban culture decimated the serious avant-garde. But Dai's concern here is the Hobson's choice that Fifth-Generation auteurs faced: either lose the elite audience, support for elite cinema production, and serious art itself (serious art being, in her view, the way back from cultural self-alienation) or sell out to the globalized film industry, where access to resources is predicated on self-Orientalization, a formulaic recycling of the archaic, and further entrenchment of the Chinese intellectual's historic self-exile initiated in the May Fourth movement. When the Fifth Generation chose the West, it cost the Chinese avant-garde culture its utopian possibility for cultural self redemption (i.e., the chance to bring the Real closer to historical representation) and it recast elite culture as a version of the "postcolonial," which is to say, an alienated condition of self-estrangement. Particularly in the film practice of Zhang Yimou, Dai argues, the cinema finds a way to represent history as mere discourse, "a mirror image of China captured in the Western gaze as Other," its dynamism lost, its subjectivity and temporality gone. Under these conditions, even when Chen Kaige, for instance, returns his work to the question of individual trauma, his male avatar is a stagy story of the Eastern individual constituted not in experience but under the gaze of the West. This process of self-Orientalizing in fact retraumatized the national body, increasing its stress fractures, opening the possibility that the national culture would simply collapse under the pressure; that is what Dai calls the "deformed fetus" of national culture in "the age of postcolonial culture" (27).

In the book's closing arguments, Dai established her own notion of the postcolonial and the dilemma of the Third World in the world system. China, in the world system, she suggested, rather resembles the relation of women in the male discourse of avant-gardists like Zhang Yimou and Chen Kaige. In postcolonial culture, what is endlessly bounced back through the reflecting mirrors, what forms a globalized city of mirrors, are the cultural representations of the Other, the West, never the self. The circular dance of fathers and sons initiated in Fifth-Generation filmcraft turns out to be a circular dance of death when it is overlaid in a neocolonial consumer culture. What had begun as an agonistic effort to rework the historical trauma of the May Fourth culture of Enlightenment just further marginalized the national culture of China in the symbolic order of the West. As the commercial booms and crazes of the 1990s unfolded and the mass culture penetrated further into popular consciousness, the touted "dialogue" of China and the West proved to be an imaginary projection of China's own lack, just as the minor genre of "women's films" exhibited nothing less than their creators' own powerlessness inside the patriarchy. The world of transnational capital presents the Third World with the problem of finding fissures in the social text to exploit. A film like *Farewell My Concubine*, so popular in the United States and Europe, on the other hand, actually inverted Huang Shuqing's strategy. Rather than finding a gap where a woman could self-authorize a historical subject women in the process of surfacing unconscious material onto the horizon of history, this film feminized the male avatar of Chinese culture. Contorting the archaisms of Beijing Opera, *Farewell My Concubine* made the male avatar of China's nationhood into a woman. Elsewhere, in other culture texts, the now empty signifier women reappears in the post-1989 avant-garde culture as the portal of male maturation. The hollowed-out, male avant-garde offers women as a blood sacrifice to history. Literary figures like Ge Hua, Su Tong, and Mo Yan turn women back into a mere signifier of passage in the stages of men's cyclical maturity. Women become the bodily entry point into history for Chinese men. Men colonize women and spatialize them, detemporalize them, pulling them into a destabilized, self-referential flux.

Dai Jinhua has said for some time now that cinema per se has a short shelf life. This is particularly the case with high-art movies. Historically, she said, their time has already passed. A persistent theme in *Breaking Out of the City of Mirrors* is precisely the ways in which the Real, as constituted in avant-garde cinema, fell into desuetude, got hollowed out or evacuated, partly because the generational psychodynamic (the father-and-son cycle or circular dance) could not complete itself adequately before the next great tectonic plate shift of history rumbled through the pieced-together map of Chinese postcolonial culture. In other words, those positioned to represent history adequately, psychoanalytically speaking, always sold out the Real for a chance to enter into the Symbolic as anointed and sanctified sons.

Chinese sons always overidentified with the father, and even that, always a generation too late. The one possible historical pathway that might have righted the national subject of China in a national narrative, women's self-authorization and women's configuration within a reciprocal gaze of heterosexuality, was precisely the path not taken in the effusive art cinema of the 1980s.[52]

After *Breaking Out of the City of Mirrors*, Dai began consolidating the newly emergent arena of popular and mass culture studies. This has drawn her to problems of how to understand mass-market commodities, spaces of consumption, cultural geography, and the psychodynamics of commercial culture that make possible local accommodation to global capital incursions. The basic problem in cultural studies, however, is "culture" itself. I do not think it is odd to find Chinese Enlightenment intellectuals like Dai re-engaging the culture question in an international cultural studies project, though her move deserves more thorough historical consideration than I am able to give it here. Some obvious links situate her in an agonistic relation to the tradition of Yan'an Maoism that in the early 1940s conditioned Ding Ling's feminist transformation practices. Recall that Yan'an Maoism rested on its own Enlightenment framework. Dai's position, however, is Maoist in the sense that the Marxism of cultural studies in Europe, Taiwan, Japan, and the United States are all indebted to Mao's shift of emphasis in Marxism from ideology to culture. Dai's creative reinvention of Lacanian-Marxism is complicated by the debts that Lacan, Althusser, Kristeva, and other influential Parisian theorists owe to the Maoisms of their own era. But here the global circuit of Maoism is less immediately concerning. I stress the question of the status of culture in Dai's thinking to underline a different difference: the distance between Li Xiaojiang's feminist theory project's grounding in social science and Dai's renegotiation of culture in global, feminist, psychodynamic cultural studies. For Dai, culture is the medium and location of the historical unconscious. It is where subjects make themselves and are made, are authorized and, in the best instance, authorize themselves.[53]

Over several years Dai has cast and recast the culture question. In "Jiushu yü xiaofei: Jiushi niandai wenhua miaoshu zhi er" (Redemption and consumption: Depicting culture in the 1990s), she grounded the culture concept in history. This argument, which links Mao fever in the early 1990s to the sudden upsurge of compulsory consumption, proposes that "culture" historically is a symptom in relation to a singular real event. For instance, books that urban, formerly "sent-down" youth, exiled to the peasant villages in the Cultural Revolution, began writing opened up nostalgic spaces. These spaces, culturally speaking, are actually ways of managing a historical and personal trauma. Unlike the empowered cadre of Ding

Ling's revolutionary generation, who saw in culture a tangible, slablike, ideological medium for recasting the voice of the people, culture in Dai's hands is pure affect. Ding Ling's problematic was character, model characters, and individual ethical practice in the Mao years. Dai, also working with the phenomenon of "Mao" signifiers, theorizes a different context. Her culture is not a coherent force open to benevolent manipulations. It is structured like an unconscious. Thus, the traces or memories of emotion, like utopian moments of GPCR mayhem, are actually traumas indelibly inscribed into the tissues of the mind, where, with effort and intelligence, they can become available to reason. The social recovery of emotional memory is what Dai calls bridging or the floating bridge. In her rhetoric, bridges are artistic or cultural desublimation projects that can cauterize an inchoate affect so as to minimize or deflect its power to annihilate. Bridging works for good and evil. As Dai has pointed out in her recent cultural studies work, a bridging over of the sacred or utopian desires of an already historically impoverished people may simply rob them of the imagination it will take to resist the numbing powers of globalized consumer society. Instead of reacting blindly against the force inflicting the trauma, Dai tends to cast the matter as a riddle. Here the puzzle is posed as a question of what is truly valuable, even sacred, in the trauma of the immediate past and consequently worth recovering and celebrating.[54]

Dai delivered another alternative in "Wu zhong fengjing: Chu du 'diliu dai' " (A scene in the fog: Reading the sixth generation films), which she used to rework an analytic definition of "culture" in a psychoanalytic frame. She zeroed in on the question of the "cultural Real." Sixth-Generation auteurs like Zhang Yuan, Qiu Yan, and Wang Xiaoshuai, who became the vaunted Sixth Generation under the benevolent and neo-Orientalist gaze of the West, created discursively anticipated commercial events. Still, despite their commodification, their films were always more than mere effects. Their art pointed to a Real lying under cultural practices these artists inherited from the 1980s. Though Dai herself can never fully see the Real but only postulate it, it might be, she supposes wryly, an "uncanny, crisis-ridden, yet vibrant cultural landscape" that is "the realization of the marginal culture hidden beneath 1980s elitism."[55] What are the symptoms that Dai claims ironically to be unable to see? Younger artists have refused the illusion of full subjectivity, for instance. They linger over aphasic sons (i.e., subjects refusing to name the father, embracing the pre-Oedipal) and their own marginality. "Polysubjects" working in a dream logic of spatialized omniscience, Dai argues, these despairing young male artists are symptomatic of the hopeful deficiencies of China in transition (again). Where the Yan'an Maoist cultural framework situated character in rigid terms, Dai's culturalism sixty years later assumes that subjects are partial and unstable because culture is the medium of psychodynamics. Culture is the place where the flow of affect or unconscious content takes place and subjects form themselves in relation to its exigencies. The cultural Real is two things, then: a hall of mirrors (i.e., the 1990s globalized Chinese urban space refracted through Western misreading) and, beneath the "fog" of ideological miscoding, what Dai sometimes calls an original picture, the "fading in of the social culture just emerging in the transformative 1990s." Under the cultural studies critic's gaze, between the hall of mirrors (i.e., the endless refraction of empty signifiers) and the original picture (history in the last instance) are the cultural actors and their unconscious traumatic affect that mediates socius through psyche.

Dai's "cultural arena" is a national entity situated in a transnational framework. That makes culture the libidinal-affective level of a national subject, too: a nation's psyche, distinguishing the nation's people from the peoples of other nations. According to another of Dai's alternatives for employing the culture concept, national subjects reside within a complex international system of geopolitical recognition that is itself structured like a convocation of subjects all possessing intrapsychic drives and intersubjective attachments. Nations in effect see or ignore others, are seen or introject others as elements of themselves. This generalization of the subject problem into international systems means that when she analyzes the nationalist, populist, bestseller genre of the diasporic narrative, Dai can argue that the Imaginary emerging into the cultural arena through the medium of novels about Chinese living in the United States is an important simulacrum. Such cultural commodities offer a symptom of something more deep-seated. Here, "culture" gives consumers symptomatic novels in place of the West's true voice (which, ever anticipated, will never arrive in any case because the West cannot see China's longing to be recognized). The diasporic Chinese narrator offers readers "at home" ersatz recognition. Chinese readers can celebrate and make the stories into the "long-awaited 'response' to the [Chinese people's] indefatigable beckoning to the West" (14). Politically, nonetheless, diasporic narrators are chauvinists who merely repackage a cultural China, forever positioned in a hostile relation to a center that will always withhold recognition. Such mass-market novels shatter the dream of authorization in the desire of the Other, while at the same time prolonging the self's drive to be authorized by an Other. This affect or bridge recycles desire endlessly. It stuffs the original trauma into the historical unconscious, cathects it into the realm of simple ideology, which effectively bridges unspeakable national trauma. Culture is nothing more than an endlessly manipulatable medium of imaginary solutions to real problems.[56]

Dai has also proposed that culture is a sacral medium. In this suggestion her critique tracked the meaning of the term "square," or *guangchang*. When the square or guangchang first registered in the political language of Maoist ideology, it substantiated Chinese modernization, she argued. It materialized the utopianism of revolutionary politics. The square was the place where citizens met together. Now the term guangchang means a shopping mall. When commercialization displaced political ideology, hollowing out even the signifier "Mao Zedong," the entire ethical political lexicon suffered a desacralization and the "pieced-together map" (another Dai metaphor) of China's urban areas was redrawn. Commercial consumption is desacralizing, profaning. It bridges over the legitimate ethical demands of citizens who cannot participate in the orgy of consumption but also can no longer be written legibly into the social text. Trauma arising out of poverty, disenfranchisement, class cruelties, and so on is bridged over in the new commercial ethic. Consumer society is momentarily stabilized only because the gulf of class differences can be bridged when middle-class consumers justify their own greed and irresponsibility against a constantly invoked opposition to G P C R cultural trauma. An affective prohibition guards against any possible re-membering of socialism. The shopping mall, earlier a sacred space for egalitarian rituals of political violence, will, Dai suggests with nausea and anticipation, surely be reconsecrated differently in yet other places at yet other times.[57]

As Dai explained in her 1997 interview with Zhou Yaqin, cultural studies is a "recovery from history, or supplement to history," by which she means the "surfacing of factors formerly consigned to oblivion, a surfacing that contributes to altering the whole picture," and the renaming of a subverted disciplinary canon. As a nondisciplinary or interdisciplinary space where theorists like Bourdieu and Foucault prevail, the project of cultural studies is to avoid simplistic formulas while at the same time breaking the enclosure of the text or diegesis with a renovated Marxism. In an interview with Candy Irmy Schweiger in September 1997, Dai said that she was explicitly modeling herself on Chinese intellectuals who made the leftward turn in the first globalization of Marxism during the 1930s.[58] To me, this raises once again the question of Ding Ling and the subject of women in Chinese feminism. At the very least, it returns Dai to the question that she and Meng first raised in *Surfacing onto the Horizon of History*, when they denounced the ham-handedness of Chinese (i.e., Maoist) Marxism. Fifteen years later, in the late 1990s, Dai was proposing that Marxism is a globalized theory of social imminence and must be reconfigured in terms of a current impasse. Her operational understanding of cultural studies echoes with Frankfurt School ambivalence. But courageous as usual, she turns resolutely to investigate the specters of the 1920s and 1980s Chinese Enlightenments and the problem of where thinking and intellectuals belong now. At the other end of the twentieth century, Dai copes with the collapse of the stable referents on which Walter Benjamin had rested his case. Cultural studies is the practice she uses to uncover layers of historical sediment previously concealed because "where fault lines appear, the original picture returns and the specters of history reemerge."[59]

## Spoken Writing and the Cultural Map

So Dai Jinhua's feminist Marxism today rests on the flexible foundation of cultural studies. Earlier I suggested that her work materializes metaphor and makes rhetorical figures into a topography that is tangible, even though the forces she describes are psychic drives. This understanding of how culture operates squeezed into spaces between mainstream, repressive, social forces (e.g., class, race, gender differentials) and the eruptive power of historical change (e.g., globalization, commercial and popular cultures) actually ends up putting a premium on praxis. Praxis means that someone or a collectivity of people is doing something in reasoned response to given conditions. Of course, the game of praxis is constrained, for Dai has read Foucault very carefully and absorbed his discourse-power into her understanding of ideology. But her position is also active or activist; for where there is a game in her work, there is also a player. Dai always attributes to cultural auteurs and to artists primary responsibility for representing the Real in the Symbolic. That keeps her in the Chinese Enlightenment tradition. Also, she has often suggested that one of the hurdles facing utopian cultural studies is the difficulty, given China's complex history of father-son dynamics and its Maoist interlude, of retaining the heterosexual couple at the center of history making, where, that is, they must be situated for the sake of the health of the national culture. In Dai's work, écriture féminine is the place where the historical headway that writers (and the rare cinema director) make inscribing the Real of women (i.e., women's gendered experience) into an indelible historical record can be registered and read back. By the logic of her own practical theories, then, Dai is empowering herself. Beyond her powers as a scholar to affect the ways canons are built, students taught, and books written, she suggests two ways that cultural studies practices give her extra authority: first, she is an inventive theoretician or theory artist and therefore an auteur of sorts; second, potentially at least, she is herself a woman, nüxing.[60]

Along with Dai's increasingly interventionist arguments in cultural criticism and her turn to performance (discussed below), she is, for understandable reasons, also rethinking her relation to socialist women's liberation. The long exegesis she wrote with an Anglophone audience in mind, "Xingbie yü xushi" (Gender and narration), laid the stress on what Chinese women gained in the de jure liberation of 1949, when they were descended into the masculine logic of the Maoist name of the father in service to modernization. Watching the loss of even that Pyrrhic victory from the perspective of postsocialism, feminists like Dai find women reexiled to the edges of social space. Social losses to women are conducted in the name of enabling men to banish the specter of Maoism and to "bury the skeleton of the catastrophic era in their imaginations" (30). The historic exigencies of development linked to the psychic demands of men are again threatening to reverse the gains of women. What can be done? Women as a collectivity must rethink their historical position, Dai argues. Rather than stressing the losses to women in the Mao Revolution's violence, she seems more inclined to emphasize the way that "precisely the same violent element that thoroughly shattered the old system of patriarchy (and with it, the Name of the Father and the husband) . . . occasioned the community of women's ascent upon the social stage" (31). Looking at the 1980s from the perspective of the 1990s, she argues that when Chinese, Marxist, New Enlightened thinking hollowed out the signifier women and refilled it with mere victims, made woman "a portal to humanity suddenly demolished by violence rather than the object of men's desire," it forgot to sexualize the gaze and properly situate gendered difference in cultural life. As there is a utopian promise buried in the revolutionary tragedies of the past, cultural studies must relocate and ground the interdisciplinary space for retranslating the terms of feminism and make good on that lost promise.[61]

Still *Caught by the Mirror*, a collection of transcribed and edited oral interviews and roundtables published in June 1999, looks back at Dai's academic career and its twists and turns and forward to her projected cultural history of Chinese film in the domain of cultural studies. In most of the interviews, her assistants, visiting scholars, and students inquire about influences on her thinking, the ways that she envisions the cultural studies of the future, what dangers (relativism, marginalization, the charge of faddishness) she anticipates emerging in her future work, and more. The roundtables find her engaged with peers in collective efforts at thinking through questions in theory like chagrin (*ganga*) and postcolonialism. The publication is an important resource. It fleshes out what Dai herself intends for her work to accomplish. She is also a remarkably voluble thinker, and interviews convey her vivacious conversational style. They are colloquial lessons in how to think in theory. But the interview is also a set genre. What distinguishes it from all the other genres in Dai's arsenal—analytic essay, cultural study, film diegesis—is the interview's performance quality.

Dai's performance of her self consolidates the promise of écriture féminine to women writing women's difference. In the genre of interview she capitalizes on the authorization that her own feminist theoretical position promised any woman daring enough to engage history. She performs nü-xing. Dai presents herself in these oral accounts as a certain kind of feminist subject. She is neither an essential woman nor a victimized empty signifier. The reactive element of personality or the sense of self that a woman might get from social pressure does not enter into her exegesis of her self except in passing, as evidence of where she can break out again. That is to say, Dai never speaks in these interviews as a subject who knows what women are by virtue of just being one; she does not embrace any socially prescribed or projected femininity; she does not pretend that the experience of womanhood is simple or stable. Unlike Li Xiaojiang, who discovered herself to be female relatively late in her life, Dai makes the point that she has always been recognized as a woman in the last instance. The debatable analytic point is what kind of woman, given the instability of the signifier woman and the prescriptions surrounding any social sanctioning of femininity. Dai is very clear in these interviews. Gendered experience is the guiding force in her descriptions of herself, no matter how traumatic and ambiguous her own experiences. The tall girl, the boyish girl, the anomalous girl, the queer girl are all irrevocably female in their own ways. Whatever she encounters, then, is *the experience of woman when, as subject, she declines to rest on the Other's definition of her.*

In other words, because woman is primarily a theoretical, cultural, historical problem its emergence out of the historical unconscious rests in the end on ex post facto evidence. There must always be more evidence, even discontinuous evidence, so that the Chinese tradition of écriture féminine can be continued into the future. Analytically speaking, women as a category (i.e., the Real of women) must be surfaced onto the historical horizon through the labor of self-signifying, self-authorizing gendered subjects. These are subjects who are gendered in the heterosexual gaze that écriture féminine chinoise presumes to be normative and who answer to the logic of sexual difference. It requires a certain historical performance on the part of women like the early Ding Ling, Ling Shuhua, and Zhang Ailing. The content of that performance can never be known until after it has ended. Perhaps interviews, because they originate in the spoken presence and in response to the questions of an Other, are another means through which the historical unconscious that is women in déréliction or abjection are brought into gendered social life. Maybe in the performance of her very own difference and anomalousness, Dai Jinhua, like the writers and auteurs whom she empathetically criticizes, is able to ratify the body of écriture féminine and show that she herself is a feminist subject: she is another example of a self-authorizing heterosexual woman. In self-disclosures that are skewed more in terms of theoretical interventions than psychoanalytic detail, she uses the interview genre to negotiate a position that is neither masculinized (Mulan) nor empty (the projection of male developmental desires) nor pre-Oedipal, but rather flexible and constrained in the immediate and chaotic present.

Of the five formal interviews and three appended dialogues and round-tables, "Nüxing zhuyi: Wenhua lichang, xingbie jingyan yü xueshu xuanze" (Feminism: Cultural standpoint, gender experience and scholarly choice) is most helpful. In this transcript Dai performs the position she has advocated for over a decade. In a history of feminism's current trek through Chinese thought during the 1980s and the 1990s, she explains both how she came to feminism and how that theoretical commitment required her to excavate herself out of the unconscious of masculine history and into a self-inventive female écriture. In what her interviewers will later try to call an ugly duckling narrative, Dai responds to a request that she explain her personal reasons for coming to feminism late and in her characteristic way. Her gendered experience conditioned her intellectual decisions, she replies. What experiences were these? In her immediate environment as a child and young adult she found herself to be anomalous in relation to male normativity, she tells Zhou and Po. She became a feminist because she grew too tall. She was always a tall girl, and because she was too big, even bigger than the boys around her, the children would not let her dance female roles in the Mao Zedong performance troupe. Of course, she could not dance the boy role either, as plenty of boys existed to fill that role. To compensate for being a gender anomaly she turned to intellectual work and to clowning. Her life course brought a whole host of other problems. Called "iron girl" or "female genius," "unsuitable" or "lesbian," she was also for many years a single woman in a society that confers femininity on married women. What Dai learned was that she did not qualify to be a woman. As an exception to the gender order, she came to understand how the unfeminine woman is masculinized, yet not masculine. People enjoined her to learn femininity; women instructed her in manipulation and wile. The problem confounded her nonetheless and led her to internalize her deviancy as a personal failing, a source of self-contempt.

When she engaged feminist theory, several things became immediately possible. First, she realized that she had found a way of understanding her own bruising experience with the social gender order. Had she not been found wanting, had she not located a theoretical resource, it is possible that she might never have found a way of bringing out from the unconscious of history an experience or set of experiences that belong to a woman, herself, yet that had fallen outside the protocols of women in her time. Rather late, after much self-reflection, Dai continued, she confronted her own self-contempt and with growing self-confidence and happiness entertained the possibility that embracing womanhood (not femininity, but the being of herself, a woman) would lead her out of the trap of anomaly. The fact that the relation of theory and consciousness to experience or preconscious dynamics has to be thought in theoretical feminism was an added bonus. It meant that in the end, she had the good fortune to do (thinking) what she loves. Also, her experience as an anomalous woman turned her on to the secret of masculinity, which is that it, too, is a role or mythology and that the differences among each gendered sex were as extensive as the logic of difference separating them. That is why, in the end, she turned to thinking about the "culture of gender."

Particularly in this interview Dai is performing herself to make herself a subject of feminism, one answer to the question of women in feminism. The fit between her experience of anomalousness and the history coded into feminism in France, a society where equality is strongly advocated but women are still the second sex, led her to see that the Chinese terms for feminism had to be translated and retranslated. She thought, she said, through film theory translations (for film is where gender difference is played out most obviously), working side by side with Zhang Jingyuan, who was just then canonizing and translating the standard references for the Chinese theoretical tradition of écriture féminine. But where others would be content to translate or think within the translation paradigm, Dai drew on anomalousness to rethink the nüxing of nüxing zhuyi. And in the same way that she herself continues to experiment with her own gendered experience, Dai showed in this transcript that the value of nüxing lies precisely in its anomalousness and its bottomless capacity for reiteration.

Feminist practice, of course, can collapse into just another advertising device unless practitioners are willing to be vigilant. The key is to continue performing one's own contradictions. Just as she willingly put on parade her early self-contempt for a larger good cause, Dai generalized from the overlap between her own self and experience and the good of the subject of feminism. During a public seminar Dai performed a self-contradictory position in relation to the sexual fantasies of the writer Lin Bai. Dai's refusal to either give up Lin's work on the grounds of merit (for Dai holds the opinion that Lin's licentiousness is demeaning to literature) and still, in response to a hypothetical question from the floor, refuse to allow her own (hypothetical) daughter to read such literature had embroiled Dai in an early controversy. The illustrative point, she argued in the interview, is that in judging écriture féminine the measure must be feminist and thus address one question: Does this writing authorize or self-authorize women to be subjects? If the answer is yes, then the writing must be admitted into the feminist canon, no matter how ugly or illicit that écriture is, no matter that Dai herself finds the piece to be unwholesome. Admission into a feminist canon means that the task of bringing onto the horizon a previously buried experience will go forward. But just as it takes a conflicted Lin Bai to go forward even under attack from the gutter press for behavior unbecoming to a woman, the feminist subject has to place her self on the line whenever necessary. The performance of ambiguity or anomaly is a correct materialization of the female Real. Women as a group include among them all kinds of possibilities and these must become visible. The woman citizen is always an outsider in the nation, and it is this anomaly that, like others, must be performed so that it can be made visible.[62]

The overriding task for feminism is the upending of phallologocentrism, in other words. Male culture cannot go unchallenged, for it is, we know from Dai's less performance-oriented work, homosocial and in the end tyrannical. And so, in a sense, Dai's interviews perform the task that began a century earlier. She has every legal means for occupying public space. Her ren'ge (public standing) is hers by state fiat. Her self-appointed task in this feminist insurgency is to perform the outsider status of the woman in relation to citizenship, woman as the aporia of humanism, woman in the logic of heterosexual difference. As the interview winds down, Dai responds to her interviewers' remark that she had been an ugly duckling who grew up to be a swan. Not at all, she replies. That is just a fairy story. In fact, I grew up to be a duck. I never was a swan. Which is to say that in the end, what feminism works with and what a subject in feminism works for is the project of difference in which the duck is not required to be a swan in disguise.

When Dai Jinhua and Meng Yue pioneered the argument that a tradition of écriture féminine was inscribing Chinese women—the unconscious of the nation—into the conscious history of the nation, they provided a way out of the dilemma that the psychoanalytic problem of female déréliction poses. They solved this problem with a historical form of national feminism. As Zhang Jingyuan noted in her review of their text, there is a central double bind constraining all critical, psychoanalytically inspired, contemporary feminist theories. If phallologocentrism demonstrates that women speak only as men, how is it possible to speak of women "existing" at all or existing as an oppressed gender? Unless some way out is found, women will remain in a condition of déréliction. But if women is in fact a historical subject, then the cultural conditions for her emergence out of déréliction and into definitive subjectivity will have to be historical. Under the current historical conditions, unless one assigns identity to oneself, others will assign it, and so the history in question must be to some degree a national history. The muted claim in Dai and Meng's first diagnostic reading of what they called écriture féminine made precisely that claim. Dai's theoretical formula—the Imaginary in the nüxing tradition is the pre-Oedipal fusion of subjects in the maternal body; the Real is gendered slavery within the patriarchal clan, the bourgeois nuclear family, and all other forms of male-organized families; the symbolic order, organized around the fantasies of men that they can control the phallus—consolidates a subject, nüren, which is a mere effect of male ideology. The subject in question is always a national subject.[63]

Nonetheless, the national question in écriture féminine chinoise abuts a long history of internationalism. Dai's work is both part of a global flow of international feminism and a very practical strategy for a theorist in her national condition. Chinese feminism, as I demonstrate in this book, has always rested on varying sets of globalizing signifiers, even for its central catachreses, and Dai's feminism is no exception. Her objective is to denote a national identity (shenfen or rentong) cast in the internationalized scope of antiessentialist feminism. Another way to see this is that Dai is really made possible as a feminist theorist because Chinese feminism is never fully provincial. It cannot be provincial because it can never claim to have originated in China. From its inception in the late nineteenth and early twentieth centuries, so-called Chinese feminism is always a vampirizing or circulating theory. This is true whether the impulse to ground it comes from theoretical eugenics, nationalism, Marxism, or self-identified "feminist theory." The Chinese tradition Dai exemplifies draws complexity and sophistication from the fact that it has routinized even translation. Contingency is built into the decision to retranslate core texts and to rename core practices of nüxing zhuyi, nüquan zhuyi, nüxing xiezuo, funü wenxue. It is not simply that catachreses women crystallize around already or foundationally internationalized subjectivities. It is also that in each case where feminist work surfaces (i.e., into the problem of citizenship, labor abuses, clan or class oppression, cultural texts, etc.) it does so in an inventive relation to a global theory. In this chapter the example is Dai Jinhua's brilliant reworking of poststructuralist or antiessentialist Marxist feminism.

# Conclusion

In their optimism and agony, 1920s–1930s progressive Chinese feminists proposed a subject in evolutionary eugenic theory, which they believed to be an indispensable ingredient of China's future. That singular subject was the collectivity of women. Nüxing's centrality in foundational Chinese feminism distinguished eugenic feminism from other contemporary, popular evolutionary schemes. General theories of evolution were circulating widely in the late nineteenth century in Europe and Asia. Translator-philosopher Yan Fu's treatment of Thomas Huxley's *Evolution and Ethics* broadcast social Darwinian thinking widely among the generation of the first Chinese Enlightenment. Many of that era's leading thinkers presumed the scientific truths of evolution. But unlike social evolutionists in this broad stream, which Charlotte Furth has called "a combination of progressive Darwinism and more traditional outlook on the times," eugenicist feminists placed women at the center of their theory. The Gao Xians and Yi Jiayues could not imagine a future without a Chinese woman who freely selected Chinese men for sexual intercourse and formed modern nuclear families with them.[1]

One of the dubious powers of general theory is its capacity to project an inevitable future out of a present truth. The relation I drew in chapter 6 between Zhang Jie's 1981 short story "The Ark" and Li Xiaojiang's 1989 thesis in "Sex Gap" is an example of this point. Creative writers and critics, women and men inclined to thinking about injustices through colloquial fiction, no doubt also appreciated Chinese progressive feminism. But Henrik Ibsen and Lu Xun, two writers often said to represent the best of Chinese feminism, did not propose a general theory. Rather, they focused on a perceived riddle of women's liberation—without liberation women are abject, but then liberated women had no way to live—through a hypothetical, the fictional subject of Nora in Ibsen's internationally significant play, *A Doll's House*.

Two central assumptions in this book are (1) that modern women is a subject inside a long and discontinuous history of political and general theory, and (2) that the placement of women in systematic or general arguments is what differentiates feminism from ordinary sympathy. Writing that sympathizes with the burdens imposed on women can be found in all times and most places. Feminism, if it is any one thing at all, is a modern globalized theoretical project that seeks to describe and eliminate the injustices that the imagined collectivity of women suffers because women are women. Literary feminists and their fellow travelers in the 1920s and 1930s have engaged and crystallized or disproved generalities, but they did not set the terms of the general debate.

Internationally, feminism, if one can speak in such terms, is precisely that highly suspect tradition of universalizing about the legitimate claims of the hallucinatory subject women and this women's claim to social justice, economic and labor parity, erotic expression, and social emancipation. I have argued that the theory of general emancipation and the subject of women are inextricably bound together. Whether the term in play was nüxing, nüren, funü, or nüzi, within the theorization project I have called Chinese progressive feminism, all analytic subject forms designating and defining women pointed to the historical fact that in colonial modernity and even more broadly in revolutionary modernity, Chinese women were being socially organized in new ways.

Gayatri C. Spivak's aphorism—"A concept-metaphor without an adequate referent is a catachresis"—may be even more useful if its terms are relocated. The historical catachresis is an inadequate (because it is incongruent and necessarily incomplete) linguistic term for an adequate, though impossibly complex social referent. What makes the notion of the historical catachresis useful in this book is that it helps to crack a code. It points out ways that theorists from Gao Xian to Dai Jinhua have redefined women as an analytic category and social subject. Successive revolutions, civil wars, wars of liberation, political mobilization, and now the neoliberalization of China's political economy have found theorists returning to the question of women's liberation. Their conditions differ. Their terms and codes have varied widely. In conditions of chronic, high-stakes political conflict, women and men have theorized or addressed theoretical formations. This thirst for social justice stands as a discontinuous and agonistic relation of successive "new women" to their redefined capacities as national breeding stock, wellspring of labor value, revolutionary exemplar, market consumer, patient workers in the task of recuperating the unconscious of history onto history's horizon. In the language they share with those who would define and those who would deny them full humanity lie many contests that must become a part of the history of the event of woman.

In 1942, when Ding Ling asked "When will it no longer be necessary to attach special weight to the word 'woman' and raise it specially?" she was locked in a specific political struggle. But as I have suggested, it is also possible that this question runs like a red line down the center of her creative life. Which is why the history of women in Chinese feminism cannot be written without reference to the projects of Ding Ling. If, in general terms, Ding Ling's early fiction is a test posed to the singular subject of Chinese progressive feminism, and if her later work is an effort to represent in Maoist revolutionary theoretical language a singular female subject *for the future*, then the projects have a commonality. Each rests on a call for justice in a future to come. Encoded in her critiques are portraits of what women will have to become. In her engagement with the Chinese feminist struggle, the present cannot be the sole measure of adequacy in women, for the present cannot be allowed to address the question of what women are. Her question to the present always concerns adequacy: When will women, whose ren'ge or personality poses a treacherous problem for them, obtain the kind of justice that will make it possible for women to stand comfortably in the society as adequate subjects? Ding Ling's question of *when* implies a future where equity and justice make eugenic difference a moot issue. Perhaps, if the question of ren'ge does turn out to be the central problematic in the history of women in Chinese feminism, Ding Ling's address to the future will take on even more importance. In any case, her Maoist writing does not appear to debate the traces of eugenicism. It proposes, rather, that responsibility for reproductive and erotic choice be a social goal that all members of the community in revolution equally seek. This is not because choice will improve the racial stock. But then again, that salutary effect is never explicitly disavowed.

Ding Ling's effort to retool the machine of feminist justice in the drive to engineer a revolutionary modernity concentrated on how and in what ways social progress ensuring this end could be institutionalized. If the burden of social reproduction is assigned exclusively to women comrades, when and how she asked, could the future where women too possess an adequate social standing and personality (to say nothing of claims and privileges) ever be achieved? Her hallmark essay "Thoughts on March 8" posed two possibilities. In a distopic future, women remain trapped in social abjection, or déréliction, where erotic choice is disallowed and revolutionary women are robbed of their right to social struggle. In the utopic future, revolutionary responsibilities rest on men and women equally, and sexual justice is openly discussed even when erotic desire finds itself at war with social justice. Ding Ling was, as I argued in chapters 4 and 5, drawing attention to the impossible project of stabilizing a ren'ge, or social personality, for nüxing. She was also fortifying the potential (while probing the instabilities) of the collective social subjects that class war and social revolution were just then gathering force to institutionalize. The more deeply engrossed in Maoist theory (the "line") Ding Ling became, the more clearly it is possible to see her ambivalent embrace of that more hopeful and egalitarian future subject, funü.

In the 1980s, Li Xiaojiang took what she and so many others felt was the Maoist Revolution's denial of sexual difference and projected its opposite— natural sexual difference—into the future. A truly natural society should be closer to nature, she argued, a nature that the Maoist Cultural Revolution (and, by extension, Marxist-Leninist revolution in general) had repressed. The sexual gap is a fact of nature, according to Li. The sacrifice of women's autonomy to the demands of nature in the interests of capital accumulation was the form in which natural sexual difference had to be expressed in the past. But in a future that women would eventually construct out of the myths and traces of the archaic past, sex difference would require no sacrifice. History would have prepared subject forms for women, not just in China but globally, allowing for the expression of difference in a condition of equity. What that equity would look like, Li seemed to be proposing, could be known only under a condition of material abundance. A great future market economy would allow the expression of natural difference. It would provide the means for women to express subjectively the affect that nature pulls out of them, in their (evolutionary?) roles as mothers and wives. Li was returning, I hinted, to the analytic problem of heteronormativity. This ideology rests on arguments that discipline erotic expression, using appeals to the natural law of species reproduction. And it rests on arguments that join the theory of the struggle of the fittest in the human species to the theory of the struggle of the fittest in a capitalist marketplace.

The agonistic relationship that the iconoclastic Li Xiaojiang struck in the 1980s, not just with the Communist government's Women's Federation bureaucracy but also with the respectable social science establishment that Den'g reforms fostered, should not hide her importance as a theorist. Her ingenious efforts at creating a "studies" around what she called the "historical" subject of women mirror the consolidation of academic disciplines. Her critique of masculine reason poked a clever stick into the gaze being stabilized in the postrevolutionary 1980s. In this analysis, her greatest significance was her reinvention of the rationale for placing women at the center of historical evolution. In the future (as in the archaic past), she argued, natural species life would join the forward development of national social life. At the end of history there would be the natural affinity, the sexual key to enlightened modernity, of women and men. Perhaps it is an overinterpretation to see in Li's crisis point of the "sexual gap" a way of readdressing the question of sexual selection and natural social development. In any case, the future is where women belong who are both different erotically from men and men's equivalent socially and economically. Only when the market has commodified social relations and created the conditions for such choices will parity be achieved.

In the disturbing transformation of Chinese cities from shabby, relatively orderly bureaucratic centers of autarkic state planning to global cities ringed with migrant workers' camps during the 1990s, the despairing optimism of Dai Jinhua points to a future that only women can create for themselves, must create for themselves. It is unclear at this point in her unfolding critique of culture where this future orientation will lead Dai. I have argued that she returns periodically to the écriture féminine chinoise as a way of tempering her pessimism and pointing toward a future that truly is being written by women for women. But in the city of mirrors, where the sign of woman is always a cathexis, a bridge, in Dai's language, and where desire is cycled through mass cultural images in film, TV, video, computer, and advertising, the future is unclear. A reconsolidation of heroic patriarchy in film culture led back to the carnival of sons and to the investment of fathers, to the detriment of women's slow surfacing into representation as themselves. Yet the future is dark. How well the project of women's feminism can point to a future that is any kind of improvement on the past Dai leaves up to women writers like those she and Meng Yue canonized. It may be a bleak future. Nonetheless (in a move that surprises when perhaps it should not), Dai remains oriented to the future.

My arguments in the book's final chapters parallel Robert Young's discussion of the debt linking psychoanalysis to nineteenth-century discourses of racism through the notion of hybridity. I drew attention to ways that eugenic and psychoanalytic reasoning, and the feminisms that have emerged out of them, mirror each other because of their shared preoccupation with human bio-social reproduction. The stages of infant development and the subject's accession into the Symbolic through the processes of attachment, cathection, castration, and so on proceed "naturally" only because the theory came to presume that heterosexual difference is the key to the acquisition of social subjectivity. The sexual instinct to cross difference in order to reproduce the species is given as the basic drive forming the male subject in its tortured relation to the disavowed, remaindered, derelict female Other. Psychoanalytic arguments like Lacan's and Dai's root themselves in the eugenic grounds of progressive feminism, because they also situate the engine of social causality at the level of species survival (at the very least, because to survive, the infant must come to terms with its instinctive drives). Psychoanalytic feminisms and evolutionary progressive feminisms hold common intellectual commitments to the ideas that the foundational drive in human social life is species reproduction; the social expression of this drive is complex and often tortured; and the achievement of adequacy among human subjects is rare and difficult. In the Lacanian version of the argument, the Oedipal drama recapitulates what is alleged to be the developmental framework of subjectivity itself.[2]

I began this book with a discussion of history writing. I argued that the future anterior tense is useful because it draws attention to the human scale of thinking. The generalizations that people make about existence are not mere representations and do not directly reflect social fact. For that reason my study is not a history of ideas as such. Rather, I have attempted to excavate and to describe the social object—so-called women—and the analytic categories that intellectuals and ideologues in the twentieth century established when they wrote feminist theory. The future anterior mode dismisses the possibility of ever knowing what women *are* (that would be a biogenetic argument) and focuses rather on what women *must have been* (a speculative, historical argument). I have sought wherever possible to write in the future anterior and to not presume that theoretical or speculative writing directly reflects or reports social fact. What Gao Xian and Ding Ling, Cai Chang and Li Xiaojiang thought in the immediate past about what women of the future would be is the datum that has particularly interested me, on a number of grounds. Because it is itself a claim and because it is a claim about the potential women embody, it refuses to ratify the position that woman is any one thing. Because feminist theoretical writing specifies its own subjects, it lays open to our scrutiny the pattern of conditioned speculation that motivated thinking people. Not claiming to be representation (mimesis), the future anterior mode in history writing is particularly useful for understanding what is happening when theorists take up enlightenment claims.[3]

Where and how the enlightened claims of women's humanity are made and who makes them all matter. I have shown in detail how theorists described the speculative and sometimes even imaginary subject of women in Chinese feminism. Particular attention has been paid to the vocabularies or lexicons in play, and to how individual theorists and cohorts of theorists naturalized these words. I documented how both the name given to the imaginary collective of women and the rationales for this subject's liberation have changed many times in the dominant traditions over the twentieth century. And I have brought the discussion back constantly to preoccupations that theorists themselves repeatedly returned to. Among these, the question of female personality and its adequacy for women's social standing proved to be one of the most pervasive and frequently reiterated. Another constantly reencountered experience for theorists has been the question of how to situate sexual difference.

Because the subject of women in Chinese feminism, like the subject of women in other national traditions, probably originated in relation to eugenic and social evolutionary theories, the question of sexual difference has had as much to do with national and racial biopower as with the search for sexual pleasure. Yet the question of sexuality—the modern disciplinization of erotic drives—has been a strong current in feminist speculation since the 1920s. In the works of Ding Ling, Li Xiaojiang, and Dai Jinhua, the topic of how an adequate female historical subject finds acceptable avenues for erotic expression is presumed and argued.

A third singularity in the Chinese iteration of the Enlightenment goal of women's emancipation is obviously its relationship to the Communist social revolution. The opinions of theorists on this matter have gyrated wildly. The great drama of Ding Ling's life was, as I have argued, the tortured, ambivalent, and at moments triumphant engagement with the unrepresented mass of illiterate, beggared rural women of the revolutionary base areas and the far reaches of the gulag state farm. At some points angry restorationists like Li Xiaojiang and her immediate post-Mao cohort argued that the socialist women's movement, far from expanding the lives of the rural poor, had interrupted and destroyed the sine qua non of any national women's movement: autonomy from the state apparatus.[4] Seen in the light of neoliberal reforms twenty years later, a critic as uncompromising as Dai Jinhua has recently argued that, on the contrary, the imposition of de jure rights on Chinese women by the state may be the only thing standing between female citizen and virtual statelessness in the postsocialist market economy.[5] Lin Chun, a Marxist feminist theorist living in London, has argued (correctly, in my view) that this more than anything will prove to be the durable contribution of Chinese feminist thinking to other streams of international liberation theory.[6]

The specificities of Chinese feminist predication of the female subject of liberation does not change one fact, however. All of the work I have read in detail here participated directly or indirectly in international flows of theory. The claims they make are universal claims. They constitute in and of themselves a claim to the universal. Yes, the Chinese feminist tradition is nationalist. All feminist traditions are, even the imperialist ones that have reached out to the unfortunate Other, which is a fact well documented since Anna Davin's pathbreaking work on imperial motherhood in the 1970s.

To a great degree, this study has approached the question of singular universals through the thesis that theory itself is a datum in history writing.

I do not suppose, in other words, that the history of philosophy is history per se. Theory is culpable. It is ideology in the last instance, as Spivak has argued.[7] But it is also the means through which we take the measure of the thinkable in our own given conditions, given because they are not subject to our own making. I have also supposed throughout this study that theory is not just abstraction but abstraction from something, some element in the world. Further, although enlightened theories are abstractions—the rights of man, the equality of women, the stature of science, the nature of society—they encapsulate the conditions of their making. These elements of the conditions that gave rise to the thinking appear in the thought, are embedded there, just as Chakrabarty says Marxism has stuck in its labor theory of value certain cultural assumptions about what a (British, male, working-class, etc.) "worker" is. To point this out is not to vitiate the claim that universals are valuable or possible. It only says that nestled in the conditions of the making of universal claims, the desire for general truths, are the specific conditions of their production. These do not travel. The assumptions or elements stuck in the theory present to the context (both the place of origination and the place of recoding) real lacunae, real aporia. They are aporia in theoretical or philosophic language, but, I have argued implicitly, they are opportunities in historical language. And that is why the historical catachresis is so useful.[8]

But the internationalism of the theory flows pursued in this history of the question of women in Chinese feminism—social evolutionary thought, eugenic theory, Hegelianism, social science theory, Marxism, French existentialism, écriture féminine—leads to a final problematic: How are these ideas universals? Whom do universals belong to? Particularly in my discussion of the contingent foundations set in the 1920s and 1930s of progressive Chinese feminism, I have suggested that consistent with the findings of Anthony Pagden, Dipesh Chakrabarty, Chetan Bhatt, and others, what Bhatt calls "inadvertent complicity" shaped not just the way theoretical subjects appeared in colonial and semicolonial contexts but how the colonizers came to make universalist arguments in the first case. Bhatt's argument is apropos because he is concerned with how Enlightenment ideas incorporated themselves around human differences. What he calls the "consideration of the differentiated places of non-Europeans in the European idea of founding civilization" means that in the process of consolidating enlightened humanism, the philosophies drew lavishly on ethnographic and textual elements from India and elsewhere. The observations and the very peoples, flora, and fauna that populate the philosophic ethnographies of philosophes, social scientists, and European anthropological sex theorists are, in this approach, constituent elements, rather than the Others, of Europe. The interpenetration of Herder's thought and the contents of his universal histories form a universal, which is to say an effort at generalization that is inclusive. This is what Bhatt calls "inadvertent complicity" in the thought of Herder, Hegel, Rousseau, Kant et al. and does not call hybridity (a psychoanalytic term developed in eugenics of racial mixing).[9] The "inadvertent complicity with European *and non-European* discourses of civilization" (Bhatt's emphasis) suggests that it is only in the presence of difference that the claim of universality became truly compelling; only when the difference is inadvertently and irreversibly present does the exploration of and explanation for sameness become compulsory. The wedding of universality to superior political or economic power may be contingent, which is only to say historical, but it is an effective means of control or social power. That would be, among others, the powers that accrued to modern intellectuals and particularly to theorists.

A great prize of enlightened thinking is, of course, that compromised and eugenic subject woman. Since the first Chinese Enlightenment and the eruption of the modern subject nüxing, rudiments of the feminist liberation movement have been a part of the Chinese international women's movement. This study stops far short of tracing out the affiliations that Chinese intellectuals and activists struck with international labor, international communism, and the international effort at population control. I have argued implicitly that even without justifying thought through good works, the subject woman in feminisms remains a valuable, an irreplaceable resource. Women is a hallucinatory subject where it appears in feminist theory, for, as decades of scholarship have established, women have virtually nothing in common when differences of class, nationality, ethnicity, sexuality, social standing, political affiliation, and cultural practices are properly calculated and described. And as the roots of women is excavated and its systematic origins in many highly questionable philosophic and theoretical projects of the modern era are also tabulated and aired, the project of feminism will necessarily still go on. Until the goal of rough equity is achieved, theoretical projects will always be necessary. Whether these projects are sustainable in responsible thought is a chronic concern; whether they are capable of reaching the goal set is questionable. The dubious and compromised subject of woman is indispensable because there is no other way to approach the problem posed in the event of women.

# Appendix to Chapter 1:
## Historiography and Catachresis

Keeping in mind the instability of all categories within the arrested contemporary moment, the historical catachresis lends stability to such singular events as the event of woman in modernity. What debates in feminist theory over the past decade suggest, then, are ways out of Dorothy Ko's impasse. Rather than conflating "gender" with "women" or women's self-consciousness, three landmark studies in women's social history suggest useful ways of writing catachrestically. Lata Mani's landmark essay "Contentious Traditions," which opened an impasse similar to Ko's, Nell Painter's "Representing Truth: Sojourner Truth's Knowing and Becoming Known," a discussion of why unmediated access to women is not possible, and Mrinalini Sinha's "Gender in the Critiques of Colonialism and Nationalism: Locating the 'Indian Woman,'" which offered the catachresis "Indian women," illustrate the general point and its resolution.[1]

In a remarkable pathbreaking essay, Lata Mani argued that to approach the question of what she called "female agency" or a "complex notion of female subjectivity" (106) in colonial India, a feminist historian would have to locate her work at the intersection of certain key discourses of modernity. This Mani did by selecting as her subject contemporary debates over sati. Mani read the debates and argued that colonial social welfare legislation regarding widow immolation, child marriage, and other social ills actually rested on a perverse *modernist* formulation of tradition that made local women's voluntarism unrepresentable because colonially imposed grids were figuring Indian womanhood through the metonym of widow burning. A "matrix of constraints" (91) shaping the debate, moreover, sanctioned the collusion of indigenous and imperialist patriarchies, reinforcing male dominance and resituating men's power in a colonial world defined by imperialism and nativism. Working in this matrix, Mani's nuanced, lavishly researched essay concluded that "official discourse forecloses any possibility of women's agency, thus providing justification for 'civilizing' colonial interventions" (98). In sum, patriarchal theorists omitted representations of women's "voices" by casting female subjects as either superslaves in colonial discourses or superhumans in nativist works, always through the metonymy of the widow on the pyre and thus always as a "currency" (119) of exchange among the men, who were just then inventing the nationalist core of Bengali colonial modernity.

For me, the question is what Mani's work made impossible with this analysis. In this sort of discourse analysis there is no way to conceive of gendered, catechresetic subjects other than as women that are affirmatively present (even if only by virtue of the metaphysics of presence) in the documents that she read. Asides scattered throughout the analysis, such as "It is difficult to know how to interpret these accounts, *for we have no independent access* to the mental or subjective states of widows outside these overdetermined colonial representations of them," and "In any case, the meaning of consent in a patriarchal context is hard to assess" (97), are symptomatic. They assume the possibility of unmediated access to indigenous women that somehow the conditions of colonialism precluded. This, of course, was exactly the element of Mani's argument that inspired Gayatri Spivak's fateful question, "Can the subaltern speak?" Unfortunately, Spivak made moot the historiographic stakes by shifting theoretical interest from what Mani would call context to what Spivak calls text. But I want to return to Mani's flat and enigmatic statement that the official colonial representations of women she read interested her because they "foreclosed any possibility of women's agency," and in doing so provide the colonists with grounds "for 'civilizing' colonial interventions" (98). When women were silenced, they apparently became the supine foundation of colonial modernity and its complex forms of governmentality.

Mani's ambivalence is extremely attractive. What she says is that an official discourse (imperialists mediating power through selected pundits) foreclosed all representation of women as agents. This is a historian's concern, just as the question of whether or not a subaltern "speaks" is a literary philosopher's conundrum. But what Mani does not say in the essay is how broadly she intended her historical point to be extended. Did she mean that such activity had continued elsewhere, out of sight of the colonizing machinery? Or did she believe that women in the Indian colonial matrix had lost the ability to represent themselves? Had they represented themselves as "women" before colonialism? Mani opens a question about simple representation, in other words: Is the silence or absence of women a foreclosure, a ban, or is it a silence in the absence of a reliable signifier? This is the question that links her study to the problematic that Ko raised at the conclusion of her monograph. At its most general level, it is the question of how women is represented and how the trope of women is defined in social or discursive terms.

This last question of historical representation is particularly well elaborated in Nell Painter's "Representing Truth." Painter investigates how a self-manumitted slave, Isabella Van Wagner, became a feminist icon, Sojourner Truth, and therefore a testament to contemporary, multicultural styles of academic feminism. The apocryphal event of Sojourner Truth, speaking before a suffrage gathering of white women in Akron, Ohio in 1851, ripping open her blouse to show her breast and declaim, "And ain't I a woman?" went unquestioned because it assured U.S. feminist historians that despite the patent racialism of the dominant feminist discourse, even a slave could assert her claims to womanhood and consequently to be like all women universally. Painter reiterates the Spivakian point that subelites are never exactly mooted, they just do not necessarily speak the same language as the more powerful discourses in which they (or elite representations of them) are embedded. Addressing the "specific historical juncture" (464) where the event of Van Wagner's transformation into Truth took place, Painter argued that though it was certainly true that white, racist feminists had used their own language to fashion an iconic slavewoman who spoke the truth of feminism, Sojourner Truth herself was not simply used or positioned by those more powerful than she: she also "used language—as self-fashioning" (462).

Feminist historians run a risk, I think, of assuming that beneath all the differences of race, class, region, and historical era women are not only similar, but should have the right to be recognized as women and to control their own representation. This logic seems to have caused the problem for Mani and led her to hesitate uncomfortably as she considered the question of so-called agency in widow self-immolation. In the end, she settled on a compromise argument: although woman appears in colonial discourses as the site of masculinist political discourse, outside patriarchal-colonial discourses real women exist, albeit silently. In Mani's view, the problems seemed to be that the women themselves had not left behind direct testimonials of their experience or self-authorized representations of themselves as women, but also that historians do not have unmediated access to women. In a word, Mani posed virtually the same question that Painter addressed when she took up the question of the history of "truth" in feminist historiography.

Painter's essay allows us to deepen Mani's problematic in some ways. She presents the reader with the story of a slavewoman who did not read or write and whose historical existence or persistence as a historical figure rests on a dominant white, middle-class U.S. radical feminist tradition in the archive. Had it not been for Frances Gage, for instance, the remarkable itinerant preacher, Sojourner Truth would no doubt have been forgotten altogether, and yet because of Gage and a string of others like her the singular subject of the evangelical, female, freed slave Isabella is remembered for things she did not do. The abolitionists and feminists who made her famous wrote about Sojourner Truth in anachronistic, racist terms and even, in some cases, fabricated stories and bogus eyewitness accounts. But in the end Painter rests her case on contingency. The very racist misrepresentations of Truth, she notes, preserved traces of Isabella into the present, where a Nell Painter could retrieve a new sense of Sojourner Truth, the historical, archival specificity. In other words, Painter declined to choose between *no representation* of the woman herself and the view that all representations of women are mediations allowing men to act out representational strategies among themselves. Sojourner Truth, in Painter's view, was not only obviously present in history, but she was just not interested in or capable of self-representation in the institutional framework of dominant categories of adequacy.[2]

Like Painter and Mani, Mrinalini Sinha takes up R. Radhakrishnan's question of how gendered historical subjects take "shape under highly determinate and limited historical circumstances."[3] Sinha moves the argument away from individuals or representation per se to political subjectivity. Her study notes that a century after the sati discussion that Mani's work analyzed, there erupted in the United States, Britain, and India in 1927 an international controversy. The controversy focused on the imperialist feminist panegyric *Mother India*, and it reiterated the opposition of imperialists versus nationalists that Mani had discovered in the sati debates. But this time, the struggle broke out internationally over how to characterize Indian women. Imperialist feminist American writer Katherine Mayo and her Indian allies took the position that Indian women needed enlightened Western women to rescue them from Indian men. On the other side were various kinds of nationalist feminist, educated, middle-class Indian women, who responded politically to Mayo's damning characterizations of their alleged social and religious practices. Sinha's point is that unlike the standoff between British imperialists and indigenous nationalists over the body of the sati, the twentieth-century debates actually mobilized a new subject called woman. What earlier had been the passive ground or body where men used to display their differences became the nationalist, activist, political "Indian woman." Moreover, Sinha argued, the historical emergence into political life of this subject woman meant two things: first, that women's struggle for the means of representation was a part of nationalist politics per se; second, that its efflorescence in the newly forming middle class as a part of what defined public and private experiences meant that by 1927 class formation offered a space for the mobilization of middle-class women themselves.

Sinha's discussion is important because "Indian womanhood" is a historical catachresis. Her "voice of Indian womanhood itself" (480) is irreducible, yet it is the product of learned or conditioned historical behavior. Her essay draws on two historiographic streams. She combines poststructuralist feminist theories of contingent foundations with the Subaltern Studies historical research agenda to focus on how one particular gendered historical subject formed itself out of the colonial detritus—nationalist ideological reaction formations, racist eugenics, imperialist feminist benevolence, bits of colonized religiosity, indigenous patriarchies reinforced by imperialist governmentality—and called itself the Indian woman. Indian woman was not a self-representation. It was not the realization of a previously obscured subject who was finally able to represent herself accurately. Sinha's central point is that middle-class "women *learned to speak in the voices of the Indian woman*" (479; emphasis added) and took up a subject form, enabled within a masculinist nationalist discourse, as a means of mobilizing themselves, for better or worse, as Indian feminists. Finally, the historical experience of becoming Indian women is occult now. In ideologies of neoliberal "international feminism," the phrase "Indian women" itself has become a multicultural modifier of essential woman.

Obviously, this leaves open the possibility that there also existed gendered subject forms that never belonged in the project of the Indian woman, that were not bhadralok or middle class. Such people may just have been too busy, as Sara Suleri put it, for "the concept of woman" to be "really part of an available vocabulary [being] . . . too busy for that, just living, and conducting precise negotiations with what it meant to be a sister or a child or a wife or a mother or a servant."[4] In other words, when a historian finds a historical subject in complex political discourses, its presence does not mean that the agency of oppressed or nonelites is obviated. Painter's study of Sojourner Truth made this case when she wrote into the story various contingencies that had played into Truth's history. To describe a subject contextually does not obviate the lives of gendered subjects unfolding somewhere outside of the dominant, masculinist, or middle-class center. Specificity, singularity, the formula of premising the historical real on positive, archival records of how gendered subject forms work and when they appear historically means that it is also possible to write about subjects that are neither foundationally oppositional (the commonly argued feminist thesis that women are always the Other of nationalism), nor constitutionally voiced (another common feminist argument based on a version of the repressive hypothesis and holding that women are silenced by men), nor just defined in relation to something called men as what enables men to be themselves.[5]

The catachristic historical subject Indian woman in Sinha's work or women in Chinese feminism in my own was mediated through conditions of great stress: imperial feminism, eugenic demographics, nationalist politics, colonial studies of subject populations, and other great events. The question now is how the efflorescence of women in colonial modernity can be exhumed and explained. Here the focus must narrow. In her influential essay "Woman as Sign," Elizabeth Cowie argued that to address the question of women in film, it is necessary to distinguish between "woman as a category and . . . film as a signifying system."[6] Cowie reread Lévi-Strauss critically, showing that analogous distinctions operated between kinship as "a structure through which men and women are put into place" and "kinship as a system of communication." Her subsequent point was particularly useful to feminist historians. "It is not that women as women are situated in the family," she argued. "But that it is in the family—as the effect of kinship structures—that women as women are produced, are defined within and by the group" (131). In semiotics, at least, there could be no one-to-one relationship between the universal woman of modernist discourse and specific signs women in signifying systems, except in biomedical discourses. Signs, in Cowie's own words, including the signs designating or signifying woman, are "only meaningful within the system of signification in which they are produced, and not as discrete units" (125).

Cowie's "productivist" argument resonates with discussions that Joan Scott and Denise Riley have pioneered in feminist historiography. When Scott first suggested that gender was the cultural clothing that women wore over their sex, she was arguing that in, historical studies, the term "gender" should refer to "a constitutive element of social relationships based on the perceived differences between the sexes." Critics pointed out that this definition left the problem of heterosexual "sex difference" intact.[7] It was Riley's Am I That Name? Feminism and the Category of "Women" that clapped the inverted commas around the noun women, arguing that Women was, in the famous phrase, "historically, discursively constructed, and always relatively to other categories which themselves change . . . a volatile collectivity in which female persons can be very differently positioned . . . [because] 'being a woman' . . . can't provide an ontological foundation."[8]

Riley's position is that the name women is itself what I am calling a historical catachresis. For Riley, Women was a term that exceeded specificity, yet somehow was a historical composite. It was consequently larger than Cowie's cultural sign system and necessarily had archival or discursive depth. Moreover, women transformed its content and significance under the shifting rules of play in subsequent discursive regimes. It was therefore only indirectly referential, because the signs and the rules of ideological play would change through time, and though women proved in her history of it to be hardy and viable, women also struck Riley as being quite "volatile." Riley's general point was historiographic. All history writing, including feminist historiography, exists in larger discursive formations such as social science or biblical exegesis, which may or may not be penned by women but do condition where the subject women appears and what role it plays at any given moment. Women and men normalize their gendered relationships—become women and men—through the ideological play of *savoir/pouvoir* in relation to modes of production, relations of production, and reproductive practices. Like Mani, Singha, Painter, and Scott, Riley sought to understand the history of how a sign women in a specific archive or argument in turn conditioned what could be considered to be a woman in a moment blasted out of the past.[9]

There is a major drawback to Riley's position. It ignored the degree to which, in Britain, the modern subject woman has been construed in relations with colonial others. In other words, it did not provide an adequate context or frame. This blindness to colonial modernity somewhat weakens her historiographic position because her history, being the history of a nation, turns into a simple teleology. When it does not consider the past in terms of the burden of imperialism, it effectively transforms women into nothing more than a direct referent to Britain's nationalist history. This does not abrogate the value of her insight. Like the work of Mani, Riley's represents a significant contribution to feminist historiography since it claims that women is a historically catechrestic figure because there can never be a consolidated signified (a "unit," in Cowie's language, a concept-metaphor without an adequate signifier, in Spivak's) leading back to the same universal thing.[10] Thus, helpful and interesting as it is, as historiography *Am I That Name?* precludes ways of reading the evidence.

In the complex historical relations and historiographic evidence of gendered subjects and domains, then, the subject women has become possible for certain kinds of people at certain moments that historians blast from the past. Writing these histories cannot be the province of one sex or another, one subject or another, one nation at the expense of colonizing another. The presumption that when women control the signification of women in social history, for instance, the true history of women will reveal itself suggests a level of direct referentiality that the historical documents do not support. This is precisely the point where the projection of anachronism into the past is most potent. That is frustrating. But it is also invigorating.

In Benjamin's writing of the redemptive power of history, the angel's backward look counters the tendency in history writing to suck all the various heterogeneous evidence of the past directly back into the ideological preoccupations of the present. As I read Benjamin, he poses a possibility for the blasting away of the shackles of the present in order that other possibilities as yet unexplored might be remembered or reclaimed. In each moment stopped in time there will turn out to be a future anterior of another human present. It may very well be the case, as I suggested in chapter 2, that women is an anachronism in the social history of Chinese women before the advent of colonial modernity. Yet when the archives reopen on this question, as in chapter 3, the figure that emerges is not women in Riley's sense or even women in the theoretical and ideological formation of an eighteenth-century Confucian like Chen Hongmou, but rather other, equally enigmatic figures, starting with the historical catachresis of nüxing in the 1920s. Women is a historical catachresis with a concrete existence in the historical archives of international feminism. "Woman," if we are historically contextual and specific, is as irredeemably and ideologically intransitive as nüxing. They are intransitive (and here is where I differ with Riley's intellectual history) because women and nüxing each represents the crystallization of specific historemes into globalized categoricals.[11]

The problem with anachronism is that it obviates historical evidence of gendered subjects who may not be women in Riley's, Mani's, or Sinha's terms but who did leave evidence of their activities. It is useful to call these agents by their proper names: funü, furen, nüren, nüxing, and so on. These proper names represent an effort in an ideological formation to think about and to regulate experience. The niceness of these distinctions and specificities is that they make it possible for the historian to register changes in sources and to pay attention to them. The fundamental point, however, is that no matter how useful or even necessary, women is not a sufficient historiographic category: it does not accommodate the historical evidence and it also has a history of its own that, as Riley points out, is highly complex and contingent. Painter shows that the empiricist's dream of direct access to historical subjects is not only unreasonable, but it also is not benign. The claim of a British social history historiography or a nineteenth-century U.S. abolitionist feminism might achieve a great deal in its moment. But even emancipatory projects that promise to authorize a universal identity for all women run the risk of burying evidence of the very social forces that have brought into existence, albeit unevenly and at great social cost, a modernity that made women a foundational social category.[12]

# Notes

Unless otherwise specified, all translations from Chinese are mine.

## Introduction

1   I credit this insight to my reading of Dipesh Chakrabarty's important essay "The Condition for Knowledge of Working Class Conditions," in Ranajit Guha and Gayatri Charavorty Spivak, eds., *Selected Subaltern Studies* (New York: Oxford University Press, 1988), 179–332.

2   Joan Wallach Scott, *Only Paradoxes to Offer: French Feminists and the Rights of Man* (Cambridge, MA: Harvard University Press, 1996).

3   Andrew Barshay, "Toward a History of the Social Sciences in Japan," *positions: east asia cultures critique* 4, no. 2 (1996): 217–52.

4   Nancy Friday, *The Power of Beauty* (New York: Harper Collins, 1996). See also Randy Thornhill and Craig T. Palmer, *A Natural History of Rape: Biological Bases of Sexual Coercion* (Cambridge, MA: MIT Press, 2000); Erica Goode, "Human Nature: Born or Made? Evolutionary Theorists Provoke an Uproar," *New York Times*, Science Times, 14 March 2000: D1, D9; Robert J. C. Young, *Colonial Desire: Hybridity in Theory, Culture and Race* (New York: Routledge, 1995). Francis Fukuyama has hinted that eugenics will continue to play a central role in theoretical work in the near future. See his "Biotechnology and the Future of Politics," *Daily Yomiuri*, 5 March 2001: D6.

5   An exciting discussion of the relationship of colonial and revolutionary modernities appears in Lin Chun, "The Transformation of Chinese Socialism: An Interpretation," unpublished manuscript, 2002.

6   Slavoj Žižek, "Psychoanalysis in Post-Marxism: The Case of Alain Badiou," in *South Atlantic Quarterly*, 97:2 (spring) 1998, 239–40: "Advocates of 'Anti-essentialist' identity politics . . . tend to stress that there is no 'women in general,' only White middle-class women, Black single mothers, lesbians and so on and so forth. . . . The problem for philosophical thought resides precisely in how the universality of 'woman' emerges from this 'infinite' multiple, a problem that also enables one to rehabilitate the Hegelian distinction between bad ('spurious') and true infinity: the first refers to the common-sense infinite complexity, while the second concerns the infinity of an Event which transcends, precisely, the 'infinite complexity' of its context. A homogolous distinction can be drawn between historicism and historicity proper: historicism refers to the set of circumstances (economic, political, cultural, etc.) whose complex interactions allow us

to account for a given event, while historicity proper involves the specific temporality of the Event and its aftermath, the span between the Event and its ultimate End." See also Lila Abu-Lughod, ed., *Remaking Women: Feminism and Modernity in the Middle East* (Princeton: Princeton University Press, 1998); Emma Perez, "Feminism-in-Nationalism: The Gendered Subaltern at the Yucatán Feminist Congresses of 1916," in *Between Woman and Nation: Nationalism, Transnational Feminisms and the State*, ed. Caren Kaplan, Norma Alarcon, and Minoo Moallemn (Durham, NC: Duke University Press, 1999), 219–39.

7   This is a version of Sylvain Lazarus's position. See Natacha Michel and Sylvain Lazarus, unpublished interview (April 1999). I thank Claudia Pozzana and Alessandro Russo for introducing me to this text. Lowe, Pozzana, and Russo created a rough translation in May 1999.

8   See Philip Corrigan and Derek Sayer, *The Great Arch: English State Formation as Cultural Revolution* (Oxford: Basil Blackwell, 1985) for a discussion of the heterogeneity of the subject Woman in the cultural modernity project of England. See Young, *Colonial Desire*, for analysis of the eugenic heritage of theoretical words like "desire" and "hybridity." Also see Laura Engelstein, *The Keys to Happiness: Sex and the Search for Modernity in Fin-de-Siècle Russia* (Ithaca, NY: Cornell University Press, 1992); Sumiko Otsubo, "Engendering Eugenics: Japanese Feminists and Marriage Restriction Legislation in the 1920s," in *Gendering Modern Japanese History*, ed. Barbara Molony and Kathleen Uno (Cambridge, MA: Council on East Asian Studies, Harvard University, forthcoming); Sumiko Otsubo and James R. Bartholomew, "Eugenics in Japan: Some Ironies of Modernity, 1883–1945," *Science in Context* 11, nos. 3–4 (1998): 545–65; Yoko Matsubara, "The Enactment of Japan's Sterilization Laws in the 1940s: A Prelude to Postwar Eugenic Policy," *Historia Scientiarum* 8–12 (1998): 187–201.

9   Tani E. Barlow, "Colonialism's Career in Postwar China Studies" and introduction in *Formations of Colonial Modernity in East Asia*, ed. Tani Barlow (Durham, NC: Duke University Press, 1997). See also Barlow, "Colonial Modernity and Semi-colonialism as Constituent Problems in Post-colonial Gender Theories" unpublished manuscript, 2002.

10  Wendy Brown, *States of Injury: Power and Freedom in Late Modernity* (Princeton: Princeton University Press, 1995).

11  See Peter Osborne, "Modernism as Translation," *Traces* 1 (2001): 319–30, for the term "real abstraction." Alain Badiou discusses his concept of the event in "Being by Numbers: Lauren Sedofsky talks with Alain Badiou," *Artforum* 33, no. 2 (October 1994): 84–87, 118, 123–24. Also see Jean-Jacques Lecercle, "Cantor, Lacan, Mao, Beckett, même combat: The Philosophy of Alain Badiou," *Radical Philosophy: A Journal of Socialist and Feminist Philosophy* 93 (January/February 1999): 6–13; Alain Badiou and Peter Hallward, "Politics and Philosophy: An Interview with Alain Badiou," *Angelaki: Journal of the Theoretical Humanities* 3, no. 3 (1998): 113–33. C. Colwell has explored the use of the category of the event in Gilles Deleuze in "Deleuze and Foucault: Series, Event and Genealogy," *theory and event* 1, no. 2 (1997): http://muse.jhu.edu/journals/theory_and_event/v001/1.2colwell.html.

12  Madhu Dubey, "The 'True Lie' of the Nation: Fanon and Feminism," *differences* 10, no. 2 (1998): 7. Dubey cites Cherfati-Merabtine as supposing that revolutionary nationalism enables women to "become subjects of history."

13  Thinking through the catachreses nüxing and funü in nature and culture allowed Ding Ling, and later critics Li Xiaojiang, Dai Jinhua, and their associates, access to truths of their era that are not available elsewhere. It is not simply that these female thinkers think as "women." They do. But a related, significant point is that their thinking, in all its persistent tentativeness and frequent failures, reveals things about contemporary events

that are commonly obscured. Buried in Ding Ling's claims to revolution, to be a revolutionary, is a further, never satisfied demand: that the feminine be recognized in its excessive inexpression precisely within the revolutionary moment. Li Xiaojiang's demand that the scandal of Reason (i.e., the exclusion of women from Humanity) be universally considered in philosophy; Dai Jinhua's demand that women be decommissioned from service in the carnival of the sons and the constellations of patriarchal transmission of culture, and that it be painfully reenlisted by women themselves in self-history; Du Fangqin's stubborn rewriting of the entire text of Confucianism through the postrevolutionary feminist mentality: each of these projects forwards the subject woman historically in trajectories followed out in this history of the catachresis woman in Chinese feminism, while at the same time allowing insight, making possible sight into a historical moment that, but for these feminist practices, would be lost and covered over.

14  See, for instance, Joan Copjec, *Read My Desire: Lacan against the Historicists* (Cambridge, MA: MIT Press, 1994).

15  See a fully developed position on this matter in Naoki Sakai, *Translation and Subjectivity: On "Japan" and Cultural Nationalism* (Minneapolis: University of Minnesota Press, 1997).

16  Yi Jiayue and Luo Dunwei, *Zhongguo jiating wenti* (The Chinese family question) (Shanghai: Taidong tushuju yinghang, 1928).

## 1.  History and Catachresis

1  Judith Butler, "For a Careful Reading," in *Feminist Contentions: A Philosophical Exchange*, ed. Seyla Benhabib et al. (New York: Routledge, 1995), 127–43.

2  The origins of the debate over gender history and representation may be seen in Joan Wallach Scott, *Gender and the Politics of History* (New York: Columbia University Press, 1988). Also see Naoki Sakai, "Modernity and Its Critique: The Problem of Universalism and Particularism," *South Atlantic Quarterly* 87, no. 3 (summer 1988): 475–504.

3  Diane Elam, *Feminism and Deconstruction* (New York: Routledge, 1994), 41. "Distinct from the three historical tenses of past, present, and future, history written in the future anterior doesn't claim to know in advance what it is women can do and be: the radical potentiality of women does not result from a break with the past, nor is it to be found in any form of assurance provided by the past or the present. Instead, the future anterior emphasizes radical uncertainty and looks to its own transformation. . . . history written in the future anterior is a message that is handed over to an unknown addressee and accepts that its meaning in part will have to depend upon that addressee."

4  A useful debate over the term "future anterior" appears in Seyla Benhabib et al., eds., *Feminist Contentions: A Philosophical Exchange* (New York: Routledge, 1995) between Judith Butler and Drucilla Cornell. Briefly, Cornell credits the inspiration for history in the future anterior to Jacques Lacan and argues that a feminist Lacanian temporality in history writing would signal the potential for a utopian feminine beyond the unequal social relations of the immediate present, which reduces femininity to a deficient version of masculinity. Cornell argues that Joan Scott is such a historian. Butler, on the other hand, points out that the Lacanian Symbolic is a simple projection of specific notions of normalized heterosexuality. So any use of the future anterior tense in history writing would need to acknowledge that sexual difference is "neither more primary than other forms of social difference, nor . . . understandable outside of a complex mapping of social power" (Butler, "For a Careful Reading," 142, and in the same volume, Cornell, "Rethinking the Time of Feminism," 145–56).

I encountered the notion of future anteriority in Diane Elam's useful outline *Feminism and Deconstruction*. It allowed me to resolve a theoretical and practical problem that I had struggled over for some time. Elam credits her insight not to Lacan but to Christina Crosby's monograph *The Ends of History: Victorians and "The Woman Question"* (New York: Routledge, 1991), in the same way that Cornell credits Scott's *Gender and History*. Elam and Cornell, in other words, each point to a historical monograph to prove their theoretical point. Elam, Cornell, and Butler are all working in the tradition established in the late 1970s in the first explosive debates among Althusserian Marxists and Lacanian psychoanalysis in, among other places, the influential theory journal *m/f*. The issue was how Women should be constructed in feminism, thus as subject in feminist histories of women. The immediate problem, then, was elemental: If women are made of more than just language (constituted discursively in today's cant), then what is the nature of the excess or exteriority of language?

Over the twenty-five years that Lacanian debates have shaped theoretical feminism, their most important contribution, in my view, has been to logic. The disruptiveness of Lacan's logical conundra has made it difficult to continue within the simple developmental logics of ego psychology or simple historical positivism. I do want to point out, however, that theorists have yet to grasp the proper strengths that historians bring to writing and thinking about history. "History" appears in the writing of many theorists as a rather amorphous entity detached from the historians who research and write it. A good example of my point is the frustration animating the exchange between Joan Scott and Gayatri Spivak in "Feminism in Decolonization," *differences* 3, no. 3 (fall 1991): 139–75, in which the latter tries but does not really meet the standard for reading evidence historically, while the former is a bit overly polite about the Spivak offering.

5   Elam, *Feminism and Deconstruction*, 41. On the importance of avoiding modernist anachronism, see Christian de Pee, "The Negotiation and Renegotiation of Premodern Chinese Marriage: Text as Practice versus Text into Practice," *positions* 9, no. 3 (winter 2001).

6   Elam, *Feminism and Deconstruction*, 41: "I want to argue that feminist analysis must be a deconstruction of representation that keeps the category of women incessantly in question, as a permanently contested site of meaning."

7   Rosemary Hennessy, *Materialist Feminism and the Politics of Discourse* (New York: Routledge, 1992).

8   A similar position explores how my reluctance to accept idealist categories can be worked through the concept of ideology. Hennessy also cautions that the feminist anxiety to locate an agent, Woman, for feminism and women's movements may be misplaced. Hennessy holds that feminism is the task of forming collectivities for the future. The project involves assuming nothing about the other women except through grounded frames of intelligibility. She phrases the problem as follows: "Rather than rush to reinstate woman's agency, feminists need to develop historical narratives whose readings of particular historical conjunctures can also account for the far-reaching economic and political effects of the historian's own frame of intelligibility and the subjectivities it produces" (ibid., 124). Also see ch. 4, "New Woman, New History."

9   Neil Diamant, "Reexamining the Impact of the 1990 Marriage Law: State Improvisation and Local Initiative," *China Quarterly*, no. 161 (March 2001): 171–98 examines weaknesses in the 1980s historiography, which relied heavily on this predictable argument. For a revisionist argument that does not fully extricate itself but provides an invaluably rich resource, see Naihua Zhang, "The All-China Women's Federation, Chinese Women and the Women's Movement, 1949–1993" (Ph.D. diss., Michigan State University, 1996). These scholars are shifting attention away from the conventional historian's peculiar, self-appointed job of policing the "logical order of determining priority," the question of

causality, within the allegedly predictable relation of past-present-future. They are more concerned with how movement thinkers and those who took advantage of the ideological and political opportunities themselves understood what they were doing. The shift is from conventional historical narrative to singular perspective and agency. For an analytical discussion of the importance of category in this regard, see Derek Sayer, *The Violence of Abstraction: The Analytic Foundations of Historical Materialism* (Oxford: Basil Blackwell, 1987).

It is also why this is a book about women *in* feminism and not a book about women *and* feminism. Because the future anterior tense in history writing is a way of allowing the historian à la Benjamin to blast out of the historical present, the book will also not do the following: it will not argue that feminism in China has had a continuous existence through women in the Chinese Communist Party (Christina Gilmartin), although that is surely the case, nor will it attempt to demonstrate a female tradition of feminist thinking in China (Dorothy Ko, Lingzhen Wang, Zheng Wang). I am primarily concerned here with the predication of the subject woman in feminist theorizing in the published accounts of modernist, revolutionary, and globalized thinkers and the discontinuous tradition of this thinking in the twentieth century.

10  Sharon Wesoky, *Chinese Feminism Faces Globalization* (New York: Routledge, 2002) is a good example of this. She is the first U.S.-based social theorist to use the Chinese women's movement as a source for generalization.

11  Peggy Kamuf, introduction to *A Derrida Reader: Between the Blinds*, ed. Peggy Kamuf (New York: Columbia University Press, 1991), xv.

12  The precis that follows is based on the findings of the following scholars: Francesca Bray, *Technology and Gender: Fabrics of Power in Late Imperial China* (Berkeley: University of California Press, 1997); Patricia Buckley Ebrey, *The Inner Quarters: Marriage and the Lives of Chinese Women in the Sung Period* (Berkeley: University of California Press, 1993); Susan Mann, *Precious Records: Women in China's Long Eighteenth Century* (Stanford: Stanford University Press, 1997); Ellen Widmer and Kang-i Sun Chang, *Writing Women in Late Imperial China* (Stanford: Stanford University Press, 1997). Also see Institute of Modern History, Academia Sinica, eds., *Family Process and Political Process in Modern Chinese History* (Taipei: Institute of Modern History, Academia Sinica, 1992) and Peking University Women's Studies Center, ed., *Beijing daxue funü disan qu guoji yantaohui lunwenji, 1994* (Proceedings of the Beijing University women's studies third international conference, 1994) (Beijing: Beijing daxue zhongwai funü wenti yanjiu zhongzin, 1995).

13  Patricia Buckley Ebrey, "Shifts in Marriage Finance from the Sixth to the Thirteenth Century," in *Marriage and Inequality in Chinese Society*, ed. Rubie S. Watson and Patricia Buckley Ebrey (Berkeley: University of California Press, 1991), 97–132. For a discussion of uxorilocal marriage, see Ebrey, *Inner Quarters*, particularly 111. Alternative interpretations are forwarded in Kathryn Bernhardt, *Women and Property in China, 960–1949* (Stanford: Stanford University Press, 1999).

14  All of the historians noted here raise this apparent contradiction that although actual textile production had long been commercialized and even masculinized, the state continued to connect women's virtue to their abilities in home textile production. Ebrey, Bray, and Mann have all proposed how this apparent anomaly should be interpreted. When, in the sixteenth century, cash taxes replaced taxes in kind, the conditions holding this ideology of gender in place vanished, transforming family production and removing the pressure the state had earlier placed on household textile producers.

15  Bray, *Technology*, chs. 5, "Economic Expansion and Changing Divisions of Labor," and 6, "Women's Work and Women's Place."

16 Mark Elvin, The Pattern of the Chinese Past (Stanford: Stanford University Press, 1973) developed the idea of the "high level equilibrium trap."

17 Mann, Precious Records.

18 Ibid. To some degree, the new historiography of Mann, Bray, Ebrey, and other historians of women in the gentry era is intended to explicitly question the "Western feminist" wave of an earlier scholarship from modernists. The new historiography targets the May Fourth movement of the 1920s for unduly influencing the hostile attitudes of later generations against the tradition. Chen Dongyuan is often cited as an exemplary negative figure who, during the 1920s and 1930s, established a caricature of tradition and traditional women.

19 Jinhua Emma Teng, "The Construction of the 'Traditional Chinese Woman' in the Western Academy: A Critical Review," Signs 22, no. 1 (autumn 1996): 115–51.

20 Geoff Eley, "Is All the World a Text? From Social History to the History of Society Two Decades Later," in The Historic Turn in the Human Sciences, ed. Terrence J. McDonald (Ann Arbor: University of Michigan Press, 1996), 226. Unsurprisingly, Eley thinks social history should resolve the problem of what he calls identity (and what I am calling the subject of a history). Although social historians may acknowledge the indeterminacy of "identity" in theory, he points out, still most write as if fixed determinations were the ones that count. Eley's example is "worker." Even if you accept the instability or multiplicity of the identity "worker," it is necessary nonetheless to figure out a way of understanding "worker" to be the paramount descriptor in a labor history narrative.

21 Paul Rouzer, Review of Writing Women in Late Imperial China, ed. Ellen Widmer and Kang-I Sun Chang, Journal of Asian Studies 57, no. 4 (November 1998): 1142–43. Also see Teng, "The Construction," who makes a similar point.

22 William T. Rowe, "Women and the Family in Mid-Qing Social Thought: The Case of Chen Hongmou," Late Imperial China 13, no. 2 (December 1992): 1. Progress then reversed itself when the Ming state (1368–1644) was decapitated and a Manchu government seized control of the bureaucracy. Prof. Rowe has since reworked some of his claims, softening and retaining them in an even more polished form. He will forgive me for reading only the pertinent elements of his grand and slightly intimidating 601-page Saving the World: Chen Hongmou and Elite Consciousness in Eighteenth Century China (Stanford: Stanford University Press, 2001); 313–25 and 446–56 directly address these matters. I think it is fair to say that Rowe's approach to the gender problem has not changed substantially.

23 Rowe, "Women and the Family," 5, 7.

24 Kai-Wing Chow, The Rise of Confucian Ritualism in Late Imperial China: Ethics, Classics, and Lineage Discourse (Stanford: Stanford University Press, 1994), 2.

25 Wan Sida's (1633–1683) monumental research paved the way for debate and innovation in the organization of the clan, its architecture (family shrines, or jiazu, and lineage halls, zongmiao), rethinking of family status hierarchies (how to value biological birth order, mother's rank, father's official degree, examination degrees within the lineage), the conjuncture of mourning and lineage, and so on.

26 Bray, Technology. Also Chow, Rise, 205.

27 Benjamin A. Elman, Classicism, Politics and Kinship: The Ch'ang-chou School of New Text Confucianism in Late Imperial China (Berkeley: University of California Press, 1990). Read in relation to Elman's earlier study, From Philosophy to Philology: Social and Intellectual Aspects of Change in Late Imperial China (Cambridge, MA: Council on East Asian Studies, Harvard University, 1990), the argument is even richer.

28 Elman, Classicism, 15.

29 Over nearly three centuries Zhang and Liu men connected their families to the Throne. The families also contributed widely to the independent scholarship of the vast, professionalized core of scholars who served as secretaries within the official system, or who declined to serve and instead spent productive lives on the class project of transforming Confucianism through critique and historical research. Elman goes so far as to draw an analogy with the European Renaissance. The strength of Elman's study lies in its concrete specificity and the attention it pays to men in lineages, yet never at the expense of methodological individualism. "Historians," he argues, "cannot isolate Chinese literati from their social setting. . . . Confucian scholars did not construct a vision of the political culture ex nihilo. Their mentalities were imbedded in larger social structures premised on the centrality of kinship ties" (Ibid., 6).

30 Dorothy Ko, *Teachers of the Inner Chambers: Women and Culture in Seventeenth-Century China* (Stanford: Stanford University Press, 1994), 68.

31 Calculated at roughly 10 percent of the population of the country in the seventeenth century, the elite—merchant and government families—were involved in new commercial undertakings effectively enabling a cloistered life for women and ironically illuminating the fact that the era's hallmark was the existence of writing women. See Widmer and Chang, *Writing*. Because her thesis rests on the emergence of a market in literacy, Ko stresses how women not only consumed and produced reading material but also were involved in publication and profit making. Further, she points out that a "market" and a "reading public" do not add up to a civil society such as the one that she argues emerged in the putative West.

32 Ko, *Teachers*, 181–82, 142.

33 Ibid., 273, 260.

34 Ibid., 6. Ko defines the fusion of "gender relations and the Confucian ethical system" as "the gender system," cross-hatched by what she terms a "non-Marxist" usage of class to mean "occupational groups and social stations differentiated by access to wealth, political power, cultural capital, and subjective perceptions."

35 Ibid., 253, 257–58. A question Ko develops is whether gender processes that make Women a heterosexual and homogeneous group overcome the conflict of interest that separates wives from courtesans. "The gulf separating courtesan from gentry wife," she argues, "was secondary to their shared position as 'woman' defined relative to 'man.' In this sense 'woman' constitutes a social category analytically distinct from class or status, although they intersect in practice." This is a complex matter. Or, as she puts it elsewhere, the "twin deployment of 'women-as-same' and 'women-as-different,' " or women as a category in relation to men, in tension with women as different from each other because they are in different relations to the same men, is "the very operating principle of the Confucian gender system." Thus, in her view, "Chinese courtesan culture had . . . integrative functions" in the sense that it enabled a public life for elite men, offered music and poetry to grease social interaction among men, integrated young men into the culture of privilege obtained through the examination system, and created a preserve of women who could be siphoned off from prostitution into concubinage within the gentry kin networks. "Chinese courtesans served an indispensable integrative function in society, bringing together the public and private lives of the male elites, as well as the oral and visual arts favored by the urban commoner and the scholar-gentry literary tradition" (ibid., 252).

36 Ibid., 256–61.

37 Ibid., 293. Here Ko seems to reconsider her earlier argument that "the restrictions and the freedoms" of Chinese women as a "gender" were "most clearly manifested among a

privileged group of educated women ... who taught each other about the vicissitudes of life through their writing," because "they ... highlight the possibilities for fulfillment and a meaningful existence even within the confines of the Confucian system imposed on women" (4). In China, Ko argues, awareness of individual subjectivity is not predicated "on the awareness of an individuated self or clearly perceived boundaries between self and others or between inner and outer."

38  Ibid., 291.

39  See Junichi Isomae, "The Space of Historical Discourse: Ishimoda Shō's Theory of the Heroic Age," *positions: east asia cultures critique* 10, no. 3 (winter 2002): 631–68 for an analogous problem of the relation of subject to historical "context" or space.

40  Kumkum Sangari and Sudesh Vaid, eds., *Recasting Women: Essays in Indian Colonial History* (New Delhi: Kali for Women, 1989), 3.

41  Angela Zito, *Of Body and Brush: Grand Sacrifice as Text/Performance in Eighteenth Century China* (Chicago: University of Chicago Press, 1997), 209, 211. Zito's work dovetails nicely with the process ontology that Judith Butler argues is gender:

    I argued that gender is not an inner core or static essence, but a reiterated enactment of norms, ones which produce, retroactively, the appearance of gender as an abiding interior depth. My point as well was that although gender is constituted performatively, through a repetition of acts (which are themselves the encoded action of norms), it is not for that reason determined. Indeed gender might be remade and restaged.... Here I focused on the transposition of two Derridean insights ... (1) that the term that claims to represent a prior reality produces retroactively that priority as an effect of its own operation and (2) that every determined structure gains its determination by a repetition and, hence, a contingency that puts at risk the determined character of that structure.... *The strategic task for feminism is to exploit those occasions of frailty as they emerge.*

    Judith Butler, "Further Reflections on Conversations of Our Time," *Diacritics* 27, no. 1 (1997): 13–16.

42  Spivak's *Outside in the Teaching Machine* can be read as a sustained discussion of catachresis.

43  Ibid., 7.

44  There is an aggressive future-oriented capacity in Spivak's conception. It rests on the ethical and political claims of nonelites in nonmetropolitan, non-European, and relatively disadvantaged geopolitical sites to lay claim to the temporality of modernity. A catachresis in this respect is a "concept-metaphor for which no *historically* adequate referent may be advanced *from postcolonial space.*" Spivak, *In Other Worlds: Essays in Cultural Politics* (New York: Routledge, 1997), 48 (my emphasis). This conception is useful because it makes moot the possibility of considering historical specificity exclusively in terms of ethical universal and cultural particularity or colonial imitation. The problem in relation to Chinese history is that the question of colonial modernity has yet to be adequately theorized or written about in intellectual historical terms.

45  In part, this notion is a play on Spivak's "negotiating with structures of violence," by which she simply means that a violent encounter, colonialism, for instance, will open possible avenues which condition and are conditioned by the given circumstances of violation. I am extending her formula to reinforce the implication that the truths of sexual difference are irreducible and yet contingent because there "is no *adequate* literal referent." Spivak's objective is theoretical in the special sense that word accrues now in cultural studies circles; that is, she seeks to write into academic practice a means of

thinking about a future postcolonial space (ibid., 213). I do not share her writing's persistent desires, though I am not excused from her ethical project.

Much as Gao Xian's eugenicist theorizing resembles that of Lester Ward, it is that much different from Ward's because it proceeds in another mother tongue, with vastly different referential strategies, in powerful neologisms, toward vastly different ends and in a national project unlike that of the United States in the first quarter of the twentieth century. A focus on the catachresis nüxing or women in Gao's work makes it possible to explain his theoretical invention as a meaningful, powerful, and typical (if exaggerated) world-making effort, and consequently to read eugenics as an important ground for feminism.

46   Gayatri Spivak, "Practical Politics of the Open End," in *The Post-Colonial Critic: Interviews, Strategies, Dialogues*, ed. Sarah Harasym (New York: Routledge, 1990), 104.

47   Walter Benjamin, *Illuminations: Essays and Reflections*, ed. Hannah Arendt, trans. Harry Zohn (New York: Harcourt, Brace and World, 1968), 262–63.

48   Benjamin, "Theses on the Philosophy of History" (16 and 17), in ibid., 262–63.

49   H. D. Harootunian, *Things Seen and Unseen: Discourse and Ideology in Tokugawa Nativism* (Chicago: University of Chicago Press, 1988), 4–5. See the appendix to this chapter, "Historiography and Catachresis."


2.   Theorizing "Women"

1   This chapter appears here at the suggestion of one of the anonymous reviewers. It is an adaptation of the previously anthologized essay "Theorizing Woman: Funü, Guojia, Jiating (Chinese Women, Chinese State, Chinese Family)," which first appeared in *Genders* 10 (spring 1991): 132–60.

2   Harootunian, *Things Seen*, 181–82.

3   See Mark Elvin, "Female Virtue and the State in China," *Past and Present* 104 (August 1984): 114–52.

4   Jean-François Billeter, "The System of Class Status," in *The System of State Power in China*, ed. Stuart R. Schram (Hong Kong: Chinese University Press, 1985), 138.

5   There are several reasons to concentrate on elementary terms in theoretical writing over the past two centuries. These words are normative, and consequently are like anchors. It is not that human experience is always reducible to their terms, but nonnormative personhood and nonnormative behaviors are linked variously to them, form variations on a powerful norm and not a domain beyond it. That is why Judith Butler, as so many other critics have, cautions that gender is not merely "cultural" in relation to nature. Nature is not the human body; it does not lie beneath a gender that is available or amenable to social scientistic method and social science categories. Also, scrutinizing the elementary terms of gendered personhood in theoretical writing invites access to the traces of what decency required of human beings at that time and place. Knowing something about the protocols stipulated in theory helps us imagine what kinds of person it was possible to be then. But the real point is that the enabling constraints of decency and the performance of it are what the archives have to offer; no others exist in the evidence itself. When the question is What are the sexed or gendered subjects and how do they depict themselves? rather than What is Women? this naturally places into the foreground acts of thinking: the thinking of the defined and of the people surrounding them, defining them.

6   By substituting the word "women" for the word "sexuality," Foucault's statement in

"Preface to *The History of Sexuality*, Volume Two" is apropos of the method I develop in this chapter. Foucault writes:

> I wanted to undertake a history in which sexuality would not be conceived as a general type of behavior whose particular elements might vary according to demographic, economic, social, or ideological conditions, any more than it would be seen as a collection of representations (scientific, religious, moral) which, though diverse and changeable, are joined to an invariant reality. My object was to analyze sexuality as a historically singular form of experience. . . . [This means] an effort to treat sexuality *as the correlation of a domain of knowledge [savoir], a type of normativity, and a mode of relation to the self*; it means trying to decipher how, in Western societies, a complex experience is constituted from and around certain forms of behavior: an experience that conjoins a field of knowledge [*connaissance*] (with its own concepts, theories, diverse disciplines), a collection of rules (which differentiate the permissible from the forbidden, natural from monstrous, normal from pathological, what is decent from what is not, and so on), and a mode of relation between the individual and himself (which enables him to recognize himself as a sexual subject amid others).

Michel Foucault, *Ethics: Subjectivity and Truth. Essential Works of Foucault, 1954–1984*, ed. Paul Rabinow (New York: New Press, 1997), 199–200; emphasis added.

7    Rouzer, Review of *Writing Women in Late Imperial China*, 1142–43.

8    Foucault, "Preface to *The History of Sexuality*," 199.

9    Mou Zhengyun, "Jiegou 'fünü': Jiu ci xin lun" (Deconstructing fünü: Old term, new discourse), in *Jindai Zhongguo fünü shi yanjiu* (Research on Women in Modern Chinese History) (Zhongyang yanjiu yuan jindai shi yanjiu suo, publication, Taibei), 6 (1998): 119–39. Mou's other objective is to correct mischaracterizations I made in the original version of this chapter published a decade ago. I gratefully accept her corrections and have readjusted accordingly.

10   Ibid., 127.

11   Mou also has her own thesis to argue. This thesis holds that the term nüxing designates a third term, outside the language of marriage and the patrilineal service ethic. Mou understands Beauvoir and Riley to be arguing that nüxing must be the matrix for fünü. Where I differ with her is over the status of women in Beauvoir, Riley, and Mou herself. For me Women is not the matrix of woman, just as nüxing is not the matrix of fünü.

12   Chen Hongmou, "Jiao nü wu gui" (Posthumous regulation on educating women), in *Wu zhong yi gui* (Five posthumous regulations), Sibubeiyao ed., vol. 3 (N.p.: Zhonghua shuju, n.d.); henceforth *WZYG*.

13   Rowe, *Saving the World*, 321. Prof. Rowe kindly acknowledges the grounds in Chen Hongmou's oeuvre for these generalizations. Rowe's note that *nan* and *nü* are well-understood lexical categories is an important point. It might be possible in the future to determine the relative weight that these various lexical categories play.

14   Chen did not have to provide his readers with charts of differential gendered positions because these constituted local common sense. For a discussion of the textual foundations of the cult of the gendered position and relation, see Hsu Dao-lin, "The Myth of the 'Five Human Relations' of Confucius," *Monumental Serica* 29 (1970–71).

15   Cowie, "Woman as Sign," 61–62.

16   See Hsu Dao-lin, "Five Human Relations," 30.

17   See Zito, *Of Body and Brush* for an eloquent analysis of these truisms.

18   The statement is emended and reromanized from Charlotte Furth's "Androgynous Males and Deficient Females: Biology and Gender Boundaries in Sixteenth and Seventeenth Century China," *Late Imperial China* 9 (December 1988): 1–31.

19  Manfred Porkert, *The Theoretical Foundations of Chinese Medicine: Systems of Correspondence* (Cambridge, MA: MIT Press, 1985), 22–23. Also see Zito, *Body and Brush.*

20  Essays on the body question are found in Angela Zito and Tani Barlow, eds., *Body, Subject and Power in China* (Chicago: University of Chicago Press, 1994). Gendering and sexing proceeded in many discourses far beyond my present scope. Many, like the *Book of Changes*, were not about persons but about abstract forces. Others placed "men" in "female" positions. Yet others appropriate the "female" position for subversive purposes. At no time was gender "a property of bodies or something originally existent in human beings"; it was always already "the set of effects produced in bodies, behaviors, and social relations: through the deployment of complex political technologies." The first part of this statement is from Teresa de Lauretis, "The Technology of Gender," in *The Technologies of Gender: Essays on Theory, Film, and Fiction* (Bloomington: Indiana University Press, 1987), 3. The second part is from Michel Foucault, cited in de Lauretis, same page.

21  Paul Rouzer, *Articulated Ladies: Gender and the Male Community in Early Chinese Texts* (Cambridge, MA: Harvard University Asia Center, 2001), 27. Rouzer argues that my insight into kinship and women applies equally to kinship and men. I take his point.

22  *WZYG*, 15.

23  Joseph Lau, "Duty, Reputation, and Selfhood in Traditional Chinese Narratives," in *Expressions of Self in Chinese Literature*, ed. Robert Hegel and Richard Henessey (New York: Columbia University Press, 1985), 46.

24  *WZYG.* Also see Rowe, *Saving the World*, 431–40 for Chen Hongmou's general attitudes toward ritual.

25  *WZYG*, 41.

26  See Ch'u T'ung-tsu, *Law and Society in Traditional China* (Paris: Mouton Pratique des Hautes Etudes, 1961). Part of family law requires service from junior women to seniors, and noblesse emanating down from senior women to their inferiors in age and rank.

27  *WZYG*, 48. Note that the relation/difference receives rationalizing and privileging not just in Chen's own texts, but in the text within the text, as it is the subject of comment between mother and daughter.

28  See Tani Barlow, "Zhishifenzi (Chinese intellectuals) and Power," *Dialectical Anthropology* 16, nos. 3–4 (winter 1991): 209–32. This paragraph is based on that paper. There I argue that peripheralizing signs involved zhishifenzi in the appropriation and redeployment of "modernity" within a nationalist, anti-imperialist economy of representation.

29  Mary Backus Rankin, "The Emergence of Women at the End of the Ch'ing: The Case of Ch'iu Chin," in *Women in Chinese Society*, ed. Margery Wolf and Roxane Witke (Stanford: Stanford University Press, 1975), 39–66.

30  Charlotte Beahan, "Feminism and Nationalism in the Chinese Women's Press, 1902–1911," *Modern China* 1, no. 4 (October 1975): 379–416, and "Mothers of Citizens: Feminism and Nationalism in the late Ch'ing," unpublished manuscript, n.d.

31  *Nüxuebao* (Women's study journal), cited in Beahan, "Feminism and Nationalism," 383.

32  Timothy Brennan, "The National Longing for Form," in *Nation and Narration*, ed. Homi K. Bhabha (London: Routledge, 1990), 44.

33  Beahan, "Feminism and Nationalism," 384.

34  Zhen Ziyang, *Nüzi xin duben* (New study book for women), 6th ed. (N.p., 1907).

35  Ibid., book 2, ch. 10, "Lolan furen" (Madame Roland), 7b–9a.

36  Ibid., ch. 13, "Fulanzhisi" (Frances), 10a–12a.

37  I am indebted to Theodore Huters for this phrase. The production of subjectivities in modern literary texts is also developed in Wendy Larson, *Literary Authority and the Modern Chinese Writer: Ambivalence and Autobiography* (Durham, NC: Duke University Press, 1991).

38 Talal Asad, "Are There Histories of People without Europe: A Review Article," *Comparative Studies in Society and History* 29 (July 1987): 606.

39 Mei Sheng, *Zhongguo funü wenti taolunji* (General discussion of the Chinese women's question) (Shanghai: Wenhua Books, 1929). Chapter 3 below draws on this multivolume collection extensively.

40 Ching-kiu Stephen Chan, "The Language of Despair: Ideological Representations of the 'New Women' (*xin nüxing*) by May Fourth Writers," in *Gender Politics in Modern China: Feminism and Literature*, ed. Tani E. Barlow (Durham, NC: Duke University Press, 1994).

41 Paraphrased from Annette Kuhn, *The Power of the Image* (London: Routledge and Kegan Paul, 1985), 19, cited in Linda Hutcheon, *The Politics of Postmodernism* (London: Routledge, 1989), 22. I address the culture of consumption in Tani Barlow, "What Is Wanting: Natural Science, Social Science, Women in the 1920s," in *Women in the Republican Period*, ed. Mechthild Leutner and Nicola Spakowski (Berlin: Lit Verlag, forthcoming).

42 Carolyn T. Brown, "Woman as a Trope: Gender and Power in Lu Xun's 'Soap,'" in *Gender Politics in Modern China*, ed. Tani Barlow (Durham, NC: Duke University Press, 1994).

43 See Suzanne Leith, "Chinese Women in the Early Communist Movement," in *Women in China*, ed. Marilyn Young (Ann Arbor: Michigan Papers in Chinese Studies, 1973), 50–51, 61. Leith summarizes three articles: "Zhongguo zhishi funü de sanpai" (Three groups of educated women), "Zhongguo zuijin funü yundong" (The contemporary Chinese women's movement), and "Shanghai nüquan yundong zhi hou ying zhuyi sanjian" (Three things the Shanghai women's rights movement should concentrate on).

44 The references are, in order of citation: Beibei'er (Bebel), *Funü yu shehui* (Woman and society), trans. Shen Ruixian (Shanghai: Kaiming Books, 1949); *Makesi, Liening, Engesi, Sidalin lun funü jiefang* (Marx, Lenin, Engels, and Stalin on women's liberation), ed. Chinese Democratic Women's Association (Hong Kong: New People's Press, 1949), 1–38; *Makesi, Engesi, Liening, Sidalin lun Funü Jiefang* (Marx, Engels, Lenin, Stalin on women's liberation), ed. Fulian (Beijing: Renmin Press, 1949). This collection has a slightly different composition. See page 39 for Stalin's "International Women's Day."

45 A history of Chinese Marxist theories on funü substantiates how thoroughly the history of Women in China by the early 1950s had become, for all intents and purposes, a subsidiary to the history of the European working class. Du Zhunhu's 1949 *Funü wenti jianghua* (Lectures on the woman problem) (Hong Kong: New China Books, 1949) exemplifies how, when Europe gets placed at the hegemonic center of "universal" theories of capital, Chinese history is inevitably reduced to being a subsidiary, local growth, possessing historical significance only as a semicolony of Europe, following a two-thousand-year dark night of feudalism. Interestingly, Du's sophisticated historical critique berates the Chinese women's movement's "failures" measured against the "universal" European women's movement. Du's strength is her insistence that funü is a social category.

46 Jiangxi sheng Funü lianhehui (Jiangxi province women's federation), eds., *Jiangxi suqu funü yundong shi xuanbian 1927–1935* (Selected historical documents of the Jiangxi Soviet women's movement, 1927–1935) (Jiangxi sheng renmin chubanshe, 1982), 21; 1931.11, items 1–7, 38; 1931.12, 231. Considering the situation, this seems totally inappropriate.

47 Ibid., 1932.2.1, 46; 1932.2.1, 43; 1932.1.2, 44–45. This is a splendid document detailing instructions governing women's organizations. It clarifies how model organizers in the women's work movement establish proper form, possess preestablished work plans, fix topics for each meeting (e.g., "opposing feudal bonds" or "enlisting men, comforting troops, doing mass work, getting literate"). See 1932.2, 52 for the statement that "mar-

riage is a relationship of two persons, male and female." See also 1932.3.2, 53 and many other subsequent documents. Women's Day and propaganda for the marriage law are the two major work areas for *ganbu* (cadres) undertaking women's work; 1933.2.7 uses it to demonstrate why woman is connected to state and suggests that workers use magazines, newspapers, and storytellers to spread the word. The effort is also reflected in regional documents numbers 1933.2, 10, 77.

48 The provisional nature of the laws and the multiplicity of subject positions are clear in ibid., 1932.6.20, 60–65, which talks about the resistance to certain laws. Its self-critical tone is significant.

49 Ibid., stipulation 5 in part 2.

50 Ibid., 1933.8.31, 104; "Provisional Central Government's Announcement Instructions to the People's Committees as regards Protecting Women's Rights and Establishing Women's Life Improvement Committees Organizations, and Work"; 1933.3.14, 87. The document gives instructions on the mechanics of representation. For example, set a time for a conference, locate the laboring women's congress inside the system of other mass organizations, recruit according to certain forms, get ten to twenty women, establish a representative, elect a presidium, capped by a party member. See p. 88 for a good discussion of how representation works.

51 Ibid., 1933.6.25, 95 suggests that quite strongly.

52 Ibid., 1933.3.28, 89.

53 See Patricia Stranahan, *Yan'an Women and the Chinese Communist Party* (Berkeley: Center for Chinese Studies Press, 1983), and "Labor Heroines of Yan'an," *Modern China* 7, no. 1 (January 1981): 83–112.

54 Lu Fu (pseud.), *Xin funü duben* (New woman's study book) (Hong Kong: Xinminshu Press, 1949), 60–61.

55 Zhou Enlai, "Lun xianqi liangmu yu muzhi" (On virtuous wife, good mother, and the mother responsibility), *Jiefang Ribao* (Liberation daily), 20 November 1942; hereafter *JFRB*. Zhou argued that not just mothers but fathers, too, had a substantial political obligation to be the best parents possible.

56 See Stranahan, *Yan'an Women*, 63–86. This is the single best empirical documentary study of the topic available in English. Stranahan argues that, in fact, given the context, CCP post-1942 policy on women's affairs was remarkably fair and probably productive both in Party terms and in the view of the women policy effected. See also Phyllis Andors, *The Unfinished Liberation of Chinese Women, 1949–1980* (Bloomington: Indiana University Press, 1983), and "Studying Chinese Women," *Bulletin of Concerned Asian Scholars* (October–December 1975): 41–43.

57 See the case histories and subject biographies in Fulian, ed., *Zhongguo jiefangqu nongcun funü fanshen yundong sumiao* (A rough sketch of the fanshen movement among rural women in the liberated regions of China) (N.p.: Xinhua Books, 1949).

58 Fulian, ed., *Zhongguo jiefangqu funü canzheng yundong* (Political participation movement of the women of the Chinese liberated areas) (Hong Kong: New Peoples' Press, n.d.), 71.

59 See Lu Fu, *New Woman's Study Book*, 74–80, particularly the chapter "Women yao yanjiu xinfa weisheng" (We want to study new hygienic methods), 78–80.

60 At least, this is how I interpret the writing on love and family construction that appeared in the 1950s. See, for example, Dan Fu, *Mantan liangxing guanxi zhong de daode wenti* (Conversation about moral questions concerning relations between the sexes) (Shanghai: Xuexi Shenghuo Press, 1956). Also see Li Di, *Zhufu shouji* (Handbook for housewives) (Beijing: Tongsu wenyi Press, 1955).

61 Fulian, ed., *Zhongguo funü disanci quanguo daibiao dahui zhongyao wenxuan* (Selected key documents of the Third National Congress of Chinese women) (Beijing: Zhongguo funü zazhi Press, 1958), 27.

62 William Parish and Martin Whyte, *Village and Family in Contemporary China* (Chicago: University of Chicago Press, 1978), 39.

63 For information on founding and early propaganda and literary outreach, see Elizabeth Croll, *Feminism and Socialism in China* (London: Routledge and Kegan Paul, 1978), and *The Women's Movement in China: A Selection of Readings, 1949–1973* (London: Anglo-Chinese Educational Institute, Modern China Series 6, 1974); Vibeke Hemmel and Pia Sindbjergh, *Women in Rural China: Policy towards Women before and after the Cultural Revolution* (Curzon: Scandinavian Institute of Asian Studies 7, 1984).

64 These luminaries and dignitaries were, in descending order, Cai Chang, Deng Yingchao, Zhang Chinqiu, Li Dechuan, Chen Shaomei, Kang Keqing, Ding Ling, and Ho Xiangning. See Fulian, ed., *Quanguo funü diyici quanguo daibiao dahui* (First congress of the All-China Women's Association) (Hong Kong: Xinmin Press, 1949), 102–8. The only real surprise here is Ding Ling, who had been dropped from women's work following the publication of the manifesto "Thoughts on March 8" in 1942.

65 Ibid., "Zhonghua quanguo minzhu funü lianhehui zhangcheng" (Regulations of the All-China Democratic Women's Association) and its various articles of incorporation, provisions, and systems, 94–100, 20–21. See also "Linqiu funü daibiaohui jieshao" (An introduction to the Linqiu County Women's Association), 73.

66 Ibid., 73–74.

67 Ibid., 28, 31. I quote this slogan because it is so outrageous. How Chinese women became "consumers" in the rhetoric of state discourse before there was anything to consume is provocative.

68 Fulian, *Selected Key Documents*, 3.

69 Nor, of course, was inscription as funü exclusionary, for a woman could at the same time be inscribed as "youth," as "worker," and as "daughter of a revolutionary martyr."

70 See David Kwok, *Scientism in Chinese Thought* (Berkeley: University of California Press, 1965).

71 See Emily Martin [Ahern], "The Power and Pollution of Chinese Women," in *Women in Chinese Society*, ed. Margery Wolf and Roxane Witke (Stanford: Stanford University Press, 1975).

72 For instances of literary representations, see Wang Zheng, "Three Interviews," in *Gender Politics in Modern China*, ed. Tani Barlow (Durham, NC: Duke University Press, 1994) for Dai Qing's and Wang Anyi's discussions about sexuality in their work. The concluding arguments are taken from my article "Politics and Protocols of funü: (Un)Making the National Woman," in *Engendering China*, ed. Christina Gilmartin et al. (Cambridge, MA: Harvard University Press, 1993).

3. Foundations of Progressive Chinese Feminism

1 Kumari Jayawardena, *Feminism and Nationalism in the Third World* (London: Zed Press, 1986), 1–24. Jayawardena correctly notes that another singularity of Chinese feminism in the context of "the East" is its inextricable link to the socialist revolution.

2 The arc from vegetation to animal life, barbaric primitivism to ascending stages of human civilization would culminate in the formation of the small, heteropatriarchal family unit. See Mei Sheng, ed., *Zhongguo funü wenti taolunji* (Collected discussions of the Chinese women question; hereafter ZFWT) (Shanghai: Shanghai New Culture Press,

1929–34): Kagawa Toyohiko 9: 23–47; Yi Jiayue 8: 166–83; and Gao Xian 7: 1–33, for a range of different approaches that make the same assumption. See the section "Mei Sheng and *The Chinese Woman Question*" in this chapter for analysis of this archive as a source.

3   For U.S. historiography on the relation of feminism and citizenship, see Candice Bred-benner, *A Nationality of Her Own: Women, Marriage and the Law of Citizenship* (Berkeley: University of California Press, 1998). The fact that internationally foundational feminist theorists were overwhelmingly male has led to reflection about how "the woman ques-tion" debate should be classified. Some historians have argued that the controversy over women is nothing more than a signifier of male insecurity in the face of colonial aggression. Others have argued that women is merely an ideological trope for nation itself in the discourse of nationalism. Still others hold that male concern over women was a thinly masked interest argument for reordering heteropatriarchy. I am not inter-ested in contesting any of the prevailing views, except to point out that whatever else it was, the controversy over the woman question was *also* very much about women.

4   Lila Abu-Lughod, "Introduction: Feminist Longings and Postcolonial Conditions," in *Remaking Women: Feminism and Modernity in the Middle East* (Princeton: Princeton University Press, 1998), 32.

5   Anthony Pagden, "The Effacement of Difference: Colonialism and the Origins of Na-tionalism in Diderot and Herder," in *After Colonialism: Imperial Histories and Postcolonial Displacements*, ed. Gyan Prakash (Princeton: Princeton University Press, 1995), 129–52, 130.

6   See Tani E. Barlow, "Spheres of Debt and Feminist Ghosts in Area Studies of Women in Asia," *Traces* 1 (2000): 195–227. For the notions of specter and debt, see Jacques Derrida, *Specters of Marx: The State of the Debt, the Work of Mourning, and the New International*, trans. Peggy Kamuf, introduction by Bernd Magnus and Stephen Cullenberg (New York: Rout-ledge, 1994).

7   Jay Geller, "Judenzopf/Chinesenzopf: Of Jews and Queues," *positions* 2, no. 3 (1994): 500–537. Also see Patricia Sieber, introduction to *Theatres of Desire: Authors, Readers, and the Reproduction of Early Chinese Song-Drama, 1300–2000* (New York: Palgrave, 2003), for a tour de force statement on the European Enlightenment's incorporation of "China" and Chinese literature as a precondition of its self-theorization.

8   Theorists of the woman question discriminated terms with precision and situated them-selves extrinsically in relation to the Anglo-American streams of suffragism (*nüquan zhuyi*) and feminism (*nüxing zhuyi*). See *Funü zazhi* (*FNZZ*) (Ladies' Journal) 8, no. 5 for an example of wide-range commentary on the woman question, feminism, and the prog-ress of women's social advancement.

9   Etienne Balibar, "The Borders of Europe," in *Cosmopolitics: Thinking and Feeling beyond the Nation*, ed. Pheng Cheah and Bruce Robbins (Minneapolis: University of Minnesota Press, 1998), 216. Balibar suggests that in the traces of thought are the traces of perfor-mance. One cannot divide the actions of thinking from the text; thus, as the discipline of cartography establishes the idea of the boundary, so, in my argument, the feminist claims to liberation on the grounds of racial progress are constitutive of a subject called women who is thought and discovered in our midst. The intellectual historian reads the archive of the effort to conceptualize the line on which anyone thinks. Roger Chartier, *On the Edge of the Cliff: History, Language, and Practices*, trans. Lydia G. Cochrane (Baltimore: Johns Hopkins University Press, 1997) defines intellectual history as "a history of the very preconditions of philosophical activity" (6).

10  See Kathy Peiss, *Hope in a Jar: The Making of America's Beauty Culture* (New York: Metro-

politan Books, 1998), particularly chs. 1, "Masks and Faces," which touches on the relation of ethnographic and advertising representation, and 4, "The Rise of the Mass Market."

11 Wen-hsing Yeh, *The Alienated Academy: Culture and Politics in Republican China, 1919–1937* (Cambridge, MA: Council on East Asian Studies, Harvard University, 1990), particularly ch. 1. Yeh's documentation clarifies the colonial quality of university instruction.

12 Christina Gilmartin, *Engendering the Chinese Revolution: Radical Women, Communist Politics, and Mass Movements in the 1920s* (Berkeley: University of California Press, 1995) makes a similar argument about influence within a frame of social history. Her point is that the May Fourth women's liberation argument was sublated in the communist movement. Mine is that eugenics are sublated in May Fourth feminism. Whether the eugenicism of population control theories and their central role in "international feminism" has been truly challenged yet in any metropolitan feminism is difficult to say. To my knowledge, there are no empirical studies available on the role of population control in women's rights feminism, for instance. For a haunting reminder of eugenic roots, see Nancy Friday, *The Power of Beauty* (New York: Harper and Collins, 1996).

13 Balibar, "Borders," 225.

14 Chen Shousun, *Shehui wenti cidian* (Dictionary of social questions) (Shanghai: Minzhu shuju, 1929), 598.

15 Li You-ning and Zhang Yu-fa, *Jindai Zhongguo nüquan yundong shiliao, 1842–1911* (Documents on the feminist movement in modern China, 1842–1911) (Taipei: Quanji wenxue she, 1975), 193–209.

16 Ibid., 211–28; Lin Yuezhi, "Lun Ouzhou gujin nüren diwei" (On the status of European women old and new) *Wangguo gongbao* 1911. Also see 183–87 and 187–92 of Lin Yuezhi's essays on the status of Indian women in the national history of India. This point is also lavishly illustrated in Hu Ying, *Tales of Translation: Composing the New Woman in China, 1899–1918* (Stanford: Stanford University Press, 2000).

17 These findings reinforce Beahan's "Feminism and Nationalism."

18 See, for instance, Qian Yunhui, "Lun nüjie jibi" (On the corrupt state of womanhood), *Funü shibao* 1:1911, 1–6.

19 See Xing Yi, "Meiguo funü zatan" (Random chat on American Women) *Funü shibao* 2:1911, 51–54.

20 I regret that William Schaefer's excellent essay "Shanghai Savage," *positions* (forthcoming) was not available when I wrote this chapter.

21 See Chu Jun, "Funü zhi weisheng yiban" (Some issues of female hygiene) *Funü shibao* 3:1911, 25–29; and Chu Jun, "Funü zhi weisheng zahua" (Miscellaneous words on female hygiene) *Funü shibao* 4:1911, 17–29.

22 Song Butian, "Jiating weisheng lun" (On family hygiene) *Funü shibao* 10:1913, 7–12.

23 Tang Chuangwo, "Shengti cao" (Rope calesthenics) *Funü shibao* 2:1911, 71; and Wu Ling "Renti mei" (Beauty of the human body) *Funü shibao* 2:1911, 7–11.

24 I have not solved the mystery of why the original cover of the publication reads *Nüxing wenti taolunji*, while the inside table of contents gives the second title. I have consulted both the original volume (in the UC Berkeley archives) and the 1977 Taiwan reissue, Fang Shih-to, ed., *Zhongguo shehui shiliao jiyao* (Abstracts of Chinese social history data) (Taipei: Tianyi chubanshe, 1977).

25 Ibid.

26 Gao Ersong and Gao Erbo, eds., *Hankou can sha an* (The case of the Hankou massacre) (1925 Reprint, Taipei: Wenhai chubanshe, 1985). This attribution and information in Xu Naixiang, *Zhongguo xiandai wenxue zuozhe biminglu* (Modern Chinese writers' pen names

index) (Changsha: Hunan weiyi chubanshe, 1988), 564–65, are the major reasons to suppose that Mei Sheng might be the two brothers, Ersong and Erbo. An annotated bibliography the brothers definitely wrote together in 1925 appears to be a precursor to the editing project. See Gao Ersong and Gao Erbo, "Zhongguo xuezhe funü wenti zhi yanjiu" (Chinese scholarship on the woman question), *Shehuixue zazhi* 2, nos. 2–3 (1925): 1–56.

27  Gao Xisheng (pseud.), *Jingji kexue da zidian* (N.p.: Kexue yanjiushe, 1935).

28  Mei Sheng, ed., *Shehui kexue da zidian* (A dictionary of social science) (Shanghai: Shijie shuju, 1929), 1.

29  Chen Shousun's *Shehui wenti cidian* (A dictionary of social problems) published the same year (1929), set the monogamy issue into an ethical framework, noting only that civilized countries, including Japan, codified morality into strict monogamy law. This suggests methods and theories related to the question of women did concur that social evolutionary theory took priority.

By 1935 pride of place had shifted. In Shi Fuliang's *Shehui kexue xiaocidian* (Junior dictionary of social science) entries began with "monism" (*yi yuan lun*), nationalist monism (*yi yuan de guojia lun*), monopartyism (*yi da zhengdang zhuyi*), mono–trade unionism (*yi da gonghui zhuyi*), and then "monogamy." The shift is away from sex drive social science theory and toward political science terms.

30  See Susan Glosser's analysis of family theory and the new periodical press in *The Contest for Family and Nation in Republican China* (Berkeley: University of California Press, 1995), ch. 1. The connection between Yi Jiayue and the journal *Jiating yanjiu* exemplifies the politics of theory in this foundational moment of the social sciences. Also note that Mei Sheng included only two articles (both by Yi Jiayue himself) from *Jiating yanjiu*. See Yeh Wen-hsing's *The Alienated Academy* for an important framing of this intellectual work.

31  Zito, *Of Body and Brush*, has illustrated what in the Qing era had become a complex editorial arsenal.

32  Some of these questions included: How did social theory explain the historical processes of women's universal derogation? How do we chart the universality of the transition of humanity from primitive marriage practices like chaotic, primeval promiscuity to the patriarchal precedents of jus primae noctis, to the regulated systems of male-dominated endogamy (*tongzu hunyin zhi*) and exogamy (*yi zu hunyin zhi*), with its three types: exchange, force, and purchase? How can we piece together a universal anthropology of man, arguing from evidence and statistical data widely scattered in Europe, Peru, North America, India, and China? How does the example of the English Pankhursts affect strategic objectives in Japanese socialism or suffragism? How has the Chinese social political economy held women in such a degraded position, not just in relation to Chinese men but also in relation to the women of other nations, such as the United States?

33  All citations to *ZFWT, 1, Tonglun* (General discussions): Feng Fei, "Funü wenti gailun" (General outline of the woman problem), 23–56; Yamakawa Kikue, "Shenshi guanyu funü jiefang" (Gentry seclusion and women's liberation),114–21; Lo Jialun, "Funü jiefang," 1–23; Beibeier, "Nüzi jianglai de diwei" (The future status of women), trans. Han Jun, from trans. Daneile de Leon, *Bebel Der Sozialismus und die Freatt*.

34  Consumers of Bebel may have been the sort of second-level educated people who did not have the high-elite language fluency that Yeh talks about in chapter 1 of *Alienated Academy*. See Edward Carpenter, *Ai shi* (History of love) (Shanghai: Wenyi chubanshe, 1920); *Funü zazhi* (Ladies' magazine) 8, no. 6 (June 1922) for a special issue devoted to the thought of Margaret Sanger. In this extremely popular issue the essays of Qiu Shiying and Se Lu and

essays translated from Japanese by Shi Ping and English by Yang Xianjiang explicitly linked the discourse of civilization to notions of birth limitation, race improvement, and neo-Malthusianism. Se Lu was particularly unequivocal. In his view, women's liberation was a matter of racial improvement, and racial improvement rested on limiting population growth. See Se Lu, "Chan er zhixian yu Zhongguo" (Birth control and China), 10–14.

35 These categories address (1) causes of women's subordination, (2) methods for addressing the crimes against women, and (3) methods of alleviating unjust living conditions (e.g., education, jobs, economic independence, and political rights, and less pronounced, the need to relieve women of the constant, enforced state of pregnancy). Feng Fei, "General Outline of the Woman Problem" speculated that marriage reform, political rights, and education would precede other forms of redress since the Industrial Revolution had in effect caused women's movements internationally in France, England, Africa, India, Canada, Italy, Germany, and Russia, and each would respond positively to similar remedies (36–39, 49). Marriage reform, educational opportunity, economic independence: this consensus is reiterated over and over in Feng's and others' articles until there is no possible dispute of their centrality. Also see Feng Fei, Nüxing lun (On women) (Shanghai: Shanghai Wenyi Chubanshe, 1931; reprint 1990).

36 As I read 1920s popular social sciences, it rapidly became clear that this very same subject of nüxing was playing a central role in the larger sphere of progressive social theory. The influential journals Funü zazhi (Ladies' journal), Qingnian zazhi (New youth), Shaonian Zhongguo (Young China), and Xin Nüxing (New women) all figured "women" either in their titles or as a problem in the pages of the publication. For general discussion of this point, see Li Chen Shen, "Contribution à l'étude de la condition feminine en Chine: L'emancipation de la femme à travers quelques revues en langue Chinoise, notamment la revue 'Funü zazhi' (Journal de la Femmes), des annèes 1915–1929," unpublished manuscript (n.d.). A valuable and excellent resource is Jacqueline Nivard, Histoire d'une revue féminine chinoise: Funü zashi, 1915–1931 (n.d.). Funü zazhi was but one of an efflorescence of journals crafted for middle-class readers on a wide range of topics (youth, education, foreign affairs, etc.) published by the Commercial Press in the 1920s and 1930s. Because so little has been written about the history of the social sciences in this period, the extent of nüxing's centrality in the institutionalized study of society is unknown.

37 Little is known about Gao. Ono Kazuko, Chinese Women in a Century of Revolution, 1850–1950, ed. Joshua Fogel, trans. Kathryn Bernhardt et al. (Stanford: Stanford University Press, 1989), 225 states that he graduated from Tokyo Imperial University, apparently in chemical engineering. He worked at the Commercial Press in Shanghai and apparently published fairly widely on Wardian social evolutionary theory. Christina Gilmartin (personal correspondence) notes that Gao published in Funü pinglun and Funü zhoubao, among other popular journals of educated opinion. Gao also published two essays in the most important journal of opinion during the 1910s and 1920s, Xin qingnian (New youth): "Shengcun jingzheng yu daode" (The competition for survival and morality) in May 1917 and "Lo shu shi shemma?" (What is the Lo syllabary?) in February 1920. Thanks to Prof. Hiroko Sakamoto for providing me with copies of these essays.

38 See Mark C. Smith, Social Science in the Crucible: The American Debate over Objectivity and Purpose, 1918–1941 (Durham, NC: Duke University Press, 1994), 88 for a characterization of Ward and his cohort. Ward began publishing in the 1880s and continued through the 1910s.

39 Were it not for the question of what is at stake in the historical catachresis nüxing, Gao might not be so useful. His work links major tropes of May Fourth feminist discourse, such as the attack on male supremacy, discussion of the social significance of anatomical

difference, and questions of ren'ge to an argument for women's liberation that is actually based on examples of female insufficiency drawn from nature. Its stark staging of these ideas also indicates that they are a "discourse" in the sense of being widely hegemonic. See Frank Dikötter, The Discourse of Race in Modern China (Stanford: Stanford University Press, 1992), chs. 4, "Race as Nation (1903–1915)," and 5, "Race as Species (1915–1949)," for background discussion. Dikötter treats sexuality in Sex, Culture, and Modernity in China: Medical Science and the Construction of Sexual Identities in the Early Republican Period (Honolulu: University of Hawai'i Press, 1995).

40 Gao Xian, "Xingzhe" (Sexual selection; hereafter, ss) in ZFWT, 7: 5; and"Lian 'ai duli" (Independence in love; hereafter IL) in ZFWT, 4: 7.

41 Lawrence Birken, "Darwin and Gender," Social Concept 4, no. 1 (December 1987): 75–88.

42 To paraphrase Gao, what more proof was necessary than evidence that culture blinded Chinese men to women's natural secondary sex characteristics? Some Chinese were so besotted that if the female did not bind her feet, males did not recognize her womanhood (ss, 18).

43 A look at the New York Times Sunday Book Review (February 13, 2000) will easily attest to this; see the review of David M. Buss, The Dangerous Passion: Why Jealousy Is as Necessary as Love and Sex (New York: Free Press, 2000), For a capsule history of current, neo-evolutionary theory, see Erica Goode, "Human Nature Born or Made," New York Times Science Times March 14, 2000, 1.

44 One of those many significances of nüxing was its centrality in the discourse of race improvement. See Funü zazhi 8, no. 6 (1922). Also see Barry Sautman, Relations in Blood: China's Racial Nationalism (Seattle: University of Washington Press, forthcoming).

45 But, as Gao points out, in conditions where women are not forced to "sell" their sexuality, in nature, for instance, or in a just social world that conforms to the laws of nature, women are (as they actually should always be) the heart of sexual and social reproduction. A female-authored, feminist, female subject who embodies the nüxing subject that Gao Xian theorizes for a Chinese feminist future is Ding Ling's Mengke, in the story of the same name. In the end, Mengke must sell the only thing of value that she owns: her sex. This is an argument forwarded by many social developmentalists, including Ellen Key.

46 Scott Lash and Jonathan Friedman, Modernity and Identity (Oxford: Blackwell, 1992).

47 See Judith Butler, "Contingent Foundations: Feminism and the Question of 'Postmodernism,'" in Linda Nicholson, ed., Feminist Contentions: A Philosophical Exchange (New York: Routledge, 1995), 15–16. As Butler has noted, "Identity categories are never merely descriptive, but always normative, and as such, exclusionary." As I am participating in a strain of deconstructive feminism, I would also agree with her concluding point: "This is not to say that the term 'women' ought not to be used, or that we ought to announce the death of the category. On the contrary, if feminism presupposes that 'women' designates an undesignatable field of differences, one that cannot be totalized or summarized by a descriptive identity category, then the very term becomes a site of permanent openness and resignifiability."

48 See particularly Foucault's discussions of biopower in Discipline and Punish (London: Allen Lane, 1977), History of Sexuality, vol. 1 (London: Allen Lane, 1979), History of Sexuality, vol. 2 (London: Viking, 1986), The Order of Things (New York: Random House, 1970), and a good analytic summary essay by David Hoy, "Foucault: Modern or Postmodern?" in After Foucault: Humanistic Knowledge, Postmodern Challenges, ed. Jonathan Arac (New Brunswick, NJ: Rutgers University Press, 1988), 12–41.

49 A view distinctly different from this appears in the work of Frank Dikötter, who appears

to find no progressive or liberatory element in racialized nationalism or eugenics theory. See Dikötter, *Discourse*, chs. 4, 5.

50 Edward Said, *Orientalism* (New York: Vintage, 1975). "Orientalism" and the colonialism debate have presented an analytic question in East Asian Studies. Over the past ten years, several lines of argument have emerged. Some have proposed, perhaps a bit too strenuously, that "colonialism"—administrative, juridical, military, cultural—is not an acceptable way to describe the conditions of multinational imperialism that China confronted in the nineteenth and the first half of the twentieth century. Among these are historians of imperialism, who have pointed to the absence of long-term, outright colonial holdings even among the big imperialists, England, Germany, Japan, and the United States. This "imperialism group" has consequently experimented with analytic openings such as imperialism without colonies, informal imperialism, subimperialism, and open door imperialism that admits imperialism into the analysis but rejects colonialism. Less compelling is the position taken by what I would call the multiculturalists, who also reject a colonialism paradigm. But multiculturalists propose that the "international settlements" established in increasing numbers after the Opium Wars of the early 1840s and institutionalization of the Unequal Treaty system were not colonies, but progressive migration events that effectively established public spheres in China. A third trend in the debates consists of scholars, largely cultural historians and humanists, who do accept the usefulness of the colonial paradigm. Among these a consensus is emerging that the Leninist-Maoist term "semicolonialism" is the most descriptive and fruitful avenue to pursue for grasping the singularity of foreign incursion in China over the century from 1840 to 1949. See Shu-mei Shih, *The Lure of the Modern: Writing Modernism in Semicolonial China, 1917–1937* (Los Angeles: University of California Press, 2001), 371–77. Shih has recently argued that semicolonialism was (1) not a binarial formation situating colonized and colonizer in hostile antagonism; (2) largely affected educated elites who created a cosmopolitanism out of relations of compliance; and (3) a cultural phenomenon that emerged as the consequence of imperialism's crushing inroads into the political, economic, juridical, and educational domains.

51 Timothy Brook and Bob Tadashi Wakabayashi, introduction to *Opium Regimes: China, Britain, and Japan, 1839–1952*, ed. Timothy Brook and Bob Tadashi Wakabayashi (Berkeley: University of California Press, 2000), 1–30. Also see Eric Tagliacozzo, review of *Opium Regimes*, *Journal of Asian Studies* 60, no. 3 (August 2001): 819–20 for a discussion of other new monograph studies of the opium trade supporting the thesis forwarded in *Opium Regimes*.

52 This is the argument forwarded in Leften Stavros Stavrianos, *The Global Rift: The Third World Comes of Age* (New York: Morrow, 1981).

53 Bryna Goodman, "Improvisations on a Semicolonial Theme, or, How to Read a Celebration of Transnational Urban Community," *Journal of Asian Studies* 59, no. 4 (November 2000): 921–23. Goodman argues that semicolonialism is not a historically adequate term because "throughout the modern period China never in fact became a subject nation, but retained sovereignty over nearly all of its territory and was recognized as a sovereign nation by international law" (889). The conclusion that she pulls from her case study is that the particular native place organizations of merchants from widespread regions who settled in Shanghai were actually the primary point of contact between foreigners in the settlement and Chinese generally. Because these native place associations and merchants generally lacked a consciousness of the nation, the contact zone led to two events. First, irritation with the British and other imperialists led native place associations to develop feelings of nationalism. Second, it was the nationalism of these

social actors that in turn stimulated the (imperialist) settlers to take a harder line on occupation and turn themselves into colonialists in the first quarter of the twentieth century. In other words, before 1911 there was no colonialism in China because the Great Powers did not successfully establish direct colonies; after 1911 there was only colonialism because the Great Powers responded to Chinese nationalism. But analytically, and this is Goodman's concluding point, the more definitive colonial relations became in the subsequent decade, the less significant they were. Why? Because in the minds of Chinese, the question was modernity and modernity was not easily identified with "either the decadent Qing dynasty or the embarassment of a foreign settlement on Chinese territory" (923).

54  Among Asianists in recent years, how to understand the event of colonial modernity or semicolonialism in China has become an increasingly urgent research agenda. Robert Bickers, Arif Dirlik, Joshua Fogel, Bryna Goodman, Gail Hershatter, Hiroko Sakamoto, James Hevia, Andrew Jones, Jurgen Osterhammel, Shu-mei Shih, Wang Hui, Rudolph Wagner, and Jeffrey Wasserstrom, as well as scholars associated with the *positions: east asia cultures critique* project, have presented research and criticism that restores the colonialism question to the heart of scholarly debate. See, for instance, *positions* special issues "Colonial Modernity" 1, no. 1 (spring 1993), and "Visual Cultures of Japanese Imperialism" 8, no. 3 (winter 2000). See Barlow, introduction to *Formations*, for an earlier attempt at formulating the notion of "colonial modernity."

55  Theorists in the China field have tended to exaggerate the teleology of imperialism (leaving little room in my view for contingencies and accreted traces) when they argue that Chinese semicolonialism is not a "real" colonialism because it does not repeat the experience of India. Modernity in China is colonial not because China resembles India, but because temporally, economically, and institutionally the experience of governance in India infused political and economic thinking about the China trade and settlement projects. The debate over Chinese colonial modernity or semicolonialism generally occludes Japan, often with the argument that Japan, a second-rate imperialist power, is not centrally significant. This is despite the fact that Japan actually held direct colonies in Taiwan (1895) and Manchuria (in 1905 the "Kwantung Leased Territory" became an experiment in colonial policy and infrastructure; in 1931 the army seized the territory outright and established the puppet state of Manchukuo). Furthermore, modernism, whether one considers modernity to be colonial by definition, as I do, or not, cannot be grasped in China without understanding how enlightenment ideas entered the treaty ports through Japan and Japanese translation. Chinese sovereignty in relation to treaty ports installed by the Great Powers (Britain, France, Germany, Russia, Japan, and the United States) through international law ignores the compromised condition of the imploding Qing dynasty and civil wars, anti-Japanese struggle, and land revolution leading to the Chinese Communist Party's seizure of power. The Treaty of Nanking may indeed have been legal under international capitulation law; it was also a colonizing strategy in a situation that opened novel opportunities for reshaping the colonial project in the shaky national conditions prevailing in China.

56  Even in area studies, by which I mean studies of places other than a home country, intellectual history is a singular form of knowledge. Accepting the transversal economy of colonial modernity changes the relation of general and particular, and it is only in the content of thought that the specificities characterizing national and subnational traditions are to be found. A good example is Claudia Pozzana, "Spring, Temporality, and History in Li Dazhao," in *New Asian Marxisms*, ed. Tani Barlow (Durham, NC: Duke University Press, 2002).

57  See Brook and Wakabayashi, *Opium Regimes*, particularly their introduction, which lays out the commodification of opium as a vehicle of capital accumulation and the impact of this commodity on governmentality. When that question is posed, the underlying problematic becomes how modernity and colonialism are historically related on a global scale. The contribution of the subaltern studies initiative broadly speaking was to establish, contra Foucault, the colonial roots of modernity. This mutuality holds as true for codifying and standardizing the English language as it does when we consider the transformative effect of colonialism on standard Chinese in the twentieth century or the financing of the Industrial Revolution from the proceeds of the Atlantic triangle trade. Indeed, if research by Timothy Brook, Bob Wakabayashi, Eguchi Keiichi, Bin Wong, and Jane Wyman holds up, modernity in China may be directly connected to the larger colonial economy through the Pacific opium trade.

58  See Louise Edwards, "Policing the Modern Woman in Republican China," *Modern China* 26, no. 2 (April 2000): 115–47; Joan Judge, "Talent, Virtue, and the Nation: Chinese Nationalisms and Female Subjectivities in the Early Twentieth Century," *American Historical Review* 106, no. 3 (June 2001): 765–803; Miriam Silverberg, "The Modern Girl as Militant," in *Recreating Japanese Women, 1600–1945*, ed. Gail Lee Bernstein (Berkeley: University of California Press, 1991), 239–66. For a discussion of the phenomenon of the New Woman and the Modern Girl, see Shih, *Lure of the Modern* (318–22), who suggests that the modern girl phenomenon is connected to Japanese urban media and theoretical projections, although this remains to be fully researched. I acknowledge with pleasure the Modern Girl Research Group (Tani Barlow, Madeleine Dong, Uta Poiger, Priti Ramamurthy, Lynn Thomas, Alys Weinbaum) at the University of Washington who are charting the global range of the modern girl phenomena. See our jointly authored essay "The Modern Girl around the World" unpublished manuscript (2004). A Tokyo-based research group (Ruri Ito, Hong Yuru, Vera Makie, Barbara Sato, Adachi Mariko, Dai Jinhua, Tachi Kaoru, Muta Kazue, Eunshil Kim, and Tani Barlow) is examining the modern girl as an East Asia, colonial modern phenomenon.

59  See Nupur Chaudhuri and Margaret Strobel, *Western Women and Imperialism: Complicity and Resistance* (Bloomington: Indiana University Press, 1992). The human sciences generally and not just the modernist history narrative established woman as a proper subject of and vehicle for describing racial, ethnic, social, national, and sexual difference. See Tomiyama Ichiro, "Colonialism and the Sciences of the Tropical Zone: The Academic Analysis of Difference in 'the Island Peoples,' " *positions* 3, no. 2 (1995): 367–91.

60  The experience of Indian women in colonial modernization discourses did not resemble that of Chinese women, nor were the conditions for their production analogous. Rather, in each case, what emerged out of the intersection of colonial-nativist-modernist discourse was the tacit agreement that women constitute a mass or subject that a history can be written about. Women were no longer imbricated within documentation or daily life but became the subjects of modernist historiography. For a discussion of history as modernist inscription, see Dipesh Chakrabarty, "The Death of History? Historical Consciousness and the Culture of Late Capitalism," *Public Culture*, 4, no. 2 (spring 1992): 47–65, and Nicholas B. Dirks, "History as a Sign of the Modern," *Public Culture* 2, no. 2 (spring 1990): 25–32.

61  I adapt the *OED* definition of predicate: 1. Logic, that which is predicated or said of the subject in a proposition or the second term of a proposition which is affirmed or denied of a first term by means of the copula, as in "this man is my father." 2. The grammatical, a statement made about a subject, including the logical copula (which in a verb is expressed in the personal suffix) or an appellation asserting something. 3. The pro-

clamatory, which is to proclaim or declare, affirm or assert, and to set forth publicly as in preaching, extolling, and commending. I am thus not so concerned with performance or performance theory in this chapter but with the special ways that theory works as a predicator of categories of social formations.

62  I have skimmed all of the issues of this journal (about twenty-five) held in the University of Washington library. In a later project I will compare the journal and Mei Sheng's collection more systematically to establish what percentages of Chinese, female, Japanese, and other contributors appear in each. This should document the processes of redaction. My hunch is that canonization weeded out most female contributors. Mei's collection appears to be more Japanese, more male, more theoretically sophisticated than the heterogeneous journal world.

63  San Si, "Women de jiemei" (Our sisters), *ZFWT*, I 1: 134–52. The author's pseudonym means "Three four."

64  See Zeng Qi, "Funü wenti yu xiandai shehui" (The woman question and contemporary society), *ZFWT*, I 1: 56–64 for another example of this sort of thinking based on the insight that "from the most primitive Africans to the most civilized Europeans, no society has ever had sex equality, and consequently, men have brainwashed women into thinking that it is women's natural lot to serve men. When men realized their oversight, they took steps to emancipate women. Chinese women are irrational (*bu holi*), not part of humanity (*fei renlei*), the playthings of men, and like animals (*rutong nüma yiban*) because of the selfishness of men." Ji Tao, "Zhongguo nüzi de diwei" (The position of Chinese women), *ZFWT* I 1: 64–68 adds the insight that Chinese women are "the governed" (*bei zhizhe*) and defined by their lack (e.g., not independent), but he at least attributes to women the desire for liberation. Lu Yi'e, "Qiuji shixue funü de genben fangfa" (The basic method for remedying the lack of education among women), *ZFWT* I 2: 180–82 expresses horror at being surrounded by millions of illiterate women. Liu Shuang, "Nannü tongxue wenti de yanjiu" (Investigation into the question of male/female coeducation), *ZFWT* I 2: 184–92 suggests that coeducation will help women accept the flaws in their biophysical makeup. The presumption of the inhumanity and deficiencies of women is so widespread and encompasses many dimensions, from literacy to social psychology to ethics and geopolitics. My object in citing these examples is to convey the repetitive quality of this presupposition and its foundational role in progressive feminism.

65  San Si, "Our Sisters," 143.

66  I will argue shortly that, when they dispute the social subjectivity of women, feminist theorists reinforce the biologism that positions women solely as the sum of their bio-genetic physiology.

67  The familiar trope of febrile emotionality in relation to will is probably a fusion of late traditional discussion of *qing* (emotion) and Victorian emphasis on women's sentiment.

68  Y. D., "Zhiye yu funü" (Occupations and women), *ZFWT* II 3: 21–26. The analysis rests heavily on Charlotte Perkins Gilman's *Women and Economics* (New York: Harper and Row, 1966), which argues that, whereas humans are like animals in respect to our rootedness in nature, we are the only animal in nature that forces the female of the species into dependency. Y. D. cites Olive Scheiner, Mabel Daggitt, and Gilman to situate the argument historically in the era of wage slavery.

69  See Li Renjie, "Nannü jiefang" (Liberation of men and women), *ZFWT*, I 1: 68–88. Given the history and persistence of the market in women, this logic is striking.

70  Y. D., "Funü jingshen shenghuo" (The spiritual life of women), *ZFWT*, III 7: 107–17.

71  See Joan Scott's *Only Paradoxes to Offer* for meditation on the centrality of the paradox of difference and equality in bourgeois feminism.

72 Shi Heng, "Lian'ai geming lun" (On the erotic love revolution), *ZFWT*, IV 9: 78. Another excellent illustration of this double bind is Li Renjie, "Liberation of Men and Women," dated 1920, which argues that the problem is so grave that it will require actors of superhuman will (*te zhi*).

73 Rosalind Coward, *Patriarchal Precedents: Sexuality and Social Relations* (London: RKP, 1983), chs. 1, "The Dissolution of the Patriarchal Theory," and 2, "The Meaning of Mother-Right."

74 In kinship, theorists sought evidence of sexual desire and the sublation of that desire. Coward notes that this theoretical event took place and even characterized the new social science of anthropology (see ibid., ch. 4, "The Impasse on Kinship"). Robert Young took up the same point later in his *Colonial Desire*.

75 Coward, *Patriarchal Precedents*, 57, 70–74.

76 Jonathan Ned Katz, *The Invention of Heterosexuality* (New York: Penguin, 1995), 92. In sum, Katz argues that historically, heterosexuality is an ideological formation that took shape (at least in the United States) in the era of the shift from monopoly to consumer capitalism; indicated an innate drive within human beings for sexualized and sexual pleasure; had attached to it subjects like the "heteroerotic" flapper of the 1920s, who aggressively sought sexual responses; and has the added benefit of seeming universal. This is consistent with Roz Coward's discussion.

77 Ibid., 92.

78 Feng Fei, *On Women*.

79 Barlow, "Zhishifenshi."

80 William Pietz, "The Problem of the Fetish, I," *Res* 9 (spring 1985); "The Problem of the Fetish, II," *Res* 13 (spring 1987): 23–45; "The Problem of the Fetish, III," *Res* 16 (autumn 1988): 105–23.

81 Edward M. Gunn, *Rewriting Chinese: Style and Innovation in Twentieth-Century Chinese Prose* (Stanford: Stanford University Press, 1991), 41. Gunn characterized the outcome as "historically sweeping, if linguistically superficial, change." See also Jingyuan Zhang, *Psychoanalysis in China: Literary Transformations, 1919–1949* (Ithaca, NY: Cornell East Asia Series, Cornell University, 1992). Interestingly, Zhang glosses "sexuality" in the Freudian context as *seiyoku* or *xingyu*, noting without comment that the term came through Japanese. My sources suggest that either this gloss is particular to Freud discourse or that the polysemy of the term was even more pronounced than Zhang is letting on here.

82 Shimamura Tamizo, "Nannü liangxing wenti" (The question of [hetero]sexuality), trans. Wang Xiangzhen, *ZFWT*, III 7: 3–42. See Wang Qingni, "Liangxing de daode" (Morality of sexuality), *ZFWT*, III 7: 42–68.

83 Yoneda Syotaro, "Lian'ai yu wenhua" (Love and civilization), VI 9: 8–17.

84 Chen Dezheng, "Xiang'ai de jiazhi" (The value of [hetero]sexual love), *ZFWT*, IV 9: 43.

85 James Reeve Pusey, *China and Charles Darwin* (Cambridge, MA: Harvard University Press, 1983), 381–82 also struggles with this question. In an important footnote on 497, Pusey traces the question of how terms like "natural selection," "hybridization," and "intercrossing" were handled in translation projects in the first decade of the twentieth century. In the process of translation itself, the power of the category "sexuality" is obvious, as it is so difficult to find terms that are abstract or extrinsic to norms and practices.

86 Keep in mind that this is "Shimamura" appearing in Chinese translation.

87 Shimamura, "The Question," 34: "What then is the liangxing wenti? We can answer this question in one sentence: it is the symmetry of the actual and conceptual in the mutual, critical relation of the male and female sexes. Or to put it another way, the elucidation of real and ideal relation of male and female sexes [*nannü liangxing*]."

88 Yi Jiayue (pseud. Axe for Transforming the Family), "Jiating yu hunyin" (Family and

marriage), *ZFWT*, III 8: 166–83: "It is not difficult to grasp that marriage is the motive force in establishing the family! Because where you have the marital relationship there you also have the relation of husband and wife; with the procreative relation, you have a parental relation and you have marriage. Husband and wife, parents, children and voilà you have a family!" (166). Yi is also the author, with Luo Dunwei, of *Zhongguo jiating wenti* (The Chinese family question) (Shanghai: Daidong, 1928).

89  Yi Jiayue, "Family and Marriage," 172.

90  Charles A. Ellwood (1873–1946) was the author of, among many other works, *The Social Problem: A Constructive Analysis* (New York: Macmillan, 1915); *Cultural Evolution: A Study of Social Origins and Development* (New York: Century, 1927); and *Recent Developments in the Social Sciences* (Philadelphia: Lippincott, 1927).

91  Yi Jiayue, "Family and Marriage," 177–78.

92  Zhou Jianren, "Jiating shenghuo de jinhua" (Evolution of family life), *ZFWT*, 8: 205. See chapter 7 below for a discussion of how Meng Yue and Dai Jinhua resumed this notion of ultrastability in their pathbreaking psychoanalytic feminism.

93  Zhou Jianren, "Zhongguo jiu jiating zhidu de biandong" (Changes in the old Chinese family system), *ZFWT*, 8: 233.

94  Chen Dezheng, "Jiazu zhidu de pochan'guan" (The bankrupt outlook of the family system), *ZFWT*, III 8: 235–43.

95  Yan Zhongyun, "Ji jüewu de nüxing duiyu nannü shejiao de zeren" (The responsibility of self-awakened women to the question of social relations between the sexes), *ZFWT*, II 6: 190–93; Zhang Meili, "Nannü shejiao guodu shidai" (The transitional period of social relations between women and men), *ZFWT*, II 6: 193–94.

96  Gao Xian, *SS*, 4–5.

97  Hoashi, Osaro, "Xin shidai zhi xin zhencao lun" (On a new chastity for a new age), trans. Yang Xianjiang, *ZFWT*, V 13: 117–27; originally published in *Funü zazhi*.

98  Xi Leng, "Yixing shejiao de taidu wenti" (The question of attitudes toward heterosexual intercourse), *ZFWT*, II 6: 151–53.

99  Chen Dezheng, "Shejiao gongkai he lian'ai" (Open social intercourse and love), *ZFWT*, II 6: 153–54.

100  [Shen] Yan Bing, "Nannü shejiao gongkai wenti guanjian" (Opinion on the question of open social intercourse between women and men), *ZFWT*, II 6: 155–59. Yan Bing is another pseudonym of Mao Dun.

101  Lin Zhaoyin, "Liangxing jiaoyu zhi yanjiu" (Investigation into sex education), *ZFWT*, III 7: 77, 80, 82.

102  Y. D., "The Spiritual Life of Women." On the question of "the biological differentiation of male and female," see 107–9.

103  Lin Zhaoyin, "Investigation." For a similar argument that the true mark of female difference is spiritual, see Yoneda, "Love and Civilization." See also Kagawa Toyohiko "Lian'ai zhi li" (The power of love) *ZFWT*, IV 9:23–32.

104  For an example of this ubiquitous phrase, see Zhu Zhengxin, "Beibei'er de funü wenti lun" (Bebel on the woman question), *ZFWT*, I: 66.

105  Chen Guyuan, "Jiazu zhidu de piping" (Critique of the clan system), *ZFWT*, III 8: 184–90. Eugenics was not the only argument in play here. Chen also felt that social progress required that the quality of sons be improved and that fathers repudiate the prerogatives of paternal tyranny.

106  Xiao Feng, "Lian'ai lun fafan" (Preface to the treatise on lian'ai), *ZFWT*, IV 9: 3.

107  This is particularly true of Japanese contributions that tend to dwell on the category of "civilization" rather than "society."

108 Yoneda, "Love and Civilization" is a relatively conservative and careful argument that love cannot be the sole determinant in marriage, because one's philosophic personal outlook (*renshengguan*) on civilization must also be strengthened, given the relative fickleness of erotic passion and the historical responsibilities of marriage. Thus, though heterosexual love should be the spark that initiates a decision to marry, it cannot be the only factor in play because part of the raison d'être of marriage is procreation and child rearing requires stability. The historical argument for the stable family is as strong as the historical argument for the natural dynamic of sexual desire. Yoneda's argument engages many of the points imported into the dispute through the aegis of Ellen Key (marriage without love is immoral), Ibsen (women should leave loveless marriages), and others.

109 The first historian to raise this term's potential significance to intellectual history in an English-language historical analysis is Roxane Witke, in her pathbreaking *Transformations of Attitudes towards Women During the May Fourth Era of Modern China* (Berkeley: University of California Press, 1970).

110 Prof. Chen Liwei, personal correspondence, 15 May 2001. Grateful acknowledgments to Prof. Sakamoto Hiroko, who solicited Chen's research finding on my behalf.

111 Gunn, *Rewriting Chinese*. Shejiao and *ren'ge* are complex catachreses à la Edward Gunn's work on translation practice. Older vernaculars were appropriated into Japanese and then into the new colloquialized common written language, *bai huawen*. I do not know yet if *jinkaku* was important in Japanese feminism. See Sharon Sievers, *Flowers in the Salt: The Beginning Feminist Consciousness in Modern Japan* (Stanford: Stanford University Press, 1983).

112 Wang Pingling, "Xin funü ren'ge wenti" (New women ren'ge question), *ZFWT*, V 14: 156–65; originally published in *Funü zazhi*.

113 *Black's Law Dictionary* (Saint Paul, MN: West Publishing, 1990).

114 Zhang Chengchang, "Nüzi renshengguan de gaizao wenti" (The question of reforming women's human outlook), *ZFWT*, 11 5: 166–72; originally published in *Nü jie zhong*.

115 Feng Fei, "General Outline."

116 Ye Shaojün, "Nüzi ren'ge wenti" (The question of women's ren'ge), *ZFWT*, 11 5: 149–56; originally published in *Xin chao*.

117 See the eleven essays collected in *ZFWT*, vol. 5, section 13, "Chastity."

118 Chen Qixiu, "Nüzi zhencao de jinqian jiazhi" (The monetary value of female chastity), *ZFWT*, V 13: 137.

119 Yi Jiayue, "Zhongguo de lihun wenti" (The question of Chinese divorce), *ZFWT*, 11 5: 5–26; originally published in *Xuedong*, 1922.

120 Mei Sheng, "Lihun wenti" (The divorce problem), *ZFWT*, 11 5: 26–39.

121 Zhou Jianren, "Zhongguo nüzi de jüewu yu dushen" (Chinese women's awakening and their celibacy), *ZFWT*, 11 5: 82–86; originally published in *Funü zazhi*. More commonly, essayists agreed with Si Zhen that the choice of celibacy was silly because nature made women as sexual as it made men and the true ren'ge of women is fully expressible only in the procreative act and the erotic pleasures of mutual heterosexual erotic satisfaction. See Si Zhen, "Aiqing yu jiehun" (Love and marriage), *ZFWT*, 11 4: 124. This is also the position that Ding Ling takes in "Shujia zhong" (Summer break); see chapter 4 below.

122 Wan Pu, "Nüzi canzheng yu guojia wenti" (Female political participation and the national question), *ZFWT*, 11 4: 80.

123 Zhang Xichen, "Dui yu zhongguo funü canzheng san da yiwen de jieshi" (An analysis of three large obstacles to Chinese women's political participation), *ZFWT*, 2: 75–78.

124 Lo, "The Question of Chinese Divorce," 17. Xi Leng, "Yixing shejiao de taidu wenti" (Question of attitudes toward heterosexual social intercourse) *ZFWT*, II 6: 151–53.

125 This line of analysis is reflected in the essay's internal chapter divisions. These are the excellence of lian'ai, the view of love among the Orientals, past and present views on love, the progress of love, ancient Nora, love and self-liberation, and the path from noncomprehension to affirmation. See Kuriyakawa Hakuson, "Jindai de lian'aiguan" (Perspectives on contemporary lian'ai), trans. Y. D., (Li Xiaofeng, Li Rongdi) *ZFWT*, II 4: 47–73, in the section "Lian'ai wenti."

126 See Charles Shiro Inouye, "In the Scopic Regime of Discovery: Ishikawa Takuboku's *Diary in Roman Script* and the Gendered Premise of Self-Identity," *positions* 2, no. 3 (winter 1994): 542–69 for another reading of the problem of lust unmediated by women's corporate standing, in the case of a man who theorizes himself from the brothel, in the mirror of the degraded prostitute.

127 Kuriyakawa, "Perspectives," 49.

128 His point is that love interrupts the utilitarian desire for sons or simple sexual release and consolidates diverse regimes of social relations from love of clan, neighbor, race to all humankind, thus connecting Ellen Key's eugenicist developmentalism, German sex theory, and what sounds a bit like Tan Sitong's treatise on benevolence.

129 Kuriyakawa, "Perspectives," 55: "Lovers are able to see the self in the relation between themselves, from the self to the nonself they join as one body and this is the unification [*jiehe*, also marriage] of personal being [*ren'ge*]."

130 Hoashi, Osaro, "On a new chastity." See also Yosano Akiko, "Zhencao lun" (On chastity), trans. Zhou Zuoren, *ZFWT*, 5: 87–93, originally published in *Xin qingnian*; Hu Shi, "Zhencao wenti" (The chastity question), *ZFWT*, V 13: 95–104, originally published in *Xin qingnian*.

131 Hoashi, Osaro, "On a New Chastity," 125. Similarly, see Pei Wei, "Lian'ai yu zhencao de guanxi" (The relation of love and chastity), *ZFWT*, V 13: 127–31, originally published in *Funü pinglun*, which reprises similar themes with an emphasis on the sexualization of the male gaze.

132 Chen Qixiu, "Monetary Value," *ZFWT*, V 13: 124–139. "In the fourth stage women can, on the one hand, have independent ren'ge, and on the other also remain elements of the society [*shehui de yige fenzi*] and so the concept of chastity has on the one hand each individual's value [measured in terms of] ren'ge and on the other a social, economic value. If for some reason a woman's chastity is despoiled, rendering her unable to have a social life or existence, this will destroy her social labor power, causing a devaluation to the social body, he writes . . . which is why men must take responsibility for their insults to society." My point in paraphrasing this is the emphasis it places on humankind's ability to make progressive history.

133 Xia Yun, "Hunyin wenti de yanjiu" (Research on the marriage questions) *ZFWT* 4: 9, 155–60.

134 Louis Althusser, *Essays in Self-Criticism*, trans. Grahame Lock (London: NLB, 1976).

135 Alessandro Russo, "The Probable Defeat: Preliminary Notes on the Chinese Cultural Revolution," *positions* 6, no. 1 (spring 1998): 180.

136 Lydia Liu, *Translingual Practice: Literature, National Culture, and Translated Modernity in China, 1900–1937* (Stanford: Stanford University Press, 1995) takes the thesis that neologism is an important phenomenon because it allows us to study change. Her central point appears to be that "trans" in translingual marks an imaginary space or middle zone that she calls "the ground for change" (40). There are three weaknesses in this position: (1) neologism is transformed into a figure of speech; (2) unless the neologism is con-

nected to a general theoretical project where the reasons for constructing new terms is explained, the existence in literary expression of the neologism is occult and ahistorical; (3) as Liu uses the term, neologism is an abstraction, a spatialism, rather similar to Bhabha's third zone, which exists as a utopian possibility only in the language itself; in this formulation, "language" becomes the actor or agent. This last is not a position that I can endorse. In general, the use of "neologism" to cover the project of language transformation is an unnecessary narrowing of my project, which asks how people undertook the intellectual-critical work of rethinking the truth. Historical catachresis is a theoretician's investigation of signifiers in a theoretical and political language where truth is at stake. It is not about "change."

137 Li Renjie, "Liberation of Men and Women," 71.

## 4. Woman and Colonial Modernity in the Early Thought of Ding Ling

1 Some of the material in this chapter has appeared, in greater scholarly detail, under the following titles: "Gender and Identity in Ding Ling's Mother," *Modern Chinese Literature* 3, no. 1 (spring 1987): 123–42, reprinted in *Modern Chinese Women Writers: Critical Appraisals*, ed. Michael Duke (Armonk, NY: M.E. Sharpe, 1989); "Feminist Genealogies: The Problem of Division in Ding Ling's *Wei Hu*," in *Woman and Literature in China*, ed. Wolfgang Kubin et al. (Berlin: Studienverlag Brockmeyer, 1985); "Feminism and Literary Technique in Ding Ling's Early Short Stories," in *Women Writers of 20th Century China* (Eugene: Asian Studies Program, University of Oregon, 1985). I thank all parties for permission to reuse the material in altered form.

2 See Corrigan and Sayer, *The Great Arch*, for a discussion of the heterogeneity of the subject woman in the cultural modernity project of England, and Young, *Colonial Desire*, for analysis of the literal sexual content of colonial and postcolonial theoretical words like "desire" and "hybridity."

3 Yi-Tsi Mei Feuerwerker, *Ding Ling's Fiction: Ideology and Narrative in Modern Chinese Literature* (Cambridge, MA: Harvard University Press, 1982).

4 I do not agree with Zhou Liangpei, who simply argues that Ding Ling is Sophia or Sophia-like because the details of the writer's life add up to the sort of life experience that Sophia must have had. My analysis is really not concerned with the narratives of autobiography but with the predication of subjects in theoretical and literary work. See particularly Zhou's "Ding Ling shi Shafei?!" (Ding Ling is Sophia?!), in *Ding Ling zhuan* (Ding Ling's biography) (Beijing: Zhongguo xiandai zuojia zhuanji congshu, Beijing shiyue wenyi chubanshe, 1993), 85–216. The other major convention in current Ding Ling studies is a newly created tradition of middle-brow, patriotic, ethical writing on communist feminist themes founded in the People's Republic at the end of the Great Proletarian Cultural Revolution (1966–1976). Description and analysis of this trend appears in chapter 5.

5 Progressive Chinese theory was not the only domain where questions in pro-feminine thinking were being raised. Quite a lot of pro-feminine writing and thinking in the 1920s and early 1930s unfolded in the world of literature, poetry, aesthetics, and literary history and criticism. My implicit point here is that literary feminism has a complex relation to theoretical or systematic analyses, such as the tradition of progressive feminism. The scholarly tradition in the United States usually studies the rise of Chinese feminism through the New Literature or colloquial language movement and its major and minor female and male writers. This historiography has generously celebrated

female writing about the individual female psychic life. But it also reinforces a conventional reading practice that opposes feminism and socialism. See Wendy Larson, *Women and Writing in Modern China* (Stanford: Stanford University Press, 1998) for an interesting attempt to shift these grounds. Larson is primarily concerned with how the new, female-dominated domain of "women's literature" (*funü wenxue* or *nüxing wenxue*) fared historically in the 1920s. Though she agrees that this women's literature had powerful male sponsors and that its lifespan was very short, she nonetheless sees its emergence as a historical turning point. That is because *funü wenxue* opened up for the first time a literary convention that "implies not only writing by women, but as developed by critics in the late 1920s and early 1930s, *writing that through style, topic, and structure was gendered as female. Funü wenxue not only meant that women could participate in literature as they could in politics or education, but that they would infuse their unique subjectivities, histories, and experiences into the literary text, and change how writing functioned, what and who it represented, in essence what writing was*" (134–35; emphasis added). This is similar to positions that Chinese literary theorists of *écriture féminine* have taken (see chapter 7, this volume).

6   Yuan Liangjun, ed., *Ding Ling yanjiu ziliao* (Ding Ling research materials) (Tianjin: Zhongguo xiandai zuojia zuopin yanjiu ziliao congshu, Tianjin renmin chubanshe, 1982), 12–13.

7   I will not reiterate the internal dynamics of this debate except as regards the overlap of heterosexual poetics in social theory and Ding Ling's high modernist literature. Her attempts to stabilize a subject women, nüxing, in fiction engages and unravels some pervading modernist assumptions of the era, including the eugenicist strain in foundational, progressive Chinese feminism. The new woman was more than the literature of female writers, as Amy D. Dooling and Kristina M. Torgeson argue in their excellent introduction to *Writing Women in Modern China: An Anthology of Women's Literature*, ed. Amy D. Dooling and Kristina M. Torgeson (New York: Columbia University Press, 1998). Also an accurate accounting of the invention of modern Chinese literature in the Republican Era (1911–1949), one that includes female writers writing about femininity, has to be made before generalizations are fully accountable. Dooling and Torgeson make this point with portraits of such new style women as Chen Xifen (1883–1923), Qiu Jin (1875–1907), Chen Hengzhe (1890–1976), Feng Yuanjun (1900–1974), Shi Pingmei (1902–1928), Lu Yin (1898–1934), Ling Shuhua (1900–1990), Yuan Changying (1894–1973), Chen Ying (1907–1986), and Luo Shu (1903–1938).

8   See Ching-kiu Stephen Chan, "The Language of Despair: Ideological Representations of the 'New Women' by May Fourth Writers," *Modern Chinese Literature* 4, nos. 1–2 (1988): 27.

9   This is also a theme in Larson, *Women and Writing*.

10  Jing Tsu, "Perversions of Masculinity: The Masochistic Male Subject in Yu Dafu, Guo Moruo, and Freud," *positions* 8, no. 2 (2000): 269–316.

11  See Shih, *The Lure of the Modern*, chs. 3, "Psychoanalysis and Cosmopolitanism: The Work of Guo Moruo," and 4, "The Libidinal and the National: The Morality of Decadence in Yu Dafu, Teng Gu, and Others." These chapters offer historical material about the ways that Guo Moruo, particularly, adapted Freudian notions into his thinking.

12  Michel Foucault, *The History of Sexuality. Vol. 1: An Introduction* (New York: Vintage Press, 1980), 47.

13  This is not a contradiction. The point that Jing Tsu makes, following the attempt of Judith Butler and other queer theorists to rethink Lacan, is that the maintenance of heterosexuality requires a painful disavowal of homosocial desires. Tsu particularly is considering heterosexuality to be a discipline, a kind of law that requires the abandonment of other, more primary or "essential" desires.

14  See Philip C. Huang, "Women's Choices under the Law: Marriage, Divorce, and Illicit Sex in the Qing and the Republic," *Modern China* 27, no. 1 (January 2001): 3–58 for a clue to the legal sources of the new feminist attention to the question of individual will and the legal imperative for self-willed action and culpability.

15  Ding Ling, "Xiao huolun shang" (On a small steamer), in *Zisha riji* (Suicide diary) (Shanghai, 1937).

16  Ding Ling, "Yi ge nüren he yi ge nanren" (A woman and a man), in *Yi ge nüren* (A woman) (Shanghai, 1930) and "Ah Mao guniang" (The girl Ah Mao), in *Zai heian zhong* (In darkness) (Shanghai, 1938).

17  See Ding Ling, "Qingyunli zhong de yijian xiaofangli" (In a small room on Qingyun Alley), in *Zisha riji*.

18  Ding Ling, "Mengke," In *Zai heian zhong*. Subsequent quotations are cited in the text.

19  Ding Ling, *Zisha riji*.

20  Ding Ling, "Shafei nüshi riji" (Sophia's diary), in *Zai heian zhong*.

21  Chang Jen-mei interpreted the protagonists's foreign names in her *Ding Ling: Her Life and Her Work* (Taipei: Institute of International Relations, 1978).

22  In an earlier published version of this analysis I use the term "authorial voice." See Tani Barlow, "Feminism and Literary Technique in Ding Ling's Early Short Stories," in *Women Writers of 20th Century China* (Eugene: Asian Studies Program, University of Oregon, 1982), reissued in Chinese translation as "Nüquan zhuyi he wenxue jishu zai Ding Ling nushi de chuqi de xiaoshuo," in *Ding Ling yanjiu zai guowai* (Foreign research on Ding Ling), ed. Sun Ruizhen (Changsha: Hunan renmin chubanshe, 1985).

23  Ding Ling, "Shujia zhong,"(Summer break), 178.

24  Translation adapted from Ruth Keene and Hal Palland, trans. in Barlow, *I Myself*, 89.

25  Ding Ling, "Ta zou hou" (After he left), in *Yige nüren*: 58–59.

26  Ding Ling, "The Girl Ah Mao."

27  Ding Ling, "Summer break," 187–88.

28  Ding Ling, "Sophia," (Barlow, trans.) in Barlow, *I Myself*, 79.

29  Ding Ling, "Wo de chuangzuo jingyan" (My creative experience), in *Ding Ling pingzhuan* (Critical biography of Ding Ling), ed. Zhang Baiyun (Shanghai, 1934), 218.

30  See Shen Congwen, *Ji Ding Ling* (Remembering Ding Ling) (Shanghai, 1934), 1: 78. Shen claimed that Ding Ling had reread Bovary many times. Ding Ling and Prof. Y. T. Feuerwerker have both rejected Shen's contention, but there seems little doubt that Ding Ling had read the novel at least once. Though ambiguous, it does seem likely to me that Ding Ling learned some narrative techniques from Flaubert. Ding Ling's own remarkable skills are on display in *Sun Shines over the Sanggan River* (Beijing: Foreign Language Press, 1984).

31  Prof. Feuerwerker has expressed reservations about this interpretation.

32  He Yubo, "Ding Ling nüshi lunping" (Critical discussion of Ms. Ding Ling), in *Ding Ling pingzhuan*. He analyzes *Zai heian zhong* (In darkness) in terms of the struggle between rational thought and emotion, noting that Ding Ling's early characters always allow sentiment to overwhelm them in the end.

33  Ding Ling, "Yecao," in *Yi ge nüren he yi ge nanren* (A woman and a man) (Shanghai, 1930), 96.

34  Ding Ling, "My creative experience," 210.

35  For a fascinating analysis of the economy of the name Sophia in the 1920s in feminist circles, see Raoul David Findeson.

36  Cao Ye, quoted in Gary Bjorge, "Sophia's Diary: An Introduction," *Tamkang Review* 5, 1974.

37  See Gilmartin, *Engendering the Chinese Revolution*; Wang Zheng, *Women in the Chinese Enlightenment* (Berkeley: University of California Press, 1999); and Neil J. Diamant, *Revolutionizing the Family: Politics, Love, and Divorce in Urban and Rural China, 1949–1968* (Berkeley: University of California Press, 2000) and "Reexamining the Impact," 171–72.

38  Xiang Jingyu, "Zhongguo zhishi funü disanpai" (The three groups of intellectual Chinese women), *Funü zhoubao*, 1923, reprinted in Zhonha guanguo funü lianhe hui, eds., *Zhongguo funü yundong lishi ziliao, 1921–1927*, 103–5 (hereafter *FYLC*). Also see her "Zhongguo funü xuanchuan yundong de xin jiyuan" (The beginning of a new epoch in the Chinese women's propaganda movement), *Funü ribao*, 1924, dated 1923, reprinted in *FYLC*, 275–77, where Xiang argues that a major failing of the Chinese women's movement is that talented women are drawn into literary and cultural studies and fail to develop any "political common sense" (*zhengzhi de changzhi*; 276).

39  Sex preoccupation, the male feminist Yun Daiying argued, was, in a certain respect, quite inevitable because of the impact biological ethics necessarily had on traditional beliefs. To Yun, sexual expression per se was not the issue. The crisis occurred when Chinese youth turned inward, toward individualistic and onanistic pleasures, away from social and mass questions and thus away from collective responsibility. So, Yun argued, the individualized conception of the "women's liberation movement" (*funü jiefang yundong*) left the real enemy—objective, material, economic oppression—unaddressed. See Yun Daiying, "Funü jiefang yundong de youlai he qi yingxiang" (The origins and influence of the women's liberation movement), *Funü zhoubao*, 1923, reprinted in *FYLC*, 94–97.

40  Yang Zhihua, "Shanghai funü yundong" (Shanghai women's movement), *Zhongguo funü*, 1926, dated 1925, reprinted in *FYLC*, 309–13.

41  Xiao Chunu, " 'Nüzi jiefang' de genbenyi" (The basic principle of "women's liberation"), *Funü xunkan*, 1923, reprinted in *FYLC*, 98–101, cited on 99.

42  Yang Zhihua, "Shanghai Women's Movement," 313.

43  Xiang Jingyu, "Jinhou Zhongguo funü guomin geming yundong" (Chinese women's future national revolutionary movement), *Funü zazhi*, 1924, reprinted in *FYLC*, 108–13.

44  It is not that Chinese women are less enthusiastic about liberation or less aware, or even less willing to expend great effort. It is simply that the conditions for liberation at the individual level are still rudimentary in colonialized, warlord-dominated China. See Xiang Jingyu, "The Beginning of the New Epoch," 275–77.

45  Xiang, "The Future of the National Revolutionary Movement," 110–11.

46  Deng Yingchao, "Zai Shantou funü lianhuanhui shang de yanshuo" (Speech at the Shantou women's federation welcome meeting), *Funü zhi sheng huibao*, 1926, reprinted in *FYLC*, 314–16.

47  Also, the combined colonial cultural economy and feudal heritage left Chinese women generally inept; see Xiang Jingyu, "The Beginning of the New Epoch," 276. Ho Xiangning's contempt for women who mistake the Ph.D. degree for true liberation is echoed in Wang Yizhi, "Funü jiefang yü laogong jiefang" (Women's liberation and liberation of labor), *Zhongguo qingnian*, 1925, reprinted in *FYLC*, 288. The idea that a leadership vacuum exists among women or that women are not equal to their historic task is common in the documents of the 1920s and resurfaced in the 1980s.

48  Cai Chang, "E'guo geming yu funü" (The Russian Revolution and women), *Guangming*, 1925, reprinted in *FYLC*. See 301 for the convergence of women's movement and revolutionary leadership and 303 for the statement of political equality. The pejorative use of *bushengchan* ("unproductive") appears to have entered the discourse through translation. It appears widely in the iconography of the socialist housewife in later CCP postliberation rhetoric. As with the earlier feminist critique, the use of liberationist categories has

the unintended side effect of casting wives and mothers as either victims, less than human, or, as here, "unproductive." Seemingly, what was initially meant was simply that women engage in "social reproduction" of the proletariat rather than "production" or wage labor for the capitalists. That is not what the term "unproductive" comes to signify in a normative register.

49  See Cai Chang, "Zhongguo gongchandang disanci zhongyang kuoda zhixing weiyuanhui guanyü funü yundong yizhuan" (Chinese Communist Party's third Central Committee resolution on enlarging the women's movement), 1926, in FYLC, 475–78. For discussion of the national and personal politics of this era, see Gilmartin, Engendering the Chinese Revolution, 157–62. See the arguments Naihua Zhang has made in her dissertation, "The All-China Women's Federation."

50  Cai Chang, "Resolution on Enlarging the Women's Movement," 476.

51  See Gilmartin, Engendering the Chinese Revolution, 231 for a capsule biography of Xiang, and Ding Ling, Muqin (Mother) (Shanghai: Liang you tushu yinshua gongsi, 1933), for a fictional portrait of Xiang. Also see Naihua Zhang, "The All-China Women's Federation" for the question of interest theory in Chinese movement feminism in the post–Great Proletariat Cultural Revolution era.

52  Xiang Jingyu, "The Future of the National Revolutionary Movement," particularly 109.

53  Xiang Jingyu, "Zai Shanghai nüjie guomin huiyi zuchenghui chengli dahui shang de jianghua" (Talk at the Shanghai women's world national conference planning committee organized general meeting), Funü zhoubao, 1924, reprinted in FYLC, 223–24.

54  Because even that would not be enough, funü activists should agitate particularly to "awaken the female masses [juewu funü qunzhong]." Xiang Jingyu, "Funü yundong yü guomin yundong" (The women's movement and the national movement), 234.

55  Xiang Jingyu, "Cong pingmin jiaoyu zhong huafen nüzi pingmin jiaoyu de wojian" (My opinion on segregating plebeian women's education from commonfolks' education), Funü zhoukan, 1924, reprinted in FYLC, 253–54. The question here again is the dual work of women, who are both persons and female: although they should be educated co-educationally with men, Chinese women are hobbled with the old lijiao education and thus are more successful in single-sex classrooms.

56  Cai Chang, "Zhongdeng yishang nüxuesheng de dushu wenti" (Study problematics for women students above the secondary level), Funü zazhi, 1924, reprinted in FYLC, 256.

57  Ibid., 260. Also see Xiang Jingyu, "Zhili di'er nüshi xuechao zai nüsi jiaoyu gexin yundongshang de jiezhi" (The value of the female education innovation movement at Zhili Second Women's Formal School), Funü zhoubao, 1924, reprinted in FYLC, 262 for a more detailed discussion of the powers of education. Cai believed that the question of female illiteracy was not as grave as the corrupting power of old-fashioned female education that filled women's heads with the notion that yield and self-sacrifice were "natural" parts of themselves.

58  See Cai Chang, "Su'E zhi funü yu ertong" (The women and children of Soviet Russia), Guangming, 1925, reprinted in FYLC, 317–21.

59  Ding Ling, "Yecao," in Yige nüren; "Busuan qingshu" (Not a love letter), in Yiwai ji (Unexpected collection) (Shanghai: Liangyu tushu yishua gongse, 1936); "Nianqian de yitian" (The day before New Year's day), in Shui (Water) (Shanghai, 1932); Wei Hu (Shanghai: Dajiang shupu, 1930). Subsequent quotations are cited in the text.

60  Yuan Liangjun, Ding Ling Research Materials, 616. Also see Ding Ling's comments about revision in her "Wo de zibai" (My confession), in Ding Ling xuanji (Selected Ding Ling) (Tianma shudian, 1933). A biographic note: Ding Ling assigned to this morally un-

impeachable figure her own "real" past. She gave herself—explicitly, without any attempt to mask or varnish the biography—a role to play in the narrative and made sure that her proxy monopolized the most valuable elements of the new female subjectivity. To her earlier, constant companion, Wang Jianhong, now conveniently dead, she assigned the wanton sexuality, romantic frenzy, and uncontrollable irresponsibility (all the qualities that Xiang Jingyu had excoriated in her review of "romantic" Chinese feminists), heaping on her own proxy the situated, calm, responsible, and nationalist female writer subject.

61 Ding Ling, "Chen Boxiang," in *Yiwai ji;* "Wo zai Xiacun de shihou," in *Wo zai Xiacun de shihou* (When I was in Xia Village) (Shanghai: Sanlian shudian, 1951).

62 Wei Hu was a character sketch of the Communist Party strategist Qu Qiubai and Li Jia a portrait of Ding Ling's friend Wang Jianhong. In fact, Wang married Qu Qiubai and died shortly thereafter. For Ding Ling's later retrospective on the *Wei Hu* story, see "Wo suo renshi de Qu Qiubai tongzhi" (The comrade Qu Qiubai I knew), in *Ding Ling sanwen jinzuoxuan* (Collection of Ding Ling's recent prose) (Kunming: Yunnan renmin chubanshe, 1983), 100–143.

63 Ding Ling's stories always frankly described female characters' sexual feelings outside the conventions of marriage. By *Wei Hu's* time, her fiction suggested a rough hierarchy that valued heterosexual, anarchist romance most highly, but ranked honest homoerotic attachment as moderately valuable and only sexual repression as "immoral." Readers valued, for instance, the honesty Sophia marshaled when she spoke of her desire to take Ling Jishi as her lover, but narrative also shaped their romance into a blind alley by making Ling such an unworthy erotic object. Before *Wei Hu,* Ding Ling's libidinal ideal appeared to be heterosexual, romantic liaisons like the one she depicted in "The Day before New Year's Day." That story unfolded in bed. Although her first female protagonists often reported from the brave new heterosexual social world, where men abandoned, tricked, exploited, and degraded them, Ding Ling herself appeared to prefer sexual experience of any sort to repression.

The notion that sexual repression sickened women's emotional life informed most of the *In Darkness* stories, but particularly "Summer Break." In that story, it will be recalled, Zhiqing finally connected her greedy lethargy to solitary sexual delirium. In the long, interesting, ambivalent passage below, Chengshu sardonically interrogates Zhiqing's view:

And Zhiqing . . . took off on a description of the childishness of certain people, and she criticized and condemned the terrible atmosphere of their alma mater; good people originally, all they had to do was be in the Wuling Women's Normal School for two months and there they would gain a kind of knowledge which did not come from textbooks, which wasn't learned at home, and which in three years at other schools they had never learned. They forgot why they had come to school. On the contrary, from dawn to dusk they indulged in kissing, hugging, writing, and placing letters secretly under somebody's pillow, and then tears, jealousies, right down to inelegant kicking and hitting—they learned it all.

"Do you still intend to carry through on your principle of staying single?" [Zhiqing asked.] Chengshu nodded her head again. Then Zhiqing started mocking the group of schoolmates, old and new, who had also vowed to sacrifice for this concept; some had been married off by their parents to farmers or businessmen who couldn't possibly satisfy them; some had let themselves be talked into becoming concubines to military men. Some had surrendered in the end and put friends in charge of their fates, let them casually go ahead and mediate a marriage. As to the rest of those who had raised high the banner of the principle of staying single, they all lay in the arms of their girl friends, the glances they gave each other of deviant tenderness, the intimate sounds they made, differing not one whit from those which passed between newly married couples. . . .

"And you?" Chengshu (who knew very well the joy such love brought) asked in an even tone.

"Only I am a true example of the principle of remaining single!" And with that statement Zhiqing seemed even more arrogant, as though nothing could command her respect, as though emotions were a laughable thing. (Ding Ling, "Summer Break," 145–46)

See also Xiang Jingyu's criticism of the "rotten atmosphere" in single-sex girls schools in her "Zhongdeng yishang nuxuesheng de dushu wenti" (The educational problems of girl students in middle school and above), in *FYLZ*, 255–56.

The moral of "Summer Break" is that we take love where we can and that nothing is worse than solitary masturbation or repression that transfigures eros into love of money. But between the stupidity of marriage slavery and the ideal of principled anarchist heterosexual romance lay homoeroticism. To my knowledge, Ding Ling never legitimated such sexual expression as an experience in itself or isolated it as "Lesbian." She consistently acknowledged sex between women, saying that it was understandable but compensatory, and her narratives chided such erotic affairs in the same tone as they criticized women's failure to will action in other life experiences.

64 Balibar, "The Borders of Europe," 216.

65 Unlike most literary Chinese feminists, Ding Ling's preoccupation with the question of new women persisted throughout a lifetime. See Wendy Larson, "The End" (*Women and writing*); Dooling and Torgeson, introduction; and Y. T. Feuerwerker, "Women as Writers in the 1920s and 1930s," in *Women in Chinese Society*, ed. Margery Wolf and Roxane Witke (Stanford: Stanford University Press, 1975). Xiang Jingyu and Ding Ling were contemporaries, after all, drawing on the same body of progressive feminism. As Ping-chun Hsiung and Yuk-lin Renita Wong have demonstrated for a later period, most characteristically Chinese protocols of womanhood coexist temporally. See Ping-chun Hsiung and Yuk-lin Renita Wong, "Jie Gui— Connecting the Tracks: Chinese Women's Activism Surrounding the 1995 World Conference on Women in Beijing," *Gender and History* 10, no. 3 (November 1998).

66 Here the analogy of India to China as "India" appears in the work of the Subaltern Studies Collective falls apart. The anticolonial nationalism of Indian nationalists differs substantially from the discourses of the nation that characterize the Chinese communist movement. As Lin Chun, "The Transformation of Chinese Socialism," unpublished manuscript (1998), has usefully pointed out, the Revolution clarifies the difference.

67 Spivak, *In Other Worlds*, 124.

68 Ding Ling, "Wo de zibai" (My confession).

69 See Ding Ling, "Wo muyin de shengping" (My mother's life), in *Muqin* (Mother) (Beijing, 1980). Later, after her incarceration, she claimed that originally she had planned *Mother* as the first third of a trilogy "describ[ing] the condition of the Chinese village before the Republic . . . the many revolutions [culminating in] the land revolution [of the 1930s and 1940s]." This trilogy form would have allowed her to paint a "picture of the world process of change and describe the bankruptcy and division of the Chinese 'Great Family' with the mother as the link of the whole story." Had she ever completed the sequence, it would have narrated the story of Chinese women "from the author's moth-

er's period to the author's own." The first quotation is from Nym Wales (pseud. Helen Snow), *The Chinese Communists: Sketches and Autobiographies of the Old Guard* (Greenwood, CT: Greenwood Press, 1972), 217, and the second is from Ding Ling, "Bianzhe houji," in *Muqin* (1980). The later statement suggests that *Sanggan River* might profitably be read as the sequel to *Mother*. As late as 1947, however, she was still dreaming that someday she might complete her historical novels conceptualized as "a trilogy dealing with the women of North China." See Robert Payne, *Journey to Red China* (London: Heinemann, 1947), 152.

70 *Mother* also "enculturated" language. This novel and Ding Ling's short stories of the early 1930s participated in early constructions of a self-consciously Chinese written language. Left-wing writers tried to recover what they theorized was a more authentic Chinese popular culture lying beneath May Fourth syntax, in popular and proletarian culture. This recovery effort is the origin of the Party's Mao Zedong language. Ding Ling was certainly an architect of literary "Maospeak" and perhaps could be accused or lauded for linguistic culturalism. Critic Li Tuo, tracing the formation of what he calls the "Mao literary language," has questioned the "Chineseness" of the final product. See Li Tuo, "Ye tan 'wei xiandaipai' ji qi piping" (On false modernism clique and its criticism), *Beijing Wenxue* 4 (1988), and "Xiandai Hanyu yu dangdai wenxue" (Modern Chinese and contemporary literature), *Xindi* 6 (1986).

71 I am suggesting alternatives to an older historiographic assumption in Anglophone feminist studies that began with Roxane Witke's belief that Chinese intellectual figures sacrificed individualism to the needs of the nationalist, revolutionary struggle. Related assumptions structure the work of critics as dissimilar as Judith Stacey and Rey Chow and feed into more current arguments that Maoism repressed normal sexual activity in Chinese society and diverted libidinal desire from its proper, natural course.

72 Ding Ling, *Muqin* (Mother) (Shanghai: Liangyou tushu yinshua gongsi, 1933); subsequent quotations are cited in the text. It is customary in Ding Ling criticism to downplay the significance of this novel in favor of the innovating short story "Shui" (Water; also translated as "Flood"). Of course, my object is slightly different here.

73 See, for instance, Gayatri C. Spivak's introduction to *Selected Subaltern Studies*, ed. Gayatri C. Spivak and Ranajit Guha (New York: Oxford University Press, 1988) for an example of what must happen for this problem to be remedied.

74 Marsten Anderson, in the chapter entitled "Beyond Realism: The Eruption of the Crowd," in *The Limits of Realism: Chinese Fiction in the Revolutionary Period* (Berkeley: University of California Press, 1990), 180–202.

75 "Ding Ling de Muqin" (Ding Ling's Mother), in Zhang Baiyun, ed., *Ding Ling Pingzhuan*, 146–47.

76 Ibid., 159.

77 Ibid., 140.

78 Ibid., 137.

79 Ibid., 163–64.

80 The narrative also drew attention to the only one of the great Qing novels that deals directly with the theme of female virtue, Li Ju-chen's *Flowers in the Mirror*, trans. and ed. Lin Tai-yi (Berkeley: University of California Press, 1965). Both narratives place a band of talented, learned women in a situation requiring them to band together and support true rulers against usurpers who would destroy the country. See Ding Ling, *Mother*, 127.

81 Andrew Plaks, *Archetype and Allegory in the Dream of the Red Chamber* (Princeton: Princeton University Press, 1976), ch. 3, "Complementary Bipolarity and Multiple Periodicity."

82 Chapter 1 spans the period of winter to spring 1909; chapter 2, spring to summer 1910;

chapter 3, late summer to lunar New Year of the solar year 1911; the novel then concludes with a careful summary of the events (inside the courtyard, not outside, in the political world) of spring and summer 1911. Of course, the passage of organic time brings the women closer to the moment of historical insurrection, but only the reader knows this.

83 Wang Shuming, "Muqin" (Mother), in Zhang Baiyun, ed., *Ding Ling Pingzhuan*, 177. Contemporary critic Wang Shuming seemed cognizant of this when he acknowledged the archaism and historicism by typing *Mother* as a "biographical novel" (*zhuanjishi de xiaoshuo*). In Wang's view, the biographical focus determined the novel's restricted specular economy. Manzhen's feudal, female consciousness perforce limited the scope of the readers' understanding because "traditional" women had little direct experience with the world beyond the garden wall.

84 Before *Mother*, Ding Ling's fiction assumed a universal sexualized category—woman or nüxing—into which Chinese, like Russian, Japanese, and English, women were naturally, hierarchically fitted according to their degree of enlightenment or oppression. *Mother* challenged this metonymy when it overtly linked women's liberation to foreign imperialism. In a conversation with her wetnurses about "Foreign Country" (the servants are too ignorant of geography to understand the term generically), Manzhen distinguishes Chinese from Western women. "All I know," she explains, "is that foreign women are different from Chinese women." The "differences" are, first, that "they don't bind their feet, they bind their waists," and second, that they are the female side of Western imperialism. The same imperialists threatening to carve China up like a melon produced a hierarchy of enlightenment that inferiorized the bound-foot woman at the moment it claimed to rescue her.

85 Manzhen's infant son does not represent the patrilineal center around whom mother and sister pivot. That would have been the case had they stayed on the farm with Yaoma. But the novel makes clear the fact that widow and children are not absorbed back into the Jiang or the Yu families.

86 See Jane Gallop, *The Daughter's Seduction: Feminism and Psychoanalysis* (Ithaca, NY: Cornell University Press, 1982) and other Lacanian-inspired criticism for the position that no relationship excludes sexual attachment. I am taking the anti-Oedipal position that eroticization is not automatically transferable.

87 Ding Ling, "Xiang Jingyu lieshi gei wo de yingxiang" (Martyr Xiang Jingyu's influence on me), in *Ding Ling jinzuo* (Ding Ling's recent writing) (Chengda: Sichuan renmin chubanshe, 1980), 88. In her personal life after Hu Yepin's death, Ding Ling appears to have been preoccupied with a choice she believed confronted her between self as lover and self as sister. Her own immediate problem was explaining why, after Hu died, she both deepened her stake in communist politics and begun a sexual affair with translator Feng Da. She was no longer a young woman and, she explained, she no longer suffered romantic fools gladly. She made every effort to strip herself of womanliness. Yet, there was no way to deny it: she was Feng's lover, not his sister. See Shen Congwen, *Remembering Ding Ling*, 189.

## 5. Woman under Maoist Nationalism in the Thought of Ding Ling

1 Yang Guixin, *Ding Ling chuangzuo zhongheng tan* (Speaking on the breadth and depth of Ding Ling's creations) (Changsha: Hunan renmin chubanshe, 1984), 45. Yang cites Feng Xuefeng's judgment that Ding Ling fiction "advances [qianjin] and alters [biandong] along with society." Yang explains that this understanding of Feng's applies to the dialectic in Ding Ling's feminism. According to Yang, foreign scholars of Ding Ling's

work have correctly privileged Ding Ling's feminism but must do so in the context of her literary realism and commitment to developing a Chinese tradition of Engelsian realism. See 45–49 for Yang's discussion. See also Feng Xuefeng, "*Taiyang zhao zai Sanggan he shang zai women wenxue fazhanshang de yiyi*" (The significance of *The Sun Shines over the Sanggan River* in the development of our literature), in Ding Ling, *Taiyang zhaozai Sanggan he shang* (The sun shines over the Sanggan River) (Beijing: Renmin wenxue chubanshe, 1955).

2   Li Daxuan, *Ding Ling yü Shafei xielie xingxiang* (Lineage of the form of Ding Ling and Sophia) (Changsha: Hunan wenyi chubanshe, 1991).

3   Of course, Ding Ling remained a writer with a writer's commitments to the Chinese revolutionary literature movement. But particularly after 1942, the Central Committee of the Communist Party and its major cultural cadre (including Ding Ling herself) set the parameters for literary production. They determined through often simple factional struggle what the correct relation of history, life, and literature would be until the subjective "opening" (*kaitou*) of the next historical epoch. Writers who misrepresented the people to each other or to the political authorities imperiled the success of strategic and tactical decisions. One could say, prosaically, that linking literature and politics raises literature's status. When literature is policy, writers are overt political operatives. When the literary text and policy are conflated, theory (*lilun*) unfolds in relation to the practices of mobilization and shares with mobilization its inherent risk of failure. See Barlow, "*Zhishifenzi* and Power" for a more focused argument on this point. I bring this up to stress the difference between linguistic subjects and policy subjects. When *funü* is the subject of a policy, its powers are qualitatively and quantitatively different than when it is the subject of an idea or critique. Policy applies subject forms in a gross fashion. Each is social in a different way.

4   Diamant, *Revolutionizing the Family* illustrates quite empirically the profusion of these unincorporated practices as well as making the point that the closer to the center, the more preoccupied with normative ideological concerns individuals become.

5   This is a process that many critics have noticed. Song Jianyuan calls it simply "describing the new person" (*miaoxie xin de renwu*). Song Jianyuan, *Ding Ling pingzhuan* (Critical biography of Ding Ling) (Xi'an: Shaanxi renmin chubanshe, 1989), 9.

6   See Gregor Benton, "The Yenan 'Literary Opposition,' " *New Left Review* 92 (July/August 1975): 93.

7   Ellen Judd, "Prelude to the 'Yan'an Talks': Problems in Transforming a Literary Intelligencia," *Modern China* 11:3 (July 1985), 379.

8   Ibid., 395.

9   This last point is made most forcefully in ibid., 397, but is suggested in Holm as well. Gregor Benton, "The Yenan 'Literary Opposition,' " 96–102 has pointed out the degree to which Ding Ling's use of the zawen was a "Maoist" phenomenon.

10   Kyna Rubin, "An Interview with Mr. Wang Ruowang," *China Quarterly* 87 (1981), 508.

11   Her 16 September 1941 essay in the Party newspaper *Jeifang ribao* (Liberation daily; hereafter *JFRB*), "Douzheng shi xiangshou" (To struggle is pleasure), endorsed the view that writers should "plunge into life" before committing words to paper. But the follow-up, an essay called "Cailiao" (Material), *JFRB* 29 September 1941, suggested that policy decisions about cultural representation should respect the gap separating high and low and should give more latitude to literary writers than to mere journalists. Trying to determine political affiliations on the basis of the public record is difficult. Liu Shaoqi's essay "On the Intra-Party Struggle," delivered to the Central China Communist Party School (July 2, 1941, in Conrad Brandt, Benjamin Schwartz, and John K. Fairbank, A

Documentary History of Chinese Communism (London: Allen and Unwin, 1952), 356–72), and later a Party Rectification document, says pretty much the same things Ding Ling's famous "Women xuyao zawen" (We need the zawen) did when she published it in the Liberation Daily on 10 October 1941. Ding Ling was sanctioned for her activities; Liu, already a member of the Politburo, was not. The difference may be that Liu did not intend to grant the sort of authority to ideological intellectuals that Ding Ling apparently assumed belonged to her. "We Need the Zawen" was part of a rash of criticism, including, among other things, a satirical cartoon exhibition that opened in February 1942. On the cartoon display, see JFRB 13, 15, 19 February 1942. Echoing points that Liu was also making, she argued that to openly criticize social inequalities made later genuine consensus possible; without it, discontent would persist. As is well-known, Lo Feng, Wang Shiwei, Xiao Jun, Cao Ming, and other literary intellectuals reacted. For instance, see Lo Feng, "Haishi zawen de shidai" (It is still the age of the zawen), JFRB 12 March 1942, and Xiao Jun, "Lun zhong shen da shi" (On marriage), JFRB 25 March 1942. For more extensive discussion of Xiao Jun's role, consult Holm and Rubin.

12  Gary Bjorge argued that because Ding Ling was appointed to this position by Lo Fu (Zhang Wentian) and worked there under the editorship of Bo Gu (Jin Bangxian), both members of the so-called 28 Bolsheviks, the Zhou Yang–Ding Ling conflict should be interpreted as the reverberation of a primary conflict between the Moscow-oriented internationalists and the China-oriented Maoists. However, I believe the politics of these years are so complex and so highly overcharged because of the significance that Yan'an came to have in later years that it is best to qualify all interpretation of particulars. See Bjorge, "Introduction: Sophia's Diary," particularly 105–6.

13  See "Zhengduan san feng yundong zhankai" (Movement to rectify the three winds launched), JFRB 8 April 1942.

14  See Liao Ying, "Ren zai jianku zhong shengzhang" (People grow through hardship), JFRB 10 June 1942.

15  Ding Ling, "Wenyi jie dui Wang Shiwei ying you de taidu ji fanxing" (The attitude and self-introspection that the literary world should take toward Wang Shiwei), JFRB 16 June 1942.

16  "In what future time will it be possible to not have to specially weight nor particularly elevate these two characters, fu nü," is the plaintive first line of Ding Ling's "San ba jie you gan" (Thoughts on March 8), JFRB 9 March 1942.

17  Gilmartin, Engendering the Chinese Revolution.

18  Naihua Zhang, "All-China Women's Federation."

19  Ho Kuo Cheng, "The Status and the Role of Women in the Chinese Communist Movement, 1946–1949" (Ph.D. diss., Indiana University, 1973), chs. 1, 2.

20  Song Jianyuan argues in an authorized biography that Ding Ling is the primary heir of Lu Xun and that her contribution to Chinese letters is not her May Fourth women's fiction but the way she mediated the turn to proletarian literatures. Song distinguishes, as Ding Ling always did, between the puluo, or idealist proletarian writers, and genuine proletarian class literature (wuchan jieji wenxue), which she claimed as her own project. Song correctly notes that Ding Ling's concern with subaltern subjects was to "extremely truthfully represent life and truthfully describe character [renwu]" (4). See the introduction and conclusion to Song Jianyuan, Ding Ling pingzhuan (Critical biography of Ding Ling) (Xian: Shaanxi renmin chubanshe, 1989).

21  Ding Ling, "Guanyu Du Wanxiang: Zai Beijing tushuguan zuzhi de yu duzhe jianmian hui shang de tanhua" (About "Du Wanxiang": A talk at the face-to-face meeting with readers organized by the Beijing Library), in Ding Ling jin zuo (Ding Ling's recent work),

166. The name of the woman who was Ding Ling's model for Du Wanxiang is Deng Wanrung. See Zheng Xiaofeng, *Ding Ling zai Beidahuang* (Ding Ling in the Great Northern Wasteland) (N.p.: Hubei renmin chubanshe, 1989), 46.

22  Ding Ling, "Xie gei nü qingnian zuozhe" (Written for a young female author), in *Shenghuo, chuangzuo, shidai linghun* (Life, creation and the soul of the times) (Changsha: Hunan renmin chubanshe, 1981), 190.

23  Ding Ling, "Du Wanxiang," in Barlow with Bjorge, *I Myself Am A Woman*, 353–54.

24  Ho Kuo Cheng (translator), "The Status," 33. Chen Boda, "Xin funü de rensheng guan" (The life philosophy of the new woman), in *Funü yundong wenxian* (Collected works on the women's movement), ed. Zhu De et al. (Hong Kong: Xin minzhu chubanshe, 1949), 79.

25  I discuss Ding Ling's position on official writers and subalterneity—the power to represent those excluded from powers of self-representation—later in this chapter.

26  Ding Ling, *Kua dao xin de shidai lai* (Stride into the new age) (Beijing: Renmin wenxue chubanshe, 1951).

27  Ding Ling, "Tan 'laolao shishi'" (Speaking on "honesty"), in *Kua dao xin de shidai lai*, 237.

28  Ding Ling, "Qingnian lian'ai wenti" (The question of young people and erotic love), in *Kua dao xin de shidai lai*, 214–35. In general, she takes the position that if "we" liberate ourselves politically and economically but suppress thinking, then the Revolution will not fulfill its future potential. Intimate affairs should be considered in a political light, not to condemn or deny individual acts but to understand and rationalize emotions.

29  Ding Ling, "Zai qianjin de daolu shang: Guanyu du wenxue shu de wenti" (On the road forward: Questions on reading literature), in *Kua dao xin de shidai lai*, 184.

30  Ding Ling, "Zhishifenzi xianxiang zhong de wenti" (Problems of intellectuals going down), in *Kua dao xin de shidai lai*, 199–224. This is a reversal of the position that Ding Ling took in 1942, when she seemed to be supporting the argument that the Party should accommodate the moods of the youth.

31  Ding Ling, afterword to *Shaanbei fengguang* (Scenes of Northern Shaanxi) (Beijing: Xinhua shuchan, 1950).

32  Ding Ling, "Buneng cong xingshi chufa" (You cannot start from form), in *Kua dao xin de shidai lai*, 17.

33  Ding Ling, "Remembering Chen Man," Jean James, trans., in Barlow with Bjorge, *I Myself Am a Woman*, 326–27. I have slightly altered James's translation.

34  Almost immediately after she arrived in Bao'an from Nanjing after eluding house arrest there in 1936, Ding Ling went to work dismantling the "new realism" that she and the League of Left-Wing Writers had promoted and supplanting it with the Communist Party's policy-mandated "national defense" models. For an important view of this war literature and theory, see Theodore Huters, ed., special issue of *Modern Chinese Literature* 5, no. 2 (fall 1989). Before her death, Ding Ling published several pieces of exculpatory writing. See particularly "Yan'an wenyi zuotanhui de qianqian houhou" (Before and after the talks at the Yan'an Forum), in *Ding Ling jinzuo (2): Wo de shengping yü chuangzuo* (Ding Ling's recent work, 2: My life and work) (Chengdu: Sichuan renmin chubanshe, 1982), 26–52. For an excellent introduction to the nonliterary arts work that Ding Ling conducted throughout her stay in the Border Regions, see Ellen Judd's two essays on dramatic arts: "Prelude to the 'Yan'an Talks': Problems in Transforming a Literary Intelligencia," *Modern China* 11:3 (July 1985); and "Cultural Articulation in the Chinese Countryside, 1937–1947," *Modern China* 16:3 (July 1990).

35  Social mobilizations really did change villages in the Border Regions, particularly after 1942, and the forms Ding Ling experimented with— reportage, records, opera,

storytelling—were instrumental forms that sought to transform lived realities. The distinction in Ding Ling's fiction between what Feuerwerker terms "life" and "literature," or representation and experience, became increasingly less clear in Ding Ling's sophisticated propaganda narratives.

36  Ding Ling, "Yi ke wei chu tang de qiangdan" (The unfired bullet), in *Wo zai Xiacun de shihou* (When I was in Xia Village) (Shanghai: Sanlian Shudian, 1951); subsequent quotations are cited in the text. For a second war story based on it, see Ding Ling, *Yi ge xiao hongjun de gushi* (Story of a little red soldier) (Shanghai, 1956).

37  Though it was not at all rare to find female symbols of resistance in Chinese wartime popular culture, the difference between Ding Ling's national defense tropes and the sort of recycled, traditionalistic, Mulan-style martial sagas that Chang-Tai Hung outlines in his "Female Symbols of Resistance in Chinese Wartime Spoken Drama," *Modern China* 15, no. 2 (April 1989): 149–77 is fairly stark. This suggests another reason why the episteme of the communist era should highlight the quality of *revolutionary modernity*. The trope of the empowered, often female victim and narratives of national political redemption were Ding Ling's signature themes of the late 1930s and early 1940s. See Feuerwerker, *Ding Ling's Fiction*, 106–8 for a brief discussion of the weak and helpless in Ding Ling's Yan'an fiction.

38  Ding Ling also wrote stories that showed how the creativity of the weak could be sapped if they languished inside patriarchal families. A cautionary story illustrating the evils of the selfish *jiazhang* (patriarch) who refuses to allow his child to serve the nation is "Xianzhang jiating" (County magistrate's family), in *Wo Zai Xiacun de shihou*, written during the Northwest Front Service Group tour.

39  Like "The Unfired Bullet," "Affair" has a magical, dreamy quality. In a postface to a later anthology that included "Dongcun shijian" (The affair in East Village), *Suchu de wenyi* (Shanghai: n.p., 1938), Ding Ling herself commented that the story "has meaning, but I think that it relies too heavily on imagination."

40  The story employed a simple class analysis to frame the economy of female sexuality in feudal relations of production. In the struggle to monopolize the virgin sexuality of the wife, the story sets the master against his slave, Zhao versus Chen, and thereby annuls any possibility that Qiqi might desire Delu and choose him as her lover. Also, obviously, the story demonstrated how female sexuality was, at least in the corrupt feudal rural village, a simple abstract commodity that the landlord could extract, exploit, or exchange. As the narrative's representative of the ruling class, Zhao had direct authority over all of his tenants, male and female. He used his power brutally to "cow" them, turn them into "beasts of burden." On top of that ability to generate surplus and accumulate capital and social wealth, the landlord magically transformed female bodies into exchange tokens, thus adding women to the other forms of wealth—labor, land, and money—that he has stolen from the poor peasants. But the Chen family is itself blameworthy because it protects its patrilineal descent line at any cost. It has already bought Qiqi once, and under pressure transforms her back into capital. Ding Ling highlighted Qiqi's economic exchangeability by introducing a long plot digression to explain how the Chen family evaluated its two capital resources: Qiqi and the ox. The ancient ox, it turns out, had years earlier saved the Chens' second son from a wolf attack. "The entire family was reluctant to kill or sell the ox," the narrator explains. "It had saved Lao Yao's life. Really they would never find anyone with enough money to buy the ox." Qiqi, by comparison, had not contributed as much to the patriline as the ox had, as she was still a virgin without a son; she represented a depletion of family resources, a frozen asset, and

was still too young to contribute anything to the corporate holding. No single person, the story suggests, could hope to alter such cruel economies. The Chen women might express anger over Qiqi's fate and visit her frequently at Zhao's compound; the decision might ruin Chen Delu. But in fact, the family as a whole has no other possible option, because to remain a "family" means precisely that wives are cashed in when fathers are threatened.

41   Ding Ling held a number of government positions in the late 1930s. She taught literature at Kang Da, acted as secretary in the Eighth Route Army, was a vice chair of the political arm of the Jingwei tuan (Guard Corps), played an active role in the Zhongguo wenyi xiehui (Chinese Arts and Literary Union), and participated, with her co-chair, Deng Yingchao, in organizing the Jiuguo funühui (National Women's Salvation Association). In 1941 she took over as editor of the literary supplement to Jiefang ribao. She also placed herself in a series of key positions as one of the very few literary figures able to speak for the patriotic youth, then arriving by the thousands from the White Areas to join the Red Army during the United Front; as a trustworthy representative of the Shanghai intellectual world to old military and political revolutionaries like Wang Ming, Po Gu, Peng Dehuai, Zhou Enlai, and Mao Zedong; and apparently acting as a political cadre inside the sophisticated community of left-wing refugee intellectuals, women and men like Wang Shiwei, Hu Ke, Bai Shuang, and He Qifang. See Yuan Liangjun, Ding Ling yanjiu ziliao (Ding Ling research materials) (Tianjin: Zhongguo xiandai zuojia zuopin yanjiu ziliao congshu, Tianjin renmin chubanshe, 1982).

42   Ding Ling, Yinian (One year) (Chongqing: Shenghuo shudian, 1939), 23–25; subsequent quotations are cited in the text. She wrote: "We held self-examination meetings [jiantao-hui] about their lives. This kind of life examination meeting [shenghuo jiantaohui] was usually called by the unit. Occasionally when an important problem arose they also held large meetings. There they regulated rewards and punishments. The comrades were affectionate to one another. This spirit of affection was even more obvious at these meetings. They criticized dispassionately and 'struggled against bad tendencies.' There was, Ding Ling claimed, love, among the comrades, and you could see expressions of this kind of loving spirit in these kinds of meetings. Dispassionately criticizing, they all struggled without prejudice, not the least bit polite with each other. But after the meeting was over, all one could see was that they all treated each other as brother and sister, and were as harmonious as ever. "How could one not be moved after witnessing that?"

43   The comrades decide to honor him with a real "thought struggle meeting" on the spot to honor his moral rearmament. " 'Comrade Wang Qi,' one female cadre began, 'you are a member of our Service Group and you should learn our spirit in order not to disgrace yourself. Your disorganized thoughts are really condemnable.' The meeting continued in that vein for three more hours and still no one was fatigued." "I think," narrator Ding Ling concluded, "that probably no one who attended that meeting will ever forget Comrade Wang Qi" (ibid., 69).

44   Ding Ling made this point quite emphatically:

> [Her] love for her sons changed completely. When they were small she had regarded them as tame kittens. Then she hoped they would grow up quickly in order to help her bear all her sufferings and hardships. Then the children grew up as strong as bears and as alert as eagles. They could not understand her at all, so she just had to love them in her heart, quietly and sadly, while feeling she might completely lose touch with them. As her sons grew up, things became more difficult and her nature hardened. They never seemed to consider their mother and she felt she hated them some-

times. Yet she needed their love even more than ever, so she became weak and nervous. . . . [But] now their feelings were unimportant. Did she not love them anymore? No, that wasn't it at all, she just looked at them from a different angle.
Ding Ling, "Xin de xinnian" (New faith), in *Wo zai Xiacun de shihou*. All translations adapted from Kung Pusheng, trans., *When I Was in Sha Chuan and Other Stories* (Poona, India: n.p., n.d.). The "angle" seems to be a combination of insight into the larger world outside family and recognition of her own personal desires, now legitimated by the authority of the Party.

45 Ibid., 55.

46 Ding Ling, "The County Magistrate's Family," 79.

47 Such optimistic and, under the circumstances, resolutely cheery Yan'an national defense fiction also reads very well as self-invention, and "The County Magistrate's Family" is an obvious vehicle for more "Ding Ling" portraiture. The piece is classified as a story (*xiaoshuo*), though Ding Ling claimed she took material directly from personal experience (an assertion that should alert the educated reader to the formation of yet another Ding Ling). In fact, early Yan'an Ding Ling emerges as the Service Group's greatest product. Alert, attentive to detail, responsible to the national interest, loving yet properly remote, passionate yet controlled, a moral authoritarian and tireless worker, cognizant of the motives of others, skilled at timing and protocol, cool under fire: the list of qualities this Ding Ling possessed proliferated uncontrollably. And unlike the child Ding Ling in *Mother*, this time Ding Ling spoke for the nation, or *guo*.

All of these narratives starring a Ding Ling who stood for the nation were also certainly part of the writer's ongoing self-mythologizing. She and others were developing a language that would reenvision a modern national community free of Japanese imperialism and Chinese feudalism. Who better to speak this inflated, synthetic, and militarized language than the widow of a revolutionary martyr, herself a former political prisoner? This version of the Ding Ling persona also claimed a talent for moral instruction. Ding Ling had never published in the zawen genre until she got to Yan'an. There she used it primarily to convey "moral lessons," or *jiaoxun*. "Fan yü zheng" (For and against) in *One Year*, for instance, begins as a homily about actors and ends with a lesson on how to behave correctly in the real world.

"Shuo huanying" (Speaking on Welcome) addresses foreign visitors, the moral issue at stake being the relative status of the Chinese and the guests. "Shuo dao 'yingxiang' " (Speaking of 'Influence') attacks the "hereditary disease" of the male, bourgeois, literary establishment at Wuhan, and "Fengci" (Satire) dismisses metaphoric writing in favor of explicit disagreements and honesty among comrades.

48 Tony Saich restates the point that the CCP has always been made up of a wide range of individuals who are "members of the society in which they live, work, form relationships, suffer hardships and experience joys." The shift of focus from histories preoccupied with Party discipline to a focus on the mundane, everyday reality of life in a flexible, albeit authoritarian, political apparatus even during the revolutionary years shifts priorities in Ding Ling research. See Tony Saich, "Introduction: The Chinese Communist Party and the Anti-Japanese War Base Areas," *China Quarterly* 140 (December 1994): 1005.

49 Yung-fa Chen, *Making Revolution: The Communist Movement in Eastern and Central China, 1937–1945* (Berkeley: University of California Press, 1985). Chen's is one of a very rich body of Border Region research. A founding monograph is Mark Selden, *The Yenan Way in Revolutionary China* (Cambridge, MA: Harvard University Press, 1971).

50  Tetsuya Kataoka, *Resistance and Revolution in China: The Communists and the Second United Front* (Berkeley: University of California Press, 1974) claims that the CCP in fact did not fully prosecute the war because to do so would have undermined the claims to sovereignty it was developing in its New Democracy institutions. Pauline Keating has more recently argued that the tension historians perceive between Selden's emphasis on democratization and Chen Yung-fa's emphasis on authoritarian state building is in fact illusory. She reconciles the Yan'an Way "to accommodate both populism and statism." I follow suit. See Pauline Keating, "The Yan'an Way of Co-operatization," *China Quarterly* 140 (December 1994): 1025–51.

See Partha Chatterjee, *Nationalist Thought and the Colonial World: A Derivative Discourse* (Tokyo: United Nations Press, 1986), 26–28 for an interesting discussion of nationalism in this expanded light for the Indian movement. Chatterjee's point is that academic discussion is reductionist. It has contracted nationalism's significance by eliding the questions of (1) nationalism as thought, (2) modernization of social-cultural codes, (3) appropriation and use in new cultural contexts, (4) relations of dominance in cultural contexts and their portability, and (5) the existing relations of power in the revolutionary country experiencing nationalist mobilization. I think that some of the questions Chatterjee raises are germane to Maoism. The intense nationalism of Chinese communism was partly a consequence of the exigencies of war, and previous historiography has stressed the importance of anti-Japanese sentiment to the CCP's seizure of power.

51  Yung-fa Chen, *Making Revolution*, 12.

52  Kataoka, *Resistance*, 201–3. Firsthand accounts of Party recruitment of cadres and soldiers routinely mention how the government's new language was a secret, coded political dialect that made it possible for peasant leaders to organize local Party cells in white territory or carry out other basic political tasks. See William Hinton, *Fanshen* (Berkeley: University of California Press, 1997). Scientific language used for keeping records and particularly the local report genre developed by Mao Zedong also required that cadres manipulate representational language in new ways. See Yung-fa Chen, *Making Revolution*, ch. 3; and see Mao Zedong, *Report from Xunwu*, trans. Roger R. Thompson (Stanford: Stanford University Press, 1990).

53  See Yung-fa Chen's section entitled "Ambiguity in Class Analysis": "To apply such an alien scheme to Chinese rural communities . . . the Party had to make changes. It defined classes and strata according to three criteria: mode of 'exploitation,' ownership of the means of production, and living standard of the individual community. Exploitative relationships were but one of the three." The most useful discussion of the empowering of individuals through this application is his discussion of the ambiguity of the category of worker (210–13).

54  David Holm, *Art and Ideology in Revolutionary China* (Oxford: Oxford University Press, 1991). I am greatly indebted to Holm for my understanding of the Yan'an cultural experience. His book is a tour de force.

55  Ibid., 54. Also see David Holm, "The Literary Rectification in Yan'an," in *Essays in Modern Chinese Literature and Literary Criticism*, ed. Wolfgang Kubin and Rudolf Wagner (Bochum: Brockmeyer, 1982), Holm expands discussion of national forms during the Rectification Campaign. He argues that although national forms was not a key term in theoretical dispute at the Yan'an Forum, it was assumed to be the main object of struggle. Why was the term suppressed? At the most superficial level, the Mao group sought to dampen fears in China proper that the Party would stifle cultural activity and thus did not explicitly theorize their view that cultural mobilization determined instrumental uses of

culture. At another level, Holm demonstrates, the Mao group sought to purge Trotsky-ists (preeminently Wang Shiwei, who was crucified ideologically and later executed), who were suggesting that Marxism was incompatible with a popular base and cultural revolutionary nationalism. Finally, the Mao group sought to win over the intellectuals and therefore was determined to shift the ground of debate from specific practices (i.e., national forms) to general nationalist mobilization. They therefore turned the argument around to argue that elites should "massify" themselves rather than forcing the view that mass culture was the exclusive touchstone for the literate. Also see Holm, *Art and Ideology in Revolutionary China*.

Until the 1942 Party rectification, the Mao group, as is well-known, did not have the decisive voice when it came to cultural theory. Euro-Marxists, "Internationalists" like Wang Ming, expressed interest in Moscow's valorization of Europe's bourgeois heri-tage. Against Mao's thesis of the two-stage bourgeois democratic revolution, the Wang Ming–Moscow version held that when the bourgeois democratic revolution in China was completed, history working teleologically would bring about modern, progressive, democratic (read Europeanized) cultural forms. Wang Ming's position was closer to that of a Gramsci or Trotsky; the CCP should take a relatively laissez-faire position on culture. China's masses (and here the difference between the Maoist and so-called Internationalist positions go back to earlier debates in the early 1930s over "populariza-tion" versus "elevation" of the proletarian reader) would eventually abandon feudal cultural forms and accept more progressive, Europeanized, bourgeois high culture. The internationalist-thinking, non-Maoist, Marxist opposition argued that China's develop-mental path necessarily included a colonial phase and therefore May Fourth cultural practices were acceptable because they represented a real progressive move away from feudalism. Peasant arts and culture, on the other hand, encapsulated the feudal forms and kept them alive. Promoting a national culture meant siding with the particular over the universal. The anti-Maoists held that the culture of Europeanized Russia represented an international, universal norm that China, too, with patience, would approximate.

See Wang Hui's discussion of these matters from the perspective of the problem of local dialects in "Local Forms, Vernacular Dialects and the War of Resistance against Japan: The 'National Forms' Debate" (parts 1 and 2), trans. Chris Berry, UTS *Review* 4:1 (1998), 25–41, and UTS *Review* 4:2 (1998), 27–56. Wang covers much of the same ground as Holm. See particularly "The Problem of the 'Local' and the 'All-Chinese,'" part 1, 34–38, focusing on the role of Ke Zhongping, a popularizer and theorist of performance, and importantly a collaborator of Ding Ling's whom she understudied.

56  What is remarkable about many of Maoism's major texts of the period is how they privilege a notion of culture that is both omnibus and unstable. See "On New Democ-racy" (106–156), "The May Fourth Movement" (9–11), "The Orientation of the Youth" (12–21), "The Chinese Revolution and the Chinese Communist Party" (72–101), and other United Front essays in *Mao Tse-tung Selected Works, Vol 3, 1939–1941* (New York: International Publisher, 1954). Because it appears in much United Front policy as a semifeudal, semicolonial country, Chinese society and economy are heterogeneous. So-cially, China possesses both bourgeois and feudal forms since its economy is feudal but leavened with colonial despots and new national capitalism. Mao argues that there are three reasons why it is theoretically and practically correct to periodize the present with an emphasis on "new democracy." First, it situates the Party in Chinese history and enables it to act out its historic role as an agent of antifeudalism. Second, the stage of New Democracy situates the Party as an agent of the nation (110–11). Finally, knowing

historically where they are situated, so to speak, liberates strategists and patriots to look at "culture as an ideological form" (107).

When Maoists said "culture," they sometimes meant May Fourth norms from the 1920s, such as the New Literature movement, language reform, and European bourgeois and Russian Bolshevik fine arts, crafts, literary projects, and theatrical performances. "On New Democracy" is an example of the second sense in which Maoists used culture in the 1930s. Here culture is an inclusive, though malleable ground of social transformation, a realm of popular signification where acute Party operatives can judge the efficacy of specific policies. In Bolshevik and Marxist terms, "Any given culture (as an ideological form) is a reflection of the politics and economy of a given society, while it has in turn a tremendous influence and effect upon the politics and economy of the given society" (107). But the Maoists posed a further question that was both specific and unstable: "We want to build up a new culture of the Chinese nation," they stated, and then asked rhetorically, "but what kind of culture is this new culture after all?" This was a specific question because, quite properly, it cited the thesis on Feuerbach to argue that the Marxist's job was to change the world. It was destabilizing when it suggested that culture was at one and the same time both a reflection of real social and economic conditions and its direct opposite (i.e., neither reflection nor sign of present conditions but rather a blueprint of the historical future to come). See "On New Democracy," 108–9.

57  The powers invested in the cultural realm charged cultural production with particular dangers. In a culturalized arena where what things mean (signification) is believed to be transitive or essentially indeterminate, political representation becomes deeply problematic.
    This bears on the question of how woman and women ought to appear in cultural forms and in social policy. Previous historians of Ding Ling and Chinese women during the Yan'an period have consistently argued that the critic was a "feminist" and the "Marxist" CCP was antifeminist; misogynists restricted what Ding Ling was allowed to say publicly about women and literature after 1942. I am building on their critique of CCP misogyny, but in a somewhat different direction. Where the cultural realm is so extraordinarily charged with power, all representation aids either, to misquote Chairman Mao, the enemy or ourselves. Ideological identification, the instability involved in saying what exactly constitutes woman, and the perceived need of the government to modernize women produced a situation where cultural representation and policy objectives were supposed to line up exactly. When they did not, the stability of all appeared to be threatened. See Patricia Stranahan, Molding the Medium: The Chinese Communist Party and the Liberation Daily (Armonk, NY: M.E. Sharpe, 1990).

58  See Marsten Anderson, The Limits of Realism: Chinese Fiction in the Revolutionary Period (Berkeley: University of California Press, 1990).

59  Ding Ling, "Guanyu lichang wenti wo jian" (My opinion on the problem of class standing), in Kua dao xin di shidai lai; subsequent quotations are cited in the text.

60  Feuerwerker, Ding Ling's Fiction, 99–104.

61  Yi Ou, "Zhongguo funü" (Chinese women), JFRB 6 January 1942.

62  See JFRB: Zhu Qing, "Yisilanjiao de hunyin" (Islamic marriage), 1 February 1942; "Wushiba ge nüxuesheng zai Suishi" (58 girl students in Suishi), 6 February 1942; untitled, 11 February 1942; Ge Lu, "Jiehun hou" (After marriage), 3 and 4 March 1942.

63  Cited in Stranahan, Molding the Medium, 57–58. Xie wrote under the pseudonym Wang Dingguo and was a vice chair of the Shaan Gan Ning Border Region Assembly.

64  Ibid., 57. The essay "Dedaole xie shenma jiaoxun" (Attaining some instruction), JFRB 16 February 1942, was unsigned.

65  Zeng Ko, "Yuanjiu muqin" (Save the mothers), JFRB 8 March 1942.

66  Cao Ming, "Chuangzuo ni de mingyun" (Create your own destiny), *JFRB* 8 March 1942.

67  Bai Shuang, "Huidao jia qu? Dao shehui lai?" (Back to the family? Or out into society?), *JFRB* 8 March 1942.

68  Ding Ling, "San ba jie you gan" (Thoughts on March 8), *JFRB* 9 March 1942.

69  Stranahan, *Yan'an Women*, 45 n. 51; emphasis added.

70  Ding Ling, "Jieda san ge wenti: Zai Beijing yuyan xueyuan waiguo liu xuexheng zuotan-hui shang de jianghua" (Answering three questions: Speech at the conference of foreign students at the Beijing Foreign Languages Academy), in *Ding Ling jin zuo* (Ding Ling's recent work), 180–83.

71  Ding Ling, "Thoughts on March 8," 319.

72  Ding Ling, "Answering Three Questions," 180. Also see "Guanyu zawen" (Regarding zawen), in *Ding Ling jin zuo (2) Wo de shengping yü chuangzuo* (My life and work), 152–56, where Ding Ling adds to her stock explanations about the genesis of the essay the information that the first person to criticize it was Cao Yi'o, a female comrade. Ding Ling also reminds readers that the essay did not gather deadly opprobrium until 1958, when it was designated a "poisonous weed" (*ducao*) and that people who were not at Yan'an in the glory years do not understand how freely comrades were allowed to criticize one another and Party policies.

73  Ding Ling, "Ye" (Night), in *Wo zai Xiacun de shihou* (When I was in Xia Village) (Shanghai: Sanlian shudian, 1951); subsequent quotations are cited in the text. Written around the same period as she drafted "Thoughts on March 8" and just ten days before she published "When I Was in Xia Village," "Night" was originally published in *JFRB* on 10 and 11 June 1942. "Thoughts on March 8" is dated 3 August 1941, though it was not published until March the following year.

74  Ding Ling, "Night," 6–7 gives a good example of how political language could be used against wives in this context: " 'This old hag is definitely not the material substructure,' he thought to himself as he lay on the kang facing the wall [waiting for his wife to serve him dinner]. 'At least the cow breeds, but this old thing is more like a "hen who can't lay eggs." ' What was the material substructure? He wasn't sure himself, but he was pretty sure it meant that the old woman couldn't have any more children. It was a new phrase he had picked up from the Deputy Secretary."

75  Ding Ling, "Shenghuo, sixiang yu renwu" (Life, thought and character), in *Ding Ling Xiju ji* (Collection of Ding Ling's dramas), ed. Zhongguo siju chubanshe bianwenbu (Beijing: Zhongguo xiju chubanshe, 1983), 174. The essay was first published in 1954.

76  Ding Ling, "When I Was in Xia Village." Translations from Y. T. Feuerwerker, "Ding Ling's 'When I Was in Sha Chuan (Cloud Village),' " *Signs* 2, no. 1 (autumn 1976): 265. Feuerwerker has written movingly about the characteristic formula Ding Ling used in this story and has brilliantly translated the piece. See *Ding Ling's Fiction*, 114–15.

77  The position Ding Ling claimed for herself in "Thoughts on March 8" is visible in this story as well, though I have chosen to exploit the question of character here. Ding Ling, a well-known female writer, invented a female narrating persona to represent a female protagonist victimized by sexual violence most frequently visited on women: rape, forced prostitution, unchastity, venereal disease, social opprobrium. She explained that she had built the short story around an incident she had heard about from a friend. The case of a young village girl who had sacrificed her health and sexuality in the war against Japan became in Ding Ling's mind an opportunity to commemorate the unsung sacrifices of ordinary women and men. For Ding Ling, the immediate question was social redemption, because the local communal ethic intransigently condemned this loss of chastity even by way of rape during wartime. See Ding Ling, "Tan ziji de chuangzuo" (Chat on my

creative work), in Ding Ling, shenghuo, chuangzuo, shidai de linghun (Life creation, spirit of the age) (Changsha: Hunan renmin chubanshe, 1981), 177–78.

78  Ding Ling, "Xia village," Y. T. Feuerwerker, trans., Signs 2:1 (1976), 266: "If there were something concerning my friend which she hadn't told me, or about which I hadn't asked her, I would never want to hear it from other people. It would hurt my friend, myself and our relationship."
    The relationship of narrator and Zhenzhen quickly deepens into a complex relation of representation between two women. (I will comment more extensively on that point later). The narrator's kang (heated brick bed) comes to serve as Zhenzhen's stable reference point. Delegations of villagers and kin arrive there to try to impose solutions on Zhenzhen. They pressure her to marry the boy whose "fault" it was that she originally refused her arranged marriage, for example. In all this flurry only the narrator remains neutral, claiming that she will accept Zhenzhen's decision no matter what it is. Of course, when the girl chooses to leave the village, the narrator expresses her satisfaction and relief. Though she has never directly intervened, in a sense she has rescued Zhenzhen from a community that at bottom values women for the terms of their sexual chastity. This is a sophisticated retelling of the narrative line in "Affair in East Village."

79  Ding Ling, "Life, Thought, Character," 182–83.

80  Chen Boda, cited in Ho Kuo Cheng, "The Status," 33.

81  Ding Ling, "Zai yiyuan zhong," in Ding Ling wenji (Collected works of Ding Ling) 3, (Changsha: Hunan renmin chubanshe, 1983), 243–65; subsequent page numbers cited in text. Lu Ping exemplifies the potential to the communist movement of the ardent petit bourgeois revolutionary girl and all the good and ill she brings with her.

82  Ding Ling, "The attitude and introspection that the literary world should take toward Wang Shiwei." I have consulted Bjorge's translation in his "Life and Literature," 157.

83  Ding Ling, "Sanbajie you gan" (Thoughts on March 8) JFRB (March 9, 1942), trans. Gregor Benton, in I Myself am a Woman, 320.

84  Ding Ling, "Zhandou shi xianghou" (Struggle is pleasure) JFRB, 16 September 1941.

85  Gu Man, "Guanyu Ding Ling pingfan" (Regarding reversing the miscarriage of justice on Ding Ling), in Ding Ling yanjiu tongxun (Ding Ling research newsletter) 13 (1999): 8–11. The sentence is: "Ding Ling shen shang jizhongle xuduo huai nüren de maobing."

86  Ding Ling, "Yan bian zhi xing tan chuangzuo" (Talking about creation on a trip to the Yan'an border region), in Ding Ling's recent work, 2: My life and work, 158–71, particularly 164, 169. In 1954 Ding Ling seemed to suggest that she was right about the rich peasant issue, and her novel was a policy corrective. With her own eyes she had seen a character in the doorway and this character became the popular Heini. Analogously, when she drafted The Sun Shines over the Sanggan River and gave it to friends to criticize, they did not like the character of Gu Yong either, and felt she had been too sympathetic to the landlord and rich peasant characters. The problem was that she had witnessed a struggle session against just such a rich peasant. She felt the line on class struggle that subjected to confiscation a hard-working peasant like Gu had to be in error. Consequently, she disregarded her critics and gave Gu Yong a history of struggle to explain his ambivalent class position. "When I wrote it," she explained, "it was for readers to comment on," and not just to fix Gu Yong's type. The question facing readers and writer was at heart normative: "How should we regard this sort of person?" (186). As she had for some years, Ding Ling seemed most comfortable with ethical ambivalence. But ambivalent or not, the question proffered and the response invited were couched in wholly normative terms. Character invited readers to engage in what are complex political parables and to pass judgment on the goodness or badness of normative characters. Her skill level had reached a point where

she could offer a realistic reflection of a life experience and expect readers to join her in the arduous process of reading character for ill or good.

87  Ding Ling, "Jiang yidian xinli hua" (Some words from the heart), in Ding Ling's recent work, 157.

88  Ding Ling, "Wode shenghuo hui yi" (Recollections on My Life) in Ding Ling zai Bei da huang (Ding Ling in the Great Northern Wasteland), ed. Zheng Xiaofeng (N.p.: Hubei renmin chubanshe, 1989), 39–41. The story appeared in 1961 in a local newspaper on the Tangyuan state farm under Ren's byline.

89  Ibid.

90  Zheng, Ding Ling, 27–28.

91  A lienü or jiefu. These are conventional terms for exemplary kinswomen. For a discussion of the late imperial usage of these terms and practices, see the work of Katherine Carlitz, including "Shrines, Governing-class Identity, and the Cult of Widow Fidelity in Mid-Ming Jiangnan," Journal of Asian Studies 56, no. 3 (1997): 612–40. I am drawing attention to a certain continuity of practice. The people on the state farms said: "When Lao Ding was among us she was not only really good at raising chickens, she was also a non-Party member who was like a Party member, a leader who was not like a leader, and a true progressive. 'She spoke the language of the Party, did the work of the Party, so where on earth can there be such an anti-Party rightist?' So, when queried every year, the masses asked why, with all the 'reform,' she had not been reformed yet?" (Zheng, Ding Ling, 20). It seems that Big Rightist was a legal-ethical category and the masses were puzzled and then happy that Ding Ling did not meet the criteria.

92  See Cheng, "The Status," 13, 32–35.

93  Wang Zhongchen and Shang Xia, Ding Ling shenghuo yu wenxue de daolu (The path of Ding Ling's life and literature) (Changchun: Jilin renmin chubanshe, 1982), 154. In fact, the charge that it was a "poisonous weed" had been trumped up in the mid-1950s, not the early 1940s, they are quite right. However, the drive to clear Ding Ling's name is fully invested in the discourse of social ethics that landed Maoist intellectuals in the character problem in the beginning. Much of Ding Ling's writing after rehabilitation centered on Yan'an and people such as Ke Zhongping, Agnes Smedley, and other comrades from the era. See Ding Ling, Ding Ling's Recent Work, 2: My Life and Work.

94  Zheng, Ding Ling, 21.

95  Feng Xuefeng, "The Significance of The Sun Shines over the Sanggan River." For a history and documentation of the various versions of the novel, reasons for revisions, and its publication history, see Gong Mingde, "Taiyang zhao zai Sanggan he shang" xiugai jianping (The Sun Shines over the Sanggan River commentary on revisions) (Changsha: Hunan renmin chubanshe, 1984).

96  Cited in Hao Shendao, "Xian tan Zhang Yumin xingxiang" (A chat on the future of Zhang Yumin), in Ding Ling zuopin pinglun ji (Collected commentary on Ding Ling's work), ed. Zhongguo wenxie chuban gongsi (Beijing: Zhongguo wenlian chuban gongsi, 1984), 258; hereafter DLZPJ. The Hao essay is dated 1982.

97  I have used the 1955 edition of the novel in Chinese and adapted Yang Hsien-yi and Gladys Yang, trans., The Sun Shines over the Sanggan River (Peking, 1954). Citations in the text refer to the original page numbers, followed by the page numbers of the Yang translation.

98  I have read this novel against other, journalistic and historical accounts of land reform politics. See Jack Belden, China Shakes the World (New York: Harper and Brothers, 1949); Hinton, Fanshen; Edwin Moise, "Radical, Moderate, and Optimal Patterns of Land Reform," Modern China 4, no. 1 (1978): 79–90; Ralph Thaxton, "The World Turned Upside

Down: Three Orders of Meaning in the Peasants' Traditional Political World," *Modern China* 3, no. 2 (1977): 185–228; C. K. Yang, *A Chinese Village in Early Communist Transition* (Cambridge, MA: MIT Press, 1959); and Ann Anagnost, *National Past-times: Narrative, Representation and Power in Modern China* (Durham, NC: Duke University Press, 1998).

99  Feng Xuefeng notes that "the Party" does not exist in the novel except in the fallible characters of individual and collective Party members. Character is the vehicle for politics.

100  See Cai Kui Chenhai, *"Taiyang zhao zai Sanggan he shang* de geming xianshi zhuyi" (The revolutionary realism of *The Sun Shines over the Sanggan River*), *Xin wenxue luncong*, 1980, reprinted in DLZPJ, particularly 229–31 for a discussion of the "bitter process of putting into motion" (*jianku de fadong guocheng*) the land reform, the "process of peasant awakening" (*nongmin de juexing guocheng*), and the "process of coming to awareness" (*juexing guocheng*).

    In considering "Maoism" in this way, what Althusserian Marxism claimed in the Mao text that Althusser read becomes more clear. It would be a pleasure to reread the peripheralization of the sign "Mao" in the Althusserian moment of what would eventually become Anglophone cultural studies and which, through the figure of Foucault, gave rise to social analysis that resembles nothing more than Ding Ling's vision of the grid of revolutionary land reform.

101  Feuerwerker has noted that political ideology determines the plot, from the introduction of Gu Yong, the representative middle peasant who has been misclassified as a rich peasant, to the triumph over Qian Wengui. See Feuerwerker, *Ding Ling*, 138. Of course, the criticism of the novel in the late 1950s took the position that it was not sufficiently ideological in the sense of true because it had not correctly represented model characters and had also mischaracterized typicalities because of Ding Ling's habit of providing each with a flaw.

102  Cai Kui, "The Revolutionary Realism," 222. The term is *jiti xingxiang*. Joe Huang notes that land reform cadres read Ding Ling's novel before going into the field. See Huang, *Heroes and Villains in Communist China: The Contemporary Chinese Novel as a Reflection of Life* (London: C. Hurst, 1973).

    The Maoist grid Ding Ling used to field her enormous cast of characters allowed the reader to do in imagination what the land reform cadre did in practice. But this grid did not invent the oppressive power. Power existed already in the hands of the despot Qian. Power, as Qian Wengui knows, is dispersed in the world, hidden in people's secrets, latent in all relationships, and manageable through clever strategies. Ding Ling established Qian as a power specialist, the only villager to correctly interpret virtually every clue that she made part of the characters arraigned against him. When Gu Yong arrives in Nuanshui with a rubber-wheeled cart, he satisfies everyone with a lie about why— except Qian. "When Qian heard that Gu Yong had borrowed Hutai's cart he chuckled to himself: 'A straightforward fellow like you, learning to tell lies, too?' " (8–9; 9). Reasoning on the basis of information—time of the year, status inside kinship, labor demands, personal habits of everyone involved—Qian correctly ferrets out a lie and he knows the lie gives him power over Gu. He can use this piece of evidence most efficiently through his kinship connection to Gu, and drawing on *qinqi pengyou, qingqi guanxi* (networks of friends and relatives) he can compromise Gu and gather more intelligence into his efforts to resist the land reform.

103  The Qian portrait resolves an important riddle because it warns that a local power holder, a "landlord," might indeed have no unusual wealth, education, or social status. Qian has never held office, never had a trade. But he knows all the ward chiefs, the

government officials, and the collaborators (chs. 1, 27, 28, 29). The "power" that Qian has and that the individual peasant characters frequently refer to circulates endlessly because no one is willing to disclose their own individual implicatedness in Qian's corruption.

104 A joke perhaps that *wen* is more valuable than *qian*. Or perhaps a joke that in feudal relations, *wen* is *qian* and *qian* is *wen*.

105 Cited in Hao Shendao, "Xian tan Zhang Yumin xingxiang" (A chat on the future of Zhang Yumin), *DLZPJ*, 258.

106 Yang Guixin, "Heini de shenbian: Dui wenxue pinglun gongzuo de yixie yijian" (Heini's self-defense: An opinion on the work of literary criticism), *Xin wenxue lucong*, 1980, reprinted in *DLZPJ*, 276; subsequent quotations are cited in the text.

107 This echoes the plaint of Yu Manzhen that she had no jia; wherever she and her children are is where her jia is.

108 Yang Guixin, *Ding Ling*, 302–5.

109 Hong Zicheng, 1956: *Baihua shidai* (1956: Era of the hundred flowers), in *Bainian Zhong-guo wenxue zong xi* (One hundred years of Chinese literature), ed. Xie Mian (Jinan: Shandong jiaoyu chubanshe, 1998), 207–8. Also see Zhou Liangpei, *Ding Ling zhuan* (Ding Ling's biography) (Beijing: Shiyue wenyi chubanshe, 1993) for republished documentation of charges and rebuttals in the late 1950s. The "struggle session" is infantile.

Ding Ling's position throughout the fifteen years between the Yan'an Forum in 1942 and her dismissal from office was consistently identical to that of Chairman Mao, even when her natural constituency of petit bourgeois readers rejected her.

110 Zhang Tianyi, "Guanyu Shafei nüshi" (On Miss Sophia), in *Ding Ling yanjiu ziliao* (Ding Ling research materials), ed. Yuan Liangjun (Tianjin: Tianjin renmin chubanshe, 1982), 403. The stone cold literalism of this argument goes to the point of specifying that Sophia did not *really* read Hu Shi's books, of course! But even as it disputes the reality of what it specifies it reinforces the sensation that Sophia is a real person.

111 Ibid., 406.

112 Ibid., 412: "So what will Sophia have done in her future [as she neither died nor could she join the Revolution]? So, regarding all of the material on Ding Ling's thoughts, words and deeds exposed in the current meetings to resist the Ding-Chen anti-Party clique . . . one can say that 'Sophia's Diary' is just another chapter [in the story of Sophia]." There are two ways to resist this charge. One is to refuse the connection between Ding Ling and Sophia, which Ding Ling had done since the late 1920s without success. The other is to argue that Sophia is not so bad, and in fact did join the Revolution. This latter argument could be made on the basis of Ding Ling's own publications, for "Sophia, Part Two" indeed does have Sophia join the Revolution! But my point is simply that no one believed the first rejoinder and the second one reinforces the structure of accusation.

113 Xia Kangda, "Zhong ping 'Wo zai Xiacun de shihou' " (A serious critique of "When I Was in Xia Village"), *DLZPJ*.

114 Zhang Naihua, "The All-China Women's Federation."

115 Zhao Yuan, "Ye tan 'Taiyang zhao zai Sanggan he shang' " (Also speaking of *The Sun Shines over the Sanggan River*), *DLZPJ*, 241–56, originally published in 1980; Hao Shendao, "Xian tan Zhang Yumin xingxiang" (A chat on the figure of Zhang Yumin), *DLZPJ*, 257–75, originally published in 1982; Yan Jiayan, "Xiandai wenxueshi shang de yi zhuang jiyuan: Zhong ping Ding Ling xiaoshuo 'Zai yiyuan zhong' " (An old case in modern literary history: A serious evaluation of Ding Ling's short story "In the Hospital"), *DLZPJ*, 208–20, first published in 1981.

116  Wang and Shang, *The Path of Ding Ling's Life and Literature*; subsequent quotations are cited in the text.

117  Yang Guixin, *Ding Ling chuangzuo zongheng tan* (Speaking on the breadth and depth of Ding Ling's creations) (Changsha: Hunan renmin chubanshe, 1984), 262; subsequent quotations are cited in the text. I want to acknowledge my indebtedness to Yang Guixin's work.

118  "Haiwai you ren chengzan Ding Ling wei Zhongguo de nüquan yundong de changdaozhe he zhichizhe."

119  Song Jianyuan, *Critical Biography of Ding Ling*.

120  Ibid., 5.

121  Ibid., 320. He also calls "Thoughts on March 8" a *sanwen* rather than a *zawen*.

122  Ibid., 12, 296.

123  Xu Huabin, *Ding Ling xiaoshuo yanjiu* (Research on Ding Ling's fiction) (Shanghai: Fudan daxue chubanshe, 1990).

124  Chen Guang, ed., *Ding Ling nüxing xiaoshuo jin zuo* (Ding Ling's golden fiction on women) (Changsha: Hunan wenyi chubanshe, 1995).

125  Li Daxuan, *Lineage of the Form of Ding Ling and Sophia*.

126  Zhou Yuanpei, *Ding Ling zhuan* (Biography of Ding Ling's Beijing) (Beijing: Shi yue wenyi chubanshe, 1993).

127  Ding Ling and Chinese Nüxing Literature Group, eds., *Ding Ling yu Zhongguo nüxing wenxue: Diqici chuangzuo Ding Ling xueshu yanjiu hui wenji* (Ding Ling and Chinese women's literature: seventh collected all-China seminar on Ding Ling scholarship) (Changsha: Hunan wenyi chubanshe, 1998).


6.  Socialist Modernization and the Market Feminism of Li Xiaojiang

1   This chapter includes research developed at several points. Some of the documentation comes from an unpublished research report, "Politics and Protocols of funü: Re-Making the National Woman," which I delivered in spring 1991 at an Association of Asian Studies panel organized by Prasenjit Duara. A shortened version of this project appeared in Christina Gilmartin et al., eds., *Engendering China: Women, Culture and the State* (Cambridge, MA: Harvard University Press, 1994). Pages analyzing Li Xiaojiang's *Xinggou* (Sex gap) appear in slightly different format and framework in "Spheres of Debt and Feminist Ghosts in Area Studies of Women in China," *Traces* 1 (2000): 195–227. A central part of the chapter appeared previously in Lisa Lowe and David Lloyd, eds., *The Politics of Culture in the Shadow of Capital* (Durham, NC: Duke University Press, 1997) under the title "Woman at the Close of the Maoist Era in the Polemics of Li Xiaojiang and Her Associates." I thank all parties for permission to reuse the material in altered form.

      I do not mean to imply here that either theorist should extricate herself from feminism's inherent statism, only that each is sometimes mischaracterized as antistatist.

2   I first encountered Li Xiaojiang's name on essays that I read in an archival publication called *Funü zuzhi yü huodong: Yinshua baokan ziliao* (Women's organizations and activities: Published press materials reader); hereafter cited as ZH. The monthly republishes articles on various women-related topics selected from the national press. I am grateful that I read Li's works from the early and mid-1990s in the popular press, before she reissued them in book form. Discovering her essays among many other documents, reports, and news articles increased my sense of her range and passions. Moreover, her

essays were usually the most provocative in context, although they were also initially difficult to interpret because of their theoretic vocabulary.

3   General background to the events of the feminist 1980s may be found in the following: Li Xiaojiang and Li Hui, "Women's Studies in China," *National Women's Studies Association* 1, no. 3 (spring 1989): 458–60; Wan Shanping, "The Emergence of Women's Studies in China," *Women's Studies International Forum* 11, no. 5 (1988): 455–64; Qu Wen, "A Brief Account of the Current Status of Research on Women" (unpublished report from the Women's Research Institute of the Women's Federation, n.d.); Wang Zheng, "Research on Women in Contemporary China: Problems and Promises," unpublished manuscript, 1993; and Liu Bohong, "Yijiujiusi: Funü yanjiu zouxiang" (1994: Towards women's studies), "Yijiujiusan: Funü yanjiu zouxiang" (1993: Towards women's studies), and "Yijiujiusan: Funü yanjiu qushi" (1993: Trends in women's studies), in *Funü Yanjiu* (Women's studies) (Beijing: Renmin daxue shubao ziliao zhongxin, 1994).

4   "Qunzhong tuanti shi guangda qunzhong de zhongyao daibiaozhe" (Mass organizations are important representatives of the great masses), "Si da" *yilai funü yundong wenxuan* ("4th Congress" women's movement documents) 9, no. 29 (1979): 1; hereafter *FYW*. I would suggest, along with many others, that Fulian on the contrary tended to "construct the interests [that] it represents." See Ernesto Laclau and Chantal Mouffe, *Hegemony and Socialist Strategy* (New York: Verso, 1985), 120.

5   For discussions of similar recovery efforts at other levels of the government, see Elizabeth Croll, *Chinese Women Since Mao* (London: Zed Books, 1983), ch. 9, "The Politics of the Women's Movement"; Derek J. Waller, *The Government and Politics of the People's Republic of China*, 3d ed. (London: Hutchison, 1981), 112–19. For Kang Keqing's claim that the restoration took place in the name of Mao Zedong, see Kang, "Xin shiqi Zhongguo funü yundong de chonggao renwu" (The lofty responsibility of Chinese women's movement in the new period), in *Cai Chang, Deng Yingchao, Kang Keqing: Funü jiefang wenti wenxuan* (Cai Chang, Deng Yingchao, Kang Keqing: Documents in the question of the women's movement), ed. Fulian (Beijing: Renmin chubanshe, 1988), 329; hereafter *CDK*. For the claim that it was Mao's concern that women be liberated, see Kang Keqing, "Mao Zhuxi shuailing women zou funü chedi jiefang de daolu" (Chairman Mao led us onto the path of women's total liberation), *CDK*, 310, 312.

6   The primary strategies put into play included a long-term campaign to rebuild the Federation, a shorter-term plan to reframe the marriage law, and a propaganda campaign for building women's self-esteem, which had its roots in the early 1960s. Some of these strategies were as old as the 1950s land reform; others, like the instrumental use of the marriage law, dated as far back as the 1930s. (Some of the leadership at the helm of the restored Federation had actually authored the very practices they now sought to reinstate.) However, recycling the Party's exclusive claims to represent women posed a greater problem than the specific elements of the restoration campaign. See Emily Honig and Gail Hershatter, *Personal Voices: Chinese Women in the 1980s* (Stanford: Stanford University Press, 1988) and Naihua Zhang "The All-China Women's Federation." Zhang's important, heavily documented dissertation calls this era the beginning of the "emergence of 'women's movement' from below" and dates the event of this movement from below to 1979–1993.

7   Deng Yingchao, "Bianxuan Zhongguo funü yundong shi de zhuxian" (Zhuxian compiling the history of Chinese women's movement), *CDK*, 366–68, and "Zhenfen geming jingshen, zuohao fuyun shi gongzuo" (Inspire revolutionary spirit, do good work on the history of the women's movement), *CDK*, 413–20. Also see Deng's "Zhongguo nü xianfeng Xiang Jingyu" (China's woman pioneer Xiang Jingyu), *CDK*, 427–32.

8  For confirmation of this perspective, see Kimberley Manning, "Sexual Equality and State Building: Gender Conflict in the Great Leap Forward" (Ph.D. diss., University of Washington, 2003).

9  Li Xiaojiang, "Gaige he Zhongguo nüxing qunti yishi de juexing" (The reforms and the awakening of mass consciousness among Chinese women), *ZH* (February 1989): 21.

10  See Honig and Hershatter, *Personal Voices* for a range of this opinion.

11  Li Xiaojiang, "Zou xiang nüren" (Toward women), *Nüxing/ren* 4 (1990), 256. Pan Suiming, "Fulian yinggai you duli de yizhi" (Fulian should have its independent will), *ZH* (March 1988): 44.

12  See "Zhongyang shuji chu yuanze pizhun 'Guanyu Fulian tizhi gaige di shexiang' " (Central committee secretariat approves in principle "Concerning suppositions for an organizational and structural reform of the Women's Association"), *ZH* (May 1988): 507.

13  Ruo Shui and Feng Yuan, "Nüxing lixiang di fansi yu qiuzheng" (Reflection on and confirmation of female ideals) *ZH* (February 1987): 31; originally published in *Zhongguo funü*, 1986.

14  See Wu Daiying, "Funü jiefang de erlü beifan" (Behind the second law of women's liberation), *ZH* (May 1987): 11; originally published in *Hunyin yü jiating* earlier in 1987. The term "xingbie zhuanhua" appears in this essay.

15  See Ruo Shui and Feng Yuan, 31. This question of difference proved the signature point in the 1980s, as I have argued. Obviously, the question of difference raised a tremendous categorical problem. That is because essential, human, sexual difference and women's humanity do not coexist in the same frame. Logically speaking, either women are people (ren), meaning that "human" as a category is always already split, or women are essentially the other of man, Human is a euphemism for man (*nanren*), and Humanism is harboring, as Li Xiaojiang would strenuously argue, a scandalous blot on the face of reason. The struggle of women to be different from men and to be human beings had proven logically impossible in the 1930s, and a similar double bind had haunted the problem of women's ren'ge over much of the century. Most commentary in the 1980s making the case for women's difference tacitly seemed to side with Wang Jinling, who introduced anthropologist Margaret Mead's notion that though sex difference seems normative and stable, it is actually historically and culturally contingent and thus amenable to directed change. Wang Jinling, "Shehui kongzhi: Ta di qidian yu zhongdian—lun xingbie wenhua" (Social controls: Their beginning and their end, a discussion of "gender culture"), *ZH* (June 1987): 15–18; originally published in *Zhongguo funü bao*, 1986. Also see Ruo and Fen, "Reflection on and Confirmation of Female Ideals."

16  Although participants expressed doubts that the concept could entirely fix the crisis that the Federation's passivity had set off, the notion of women's culture (nüxing wenhua) made two familiar moves: first, it set into predication the sexed subject nüxing; second, it reopened the question of how the dialectic of women's oppression and liberation should work. It does not, of course, abandon the humanist subject man but simply complicates it. See Huang Hongyun, "Nüxing zhuti yishi ji qi jianguo tujing" (Essential female subject consciousness and the constructed path), *ZH* (March 1988): 21–23; originally published in *Wuhan Xuexi yu shixian*. The consensus among Huang and her colleague Jin Hong was strategic. They argued that remedial work should dwell not on reconstructing a "women's culture" but on attacking chauvinism and cultivating a transcending sense of female self (*nüxing di ziwo*). This self would recognize gender difference and eschew masculinist culturalism.

17  Ling Gang, "Xiandai nüxing jiefang zhi lu zai nali" (Where is the path to modern women's liberation?) *ZH* (January 1986), 15–18.

18   Ruo and Fen, "Reflection on and Confirmation of Female Ideals," 30.

19   By the mid-1980s, broad campaigns to institutionalize legal culture had begun to re-shape the ways policy on women worked and the term "ren'ge" resurfaced into everyday language. For the most part it signified questions of legal standing and personality reform. See, for instance, Meng Xiaoyun, "Dangdai Zhongguo funü mian mian guan" (Today's Chinese women see everything) *ZH* (January 1986): 16–19; Lin Gang, "Where is the path to modern women's liberation?"; Luo Xiaolu, "Zhongguo funü wenti lilun yanjiu de xianzhuang yu fashan" (The situation and development of research into theories of the Chinese women's question) *ZH* (January 1987): 11–12; Guan Xiaotong, "Nüzi yao baochi zai hunyin jiating zhong de dulixing" (Women want to maintain their independence within the marital family) *ZH* (January 1988): 15–16.

20   Liu Lihua, "Huashuo Zhongguo nannü pingdeng" (Speaking of equality between Chinese men and women), *ZH* (March 1990): 17–21.

21   Beijingshi funü lianhehui and Beijing funü wenti lilun yanjiuhui, eds., *Zhongguo funü lilun yanjiu shinian* (Women's theoretical studies in China, 1981–1990) (Beijing: Zhongguo funü chubanshe, 1991), 1. See also Zhang Yanxia, ed., *"Funü yanjiu zai Zhongguo" quanti yantaohui lunwenji* (Complete seminar papers on Women's studies in China) (Beijing/Huairou: Quan fulian funü yanjiu suo zhubian, 1995) for further writing of this kind. In the latter collection, Jin Yihong argues that the 1980s constituted a "predisciplinary" moment in the development of gender studies, the 1990s a more mature disciplined praxis. See "Zhongguo funüxue yanjiu tedian ji yingxiang qi shehui tiaoyong de yinsi fenxi" (Characteristics of China's women's studies and analysis of factors affecting their social effects), 1–5. This periodization is consistent with the positions expressed in the longer essays collected in the earlier compendium. *Women's Theoretical Studies in China from 1981 to 1990* is valuable for several reasons: it is canonical; it is retrospective, providing a coda to the "1980s" by the very activists who shaped the decade's intellectual politics; and it is respectable.

22   Yu Yan, "Nüxing renleixue: jian'gou yü zhanwang" (Anthropology of women's establishment and outlook), in *Zhongguo funü lilun yanjiu shinian*, 1–20. The role of Beauvoir's work particularly remains to be traced through the careers of the founders. Du Fanqin, a founder and historian, has acknowledged that the book's impact has been great. See Du Fangqin, "Shinian huiyin: Zhongguo funü yanjiu de duiwai jiaoliu," in *"Funü yanjiu zai Zhongguo" quanti yantaohui lunwenji*, ed. Zhang Yanxia (Beijing/Huairou: Quan fulian funü yanjiu suo zhubian, 1995), 69–72. Li Huiying's "Nüxing wenxue yanjiu shuping" (Commentary on research in women's literature), in *Women's Theoretical Studies in China from 1981 to 1990*, is less circumspect about the sources of theoretical insight. Li pointed out that feminist theory had already infused studies of female literature globally and, increasingly, in China, too. She expressed some discomfort about feminist criticism given scholars' incommensurate contexts. How can feminist critique from the West be "applied" in China when Chinese women secured their basic political rights (the sine qua non of Western feminism) long ago? To bolster her points, Li pointed to the two canonical texts most commonly found in this cohort's central bibliography, Simone de Beauvoir and Betty Friedan. This may be a place where the popular and the elite educated women's movements drew on the same sources for inspiration.

23   Li Meige, "Nüxing xinlixue yanjiu jianjie" (A brief introduction to research on female psychology), in *Zhongguo funü lilun yanjiu shinian*, 81–94.

24   For Tan Shen's review of the inroads that women's studies sociologists are actually making in Chinese university departments, see "Funü yanjiu zai shehui xuejia de diwei" (Status of women's studies in the world of sociology), in *"Funü yanjiu zai Zhongguo" quanti*

*yantaohui lunwenji*, ed. Zhang Yanxia (Beijing/Huairou: Quan fulian funü yanjiu suo zhubian, 1995), 36–38. For Chen Ping, see "Zhongguo nüxing renkou yanjiu de qibu" (First steps in the study of Chinese female population), in *Zhongguo funü lilun yanjiu shinian*, 21–51.

25  Wan Shanping, "The Emergence of Women's Studies in China," 458–59.

26  "Funü wenti: Wanshan he fazhan" (Women's studies questions: Excellence and progress), *zh* (February 1985): 10.

27  Yang Xingnan, "Lilun tansuo, shi nüxing chengwei da xie de ren" (Theoretical exploration makes woman into a person writ large) *zh* (April 1988): 34–38.

28  Li Min and Wang Fukang, *Zhongguo funüxue* (Chinese women studies) (Nanchang: Jiangxi renmin chubanshe, 1988), 33–34. Note that in comparison to Li Min, Li Xiaojiang appears to have argued for more interventionism. Though she shared the notion that women's studies is a social science, she also stressed more immediate social factors to explain the emergence of Chinese women's studies. "Just as in the West women's studies derived from the 1960s decade for the women's rights movement, the present Chinese women's studies is a direct product of China's 'woman liberation question,'" which abuses attendant on the economic reforms of the early 1980s was causing. See Li Xiaojiang, "Zenyang kan dangqian funü wenti he funü yanjiu" (How to look at the present woman question and women's research), *zh* (January 1989): 5–9. Li Min and Wang Fukang ground their argument about historical truth in a complex series of national historical periods. They trace the "voice" of Chinese women through five stages of historical development and connect the evolution of the "voice of women" to the birth of a self-conscious or reflexive social science study of "women in China." Praising the early twentieth-century bourgeois women's movement, Li and Wang also note that historically, the movement to accurately represent women (which, in their scheme, is "women's studies" broadly speaking) had always been linked to Western theory. Indeed, according to Li and Wang, the same May Fourth movement that had initiated the first genuine "women's voice" had also been largely Western-inspired.

29  Xiao Li and Xiao Yu, "Zhongguo jindaishi shang guanyu funü jiefang de sanci lunzheng" (Chinese modernity's three debates over women's liberation), *zh* (March 1986): 53–54.

30  Cai Yu, "Zhongshi he jiaqiang funüshi yanjiu" (Take seriously and strengthen the study of women's history), *zh* (March 1987): 52–54.

31  Chang Ying, "Zhongguo jindai funü yundongshi xueshu taolunhui zongshu" (Synthesis of the symposium on the history of the modern Chinese women's movement), *zh* (January 1988): 39–40. These are notes of a meeting of historians from all over China who met at Henan University in September 1987, presumably at Li Xiaojiang's instigation, as it was her work unit at that time.

32  Qing Ren, "Funü wenti yanjiu zongshu" (Summary of research into the woman question), *zh* (April 1989): 11–14; emphasis added. This, like several other articles in the same volume, is written in direct response to Wei Shiqing's key article on the path of women's future, published in 1988.

33  In Barlow, "Politics and Protocols of Funü," I particularly stressed the formation of the subject nüren. For a contemporary document that makes the case well, see Tao Tiezhu and Tan Shen, "Nannü tongbu shidai de lilun tan jiu" (Theoretical investigation into the era of men and women stepping together), *zh* (June 1987): 12–14. That document lists major figures and programs such as Li Xiaojiang at Zhengzhou University, Henan, Zhu Qi's work at Tianjin University on matriarchy, Li Zhongming's investigation of patriarchy in Hubei, and Nan Xi's scholarship at Sichuan Foreign Languages Academy. In each case, the subject is nüren.

34 This exposition of her thinking draws on the first three. I will not address the issues raised in *Inquiry into Women's Aesthetic Consciousness*.

35 Liu Kang, "Subjectivity, Marxism, and Cultural Theory in China," in *Politics, Ideology, and Literary Discourse in Modern China: Theoretical Interventions and Cultural Critique*, ed. Liu Kang and Xiaobing Tang (Durham, NC: Duke University Press, 1993).

36 But, as Jing Wang has demonstrated, Li Zehou also recuperated into post-Mao Chinese Marxism key elements of the Confucian scholastic heritage. When Li Zehou retooled hoary textual strategies of the Confucian scholastic tradition, he in effect bolstered, at least for the duration of the era, the powers that conventionally accrued to theorizers under Maoism. To take one of Jing Wang's examples, Li Zehou systematically eschewed binary difference in favor of reconcilable polarities on the neo-Confucian analogy of the "unity of Heaven and Man" (*tian ren he yi*). This textual strategy provided Li with a theoretical tool for abrogating incommensurability, because in neo-Confucian logics of unity, all differences (past and present, traditional and modern, East and West, male and female) are remediable, are in effect manageable, because differences interpenetrate and thus are simply moments on tangible continua. Jing Wang, *High Culture Fever: Politics, Aesthetics, and Ideology in Deng's China* (Berkeley: University of California Press, 1996).

37 This paragraph is heavily indebted to Liu Kang, "Subjectivity, Marxism, and Cultural Theory in China," 23–55, and Jing Wang, *High Culture Fever*. The quote is from Liu, 25–26.

38 Li Xiaojiang, "Economic Reform and the Awakening of Chinese Women's Collective Consciousness," in *Engendering China*, 374–75.

39 Michael Dutton and Paul Healy, "Marxist Theory and Socialist Transition: The Construction of an Epistemological Relation," in *Chinese Marxism in Flux, 1978–84: Essays on Epistemology, Ideology and Political Economy*, ed. Bill Brugger (Armonk, NY: M.E. Sharpe, 1985), 38.

40 Ibid., 46. Both agree on "the real as the raw material, the starting point of knowledge production . . . [and] the subject abstracting the essence (the quintessential, the true) of the real object, eliminating all that is inessential (the coarse, the false), thus producing knowledge."

41 Meng Yue, "Female Images and National Myth," in *Gender Politics in Modern China*, 118–36.

42 See Lingzhen Wang, "Retheorizing the Personal: Identity, Writing and Gender in Yu Luojin's Autobiographical Acts," *positions: east asia culture critique* 6, no. 2 (fall 1998): 395–438.

43 This paragraph is adapted from Barlow, "Politics and Protocols of Funü," 344–45.

44 Li Xiaojiang, *Xiawa de tansuo* (Eve's exploration) (Changsha: Henan renmin chubanshe, 1988), 8; hereafter cited as *Eve*. Subsequent quotations are cited in the text.

45 The hierarchy of differences is central to Li's notion of the universal female subject and the teleology of the emancipation of nüren in the movement of the split world subject of Humanity. So, while the series incited discourse on the sexual subject, it has from its founding felt impelled to manage national difference within an unstable universalizing Chinese academic theory. This mediation is a constituting part of the field of women's scholarship, and differences of many kinds—local and global, Chinese and other, modern and feudal, national and international, man and woman—are endemic in Li's thought. See, for instance, the Zhengzhou University Women's Center collection *Dangdai shijie nüchao yu nüxue* (Woman tide and women's studies) (n.p., 1990); Du Fangqin's *Nüxing guannian de yanbian* (Evolution of the female concept) (Zhengzhou: Henan renmin chubanshe, 1988); and Zheng Huisheng's *Shanggu Huaxia funü yu hunyin* (Ancient Chinese woman and marriage) (Zhengzhou: Henan renmin chubanshe, 1988).

This competing claim for women's studies as simultaneously universal and particular is not directly argued out. A similar riddle is at work in Pan Suiming's volume *Shenmi de shenghuo: Xing de shehui shi* (The sacred flame: A social history of sex) (Zhengzhou: Henan renmin chubanshe, 1988). The academic study of female sexuality thus can be diagrammed without cultural inflection, as Pan does on page 12. The universal science of sex applies equally well across the board. Even so, Pan finds himself almost interminably caught up in renegotiating national difference. Take, for instance, the chapter entitled "Man and Beast," which begins with an amusing anecdote about a foreign friend whose Chinese is poor and who misuses categories by referring to animals using the human gendering terms *nanniu* and *nüniu*, or "human male cow" and "human female cow." Although the friend was syntactically in error, Pan reflects, the confusion actually revealed a weakness in the gender-signifying system endemic to *Chinese* in which animals each have an always already gendered proper noun of their own, the equivalent of "cock" and "hen" in English. In Pan's view, this makes it difficult to articulate an abstract, universal sex binary as a separate category in colloquial Chinese. The resolution that Pan settles on is interrogative. Drawing out of Chinese informants what he takes to be a crippling inability to talk directly about sexual life, he encourages them to think of the "sacred fire" in terms of a new sexual science of "frontal copulation," "rear entry," "foreplay," "instinctive drives," and so on, that is, providing the standard rhetoric of sexological discourses. Thus, in Pan's work women's studies discourse poses a problem and a solution: the problem is how the national discourse at the popular level can accommodate the universal science of sex; the solution is pedagogy. Pan, the avuncular enlightened scholar, teaches scientific discourse on sex until it can be "spoken" in the colloquial languages of the Chinese citizen.

It is also possible that Li Xiaojiang foregrounded the national problem for women's studies to foreclose chauvinist charges that she was nothing but a recycled Western feminist. Such a tag, had it stuck, would have defeated her long-term objectives immediately, for the disavowal of "Western feminism" is one of the foundations of most women's liberation arguments in Chinese venues since at least the 1940s.

46  "Longzhao zai nüjie de mituan" (The enigma veiled within the world of women), in *Eve*, 14–34.

47  Liu Kang, "Subjectivity, Marxism and Cultural Theory," 32. For Li's assertion that woman theory belongs in the human sciences, see *Eve*, 25, and "The Sublime," in *Eve*, 74–107.

48  Li Xiaojiang, "Nüxing ziwo renshi" (The self-comprehension of women), in *Funü yu jiazheng* (Woman and domestic science), Li Xiaojiang, Liang Jun, Wang Hong, eds. (Zhengzhou: Henan renmin chubanshe, 1988), 1–46.

49  Untroubled, that is, by "unnatural" government policy such as those promulgated under the Gang of Four during the period of the ultraleftist high tide.

50  Li, *Domestic Science*, 40; subsequent quotations are cited in the text.

51  The full quote is: " 'Female self-consciousness' [*nüxing ziwo yishi*] is like a woman who asks herself: what am I? whereas female self-comprehension [*nüxing ziwo renshi*] is more like an exploration of the question 'what is woman' [*nüren*]" (*Domestic Science*, 3; original emphasis).

52  For the autobiographic roots of this belief, see her "Zuoxiang nüren" (Towards woman), in *Nüxingren*, ed. Chen Yu-shih. Li herself first saw menstruation as a betrayal and later claimed to have come into full comprehension of her true femininity while pregnant and breast feeding.

53  Li Xiaojiang is by no means alone in this view. See Wang Zheng, "Three Interviews: Wang Anyi, Zhu Lin, Dai Qing," in *Gender Politics in Modern China*, 159–208.

54  See Li Xiaojiang, "Lishi – dongfang nüxing zhi mi" (History: The Riddle of the Oriental Woman), in *Eve*, 135–57.

55  In the later definition she was apparently influenced by Betty Friedan.

56  At her most lucid, Li balances what she calls woman's three great responsibilities against her three great pursuits. Women are responsible to husband, children, and work but they desire or pursue, as a consequence of their responsibilities, sexual love, mother love, and self-love through relations with husband, child, and creative work. Of course, the woman who sacrifices work imperils her self-love and thereby threatens to undermine her pursuit of individual being. Also see Li, *Domestic Science*, 27 and *Eve*, 125–35.

57  Li Xiaojiang, *Nüren: Yi ge yaoyuan meili de chuanshuo* (Woman: A distant, beautiful legend) (Shanghai: Renmin chubanshe, 1989), 3–4.

58  Ibid.

59  Expatriot scholars formed an organization called Chinese Society for Women's Studies (CSWS) in the late 1980s, which made it possible for them (Ma Yuanxi, Zuo Jiping, Bao Xiaolan, Zhong Xueping, and Wang Zheng were the most active organizers in the early years) to apply for funds to subsidize their scholarship. In 1992 at the Harvard-Wellesley Conference organized by Christina Gilmartin, Lisa Rofel, Gail Hershatter, Tyrene White, and Emily Honig, a conflict broke out in a closed-door session limited to China-born scholars between Li Xiaojiang and the central leadership of the CSWS. The point of conflict is not clear. However, the struggle that emerged between Li and the CSWS appears to have focused on the question of how difference would be theorized—as sexual or as social. This conflict has taken shape in the scholarship of the cohort involved in it, as the alleged contradiction between "essentialism" (putatively Li's position) and "the gender analytic" (the name CSWS gives to its own formula). For a rather allusive version of the conflict, see Wang Zheng, "Research on Women in Contemporary China," in *Guide to Women's Studies in China*, ed. Gail Hershatter, Emily Honig, Susan Mann, and Lisa Rofel (Berkeley: Institute of East Asian Studies, University of California, 1998).

60  Li Xiaojiang, "Towards Women," 258–60.

61  Li made a similar claim about realization of herself as a woman in relation to the onset of her menarche during a troubling political moment. See ibid.

62  Li Xiaojiang, *Xinggou* (Sex gap) (Beijing: Sanlian shudian, 1989); subsequent quotations are cited in the text. Also see Barlow, "Woman at the Close of the Maoist Era."

63  Barlow, "Spheres of Debt." The power of Beauvoir for the influential Li seems to have lain in a logic of the particular and universal that fueled Li's critique of the Chinese revolutionary and women's movements. This preoccupation is one of the reasons I am designating her thinking as a form of "liberal feminism."

64  Their stunning insistence on the primacy of gendered difference over all other codes and grids of difference certainly leads them to similar repudiations of what each decrees to be pseudoliberation and the inauthenticity of women's gestures. This sacrifices all other conceivable intersections of difference to the Big One of sex. See Simone de Beauvoir, *The Second Sex* (New York: Knopf, 1993), 77–78 for the parable of the polygamous Oriental "idol" and his harem of wives in various states of decay for a sense of how race plays out in Beauvoir's thesis concerning the "submergence" of the feminine in the patriarchal social form. The colonial contempt of the parable is vivid and excruciating.

7.  Dai Jinhua, Globalization, and 1990s Poststructuralist Feminism

1   Dai Jinhua, "Zhongguo nüxingxue yu nüxing zhuyi, zuotian yu jintian" (Chinese women's studies and feminism, yesterday and today), in *You zai jing zhong* (Still caught by the mirror) (Beijing: Zhishi chubanshe, 1999), 136.

2   See Jing Wang and Tani E. Barlow, eds., introduction to *Cinema and Desire: Feminist*

*Marxism and Cultural Politics in the Work of Dai Jinhua* (London: Verso, 2002). Also Hong Juan, "Yi pingdeng de xintai shuxie xingbie: Fang xuezhe Dai Jinhua" (Writing gender with a balanced mentality: Interviewing scholar Dai Jinhua), *Zhonghua dushu bao* (Chinese reader's newspaper), 2 February 1996.

3   This is the view of Chen Xunxing in "Zhongguo dalu lunshu zhong de 'nüxing xuezuo' " (Écriture féminine in the Mainland China discussions), paper delivered at Qinghua University, Taiwan, 10–11 July 1998. Chen lists as the second most significant book in this stream of theoretical feminism Zhang Jingyuan's translated and edited volume, *Dangdai nüxing zhuyi wenxue piping* (Contemporary literary criticism) (Beijing: Beijing University Press, 1992). This now classic volume consists of key articles in translation from the following scholars: Mary Jacubus, Jonathan Culler, Rosalind Coward, Barbara Johnson, Barbara Smith, Adrienne Rich, Simone de Beauvoir, Susan Gubar, Hélène Cixous, Elaine Showalter, Susan Gilbert, Gayatri Spivak, Mary Poovey, Julia Kristeva, Luce Irigaray, Jaqueline Rose, Michele Montrelay, and Juliet Mitchell. It also includes Zhang Jingyuan's own important, twenty-page introduction. For the development of theoretical feminist research method focusing on Chinese literature, see Chen Xunxing, *Zhongguo dangdai wenxue de xushi yü xingbie* (Gender and narrative in Chinese contemporary literature) (Beijing: Beijing University Press, 1995).

4   Dai Jinhua, *Jingcheng tuwei: Nüxing, dianying, wenxue* (Breaking out of the city of mirrors: Women film literature) (Beijing: Zuojia chubanshe, 1995).

5   An excellent introduction to questions of Chinese popular culture is Jing Wang, "Culture as Leisure and Culture as Capital," in "Chinese Popular Culture and the State," ed. Jing Wang, special issue of *positions* 9, no. 1 (2001): 69–104. A comprehensive discussion of economic policy and implementation is Shaoguang Wang and Angang Hu, *The Political Economy of Uneven Development: The Case of China* (Armonk, NY: M.E. Sharpe, 1999). A useful discussion of the rural foundations of the urban reforms and the commercialization of agriculture through the Deng policy is Jean Oi, *China Takes Off: Institutional Foundations of Economic Reform* (Berkeley: University of California Press, 1999). For the urban cultural scene in the 1990s, see Geremie R. Barme, *In the Red: On Contemporary Chinese Culture* (New York: Columbia University Press, 1999) and Zha Jianying, *China Pop: How Soap Operas, Tabloids, and Bestsellers Are Transforming a Culture* (New York: New Press, 1995). Claire Huot, *A Handbook of Changes: China's New Cultural Scene* (Durham, NC: Duke University Press, 2000) is a detailed discussion of cultural circles and products. Each of these volumes provides good background for understanding Dai Jinhua's thinking.

6   Dai Jinhua, *Yingxing shuxie: Jiushi niandai Zhongguo wenhua yanjiu* (Invisible writing: Research in Chinese cultural studies in the 1990s) (Nanjing: Jiangsu renmin chubanshe, 1999); Dai Jinhua, *Shuxie wenhua yingxiong: Shiji zhi jiao de wenhua yanjiu* (Writing culture heroes: Cultural studies in centenary exchange) (Nanjing: Jiangsu renmin chubanshe, 2000); Dai Jinhua, ed., *You zai jing zhong: Dai Jinhua fangtanlu* (Still caught by the mirror) (Beijing: Zhishi chubanshe, 1999); Dai Jinhua, *Pintu youxi* (Piecing together the map/ Playing the game) (Jinan: Taishan chubanshe, 1999); Dai Jinhua, *Shiji zhi men: Nüxing xiaoshuo juan* (Gates of the century: Volume of women's fiction) (Beijing: Shehui kexue wenxian chubanshe, 1998).

   Dai Jinhua, *Breaking out of the City of Mirrors* includes elements from essays and book chapters that Dai had been working on in her early, heroic efforts at establishing a theoretical film criticism in elite academic circles. For this period of her work, see Dai Jinhua, *Dianying lilun yü piping shouce* (Film theory and criticism handbook) (Beijing: Kexue jishu wenxian chubanshe, 1993). I want to thank Lau Kinchi for making this early material available to me in the mid-1990s.

7  In hindsight, the connection between the high culture fever of the late 1980s, including Li Xiaojiang's critique of masculine reason, and the dominant neoliberalism of the late 1990s has become clear. See Wang Hui, "The 1989 Social Movement and the Historical Root of 'Neo-Liberalism' in China," trans. Rebecca Karl, *positions* (forthcoming).

8  To some degree, this is an overstatement because the two theory streams coexist uncomfortably, in different academic communities and institutional settings. Li Xiaojiang's sexualist, philosophic humanism was tightly bound to the self-reflection movements of the late 1980s and she still contributes to a critical humanist current in the Chinese women's movement. When the journal *Dongfang* (Orient) ran a special issue on feminism in early 1995, Li's essay "Rebuilding the Bridge over the Sexual Gap" appeared and retracted some of the most extreme positions that she had taken in *Sex Gap*. See Li Xiaojiang, "Zhong jian kuyue 'xing gou' zhi qiao," *Dongfang* 4 (1995): 14–17. Thanks to Madeleine Yue Dong for bringing this special issue to my attention. See also Li Xiaojiang, "Shijimo kan 'Di er xing' " (*The Second Sex* at the end of the century), *Dushu* 12 (1999): 98–103. Most recently, Li has developed the Center of Gender Studies (Xingbie yanjiu zhongxin) at Dalian University and has resumed her work as a scholar.

9  Dai Jinhua had not read the work of Luce Irigaray (private correspondence, 19 December 1999). My point is that Dai is as invested as any humanist (e.g., Li Xiaojiang) in the eugenic roots of feminism because her psychoanalytic problematics install her in this global project in two ways. First, her inventive rewriting of Lacanian, Kristevan, and Althusserian insights promotes a certain style of foundational heterosexuality in *theory itself*. This part of her argument has unfolded in the domain of Chinese elite scholarship for exigencies that are local in nature: it is a creative response to the continuing trauma of a revolutionary century and the perception that socialism turned nature and culture inside out. Though in the end it may be as ideological as the theoretical positions it criticizes (I am drawing a different line between "theory" and "ideology" than Dai does), she emphasizes the knot that agonistically opposes sexual difference and human liberation. This has a family resemblance to the agonistic contradiction that Joan Scott drew attention to between difference and equality. In the last instance, Dai's point seems to be that only the full expression of sexual (i.e., intrapsychic) difference between women's and men's experience will bring an end to the oppressions of capitalist patriarchy. Second, Dai works at the international level of the world of cultural studies. This is a level where questions of national historiography and national subjectivity are increasingly exchanged. Consequently, she is a collaborator and contributor to a scholastic style of elite feminism that exceeds the national framework. Because of its recuperation of Marxism in the face of economic globalization, it is also international in the communist sense. That makes Dai's theoretical project utopian. For an essay that also suggests a historical link between eugenicist theory and Freudian formulas, see Geller, "Judenzopf/Chinesenzopf."

10 Some of the generalizations appearing here are based on my unpublished genealogy of Lacanian feminism's dissemination and its guiding assumptions. This theory stream in feminism is all about sexuality because it sees socius in terms of reproductive labor, introjection, projection, and relational erotic drives that are allegedly fed by desiring attachments and infantile imprinting.

11 An early, vernacular, inventive précis of this story or "theory" occurs in Mary Kelly, *Post-Partum Document* (London: Routledge and Kegan Paul, 1983). For more deeply engaged elite discussions, see Kaja Silverman, Teresa Brennan, Jane Gallop, Luce Irigaray, and Judith Butler. Although Butler's *Bodies That Matter* (New York: Routledge, 1993) contests some of the foundational assumptions in the Lacan story, it is highly indebted to Laca-

nian theories of desire. Butler's insight is that homosexual and heterosexual desires are versions of a similar formation but are valued differentially.

12　In the mid-1990s in the United States, Joan Copjec argued that two antithetical currents had come to structure and dominate contemporary feminist criticism. These were, she claimed, "Lacan and Foucault," or "psychoanalysis and historicism." Certainly, what Copjec revealed in her exaggerated pairing of polar differences in the feminist theory project was actually—no matter where you stand in relation to the alleged war of psychoanalysis and historicism—the degree to which Lacan and Foucault had become international figures of cultural criticism. Copjec tagged as Foucauldian "the reduction of society to its indwelling network of relations of power and knowledge." For Copjec, this is the project of history. Lacanianism, because of what it *does* (which is to say actual cultural therapy), is for her the more realistic, ethical, and superior theory. She argues that Lacanian psychoanalytic theory projects can address what "historicism" cannot, because history is preoccupied with surface description. Only the other of historicism, psychoanalysis, can "speak the whole unvarnished truth directly." Yet, as she is insinuating, a gendered dynamic between psychoanalysis (truth) and history (representation) was coming to fruition in the 1990s. See Copjec, *Read My Desire*. The most sustained argument for the cultural therapeutic power of Lacanian cultural critique is Juliet Flower MacCannell, *Figuring Lacan: Criticism and the Cultural Unconscious* (Lincoln: University of Nebraska Press, 1986). However, opposing pairs of "Lacan and Foucault," psychoanalysis and historicism, psychoanalysis and Marxism, psyche and social, are standard fare in the feminist project of the 1990s. For examples, see Jacqueline Rose, *Sexuality in the Field of Vision* (London: Verso, 1986) and Kaja Silverman, *Male Subjectivity at the Margins* (London: Routledge, 1992). Both were influential texts among feminist high theorists in the 1990s in the United States.

13　The global impact of the Chinese Great Proletarian Cultural Revolution of the 1970s infused the culturalism of Lacan, Althusser, Foucault, and Derrida (and in the United States, Fredric Jameson). (The Maoist-inspired, European theoretical shift to culture resurfaced into Chinese post-Maoism in the 1980s and particularly the 1990s.) A helpful study that touches on this theme is Liu Kang, *Aesthetics and Marxism: Chinese Aesthetic Marxists and Their Western Contemporaries* (Durham, NC: Duke University Press, 2000).

14　Julia Kristeva, *About Chinese Women*, trans. Anita Barrow (New York: Marion Boyars, 1977). I am indebted to Lisa Lowe, *Critical Terrains: French and British Orientalisms* (Ithaca, NY: Cornell University Press, 1991) for this view of Kristeva on woman, matriarchy, and joissance. See particularly 140–52. Glossolalia is the opposite of phallologocentrism, because it means utterances and verbal ejaculations that exceed or evade the power of male, totalitarian schemes to reduce language to a one-to-one relation between a signifier and a signified.

15　Kristeva's importance in Europe was as a protagonist in the "second debate" over Freud and femininity. The first debate had unfolded earlier, in the 1930s. In this second debate, which seems to have stretched out over the late 1970s to the late 1980s, the stakes were Lacan's effort to restore the centrality of the role of the father and the phallus in the structuring of the symbolic order. It was held that the centrality of the father to the structuring of the Symbolic was more accurate in a worldly sense. Reflecting this in theory was held to deepen the capacity of theory to correctly diagnose cultural symptoms at large because it moved the critique beyond a parochial, American preoccupation with so-called maternal object-relations theory. See Teresa Brennan, *The Interpretation of the Flesh: Freud and Femininity* (London: Routledge, 1992), chs. 1, 2 for a history of the first and second debates on femininity and female sexuality in Freud.

16 This discussion of Dai in relation to global trends in écriture féminine rests on her 1998 interview with Zhou Yaqin and Po Zhenji, "Feminism: Cultural Standpoint, Gender Experience, and Scholarly Choice," in *Still Caught by the Mirror*. Historical background for the emergence of feminist psychoanalytic concepts into circulation in Beijing, in translation in the late 1980s, is laid out in Zhang Jingyuan, *Contemporary Literary Criticism* and Chen Shunxing, *Gender and narrative in Chinese contemporary literature* and in Chen's essay "Écriture Féminine in the Mainland China Discussions." The point is that around the time French feminism's influence was cycling through Anglophone feminism, it was also deeply influencing the work of a significant elite community in Chinese theory circles. Elite literary criticism in the PRC in 1980s psychoanalytic theories made it possible to address the question of the "sexual gap" in a nuanced, articulate way. I am grateful to Zhang Jingyuan and Chen Shunxing for making these important texts available to me.

17 Alys Eve Weinbaum, "Marx, Irigaray, and the Politics of Reproduction," in *Is Feminist Philosophy Philosophy?* ed. Emma Bianchi (Evanston, IL: Northwestern University Press, 1999), 161 nn. 21, 23.

18 In the United States the Lacanian feminist thread has stalemated over what is alleged to be an impenetrable binary contradiction of socius and psyche. The crude opposition of Lacan and Foucault is a problem that even Teresa Brennan has had difficulty exceeding. See Brennan, *History after Lacan* (London: Routledge, 1993).

19 Meng Yue and Dai Jinhua, *Fuchu lishi dibiao: Xiandai funü wenxue yanjiu* (Surfacing onto the horizon of history: A study in modern women's literature) (Zhengzhou: Henan renmin chubanshe, 1980), 7; subsequent quotations are cited in the text.

20 Meng and Dai are quick to point out that in feudal culture women developed their own countermeasures and undertook a female language of dreams and signification. However, the main ideological current is the double bind or impossible situation that the lijiao and other cultural practices set out for women in the male-ordered symbolic trap female presubjects or ersatz subjects fall into. This works in much the same way as the Communist Party's emphasis on providing women with a ready-made ren'ge or personal standing by fiat. See ibid., 32, 43.

21 That is, analytically because men have colonized their own phallicized signifiers. The examples that Dai and Meng provide (and that preoccupied Dai in later work) are Hua Mulan (a man's woman, dressed as a man, eventually undressed and recycled to another man as a wife) and Cui Yingying, who dies for a passion (*qing*) that the symbolic order simply cannot accommodate.

22 A more fully developed discussion of this point is made in the book's second chapter, "Liang ge sizhe, yige jingxiang" (Two corpses and a mirror). There the critics identify Nora as icon of the mirror stage of female subject formation in China because when "women as a group" stare at Nora, what they actually see is their own "self" as this so-called self is refracted through a male Symbolic. Dai would later submerge this point into her extraordinary discussions of Nora, Mulan, and the "city of mirrors" in her later film and cultural studies.

23 See Dai and Meng, *Horizon*, 25–26, 44–45 for this discussion. I raise this point to underline the fact that ren'ge is a problem or question for Meng and Dai, but it is not an objective. These critics place quotations around the question of women's personal being on the grounds that women themselves must establish a sense of self and cannot be advised in this quest.

24 When they use the term "gendered perspective" Dai and Meng mean a way of looking that clearly distinguishes the women's view and the men's view.

25 Meng and Dai, *Horizon*, 54: "They lacked their own perspective, their own mode of

thinking, a critical tradition of their own, a standard of their own for praising themselves, and a systematic conceptual language. The problem for [Feng] Yuanjun and her female protagonists is that they are acculturated to this delimitation of rights, personality, romantic love, the conflict of fathers and sons and so on and are in fact irrelevant to the new ideological formation."

26  The argument is laid out on pages 14–47 of the main body of the book. The introduction and the book do not share the same pagination.

27  The discussion appears under the rubric of "Munü niudai" (The bond of mother and daughter), 57–61.

28  The link between this foundational move in the écriture féminine tradition and the betrayal of the new historical subject it created is Ling Shuhua, whose literature illustrated the crisis women actually confronted in their real existence. To Meng and Dai, Ling shows women confronting the double bind of history. Women are finding themselves differently eroticized in the great rupture of Chinese traditional patriarchal clan organization and are being resituated as wives in nuclear families. The problem is that they do not control the way sexual difference is being represented, nor do they control or really even accept, at least in this initial stage, the great burdens of a subjectivity that is rooted in recognition of the singularity of female sexual desire. See Meng and Dai, Horizon, 76–96.

29  Ibid., 115.

30  I am consolidating what is a far more complex, nuanced argument. Chapter 8, for instance, traces the contributions of Xie Bingyin, Feng Keng, and Ge Qin, women warrior writers who are significant literature figures but enter the Symbolic as men. Chapter 9 develops the significance of underrated figures like Su Xueling, Lin Peizhi, Chen Yingdeng, and Lin Huiyin, who kept alive the project of écriture féminine in an urban context and in a narrow bourgeois frame. They belong in the female pantheon because, unlike Cao Ming, Bai Lang, Lo Shu, and others who abandoned the historical female group (nüxing qunti), they accepted what history had allotted to women. They embraced the transition of daughter to woman and kept alive an important psychodynamic portal for women in this nascent tradition in later decades. Chapter 10 is concerned with Bai Wei, another often undertheorized figure. Meng and Dai find attractive Bai's lonely, stubborn, demystified femininity and the spiritual integrity that kept this writer committed to the fruitless task of writing woman.

31  Ibid., 214–15.

32  Ibid., 235–36; emphasis added.

33  Zhang Jingyuan, "Guonei nüxing wenxue (shi) yanjiu de xianzhuang" (The situation of the study of national women's literature['s history]), Xueren 2, no. 2 (1992): 382–89. I think it is important to point out that the book has never been reviewed in English. Also, although its influence is frequently not attributed, scholars publishing in English in the mid-1990s often show the influence of this pioneering work.

34  Dai, Gates of the Century, 1–27. The introductory essay is "Qiyü yu tuwei: Jiushi niandai de nüxing xiezuo" (Unexpected encounter and breaking out: 1990s women's culture and écriture féminine). The piece reprises and forwards themes long part of her analysis and enriched with the spatialized perspective that she developed through film criticism over the course of the 1990s.

35  Ibid., 13.

36  On the centrality of game logics in Dai's writing on "the 1990s," see "Zhizhe xixue: Shuo du Wang Xiaobo" (The sage's jest: Reading Wang Xiaobo), Contemporary Writer's Review, no. 1 (1998). (This essay is also published in Piecing Together the Map/Playing the Game, 136–

66.) See also the "Foucault, Power and the Game" section of Dai, *Still Caught by the Mirror*, interview entitled "Qingxing de lichang" (The awakened position), 12–16.

37 Dai, "Dianying shi de wenhua jingshen fansi ji qita" (Reflections on the spiritual culture of cinema history and other things), in *Still Caught by the Mirror*, 28. Lau Kinchi, trans. "Rethinking the Cultural History of Chinese Films" in *Cinema and Desire*.

38 If (to mimic Dai's own idiom) it is possible to say that Dai Jinhua was in British terms a *Screen*-style feminist film critic during the 1980s, then one might say that in the 1990s the analogy could be drawn to a Frankfurt School critique of mass culture style. In neither case was Dai directly influenced. Rather, given the internationally circulating theoretical resources and the structural transformation of Chinese urban and rural political economies, the consequences were not unlike these European theoretical projects.

39 Dai, "Zhongguo nüxingxue yu nüxing zhuyi, zuotian yu jintian" (Feminism: Cultural standpoint, gender experience and scholarly choice), in *Still Caught by the Mirror*, 147.

40 Dai Jinhua, "Dianying: Yannise shidai" (Cinema: The Janus period), *Dianying yishu*, no. 4 (1988): 12. See also her brief suggestion in this essay that film theorists contribute to the project of cinema because they have the capacity to work with the unconscious content of work.

41 Dai, *Still Caught by the Mirror*; see the 1996 essay "Man tan wenhua yanjiu zhong de xiandaixing wenti" (A chat about the modernist question at the heart of cultural studies), 215–47, and the 1997 interview "An Awakened Position," 1–27.

42 Dai, *Gates of the Century*, 17.

43 Ibid., 16.

44 Dai, *Still Caught by the Mirror*, 3.

45 Ibid., 50; emphasis added. See Lau, trans. "Rethinking," 256.

46 In Dai's view this is because literature is open to aesthetic judgment. Even in the relatively "young" language of contemporary Chinese, literature is an aesthetic and a psychodynamic medium. This would appear to be an expression of Dai's elitism. It may also be an effect of the social histories of the two media in the era since liberation. Film, more securely ensconced in the state's ideological apparatus, did not lend itself as easily as literature to social contestations. Literature, on the contrary, held a sacrosanct place in the People's Republic precisely because it was a medium where intellectuals made political demands on policymakers.

47 Dai, *Still Caught by the Mirror*, 33; Lau, trans. "Rethinking," 240.

48 Dai, *Handbook*, 218–32. The film's commercial title in Anglophone markets is *Woman, Demon, Human* and is obviously not a direct translation of *Ren, gui, qing*, which might be closer to "(hu)Man, specter, passion." The argument that Chinese film history does not have an analogue for écriture féminine appears in chapter 3 of *City of Mirrors*. Dai has reworked the same material for an essay she wrote for the English-language anthology, *Cinema and Desire*. It appears there in a translation by Jonathan Noble under the title "Gender and Narration: Women in Contemporary Chinese Film." In this line of argument, Dai proposes three conjunctions of "women" and "film": socialist directors in male drag whose female characters are empty signifiers or earth mothers of the people or are simply victims; post-Mao female directors whose fallback position in the commercializing world of Chinese film was to create a sentimental style called "the women's film"; and directors who, like Zhang Nuanxin, Hu Mei, and Huang Shiqing, tried honestly to represent the dilemma of female lived experience. *Woman, Demon, Human* is the only fully successful effort. Dai gives this analysis to illustrate how much more difficult it is for film auteurs to "break out" of the symbolic order.

49 Dai Jinhua, "The Invisible Woman: Women and Cinema," trans. Mayfair Yang, *positions:*

east asia cultures critique 3, no. 1 (spring 1995): 255–80. "As a woman playing a man . . . she [Qiu] intensifies both the conscious and unconscious confusion she feels in her own gender identity. Moreover, because the person of the role (a man) and the person of the performer (a woman) cannot coexist, this role-playing also plays havoc with, first, the construction 'female desire/object of men' and, then, the construction 'women as the saved/man as the savior' " (177–78). Yang translated a version of the essay that Dai had given her; Dai later revised the manuscript. It appears in a more elaborated form in *City of Mirrors* under the same name but in three sections that bear the titles "History's Travails and the Perversity of Culture," "Women in the Cinema," and "Women's Cinema." In the final version Dai stresses the rift between history and cultural representation and the logical error in women's encounter with the masculine Real. Her primary analytic point seems to be that in cinema practice, once women enter into History (i.e., move out of the historical unconscious of film into its representational order or "consciousness") they simply fall out of the field of vision. Yang included the illuminating interview that Dai and she staged with the filmmaker, a long discussion of Huang's motives in filming this particular story.

50 This is the logic of the place Dai makes into a material metaphor and calls "the city of mirrors." In her intricate, detailed analyses she puts a great deal of emphasis on where the metaphoric drama is unfolding. She characterizes the diegetic as a disintegrated landscape, a window broken out into a Real that, bereft of its cloaking ideologies, now reveals interlocking fissures in a ruined map. Perhaps landscape is inadequate to describe Dai's analytic strategy. The material moment that film represents to the viewer involves not simply narrative, but a visual text, and not just a visual text but also a temporal one. Not only does Huang demonstrate the incontrovertibility of Qiu Yun's sex by having her mistaken for a boy in the girl's latrine, but also, in Dai's view, Huang shows how the temporality of change has actually worked in the history of contemporary China. It is the metanarrative of gender that provides an ideological mirage in an older, more stable time.

51 Dai Jinhua, "Duan giao: zi yi dai de yishu" (Severed bridge: the art of the son's generation), in *Jing cheng tuwei* (Breaking out of the city of mirrors), 4–47, is heavily indebted to structuralist theory. Dai explained in the interview "Awakened Position" that she began seriously reading structuralism in 1983. As has always been her practice, she has read widely and randomly. She attributes her greatest insights to a volume titled *Structuralism: Moscow, Prague, Paris* by Jan Broekman, trans. Jan F. Beekman and Brunhilde Helm (Dordrecht: D. Reidel, 1974) and Christian Metz's *Film Language: A Semiotics of the Cinema*, Michael Taylor, trans. (New York: Oxford University Press, 1974).

52 I would like to credit the impulse in this part of my argument to Claudia Pozzana's brilliant retranslation of *zijue* from the banal "self-realization" to the more illuminating "self-authorization" (Project for Critical Asian Studies workshop, spring 1998). Dai Jinhua is in the Chinese Enlightenment tradition. Her use of its rhetoric of awakening, realization, and self-awareness is redolent of the 1920s when, in Pozzana's argument, this novel use arose.

53 Dai, "Awakened Position," 2–25 provides a discussion of how Dai moved into cultural studies. She explains that it was a natural step because her students and colleagues abruptly abandoned the high culture theory that she had spent ten years developing. In 1992–1993 she had to rethink her position. She began to doubt her own avant-gardism. She remains, she says, a confirmed elitist but one open to class analysis, the special strength of cultural studies. Cultural studies, in other words, legitimates for Dai the psychoanalytic study of identity forms in relation to class and social studies.

54  Dai Jinhua, "Redemption and Consumption: Depicting Culture in the 1990s" (Jiushu yu xiaofei: Jiushi niandai wenhua miaoshu zhi er), trans. Edward Gunn, in *Cinema and Desire*, 172–88.

55  Dai Jinhua, "A Scene in the Fog: Reading the Sixth Generation Films" (Wu zhong fengjing: Chu du "diliu dai"), *Frontiers*, 1996, trans. Yiman Wang, in *Cinema and Desire*, 2; subsequent quotations are cited in the text.

56  Dai Jinhua, "National Identity in the Hall of Mirrors" (Jingxiang wuliang zhong de minzu shenfen), *Guangzhou Literature and Arts*, 1998, trans. Eileen Cheng and Shu-mei Shih, in *Cinema and Desire*, 189–212.

57  Dai Jinhua, "Invisible Writing: The Politics of Chinese Mass Culture in the 1990s" (Yingxing shuxie: Jiushi niandai dazhong wenhua de zhengzhixue), *Frontiers*, 1999, trans. Jingyuan Zhang, in *Cinema and Desire*, 213–34.

58  Dai, "Rethinking," 239; and "Dushi wenxue, wenxue piping he zhishifenzi jiaose" (Urban literature, literary theory and the role of intellectuals), in *Still Caught by the Mirror*, 85.

59  Dai, "Rethinking," 243.

60  It is possible that the culture concept in cultural studies in the PRC is now shaped in relation to censorship politics. Attributing so much to a concept, culture, so Promethean and amorphous, is a useful strategy, and it maximizes Dai's already considerable powers of political allusion. For Dai's statements on Foucault's influence, see *Still Caught by the Mirror*, 12–14. From Foucault she took the lesson that when you are unsure of the rules, don't play the game. Also see 22–25 for her comments on the Promethean power of "Western theory" and the naturalization in China of Hegel and Kant.

61  Dai, "Gender and Narration." I interpret the sections that are advances in her theoretical position. See "Rewriting Woman," "The Vicious Cycle of History," and "Genderless Narratives and Gender Landscapes." This essay ends on a melancholy note: it seems as if China's historical progress can complete its course only at the expense of the regression of women's culture. Only the woman who can perform the new double bind, illustrate the new trap, can "win" in this long, losing game. All other versions of women in the 1990s are bridges for pasting over rifts in the new Enlightenment discourse of modernization and development. Women is always ex post facto. Just as in high Maoism it signified the oppressed, now women is a screen projected to conceal class structure and class differentiation. See also "Feminism: Cultural Standpoint."

62  Dai, "Feminism: Cultural Standpoint," 164–75.

63  Dai, "Cinema: The Janus Period." In this dialogue Dai made the explicit claims for theory. The theoretical claims of psychoanalysis are always grandiose, of course. Psychoanalytic critics read écriture féminine just as the physician reads the corporeal body, for signs of normativity and dis-ease. This places the theoretician into a remarkable relation to what he or she alleges to be the body politic.

## Conclusion

1  Charlotte Furth, "Culture and Politics in Modern Chinese Conservatism," in *The Limits of Change: Essays on Conservative Alternatives in Republican China*, ed. Charlotte Furth (Cambridge, MA: Harvard University Press, 1976), 51. They include theorists from the 1890s through the 1950s such as Li Dazhao, Kang Youwei, Zhao Binglin, Tao Xisheng, and Feng Youlan. See also Furth's study in the volume, "The Sage as Rebel: The Inner World of Chang Ping-lin," 113–50. Huxley published *Evolution and Ethics* in 1893 and Yan Fu translated it in 1896.

2  I am not denying the role that social evolution has played in the arrival of human dominion over the earth. But I also do not hold the view that (1) heterosexuality and species survival are the same thing; (2) instinctive drives cause human social expression; or (3) the recapitulation of erotic survival drives in the development of infants causes social expression in adults.

3  As part of a self-denoted Enlightenment in China, the history of the subject woman in Chinese feminism may prove in the end to have much in common with histories of the subject woman in other national projects of capitalist, colonial modernity. If my suggestion is correct and the event of women globally comes concurrently with the advent of arguments for women's liberation, national histories of enlightened feminism will be particularly valuable. But it is also the case, as Lata Mani noted years ago, that although the colonial encounter itself may be the hothouse where various enlightened feminist claims to women's essential humanity were developed, the particulars of how feminist theoretical initiatives emerged are more significant than generalizations that mark them all as modern. Which only means that the "Chinese" part of the history of the subject woman is significant because all politics are local and all human social claims specific; but the commonalities suggest that in the last instance, the subject woman in Chinese feminism is not a matter of identity and cannot claim a stable national essence. See Lata Mani, "Cultural Theory, Colonial Texts: Reading Eyewitness Accounts of Widow Burning," in Cultural Studies, ed. Lawrence Grossberg, Cary Nelson, and Paula Treichler (London: Routledge, 1992), 392–408.

4  See Naihua Zhang, "The All-China Women's Federation" for how this discussion has played out within the Communist Party Women's Federation.

5  Dai Jinhua, "Gender and Narration: Women in Contemporary Chinese Film."

6  Lin Chun, "Transformation of Chinese Socialism."

7  The earliest versions of Spivak's "Can the Subaltern Speak?" in Marxism and the Interpretation of Culture, Cary Nelson and Lawrence Grossberg, eds. (Chicago: University of Illinois Press, 1988), 271, are, it is sometimes forgotten, primarily focused on showing how the "postmodern theories" of French male intellectuals are ideological reflections of their privilege. Spivak notes the essay's original title was "Power, Desire, Interest."

8  Reading in the archives of theory is like reading intellectual history, except that theories are the social sciences' claim to truth in the modern era.

9  Chetan Bhatt, "Primordial Being: Enlightenment, Schopenhauer and the Indian Subject of Postcolonial Theory," Radical Philosophy 100 (March–April 2000): 37.

Appendix

1  Dorothy Ko, Teachers of the Inner Chambers; Lata Mani, "Contentious Traditions: The Debate on Sati in Colonial India," in Recasting Women: Essays in Indian Colonial History, ed. Kumkum Sangari and Sudesh Vaid (New Delhi: Kali for Women, 1989); Nell Irvin Painter, "Representing Truth: Sojourner Truth's Knowing and Becoming Known," Journal of American History 81, no. 2 (September 1994): 461–92; Mrinalini Sinha, "Gender in the Critiques of Colonialism and Nationalism: Locating the 'Indian Woman,' " in Feminists Revision History, Anne-Louise Shapiro, ed. (New Brunswick: Rutgers University Press, 1994). Subsequent quotations of each are cited in the text.

2  I develop this criticism of feminist multiculturalism further in "Teaching International Feminism in a Global Frame," unpublished manuscript, 1998.

3  R. Radhakrishnan, "Nationalism, Gender, and the Narrative of Identity," in Nationalisms and Sexualities, ed. Andrew Parker et al. (New York: Routledge, 1992), 77. Although I will

not pursue this, I cite Radhakrishnan because his phrase neatly encapsulates the problematic I am working in. The full citation is: "What remains concealed in . . . universalization is of course the fact that Western nationalism itself took shape under highly determinate and limited historical circumstances." It is thus not the case that the "West's" universalism stands adjacent to colonial specificities but rather that each universalism is itself heterogeneous in its composition.

4   Sara Suleri, *Meatless Days* (Chicago: University of Chicago Press, 1989), 1.

5   It suggests that women are imbricated in the present field of contradictions and still mobile enough to leave their traces everywhere, and thus are irreducible to a multicultural version of the subject woman/women produced in the matrix of colonial class politics in Britain, among British citizens, in the eighteenth and particularly the nineteenth centuries. For relevant historiography that examines the historical constitution of the catachresis woman in classed, raced, and colonially modern Europe, see the following influential studies: Denise Riley, *Am I That Name? Feminism and the Category of "Women" in History* (Basingstoke, England: Macmillan, 1988); Nancy Armstrong, *Desire and Domestic Fiction: A Political History of the Novel* (New York: Oxford University Press, 1987); Mary Poovey, *Uneven Developments: The Ideological Work of Gender in Mid-Victorian England* (Chicago: University of Chicago Press, 1988); Anna Davin, "Imperialism and Motherhood," *History Workshop Journal* 5 (1978): 9–65; Genevieve Lloyd, *The Man of Reason: "Male" and "Female" in Western Philosophy* (London: Routledge, 1993); Emily Apter, *Feminizing the Fetish: Psychoanalysis and Narrative Obsession in Turn-of-the-Century France* (Ithaca: Cornell University Press, 1991); and most recently, Anne McClintock, *Imperial Leather: Race, Gender and Sexuality in the Colonial Conquest* (New York: Routledge, 1995).

6   Elizabeth Cowie, "Woman as Sign," *m/f*, 1978, reprinted in *The Woman in Question*, ed. Parveen Adams and Elizabeth Cowie (Cambridge, MA: MIT Press, 1990); subsequent quotations are cited in the text.

7   Joan Scott, "Gender: A Useful Category of Historical Analysis," in *Gender and the Politics of History* (New York: Columbia University Press, 1988), 42. Also see Scott, *Only Paradoxes to Offer*, which has shifted more firmly into the notion that women is nothing more nor less than the subject of feminism. For the earlier arguments, see Scott, *Gender and the Politics of History*.

8   Riley, *Am I That Name?*, 1–2.

9   Differences of discipline condition how Riley's initiative has been understood. Whereas Riley seems to me quite significant historiographically, Diane Elam, undervaluing the project of the historiographer, judges the book to be "a fairly straightforward traditional history of the category of women at selected moments in Western cultures" (*Feminism and Deconstruction*, 38).

In the end, for feminist theorists, Judith Butler finally extended this line of argument to conclude that not only is signification (which she expanded into iterability or performativity) the key problem, but the agents who perform in and via signifying systems or cultural codes or grids constitute or actually materialize themselves. Subjects act out or reiterate commonplace norms and bring themselves into being. Many of these ideas have not become commonplace. They are a good way to think about evidence of the past. Right here, however, I am more concerned with the question of how historiographic regimes condition what can be said about the categories of women, and how historians decide what is a gendered subject, not how agency in general works.

10  Since the publication of Riley's book other scholars have shown how the category woman in British history was in fact a convention of colonial modernity. Postcolonial scholarship has also systematically undermined the capacity of national histories of

Europe to ignore what colonialism did in shaping the profiles of the metropolitan or colonizer's homeland. These studies include Gauri Viswanathan, *Masks of Conquest: Literary Study and British Rule in India* (New York: Columbia University Press, 1989), which demonstrates how English studies and cultural studies emerged out of the colonial "laboratory"; Billie Melman, *Women's Orient: English Women and the Middle East, 1718–1918: Sexuality, Religion and Work* (Ann Arbor: University of Michigan Press, 1992), which conclusively shows how "the colonies and the colonial experience constituted the gendered British identity and the experience of women and men, mainly of the middle classes" (xxi); Lila Abu-Lughod, *Remaking Women*, which argues that "women, the subject of feminism" in Britain, is implicated in the colonial politics of representation in Egypt and the Middle East; Mrinalini Sinha's monograph, *Colonial Masculinity: The "Manly Englishman" and the "Effeminate Bengali" in the Late Nineteenth Century* (New York: St. Martin's Press, 1995), where the gender in question is "man" and the stress is discourses gendering masculinity in the colonial interchanges of governmentality; and Partha Chatterjee, *The Nation and Its Fragments: Colonial and Postcolonial Histories* (Princeton: Princeton University Press, 1993), particularly ch. 6, "The Nation and Its Women," which situates women within the colonial nationalist social framework.

11   Truly historical writing, then, blasts specificity out of a present where time stands still and carefully notes the double bind of all historical work: that specificity is always compromised because it is meditated historiographically through the present of the historian. Nontranscendence or the mutual implication of history and historiography is what William Haver calls "historical consciousness." His point is simple: "Historical consciousness is at once the consciousness *of* history . . . that 'there is history rather than nothing,' and a consciousness that is itself specifically historical, an effect of, and subject to, the vicissitudes of history. . . . [If] 'historical consciousness' is to be that which enables political acting in the present, it cannot abstract itself from the 'present field of contradictions.' Therefore, 'historical consciousness' must also be the acknowledgement of its own nontranscendence." William Haver, *The Body of This Death: Historicity and Sociality in the Time of AIDS* (Stanford: Stanford University Press, 1997), 47.
    What we know of history is mediated through, is of the same stuff that we want to establish as our truth. Consciousness "*of* history," for historians at least, is mediated through previous written *accounts of the past* as much as through new archives or fresh evidence.
    "In history," Collingwood says, "as in all serious matters, no achievement is final." And that is in great part because "the historian himself, together with the here-and-now . . . is part of the process he is studying." Historians do not transcend "history." Only an ideologist or an empiricist would pretend that we do. That is why "every new generation must rewrite history in its own way" for the simple reason that "*the historian . . . is a part of the process he is studying.*" A history text, as distinct from literary criticism or sociology, emerges in relation to immediate events, under the weight of historiographic conventions and in response to perceived historiographic deficiencies. R. G. Collingwood, *The Idea of History* (Oxford: Clarendon, 1946), 248; emphasis added.

12   I am adapting the insight from Partha Chatterjee's argument in ch. 1, "Whose Imagined Community," of *The Nation and Its Fragments*. What is usually obscured because it is already assumed to be universally and always in existence is evidence of the rise of women as a category onto the horizon of history, in the words of Dai Jinhua and Meng Yue. See chapter 7 for an examination of how two Chinese theorists have thought about this point. The point for Chatterjee in the context of the relation of colonial India and colonizing Britain is that colonial modernist biopower does not just "happen." People

choose to struggle within contexts that are not of their own making but that would not exist in their absence. Among these given conditions, subjects, and subject categories is "the category of 'women,' the subject of feminism," and what is particularly germane about "women, the subject of feminism" is that it "is produced and restrained by the very structures of power through which [the] emancipation [of women] is sought." See Judith Butler, *Gender Trouble: Feminism and the Subversion of Identity* (New York: Routledge, 1990), 2, cited in Antoinette Burton, *Burdens of History: British Feminists, Indian Women, and Imperial Culture, 1865–1915* (Chapel Hill: University of North Carolina Press, 1994), 21.

# Works Cited

Abu-Lughod, Lila. "Introduction: Feminist Longings and Postcolonial Conditions." In *Remaking Women: Feminism and Modernity in the Middle East*, ed. Lila Abu-Lughod. Princeton: Princeton University Press, 1998.

——. ed. *Remaking Women: Feminism and Modernity in the Middle East*. Princeton: Princeton University Press, 1998.

Althusser, Louis. *Essays in Self-Criticism*. Trans. Grahame Lock. London: NLB, 1976.

Anagnost, Ann. *National Past-times: Narrative, Representation and Power in Modern China*. Durham, NC: Duke University Press, 1998.

Anderson, Marsten. "Beyond Realism: The Eruption of the Crowd." In *The Limits of Realism: Chinese Fiction in the Revolutionary Period*. Berkeley: University of California Press, 1990.

——. *The Limits of Realism: Chinese Fiction in the Revolutionary Period*. Berkeley: University of California Press, 1990.

Andors, Phyllis. "Studying Chinese Women." *Bulletin of Concerned Asian Scholars* 7, no. 4 (October–December 1975): 41–43.

——. *The Unfinished Liberation of Chinese Women, 1949–1980*. Bloomington: University of Indiana Press, 1983.

Apter, Emily. *Feminizing the Fetish: Psychoanalysis and Narrative Obsession in Turn-of-the-Century France*. Ithaca, NY: Cornell University Press, 1991.

Armstrong, Nancy. *Desire and Domestic Fiction: A Political History of the Novel*. New York: Oxford University Press, 1987.

Asad, Talal. "Are There Histories of People without Europe: A Review Article." *Comparative Studies in Society and History* 29 (July 1987).

Badiou, Alain. "Being by Numbers: Lauren Sedofsky Talks with Alain Badiou." *Artforum* 33, no. 2 (October 1994): 84–87, 118, 123–24.

Badiou, Alain, and Peter Hallward. "Politics and Philosophy: An Interview with Alain Badiou." *Angelaki: Journal of the Theoretical Humanities* 3, no. 3 (1998): 113–33.

Bai Shuang. "Huidao jia qu? Dao shehui lai?" (Back to the family? Or out into society?). *Jiefang Ribao* (Liberation daily), 8 March 1942.

Balibar, Etienne. "The Borders of Europe." In *Cosmopolitics: Thinking and Feeling beyond the Nation*, ed. Pheng Cheah and Bruce Robbins. Minneapolis: University of Minnesota Press, n.d.

Barlow, Tani E. "Colonial Modernity and Semicolonialism as Constituent Problems in Postcolonial Gender Theories." Unpublished manuscript, 2002.

——. "Colonialism's Career in Postwar China Studies." In *Formations of Colonial Modernity in East Asia*, ed. Tani E. Barlow. Durham, NC: Duke University Press, 1997.

——. "Feminism and Literary Technique in Ding Ling's Early Short Stories." In *Women Writers of 20th Century China*. Eugene: Asian Studies Program, University of Oregon, 1982. Reissued in Chinese translation as "Nüquan zhuyi he wenxue jishu zai Ding Ling nushi de chuqi de xiaoshuo." In *Ding Ling yanjiu zai guowai* (Research on Ding Ling outside China), ed. Sun Ruizhen. Changsha: Hunan renmin chubanshe, 1985.

——. "Feminist Genealogies: The Problem of Division in Ding Ling's *Wei Hu*." In *Woman and Literature in China*, ed. Wolfgang Kubin et al. Berlin: Studienverlag Brockmeyer, 1985.

——. "Gender and Identity in Ding Ling's *Mother*." *Modern Chinese Literature* 3, no. 1 (spring 1987): 123–42. Reprinted in *Modern Chinese Women Writers: Critical Appraisals*, ed. Michael Duke. Armonk, NY: M.E. Sharpe, 1989.

——. Introduction to *Formations of Colonial Modernity in East Asia*, ed. Tani Barlow. Durham, NC: Duke University Press, 1997.

——. "Politics and Protocols of funü: Re-Making the National Woman." Unpublished research report, 1991.

——. "Politics and Protocols of funü: (Un)Making the National Woman." In *Engendering China: Women, Culture and the State*, ed. Christina Gilmartin et al. Cambridge, MA: Harvard University Press, 1993.

——. Madeleine Dong, et al. "The Modern Girl around the World." Unpublished manuscript, 2004.

——. "Spheres of Debt and Feminist Ghosts in Area Studies of Women in China." *Traces* 1 (2000): 195–227.

——. "Theorizing Woman: Funü, Guojia, Jiating (Chinese Women, Chinese State, Chinese Family)." *Genders* 10 (spring 1991): 132–60.

——. "What Is Wanting: Natural Science, Social Science, Women in the 1920s." In *Women in the Republican Period*, ed. Mechthild Leutner and Nicola Spakowski. Berlin: LIT Verlag, forthcoming.

——. "Woman at the Close of the Maoist Era in the Polemics of Li Xiaojiang and Her Associates." In *The Politics of Culture in the Shadow of Capital*, ed. Lisa Lowe and David Lloyd. Durham, NC: Duke University Press, 1997.

——. "Zhishifenzi (Chinese Intellectuals) and Power." *Dialectical Anthropology* 16, nos. 3–4 (winter 1991): 209–32.

Barlow, Tani E., with Gary J. Bjorge, eds. *I Myself Am a Woman: Selected Writings of Ding Ling*. Boston: Beacon Press, 1989.

Barme, Geremie R. *In the Red: On Contemporary Chinese Culture*. New York: Columbia University Press, 1999.

Barshay, Andrew. "Toward a History of the Social Sciences in Japan." *positions: east asia cultures critique* 4, no. 2 (1996): 217–52.

Beahan, Charlotte. "Feminism and Nationalism in the Chinese Women's Press, 1902–1911." *Modern China* 1, no. 4 (October 1975): 379–416.

——. "Mothers of Citizens: Feminism and Nationalism in the Late Ch'ing." Unpublished manuscript, n.d.

Beauvoir, Simone de. *The Second Sex*. New York: Knopf, 1993.

Beibei'er [Bebel, Auguste]. *Funü yu shehui* (Woman and society). Trans. Shen Ruixian. Shanghai: Kaiming Books, 1949.

——. "Nüzi jianglai de diwei." (The future status of women). Trans. Han Jun from trans., Daneile de Leon, *Bebel Der Sozialismus und die Freatt* (Bebel's women under socialism). N.p., n.d.

Beijingshi funü lianhohui and Beijing funü wenti lilun yanjiuhui, eds. *Zhongguo funü lilun yanjiu shinian* (Women's theoretical studies in China from 1981 to 1998). Beijing: Zhong-guo funü chubanshe, 1991.

Belden, Jack. *China Shakes the World*. New York: Harper and Brothers, 1949.

Benhabib, Seyla, et al., eds. *Feminist Contentions: A Philosophical Exchange*. New York: Routledge, 1995.

Benjamin, Walter. *Illuminations: Essays and Reflections*. Ed. Hannah Arendt. Trans. Harry Zohn. New York: Harcourt, Brace and World, 1968.

Benton, Gregor. "The Yenan 'Literary Opposition.'" *New Left Review* 92 (July/August 1975): 93–96.

Bernhardt, Kathryn. *Women and Property in China, 960–1949*. Stanford: Stanford University Press, 1997.

Bhatt, Chetan. "Primordial Being: Enlightenment, Schopenhauer and the Indian Subject of Postcolonial Theory." *Radical Philosophy* 100 (March–April 2000): 28–41.

Billeter, Jean-François. "The System of Class Status." In *The System of State Power in China*, ed. Stuart R. Schram. Hong Kong: Chinese University Press, 1985.

Birken, Lawrence. "Darwin and Gender." *Social Concept* 4, no. 1 (December 1987): 75–88.

Bjorge, Gary J. "'Sophia's Diary': An Introduction." *Tamkang Review* 5 (1974).

*Black's Law Dictionary*. Saint Paul, MN: West Publishing, 1990.

Boorman, Howard. *Biographical Dictionary of Republican China*. New York: N.p., 1971.

Brandt, Conrad, Benjamin Schwartz, and John Fairbank, eds. *A Documentary History of Chinese Communism*. London: Allen and Unwin, 1952.

Bray, Francesca. *Technology and Gender: Fabrics of Power in Late Imperial China*. Berkeley: University of California Press, 1997.

Bredbenner, Candice. *A Nationality of Her Own: Women, Marriage and the Law of Citizenship*. Berkeley: University of California Press, 1998.

Brennan, Teresa. *History after Lacan*. London: Routledge, 1993.

——. *The Interpretation of the Flesh: Freud and Femininity*. London: Routledge, 1992.

Brennan, Timothy. "The National Longing for Form." In *Nation and Narration*, ed. Homi K. Bhabha. London: Routledge, 1990.

Broekman, Jan. *Structuralism: Moscow, Prague, Paris*. Trans. Jan F. Beekman and Brunhilde Helm. Dordrecht: D. Reidel, 1974.

Brook, Timothy, and Bob Tadashi Wakabayashi, eds. *Opium Regimes: China, Britain, and Japan, 1839–1952*. Berkeley: University of California Press, 2000.

Brown, Carolyn T. "Woman as a Trope: Gender and Power in Lu Xun's 'Soap.'" In *Gender Politics in Modern China*, ed. Tani E. Barlow. Durham, NC: Duke University Press, 1994.

Brown, Wendy. *States of Injury: Power and Freedom in Late Modernity*. Princeton: Princeton University Press, 1995.

Burton, Antoinette. *Burdens of History: British Feminists, Indian Women, and Imperial Culture, 1865–1915*. Chapel Hill: University of North Carolina Press, 1994.

Buss, David M. *The Dangerous Passion: Why Jealousy Is as Necessary as Love and Sex*. New York: Free Press, 2000.

Butler, Judith. *Bodies That Matter: On the Discursive Limits of "Sex."* New York: Routledge, 1993.

——. "Contingent Foundations: Feminism and the Question of 'Postmodernism.'" In Linda Nicholson, ed. *Feminist Contentions: A Philosophical Exchange*. New York: Routledge, 1995.

——. "For a Careful Reading." In *Feminist Contentions: A Philosophical Exchange*, ed. Seyla Benhabib et al. New York: Routledge, 1995.

——. "Further Reflections on Conversations of Our Time." *diacritics: a review of contemporary criticism* 27, no. 1 (1997): 13–16.

——. *Gender Trouble: Feminism and the Subversion of Identity*. New York: Routledge, 1990.

Cai Chang. "E'guo geming yu funü" (The Russian Revolution and women). *Guangming*, 1925. Reprinted in *Zhongguo funü yundong lishi cailiao, 1921–1927* (Historical research materials for the Chinese women's movement, 1921–1927), 300–305.

——. "Su'E zhi funü yu ertong" (The women and children of Soviet Russia). *Guangming*, 1925. Reprinted in *Zhongguo funü yundong lishi ciliao, 1921–1927* (Historical research materials for the Chinese women's movement, 1921–1927), 317–21.

——. "Zhongdeng yishang nuxuesheng de dushu wenti" (Study problematics for women students above the secondary level). *Funü zazhi*, 1924. Reprinted in *Zhongguo funü yundong lishi cailiao, 1921–1927* (Historical research materials for the Chinese women's movement, 1921–1927), 255–61.

——. "Zhongguo gongchandang disanci zhongyang kuoda zhixing weiyuanhu guanyu funü yundong yizhuan" (Chinese Communist Party's third Central Committee resolution on enlarging the women's movement). In *Zhongguo funü yundong lishi ciliao, 1921–1927* (Historical research materials for the Chinese women's movement, 1921–1927), 475–78.

Cai Chang, Deng Yingchao, and Kang Keqing. *Funü jiefang wenti wenxuan, 1938–1987* (Selected documents on the question of women's liberation). Ed. All-China Women's Federation. Beijing: Renmin chubanshe, 1988.

Cai Chang, et al., eds. *Quanguo funü diyici quanguo daibiao dahui* (First Congress of the All-China Women's Association). Hong Kong: Xinmin Press, 1949.

Cai Kui Chenhai. "*Taiyang zhao zai Sanggan he shang de geming xianshi zhuyi*" (The revolutionary realism of *The Sun Shines over the Sanggan River*). *Xin wenxue luncong*, 1980. Reprinted in *Ding Ling zuopin pinglun ji* (Collected commentary on Ding Ling's work), ed. Zhongguo wenxie chuban gongsi. Beijing: Zhongguo wenlian chuban gongsi, 1984.

Cai Yu. "Zhongshi he jiaqiang funüshi yanjiu" (Take seriously and strengthen the study of women's history). In *Funü zuzhi yu huodong: Yinshua baokan ziliao* (Women's organizations and activities: Published press materials reader) 3 (1987): 52–54.

Cao Ming. "Chuangzuo ni de mingyun" (Create your own destiny). *Jiefang Ribao* (Liberation daily), 8 March 1942.

Carlitz, Katherine. "Shrines, Governing-class Identity, and the Cult of Widow Fidelity in Mid-Ming Jiangnan." *Journal of Asian Studies* 56, no. 3 (1997): 612–40.

Carpenter, Edward. *Ai shi* (History of Love). Shanghai: Wenyi chubanshe, 1920.

Cavanaugh, Carole. "Text and Textile: Unweaving the Female Subject in Heian Writing." *positions* 4, no. 3 (1996): 595–636.

Chakrabarty, Dipesh. "The Condition for Knowledge of Working Class Conditions." In *Selected Subaltern Studies*, ed. Ranajit Guha and Gayatri Chakravorty Spivak. New York: Oxford University Press, 1988.

——. "The Death of History? Historical Consciousness and the Culture of Late Capitalism." *Public Culture* 4, no. 2 (spring 1992): 47–65.

Chan, Ching-kiu Stephen. "The Language of Despair: Ideological Representations of the 'New Woman' by May Fourth Writers." *Modern Chinese Literature* 4, nos. 1–2 (1988): 19–38. Reprinted in *Gender Politics in Modern China: Feminism and Literature*, ed. Tani E. Barlow. Durham, NC: Duke University Press, 1994.

Chang Jen-mei. *Ding Ling: Her Life and Her Work*. Taipei: Institute of International Relations, 1978.

Chang Ying. "Zhongguo jindai funü yundongshi xueshu taolunhui zunshu" (Synthesis of the symposium on the history of the modern Chinese women's movement). In *Funü zuzhi yu huodong: Yinshua baokan ziliao* (Women's organizations and activities: Published press materials reader) (January 1988): 39–40.

Chartier, Roger. *On the Edge of the Cliff: History, Language, and Practices*. Trans. Lydia G. Cochrane. Baltimore: Johns Hopkins University Press, 1997.

Chatterjee, Partha. *The Nation and Its Fragments: Colonial and Postcolonial Histories*. Princeton: Princeton University Press, 1993.

———. *Nationalist Thought and the Colonial World: A Derivative Discourse*. Tokyo: United Nations Press, 1986.

Chaudhuri, Nupur, and Margaret Strobel, eds. *Western Women and Imperialism: Complicity and Resistance*. Bloomington: Indiana University Press, 1992.

Chen Boda. "Xin funü de rensheng guan" (The life philosophy of the new woman). In *Funü yundong wenxian* (Collected works of the women's movement), ed. Zhu De et al. Hong Kong: Xin minzhu chubanshe, 1949.

Chen Dezheng. "Jiazu zhidu de pochanguan" (The bankruptcy of the family system). In *Mei Sheng*, ed. *Zhongguo funü wenti taolunji* (Collected discussions of the Chinese woman question). Shanghai: Shanghai New Culture Press, 1929–34, III 8: 235–43.

———. "Shejiao gongkai he lian'ai" (Open social intercourse and love). In *Zhongguo funü wenti taolunji* (Collected discussions of the woman question), ed. Mei Sheng. Shanghai: Shanghai New Culture Press, 1929–34, III 6: 153–54.

———. "Xiang'ai de jiazhi" (The value of [hetero]sexual love). In *Zhongguo funü wenti taolunji* (Collected discussions of the woman question), ed. Mei Sheng. Shanghai: Shanghai New Culture Press, 1929–34, VI 9: 43.

Chen Guang, ed. *Ding Ling nüxing xiaoshuo jin zuo* (Ding Ling's golden fiction on women). Changsha: Hunan wenyi chubanshe, 1995.

Chen Guyuan. "Jiazu zhidu de piping" (Critique of the clan system). In *Zhongguo funü wenti taolunji* (Collected discussions of the woman question), ed. Mei Sheng. Shanghai: Shanghai New Culture Press, 1929–34, III 8: 184–90.

Chen Hongmou. "Jiao nü yi gui" (Posthumous regulation on educating women). In *Wu zhong yi gui* (Five posthumous regulations). Sibubeiyao ed. (N.p.: Zhonghua shuju, n.d.), vol. 3.

Chen Ping. "Zhongguo nüxing renkou yanjiu de qibu." In *Zhongguo funü lilun yanjiu shinian* (First steps in the study of Chinese female population). Beijing: Zhongguo funü chubanshe, 1991.

Chen Qixiu. "Nüzi zhencao de jinqian jiazhi" (The monetary value of female chastity). In *Zhongguo funü wenti taolunji* (Collected discussions of the woman questions), ed. Mei Sheng. Shanghai: Shanghai New Culture Press, 1929–34, V 13: 124–39.

Chen Shousun. *Shehui wenti cidian* (Dictionary of Chinese social questions). Shanghai: Minzhi shuju, 1929.

Chen Xunxing. *Zhongguo dangdai wenxue de xushi yu xingbie* (Gender and narrative in Chinese contemporary literature). Beijing: Beijing University Press, 1995.

———. "Zhongguo dalu lunshu zhong de 'nüxing xuezuo' " (Écriture féminine in the Mainland China discussions). Paper delivered at Qinghua University, Taiwan, 10–11 July 1998.

Chen Yudang. *Zhonggui jinxiandai renwu minghao dacidian* (Dictionary of contemporary and modern figures' names). Hangzhou: Zhejiang guji chubanshe, 1993.

Chen, Yung-fa. *Making Revolution: The Communist Movement in Eastern and Central China, 1937–1945*. Berkeley: University of California Press, 1985.

Cheng, Ho Kuo. "The Status and the Role of Women in the Chinese Communist Movement, 1946–1949." Ph.D. diss., Indiana University, 1973.

Chinese Democratic Women's Association, ed. *Makesi, Liening, Engesi, Sidalin lun funü jiefang* (Marx, Lenin, Engels, and Stalin on Women's Liberation). Hong Kong: New People's Press, 1949.

Chow, Kai-Wing. *The Rise of Confucian Ritualism in Late Imperial China: Ethics, Classics, and Lineage Discourse.* Stanford: Stanford University Press, 1994.

Chu Jun. "Funüzhi weisheng yiban" (Some issues of female hygiene). *Funü shibao* 3 (1911): 25–29.

——. "Funüzhi weisheng zahua" (Miscellaneous words on female hygiene). *Funü shibao* 4 (1911): 17–29.

Ch'u T'ung-tsu. *Law and Society in Traditional China.* Paris: Mouton Pratique des Hautes Etudes, 1961.

Collingwood, R. G. *The Idea of History.* Oxford: Clarendon, 1946.

Colwell, C. "Deleuze and Foucault: Series, Event and Genealogy." *theory and event* 1, no. 2 (1997): http://muse.jhu.edu/journals/theory__and__event/voo1/1.2colwell.html.

Copjec, Joan. *Read My Desire: Lacan against the Historicists.* Cambridge, MA: MIT Press, 1994.

Cornell, Drucilla. "Rethinking the Time of Feminism." In *Feminist Contentions: A Philosophical Exchange*, ed. Seyla Benhabib et al. New York: Routledge, 1995.

Corrigan, Philip, and Derek Sayer. *The Great Arch: English State Formation as Cultural Revolution.* Oxford: Basil Blackwell, 1985.

Coward, Rosalind. *Patriarchal Precedents: Sexuality and Social Relations.* London: RKP, 1983.

Cowie, Elizabeth. "Woman as Sign." *m/f* 1 (1978). Reprinted in *The Woman in Question*, ed. Parveen Adams and Elizabeth Cowie. Cambridge, MA: MIT Press, 1990.

Croll, Elizabeth. *Chinese Women Since Mao.* London: Zed Books, 1983.

——. *Feminism and Socialism in China.* London: Routledge and Kegan Paul, 1978.

——. *The Women's Movement in China: A Selection of Readings, 1949–1973.* London: Anglo-Chinese Educational Institute, Modern China Series 6, 19.

Crosby, Christina. *The Ends of History: Victorians and "The Woman Question."* New York: Routledge, 1991.

Dai Jinhua. *Dianying lilun yu piping shouce* (Film theory and criticism handbook). Beijing: Kexue jishu wenxian chubanshe, 1993.

——. "Dianying shi de wenhua jingshen fansi ji qita" (Reflections on the spiritual culture of cinema history and other things). In *You zai jing zhong* (Still caught by the mirror). Beijing: Zhishi chubanshe, 1999.

——. "Dianying: Yannise shidai" (Cinema: The Janus period). *Dianying yishu*, no. 4 (1988): 3–14.

——. "Duan qiao: zi yi dai de yishu" (Severed bridges: the art of the son's generation). In *Jingcheng tuwei: Nüxing, chanying, wenxue* (Breaking out of the city of mirrors: Women, film, literature). Beijing: Zuojia chubanshe, 1995.

——. "Dushi wenxue, wenxue piping he zhishifenzi jiaose" (Urban literature, literary theory and the role of intellectuals). In *You zai jing zhong* (Still caught by the mirror). Beijing: Zhishi chubanshe, 1999.

——. "Gender and Narration: Women in Contemporary Chinese Film." Trans. Jonathan Noble. In *Cinema and Desire: The Essays of Dai Jinhua*, ed. Jing Wang and Tani Barlow. London: Verso, 2002.

——. "The Invisible Woman: Women and Cinema." Trans. Mayfair Yang. *positions: east asia cultures critique* 3, no. 1 (spring 1995): 255–80.

——. "Invisible Writing: The Politics of Chinese Mass Culture in the 1990s" (Yingxing shuxie: Jiushi niandai dazhong wenhua de zhengzhixue). Trans. Jingyuan Zhang. *Frontiers*, no. 2 (1999). Reprinted in *Cinema and Desire*, ed. Jing Wang and Tani E. Barlow. London: Verso, 2002.

——. *Jingcheng tuwei: Nüxing, dianying, wenxue* (Breaking out of the city of mirrors: Women, film, literature). Beijing: Zuojia chubanshe, 1995.

———. "Man tan wenhua yanjiu zhong de xiandaixing wenti" (A chat about the modern question at the heart of cultural studies). In *You zai jing zhong* (Still caught by the mirror). Beijing: Zhishi chubanshe, 1999.

———. "National Identity in the Hall of Mirrors" (Jingxiang wuliang zhong de minzu shenfen). *Guangzhou Literature and Arts*, nos. 3–4 (1998). Reprinted in *Cinema and Desire*, ed. Jing Wang and Tani E. Barlow, trans. Eileen Cheng and Shu-mei Shih. London: Verso, 2002.

———. "Nüxing zhuyi: Wenhua lichang, xingbie jingyan yu xueshu xuanze" (Feminism: Cultural standpoint, gender experience and scholarly choice). In *You zai jing zhong* (Still caught by the mirror). Beijing: Zhishi chubanshe, 1999.

———. *Pintu youxi* (Piecing together the map/Playing the game). Jinan: Taishan chubanshe, 1999.

———. "Qingxing de lichang" (The awakened position). In *You zai jing zhong* (Still caught by the mirror). Beijing: Zhishi chubanshe, 1999.

———. "Redemption and Consumption: Depicting Culture in the 1990s" (Jiushu yu xiaofei: Jiushi niandai wenhua miaoshu zhi er). Trans. Edward Gunn. In *Cinema and Desire*, ed. Jing Wang and Tani E. Barlow. London: Verso, 2002.

———. "Rethinking the Cultural History of Chinese Films." Trans. Lau Kin Chi. In *Cinema and Desire*, ed. Jing Wang and Tani E. Barlow. London: Verso, 2002.

———. "A Scene in the Fog: Reading the Sixth Generation Films" (Wu zhong fengjing: chu du "diliu dai"). Trans. Yiman Wang. *Frontiers*, no. 1 (1996). Reprinted in *Cinema and Desire*, ed. Jing Wang and Tani E. Barlow. London: Verso, 2002.

———. *Shiji zhi men: Nüxing xiaoshuo juan* (Gates of the century: Volume of women's fiction). Beijing: Shehui kexue wenxian chubanshe, 1998.

———. *Shuxie wenhua yingxiong: Shiji zhi jiao de wenhua yanjiu* (Writing culture heroes: Cultural studies in centenary exchange). Nanjing: Jiangsu renmin chubanshe, 2000.

———. *Yingxing shuxie: Jiushi nian dai Zhongguo wenhua yanji* (Invisible writing: Research in Chinese cultural studies in the nineties). Nanjing: Jiangsu renmin chubanshe, 1999.

———. *You zai jing zhong* (Still caught by the mirror). Beijing: Zhishi chubanshe, 1999.

———. "Zhizhe xixue: Shuo du Wang Xiaobo" (The sage's jest: Reading Wang Xiaobo). *Contemporary Writer's Review*, no. 1 (1998). Also published in *Pintu youxi* (Piecing together the map/Playing the game). Jinan: Taishan chubanshe, 1999.

———. "Zhongguo nüxingxue yu nüxing zhuyi, zuotian yu jintian" (Feminism: Cultural standpoint, gender experience, and scholarly choice). (Interview with Zhou Yaqin and Po Zhenji, 1998). In *You zai jing zhong* (Still caught by the mirror). Beijing: Zhishi chubanshe, 1999.

Dan Fu. *Mantan liangxing guanxi zhong de daode wenti* (Conversation about moral questions concerning relations between the sexes). Shanghai: Xuexi Shenghuo Press, 1956.

Davin, Anna. "Imperialism and Motherhood." *History Workshop Journal* 5 (1978): 9–65.

de Lauretis, Teresa. *The Technologies of Gender: Essays on Theory, Film, and Fiction*. Bloomington: Indiana University Press, 1987.

de Pee, Christian. "The Negotiation and Renegotiation of Premodern Chinese Marriage: Text as Practice versus Text into Practice." *positions* 9, no. 3 (winter 2001): 559–84.

Deng Yingchao. "Bianxuan Zhongguo funü yundong shi de zhuxian" (Compiling the history of Chinese women's movement). In *Cai Chang, Deng Yingchao, Kang Keqing: Funü jiefang wenti wenxuan* (Cai Chang, Deng Yingchao, Kang Keqing: Documents on the question of the women's movement), ed. Fulian. Beijing: Renmin chubanshe, 1988.

———. "Zai Shantou funü lianhehui shang de yanshuo" (Speech at the Shantou women's federation welcome meeting). *Funü zhi sheng huibao*, 1926. Reprinted in *Zhongguo funü yundong lishi cailiao, 1921–1927* (Historical research materials for the Chinese women's movement, 1921–1927), 314–16.

——. "Zhenfen geming jingshen, zuohao fuyun shi gongzuo" (Inspire revolutonary spirit, do good work on the history of the women's movement). In *Cai Chang, Deng Yingchao, Kang Keqing: Funü jiefang wenti wenxuan* (Cai Chang, Deng Yingchao, Kang Keqing: Documents on the question of the women's movement), ed. Fulian. Beijing: Renmin chubanshe, 1988.

——. "Zhongguo nü xianfeng Xiang Jingyu" (China's woman pioneer Xiang Jingyu). In *Cai Chang, Deng Yingchao, Kang Keqing: Funü jiefang wenti wenxuan* (Cai Chang, Deng Yingchao, Kang Keqing: Documents on the question of the women's movement), ed. Fulian. Beijing: Renmin chubanshe, 1988.

Derrida, Jacques. *Specters of Marx: The State of the Debt, the Work of Mourning, and the New International.* Trans. Peggy Kamuf. Introduction by Bernd Magnus and Stephen Cullenberg. New York: Routledge, 1994.

Diamant, Neil. "Reexamining the Impact of the 1990 Marriage Law: State Improvisation and Local Initiative." *China Quarterly*, no. 161 (March 2000): 171–98.

——. *Revolutionizing the Family: Politics, Love, and Divorce in Urban and Rural China, 1949–1968.* Berkeley: University of California Press, 2000.

Dikötter, Frank. *The Discourse of Race in Modern China.* Stanford: Stanford University Press, 1992.

——. *Sex, Culture, and Modernity in China: Medical Science and the Construction of Sexual Identities in the Early Republican Period.* Honolulu: University of Hawai'i Press, 1995.

Ding Ling. "Autumn Harvest Day." In *When I Was in Sha chuan, and Other Stories,* trans. Kung Pusheng. Poona, India: N.p., n.d.

——. "Ah Mao guniang" (The girl Ah Mao). In *Zai heian zhong* (In darkness). Shanghai, 1938.

——. "Bianzhe houji." In *Muqin* (Mother). Beijing, 1980.

——. "Buneng cong xingshi chufa" (You cannot start from form). In *Kua dao xin di shidai lai* (Stride into the new age). Beijing: Renmin wenxue chubanshe, 1951.

——. "Busuan qingshu" (Not a love letter). In *Yiwai ji* (Unexpected collection). Shanghai: Liangyu tushu yishua gongsi, 1936.

——. "Cailiao" (Material). *Jiefang Ribao* (Liberation daily), 29 September 1941.

——. "Chen Boxiang." In *Yiwai ji* (Unexpected collection). Shanghai: Liangyu tushu yishua gongsi, 1936.

——. "Cong qunzhong lai, dao qunzhong qu" (From the masses, to the masses). In *Kuadao xin de shidai lai* (Leap into the new age). Beijing: Renmin wenxxue chubanshe, 1951.

——. *Ding Ling sanwen jin zuo xuan* (Collection of Ding Ling's recent prose). Kumming: Yunan renmin chubanshe, 1983.

——. "Douzheng shi xiangshou" (To struggle is pleasure). *Jiefang Ribao* (Liberation daily), 16 September 1941.

——. "Du Wanxiang." In *I Myself Am a Woman: Selected Writings of Ding Ling,* ed. Tani E. Barlow with Gary J. Bjorge. Boston: Beacon Press, 1989.

——. "Fan yu zheng" (For and against). In *Yinian* (One year). Chongqing: Shenghuo shudian, 1939.

——. "Fengci" (Satire). In *Yinian* (One year). Chongqing: Shenghuo shudian, 1939.

——. "Guanyu Du Wanxiang: Zai Beijing tushuguan zuzhi de yu duzhe jianmian hui shang de tanhua" (About "Du Wanxiang": A talk at the face-to-face meeting with readers organized by the Beijing Library). In *Ding Ling jin zuo* (Ding Ling's recent work). Chengdu: Sichuan renmin chubanshe, 1980.

——. "Guanyu lichang wenti wo jian" (My opinion on the problem of class standing). In *Kua dao xin di shidai lai* (Stride into the new age). Beijing: Renmin wenxue chubanshe, 1951.

——. "Guanyu zawen" (Regarding zawen). In *Ding Ling jinzuo (2): Wo de shengping yu chuangzuo*

(Ding Ling's recent work, 2: My life and work). Chengdu: Sichuan renmin chubanshe, 1982.

———. "Haizimen" (Children). In *Yinian* (One year). Chongging: Shenghuo shudian, 1939.

———. "Jiang yidian xinli hua" (Some words from the heart). In *Ding Ling jin zuo* (Ding Ling's recent work). Chengdu: Sichuan renmin chubanshe, 1980.

———. "Jieda san ge wenti: Zai Beijing yuyan xueyuan waiguo liu xuesheng zuotanhui shang de jianghua" (Answering three questions: Speech at the conference of foreign students at the Beijing Foreign Languages Academy). In *Ding Ling jin zuo* (Ding Ling's recent work). Chengdu: Sichuan renmin chubanshe, 1980.

———. *Kua dao xin de shidai lai* (Stride into the new age). Beijing: Renmin wenxue chubanshe, 1951.

———. "Lian'ai yu wenyi chuangzuo" (Love and artistic creation). In *Shenghuo, chuangzuo, shidai linghun* (Life, creation and the soul of the times). Changsha: Hunan renmin chubanshe, 1981.

———. "Mengke." In *Zai heian zhong* (In darkness). Shanghai, 1938.

———. *Muqin* (Mother). Shanghai: Liangyou tushu yinshua gongsi, 1933.

———. "Nianqian de yitian" (The day before New Year's day). In *Shui* (Water). Shanghai, 1932.

———. "Qingnian lian'ai wenti" (The question of young people and erotic love). In *Kua dao xin di shidai lai* (Stride into the new age). Beijing: Renmin wenxue chubanshe, 1951.

———. "Qingyunli zhong de yijian xiaofangli" (In a small room on Qingyun Alley). In *Zisha riji* (Suicide diary). Shanghai, 1937.

———. "Qiu shou de yitian" (Autumn harvest day). In *Wo Zai xia cun de shihou* (When I was in Xia village). Shanghai: San lian shudlan, 1951.

———. "San bajie you gan" (Thoughts on March 8). In *Jiefang ribao*, March 9, 1942.

———. "San be jie you gan" (Thoughts on March 8). *Jiefang Ribao* (Liberation daily), 9 March 1942.

———. Satirical cartoon exhibition. *Jiefang Ribao* (Liberation daily), 13, 15, 19 February 1942.

———. *Shaanbei fengguang* (Scenes of Northern Shaanxi). Beijing: Xinhua shudian, 1950.

———. "Shafei nüshi riji" (Sophia's diary). In *Zai heian zhong* (In darkness). Shanghai, 1938.

———. "Shafei nüshi riji di erbu (Miss Sophia's diary part two). In *Yiwaiji* (Unexpected collection), ed. Ding Ling. Shanghai: Liangyou tushu yinshua gongsi, 1936.

———. *Shenghuo, chuangzuo, shidai linghuan* (Life, creation, spirit of the age). Changsha: Hunan renmin chubanshe, 1981.

———. "Shenghuo, sixiang yu renwu" (Life, thought and character). In *Ding Ling Xiju ji* (Collection of Ding Ling's dramas), ed. Zhongguo xiju chubanshe bianwenbu. Beijing: Zhongguo xiju chubanshe, 1983.

———. "Shenghuo huanying" (Speaking on welcome). In *Yinian* (One year). Chongqing: Shenghuo shuchan, 1939.

———. "Shujia zhong" (Summer break). In *Zai heian zhong* (In darkness). Shanghai, 1938.

———. "Shuo dao 'ying xiang'" (Speaking of "influence"). In *Yinian* (One year). Chongqing: Shenghuo shudian, 1939.

———. "Shuo huanying" (Speaking on welcome). In *Yinian* (One year). Chongqing: Shenghuo shudian, 1939.

———. "Sophia's Diary." Trans. Tani E. Barlow. In *I Myself Am a Woman*, ed. Tani E. Barlow with Gary J. Borge. Boston: Beacon Press, 1989.

———. *The Sun Shines over the Sanggan River*. Trans. Yang Hsien-yi and Gladys Yang. Peking, 1954.

———. *Sun Shines over the Sanggan River*. Beijing: Foreign Language Press, 1984.

———. *Suqu de wenyi* (Literature of the Soviet area). Shanghai: n.p., 1938.

———. "Ta zou hou" (After he left). In *Yige nüren* (A woman). Shanghai: Zhonghua shuju, 1930.

——. "Tan 'laolao shishi'" (Speaking on "honesty"). In *Kua dao xin di shidai lai* (Stride into the new age). Beijing: Renmin wenxue chubanshe, 1951.

——. "Tan ziji de chuangzuo" (When I was in Xia village). In *Ding Ling yu Zhongguo nüxing wenxue: Diqici chuangzuo Ding Ling xueshu yanjiuhui wenji*, ed. Ding Ling and Chinese Nü-xing Literature Group. Changsha: Hunan wenyi chubanshe, 1998.

——. *Wei Hu*. Shanghai: Dajiang shupu, 1930.

——. "Wenyi jie dui Wang Shiwei ying you de taidu ji fanxing" (The attitude and self-introspection that the literary world should take toward Wang Shiwei). *Jiefang Ribao* (Liberation daily), 16 June 1942.

——. "Wo de chuangzuo jingyan" (My creative experience). In *Ding Ling pingzhuan* (Critical biography of Ding Ling), ed. Zhang Baiyun. Shanghai, 1934.

——. "Wo de shenghuo huiyi" (Recollections on my life). In *Ding Ling zai Bei da huang* (Ding Ling in the great northern wasteland). N.p.: Hubei renmin chubanshe, 1989.

——. "Wo de zibai" (My confession). In *Ding Ling xuanji* (Selected Ding Ling). N.p.: Tianma shudian, 1933.

——. "Women xuyao zawen" (We need the zawen). *Jiefang Ribao* (Liberation daily), 10 October 1941.

——. "Wo muqin de shengping" (My mother's life). In *Muqin* (Mother). Beijing, 1980.

——. "Wo suo renshi de Qu Qiubai tongzhi" (The comrade Qu Qiubai I knew). In *Ding Ling sanwen jinzuoxuan* (Collection of Ding Ling's recent prose). Kunming: Yunnan renmin chubanshe, n.d.

——. "Wo zai Xiacun de shihou." In *Wo zai Xiacun de shihou* (When I was in Xia Village). Shanghai: Sanlian shudian, 1951.

——. "Xianzhang jiating" (County magistrate's family). In *Wo zai Xiacun de shihou* (When I was in Xia Village). Shanghai: Sanlian shudian, 1951.

——. "Xiang jingyu lieshi gei wo de yingxiang" (Martyr Xiang jingyu influence on me). In *Ding Ling jinzuo* (Ding Ling's recent writing). Chengdu: Sichuan renmin chubanshe, 1980.

——. "Xiao huolun shang" (On a small steamer). In *Zisha riji* (Suicide diary). Shanghai, 1937.

——. "Xie gei nü qingnian zuozhe" (Written for a young female author). In *Shenghuo, chuangzuo, shidai linghuan* (Life, creation and the soul of the times). Changsha: Hunan renmin chubanshe, 1981.

——. "Xin de xin nian" (New faith). In *Wo zai Xiacun de shihou* (When I was in Xia Village). Shanghai: Sanlian shudian, 1951.

——. "Yan'an wenyi zuotanhui de qianqian houhou" (Before and after the talks at the Yan'an Forum). In *Ding Ling jin zuo (2): Wo de shengping yu chuangzuo* (Ding Ling's recent work, 2: My life and work). Chengdu: Sichuan renmin chubanshe, 1982.

——. "Yan bian zhi xing tan chuangzuo" (Talking about creation on a trip to the Yan'an border region). In *Ding Ling jin zuo (2) Wo de shengping yu chuangzuo* (Ding Ling's recent work, 2: My life and work). Chengdu: Sichuan renmin chubanshe, 1982.

——. "Ye" (Night). *Jiefang jibao* (Liberation daily), 1942. Reprinted in *Wo zai Xiacun de shihou* (When I was in Xia Village). Shanghai: Sanlian shudian, 1951.

——. "Yecao." In *Yi ge nüren he yi ge nanren* (A woman and a man). Shanghai, 1930.

——. "Yecao." In *Yi ge nüren he yi ge nanren* (A woman and a man). Shanghai, 1930.

——. "Yecao." In *Yi ge nüren* (A woman). Shanghai: Zhonghua shuju, 1940.

——. "Yi ge nüren he yi ge nanren" (A woman and a man). In *Yi ge nüren* (A woman). Shanghai, 1930.

——. *Yi ge xiao hongjun de gushi* (Story of a little red soldier). Shanghai, 1956.

——. "Yi jiu san lingnian, Shanghai" (Shanghai, spring 1930). In *Yige ren de dan sheng* (The birth of a person). Shanghai: Xinyue shudian, 1931.

—. "Yi ke wei chu tang de qiangdan" (The unfired bullet). In *Wo zai Xiacun de shihou* (When I was in Xia Village). Shanghai: Sanlian shudian, 1951.

—. *Yi waiji* (Unexpected collection). Shanghai: Liangyou tushu yinshua gongsi, 1936.

—. *Yi nian* (One year). Chongqing: Shenghuo shudian, 1939.

—. "Yongyuan huozai women de xin zhong de renmen – guan yu Chen Man de jizai (A person who will live forever in our hearts – remembering Chen Man). In *Kuadao xin de shidai lai* (Stride to the new age). Beijing: Renmin wenxue chubanshe, 1951.

—. "Zai qianjin de daolu shang: Guanyu du wenxue shu de wenti" (On the road forward: Questions on reading literature). In *Kua dao xin de shidai lai* (Stride into the new age). Beijing: Renmin wenxue chubanshe, 1951.

—. "Zai yiyuan zhong" (In the hospital). In *Ding Ling weiji* (Collected works of Ding Ling) 3. Changsha: Hunan renmin chubanshe, 1983.

—. "Zhandou shi xiangshou" (Struggle is pleasure). *Jiefang Ribao* (Liberation daily), 16 September 1941.

—. "Zhengduan san feng yundong zhankai" (The rectification movement begins). *Jiefang Ribao* (Liberation daily), 8 April 1942.

—. "Zhishifenzi xiaxiang zhong de wenti" (Problems of intellectuals going down). In *Kua dao xin de shidai lai* (Stride into the new age). Beijing: Renmin wenxue chubanshe, 1951.

—. *Zisha riji* (Suicide diary). Shanghai, 1937.

Ding Ling and Chinese Nüxing Literature Group, eds. *Ding Ling yu Zhongguo nüxing wenxue: Diqici chuangzuo Ding Ling xueshu yanjiu hui wenji* (Ding Ling and Chinese literature: 7th collected all-China seminar on Ding Ling scholarship). Changsha: Hunan wenyi chubanshe, 1998.

Dirks, Nicholas B. "History as a Sign of the Modern." *Public Culture* 2, no. 2 (spring 1990): 25–32.

Dong Fang Wei Ming, "Ding Ling de Muqin" (Ding Ling's Mother). In *Ding Ling pingzhuan* (Critical biography of Ding Ling), ed. Zhang Baiyun. Qunguang shudian, 1934.

Dooling, Amy D., and Kristina M. Torgeson. Introduction to *Writing Women in Modern China: An Anthology of Women's Literature*, ed. Amy D. Dooling and Kristina M. Torgeson. New York: Columbia University Press, 1998.

Du Fangqin. *Nüxing guannian de yanbian* (Evolution of the female concept). Zhengzhou: Henan renmin chubanshe, 1988.

—. "Shinian huiyi: Zhongguo funü yanjiu de duiwai jiaoliu." In *"Funü yanjiu zai Zhongguo" quanti yantaohui lunwenji*, ed. Zhang Yanxia. Beijing/Huairou: Quan fulian funü yanjiu suo zhubian, 1995.

Du Zhunhui. *Funü wenti jianghua* (Lectures on the woman problem). Hong Kong: New China Books, 1949.

Dubey, Mahu. "The 'True Lie' of the Nation: Fanon and Feminism." *differences* 10, no. 2 (1998): 1–29.

Dutton, Michael, and Paul Healy. "Marxist Theory and Socialist Transition: The Construction of an Epistemological Relation." In *Chinese Marxism in Flux, 1978–84: Essays on Epistemology, Ideology and Political Economy*, ed. Bill Brugger. Armonk, NY: Sharpe, 1985.

Ebrey, Patricia Buckley. *The Inner Quarters: Marriage and the Lives of Chinese Women in the Sung Period*. Berkeley: University of California Press, 1993.

—. "Shifts in Marriage Finance from the Sixth to the Thirteenth Century." In *Marriage and Inequality in Chinese Society*, ed. Rubie S. Watson and Patricia Buckley Ebrey. Berkeley: University of California Press, 1991.

Edwards, Louise. "Policing the Modern Woman in Republican China." *Modern China* 26, no. 2 (April 2000): 115–47.

Elam, Diane. *Feminism and Deconstruction*. New York: Routledge, 1994.

Eley, Geoff. "Is All the World a Text? From Social History to the History of Society Two Decades Later." In *The Historic Turn in the Human Sciences*, ed. Terrence J. McDonald. Ann Arbor: University of Michigan Press, 1996.

Ellwood, Charles A. *Cultural Evolution: A Study of Social Origins and Development*. New York: Century, 1927.

———. *Recent Developments in the Social Sciences*. Philadelphia: Lippincott, 1927.

———. *The Social Problem: A Constructive Analysis*. New York: Macmillan, 1915.

Elman, Benjamin A. *Classicism, Politics and Kinship: The Ch'ang-chou School of New Text Confucianism in Late Imperial China*. Berkeley: University of California Press, 1990.

———. *From Philosophy to Philology: Social and Intellectual Aspects of Change in Late Imperial China*. Cambridge, MA: Council on East Asian Studies, Harvard University, 1990.

Elvin, Mark. "Female Virtue and the State in China." *Past and Present* 104 (August 1984): 114–52.

———. *The Pattern of the Chinese Past*. Stanford: Stanford University Press, 1973.

Engelstein, Laura. *The Keys to Happiness: Sex and the Search for Modernity in Fin-de-Siècle Russia*. Ithaca, NY: Cornell University Press, 1992.

Fang Shih-to, ed. *Zhongguo shehui shiliao jiyao* (Abstracts of Chinese social history data). Taipei: Tianyi chubanshe, 1977.

Feng Fei. "Funü wenti gailun" (General outline of the woman problem). In *Zhongguo funü wenti taolunji* (Collected discussions of the woman question), ed. Mei Sheng. Shanghai: Shanghai New Culture Press, 1929–34, I 1: 23–56.

———. *Nüxing lun* (On women in Shanghai). 1931. Reprint, Shanghai: Wenyi chubanshe, 1990.

Feng Xuefeng. "Taiyang zhao zai Sanggan he shang zai women wenxue fazhanshang de yiyi" (The significance of *The Sun Shines over the Sanggan River* in the development of our literature). In *Taiyang zhao zai Sanggan he shang*, by Ding Ling. Beijing: Renmin wenxue chubanshe, 1955.

Feuerwerker, Yi-Tsi Mei. *Ding Ling's Fiction: Ideology and Narrative in Modern Chinese Literature*. Cambridge, MA: Harvard University Press, 1982.

———. "Ding Ling's 'When I Was in Sha Chuan (Cloud Village)." *Signs* 2, no. 1 (autumn 1976): 255–79.

———. "Women as Writers in the 1920s and 1930s." In *Women in Chinese Society*, ed. Margery Wolf and Roxane Witke. Stanford: Stanford University Press, 1975.

Foucault, Michel. *Discipline and Punish*. London: Allen Lane, 1977.

———. *Ethics: Subjectivity and Truth. Essential Works of Foucault, 1954–1984*. Ed. Paul Rabinow. New York: New Press, 1997.

———. *History of Sexuality*. Vol. 1. London: Allen Lane, 1979.

———. *The History of Sexuality: Vol. 1: An Introduction*. New York: Vintage Press, 1980.

———. *History of Sexuality*. Vol. 2. London: Viking, 1986.

———. *The Order of Things*. New York: Random House, 1970.

Friday, Nancy. *The Power of Beauty*. New York: Harper Collins, 1996.

Fujita Masanori. *Gendai chugoku jinbutsu bessho sorean* (A catalog of alternate names for well-known modern Chinese persons). Tokyo: Kyuko shoin, 1986.

Fukuyama, Francis. "Biotechnology and the Future of Politics." *Daily Yomiuri*, 5 March 2001: D6.

Fulian, ed. *Makesi, Engesi, Liening, Sidalin lun Funü jiefang* (Marx, Engels, Lenin, Stalin on women's liberation). Beijing: Renmin Press, 1949.

———, ed. *Quanguo funü diyici quanguo daibiao dahui* (First congress of the All-China Women's Association). Hong Kong: Xinmin Press, 1949.

———, ed. *Zhongguo funü disanci quanguo daibiao dahui zhongyao wenxuan* (Selected key documents of the third National Congress of Chinese women). Beijing: Zhongguo Funü Zazhi Press, 1958.

———, ed. *Zhongguo jiefangqu funü canzheng yundong* (Political participation movement of the women of the Chinese liberated areas). Hong Kong: New Peoples' Press, n.d.

———, ed. *Zhongguo jiefangqu nongcun funü fanshen yundong sumiao* (A rough sketch of the fanshen movement among rural women in the liberated regions of China). N.p.: Xinhua Books, 1949.

"Funü wenti: Wanshan he fazhan" (Women's studies questions: Excellence and progress). In *Funü zuzhi yu huodong: Yinshua baokan ziliao* (Women's organizations and activities: Published press materials reader) (February 1985): 10.

Furth, Charlotte. "Androgynous Males and Deficient Females: Biology and Gender Boundaries in Sixteenth and Seventeenth Century China." *Late Imperial China* 9 (December 1988): 1–31.

———. "Culture and Politics in Modern Chinese Conservatism." In *The Limits of Change: Essays on Conservative Alternatives in Republican China*, ed. Charlotte Furth. Cambridge, MA: Harvard University Press, 1976.

———. "The Sage as Rebel: The Inner World of Chang Ping-lin." In *The Limits of Change: Essays on Conservative Alternatives in Republican China*, ed. Charlotte Furth. Cambridge, MA: Harvard University Press, 1976.

Fuss, Diane. "Interior Colonies: Frantz Fanon and the Politics of Identification." *Critical Crossings*. Special issue of *diacritics: a review of contemporary criticism* 24, nos. 2–3 (summer–fall 1994): 20–42.

Gallop, Jane. *The Daughter's Seduction: Feminism and Psychoanalysis*. Ithaca, NY: Cornell University Press, 1982.

Gao Ersong and Gao Erbo. "Zhongguo xuezhe funü wenti zhi yanjiu" (Chinese scholarship on the woman question). *Shehuixue zazhi* 2, nos. 2–3 (1925): 1–56.

Gao Ersong and Gao Erbo, eds. *Hankou can sha an* (The case of the Hankou massacre). 1925. Reprint, Taipei: Wenhai chubanshe, 1985.

Gao Xian. "Lian'ai duli" (Independence in love). In *Zhongguo funü wenti taolunji* (Collected discussions of the woman question), ed. Mei Sheng. Shanghai: New Culture Press, 1929–34, IV 7: 56–72.

———. "Lo shu shi shemma?" (What is the Lo syllabary?). *Xin Qingnian* 7, no. 3 (February 1920).

———. "Shengcun jingzheng yu daode" (The competition for survival and morality). *Xin Qingnian* 3, no. 3 (May 1917).

———. "Xing zhe" (Sexual selection). In *Zhongguo funü wenti taolunji* (Collected discussions of the woman question), ed. Mei Sheng. Shanghai: Shanghai New Culture Press, 1929–34, VII 5.

Gao Xisheng [pseud.]. *Jingji kexue da zidian*. N.p.: Kexue yanjiushe [1935?].

Ge Lu. "Jiehun hou" (After marriage). *Jiefang Ribao* (Liberation daily), 3, 4 March 1942.

Geller, Jay. "Judenzopf/Chinesenzopf: Of Jews and Queues." *positions: east asia cultures critique* 2, no. 3 (winter 1994): 500–537.

Gilman, Charlotte Perkins. *Women and Economics*. New York: Harper and Row, 1966.

Gilmartin, Christina. *Engendering the Chinese Revolution: Radical Women, Communist Politics, and Mass Movements in the 1920s*. Berkeley: University of California Press, 1995.

Gilmartin, Christina, et al., eds. *Engendering China: Women, Culture, and the State*. Cambridge: Harvard University Press, 1994.

Glosser, Susan. *The Contest for Family and Nation in Republican China*. Berkeley: University of California Press, 1995.

Gong Mingde. "*Taiyang zhao zai Sanggan he shang*" xiugai jianping (*The Sun Shines over the Sanggan River* commentary on revisions). Changsha: Hunan renmin chubanshe, 1984.

Goode, Erica. "Human Nature: Born or Made? Evolutionary Theorists Provoke an Uproar." *New York Times*, Science Times, 14 March 2000: D1, D9.

Goodman, Bryna. "Improvisations on a Semicolonial Theme, or, How to Read a Celebration of Transnational Urban Community." *Journal of Asian Studies* 59, no. 4 (November 2000): 889–926.

Gu Man. "Guanyu Ding Ling pingfan" (Regarding reversing the miscarriage of justice on Ding Ling). *Ding Ling yanjiu tongxun* (Ding Ling research newsletter) 13, no. 4 (1999): 8–11.

Gunn, Edward M. *Rewriting Chinese: Style and Innovation in Twentieth-Century Chinese Prose.* Stanford: Stanford University Press, 1991.

Hao Shendao. "Xian tan Zhang Yumin xingxiang" (A chat on the future of Zhang Yumin). In *Ding Ling zuopin pinglun ji* (Collected commentary on Ding Ling's work), ed. Zhongguo wenxie chuban gongsi. Beijing: Zhongguo wenlian chuban gongsi, 1984.

Haraway, Donna. "A Manifesto for Cyborgs: Science, Technology and Socialist Feminism in the 1980s." *Socialist Review* 15, no. 80 (1985): 63–107.

Harootunian, H. D. *Things Seen and Unseen: Discourse and Ideology in Tokugawa Nativism.* Chicago: University of Chicago Press, 1988.

Haver, William. *The Body of This Death: Historicity and Sociality in the Time of AIDS.* Stanford: Stanford University Press, 1997.

He Yubo. "Ding Ling nüshi lunping" (Critical discussion of Ms. Ding Ling). In *Ding Ling pingzhuan* (Critical biography of Ding Ling), ed. Zhang Baiyun. Shanghai, 1934.

Hemmel, Vibeke, and Pia Sindbjergh. *Women in Rural China: Policy towards Women before and after the Cultural Revolution.* Curzon: Scandinavian Institute of Asian Studies 7, 1984.

Hennessy, Rosemary. *Materialist Feminism and the Politics of Discourse.* New York: Routledge, 1992.

Hinton, William. *Fanshen: A Documentary of Revolution in a Chinese Village.* Berkeley: University of California Press, 1997.

Hoashi, Osaro. "Xin shidai zhi xin zhencao lun" (On a new chastity for a new age). Trans. Yang Xianjiang. In *Zhongguo funü wenti taolunji* (Collected discussions of the woman question), ed. Mei Sheng. Shanghai: Shanghai New Culture Press, 1929–34, 13: 117–27.

Holm, David. *Art and Ideology in Revolutionary China.* Oxford: Oxford University Press, 1991.

——. "The Literary Rectification in Yan'an." In *Essays in Modern Chinese Literature and Literary Criticism*, ed. Wolfgang Kubin and Rudolf Wagner. Bochum: Brockmeyer, 1982.

Hong Juan. "Yi pingdeng de xintai shuxie xingbie: Fang xuezhe Dai Jinhua" (Writing gender with a balanced mentality: Interviewing scholar Dai Jinhua). *Zhonghua dushu bao* (Chinese reader's newspaper), 2 February 1996.

Hong Zicheng. 1956: *Baihua shidai* (1956: Era of the hundred flowers). In *Bainian Zhongguo wenxue zong xi* (One hundred years of Chinese literature), ed. Xie Mian. Jinan: Shandong jiaoyu chubanshe, 1998.

Honig, Emily, and Gail Hershatter. *Personal Voices: Chinese Women in the 1980s.* Stanford: Stanford University Press, 1988.

Hoy, David. "Foucault: Modern or Postmodern?" In *After Foucault: Humanistic Knowledge, Postmodern Challenges*, ed. Jonathan Arac. New Brunswick, NJ: Rutgers University Press, 1988.

Hsiung Ping-chun, and Yuk-lin Renita Wong. "Jie Gui—Connecting the Tracks: Chinese Women's Activism Surrounding the 1995 World Conference on Women in Beijing." In *Gender and History* 10, no. 3 (November 1998).

Hsu, Dao-lin. "The Myth of the 'Five Human Relations' of Confucius." *Monumental Serica* 29 (1970–71).

Hu Shi. "Zhencao wenti" (The chastity question). In *Zhongguo funü wenti taolunji* (Collected discussions of the woman question), ed. Mei Sheng. Shanghai: Shanghai New Culture Press, 1929–34, 13: 95–104.

Hu Ying. *Tales of Translation: Composing the New Woman in China, 1899–1918*. Stanford: Stanford University Press, 2000.

Huang Hongyun. "Nüxing zhuti yishi ji qi jianguo tujing" (Essential female subject consciousness and the constructed path). In *Funü zuzhi yu huodong: yinshua baokan ziliao* (Women's organizations and activities: Published press materials reader) (March 1988): 21–23.

Huang, Joe. *Heroes and Villains in Communist China: The Contemporary Chinese Novel as a Reflection of Life*. London: C. Hurst, 1973.

Huang, Philip C. "Women's Choices under the Law: Marriage, Divorce, and Illicit Sex in the Qing and the Republic." *Modern China* 27, no. 1 (January 2001): 3–58.

Hung, Chang-tai. "Female symbols of Resistance in Chinese Wartime Spoken Drama." *Modern China* 15, no. 2 (April 1989): 149–77.

Huot, Claire. *A Handbook of Changes: China's New Cultural Scene*. Durham, NC: Duke University Press, 2000.

Hutcheon, Linda. *The Politics of Postmodernism*. London: Routledge, 1989.

Huters, Theodore, ed. Introduction to *Modern Chinese Literature* 5, no. 2 (fall 1989): 175–78.

Inouye, Charles Shiro. "In the Scopic Regime of Discovery: Ishikawa Takuboku's Diary in Roman Script and the Gendered Premise of Self-Identity." *positions* 2, no. 3 (winter 1994): 542–69.

Institute of Modern History, Academia Sinica, eds. *Family Process and Political Process in Modern Chinese History*. Taipei: Institute of Modern History, Academia Sinica, 1992.

Jayawardena, Kumari. *Feminism and Nationalism in the Third World*. London: Zed Press, 1986.

Ji Tao. "Zhongguo nüzi de diwei" (The position of Chinese women). In *Zhongguo funü wenti taolunji* (Collected discussions of the Chinese woman question), ed. Mei Sheng. Shanghai: Shanghai New Culture Press, 1929–34, I 1: 64–68.

Jiangxi sheng Funü lianhehui (Jiangxi province women's federation), eds. *Jiangxi suqu funü yundong shi xuanbian, 1927–1935* (Selected historical documents of the Jiangxi Soviet women's movement, 1927–1935). Jiangxi sheng renmin chubanshe, 1982.

Jin Yihong. "Zhongguo funüxue yanjiu tedian ji yingxiang qi shehui tiaoyong de yinsi fenxi" (Characteristics of China's women's studies and analysis of factors affecting their social effects). In *"Funü yanjiu zai Zhongguo" quanti yantaohui lunwenji* (Complete seminar papers on women's studies in China). Beijing/Huairou: Quan fulian funü yanjiu suo zhubian, 1995.

Judd, Ellen. "Prelude to the 'Yan'an Talks': Problems in Transforming a Literary Intelligentsia." *Modern China* 2, no. 3 (July 1985).

——. "Cultural Articulation in the Chinese Countryside, 1937–1947." *Modern China* 16, no. 3 (July 1990).

Judge, Joan. "Talent, Virtue, and the Nation: Chinese Nationalisms and Female Subjectivities in the Early Twentieth Century." *American Historical Review* 106, no. 3 (June 2001): 765–803.

Junichi Isomae. "The Space of Historical Discourse: Ishimoda Shô's Theory of the Heroic Age." *positions: east asia cultures critique* 10, no. 3 (winter 2002): 631–68.

Kagawa Toyohiko. "Lian'ai li" (The power of love). In *Zhongguo funü wenti taolunji* (Collected discussions of the woman question), ed. Mei Sheng. Shanghai: Shanghai New Culture Press, 1929–34, IV 9: 23–47.

Kamuf, Peggy. Introduction to *A Derrida Reader: Between the Blinds*, ed. Peggy Kamuf. New York: Columbia University Press, 1991.

Kang Keqing. "Mao Zhuxi shuailing women zou funü chedi jiefang de daolu" (Chairman Mao led us onto the path of women's total liberation). In *Cai Chang, Deng Yingchao, Kang Keqing: Funü jiefang wenti wenxuan* (Cai Chang, Deng Yingchao, Kang Keqing: Documents in the question of the women's movement), ed. Fulian. Beijing: Renmin chubanshe, 1988.

——. "Xin shiqi Zhongguo funü yundong de chonggao renwu" (The lofty responsibility of the Chinese women's movement in the new period). In *Cai Chang, Deng Yingchao, Kang Keqing: Funü jiefang wenti wenxuan* (Cai Chang, Deng Yingchao, Kang Keqing: Documents in the question of the women's movement), ed. Fulian. Beijing: Renmin chubanshe, 1988.

Kataoka, Tetsuya. *Resistance and Revolution in China: The Communists and the Second United Front.* Berkeley: University of California Press, 1974.

Katz, Jonathan Ned. *The Invention of Heterosexuality.* New York: Penguin, 1995.

Keating, Pauline. "The Yan'an Way of Co-operatization." *China Quarterly* 140 (December 1994): 1025–51.

Kelly, Mary. *Post-Partum Document.* London: Routledge and Kegan Paul, 1983.

Klein, Donald. W., and A. B. Clark. *Biographic Dictionary of Chinese Communism, 1921–1965.* Cambridge, MA: Harvard University Press, 1971.

Ko, Dorothy. *Teachers of the Inner Chambers: Women and Culture in Seventeenth-Century China.* Stanford: Stanford University Press, 1994.

Kristeva, Julia. *About Chinese Women,* Anita Barrow, trans. New York: Marion Boyars, 1977.

Kuhn, Annette. *The Power of the Image.* London: Routledge and Kegan Paul, 1985.

Kung Pusheng, trans. *When I Was in Sha Chuan and Other Stories,* by Ding Ling. Poona, India: n.p., n.d.

Kuriyakawa Hakuson. "Jindai de lian'aiguan" (Perspectives on contemporary lian'ai), trans. Y. D. In *Zhongguo funü wenti taolunji* (Collected discussion of the Chinese woman questions), Mei Sheng, ed. Shanghai: Shanghai New Culture Press, 1929–34, II 4.

Kwok, David. *Scientism in Chinese Thought.* Berkeley: University of California Press, 1965.

LaCapra, Dominick. *History and Criticism.* Ithaca, NY: Cornell University Press, 1985.

Laclau, Ernesto, and Chantal Mouffe. *Hegemony and Socialist Strategy.* New York: Verso, 1985.

Larson, Wendy. *Literary Authority and the Modern Chinese Writer: Ambivalence and Autobiography.* Durham, NC: Duke University Press, 1991.

——. *Women and Writing In Modern China.* Stanford: Stanford University Press, 1998.

Lash, Scott, and Jonathan Friedman. *Modernity and Identity.* Oxford: Blackwell, 1992.

Lau, Joseph. "Duty, Reputation, and Selfhood in Traditional Chinese Narratives." In *Expressions of Self in Chinese Literature,* ed. Robert Hegel and Richard Henessey. New York: Columbia University Press, 1985.

Lecercle, Jean-Jacques. "Cantor, Lacan, Mao, Beckett, même combat: The Philosophy of Alain Badiou." *Radical Philosophy: A Journal of Socialist and Feminist Philosophy* 93 (January/February 1999): 6–13.

Leith, Suzanne. "Chinese Women in the Early Communist Movement." In *Women in China,* ed. Marilyn Young. Ann Arbor: Michigan Papers in Chinese Studies, 1973.

Li Chen Shen. "Contribution à l'étude de la condition féminine en Chine: L'emancipation de la femme à travers quelques revues en langue Chinoise, notamment la revue 'Funü zazhi' (Journal de la Femmes), des années 1915–1929." Unpublished manuscript.

Li Daxuan. *Ding Ling yu Shafei xielie xingxiang* (Lineage of the form of Ding Ling and Sophia). Changsha: Hunan wenyi chubanshe, 1991.

Li Di. *Zhufu shouji* (Handbook for housewives). Beijing: Tongsu wenyi Press, 1955.

Li Huiying. "Nüxing wenxue yanjiu shuping" (Commentary on research in women's literature). In *Zhongguo funü lilun yanjiu shinian 1981–1990* (Women's theoretical studies in China, 1981–1990). Beijing: Zhongguo funü chubanshe, 1992.

Li Ju-chen. *Flowers in the Mirror.* Trans. and ed. Lin Tai-yi. Berkeley: University of California Press, 1965.

Li Min and Wang Fukang. *Zhongguo fünüxue* (Chinese women's studies). Nanchang: Jiangxi chubanshe, 1988.

Li Meige. "Nüxing xinlixue yanjiu jianjie" (A brief introduction to research on female psychology). In *Zhongguo fünü lilun yanjiu shinian 1981–1990* (Women's theoretical studies in China, 1981–1990). Beijing: Zhongguo fünü chubanshe, 1992.

Li Renjie. "Nannü jiefang" (Liberation of men and women). In *Zhongguo fünü wenti taolunji* (Collected discussions of the woman question), ed. Mei Sheng. Shanghai: Shanghai New Culture Press, 1929–34, 1: 68–88.

Li Tuo. "Xiandai Hanyu yu dangdai wenxue" (Modern Chinese and contemporary literature). *Xindi* 6 (1986).

——. "Ye tan 'wei xiandaipai' ji qi piping" (On false modernism clique and other criticisms). *Beijing Wenxue* 4 (1988).

Li Xiaojiang. "Economic Reform and the Awakening of Chinese Women's Collective Consciousness." In *Engendering China*, ed. Christina K. Gilmartin et al. Cambridge, MA: Harvard University Press, 1995.

——. *Fünü yu jiazheng* (Woman and domestic science). N.p., 1986.

——. "Gaige he Zhongguo nüxing qunti yishi de juexing" (The reforms and the awakening of mass consciousness among Chinese women). In *Fünü zuzhi yu huodong: Yinshua baokan ziliao* (Women's organizations and activities: Published press materials reader) (February 1989): 12–27.

——. "Lishi: dongfang nüxing zhi mi" (History: The riddle of oriental woman). In *Xiawa de tansuo* (Eve's exploration). Zhengzhou: Henan renmin chubanshe, 1988.

——. "Lixing de shuluo" (The oversight of reason). In *Xiawa de tansuo* (Eve's exploration). Zhengzhou: Henan renmin chubanshe, 1988.

——. *Nüren: Yi ge yaoyuan meili de chuanshuo* (Woman: A distant, beautiful legend). Shanghai: Renmin chubanshe, 1989.

——. *Nüxing shenmei yishi tanwei* (Inquiry into women's aesthetic consciousness). N.p., 1989.

——. "Shijimo kan 'Di er xing' " (*The Second Sex* at the end of the century). *Dushu* 20 (1999): 98–103.

——. *Xiawa de tansuo* (Eve's exploration). Zhengzhou: Henan renmin chubanshe, 1988.

——. *Xinggou* (Sex gap). Beijing: Sanlian shudian, 1989.

——. "Yin yang da liebian" (The great fissure of yin and yang). In *Xinggou* (Sex gap), Li Xiaojiang, ed. Beijing: Sanlian shuchan, 1989.

——. "Zenyang kan dangqian fünü wenti he fünü yanjiu" (How to look at the present woman question and women's research). In *Fünü zuzhi yu huodong: Yinshua baokan ziliao* (Women's organizations and activities: Published press materials reader) (January 1989): 5–9.

——. "Zhong jian kuyue 'xing gou' zhi qiao" (Rebuilding the bridge over the sexual gap). *Dongfang*, no. 4 (1995): 14–17.

——. "Zuoxiang nüren" (Towards woman). In *Nüxing ren*, ed. Chen Yu-shih. Taipei: Shibao chubanshe, 1990.

Li Xiaojiang and Li Hui. "Women's Studies in China." *National Women's Studies Association* 1, no. 3 (spring 1989): 458–60.

Li You-ning and Chang Yu-fa. *Jindai Zhongguo nüquan yundong shiliao, 1842–1911* (Documents on the feminist movement in modern China, 1842–1911). Taipei: Quanji wenxue she, 1975.

Liao Ying. "Ren zai jianku zhong shengzhang" (People grow through hardship). *Jiefang ribao* (Liberation daily), 10 June 1942.

Lin Chun. "The Transformation of Chinese Socialism: An Interpretation." Unpublished manuscript, 1998.

Lin Gang. "Xiandai nüxing jietang zhi lu zai nali" (Where is the path to modern women's liberation?) *ZH* (January 1986): 15–18.

Lin Yuezhi. "Liun Ouzhou gujin nüren diwei" (On the status of European women old and new). In *Jindai Zhongguo nüquan yundong shiliao, 1842–1911* (Documents on the feminist movement in modern China, 1842–1911), Li You-ning and Chang Yu-fa, eds. Taipei: Quanjir wenxue she, 1975.

Lin Zhaoyin. "Liangxing jiaoyu zhi yanjiu" (Investigation into sex education). In *Zhongguo funü wenti taolunji* (Collected discussions of the woman question), ed. Mei Sheng. Shanghai: Shanghai New Culture Press, 1929–34, III 7: 77–106.

Liu Bohong. "Yijiujiusan: Funü yanjiu qushi" (1993: Trends in women's studies). In *Funü Yanjiu*. Beijing: Renmin daxue shubao ziliao zhongxin, 1994, 24–25.

———. "Yijiujiusi: Funü yanjiu zouxiang" (1994: Towards woman studies). In *Funü Yanjiu*. Beijing: Renmin daxue shubao ziliao zhongxin, 1994.

Liu Kang. *Aesthetics and Marxism: Chinese Aesthetic Marxists and Their Western Contemporaries.* Durham, NC: Duke University Press, 2000.

———. "Subjectivity, Marxism, and Cultural Theory in China." In *Politics, Ideology, and Literary Discourse in Modern China: Theoretical Interventions and Cultural Critique,* ed. Liu Kang and Xiaobing Tang. Durham, NC: Duke University Press, 1993.

Liu Lihua. "Huashuo Zhongguo nannü pingdeng" (Speaking of equality between Chinese men and women). In *Funü zuzhi yu huodong: Yinshua baokan ziliao* (Women's organizations and activities: Published press materials reader) (March 1990): 17–21.

Liu, Lydia. *Translingual Practice: Literature, National Culture, and Translated Modernity China, 1900–1937.* Stanford: Stanford University Press, 1995.

Liu Shaoqi. "On the intra-Party struggle." In *A Documentary History of Communism,* Conrad Brandt, Benjamin Schwarz, and John K. Fairbank, eds. London: Allen and Unwin, 1952.

Liu Shuang. "Nannü tongxue wenti de yanjiu" (Investigation into the question of male/female coeducation). In *Zhongguo funü wenti taolunji* (Collected discussions of the woman question), ed. Mei Sheng. Shanghai: Shanghai New Culture Press, 1929–34, 2: 184–92.

Lloyd, Genevieve. *The Man of Reason: "Male" and "Female" in Western Philosophy.* London: Routledge, 1993.

Lowe, Lisa. *Critical Terrains: French and British Orientalisms.* Ithaca, NY: Cornell University Press, 1991.

Luo Feng. "Haishi zawen de shidai" (It is still the age of the zawen). *Jiefang ribao* (Liberation daily), 12 March 1942.

Luo Jialun. "Funü jiefang" (Women's liberation). In *Zhongguo funü wenti taolunji* (Collected discussions on the woman question), ed. Mei Sheng. Shanghai: Shanghai New Culture Press, 1928–34, 1: 1–23.

Luo Xiaolu. "Zhongguo funü wenti lilun yanjiu de xianzheang yu tazhan" (The situation and development of research into theories of the Chinese woman question). *ZH* (January 1987): 11–12.

Lowe, Lisa. *Critical Terrains: French and British Orientalisms.* Ithaca, NY: Cornell University Press, 1991.

Lu Fu (pseud.). *Xin funü duben* (New woman's study book). Hong Kong: Xinminshu Press, 1949.

Lu I'e. "Qiuji shixue funü de genben fangfa" (The basic method for remedying the lack of education among women). In *Zhongguo funü wenti taolunji* (Collected discussions of the woman question), ed. Mei Sheng. Shanghai: Shanghai New Culture Press, 1928–34, I 2: 180–82.

MacCannell, Juliet Flower. *Figuring Lacan: Criticism and the Cultural Unconscious*. Lincoln: University of Nebraska Press, 1986.

Mani, Lata. "Contentious Traditions: The Debate on Sati in Colonial India." In *Recasting Women: Essays in Indian Colonial History*, ed. Kumkum Sangari and Sudesh Vaid. New Delhi: Kali for Women, 1989.

—. "Cultural Theory, Colonial Texts: Reading Eyewitness Accounts of Widow Burning." In *Cultural Studies*, ed. Lawrence Grossberg, Cary Nelson, and Paula Treichler. London: Routledge, 1992.

Mann, Susan. *Precious Records: Women in China's Long Eighteenth Century*. Stanford: Stanford University Press, 1997.

Mann, Susan, and Yu-yin Cheng, eds. *Under Confucian Eyes: Writings on Gender in Chinese History*. Berkeley: University of California Press, 2001.

Manning, Kimberly. "Sexual Equality and State Building: Gender Conflict in the Great Leap Forward." Ph.D. diss., University of Washington, 2003.

Mao Zedong. "The Chinese Revolution and the Chinese Communist Party". In *Mao Zedong Selected Works, 1939–1941*. New York: International Publisher, 1954.

—. "May Fourth movement." In *Mao Zedong Selected Works, 1939–1941*. New York: International Publisher, 1954.

—. "On new democracy." In *Mao Zedong Selected Works, 1939–1941*. New York: International Publisher, 1954.

—. "The orientation of the youth." In *Mao Zedong Selected Works, 1939–1941*. New York: International Publisher, 1954.

—. *Report from Xunwu*. Trans. Roger R. Thompson. Stanford: Stanford University Press, 1990.

Martin [Ahern], Emily. "The Power and Pollution of Chinese Women." In *Women in Chinese Society*, ed. Margery Wolf and Roxane Witke. Stanford: Stanford University Press, 1975.

Matsubara, Yoko. "The Enactment of Japan's Sterilization Laws in the 1940s: A Prelude to Postwar Eugenic Policy." *Historia Scientiarum* 8, no. 12 (1998): 187–201.

McClintock, Anne. *Imperial Leather: Race, Gender and Sexuality in the Colonial Conquest*. New York: Routledge, 1995.

Mei Sheng. "Lihun wenti" (The divorce problem). In *Zhongguo funü wenti taolunji* (Collected discussions of the Chinese women question), ed. Mei Sheng. Shanghai: Shanghai New Culture Press, 1929–34, II: 26–39.

—, ed. *Shehui kexue da zidian* (A dictionary of social science). Shanghai: Shijie shuju, 1929.

—, ed. *Zhongguo funü wenti taolunji* (Collected discussions of the Chinese women question). Shanghai: Shanghai New Culture Press, 1929–34.

Melman, Billie. *Women's Orients: English Women and the Middle East, 1718–1918: Sexuality, Religion and Work*. Ann Arbor: University of Michigan Press, 1992.

Meng Xiaoyun, "Dangdai Zhongguo funü mian mian guan" (Today's Chinese women see everything) *ZH* (January 1986): 16–19.

Meng Yue. "Female Images and National Myth." In *Gender Politics in Modern China*, ed. Tani E. Barlow. Durham, NC: Duke University Press, 1993.

Meng Yue and Dai Jinhua. *Fuchu lishi dibiao: Xiandai funü wenxue yanjiu* (Surfacing onto the horizon of history: A study in modern women's literature). Zhengzhou: Henan renmin chubanshe, 1980.

Metz, Christian. *Film Language: A Semiotics of the Cinema*, Michael Taylor, trans. New York: Oxford University Press, 1974.

Moise, Edwin. "Radical, Moderate, and Optimal Patterns of Land Reform." *Modern China* 4, no. 1 (1978): 79–90.

Mou Zhengyun. "Jiegou 'funü': Jiu ci xin lun" (Deconstructing funü: Old term, new discourse). *Jindai Zhongguo funü shi yanjiu* 6 (1998): 119–39.

Nivard, Jacqueline. *Histoire d'une revue féminine chinoise: Funü zashi, 1915–1931.* Unpublished manuscript, n.d.

Oi, Jean. *China Takes Off: Institutional Foundations of Economic Reform.* Berkeley: University of California Press, 1999.

Ono Kazuko. *Chinese Women in a Century of Revolution, 1850–1950.* Ed. Joshua Fogel. Trans. Kathryn Bernhardt et al. Stanford: Stanford University Press, 1989.

Osborne, Peter. "Modernism as Translation." *Traces* 1 (2001): 319–30.

Otsubo, Sumiko. "Engendering Eugenics: Japanese Feminists and Marriage Restriction Legislation in the 1920s." In *Gendering Modern Japanese History,* ed. Barbara Molony and Kathleen Uno. Cambridge, MA: Council on East Asian Studies, Harvard University, forthcoming.

Otsubo, Sumiko, and James. R. Bartholomew. "Eugenics in Japan: Some Ironies of Modernity, 1883–1945." *Science in Context* 11, nos. 3–4 (1998).

Pagden, Anthony. "The Effacement of Difference: Colonialism and the Origins of Nationalism in Diderot and Herder." In *After Colonialism: Imperial Histories and Postcolonial Displacements,* ed. Gyan Prakash. Princeton: Princeton University Press, 1995.

Painter, Nell Irvin. "Representing Truth: Sojourner Truth's Knowing and Becoming Known." *Journal of American History* 81, no. 2 (September 1994): 461–92.

Pan Suiming. "Fulian yinggai you duli de yizhi" (Fulian should have its independent will). In *Funü zuzhi yu huodong: Yinshua baokan ziliao* (Women's organizations and activities: Published press materials reader) (March 1988): 44.

——. *Shenmi de shenghuo: Xing de shehui shi* (The sacred flame: A social history of sex). Zhengzhou: Henan renmin chubanshe, 1988.

Parish, William, and Martin Whyte. *Village and Family in Contemporary China.* Chicago: University of Chicago Press, 1978.

Payne, Robert. *Journey to Red China.* London: Heinemann, 1947.

Pei Wei. "Lian'ai yu zhencao de guanxi" (The relation of love and chastity). In *Zhongguo funü wenti taolunji* (Collected discussions of the woman question), ed. Mei Sheng. Shanghai: Shanghai New Culture Press, 1929–34, 13: 127–31.

Peiss, Kathy. *Hope in a Jar: The Making of America's Beauty Culture.* New York: Metropolitan Books, 1998.

Peking University Women's Studies Center, ed. *Beijing daxue funü disan qu guoji yantaohui lunwenji,* 1994 (Proceedings of the Beijing University women's studies third international conference, 1994). Beijing: Beijing daxue zhongwai funü wenti yanjiu zhongxin, 1995.

Perez, Emma. "Feminism-in-Nationalism: The Gendered Subaltern at the Yucatán Feminist Congresses of 1916." In *Between Woman and Nation: Nationalism, Transnational Feminisms and the State,* ed. Caren Kaplan, Norma Alarcon, and Minoo Moallemn. Durham, NC: Duke University Press, 1999.

Pietz, William. "The Problem of the Fetish, I." *Res* 9 (spring 1985).

——. "The Problem of the Fetish, II." *Res* 13 (spring 1987): 23–45.

——. "The Problem of the Fetish, III." *Res* 16 (autumn 1988): 105–23.

Plaks, Andrew. *Archetype and Allegory in the Dream of the Red Chamber.* Princeton: Princeton University Press, 1976.

Poovey, Mary. *Uneven Developments: The Ideological Work of Gender in Mid-Victorian England.* Chicago: University of Chicago Press, 1988.

Porkert, Manfred. *The Theoretical Foundations of Chinese Medicine: Systems of Correspondence.* Cambridge, MA: MIT Press, 1985.

Pozzana, Claudia. "Spring, Temporality, and History in Li Dazhao." In *New Asian Marxisms*, ed. Tani E. Barlow. Durham, NC: Duke University Press, 2002.

Pusey, James Reeve. *China and Charles Darwin.* Cambridge, MA: Harvard University Press, 1983.

Qian Yunhui. "Lun nujie jibi" (On the corrupt state of womanhood). *Funü shibao* 1 (1911): 1–6.

Qing Ren. "Funü wenti yanjiu zongshu" (Summary of research into the woman question). In *Funü zuzhi yu huodong: Yinshua baokan ziliao* (Women's organizations and activities: Published press materials reader) (April 1989): 11–14.

Qu Wen. "A Brief Account of the Current Status of Research on Women." Unpublished report from the Women's Research Institute of the Women's Federation, n.d.

Radhakrishnan, R. "Nationalism, Gender, and the Narrative of Identity." In *Nationalisms and Sexualities*, ed. Andrew Parker et al. New York: Routledge, 1992.

Rankin, Mary Backus. "The Emergence of Women at the End of the Ch'ing: The Case of Ch'iu Chin." In *Women in Chinese Society*, ed. Margery Wolf and Roxane Witke. Stanford: Stanford University Press, 1975.

Riley, Denise. *Am I That Name? Feminism and the Category of "Women" in History.* Basingstoke, England: Macmillan, 1988.

Rose, Jacqueline. *Sexuality in the Field of Vision.* London: Verso Press, 1986.

Rouzer, Paul. *Articulated Ladies: Gender and the Male Community in Early Chinese Texts.* Cambridge, MA: Harvard University Asia Center, 2001.

——. Review of *Writing Women in Late Imperial China*, by Ellen Widmer and Kang-I Sun Chang. *Journal of Asian Studies* 57, no. 4 (November 1998): 1142–43.

Rowe, William T. *Saving the World: Chen Hongmou and Elite Consciousness in Eighteenth Century China.* Stanford: Stanford University Press, 2001.

——. "Women and the Family in Mid-Qing Social Thought: The Case of Chen Hongmou." *Late Imperial China* 13, no. 2 (December 1992): 1–41.

Rubin, Kyna. "An interview with Mr. Wang Ruowang." *China Quarterly* 87, (1981).

Ruo Shui and Feng Yuan. "Nüxing lixiang di fansi yu qiuzheng" (Reflection and confirmation of female ideals). In *Funü zuzhi yu huodong: Yinshua baokan ziliao* (Women's organizations and activities: Published press materials reader) (February 1987): 29–33. Originally published in *Zhongguo funü*, 1986.

Russo, Alessandro. "The Probable Defeat: Preliminary Notes on the Chinese Cultural Revolution." *positions* 6, no. 1 (spring 1998): 179–202.

Saich, Tony. "Introduction: The Chinese Communist Party and the Anti-Japanese War Base Areas." *China Quarterly* 140 (December 1994): 1000–1006.

Said, Edward. *Orientalism.* New York: Vintage, 1975.

Sakai, Naoki. "Modernity and Its Critique: The Problem of Universalism and Particularism." *South Atlantic Quarterly* 87, no. 3 (summer 1988): 475–504.

——. *Translation and Subjectivity: On "Japan" and Cultural Nationalism.* Minneapolis: University of Minnesota Press, 1997.

San Si. "Women de jiemei" (Our sisters). In *Zhongguo funü wenti taolunji* (Collected discussions of the woman question), ed. Mei Sheng. Shanghai: Shanghai New Culture Press, 1929–34, 1 1: 134–52.

Sangari, Kumkum and Sudesh Vaid, eds. *Recasting Women: Essays in Indian Colonial History.* New Delhi: Kali for Women, 1989.

Sautman, Barry. *Relations in Blood: China's Racial Nationalism.* Seattle: University of Washington Press, forthcoming.

Sayer, Derek. *The Violence of Abstraction: The Analytic Foundations of Historical Materialism.* Oxford: Basil Blackwell, 1987.

Schaefer, William. "Shanghai Savage." *positions* (forthcoming).

Scott, Joan Wallach. *Gender and the Politics of History.* New York: Columbia University Press, 1988.

———. *Only Paradoxes to Offer: French Feminists and the Rights of Man.* Cambridge, MA: Harvard University Press, 1996.

Scott, Joan, and Gayatri Spivak. "Feminism in Decolonization." *differences* 3, no. 3 (fall 1991): 139–75.

Se Lu. "Chan er zhixian yü Zhongguo" (Birth control and China). *Funü zazhi* (Ladies' magazine) 8, no. 6 (June 1922): 10–14.

Seivers, Sharon. *Flowers in the Salt: The Beginning Feminist Consciousness in Modern Japan.* Stanford: Stanford University Press, 1983.

Selden, Mark. *The Yenan Way in Revolutionary China.* Cambridge, MA: Harvard University Press, 1971.

Shen Congwen. *Ji Ding Ling* (Remembering Ding Ling). Vol. 1. Shanghai, 1934.

[Shen] Yan Bing. "Nannü shejiao gongkai wenti guanjian" (Opinion on the question of open social intercourse between women and men). In *Zhongguo funü wenti taolunji* (Collected discussions of the woman question), ed. Mei Sheng. Shanghai: Shanghai New Culture Press, 1929–34, II 6: 155–59.

Shi Fuliang. *Shehui kexue xiaocidian* (Junior dictionary of social science). N.p., 1935.

Shi Heng. "Lian'ai geming lun" (On the erotic love revolution). In *Zhongguo funü wenti taolunji* (Collected discussions of the woman question), ed. Mei Sheng. Shanghai: Shanghai New Culture Press, 1929–34, IV 9: 73–81.

Shih, Shu-mei. *The Lure of the Modern: Writing Modernism in Semicolonial China, 1917–1937.* Los Angeles: University of California Press, 2001.

Shimamura Tamizo. "Nannü liangxing wenti" (The question of heterosexuality), trans. Wang Xiangzhen. In *Zhongguo funü wenti taolunji* (Collected discussions of the woman question), ed. Mei Sheng. Shanghai: Shanghai New Culture Press, 1929–34, III 7: 33–42.

Shu Wu. *Nüxing de faxian* (The discovery of women). Beijing: Xinhua shuchan, 1990.

Si Zhen. "Aiqing yu jiehun" (Love and marriage). In *Zhongguo funü wenti taolunji* (Collected discussions of the woman question), ed. Mei Sheng. Shanghai: Shanghai New Culture Press, 1929–34, II 4: 124.

Sieber, Patricia. *Theatres of Desire: Authors, Readers, and the Reproduction of Early Chinese Song-Drama, 1300–2000.* New York: Palgrave, 2003.

Silverberg, Miriam. "The Modern Girl as Militant." In *Recreating Japanese Women, 1600–1945,* ed. Gail Lee Bernstein. Berkeley: University of California Press, 1991.

Silverman, Kaja. *Male Subjectivity at the Margins.* London: Routledge, 1992.

Sinha, Mrinalini. *Colonial Masculinity: The "Manly Englishman" and the "Effeminate Bengali" in the Late Nineteenth Century.* New York: St. Martin's Press, 1995.

———. "Gender in the Critiques of Colonialism and Nationalism: Locating the 'Indian Woman.'" In *Feminist Revision History,* Anne-Louise Shapiro, ed. New Brunswick: Rutgers University Press, 1994.

Smith, Mark C. *Social Science in the Crucible: The American Debate over Objectivity and Purpose, 1918–1941.* Durham, NC: Duke University Press, 1994.

Song Butian, "Jiating weisheng lun" (On family hygiene). *Funü shibao* 10 (1993): 7–12.

Song Jianyuan. *Ding Ling Pingzhuan* (Critical biography of Ding Ling). Xi'an: Shaanxi renmin chubanshe, 1989.

Spivak, Gayatri C. "Can the Subaltern Speak?" In *Marxism and the Interpretation of Culture*, Cary Nelson and Lawrence Grossberg, eds. Chicago: University of Illinois Press, 1988.

———. *In Other Worlds: Essays in Cultural Politics*. New York: Routledge, 1988.

———. Introduction to *Selected Subaltern Studies*, ed. Gayatri C. Spivak and Ranajit Guha. New York: Oxford University Press, 1988.

———. *Outside in the Teaching Machine*. New York: Routledge, 1993.

———. "The Practical Politics of the Open End." In *The Post-Colonial Critic: Interviews, Strategies, Dialogues*, ed. Sarah Harasym. New York: Routledge, 1990.

Stavrionos, Leften Stavros. *The Global Rift: The Third World Comes of Age*. New York: Morrow, 1981.

Stranahan, Patricia. "Labor Heroines of Yan'an." *Modern China* 7, no. 1 (January 1981): 83–112.

———. *Molding the Medium: The Chinese Communist Party and the Liberation Daily*. Armonk, NY: M.E. Sharpe, 1990.

———. *Yan'an Women and the Chinese Communist Party*. Berkeley: Center for Chinese Studies Press, 1983.

Suleri, Sara. *Meatless Days*. Chicago: University of Chicago Press, 1989.

Tagliacozzo, Eric. Review of *Opium Regimes*. *Journal of Asian Studies* 60, no. 3 (August 2001): 819–20.

Tan Shen. "Funü yanjiu zai shehui xuejia de diwei" (Status of women's studies in the world of sociology). In *"Funü yanjiu zai Zhongguo" quanti yantaohui lunwenji*, Zhang Yanxia, ed. Beijing/Huairou: Quan fulian funü yanjiu suo zhubian, 1995.

Tan Zhengbi. *Zhongguo nüxing wenxue shi* (History of Chinese women's literature). 1935. Reprinted Tianjin: Baihua wenyi chubanshe, 2001.

Tang Chuangwo. "Shengticao" (Rope calesthenics). *Funü shibao* 2 (1911): 17.

Tao Quiying. *Zhongguo fanü yu wenxue* (Chinese women and literature). 1933. Reprinted Taizhong: Landeng chubanshe, 1975.

Teng, Jinhua Emma. "The Construction of the 'Traditional Chinese Woman' in the Western Academy: A Critical Review." *Signs* 22, no. 1 (autumn 1996): 115–51.

Thaxton, Ralph. "The World Turned Upside Down: Three Orders of Meaning in the Peasants' Traditional Political World." *Modern China* 3, no. 2 (1977): 185–228.

Thornhill, Randy, and Craig T. Palmer. *A Natural History of Rape: Biological Bases of Sexual Coercion*. Cambridge, MA: MIT Press, 2000.

Tomiyama, Ichiro. "Colonialism and the Sciences of the Tropical Zone: The Academic Analysis of Difference in 'the Island Peoples.'" *positions* 3, no. 2. (winter 1994): 542–69.

Tsu, Jing. "Perversions of Masculinity: The Masochistic Male Subject in Yu Dafu, Guo Moruo, and Freud." *positions* 8, no. 2 (2000): 269–316.

Viswanathan, Gauri. *Masks of Conquest: Literary Study and British Rule in India*. New York: Columbia University Press, 1989.

Wales, Nym (pseud. Helen Snow). *The Chinese Communists: Sketches and Autobiographies of the Old Guard*. Greenwood, CT: Greenwood Press, 1972.

———. *Women in Modern China*. Paris: Mouton, 1967.

Waller, Derek J. *The Government and Politics of the People's Republic of China*. 3rd ed. London: Hutchison, 1981.

Wan Pu. "Nüzi can zheng yu guojia wenti" (Female political participation and the national question). In *Zhongguo fanü wenti taolunji* (Collected discussions of the Chinese women question), ed. Mei Sheng. Shanghai: Shanghai New Culture Press, 1929–34, 11 4: 80.

Wan Shanping. "The Emergence of Women's Studies in China." *Women's Studies International Forum* 2, no. 5 (1988): 455–64.

Wang, Hui. "Local Forms, Vernacular Dialects and the War of Resistance against Japan: The 'National Forms' Debate" (Parts 1, 2), trans. Chris Berry. UTS Review 4, no. 1 (1998) and 4, no. 2 (1998).

———. "The 1989 Social Movement and the Historical Root of 'Neo-Liberalism' in China." Trans. Rebecca Karl. positions (forthcoming).

Wang, Jing. "Culture as Leisure and Culture as Capital." In Chinese Popular Culture and the State, ed. Jing Wang, special issue of positions 9, no. 1 (2001): 69–104.

———. High Culture Fever: Politics, Aesthetics, and Ideology in Deng's China. Berkeley: University of California Press, 1996.

Wang, Jing, and Tani E. Barlow. Introduction to Cinema and Desire: Feminist Marxism and Cultural Politics in the Work of Dai Jinhua, ed. Jing Wang and Tani E. Barlow. London: Verso, 2002.

Wang Jinling. "Shehui kongzhi: Ta di qidian yu zhongdian—lun xingbie wenhua" (Social controls: Their beginning and their end, a discussion of "gender culture"). In Funü zuzhi yu huodong: yinshua baokan ziliao (Women's organizations and activities: Published press materials reader) (June 1987): 15–18. Originally published in Zhongguo funü bao, 1986.

Wang, Lingzhen. "Retheorizing the Personal: Identity, Writing and Gender in Yu Luojin's Autobiographical Acts." positions: east asia culture critique 6, no. 2 (fall 1998): 395–438.

Wang Pingling. "Xin funü ren'ge wenti" (New woman ren'ge question). In Zhongguo funü wenti taolunji (Collected discussions of the woman question), ed. Mei Sheng. Shanghai: Shanghai New Culture Press, 1929–34, V 14: 156–65.

Wang Qingni. "Liangxing de daode" (Morality of sexuality). In Zhongguo funü wenti taolunji (Collected discussions of the woman question), ed. Mei Sheng. Shanghai: Shanghai New Culture Press, 1929–34, III 7: 42–68.

Wang Shaoguang and Angang Hu. The Political Economy of Uneven Development: The Case of China. Armonk, NY: M.E. Sharpe, 1999.

Wang Shuming. "Muqin" (Mother). In Ding Ling ping-zhuan (Critical biography of Ding Ling), Zhang Baiyun, ed. Shanghai: Qunguang shudian, 1934.

Wang Yizhi. "Funü jiefang yu laogong jiefang" (Women's liberation and liberation of labor). Zhongguo qingnian, 1925. Reprinted in Zhongguo funü yundong lishi cailiao, ed. N.p., n.d.

Wang Zheng. "Research on Women in Contemporary China." In Guide to Women's Studies in China, ed. Gail Hershatter, Emily Honig, Susan Mann, and Lisa Rofel. Berkeley: Institute of East Asian Studies, University of California, 1998.

———. "Research on Women in Contemporary China: Problems and Promises." Unpublished manuscript, 1993.

———. "Three Interviews: Wang Anyi, Zhu Lin, Dai Qing." In Gender Politics in Modern China, ed. Tani E. Barlow. Durham, NC: Duke University Press, 1993.

———. Women in the Chinese Enlightenment. Berkeley: University of California Press, 1999.

Wang Zhongchen and Shang Xia. Ding Ling shenghuo yu wenxue de daolu (The path of Ding Ling's life and literature). Changchun: Jilin renmin chubanshe, 1982.

Weinbaum, Alys Eve. "Marx, Irigaray, and the Politics of Reproduction." In Is Feminist Philosophy Philosophy?, ed. Emma Bianchi. Evanston, IL: Northwestern University Press, 1999.

Wesoky, Sharon. Chinese Feminism Faces Globalization. New York: Routledge, 2002.

Widmer, Ellen, and Kang-i Sun Chang. Writing Women in Late Imperial China. Stanford: Stanford University Press, 1997.

Witke, Roxane. "Transformations of Attitudes towards Women During the May Fourth Era of Modern China." Unpublished dissertation. Berkeley: University of California Press, 1970.

Wu Daiying. "Funü jiefang de erlu beifan" (Behind the second law of women's liberation). In Funü zuzhi yu huodong: Yinshua baokan ziliao (Women's organizations and activities: Published press materials reader) (May 1987): 11. Originally published in *Hunyin yu jiating*, 1987.

Wu Ling. "Renti mei" (Beauty of the human body). *Funü shibao* 2 (1911): 7–11.

Xi Leng. "Yixing shejiao de taidu wenti" (The question of attitudes toward heterosexual intercourse). In *Zhongguo funü wenti taolunji* (Collected discussions of the woman question), ed. Mei Sheng. Shanghai: Shanghai New Culture Press, 1929–34, II 6: 151–53.

Xia Kangda. "Zhong ping 'Wo zai Xiacun de shihou' " (A serious critique of "When I was in Xia Village"). In *Ding Ling zuopin pinglun ji* (Collected commentary on Ding Ling's work), ed. Zhongguo wenxie chuban gongsi. Beijing: Zhongguo wenlian chuban gongsi, 1984.

Xia Yun (C. C.). "Hunyin wenti de yanjiu" (Research on the marriage question). *ZFWT* IV 9: 155–60.

Xiang Jingyu. "Cong pingmin jiaoyu zhong huifen nüzi pingmin jiaoyü de wo jian" (My opinion on segregating plebeian women's education from commonfolks' education). *Funü zoukan*, 1924. Reprinted in *Zhongguo funü yundong lishi ziliao* (Historical materials on the Chinese women's movement), Zhonghua guanguo funzü liangeguo, eds. Beijing: Renmin chubanshe, 1986 (hereafter *ZFYLZ*).

——, "Funü yundong yü guomin yundong" (The women's question and the national movement). In *ZFYLZ*.

——. "Jinhou Zhongguo funü guomin geming yundong" (Chinese women's future national revolutionary movement). *Funü zazhi*, 1924. Reprinted in *ZFYLZ*.

——. "Zai Shanghai nüjie guomin huiyi zuchenghui chengli dahuishang de jianghua" (Talk at the Shanghai women's world national conference planning committee organized general meeting). *Funü zhoubao*, 1924. Reprinted in *ZFYLZ*.

——. "Zhongdeng yishang nüxuesheng de dushu wenti" (The education problems of girl students in the middle school and above). In *ZFYLZ*.

——. "Zhongguo funü xuanquan yundong de xin jiyuan" (The beginning of the new epoch in the Chinese women's propaganda movement). *Funü ribao*, 1924. Reprinted in *ZFYLZ*.

——. "Zhongguo zhishi funü disanpai" (The three groups of intellectual Chinese women). *Funü zhoubao*, 1923. Reprinted in *ZFYLZ*.

Xiao Chunu. " 'Nüzi jiefang' di genbenyi" (The basic principle of "women's liberation"). *Funü xunkan*, 1923. Reprinted in *ZFYLZ*.

Xiao Feng. "Lian'ai lun fafan" (Preface to the treatise on lian'ai). In *Zhongguo funü wenti taolunji* (Collected discussions of the woman question), ed. Mei Sheng. Shanghai: Shanghai New Culture Press, 1929–34, IV 9: 3.

Xiao Jun. "Lun zhong shen da shi" (On marriage). *Jiefang ribao* (Liberation daily), 25 March 1942.

Xiao Li and Xiao Yu. "Zhongguo jindaishi shang guanyu funü jiefang de sanci lunzheng" (Chinese modernity's three debates over women's liberation). In *Funü zuzhi yu huodong: Yinshua baokan ziliao* (Women's organizations and activities: Published press materials reader) (March 1986): 53–54.

Xing Yi. "Meiguo funü zatan" (Random chat on American women). *Funü shibao* 2 (1911): 51–54.

Xu Huabin. *Ding Ling xiaoshuo yanjiu* (Research on Ding Ling's fiction). Shanghai: Fudan daxue chubanshe, 1990.

Xu Naixiang. *Zhongguo xiandai wenxue zuozhe biminglu* (A list of pen names of modern Chinese literary writers). Changsha: Hunan weiyi chubanshe, 1988.

Y. D. "Funü jingshen shenghuo" (The spiritual life of women). In *Zhongguo funü wenti taolunji* (Collected discussions of the woman question), ed. Mei Sheng. Shanghai: Shanghai New Culture Press, 1929–34, III 7: 107–17.

——. "Zhiye yu funü" (Occupations and women). In *Zhongguo funü wenti taolunji* (Collected discussions of the woman question), ed. Mei Sheng. Shanghai: Shanghai New Culture Press, 1929–34, II 3: 21–26.

Yamakawa Kikue. "Shenshi guanyü funü jiefang" (Gentry seclusion and women's liberation). In *Zhongguo funü wenti taolunji* (Collected discussions of the woman question), ed. Mei Sheng. Shanghai: Shanghai New Culture Press, 1929–34, I 1: 114–21.

Yan Jiayan. "Xiandai wenxueshi shang de yi zhuang jiyuan: Zhong ping Ding Ling xiaoshuo 'Zai yiyuan zhong' " (An old case in modern literary history: A serious evaluation of Ding Ling's short story 'In the hospital'). In *Ding Ling zuopin pinglun ji* (Collected commentary on Ding Ling's work), ed. Zhongguo wenxie chuban gongsi. Beijing: Zhongguo wenlian chuban gongsi, 1984, 208–20.

Yan Zhongyun. "Ji jüewu de nüxing duiyü nannü shejiao de zeren" (The responsibility of self-awakened women to the question of social relations between the sexes). In *Zhongguo funü wenti taolunji* (Collected discussions of the woman question), ed. Mei Sheng. Shanghai: Shanghai New Culture Press, 1929–34, II 6: 190–93.

Yang, C. K. *A Chinese Village in Early Communist Transition*. Cambridge, MA: M.I.T. Press, 1959.

Yang Guixin. *Ding Ling chuangzuo zongheng tan* (Speaking on the breadth and depth of Ding Ling's creations). Changsha: Hunan renmin chubanshe, 1984.

——. "Heini de shenbian: Dui wenxue pinglun gongzuo de yixie yijian" (Heini's self-defense: An opinion on the work of literary criticism). *Xin wenxue lucong*, 1980. Reprinted in *Ding Ling zuopin pinglun ji* (Collected commentary on Ding Ling's work), ed. Zhongguo wenxie chuban gongsi. Beijing: Zhongguo wenlian chuban gongsi, 1984.

Yang Xingnan. "Lilun tansuo shi nüxing chengwei da xie de ren" (Theoretical explorations make women into a person writ large) *ZH* (April 1988): 34–38.

Yang Zhihua. "Shanghai funü yundong" (Shanghai women's movement). *Zhongguo funü*, 1926. Reprinted in *Zhongguo funu yundong lishi cailiao*. N.d., n.p.

Ye Shaojün. "Nüzi ren'ge wenti" (The question of women's ren'ge). In *Zhongguo funü wenti taolunji* (Collected discussions of the woman question), ed. Mei Sheng. Shanghai: Shanghai New Culture Press, 1929–34, II 5: 149–56.

Yeh, Wen-hsing. *The Alienated Academy: Culture and Politics in Republican China 1919–1937*. Cambridge, MA: Council on East Asian Studies, Harvard University, 1990.

Yi Jiayue. "Jiating yu hunyin" (Family and marriage). In *Zhongguo funü wenti taolunji* (Collected discussions of the woman question), ed. Mei Sheng. Shanghai: Shanghai New Culture Press, 1929–34, III 8: 166–83.

——. "Zhongguo de lihun wenti" (The question of Chinese divorce). *Xuedong*, 1922. Reprinted in *Zhongguo funü wenti taolunji* (Collected discussions of the woman question), ed. Mei Sheng. Shanghai: Shanghai New Culture Press, 1929–34, II 5: 5–26.

Yi Jiayue and Luo Dunwei. *Zhongguo jiating wenti* (The Chinese family question). Shanghai: Daidong, 1928.

Yi Ou. "Zhongguo funü" (Chinese women). *Jiefang Ribao* (Liberation daily), 6 January 1942.

Yoneda Syotaro. "Lian'ai yü wenhua" (Love and civilization). In *Zhongguo Funü wenti taolunji* (Collected discussion of the woman questions), Mei Sheng, ed. Shanghai: Shanghai New Culture Press, 1929, VI 9.

Yosano Akiko. "Zhencao lun" (On chastity), trans. Zhou Zuoren. In *Zhongguo funü wenti taolunji* (Collected discussions of the woman question), ed. Mei Sheng. Shanghai: Shanghai New Culture Press, 1929–34, 5: 87–93.

Young, Robert J. C. *Colonial Desire: Hybridity in Theory, Culture and Race*. New York: Routledge, 1995.

Yu Yan. "Nüxing renleixue: Jian'gou yu zhanwang" (Anthropology of women: establishment and outlook). In *Zhongguo funü lilun yanjiu shinian 1981–1990* (Women's theoretical studies in China, 1981–1990). Beijing: Zhongguo funü chubanshe, 1992.

Yuan Liangjun, ed. *Ding Ling yanjiu ziliao* (Ding Ling research materials). Tianjin: Zhongguo xiandai zuojia zuopin yanjiu ziliao congshu, Tianjin renmin chubanshe, 1982.

Yun Daiying. "Funü jiefang yundong di youlai he qi yingxiang" (The origins and influence of the women's liberation movement). *Funü zhoubao*, 1923. Reprinted in *Zhongguo funü yundong lishi cailiao, 1921–1927* (Historical research materials for the Chinese women's movement, 1921–1927).

Zeng Ko. "Yuanjiu muqin" (Save the mothers). *Jiefang Ribao* (Liberation daily), 8 March 1942.

Zeng Qi. "Funü wenti yu xiandai shehui" (The woman question and contemporary society). In *Zhongguo funü wenti taolunji* (Collected discussions of the woman question), ed. Mei Sheng. Shanghai: Shanghai New Culture Press, 1929–34, I 1: 56–64.

Zha Jianying. *China Pop: How Soap Operas, Tabloids, and Bestsellers Are Transforming a Culture.* New York: New Press, 1995.

Zhang Baiyun, ed. *Ding Ling pingzhuan* (Critical biography of Ding Ling). Shanghai: Qunguang shudia, 1934.

Zhang Chengchang. "Nüzi renshengguan de gaizao wenti" (The question of reforming women's human outlook). In *Zhongguo funü wenti taolunji* (Collected discussions of the woman question), ed. Mei Sheng. Shanghai: Shanghai New Culture Press, 1929–34, II 5: 166–72.

Zhang Jingru. *Wusi yilai lishi renwu biming bieming lu* (A pen name index for modern Chinese literary arena). Chongqing: Chongqing chubanshe, 1986.

Zhang Jingyuan. trans. and ed. *Dangdai nüxing zhuyi wenxue piping* (Contemporary literary criticism). Beijing: Beijing University Press, 1992.

——. "Guonei nüxing wenxue (shi) yanjiu de xianzhuang" (The situation of the study of national women's literature['s history]). *Xueren* 2, no. 2 (1992): 382–89.

——. *Psychoanalysis in China: Literary Transformations, 1919–1949.* Ithaca, NY: Cornell East Asia Series, Cornell University, 1992.

Zhang Meili. "Nannü shejiao guodu shidai" (The transitional period of social relations between women and men). In *Zhongguo funü wenti taolunji* (Collected discussions of the woman question), ed. Mei Sheng. Shanghai: Shanghai New Culture Press, 1929–34, II 6: 193–94.

Zhang, Naihua. "The All-China Women's Federation, Chinese Women and the Women's Movement: 1949–1993." Ph.D. diss., Michigan State University, 1996.

Zhang Tianyi. "Guanyu Shafei nüshi" (On Miss Sophia). Reprinted in *Ding Ling yanjiu ziliao* (Ding Ling research materials), ed. Yuan Liangjun. Tianjin: Tianjin renmin chubanshe, 1982.

Zhang Xichen. "Dui yu zhongguo funü canzheng san da yiwen de jieshi" (An analysis of three large obstacles to Chinese women's political participation). In *Zhongguo funü wenti taolunji* (Collected discussions of the woman question), ed. Mei Sheng. Shanghai: Shanghai New Culture Press, 1929–34, II 4: 75–78.

Zhang Yanxia, ed. *"Funü yanjiu zai Zhongguo" quanti yantaohui lunwenji* (Complete seminar papers on women's studies in China). Beijing: Quan fulian funü yanjiu suo zhubian, 1995.

Zhao Yuan. "Ye tan 'Taiyang zhao zai Sanggan he shang' " (Also speaking of *The Sun Shines over the Sanggan River*). 1980. Reprinted in *Ding Ling Zuopin Pinglun Ji*, ed. Zhongguo wenxie chuban gongsi. Beijing: Zhongguo wenlian chuban gongsi, 1984.

Zhen Ziyang. *Nüzi xin duben* (New study book for women). 6th ed. N.p.: n.p., 1907.

Zheng Huisheng. *Shanggu Huaxia funü yu hunyin* (Ancient Chinese woman and marriage). Zhengzhou: Henan renmin chubanshe, 1988.

Zheng Xiaofeng. *Ding Ling zai Beidahuang* (Ding Ling in the Great Northern Wasteland). N.p.: Hubei renmin chubanshe, 1989.

Zhengzhou University Women's Center. *Dangdai shijie nüchao yü nüxue* (Woman tide and women's studies in the current century). N.p., 1990.

Zhonghua guanguo funü lianhehui, ed. *Zhongguo funü yundong lishi ziliao, 1921–1927* (Historical material on the Chinese women's movement, 1921–1927). Beijing: Renmin chubanshe, 1986.

Zhou Enlai. "Lun xianqi liangmu yu muzhi" (On virtuous wife, good mother, and the mother responsibility). *Jiefang ribao* (Liberation daily), 20 November 1942.

Zhou Jianren. "Jiating shenghuo de jinhua" (Evolution of family life). In *Zhongguo funü wenti taolunji* (Collected discussions of the woman question), ed. Mei Sheng. Shanghai: Shanghai New Culture Press, 1929–34, 8: 203–9.

———. "Zhongguo jiu jiating zhidu de biandong" (Changes in the old Chinese family system). In *Zhongguo funü wenti taolunji* (Collected discussions of the woman question), ed. Mei Sheng. Shanghai: Shanghai New Culture Press, 1929–34, 8: 228–35.

———. "Zhongguo nüzi de jüewu yu dushen" (Chinese women's awakening and their celibacy). In *Zhongguo funü wenti taolunji* (Collected discussions of the woman question), ed. Mei Sheng. Shanghai: Shanghai New Culture Press, 1929–34, II 5: 82–86.

Zhou Liangpei. "Ding Ling shi Shafei?!" (Ding Ling is Sophia?!). In *Ding Ling zhuan* (Ding Ling's biography). Beijing: Zhongguo xiandai zuojia zhuanji congshu (Modern Chinese writer's biographies series), Beijing shiyue wenyi chubanshe, 1993.

Zhou Yuanpei. *Ding Ling zhuan* (Biography of Ding Ling) Beijing: Beijing shiyue wenyi chubanshe, 1993.

Zhu Qing. Untitled. *Jiefang ribao* (Liberation daily), 11 February 1942.

———. "Wushiba ge nüxuesheng zai Suishi" (58 girl students in Suishi). *Jiefang Ribao* (Liberation daily), 6 February 1942.

———. "Yisilanjiao de hunyin" (Islamic marriage). *Jiefang Ribao* (Liberation daily), 1 February 1942.

Zhu Zhengxin. "Beibei'er de funü wenti lun" (Bebel on the woman question). In *Zhongguo funü wenti taolunji* (Collected discussions of the woman question), ed. Mei Sheng. Shanghai: Shanghai New Culture Press, 1929–34, 1: 66.

Zito, Angela. *Of Body and Brush: Grand Sacrifice as Text/Performance in Eighteenth Century China*. Chicago: University of Chicago Press, 1997.

Zito, Angela, and Tani Barlow, eds. *Body, Subject and Power in China*. Chicago: University of Chicago Press, 1994.

Žižek, Slavoj. "Psychoanalysis in Post-Marxism: The Case of Alain Badiou." *South Atlantic Quarterly* 97, no. 2 (spring 1998): 239–40.

# Index

CCP (Chinese Communist Party): Ding Ling's writing on, 198; *funü* in, 37–38, 55–59, 190; Li Xiaojiang on, 259
Celibacy, and *ren'ge*, 119
Chakrabarty, Dipesh, 90, 362
Chan, Ching-kiu Stephen, 54, 130
Chang, Kang-I Sun, 24
Chang Yu-fa, 67
Characters, female: Ding Ling's, 137–139, 148, 173, 225–227, 232–233; Lu Xun's, 318; Mao Dun's, 318; positive progressive, 238; Su Qing's, 325–326. *See also names of specific characters*
Characters, normative, 216, 227, 230
Chen Boda, 193, 198, 210–211
"Chen Boxiang" (Ding Ling), 161
Chen Dezheng, 103–114, 296
Chen Guyuan, 113
Chen Hengzhe, 321
Chen Hongmu, 49, 58, 230, 372; on behavior of women, 45–46; definition of "women," 41–42; on family, 46–47; on female literacy, 44–45; Rowe on, 25–26; and yin/yang logic, 43–44
Chen Kaige, 339, 342–343
Chen Liwei, 114
"Chen Man" (Ding Ling), 200–201, 218, 234
Chen Ming, 194
Chengshu, from "Summer Break," 142–143
Chen Ping, 265–266
Chen Qixiu, 118, 123
Chen Ran, 328
Chen Shousun, 67
Chen Xunxin, 303
Chen Yun, 274
Chen Yung-fa, 209, 212, 223, 238
Cherifati-Merabtine, Doria, 11
Chi Li, 328
"Children" (Ding Ling), 206
Chi Zijian, 328
China, traditional: "women" in, 19–23
"Chinese" and "other" stories, 51–52
Chinese Communist Party. *See* CCP (Chinese Communist Party)
Chinese Communist Women's Movement: Ding Ling as icon of, 244–252; *funü* in, 172; and *nüxing* formula, 152
Chinese feminism. *See* Feminism, Chinese

Chinese Marxism. *See* Marxism, Chinese
Chow, Kai-Wing, 26–27, 29, 40
Cinema theory, of Dai Jinhua, 333–343
Citizenship, and feminism, 67–71
Class, and women, 29, 158
*Collected Discussions of the Chinese Women Question* (Mei Sheng), 71–78
Colonial modernity, 7–8, 87–91; defined, 87–89; and Ding Ling, 127–189; and intellectual history, 90; and modern Chinese literature, 131
Confucian doctrine, *funü* in, 37
*The Contemporary History of Western Women*, 68–69
*Contemporary Mass Culture Critique* (Li Tuo), 304–305
Copjec, Joan, 308
Cornell, Drucilla, 17
Corrigan, Philp, 11
"The County Magistrate's Family" (Ding Ling), 208
Coward, Rosalind, 96, 103
Cowie, Elizabeth, 43, 370
Criticism of Dai Jinhua. *See* Dai Jinhua
Cultural Revolution: Ding Ling during, 194, 196; and Li Xiaojiang, 254
Culture: Gao Xian on, 80, 84; Maoist emphasis on, 211, 212
Culture studies, Dai Jinhua on, 330–348
Culture of consumption, Dai Jinhua on, 304

Dai Houying, 275
Dai Jinhua, 8–10, 17, 86, 127, 189, 231, 247, 300, 356; background of, 303, 351; cinema theory of, 333–343; on cultural critique, 306; cultural studies of, 306, 330–348; on culture, 344–345, 346–347; on Ding Ling, 324; and *écriture féminine chinoise* (*see écriture féminine chinoise*); feminism of, 302–372; film criticism of, 321; and Meng Yue, 302–303, 314; and "the 1990s," 303–304; as *nüxing*, 349–350; on sexuality, 319; as subject of feminism, 352; on woman as category, 350; on women's history, 306; writing of, 307. *See also under titles of specific works*
Dai Qing, 276
Darwin, Charles, 54, 79, 83, 307
Darwinism, 4

Index  475

214–219; and Stalinism, 273–274; state policies of, 279–280; and *The Sun Shines over the Sanggan River*, 239, 241–242. See also Yan'an Maoism

Mao Zedong, 190, 193; *On Democracy*, 211; and Fifth Generation directors, 339

Market feminism, 254; and Dai Jinhua, 305; and Li Xiaojiang, 253–301; and 1980s liberal theory, 268–295

Marriage: and evolution arguments, 106; and terms *fu* and *nü*, 40i Sheng on, 119; and *ren'ge*, 121–123

Marriage portraits, 69–70; Chinese old fashioned, 70, 74; European-style, 70, 74; of Javanese nobility, 70, 72

Marx, Karl, 123, 190

Marxism, Chinese: and Dai Jinhua, 347; *funü* in, 55–56; and Li Xiaojiang, 270–272, 280; and Li Zehou, 271; women's studies in, 283

Marxist feminism, subject of, 151–189

Maternity, and "mother-right" theory, 107

Matriarchy, fall of: and women's liberation, 262

May Fourth movement, 317; and Gao Xian, 79, 82; Meng Yue and Dai Jinhua on, 323; women's writing since, 319

McLennan, John F., 86, 96, 105

Mei Sheng, 91–92, 113; biographic information about, 74; and *The Chinese Women Question*, 71–78; essays selected by, 107; on marriage, 119; on *ren'ge* (personal standing), 114, 118; on sexuality, 99; social science theory of, 76

Meng Hui, 328

Meng Yue, 231, 247, 275, 300; and Dai Jinhua, 302–303, 314, 319; on Ding Ling, 324; on sexuality, 319

"Mengke" (Ding Ling), 133–134, 136, 137, 141, 146, 148, 160, 166

Metz, Christian, 307, 312

Ming dynasty, women in, 21–22, 40

Modernity, colonial: defined, 87–89; and early thought of Ding Ling, 127–189; and intellectual history, 90

Morgan, Edward, 96, 104, 105

*Mother* (Ding Ling), 161, 172, 174, 237; and Chinese nationalism, 175–176; Ding Ling on, 174; and *Dream of the Red Chamber*, 178;

kin in, 182, 187; *lishu* in, 182–183, 184; mother-daughter relationship in, 188; narrative of, 178, 179; political sisterhood in, 184; story of, 174–175

Motherhood, Dai Jinhua and Meng Yue on, 326–327

"Mother-right" theory, 96–97, 107

Mou Zhengyun, 39, 40

Mo Yan, 343

Mu (mother), Chen Hongmou's, 42

Mulan, myth of, 337

Mulvey, Laura, 307, 312, 336

*Muqin* (Ding Ling). See *Mother* (Ding Ling)

"My Opinion" (Ding Ling), 215

Narrative, in Ding Ling's stories, 146, 151, 178, 179

Nation. See *Guo* (state)

National Defense stories, Ding Ling's, 202–205, 213

Nationalism, Maoist: and Chinese feminism, 64–65; and Ding Ling, 175, 190–252; *funü* in, 194–213

Nature, and sex selection, 83–84

"New Faith" (Ding Ling), 206

"New woman": Ding Ling as, 144; and Mao Dun's characters, 318; in "Sophia's Diary," 145

"Nianqian de yitian" (Ding Ling), 159

"Night" (Ding Ling), 221, 222

1920s feminism, 78–87, 156, 157, 355

1930s feminism, 355

1940s feminism, 195, 216

1980s feminism, 253, 358; debates on sexuality, 289; foundations of, 255–264; *funü* in, 257; and Li Xiaojiang, 268–295, 276, 285; and social role of women, 261–262; women's studies in, 264–268

1990s feminism, 8–9, 302–372

Nora, from *A Doll's House*, 121, 317, 355

Normative characters, 216, 227, 230

"Not a Love Letter" (Ding Ling), 159

*Nüzi xin duben* (New study book for women), 50–51

*Nüxing* (women): as category, 53; characters (*see* characters, female); and Chinese feminism, 6, 53, 152; Dai Jinhua as, 349–350; and *ren'ge*, 85, 86, 171; in Ding Ling's writing, 132–133, 134; and identity, 86;

Tani E. Barlow is Associate Professor of Women's Studies
at the University of Washington.

Library of Congress Cataloging-in-Publication Data
Barlow, Tani E.
The question of women in Chinese feminism / Tani Barlow.
p. cm. — (Next wave)
Includes bibliographical references and index.
ISBN 0-8223-3281-7 (cloth : alk. paper)
ISBN 0-8223-3270-1 (pbk. : alk. paper)
1. Feminism—China—History. 2. Feminist theory—China. I. title.
II. Series.
HQ1767.B37 2004    305.42'0951—dc22    2003019780